Wrightslaw: Special Education Law

2ⁿᵈ Edition

PETER W. D. WRIGHT, ESQ.

PAMELA DARR WRIGHT, MA, MSW

Harbor House Law Press, Inc.
Hartfield, Virginia

Wrightslaw: Special Education Law, 2nd Edition by Peter W. D. Wright and Pamela Darr Wright

Library of Congress Cataloging-in-Publication Data

Wright, Peter W. D. and Pamela Darr Wright

Wrightslaw: Special Education Law,/2nd ed.

p. cm.

Includes bibliographic references and index.

ISBN 13: 978-1-892320-16-2

ISBN: 1-892320-16-9

1. Law — special education — United States.   I. Title

2. Special education — parent participation — United States.

Library of Congress Control Number: 2006931152

14 13 12 11 10 9 8 7

Cover Design and Interior Design by Mayapriya Long, Bookwrights Design Studio.

Printed in the United States of America by Victor Graphics, Inc.

Printing History

Harbor House Law Press, Inc. issues new printings and new editions to keep our publications current. New printings include technical corrections and minor changes. New editions include major revisions of text and/or changes.

First Edition	November 1999
Second Edition	March 2007
Seventh Printing	April 2009

Disclaimer

Law is always changing. The information contained in this book is general information and may or may not reflect current legal developments. For changes in the law and regulations, and new decisions from the Supreme Court, please check the Updates page at www.wrightslaw.com/bks/selaw2/updates.htm It is sold with the understanding that the publisher and authors are not rendering legal or other professional services. For legal advice about a specific set of facts, you should consult with an attorney.

 The purpose of this book is to educate and inform. While every effort has been made to make this book as complete and accurate as possible, there may be mistakes, both typographical and in content. The authors and Harbor House Law Press, Inc. shall have neither liability nor responsibility to any person or entity with respect to any loss or damage caused, or alleged to be caused, by the information contained in this book. If you do not wish to be bound by the above, you may return the book to the publisher for a full refund. Every effort has been made to ensure that no copyrighted material has been used without permission. The authors regret any oversights that may have occurred and are happy to rectify them in future printings of this book.

Bulk Purchases

Harbor House Law Press books are available at discounts for bulk purchases, academic sales or textbook adoptions. For information, contact Harbor House Law Press, P. O. Box 480, Hartfield VA 23071. Please provide the title of the book, ISBN number, quantity, how the book will be used, and date needed.

Toll Free Phone Orders: (877) LAW IDEA or (877) 529-4332

Toll Free Fax Orders: (800) 863-5348.

Internet Orders: http://www.wrightslaw.com/store/

Contents

Acknowledgements

We were fortunate to receive assistance from several individuals who gave their time to read large portions of the manuscript. **Anne Eason**, an attorney from Norwalk, Connecticut, and co-author of *IEP and Inclusion Tips for Parents and Teachers*, reviewed the entire manuscript and offered dozens of useful suggestions.

Suzanne Heath, co-author of *Wrightslaw: No Child Left Behind*, guest lecturer at Rivier College Department of Education, and member of New Hampshire Special Education Advisory Committee, reviewed the manuscript and offered advice about reading research and the alignment of IDEA 2004 and No Child Left Behind. Sue compiled the extensive list of resources and references in Appendix A.

John Willis, Assessment Specialist and Senior Lecturer in Assessment at Rivier College in New Hampshire, and co-author of *Guide to Identification of Learning Disabilities*, reviewed the entire manuscript and offered invaluable advice about assessments.

We wish to acknowledge the contributions of individuals who read one or more chapters of the manuscript. Their recommendations were enormously helpful in making the book more accurate and readable. ·

Loni Allen, education resource specialist with Parents Helping Parents and parent advocate in California

Candace Cortiella, Director of the Advocacy Institute and advocate for students with disabilities

Pam Cook, special education advocate in Pittsburgh, Pennsylvania

Barbara J. Ebenstein, Esq., attorney and hearing officer in New York

Sharon England, Esq., attorney in Richmond, Virginia

Ruth Heitin, Ph.D, educational consultant in Alexandria, Virginia

Pat Howey, Wrightslaw speaker, special education consultant and advocate in West Point, Indiana

Scott Johnson, Esq., law professor at Concord University School in Concord and founder of The Educational Law Resource Center in New Hampshire

Sonja Kerr, Esq., attorney in Anchorage, Alaska

Dr. John McCook, director of special education, Knox County Schools, Tennessee

Rosemary N. Palmer, Esq., attorney in Tallahassee, Florida

Jane B. Ross, Executive Director, Smart Kids with Learning Disabilities at www.SmartKidswithLD.org

Jamie Ruppman, Associate Director of The Advocacy Institute and advocate for children with disabilities

Wayne Steedman, Esq., attorney in Baltimore, Maryland and Wrightslaw speaker

Charlotte Temple, Advocacy Director, The Arc of Jacksonville, Florida

Adrienne Volenik, Esq., Director of the Disability Law Clinic and Clinical Professor of Law at the University of Richmond School of Law

We thank **Mayapriya Long** who designed the wonderful cover for *Wrightslaw: Special Education Law, 2nd Edition*.

Finally, we thank **Debra Pratt**, **Tim Bowman**, **Sue O'Connor**, and **Jackie Igafo-Te'o**, the creative, resourceful folks who make the Wrightslaw office a warm, wonderful and fun place to work.

Dedication

We dedicate this book to our parents, **Virginia Bowen Darr, Robert William Darr, Penelope Ladd Wright**, and **Thomas W. D. Wright**. From these remarkable people, we inherited our passion and commitment to make the world a better place for all children.

We also dedicate this book to our children, **Hillary, Damon, Stephanie, Jason**, and **Sara**, and to our grandchildren, **Kelsey, Dylan**, and **Owen**, who will carry on the legacy.

Finally, we dedicate this book to **Diana Hanbury King** and **Roger Saunders** who taught Peter how to read, write, spell, and do arithmetic.

Updates

Special education law is always changing. Since the second edition of *Wrightslaw: Special Education Law* was published in 2007, the U. S. Department of Education issued new regulations (effective December 31, 2008) and the U. S. Supreme Court issued decisions in two cases, with oral argument scheduled in another case.

Changes to the law and/or regulations and new decisions from the U. S. Supreme Court will be available on the **Updates Page** at:

http://www.wrightslaw.com/bks/selaw2/updates.htm

Please check the **Updates Page** often.

Section One

Law and History

CHAPTER 1

Introduction

The reauthorized Individuals with Disabilities Education Act of 2004 is confusing to most parents, educators, related services providers, and even to many advocates and attorneys. Ignorance of the law can be as damaging as the child's disability.

What Changed in IDEA 2004?

What are the requirements for highly qualified special education teachers? How can special education teachers meet the highly qualified teacher requirements?

What does the Individuals with Disabilities Education Act say about child find? Are children who attend private schools and charter schools entitled to special education and related services? What does the law say about least restrictive environment and inclusion?

What does the law say about evaluations, reevaluations and parental consent? What does the law say about the use of discrepancy formulas and Response to Intervention (RTI) to identify children with specific learning disabilities?

What does the law say about Individualized Education Programs (IEPs) and IEP teams? Transition plans? How did the law about reviewing and revising IEPs change? Which IEP Team members may be excused from IEP meetings, and under what circumstances? What are "multi-year IEPs"?

What are early intervening services and who is eligible for early intervening services? What does the law say about who must be tested on state and district assessments? Who is entitled to accommodations? Who is eligible to take an alternate assessment? Who makes decisions about assessments?

What does the law say about Independent Educational Evaluations and parental access to educational records? What changes were made to procedural safeguards notice, prior written notice, and the new due process complaint notice? What are the new requirements and timelines for due process hearings? Resolution sessions? Qualifications of hearing officers? How did the law about attorneys' fees change?

What does the law say about discipline? Manifestation review hearings? Who has the authority to decide that a child will be placed in an interim alternative educational setting? For how long? What does the law say about functional behavioral assessments and behavior intervention plans?

Wrightslaw: Special Education Law, 2nd Edition will help you find answers to your questions in the Individuals with Disabilities Education Act of 2004 and other federal education laws.

Who Should Read This Book?

If you are the parent of a child with a disability, you represent your child's interests. To effectively advocate for your child, you need to learn about your child's rights, your rights and responsibilities under the Individuals with Disabilities Education Act, and how the law will affect your child's education.

If you work as a teacher, related services provider, or school administrator, the Individuals with Disabilities Education Act of 2004 will have a profound impact on you and your job. You may receive conflicting information and advice about this law. You need to know what the law actually says.

If you teach special education, school psychology, school administration, or education law courses, your students need to know how to find answers to their questions about what the law requires of them. If you are an employee of a state department of education, you may be responsible for investigating complaints, collecting data, or other activities to improve educational results for children with disabilities. You need to be aware of new requirements in IDEA 2004 that will affect your work.

If you are an attorney or advocate who represents children with disabilities, you need to have the Individuals with Disabilities Education Act of 2004 on your desk, in your briefcase, and in your computer.

Wrightslaw: Special Education Law, 2nd Edition is the instruction manual for bringing more than 90 percent of children with disabilities up to grade level.[1]

How This Book is Organized

Wrightslaw: Special Education Law, 2nd Edition is organized into five sections.

Section One is **Learning About the Law.** This section includes an overview of law, how law evolves, and background information about special education and the Individuals with Disabilities Education Act. Chapter 2 is **Statutes, Regulations, Commentary to the Regulations and Caselaw.** You will learn about legislative intent, how law evolves, and why it is important that you do your own legal research. Chapter 3 is **History of Special Education.** In this chapter, you learn about the evolution of public education and special education and several landmark discrimination cases that led Congress to enact Public Law 94-142 in 1975.

Section Two is the **Individuals with Disabilities Education Improvement Act of 2004.** Chapter 4 is an **Overview of IDEA 2004** that describes how the law is organized and new requirements in the reauthorized statute. Chapter 5, the **Individuals with Disabilities Education Improvement Act of 2004**, begins with a Table of Statutes, followed by the full text of the the Individuals with Disabilities Education Act, with commentary, cross-references and strategies. You will find the **IDEA 2004 Regulations** in Chapter 6.

Section Three is **Other Federal Education Statutes.** Chapter 7, **Section 504 of the Rehabilitation Act**, explains how Section 504 differs from the Individuals with Disabilities Education Act. Section 504 relates to accommodations and modifications and improved building accessibility to provide access to education. Chapter 8, **No Child Left Behind**, provides requirements for highly qualified special education teachers, annual proficiency testing, research-based reading programs, and the legal definitions of reading, scientifically based reading research, diagnostic reading assessments, and the essential components of reading instruction. Chapter 9, the **Family Educational Rights and Privacy Act,** is about privacy and confidentiality, access, amendment, and destruction of education records. Chapter 10, the **McKinney-Vento Homeless Assistance Act,** requires all school districts to ensure that all children whose families are homeless have access to school. This chapter includes highlights from the McKinney-Vento Act, including the requirement that school districts *shall* make decisions in the best interest of the child.

Section Four is **Special Education Caselaw.** Chapter 11 is **An Overview of Special Education Caselaw.** In this chapter, you learn about special education cases decided by the United States Supreme Court. Chapter 12 is the **Special Education Law Casebook.** This chapter includes the full text of eight decisions from the U. S. Supreme Court. As you read these decisions, you will see how issues have changed since the Supreme Court issued its first decision in 1982.

Section Five, References and Resources, includes two Appendices and the Bibliography. Appendix A is a **List of Resources and References** on topics in the Individuals with Disabilities Education Act and other federal education laws. Appendix B is a **Glossary of Special Education Acronyms, Abbreviations and Terms.** Following the appendices are a **Bibliography** and a comprehensive **Index.**

---

1   See the No Child Left Behind regulation about alternate assessments in the *Federal Register* (December 9, 2003) at www.ed.gov/legislation/FedRegister/finrule/2003-4/120903a.pdf (Retrieved October 11, 2006)

Strategies to Help You Use This Book

Wrightslaw: Special Education Law, 2ⁿᵈ Edition includes the full text of the IDEA statute and regulations. The authors used **bold type** to emphasize important words and phrases in the statutes. Commentary and cross-references are in footnotes.

Look at the example below. The statute begins with (d) Purposes.

> **(d) Purposes**. The purposes of this title are–
>
> (1)
>
> (A) to ensure that all children with disabilities have available to them a free appropriate public education that emphasizes special education and related services designed to meet their **unique needs and prepare them for further education,**[2] **employment, and independent living;**[3]

The authors used bold type to draw your attention to the phrase "**unique needs and prepare them for further education, employment and independent living.**" The footnotes (see below) are commentary by the authors.

Additional Documents

We encourage readers to download additional documents that will help to answer your questions. You may also want to print these documents and attach them to this book.

Federal Regulations

On August 14, 2006, the Department of Education published the Final Regulations for IDEA 2004 in the *Federal Register* (page 46540 to page 46845). The IDEA regulations are in Chapter 6 of *Wrightslaw: Special Education Law, 2ⁿᵈ Edition*.

Analysis and Commentary

In earlier reauthorizations of the Individuals with Disabilities Education Act, the Education Department published Appendices that answered questions about IEPs and other issues. The Education Department did not publish an Appendix of questions and answers with the IDEA 2004 regulations. However, they did publish an "Analysis of Comments and Changes" (Commentary) to the regulations. The Commentary in the *Federal Register* begins at page 46547 and continues through page 46743.

The Commentary provides definitions and discussions of legal terms in the IDEA 2004 statute and regulations, and often clarifies the "plain meaning" of a term. If you are doing legal research or looking for the answer to a specific question, the Commentary will be an invaluable resource.

You can download the full text of the Commentary as one document or as eight files on different topics from www.wrightslaw.com/idea/commentary.htm

Model Forms

When Congress reauthorized the IDEA, they required the Education Department to develop and publish model IEP, Procedural Safeguard Notice, and Prior Written Notice forms. When the Education Department

---

2 The phrase "further education" is new in IDEA 2004, as is the emphasis on effective transition services. Section 1400(c)(14) describes "effective transition services to promote successful post-school employment or education."

3 Purposes in Section 1400(d) is the mission statement of IDEA. The purpose of special education is to prepare children with disabilities for **further education, employment, and independent living**. In developing IEPs, use this "mission statement" as your long-term goal.

published the federal special education regulations on August 14, 2006, they published these model forms. We encourage you to download, print and read these forms.

Individualized Education Program (IEP): www.wrightslaw.com/idea/law/model.iep.form.pdf

Procedural Safeguards Notice: www.wrightslaw.com/idea/law/model.safeguard.form.pdf

Prior Written Notice: www.wrightslaw.com/idea/law/model.pwn.form.pdf

When references to other works are cited, you will find the citation in a footnote. Additional references and resources are included in Appendix A at the end of this book.

Updates

For updates on the Individuals with Disabilities Education Act, go to www.wrightslaw.com/idea/index.htm

To learn more about special education law and advocacy, subscribe to *The Special Ed Advocate*, the free online newsletter that is published weekly by Wrightslaw.

CHAPTER 2

Statutes, Regulations, Commentary, and Caselaw

In this chapter, you will learn about statutes, regulations, commentary to the regulations, and caselaw. You will learn about legislative intent and how law evolves through judicial interpretations. You will also learn why it is important to do your own legal research.

Congress enacted Public Law 94-142 in 1975. The statute was known as the Education for All Handicapped Children Act. Over the years, the Act was amended and renamed. The last revision enacted by Congress on November 19, 2004 is known as the Individuals with Disabilities Education Improvement Act of 2004 (IDEA 2004). The President signed the Act into law on December 3, 2004. IDEA 2004 went into effect on July 1, 2005.

When Congress reauthorized the Individuals with Disabilities Education Act in 2004, they made significant changes to the law. **Purposes** is the most important statute because it is the mission statement. The Purpose is:

> . . . to ensure that all children with disabilities have available to them a free appropriate public education that emphasizes special education and related services **designed to meet their unique needs** and **prepare them for further education, employment and independent living** . . . [and] to ensure that the rights of children with disabilities and parents of such children are protected . . . [1]

The authorization of any new law brings about a spate of interpretations and questions. Self-styled experts may spread wrong interpretations, misinformation and disinformation. Do not rely on the opinions of others or advice you may read in articles.

To find answers to your questions about the Individuals with Disabilities Education Act, *you need to do your own legal research*. The intention of this book is to bridge the gap between the law and one's understanding of the legal language within it, in an accurate, objective manner and through direct reference to the law itself.

In this book, you will read the law. In the beginning, this is more difficult than reading articles about the law or having the law explained to you. As you continue to read and become accustomed to the language and structure of the law, the law itself will become more meaningful to you. When you learn how the law is organized, you can quickly find sections or regulations that are relevant to your questions.

Statutes

Individuals with Disabilities Education Act

Statutes are laws passed by federal, state and local legislatures. The original federal special education law was "The Education of All Handicapped Children Act." When Congress reauthorized the law in 2004, they renamed it as "The Individuals with Disabilities Education Improvement Act of 2004."[2]

Congress first publishes a law as an "Act" in the *Statutes at Large*, then organizes laws by subject in the *United States Code* (U. S. C.) The Individuals with Disabilities Education Act is printed in the *Statutes at Large* and in the *United States Code*. The numbering system used to categorize an *Act* in the *Statutes at Large* is different from the system used in the *United States Code*.

---

1   20 U. S. C. §1400(d)
2   IDEA 2004 is Public Law 108-446 and is cited as Pub. L. 108-446

The *United States Code* has fifty subject classifications called Titles. For example, Title 20 is about education, Title 26 is the Internal Revenue Code, and Title 42 is about public health and welfare. In each title, laws are indexed and assigned section numbers. The Individuals with Disabilities Education Act is cited as 20 U. S. C. § 1400, *et seq.*[3] Statutes published in the *Statutes at Large* have sections (section 1, 2, 3, 4, etc.) and may have subsections (i.e., (a), (b), (c), (d)).

The "Act" begins with Section 600. When the Act is published in the *United States Code* (U. S. C.), the numbers change. IDEA 2004 is in Title 20 of the *United States Code,* beginning with Section 1400. For example, "Definitions" are in Section 1401 of the *United States Code* (cited as 20 U. S. C. § 1401) and are in Section 602 of "the Act."

Other Federal Statutes

Other important federal education statutes are:

- The No Child Left Behind Act of 2001, a reauthorization of the Elementary and Secondary Education Act of 1965 (ESEA) which begins at 20 U. S. C. § 6301 *et seq.*
- Section 504 of the Rehabilitation Act of 1973 which begins at 29 U. S. C. §794 *et seq.*
- The Family Educational and Rights and Privacy Act which begins at 20 U. S. C. § 1232 *et seq.*
- The McKinney-Vento Homeless Assistance Act which begins at 42 U. S. C. § 11431 *et seq.*

States must ensure that their statutes and regulations are consistent with the *United States Code* (U. S. C.) and the *Code of Federal Regulations* (CFR). While state statutes and regulations may provide more rights than federal laws, they cannot provide fewer rights than guaranteed by federal law. If a state law or regulation is in direct conflict with a federal law, the federal law controls, pursuant to the "Supremacy Clause" of the U. S. Constitution.

Regulations

The U. S. Department of Education develops and publishes the federal special education regulations. Regulations clarify and explain the United States Code. A regulation must be consistent with the United States Code and has the same force of law. Before the Department publishes the regulations, the agency must publish the proposed regulations in the *Federal Register* (F. R.) and solicit comments from citizens about the proposed regulations. The special education regulations are published in Volume 34, Part 300 of the Code of Federal Regulations. The legal citation for the regulations is 34 CFR § 300.

Commentary to the Regulations

When the Education Department published the regulations for IDEA 2004, they included an "Analysis and Commentary" with the document. In the Commentary, the Department described the comments they received about the proposed regulations and what changes were made.

In the Commentary, terms, definitions and requirements are described and explained in clear language.[4] When you read a regulation, these comments will help you understand why the Department used specific language. In earlier reauthorizations of the Individuals with Disabilities Education Act, the Education Department published a Question and Answer Appendix to the Regulations that answered questions about IEPs and other issues. The IDEA 2004 Regulations do not include such an Appendix. However, the Commentary will help you understand the different perspectives and interpretations that can be made about a regulation.

---

3   *et seq.*, an abbreviation of the Latin phrase *et sequentia* meaning "and the following ones," is a legal term indicating that a writer is citing a page and the pages that follow.
4   Download portions of the Commentary from Wrightslaw.

Judicial Interpretations and Caselaw

Evolving Caselaw

Caselaw is always changing and evolving. The Individuals with Disabilities Education Act will continue to evolve and be re-defined by caselaw. Special education litigation usually starts with a special education due process hearing. In some states, the losing party can appeal directly to state court or federal court. In other states, the appeal is initially for a review hearing, then an appeal to court.

State courts and federal courts are different judicial systems. In general, after a case is filed in state or federal court, it remains within that system. For example, cases filed in state court remain within the state court system while cases filed in U. S. District Courts generally remain in the federal court system. A state court case may be "removed" to federal court and a federal case may be remanded back to state court.

When a state court issues a decision, the decision may be appealed to a higher state court. For example, a Virginia trial judge's interpretation of a statute is governed by earlier rulings from the highest state court in Virginia. The highest state court is usually the state Supreme Court. In general, a party who loses in state court cannot appeal to the federal court, but must follow the appellate process outlined in the state's judicial system.

Federal judges are bound by rulings of their Circuit Court of Appeals. There are twelve circuit courts.[5] For example, Virginia, Maryland, North Carolina, South Carolina, and West Virginia are in the Fourth Circuit. A U. S. District Court judge in those states must follow rulings from the United States Court of Appeals for the Fourth Circuit. The judge is not required to follow legal rulings from other circuits, although these opinions may be cited as persuasive authority.

All state and federal courts must follow rulings issued by the U. S. Supreme Court. If the U. S. Supreme Court issues a ruling with which Congress disagrees, Congress may enact a new law to change the impact of a decision of the Supreme Court.

Legislative Intent

Judges often look at legislative history and legislative intent when they analyze the meaning of a statute. When you read decisions by the U. S. Supreme Court,[6] you will see that the Justices often discuss legislative history and legislative intent in their decisions. Legislative intent is usually found in Committee Reports, transcripts of debates in the *Congressional Record* and other sources.[7]

Legal Interpretations

Law is always subject to different interpretations. Attorneys and judges will interpret a section of the law differently, depending on their perspectives. If you read an article about special education law, the interpretations and conclusions are likely to represent the opinions of the author. If you read the law and regulations on your own, you will form your own interpretations and conclusions about the law and the impact it is likely to have on you.

Compelling facts may cause a judge to want to rule in one direction, even if the ruling is contrary to current caselaw. The decision-maker in this situation will often find and use unique facts in the case to create an exception to general caselaw. These "exceptions to the rule" decisions cause the body of law to change and grow.

How a court interprets a law or regulation may be dictated by a single word, for example, "may" instead of "shall." When Congress wants to pass a bill but cannot agree on the wording of a statute, compromise is achieved by using vague language. Vague and confusing words or phrases lead to litigation. For example, in special education law, the term "appropriate education" has been litigated for more than thirty years.

---

5   To find out what circuit your state is in, go to www.uscourts.gov/images/CircuitMap.pdf
6   Section Four includes key decisions in special education cases by the U. S. Supreme Court.
7   Find legislative information at http://thomas.loc.gov/

Over time, when courts agree on the same interpretation, a majority rule evolves. A minority rule may also develop. If a majority rule does not develop, the legal issue becomes more confusing. U. S. Courts of Appeal in different circuits around the country often issue conflicting rulings, leading to a "split among circuits." When there is a split among circuits, the U. S. Supreme Court may agree to hear the case to clarify the issue and resolve the split.

Legal Research

When you research a special education legal issue, you should study:

- United States Code
- State and Federal Regulations
- U.S. Department of Education's Analysis and Commentary about the Regulations
- Judicial decisions and caselaw

If you have questions about a legal issue, read the United States Code section related to your issue. Next, read the regulation that discusses or clarifies your issue. Read the Commentary to understand the disputed issues about a regulation. Expect to read the Code and regulation several times. Then find out if there are any cases about your legal issue.[8]

If you find cases about your issue, read the earlier decisions first, then tackle the recent decisions. If you know a case was appealed, read the earlier decision that was appealed and reversed (or appealed and affirmed). When you read earlier decisions, you will see how law in that area is evolving. For every position taken by one court that the law is clear, another court is likely to interpret the law differently and arrive at a different opinion. This is the nature of law.

Legal Citations

References to law are called legal citations. Legal citations are standardized formats that explain where you will find a particular statute, regulation, or case. When you see a legal citation such as 20 U. S. C. § 1400 *et seq.*, the term "*et seq.*" means beginning at Section 1400 and continuing thereafter.

In the *United States Code,* "Findings and Purposes" are in Section 1400 of Title 20. The legal citation for Findings and Purposes is 20 U. S. C. § 1400. You may refer to Findings and Purposes as "20 U. S. C. § 1400" or "Section 1400." In *Wrightslaw: Special Education Law, 2nd Edition,* legal citations do not include the Title. For example, the full legal citation for the law about IEPs is 20 U. S. C. § 1414(d). In most cases, the authors will use a simpler format for citations, such as Section 1414(d).

In Summation

In this chapter, you learned about statutes, regulations, commentary, and caselaw. You learned about legal research, legislative intent, judicial interpretations and how law evolves. The next chapter, *A Short History of Special Education Law,* will give you an overview of the history and traditions associated with public schools and special education, and the impact of landmark legal decisions about discrimination.

---

8 Selected special education cases are in the Wrightslaw Caselaw Library at http://www.wrightslaw.com/caselaw.htm

Good sources of legal information are Findlaw.com, Versuslaw.com, and the *Individuals with Disabilities Education Law Reporter* (*IDELR*) and other publications by LRP. Many cases are not available online and must be located in a court, academic law library, or *IDELR.*

CHAPTER 3

History of Special Education Law

In these days, it is doubtful that any child may reasonably be expected to succeed in life if he is denied the opportunity of an education.[1]

To understand the battles being fought today for children with disabilities, it is important to understand the history and traditions associated with public schools and special education. In this chapter, you will learn about the evolution of public education and special education, the impact of several landmark discrimination cases, and the circumstances that led Congress to enact Public Law 94-142 in 1975.

Common Schools Teach Common Values

Waves of poor, non-English speaking, Catholic and Jewish immigrants poured into the United States during the 19th and early 20th centuries. Citizens were afraid that these new immigrants would bring class hatreds, religious intolerance, crime, and violence to America. Social and political leaders searched for ways to "reach down into the lower portions of the population and teach children to share the values, ideals and controls held by the rest of society."[2]

An educational reformer named Horace Mann proposed a solution to these social problems. He recommended that communities establish common schools funded by tax dollars. He believed that when children from different social, religious and economic backgrounds were educated together, they would learn to accept and respect each other. Common schools taught common values that included self-discipline and tolerance for others. These common schools would socialize children, improve interpersonal relationships, and improve social conditions.[3]

For public schools to succeed in the mission of socializing children, all children had to attend school. Poor children attended school sporadically, quit early, or didn't enter school at all. Public school authorities lobbied their legislatures for compulsory school attendance laws. Compulsory attendance laws gave school officials the power to prosecute parents legally if they failed to send their children to school.[4]

Early Special Education Programs

The first special education programs were delinquency prevention programs for "at risk" children who lived in urban slums. Urban school districts designed manual training classes as a supplement to their general education programs. By 1890, hundreds of thousands of children were learning carpentry, metal work, sewing, cooking and drawing in manual classes. Children were also taught social values in these classes. Early special education programs also focused on the "moral training" of African-American children.[5]

Special schools and special classes for children with disabilities, especially deafness, blindness, and mental retardation did exist in 19th century America and gradually increased during the 20th century.[6] Programs for

---

1 *Brown v. Board of Education*, 347 U.S. 483 (1954)
2 Church, Robert L. (1976) *Education in the United States*, page 81 (New York: The Free Press)
3 Cremin, Lawrence A. (1967) *The Transformation of the School: Progressivism in American Education, 1876-1957*, pages 183-194 (New York: Knopf)
4 Sperry, David, Philip T. K. Daniel, Dixie Snow Huefner, E. Gordon Gee. (1998) *Education Law and the Public Schools: A Compendium*, pages 139-145 (Norwood, MA: Christopher-Gordon Publishers, Inc.); Cremin, pages 182-226
5 Cremin, pages 182-226
6 See, for example, *History of the Vineland Training School* at www.vineland.org/history/training school/history/history. html for children with mental retardation, *Perkins School for the Blind* at www.massmoments.org/index.cfm?mid=68, and *The American School for the Deaf* at www.asd-1817.org/about/index.html. (Retrieved on October 11, 2006)

children with specific learning disabilities (called "brain injury," "minimal brain dysfunction," and other terms) became more common in the 1940's.[7]

However, many early special education programs were private and/or residential. The quality and availability of programs varied between and within states. Good special education programs were rare and difficult to access. For most children with disabilities, special education programs were simply not available. [8]

Brown v. Board of Education (1954)

In 1954, the U. S. Supreme Court issued a landmark civil rights decision in *Brown v. Board of Education*.[9] In *Brown*, school children from four states argued that segregated public schools were inherently unequal and deprived them of equal protection of the laws. The Supreme Court found that African-American children had the right to equal educational opportunities and that segregated schools "have no place in the field of public education." The Court wrote:

> Today, education is perhaps the most important function of state and local governments. Compulsory school attendance laws and the great expenditures for education both demonstrate our recognition of the importance of education to our democratic society. It is required in the performance of our most basic public responsibilities, even service in the armed forces. It is the very foundation of good citizenship. Today, it is a principal instrument in awakening the child to cultural values, in preparing him for later professional training, and in helping him to adjust normally to his environment. In these days, it is doubtful that any child may reasonably be expected to succeed in life if he is denied the opportunity of an education. Such an opportunity, where the state has undertaken to provide it, is a right that must be made available to all on equal terms.[10]

> We come then to the question presented: Does segregation of children in public schools solely on the basis of race, even though the physical facilities and other "tangible" factors may be equal, deprive the children of the minority group of equal educational opportunities? We believe that it does.[11]

In *Brown*, the Supreme Court described the emotional impact that segregation has on children, especially when segregation "has the sanction of the law:"

> To separate them from others of similar age and qualifications solely because of their race generates a feeling of inferiority as to their status in the community that may affect their hearts and minds in a way unlikely ever to be undone. The effect of this separation on their educational opportunities was well stated by a finding in the Kansas case by a court that nevertheless felt compelled to rule against the Negro plaintiffs:

> > Segregation of white and colored children in public schools has a detrimental effect upon the colored children. The impact is greater when it has the sanction of the law; for the policy of separating the races is usually interpreted as denoting the inferiority of the Negro group. A sense of inferiority affects the motivation of a child to learn. Segregation with the sanction of law, therefore, has a tendency to [retard] the educational and mental development of Negro children and to deprive them of some of the benefits they would receive in a racially integrated school system.[12]

7 Hallahan, Daniel P. and Cecil D. Mercer (2001) Learning Disabilities: Historical Perspectives. *Learning Disabilities Summit: Building a Foundation for the Future* at www.nrcld.org/html/information/articles/ldsummit/hallahan.html (Retrieved on October 11, 2006)

8 See *History of Crotched Mountain School for the Deaf* at www.crotchedmountain.org/crotchedmountain/html/deafschool.htm (Retrieved on October 11, 2006)

9 *Brown v. Board of Education*, 347 U.S. 483 (1954) www.wrightslaw.com/law/caselaw/ussupct.brown.bd.ed.htm

10 *Id.*, at page 493

11 *Id.*, at page 493

12 *Id.*, at page 494

After the decision in *Brown*, parents of children with disabilities began to bring lawsuits against their school districts for excluding and segregating children with disabilities. The parents argued that, by excluding these children, schools were discriminating against the children because of their disabilities.

Elementary and Secondary Education Act of 1965 (ESEA)

Congress enacted the Elementary and Secondary Education Act (ESEA) in 1965 to address the inequality of educational opportunity for underprivileged children. This landmark legislation provided resources to help ensure that disadvantaged students had access to quality education. [13]

In 1966, Congress amended the ESEA to establish a grant program to help states in the "initiation, expansion, and improvement of programs and projects . . . for the education of handicapped children."[14] In 1970, Congress enacted the Education of the Handicapped Act (P.L. 91-230) in an effort to encourage states to develop educational programs for individuals with disabilities. According to the National Council on Disability:

> Congress first addressed the education of students with disabilities in 1966 when it amended the Elementary and Secondary Education Act of 1965 to establish a grant program to assist states in the "initiation, expansion, and improvement of programs and projects . . . for the education of handicapped children." In 1970, that program was replaced by the Education of the Handicapped Act (P.L. 91-230) that, like its predecessor, established a grant program aimed at stimulating the States to develop educational programs and resources for individuals with disabilities. Neither program included any specific mandates on the use of the funds provided by the grants; nor could either program be shown to have significantly improved the education of children with disabilities.[15]

PARC and *Mills*

During the early 1970s, two cases were catalysts for change: *Pennsylvania Assn. for Retarded Children v. Commonwealth of Pennsylvania (PARC),*[16] and *Mills v. Board of Education of District of Columbia.*[17]

PARC dealt with the exclusion of children with mental retardation from public schools. In the subsequent settlement, it was agreed that educational placement decisions must include a process of parental participation and a means to resolve disputes.[18]

Mills involved the practice of suspending, expelling and excluding children with disabilities from the District of Columbia public schools. The school district's primary defense in *Mills*[19] was the high cost of educating children with disabilities.[20]

> The genesis of this case is found (1) in the failure of the District of Columbia to provide publicly supported education and training to plaintiffs and other "exceptional" children, members of their class,

---

13 See *Wrightslaw: No Child Left Behind*, page 9.

14 *Back to School on Civil Rights*, published by the National Council on Disability (2000). URL: www.ncd.gov/newsroom/ publications/2000/backtoschool_1.htm (Retrieved on October 11, 2006)

15 *Id.*

16 334 F. Supp. 1257 (E. D. Pa, 1971) and 343 F. Supp. 279 (E. D. Pa. 1972)

17 348 F. Supp. 866 (D. DC 1972)

18 *PARC* at page 303

19 Financial cost is often the primary defense in special education cases before the U.S. Supreme Court.

20 In 2005, the National Council on Disabilities commissioned this author to write a comprehensive Position Statement about the Burden of Proof issues that were pending before the U.S. Supreme Court in *Schaffer v. Weast*. This Statement was filed with the Court. See *IDEA Burden of Proof: On Parents or Schools?* www.ncd.gov/newsroom/publications/2005/burdenofproof.htm (Retrieved on October 11, 2006) The history of the *Mills* case and the unique rulings by the District Court Judge Waddy were discussed in depth in the Position Statement. Many procedural safeguards in Section 1415 were taken almost verbatim from his Orders.

and (2) the excluding, suspending, expelling, reassigning and transferring of "exceptional" children from regular public school classes without affording them due process of law.[21]

Congressional Investigation (1972)

After *PARC* and *Mills*, Congress launched an investigation into the status of children with disabilities and found that millions of children were not receiving an appropriate education:

> Yet, the most recent statistics provided by the Bureau of Education for the Handicapped estimated that of the more than 8 million children . . . with handicapping conditions requiring special education and related services, only 3.9 million such children are receiving an appropriate education. 1.75 million handicapped children are receiving no educational services at all, and 2.5 million handicapped children are receiving an inappropriate education.[22]

The investigation so moved members of Congress that they wrote:

> The long-range implications of these statistics are that public agencies and taxpayers will spend billions of dollars over the lifetimes of these individuals to maintain such persons as dependents and in a minimally acceptable lifestyle. With proper education services, many would be able to become productive citizens, contributing to society instead of being forced to remain burdens. Others, through such services, would increase their independence, thus reducing their dependence on society.[23]

> There is no pride in being forced to receive economic assistance. Not only does this have negative effects upon the handicapped person, but it has far-reaching effects for such person's family.[24]

> Providing educational services will ensure against persons needlessly being forced into institutional settings. One need only look at public residential institutions to find thousands of persons whose families are no longer able to care for them and who themselves have received no educational services. Billions of dollars are expended each year to maintain persons in these subhuman conditions . . . .[25]

> Parents of handicapped children all too frequently are not able to advocate the rights of their children because they have been erroneously led to believe that their children will not be able to lead meaningful lives . . . . It should not . . . be necessary for parents throughout the country to continue utilizing the courts to assure themselves a remedy . . . .[26]

In 1972, legislation was introduced in Congress after several "landmark court cases establishing in law the right to education for all handicapped children."[27]

Public Law 94-142: The Education for All Handicapped Children Act of 1975

On November 19, 1975, Congress enacted Public Law 94-142, also known as The Education for All Handicapped Children Act of 1975. Congress intended that all children with disabilities would "have a right to education, and to establish a process by which State and local educational agencies may be held accountable for providing educational services for all handicapped children."[28]

Initially, the law focused on ensuring that children with disabilities had access to an education and due process of law. Congress included an elaborate system of legal checks and balances called "procedural safeguards" that are designed to protect the rights of children and their parents.

---

21 *Mills* at page 868
22 U. S. C. C. A. N. 1975 at page 1433
23 *Id.*, at page 1433
24 *Id.*, at page 1433
25 *Id.*, at page 1433
26 *Id.*, at page 1433
27 *United States Code Congressional and Administrative News 1975* (U. S. C. C. A. N. 1975) at page 1430
28 *Id.*, at page 1427

Individuals with Disabilities Education Improvement Act of 2004

Congress has amended and renamed the special education law several times since 1975. On December 3, 2004, the Individuals with Disabilities Education Act was amended again. The reauthorized statute is the Individuals with Disabilities Education Improvement Act of 2004 and is known as IDEA 2004. The statute is in Volume 20 of the United States Code (U. S. C.), beginning at Section 1400. The special education regulations are published in Volume 34 of the Code of Federal Regulations (CFR) beginning at Section 300.

In reauthorizing the IDEA, Congress increased the focus on accountability and improved outcomes by emphasizing reading, early intervention, and research-based instruction by requiring that special education teachers be highly qualified.

Purposes

The Individuals with Disabilities Education Act of 2004 has two primary purposes. The first purpose is to provide an education that meets a child's unique needs and prepares the child for further education, employment, and independent living. The second purpose is to protect the rights of both children with disabilities and their parents. [29]

Overrepresentation of Minority Children

In 1975, Congress found that poor African-American children were over-represented in special education. These problems have persisted. In the Findings of IDEA 2004, Congress described ongoing problems with the over-identification of minority children, including mislabeling and high dropout rates:

(A) Greater efforts are needed to prevent the intensification of problems connected with mislabeling and high dropout rates among minority children with disabilities.

(B) More minority children continue to be served in special education than would be expected from the percentage of minority students in the general school population.

(C) African-American children are identified as having mental retardation and emotional disturbance at rates greater than their White counterparts.

(D) In the 1998-1999 school year, African-American children represented just 14.8 percent of the population aged 6 through 21, but comprised 20.2 percent of all children with disabilities.

(E) Studies have found that schools with predominately White students and teachers have placed disproportionately high numbers of their minority students into special education. [30]

Aligning IDEA and NCLB

The IDEA 2004 reauthorization emphasized the need to align IDEA with other school improvement efforts, specifically "improvement efforts under the Elementary and Secondary Education Act of 1965." [31] Congress found that:

... the education of children with disabilities can be made more effective by ... having high expectations for such children and ensuring their access to the general education curriculum in the regular classroom ... to meet developmental goals and ... the challenging expectations that have been established for all children .... [32]

---

29 20 U. S. C. §1400(d)(1)
30 20 U. S. C. §1400(c)(12)
31 20 U. S. C. §1400(c)(5)(C)
32 20 U. S. C. §1400(c)(5)(A)

The purpose of the No Child Left Behind Act of 2001 is "to ensure that **all children have a fair, equal, and significant opportunity** to obtain a high-quality education and reach, at a minimum, proficiency on challenging State academic achievement standards and state academic assessments."[33]

IDEA requires states to establish goals for the performance of children with disabilities that are consistent with the goals and standards for nondisabled children. States are also required to improve graduation rates and dropout rates, and to report the progress of children with disabilities on state and district assessments. [34]

In Findings, Congress described a critical need for adequately trained personnel and that "high quality, comprehensive professional development programs are essential to ensure that the persons responsible for the education or transition of children with disabilities possess the knowledge and skills necessary to address the educational and related needs of those children."[35] Special education teachers who teach core academic subjects must meet the highly qualified teacher requirements in NCLB and must demonstrate competence in the subjects they teach.[36] These requirements for highly qualified special education teachers bring IDEA into conformity with the No Child Left Behind Act.

In Summation

In this chapter, you learned how public education and special education evolved, the impact of landmark cases about racial and disability discrimination, the circumstances that led Congress to enact Public Law 94-142 in 1975, and how the law has evolved over the past thirty years.

In Section Two, you will learn about the Individuals with Disabilities Education Act of 2004. Chapter 4 provides an overview of IDEA 2004, how the law is organized, and new requirements in the law. Chapter 5 begins with a Table of Statutes, followed by the full text of the Individuals with Disabilities Education Act with commentary, cross-references and resources. Chapter 6 is the full text of the federal special education regulations.

---

33 20 U. S. C. § 6301

34 20 U. S. C. § 1412(a)(15)

35 20 U. S. C. § 1450(6)

36 The definition of a "highly qualified teacher" is in Title IX of No Child Left Behind at Section 7801(23) and is also referenced in Section 6319 of NCLB. In IDEA, the definition of "highly qualified" is in Section 1401(10).

Section Two

Individuals with Disabilities Education Act of 2004

CHAPTER 4

An Overview of IDEA 2004

The Individuals with Disabilities Education Act of 2004 includes significant changes from the previous authorization in 1997. This chapter provides an overview of the law, how the law is organized, and new requirements in IDEA 2004.

Accountability, Improved Outcomes, Research Based Instruction

When Congress reauthorized the law, it focused on accountability and improved outcomes by bringing IDEA 2004 into conformity with the No Child Left Behind Act (NCLB).

IDEA 2004 requires schools to use "proven methods of teaching and learning" based on "replicable research." Many schools continue to use educational methods that are not research-based. Pressure from litigation and No Child Left Behind requirements are forcing school districts to adopt research-based methods of teaching. IDEA 2004 also includes new requirements for early intervening services and highly qualified special education teachers.

The Individuals with Disabilities Education Act of 2004 is divided into five parts:

Part A – General Provisions (Sections 1400 – 1409)

Part B – Assistance for Education of All Children with Disabilities (Sections 1411 – 1419)

Part C – Infants and Toddlers with Disabilities (Sections 1431 – 1444)

Part D – National Activities to Improve Education of Children with Disabilities (Sections 1450 – 1482)

Part E – National Center for Special Education Research (Section 9567)

Parents, advocates, attorneys, and educators will refer most often to the following sections:

Section 1400 – Findings and Purposes

Section 1401 – Definitions

Section 1412 – State Responsibility (the Catch-all Section)

Section 1414 – Evaluations, Eligibility, Individual Education Programs, Educational Placements

Section 1415 – Procedural Safeguards

Part A – General Provisions

Part A of the Individuals with Disabilities Education Act of 2004 includes Sections 1400 through Section 1409 of Title 20 of the United States Code (U. S. C.). Section 1400 describes the Findings and Purposes of the law. The legal definitions in alphabetical order are in Section 1401. Section 1403 advises that states are not immune from suit if they violate IDEA. Section 1408 is a new section about paperwork reduction.

Section 1400: Findings & Purposes

The most important section in the Individuals with Disabilities Education Act is Section 1400 which describes the Findings and Purposes of the law.

Findings

The history and findings that led Congress to pass the federal special education law that is now the Individuals with Disabilities Education Improvement Act (IDEA 2004) are in Section 1400(c). When Congress enacted the Education for All Handicapped Children Act (Public Law 94-142) in 1975, fewer than half of all children with disabilities were receiving an appropriate education. More than one million children were excluded from school.[1] Initially, the law focused on ensuring that children had *access* to an education and due process of law.

In Findings of IDEA, Congress described obstacles to implementation of the law:

. . . implementation of this title has been impeded by low expectations, and an insufficient focus on applying replicable research on proven methods of teaching and learning for children with disabilities.[2]

Congress reported that "over 30 years of research and experience" demonstrated that special education would be more effective by:

. . . having high expectations for such children and ensuring their access to the general education curriculum in regular classrooms, to the maximum extent possible . . . to meet the challenging expectations that have been established for all children; and be prepared to lead productive and independent lives to the maximum extent possible.[3]

When Congress reauthorized the Individuals with Disabilities Education Act in 2004, they added new language to Findings about meeting the "developmental goals" and "challenging expectations that have been established for nondisabled children" so children will "be prepared to lead productive and independent adult lives."[4]

Purposes

The most important statute in IDEA is Purposes in Section 1400(d). The main purposes are:

. . . to ensure that all children with disabilities have available to them a free appropriate public education that emphasizes special education and related services designed to **meet their unique needs** and **prepare them for further education, employment and independent living**" and "to ensure that the **rights of children** with disabilities **and parents** of such children **are protected** . . .[5]

Purposes is the mission statement of IDEA. When you are developing IEPs, use this mission statement as your long-term goal. If you are confused about a term or section in the law, go back and re-read Section 1400, especially Purposes in Section 1400(d).

Section 1401: Definitions

Section 1401 of IDEA 2004 includes thirty-six legal definitions. Read these definitions carefully, especially the definitions of child with a disability, free appropriate public education, highly qualified teacher, special education, and transition services (below). Six new definitions were added to IDEA 2004: core academic subjects, highly qualified teacher, homeless children, limited English proficient, universal design, and ward of the state.

Child with a Disability

If you are a parent, the most important definition is likely to be "child with a disability."[6] Your child's classification as a "child with a disability" determines whether your child is eligible for special education and related services under the law.

---

1 20 U. S. C. § 1400(c)(2)
2 20 U. S. C. § 1400(c)(4)
3 20 U. S. C. § 1400(c)(5)
4 20 U. S. C. § 1400(c)(4)(A)
5 20 U. S. C. § 1400(d)(1)
6 20 U. S. C. § 1401(3)

A child with a disability is *not* automatically eligible for special education and related services under IDEA. The key phrase is "who, by reason thereof, *needs special education and related services*." Does the child's disability adversely affect educational performance? To be eligible for a free, appropriate public education under the IDEA, the child must meet both criteria.

If a child has a disability but does not need "special education and related services," the child will not be eligible under IDEA but may be eligible for protections under Section 504 of the Rehabilitation Act.

Free Appropriate Public Education (FAPE)

The definition of a "free appropriate public education"[7] is special education and related services that are provided at public expense, meet state standards, are appropriate, and are provided in conformity with an IEP. Because the definition is vague, the term has been litigated extensively since the law was enacted. In *Board of Education v. Rowley*, 458 U.S. 176 (1982), the U. S. Supreme Court concluded that the child with a disability is not entitled to the "best" education, nor to an education that maximizes the child's potential.[8]

Highly Qualified

The requirements for "highly qualified" special education teachers are new and bring IDEA into conformity with the No Child Left Behind Act (NCLB). Special education teachers who teach core academic subjects must meet the highly qualified teacher requirements in NCLB and must demonstrate competence in the subjects they teach. Special educators who do not provide instruction in core academic subjects are not required to meet the highly qualified teacher requirements.[9]

The full definition of "highly qualified teacher" is in Title IX of NCLB at Section 7801(23) and is also referenced in Section 6319 of NCLB.[10]

Special Education

The law defines "special education" as "specially designed instruction, at no cost to the parents, to meet the unique needs of a child with a disability . . . ." Special education encompasses a range of services and may include one-on-one tutoring, intensive academic remediation, services in the general education classroom, and 40-hour Applied Behavioral Analysis (ABA) programs. Special education is provided in different settings, including the child's home.[11]

Specific Learning Disability

Congress did not change the definition of "specific learning disability"[12] but did change the requirements for evaluations of children who may have specific learning disabilities. Schools "shall not be required to take into consideration whether a child has a severe discrepancy between achievement and intellectual ability . . . ." to find a child eligible for special education services as a child with a specific learning disability.[13]

Transition Services

The definition of "transition services" was changed to emphasize that transition is "a results-oriented process" to improve "the academic and functional achievement of the child with a disability." The goal of transition

---

7 20 U. S. C. § 1401(9)

8 The full text of the *Rowley* decision is in Chapter 12.

9 20 U. S. C. § 1401(10)

10 For No Child Left Behind definitions, see the Glossary of Terms in *Wrightslaw: No Child Left Behind*.

11 20 U. S. C. § 1401(29)

12 20 U. S. C. § 1401(30)

13 20 U. S. C. § 1414(b)(6)

is to facilitate the child's transition from school to employment and further education. Transition services must be based on "the individual child's needs, taking into account the child's strengths, preferences, and interests."[14]

Part B – Assistance for Education of All Children with Disabilities

Part B governs special education and related services for children with disabilities between the ages of 3 and 21. For most readers, the most important statutes in Part B are Section 1412, Section 1414, and Section 1415.

Section 1412 includes child find, least restrictive environment, unilateral placements, reimbursement, and state and district assessments. Section 1414 describes requirements for initial evaluations, parental consent, re-evaluations, eligibility, IEPs, and educational placements.

Section 1415 describes the procedural safeguards designed to protect the rights of children and their parents. These safeguards include the right to examine educational records and obtain an independent educational evaluation, and the legal requirements for prior written notice, procedural safeguard notice, due process complaint notice, due process hearings, resolution sessions, mediation, attorney's fees, and discipline.

Section 1412: State Eligibility ("Catch-All Statute")

Section 1412 about State Eligibility is often called the "Catch-All" statute because it includes such diverse topics: child find, least restrictive environment, transition to preschool programs, equitable services for children in private schools, unilateral placements in private programs, tuition reimbursement, and new requirements about participation in assessments, accommodations guidelines, and alternate assessments. Although Extended School Year (ESY) is not cited in the IDEA statute, the special education regulations that interpret Section 1412 describe and clarify Extended School Year.[15]

Free Appropriate Public Education (FAPE)

To receive federal funds, states must provide assurances to the U. S. Department of Education that they have policies and procedures in place to ensure that all children with disabilities receive a free appropriate public education. The right to a free appropriate public education extends to children with disabilities who have been suspended or expelled from school.[16] To remedy problems with evaluations that led to over-representation of minority children in special education, evaluations must be administered in the child's native language or mode of communication and "no single procedure shall be the sole criterion" for eligibility.[17]

Child Find

Child find requires school districts to identify, locate, and evaluate *all* children with disabilities, including children who are home schooled, homeless, wards of the state, and children who attend private schools and determine which children are and are not receiving special education and related services.[18]

If a child has a disability and is eligible for special education services, the school does not have to give the child a "label" before providing services.[19] School districts must report data about the number of children who are evaluated, found eligible and provided services. These requirements apply to children who attend private and religious schools in the district.[20]

Children Who Attend Private Schools

The law includes new requirements about equitable participation of children who attend private schools and consultation between public and private school officials. Children who attend private school are entitled

---

14 20 U. S. C. § 1401(34)
15 34 CFR 300.106
16 20 U. S. C. § 1412(a)(1)(A)
17 20 U. S. C. § 1412(a)(6)(B)
18 20 U. S. C. § 1412(a)(3)
19 20 U. S. C. § 1412(a)(3)(B)
20 20 U. S. C. § 1412(a)(10)(A)(ii)

to equitable services. Special education and related services may be provided on the premises of private school, including religious schools.[21]

Tuition Reimbursement

The law about reimbursement for parental placements in private schools is unchanged. If the parent removes the child from a public school program and places the child into a private program, the parent may be reimbursed for the costs of the private program if a hearing officer or court determines that the public school did not offer a free, appropriate public education (FAPE) "in a timely manner."[22]

If you are a parent and you plan to request a due process hearing for tuition reimbursement, you need to be familiar with the federal statute and regulations, and your state statute and regulations. You should also read the Rules of Adverse Assumptions.[23]

Before you remove your child from the public school program, you must take specific steps if you hope to be reimbursed for the child's tuition in the private program. At the most recent IEP meeting before you remove your child from the public school program:

You must state your concerns

You must state your intent to enroll your child in a private program at public expense

    OR

Ten business days before you remove your child from the public school program, you must write a letter to the school that states:

Your specific concerns, in detail, about the inadequacy of the school's IEP and/or placement

Your basis for rejecting the IEP

Why your child will be damaged if placed in the school's proposed program

A statement of your intent to enroll your child in a private program at public expense[24]

Least Restrictive Environment (LRE), Inclusion and Mainstreaming

The description of "least restrictive environment" did not change in IDEA 2004. Schools are required to educate children with disabilities with children who are not disabled, "to the maximum extent appropriate." A child may only be removed from the regular educational setting if the nature or severity of the disability is such that the child cannot be educated in regular classes, even with the use of supplementary aids and services.[25] Judicial decisions about mainstreaming, inclusion, and least restrictive environment vary, even within the same state.

Qualifications of Special Education Teachers

The requirements about qualifications of special education teachers are new and track the highly qualified teacher requirements in the No Child Left Behind Act.[26] Teachers of core academic subjects must be highly qualified by the end of the 2005-2006 school year.[27] The requirements for related services providers and paraprofessionals did not change.

IDEA 2004 requires states to take measurable steps "to recruit, hire, train, and retain highly qualified personnel to provide special education and related services."[28] There is no "right of action," such as the right to sue a state or school district, because a teacher is not highly qualified. However, parents may file complaints about inadequately trained teachers with their State Department of Education.

---

21 20 U. S. C. § 1412(a)(10)
22 20 U. S. C. § 1412(a)(10)(C)
23 Chapter 21, *Wrightslaw: From Emotions to Advocacy.*
24 20 U. S. C. § 1412(a)(10)(C)
25 20 U. S. C. § 1412(a)(5)
26 20 U. S. C. § 1412(a)(14)
27 20 U. S. C. § 6319(a)
28 20 U. S. C. § 1412(c)(14)

Participation in State and District Assessments

Congress changed the language in IDEA about participation in assessments to "*All* children with disabilities are included in *all* general State and district wide assessment programs . . . with appropriate accommodations, where necessary and as indicated in their respective individualized education programs." [29] (emphasis added)

The requirements that schools include all children with disabilities in all state and district assessments may have a negative impact on schools that refuse to use research-based methods to teach children to read, write, spell, and do arithmetic, because these schools are less likely to meet their annual progress goals.

The requirements for accommodation guidelines and alternate assessments are new in IDEA 2004. [30] States and districts must issue reports to the public about state and district assessments, alternate assessments, and the performance of children with disabilities on these assessments. [31]

Over-Identification of Minority Children

Congress found that African-American children are identified with mental retardation and emotional disturbances at far greater rates than white children. "Studies have found that schools with predominately White students and teachers place disproportionately high numbers of minority students into special education." [32] Congress required States to develop policies and procedures "to prevent the inappropriate over identification or disproportionate representation by race and ethnicity as children with disabilities . . . ." [33]

Mandatory Medication Prohibited

IDEA 2004 prohibits school personnel from requiring a child to obtain a prescription for a controlled substance (i.e., Ritalin, Adderal) in order to attend school, receive an evaluation, or receive special education. [34]

Section 1413: Local Educational Agency Eligibility

Section 1413 includes requirements for school district (LEA) and charter school eligibility. IDEA includes new requirements about purchasing instructional materials, records of migratory children, and early intervening services.

Services to Children Who Attend Charter Schools

School districts must serve children with disabilities who attend charter schools in the same manner as children who attend other public schools, and must provide supplementary services and related services on site at the charter school. [35]

Early Intervening Services

Early intervening services are new in IDEA 2004. Early intervening services require that schools use "proven methods of teaching and learning" based on "replicable research." [36] School districts may use a portion of their Part B funds to provide early intervening services for students who need academic and behavioral assistance but have not been identified as needing special education services. Funds may also be used for professional development so teachers have the knowledge and skills to deliver scientifically based academic and literacy instruction. [37]

---

29 20 U. S. C. § 1412(c)(16)(A)
30 20 U. S. C. § 1412(a)(16)
31 20 U. S. C. § 1412(a)(16)(D)
32 20 U. S. C. § 1400(c)(12)(E)
33 20 U. S. C. § 1412(c)(24)
34 20 U. S. C. § 1412(c)(25)
35 20 U. S. C. § 1413(a)(5)
36 20 U. S. C. § 1400(c)(4)
37 20 U. S. C. § 1413(f)

Section 1414: Evaluations, Eligibility, Individualized Education Programs, and Educational Placements

The second most important statute in IDEA 2004 is Section 1414 about Evaluations, Consent, Reevaluations, Eligibility, IEPs and IEP Meetings, and Educational Placements.

Initial Evaluations

Parents, state departments of education, state agencies, and school district staff may request an initial evaluation of a child.[38] IDEA 2004 includes a new requirement that initial evaluations and eligibility be completed within 60 calendar days of receiving parental consent[39] unless a state has statutes or regulations that permit longer timelines.

Parental Consent

The school must obtain informed parental consent before conducting an initial evaluation. If the parent does not consent to an initial evaluation, or does not respond to a request to provide consent, the district may pursue a due process hearing against the parent. Parental consent for an evaluation is not consent for the child to receive special education services.[40]

The school must obtain informed parental consent before providing special education services. If the parent does not consent to special education services, the district may not pursue a due process hearing against the parent. If the parent refuses consent for services, the district has not violated the IDEA, and is not required to convene an IEP meeting or develop an IEP for the child.[41]

Reevaluations

The language about reevaluations changed in IDEA 2004. The school is not required to reevaluate a child more often than once a year, unless the parent and school agree to more frequent evaluations. The school shall evaluate at least every three years, unless the parent and school agree that a reevaluation is unnecessary. The school must reevaluate if the child's educational needs change *or* if the child's parent or teacher requests a reevaluation.[42]

Placing limits on the frequency of evaluations is likely to create difficulties in developing appropriate IEPs. IDEA 2004 requires the IEP to include "a statement of the child's present levels of academic achievement and functional performance."[43] If a child has not been evaluated for a year or more, the IEP team will not have current information about the child's present levels of academic achievement and functional performance on which to base the IEP.

Evaluation Procedures

The language about evaluation procedures changed in IDEA 2004. The school shall "use a variety of assessment tools and strategies to gather relevant functional, developmental, and academic information" about the child. Information from evaluations will be used to determine the content of the child's IEP and to help the child make progress in the general education curriculum.[44]

The school shall "not use any single measure or assessment as the sole criterion" for determining if a child is eligible for special education services. The language about assessing children "in all areas of suspected disability" and that assessments shall provide relevant information to determine the child's educational needs did not

---

38 20 U. S. C. § 1414(a)(1)(B)
39 20 U. S. C. § 1414(a)(1)(C)
40 20 U. S. C. § 1414(a)(1)(D)(i)
41 20 U. S. C. § 1414(a)(1)(D)(ii)
42 20 U. S. C. § 1414(a)(2)
43 20 U. S. C. § 1414(d)(1)(A)(i)
44 20 U. S. C. § 1414(b)(2)(A)

change.[45] A "screener"[46] by a teacher or educational diagnostician to determine instructional strategies does not comply with the requirements for evaluations.

IDEA 2004 includes new requirements for assessments. The school must ensure that assessments are not "discriminatory on a racial or cultural basis . . . are provided and administered in the language and form most likely to yield accurate information on what the child knows and can do academically, developmentally, and functionally . . . [and] are administered by trained and knowledgeable personnel."[47]

When a child transfers to a new school, the receiving school must complete assessments "as expeditiously as possible to ensure prompt completion of full evaluations."[48]

Eligibility and Educational Need

In IDEA 2004, the heading "Determination of Eligibility" was changed to "Determination of Eligibility and Educational Need."[49] A team of qualified professionals and the child's parent determine "whether the child is a child with a disability . . . and the educational needs of the child . . . ." The school shall give the parents copies of the evaluation report and documentation of eligibility.[50]

If the school decides that a child with a disability is not eligible for special education services under IDEA, or the parent disagrees with the school's classification or label, the parent should consider obtaining a comprehensive psycho-educational evaluation by an expert in the private sector.

Lack of Appropriate Instruction

Many experts in the field of learning disabilities believe that a majority of children identified with specific learning disabilities are "victims of poor teaching." Almost all children can learn to read if taught appropriately, but many do not get appropriate instruction because teachers are not adequately prepared.[51]

A child shall not be found eligible if the child's problems are due to "lack of appropriate instruction in reading, including in the essential components of reading instruction, lack of instruction in math, or limited English proficiency."[52] This language about "lack of appropriate instruction in reading, including the essential components of reading instruction" is new and brings IDEA into conformity with NCLB.

The essential components of reading instruction are defined as explicit and systematic instruction in (A) phonemic awareness; (B) phonics; (C) vocabulary development; (D) reading fluency, including oral reading skills; and (E) reading comprehension strategies.[53]

Identifying Children with Specific Learning Disabilities

The school is not required to consider if a child has a severe discrepancy between achievement and intellectual ability to determine if the child has a specific learning disability and needs special education services. The school district may use Response to Intervention (RTI)[54] to determine if the child responds to scientific, research-based

---

45 20 U. S. C. § 1414(b)(3)

46 20 U. S. C. § 6368(7)(B); see *Wrightslaw: No Child Left Behind*.

47 20 U. S. C. § 1414(b)(3)

48 20 U. S. C. § 1414(b)(3)(D)

49 20 U. S. C. § 1414(b)(4)

50 20 U. S. C. § 1414(b)(4)

51 Lyon, G. Reid and Jack M. Fletcher. Early Warning System. www.educationext.org/20012/22.html (Retrieved October 11, 2006)

52 20 U. S. C. § 1414(b)(5)

53 See 20 U. S. C. § 6368 in *Wrightslaw: No Child Left Behind*.

54 20 U. S. C. § 1414(b)(6)

intervention as part of the evaluation process.[55, 56] The legal definition of "scientifically based reading research" is in No Child Left Behind.[57]

The law includes new language that allows school personnel to decide that "no additional data are needed" to determine the child's educational needs or eligibility.[58] This language appears to be at odds with the requirement that the school reevaluate "at least once every three years."[59]

Additional Requirements for Evaluations and Reevaluations

Information from evaluations and reevaluations shall be used to determine "the educational needs of the child" and "the present levels of academic achievement and related developmental needs of the child." The school must review evaluations and information provided by the parents.[60]

"Additional Requirements for Evaluations and Reevaluations" changed in IDEA 2004. If the IEP team and other qualified professionals decide they do not need additional data to determine if the child is eligible or the child's educational needs, the school can notify the parents that they do not intend to reevaluate. The school must provide the reasons for this decision. Under these circumstances, the parent must specifically request a reevaluation.[61]

The school must evaluate the child before terminating the child's eligibility for special education services. The school is not required to evaluate when the child graduates from high school with a regular diploma or "ages out" of special education.[62] However, if the child graduates with a regular diploma or is no longer eligible for services because of age, the school must provide the child with a summary of "academic and functional performance" and recommendations to help the child meet postsecondary goals.[63]

Individualized Education Programs (IEPs)

Present Levels of Academic Achievement and Functional Performance

Your child's IEP must include a statement of the child's present levels of academic achievement and functional performance, including how the child's disability affects the child's involvement and performance in the general education curriculum.[64]

Measurable Goals

Your child's IEP must also include "a statement of measurable annual goals" to address the child's present levels of academic achievement and functional performance.[65]

Congress added new language about research-based instruction to IDEA 2004. The child's IEP must include "a statement of the special education and related services and supplementary aids and services, based on peer-reviewed research to the extent practicable, to be provided to the child . . . and a statement of program modifications or supports for school personnel that will be provided for the child."[66]

---

55 See "Responsiveness to Intervention in the SLD Determination Process" in *Tool Kit on Teaching and Assessing Students with Disabilities* published by the U. S. Department of Education at www.osepideasthatwork.org/toolkit/pdf/RTI_SLD.pdf
56 For more articles, publications and other resources about Response to Intervention, go to: http://www.wrightslaw.com/info/rti.index.htm
57 20 U. S. C. § 6368(6); see also the "Glossary of Terms" in this book.
58 20 U. S. C. § 1414(c)(4)
59 20 U. S. C. § 1414(a)(2)(B)(ii)
60 20 U. S. C. § 1414(c)(1)
61 20 U. S. C. § 1414(c)(4))
62 20 U. S. C. § 1414(c)(5)
63 20 U. S. C. § 1414(c)(5)(B)
64 20 U. S. C. § 1414(d)(1)(A)
65 20 U. S. C. § 1414(d)(1)(A)
66 20 U. S. C. § 1414(d)(1)(A)

Educational Progress

The IEP must include "a description of how the child's progress toward meeting the annual goals . . . will be measured and when periodic reports on the progress the child is making toward meeting the annual goals (such as through the use of quarterly or other periodic reports, concurrent with the issuance of report cards) will be provided."[67]

Appropriate Accommodations and Alternate Assessments

IDEA contains new language about "individual appropriate accommodations" on state and district testing and new requirements for alternate assessments. Your child's IEP must include "a statement of any individual appropriate accommodations that are necessary to measure the academic achievement and functional performance of the child on State and districtwide assessments . . . ."

If the IEP Team recommends that your child take an alternate assessment, the team must include a statement about "why the child cannot participate in the regular assessment" and why "the particular alternate assessment selected is appropriate for the child . . . ."[68]

Transition Requirements

The requirements for transition in IEPs changed in IDEA 2004. The "first IEP to be in effect when the child is 16, and updated annually thereafter [must include] appropriate measurable postsecondary goals based upon age appropriate transition assessments related to training, education, employment, and, where appropriate, independent living skills . . . and the transition services (including courses of study) needed to assist the child in reaching these goals."[69]

IEP Team Meetings

A member of the IEP team may be excused from attending an IEP meeting if the member's area of curriculum or service will not be discussed or modified and if the parent and school agree. An IEP team member may also be excused from an IEP meeting that involves their area of curriculum or service if they submit input in writing and if the parent and school consent. The parent's consent must be in writing.[70]

Children Who Transfer Schools

The subsection about IEPs for children who transfer is new. If the child transfers to a district in the same state or another state, the receiving school must provide comparable services to those in the sending district's IEP until they develop and implement a new IEP.[71]

Developing the IEP

In developing the IEP, the IEP team *shall* (i.e. must) consider:

- the child's strengths

- the parent's concerns for enhancing the child's education

- the results of the initial evaluation or most recent evaluation

- the child's academic, developmental, and functional needs[72]

---

67 20 U. S. C. § 1414(d)(1)(A)
68 20 U. S. C. § 1414(d)(1)(VI)
69 20 U. S. C. § 1414(d)(1)(A)(i)(VIII)
70 20 U. S. C. § 1414(d)(1)(C)
71 20 U. S. C. § 1414(d)(2)(C)
72 20 U. S. C. § 1414(d)(3)(A)

The IEP team *shall* consider special factors for children:

- whose behavior impedes learning
- who have limited English proficiency
- who are blind or visually impaired
- who are deaf or hard of hearing[73]

Reviewing and Revising IEPs

The child's IEP must be reviewed at least once a year to determine if the child is achieving the annual goals. In addition, the IEP team must revise the IEP to address:

- any lack of expected progress
- results of any reevaluation
- information provided by the parents
- anticipated needs[74]

IDEA 2004 also changed how IEPs may be revised. If the parent and school decide to amend or modify the IEP that was developed at an annual IEP meeting, and they do not want to convene another IEP Team meeting, they may revise the IEP by agreement. The IEP Team must create a written document to amend or modify the IEP. This document must describe the changes or modification in the IEP and note that, by agreement of the parties, an IEP meeting was not convened. [75] The parent should be provided with a copy of the revised IEP.

Multi-Year IEPs

IDEA 2004 includes a multi-year IEP pilot project. States may request approval to implement "comprehensive, multi-year IEPs" for periods of no longer than three years. IEP review dates must be based on "natural transition points." Parents have the right to opt-out of this program and can request a review of the IEP without waiting for the natural transition point.[76]

Placement Decisions

Parents are members of the team that decides the child's placement. Decisions about the child's placement cannot be made until after the IEP team, which includes the parent, reaches consensus about the child's needs, program, and goals.

Although the law is clear on this issue, the child's "label" or eligibility category often drives decisions about services and placement, leading school personnel to determine the child's placement before the IEP meeting. These unilateral actions prevent parents from "meaningful participation" in educational decision-making for their child.[77]

New Ways to Meet

School meetings do not have to be face-to-face. IEP and placement meetings, mediation meetings, and due process (IEP) resolution sessions may be convened by conference calls or videoconferences.[78]

---

73 20 U. S. C. § 1414(d)(3)(B)
74 20 U. S. C. § 1414(d)(4)
75 20 U. S. C. § 1414(d)(3)(D)
76 20 U. S. C. § 1414(d)(5)
77 20 U. S. C. § 1414(e)
78 20 U. S. C. § 1414(f)

Section 1415: Procedural Safeguards

Section 1415 describes the safeguards designed to protect the rights of children with disabilities and their parents. These safeguards include the right to participate in all meetings, to examine all educational records, and to obtain an Independent Educational Evaluation (IEE) of the child. Section 1415 includes requirements for prior written notice, procedural safeguards notice, mediation, resolution sessions, due process hearings, the new two-year statute of limitations, appeals, discipline, and age of majority.

Prior Written Notice (PWN)

If the school district proposes to change or refuses to change the identification, evaluation, or educational placement of a child, the school must provide the parent with written notice.[79] The written notice must:

- describe the action proposed or refused

- explain why the school proposed or refused to take action

- describe each evaluation procedure, assessment, record, or report used as a basis for the proposed or refused action

- provide sources the parent can contact to obtain assistance

- describe other options considered and why these options were rejected

- describe the factors that were relevant to the school's proposal or refusal[80], [81]

Due Process Complaint Notice

The party who requests a due process hearing must provide a detailed notice to the other party that includes identifying information about the child, the nature of the problem, facts, and a proposed resolution.[82] A Due Process Complaint Notice can be a letter to request a due process hearing that includes the required components.[83] A due process hearing may not be held until after this notice has been filed.

Procedural Safeguards Notice

The Procedural Safeguards Notice[84] provides parents with specific information about their rights and protections under the law, including the right to an Independent Educational Evaluation (IEE), prior written notice, the right to examine all educational records, notice of the time period (statute of limitations) within which "to make a complaint," mediation, due process, current educational placement, discipline, reimbursement for private placements, and attorneys' fees.[85]

Independent Educational Evaluation (IEE)

Parents have a right to obtain an Independent Educational Evaluation of their child.[86] School districts often attempt to restrict the parent's choice to a list of approved evaluators selected by the district. In 2004, the Office of Special Education Programs issued a policy letter to clarify that parents have the right to choose their independent evaluator.[87]

---

79 20 U. S. C. §1415(b)(3)

80 20 U. S. C. §1415(c)(1)

81 The U. S. Department of Education published a Model Prior Written Notice Form at www.ed.gov/policy/speced/guid/idea/modelform-notice.pdf (Retrieved on October 12, 2006)

82 20 U. S. C. §1415(b)(7); 20 U. S. C. §1415(c)(2)

83 To learn how to write persuasive letters, read Chapter 24, "Letter to the Stranger, in *Wrightslaw: From Emotions to Advocacy.*

84 20 U. S. C. § 1415(d)

85 The U. S. Department of Education published a Model Procedural Safeguards Form at: www.ed.gov/policy/speced/guid/idea/modelform-safeguards.pdf (Retrieved on October 11, 2006)

86 20 U. S. C. §1415(b(1)

87 See "Letter to Parker" www.wrightslaw.com/info/test.eval.choice.osep.htm

Mediation

The right to use mediation to resolve disputes was added to IDEA in 1997. Mediation must be voluntary, may not be used to deny or delay a parent's right to a due process hearing, and must be conducted by a qualified, impartial mediator.

Mediation is a confidential process in which the parties meet with a disinterested party in an effort to resolve their dispute. A successful mediation requires the parties to discuss their views and differences frankly. Before entering into mediation, both parties should understand their rights and the law. A due process hearing does not have to be pending for a party to request mediation.[88]

Written Settlement Agreements

The requirements for legally binding written settlement agreements are new in IDEA 2004. Previously, when a party breached or failed to honor a mediation agreement, the other party had to file suit under a breach of contract theory to enforce the agreement. Now, a party can use the power of federal courts to ensure that settlement agreements are honored.[89]

Due Process Hearings

Many pre-trial procedures and timelines for due process hearings are new in IDEA 2004, including the resolution session,[90] due process complaint notice, amended complaint notice, statute of limitations and timelines.

Statute of Limitations

The two-year statute of limitations to present a complaint is new.[91] If your state does not have a statute of limitations, you must request a due process hearing within two years. If a due process hearing may be on the horizon, you need to know the statute of limitations in your state.

Because IDEA 2004 includes new, different procedural requirements for pretrial matters in due process hearings, you should assume that your state revised the state special education law and regulations. You should contact your State Department of Education / State Education Agency (SEA) to request the statute of limitations in your state. Be sure to get this information in writing.

New Procedures and Timelines

If the school did not provide prior written notice to the parents previously, the school must send that notice within 10 days. After receiving the due process complaint notice, the other party must file a response that specifically addresses the issues raised in the complaint within 10 days. If the notice is insufficient, the receiving party must complain to the hearing officer within 15 days.[92]

The hearing officer must determine if the complaint is sufficient within 5 days.[93] A party may only amend its due process complaint notice if the other party consents in writing and is given the opportunity to resolve the dispute by using a resolution session.[94] This requirement is similar to the "12(b)(6)" Motion to Dismiss proceeding in the Federal Rules of Civil Procedure (FRCP).[95]

---

88 20 U. S. C. § 1415(e)
89 20 U. S. C. § 1415(e)(2)(F)
90 20 U. S. C. § 1415(f)(B)
91 20 U. S. C. § 1415(b)(6)(B)
92 20 U. S. C. § 1415(c)(2)
93 20 U. S. C. § 1415(c)
94 20 U. S. C. § 1415(c)(2)(E); 20 U. S. C. §1415(f)(1)(B)
95 20 U. S. C. § 1415(c)(2)

Resolution Session

After the school district receives the parent's due process complaint notice, it is required to convene a resolution session within 15 days, even if the Notice is insufficient. The resolution session provides the parties with an opportunity to resolve their dispute before a due process hearing. The school district must send the "relevant member or members of the IEP team" who have knowledge about the facts in the parent's complaint and a district representative who has decision-making authority (settlement authority).[96] The school board attorney may not attend the resolution session unless an attorney accompanies the parent.

The parent and the district may agree to waive the resolution session or use mediation. If the district has not resolved the complaint to the parents' satisfaction within 30 days of receiving the Complaint, the due process hearing can be held.[97]

"Five-Day Rule"

The law requires that evaluations and recommendations be disclosed within 5 business days before a due process hearing.[98] Most state statutes and regulations, and standards of practice, require that all exhibits, exhibit lists, and witness lists be disclosed at least 5 days before a hearing.[99] Failure to comply with these requirements about disclosure often causes hearing officers to dismiss cases.[100]

Substantive v. Procedural Issues

IDEA 2004 clarifies that "a decision made by a hearing officer shall be made on substantive grounds based on a determination of whether the child received a free appropriate public education."[101] Examples of substantive issues include determining if the child has a disability that adversely affects educational performance (eligibility) or if the child received a free appropriate education (FAPE). Examples of procedural issues include delays in scheduling evaluations or convening meetings, or not having all appropriate personnel at an IEP meeting.

Minimum Standards for Hearing Officers

IDEA now requires that hearing officers be knowledgeable about the law, federal and state regulations, and caselaw. Hearing officers must also have the knowledge and ability to "conduct hearings and write decisions in accordance with appropriate standard legal practice."[102]

Attorneys' Fees from Parents and Their Attorneys

Parents who prevail can recover attorneys' fees from school districts. Under IDEA 2004, school districts may recover attorneys' fees from the parent or the parent's attorney under specific limited circumstances. If the parent or parent's attorney files a complaint that is frivolous, unreasonable, or for an improper purpose, or to harass, cause unnecessary delay, or needlessly increase the cost of litigation, the Court may award attorneys' fees to the school district.[103]

Discipline

Section 1415(k) includes requirements for disciplinary placements in interim alternative educational settings, manifestation determinations, placements, appeals, and authority of the hearing officer.

---

96 20 U. S. C. § 1415(f)(1)(B)

97 20 U. S. C. § 1415(f)(1)(B)(ii)

98 20 U. S. C. § 1415(f)(2)

99 In addition to evaluations and other documents specific to the child, the exhibit list should include research reports, learned treatises, relevant journal articles, book chapters, and other documents that are relevant to the issues in the case.

100 *Surviving Due Process: Stephen Jeffers v. School Board* is a DVD that takes you through a due process hearing, from initial preparations to testimony by the final witness. See direct examination and dramatic cross-examination of witnesses, objections, arguments between counsel, and rulings by the hearing officer. *Surviving Due Process* is based on a true story.

101 20 U. S. C. § 1415(f)(3)(E)

102 20 U. S. C. § 1415(f)(3)(A)

103 20 U. S. C. § 1415(i)(3)

IDEA 2004 allows schools to place a child with a disability in an interim alternative setting if the child violates a code of student conduct.[104] To prevent zero-tolerance abuses, Congress added new language to the law that school personnel "consider any unique circumstance on a case-by-case basis" in determining whether to change a child's placement.

Suspensions & Placements in Interim Alternative Educational Settings

If a child with a disability violates a code of student conduct, school officials may suspend the child for up to 10 days. If the school removes a child for 10 days or more, regardless of the severity of the child's misconduct (i.e., violation of a code of conduct v. possession of a weapon), the school must continue to provide the child with FAPE.[105] The child will continue to receive educational services, participate in the general education curriculum, and make progress on the IEP goals. The child will receive "as appropriate, functional behavioral assessment, behavioral intervention services and modifications" to prevent the behavior from reoccurring.[106]

Manifestation Determination

The law requires the IEP team, which includes the child's parent, to review all relevant information in the child's file, including information provided by the parent, to determine if the negative behavior was caused by the disability, had a direct and substantial relationship to the disability, or was a result of the school's failure to implement the IEP.[107]

Functional Behavioral Assessments and Behavior Intervention Plans

If the IEP team determines that the child's behavior was a manifestation of the disability, the IEP Team "shall conduct a functional behavioral assessment and implement a behavioral intervention plan." If the child already has a behavior intervention plan, the IEP Team shall modify the plan to address the child's behavior.[108]

45-Day Suspension: Dangerous Weapon, Drugs, and Serious Bodily Injury

If the child carries a dangerous weapon to school, knowingly possesses or uses illegal drugs at school, or inflicts serious bodily injury upon another person while at school, the school may remove the child to an interim alternative placement for not more than 45 school days.[109] The school must continue to provide the child with FAPE.

Part C: Infants and Toddlers with Disabilities

Part C governs early intervention services for infants and toddlers under the age of 3, with some exceptions. Part C includes Section 1431 through Section 1444 of Title 20 of the United States Code (U. S. C.).

Findings and Policy

Congress made significant changes to Findings and Policy in Section 1431 and added new language about the "urgent and substantial need . . . to recognize the significant brain development that occurs during a child's first 3 years of life." Congress also found that there is an "urgent and substantial need to maximize the potential for individuals with disabilities to live independently in society."[110] According to the Policy Statement:

It is the policy of the United States to provide financial assistance to States to develop and implement a **statewide, comprehensive, coordinated, multidisciplinary, interagency system that provides early**

104 20 U. S. C. § 1415 (k)
105 20 U. S. C. § 1415(k)(1)
106 20 U. S. C. § 1415(k)(1)(D)
107 20 U. S. C. § 1415(k)(1)(E)
108 20 U. S. C. § 1415(k)(1)(F)
109 20 U. S. C. § 1415(k)(1)(G)
110 20 U. S. C. § 1431(a)

intervention services for infants and toddlers with disabilities and their families . . . .[111] (emphasis added)

Definitions

Infant or Toddler with a Disability

An infant or toddler with a disability is "an individual under 3 years of age who needs early intervention services because the individual is experiencing developmental delays, as measured by appropriate diagnostic instruments and procedures" in one or more areas of development. At the state's discretion, an infant or toddler with a disability may also include "at-risk infants and toddlers" and children who previously received early intervention services until they enter kindergarten or elementary school.[112]

Early Intervention Services

Early intervention services must be designed to meet the child's developmental needs, including physical, cognitive, communication, social and emotional, and adaptive areas, and must be provided by qualified personnel.[113] Many school districts offer one-size-fits-all school-based programs that are not "designed to meet the developmental needs" of a particular infant or toddler. Early intervention services "are provided at no cost except where a federal or State law provides for payments by families, including a schedule of sliding fees . . . ."[114]

Requirements for Early Intervention Programs

Part C describes the minimum requirements for early intervention programs.[115] States must have policies to ensure that early intervention services are based on scientifically based research. The evaluation of the child must be timely, comprehensive and multidisciplinary and must include "a family-directed identification of the needs of each family." States must have comprehensive child find systems and public awareness programs and must maintain central information directories about early intervention services, resources, and experts, and demonstration programs.

States must have comprehensive systems of personnel development, including training for paraprofessionals and primary referral sources, policies and procedures to ensure that personnel are appropriately and adequately trained, and that early intervention services are provided in natural environments.

The subsection about "Flexibility to Serve Children 3 Years of Age Until Entrance into Elementary School" is new.[116] States may continue to provide early intervention services to young children with disabilities until they enter or are eligible to enter kindergarten. These early intervention services must "include an educational component that promotes school readiness and incorporates pre-literacy, language and numeracy skills."[117]

Individualized Family Service Plan (IFSP)

The legal requirements for Individualized Family Service Plans (IFSPs) are similar to the requirements for Individualized Education Plans, but with some important differences. The assessment and program development process includes a "family-directed assessment" of the family's resources, priorities, and concerns. Congress added new requirements for Individualized Family Service Plans which must now include "measurable results or outcomes expected to be achieved . . . including pre-literacy and language skills" and the "criteria, procedures, and timelines" that will be used to measure the child's progress. IDEA 2004 includes a new requirement that the

111 20 U. S. C. § 1431(b)
112 20 U. S. C. § 1432(5)
113 20 U. S. C. § 1432(4)
114 20 U. S. C. § 1432(4)(B)
115 20 U. S. C. § 1435
116 20 U. S. C. § 1435(c)
117 20 U. S. C. § 1435(c)(2)

IFSP include "a statement of specific early intervention services based on peer-reviewed research . . . necessary to meet the unique needs" of the child and family.[118]

Procedural Safeguards

The protections and safeguards for young children with disabilities and their parents in the Procedural Safeguards section of Part C are similar to those in Part B, but with some important differences. Parents of young children have a right to accept or decline any early intervention service without jeopardizing their right to other early intervention services.[119] The law includes a procedure to protect the rights of the child when the parents are not known or cannot be found by appointing an individual to act as a surrogate for the parents.

Part D – National Activities to Improve Education of Children with Disabilities

Part D has been revised and reorganized into four subparts. Subpart 1 about State Personnel Development Grants includes purpose, definition of personnel, eligibility, applications, and how funds may be used. Subpart 2 about Personnel Preparation focuses on improving educational outcomes and results by improving teacher training and professional development. Subpart 3 describes requirements for Parent Training and Information Centers and Community Resource Centers. Subpart 4 contains General Provisions.

Findings

Congress made significant changes to Findings in Part D. Section 1450 describes the critical need for adequately trained personnel[120] and for "high quality, comprehensive professional development programs . . . to ensure that the persons responsible for the education or transition of children with disabilities possess the skills and knowledge necessary to address the needs of those children."[121]

Personnel Development

Section 1462 about Personnel Development to Improve Services and Results for Children with Disabilities focuses on the need to ensure that all teachers "have the necessary skills and knowledge, derived from practices that have been determined, through scientifically based research, to be successful in serving those children . . ."[122]

Parent Training and Information Centers (PTI) and Parent Resource Centers (CPRC)

The Education Department shall award grants to at least one parent organization in each state for a Parent Training and Information Center. These Centers are to help parents learn about their children's disabilities and educational needs, their legal rights and responsibilities, how to communicate effectively with school personnel, and how to participate in educational decision-making.[123]

The Education Department may also award grants to parent organizations that do not meet the criteria for a PTI but focus on helping under-served parents. For example, a center may focus on helping low-income parents, parents with limited English proficiency, and parents with disabilities.

Part E – National Center for Special Education Research

Part E is new in IDEA 2004 and establishes the National Center for Special Education Research, referred to as the Special Education Research Center. The duties of the Center include improving services, identifying

---

118 20 U. S. C. § 1436
119 20 U. S. C. § 1439
120 20 U. S. C. § 1450(5)
121 20 U. S. C. § 1450(6)
122 20 U. S. C. § 1462(a)
123 20 U. S. C. § 1471

scientifically based educational practices that improve academic achievement and educational results, and identifying scientifically based related services and interventions that promote participation and progress in general education.[124]

In Summation

In this chapter, you learned how the Individuals with Disabilities Education Act is organized. You learned about important changes Congress made when the law was reauthorized. The next chapter includes the full text of the Individuals with Disabilities Education Act of 2004 with commentary and analysis.

---

124 20 U. S. C. § 9567

CHAPTER 5

Individuals with Disabilities Education Improvement Act of 2004

Table of Statutes

Part A — General Provisions

20 U. S. C. § 1408. Paperwork Reduction
    (a) Pilot Program.
    (b) Report.

20 U. S. C. § 1409. Freely Associated States

Part B – Assistance for Education of All Children with Disabilities

20 U. S. C. § 1411. Authorization; Allotment; Use of Funds; Authorization of Appropriations
    (a) Grants to States.
    (b) Outlying Areas and Freely Associated States, Secretary of the Interior.
    (c) Technical Assistance.
    (d) Allocations to States.
    (e) State Level Activities.
    (f) Subgrants to Local Educational Agencies.
    (g) Definitions.
    (h) Use of Amounts by Secretary of the Interior.
    (i) Authorizations of Appropriations.

20 U. S. C. § 1412. State Eligibility
    (a) In General.
    (b) State Educational Agency as Provider of Free Appropriate Public Education or Direct Services.
    (c) Exception for Prior State Plans.
    (d) Approval by the Secretary.
    (e) Assistance Under Other Federal Programs.
    (f) By-Pass for Children in Private Schools.

20 U. S. C. § 1413. Local Educational Agency Eligibility
    (a) In General.
    (b) Exception for Prior Local Plans.
    (c) Notification of Local Educational Agency or State Agency in Case of Ineligibility.
    (d) Local Educational Agency Compliance.
    (e) Joint Establishment of Eligibility.
    (f) Early Intervening Services.
    (g) Direct Services by the State Educational Agency.
    (h) State Agency Eligibility.
    (i) Disciplinary Information.
    (j) State Agency Flexibility.

20 U. S. C. § 1414. Evaluations, Eligibility Determinations, Individualized Education Programs, and Educational Placements
    (a) Evaluations, Parental Consent, and Reevaluations.
    (b) Evaluation Procedures.
    (c) Additional Requirements for Evaluation and Reevaluations.
    (d) Individualized Education Programs.
    (e) Educational Placements.
    (f) Alternative Means of Meeting Participation.

20 U. S. C. § 1415. **Procedural Safeguards**

(a) Establishment of Procedures.
(b) Types of Procedures.
(c) Notification Requirements.
(d) Procedural Safeguards Notice.
(e) Mediation.
(f) Impartial Due Process Hearing.
(g) Appeal.
(h) Safeguards.
(i) Administrative Procedures.
(j) Maintenance of Current Educational Placement.
(k) Placement in Alternative Educational Setting.
(l) Rule of Construction.
(m) Transfer of Parental Rights at Age of Majority.
(n) Electronic Mail.
(o) Separate Complaint.

20 U. S. C. § 1416. **Monitoring, Technical Assistance, and Enforcement**

(a) Federal and State Monitoring.
(b) State Performance Plans.
(c) Approval Process.
(d) Secretary's Review and Determination.
(e) Enforcement.
(f) State Enforcement.
(g) Rule of Construction.
(h) Divided State Agency Responsibility.
(i) Data Capacity and Technical Assistance Review.

20 U. S. C. § 1417. **Administration**

(a) Responsibilities of Secretary.
(b) Prohibition Against Federal Mandates, Direction, or Control.
(c) Confidentiality.
(d) Personnel.
(e) Model Forms.

20 U. S. C. § 1418. **Program Information**

(a) In General.
(b) Data Reporting.
(c) Technical Assistance.
(d) Disproportionality.

20 U. S. C. § 1419. **Preschool Grants**

(a) In General.
(b) Eligibility.
(c) Allocations to States.
(d) Reservation for State Activities.
(e) State Administration.
(f) Other State-Level Activities.
(g) Subgrants to Local Educational Agencies.

Part C – Infants and Toddlers with Disabilities

20 U. S. C. § 1431. Findings and Policy
(a) Findings.
(b) Policy.

20 U. S. C. § 1433. General Authority

20 U. S. C. § 1434. Eligibility

20 U. S. C. § 1435. Requirements for Statewide System
(a) In General.
(b) Policy.
(c) Flexibility To Serve Children 3 Years of Age Until Entrance Into Elementary School.

20 U. S. C. § 1436. Individualized Family Service Plan
(a) Assessment and Program Development.
(b) Periodic Review.
(c) Promptness After Assessment.
(d) Content of Plan.
(e) Parental Consent.

20 U. S. C. § 1437. State Application and Assurances
(a) Application.
(b) Assurances.
(c) Standard for Disapproval of Application.
(d) Subsequent State Application.
(e) Modification of Application.
(f) Modifications Required by the Secretary.

20 U. S. C. § 1438. Uses of Funds

20 U. S. C. § 1439. Procedural Safeguards
(a) Minimum Procedures.
(b) Services During Pendency of Proceedings.

20 U. S. C. § 1440. Payor of Last Resort
(a) Nonsubstitution.
(b) Obligations Related to and Methods of Ensuring Services.
(c) Reduction of Other Benefits.

20 U. S. C. § 1441. State Interagency Coordinating Council
(a) Establishment.
(b) Composition.
(c) Meetings.
(d) Management Authority.
(e) Functions of Council.
(f) Conflict of Interest.

20 U. S. C. § 1442. Federal Administration

Part D – National Activities to Improve Education of Children with Disabilities

Subpart 1 – State Personnel Development Grants

Subpart 2 – Personnel Preparation, Technical Assistance, Model Demonstration Projects, and Dissemination of Information

20 U. S. C. § 1462. Personnel Development to Improve Services and Results for Children with Disabilities

(a) In General.

(b) Personnel Development; Enhanced Support for Beginning Special Educators.

(c) Low Incidence Disabilities; Authorized Activities.

(d) Leadership Preparation; Authorized Activities.

(e) Applications.

(f) Selection of Recipients.

(g) Scholarships.

(h) Service Obligation.

(i) Authorization of Appropriations.

20 U. S. C. § 1463. Technical Assistance, Demonstration Projects, Dissemination of Information and Implementation of Scientifically Based Research

(a) In General.

(b) Required Activities.

(c) Authorized Activities.

(d) Balance Among Activities and Age Ranges.

(e) Linking States to Information Sources.

(f) Applications.

20 U. S. C. § 1464. Studies and Evaluations

(a) Studies and Evaluations.

(b) Assessment of National Activities.

(c) Study on Ensuring Accountability for Students Who Are Held to Alternative Achievement Standards.

(d) Annual Report.

(e) Authorized Activities.

(f) Study.

20 U. S. C. § 1465. Interim Alternative Educational Settings, Behavioral Supports, and Systematic School Interventions

(a) Program Authorized.

(b) Authorized Activities.

(c) Definition of Eligible Entity.

(d) Applications.

(e) Report and Evaluation.

20 U. S. C. § 1466. Authorization of Appropriations

(a) In General.

(b) Reservation.

Subpart 3 – Supports to Improve Results for Children with Disabilities

20 U. S. C. § 1470. Purposes

20 U. S. C. § 1471. Parent Training and Information Centers

(a) Program Authorized.

(b) Required Activities.

(c) Optional Activities.

(d) Application Requirements.

(e) Distribution of Funds.

(f) Quarterly Review.

20 U. S. C. § 1472. Community Parent Resource Centers
(a) Program Authorized.
(b) Required Activities.

20 U. S. C. § 1473. Technical Assistance for Parent Training and Information Centers
(a) Program Authorized.
(b) Authorized Activities.
(c) Collaboration with Resource Centers.

20 U. S. C. § 1474. Technology Development, Demonstration and Utilization; Media Services; and Instructional Materials
(a) Program Authorized.
(b) Technology Development, Demonstration, and Use.
(c) Educational Media Services.
(d) Applications.

20 U. S. C. § 1475. Authorization of Appropriations

Subpart 4 – General Provisions

20 U. S. C. § 1481. Comprehensive Plan for Subparts 2 and 3
(a) Comprehensive Plan.
(b) Assistance Authorized.
(c) Special Populations.
(d) Priorities.
(e) Eligibility for Financial Assistance.

20 U. S. C. § 1482. Administrative Provisions
(a) Applicant and Recipient Responsibilities.
(b) Application Management.
(c) Program Evaluation.
(d) Minimum Funding Required.

Part E – National Center for Special Education Research

20 U. S. C. § 9567. Establishment
(a) Establishment.
(b) Mission.
(c) Applicability of Education Sciences Reform Act of 2002.

20 U. S. C. § 9567a. Commissioner for Special Education Research
(a) General Duties.
(b) Standards.
(c) Plan.
(d) Grants, Contracts, and Cooperative Agreements.
(e) Dissemination.
(f) Authorization of Appropriations.

20 U. S. C. § 9567b. Duties

The Individuals with Disabilities Education Act of 2004

Part A – General Provisions

WRIGHTSLAW OVERVIEW: Part A of the Individuals with Disabilities Education Act, General Provisions, includes Sections 1400 through Section 1409 of Title 20 of the United States Code (U. S. C.):

20 U. S. C. § 1400. Congressional Findings and Purposes
20 U. S. C. § 1401. Definitions
20 U. S. C. § 1402. Office of Special Education Programs
20 U. S. C. § 1403. Abrogation of State Sovereign Immunity
20 U. S. C. § 1404. Acquisition of Equipment; Construction or Alteration of Facilities
20 U. S. C. § 1405. Employment of Individuals with Disabilities
20 U. S. C. § 1406. Requirements for Prescribing Regulations
20 U. S. C. § 1407. State Administration
20 U. S. C. § 1408. Paperwork Reduction
20 U. S. C. § 1409. Freely Associated States

The most important section in IDEA 2004 is Section 1400(d) that describes the purposes of the law. Section 1401 includes the legal definitions in alphabetical order. Section 1403 advises that states are not immune from suit if they violate IDEA. Section 1406 describes the requirements and timelines for the federal special education regulations. Sections 1407, Section 1408, and Section 1409 are new in IDEA 2004.

20 U. S. C. § 1400. Short Title; Table of Contents; Findings; Purposes

WRIGHTSLAW OVERVIEW: Section 1400 is Findings and Purposes. Section 1400(c) describes the history and findings that led Congress to pass the Education for All Handicapped Children Act of 1975 (Public Law 94-142) which is now the Individuals with Disabilities Education Act of 2004. The most important statute is Purposes in Section 1400(d): "to ensure that all children with disabilities have available to them a free appropriate public education that emphasizes special education and related services designed to meet their unique needs and prepare them for further education, employment and independent living" and "to ensure that the rights of children with disabilities and parents of such children are protected . . ." When you have questions about a confusing term or section in the law, re-read Section 1400, especially Purposes in Section 1400(d). This will help you understand how the confusing portion fits into the overall purpose of the law.

(a) **Short Title.** This title may be cited as the 'Individuals with Disabilities Education Act'.

(b) **Table of Contents.** [1,2]

(c) **Findings.** Congress finds the following:

(1) Disability is a natural part of the human experience and in no way diminishes the right of individuals to participate in or contribute to society. Improving educational results for children with disabilities is an essential element of our national policy of **ensuring equality of opportunity, full participation, independent living, and economic self-sufficiency for individuals with disabilities.**

(2) Before the date of enactment of the Education for All Handicapped Children Act of 1975 (Public Law 94-142), the educational needs of millions of children with disabilities were not being fully met because–

(A) the children did not receive appropriate educational services;

---

1   The Overviews and footnotes in this book are by the authors and are not a part of the statute.

2   Section 1400(b) lists the sections and subsections of Parts A, B, C, D, and E of the Individuals with Disabilities Education Act in a table of contents format.

(B) the children **were excluded entirely from the public school system** and from being educated with their peers;

(C) **undiagnosed disabilities** prevented the children from having a successful educational experience; or

(D) a **lack of adequate resources** within the public school system forced families to find services outside the public school system.[3]

(3) Since the enactment and implementation of the Education for All Handicapped Children Act of 1975, this title has been successful in ensuring children with disabilities and the families of such children access to a free appropriate public education and in improving educational results for children with disabilities.

(4) However, the implementation of this title has been impeded by **low expectations, and an insufficient focus on applying replicable research on proven methods of teaching and learning** for children with disabilities.[4]

(5) Almost **30 years of research and experience** has demonstrated that the **education of children with disabilities can be made more effective** by-

(A) having **high expectations** for such children and ensuring their **access to the general education curriculum** in the regular classroom, to the maximum extent possible, in order to-

(i) **meet developmental goals** and, to the maximum extent possible, the **challenging expectations that have been established for all children**; and

(ii) be **prepared to lead productive and independent adult lives**, to the **maximum extent possible**;[5]

(B) **strengthening the role and responsibility of parents** and ensuring that families of such children have meaningful opportunities to participate in the education of their children at school and at home;

(C) **coordinating this title** with other local, educational service agency, State, and Federal school improvement efforts, including improvement efforts under the **Elementary and Secondary Education Act of 1965**,[6] in order to ensure that such children benefit from such efforts and that **special education can become a service for such children rather than a place where such children are sent**;[7]

(D) providing appropriate special education and related services, and aids and supports in the regular classroom, to such children, whenever appropriate;

(E) supporting **high-quality, intensive preservice preparation and professional development** for all

---

3 Before Congress passed the Education for All Handicapped Children Act (Public Law 94-142) in 1975, more than one million handicapped children were excluded from school. Initially, the law focused on ensuring that children had access to an education and due process of law. When Congress reauthorized the law in 1997, they emphasized accountability and improved outcomes while maintaining the goals of access and due process. IDEA 2004 increased the focus on accountability and improved outcomes by bringing IDEA into conformity with the No Child Left Behind Act, and adding requirements for early intervening services, research-based instruction, and highly qualified special education teachers.

4 IDEA 2004 addresses poor educational outcomes for children with disabilities by requiring "proven methods of teaching and learning" based on "replicable research." These terms are important. "Research based methods" are also referred to as "evidence-based." Pressure from litigation, legal rulings requiring schools to use research based methods, and No Child Left Behind are forcing school districts to adopt research based or evidence-based methods.

5 The language about meeting the developmental goals and challenging expectations established for nondisabled children so children are "prepared to lead productive and independent adult lives to the maximum extent possible" is important.

6 IDEA is the federal law that requires schools to provide special education and related services to qualifying children with disabilities. The Elementary and Secondary Education Act of 1965 (ESEA) is the federal law that was enacted to help schools educate disadvantaged children. When the ESEA was reauthorized in 2001, it was renamed "No Child Left Behind." The "improvement efforts under the ESEA" refers to No Child Left Behind (NCLB). NCLB and IDEA often use the same terms or incorporate identical language, definitions and requirements of the other statute by reference.

7 Special education is a service, not a place. Special education is not the classroom in the trailer or the special school across town. Pursuant to the least restrictive environment requirement in Section 1412(a)(5), special education services should be delivered in general education settings except "when the nature or severity of the disability of the child is such that education in regular classes with the use of supplementary aids and services cannot be achieved satisfactorily." When school personnel view special education as a "place," they often fail to evaluate the child's unique needs and how the school can meet these needs. Coordinating IDEA and NCLB will help to ensure that special education is "a service for such children rather than a place where such children are sent."

personnel who work with children with disabilities in order to ensure that such personnel have the skills and knowledge necessary to improve the academic achievement and functional performance of children with disabilities, including the use of scientifically based instructional practices, to the maximum extent possible;

(F) providing incentives for whole-school approaches, **scientifically based early reading programs, positive behavioral interventions and supports**, and **early intervening services**[8] to **reduce the need to label children as disabled** in order to address the learning and behavioral needs of such children;[9]

(G) focusing resources on teaching and learning while reducing paperwork and requirements that do not assist in improving educational results; and

(H) supporting the development and use of technology, including assistive technology devices and assistive technology services, to maximize accessibility for children with disabilities.

(6) While States, local educational agencies, and educational service agencies are primarily responsible for providing an education for all children with disabilities, it is in the national interest that the Federal Government have a supporting role in assisting State and local efforts to educate children with disabilities in order to improve results for such children and to ensure equal protection of the law.

(7) A more equitable allocation of resources is essential for the Federal Government to meet its responsibility to **provide an equal educational opportunity** for all individuals.

(8) Parents and schools should be given expanded **opportunities to resolve their disagreements in positive and constructive ways.**

(9) Teachers, schools, local educational agencies, and States should be relieved of **irrelevant and unnecessary paperwork** burdens that do not lead to improved educational outcomes.

(10)
(A) The Federal Government must be responsive to the growing needs of an **increasingly diverse society.**

(B) America's **ethnic profile is rapidly changing**. In 2000, 1 of every 3 persons in the United States was a member of a **minority group** or was **limited English proficient.**

(C) Minority children comprise an increasing percentage of public school students.

(D) With such changing demographics, recruitment efforts for special education personnel should focus on **increasing** the participation of **minorities in the teaching profession** in order to provide appropriate role models with sufficient knowledge to address the special education needs of these students.

(11)
(A) The **limited English proficient population** is the fastest growing in our Nation, and the growth is occurring in many parts of our Nation.

(B) Studies have documented apparent **discrepancies in** the levels of **referral and placement of limited English proficient children in special education.**

(C) Such discrepancies pose a special challenge for special education in the referral of, assessment of, and provision of services for, our Nation's students from non-English language backgrounds.

(12)
(A) Greater efforts are needed to **prevent** the intensification of problems connected with **mislabeling and high dropout rates among minority children with disabilities.**

(B) More minority children continue to be served in special education than would be expected from the

---

8 Congress added early intervening services (EIS) to IDEA 2004. Early intervening services are for children who have not been identified as needing special education or related services, but who need additional academic and behavioral support to succeed in a general education environment. See 20 U. S. C. § 1413(f)(1).

9 Many school districts refuse to evaluate or provide special education services until after a child fails. This "wait to fail" model has tragic results. The neurological "window of opportunity" for learning to read begins to close during elementary school. Late remediation is more difficult and carries a high price tag, emotionally and economically.

percentage of minority students in the general school population.

(C) **African-American children** are **identified as having mental retardation and emotional disturbance** at rates greater than their White counterparts.

(D) In the 1998-1999 school year, African-American children represented just 14.8 percent of the population aged 6 through 21, but comprised 20.2 percent of all children with disabilities.

(E) Studies have found that schools with predominately White students and teachers have placed **disproportionately high numbers of their minority students into special education**.

(13)

(A) As the number of **minority students** in special education **increases,** the number of **minority teachers** and related services pexrsonnel produced in colleges and universities **continues to decrease**.

(B) The **opportunity for full participation** by minority individuals, minority organizations, and Historically Black Colleges and Universities in awards for grants and contracts, boards of organizations receiving assistance under this title, peer review panels, and training of professionals in the area of special education is essential to obtain greater success in the education of minority children with disabilities.

(14) As the graduation rates for children with disabilities continue to climb, providing **effective transition services** to promote **successful post-school employment or education** is **an important measure of accountability** for children with disabilities.

(d) Purposes. The purposes of this title are–

(1)

(A) to ensure that all children with disabilities have available to them a free appropriate public education that emphasizes special education and related services designed to meet their **unique needs and prepare them for further education,**[10] **employment, and independent living;**[11]

(B) to ensure that the **rights of children** with disabilities **and parents** of such children **are protected**; and

(C) to assist States, localities, educational service agencies, and Federal agencies to provide for the education of all children with disabilities;

(2) to assist States in the implementation of a statewide, comprehensive, coordinated, multidisciplinary, interagency system of **early intervention services** for infants and toddlers with disabilities and their families;

(3) to ensure that educators and parents have the **necessary tools to improve educational results** for children with disabilities by supporting system improvement activities; coordinated research and personnel preparation; coordinated technical assistance, dissemination, and support; and technology development and media services; and

(4) to **assess, and ensure the effectiveness of, efforts to educate children with disabilities**.[12]

---

10 The phrase "further education" and the emphasis on effective transition services is new. Section 1400(c)(14) describes "effective transition services to promote successful post-school employment or education." The definition of "transition services" was changed to a "results-oriented process that is focused on improving the academic and functional achievement of the child" to facilitate "movement from school to post-school activities, including post-secondary education ..."

11 Purposes in Section 1400(d) is the mission statement of IDEA. The purpose of special education is to prepare children with disabilities for **further education, employment, and independent living**.

12 IDEA 2004 requires that all children with disabilities participate in all state and district assessments, with appropriate accommodations as determined by the IEP team. Section 1412(a)(16) includes new requirements about accommodations guidelines and alternate assessments.

20 U. S. C. § 1401. Definitions

WRIGHTSLAW OVERVIEW: Read these definitions carefully, especially the definitions of child with a disability, free appropriate public education, highly qualified teacher, least restrictive environment, IEP, related services, special education, and specific learning disability. The definitions are in alphabetical order. One definition often takes you to another section of the law that provides additional information on the subject. IDEA 2004 added six new definitions: core academic subjects, highly qualified teacher, homeless children, limited English proficient, universal design, and ward of the state. In the regulations, Definitions begin at 300.4 and continue to 300.45.

Except as otherwise provided, in this title:

(1) Assistive Technology Device.

(A) In General. The term 'assistive technology device' means any item, piece of equipment, or product system, whether acquired commercially off the shelf, modified, or customized, that is used to increase, maintain, or improve functional capabilities of a child with a disability.

(B) Exception. The term does not include a medical device that is surgically implanted, or the replacement of such device. [13]

(2) Assistive Technology Service. The term 'assistive technology service' means any service that **directly assists a child** with a disability in the selection, acquisition, or use of an assistive technology device. Such term includes–

(A) the evaluation of the needs of such child, including a functional evaluation of the child in the child's customary environment; [14]

(B) purchasing, leasing, or otherwise providing for the acquisition of assistive technology devices by such child;

(C) selecting, designing, fitting, customizing, adapting, applying, maintaining, repairing, or replacing assistive technology devices;

(D) coordinating and using other therapies, interventions, or services with assistive technology devices, such as those associated with existing education and rehabilitation plans and programs;

(E) training or technical assistance for such child, or, where appropriate, the family of such child; and

(F) training or technical assistance for professionals (including individuals providing education and rehabilitation services), employers, or other individuals who provide services to, employ, or are otherwise substantially involved in the major life functions of such child. [15]

(3) Child With A Disability.

(A) In General. The term 'child with a disability' means a child–

(i) with mental retardation, hearing impairments (including deafness), speech or language impairments, visual impairments (including blindness), serious emotional disturbance (referred to in this title as 'emotional disturbance'), orthopedic impairments, autism, traumatic brain injury, other health impairments, or specific learning disabilities; and

---

13 See regulations 300.5, 300.6, 300.34(b), and 300.113 about hearing aids and cochlear implants.

14 An assistive technology evaluation may be conducted in the home, which is a customary environment for a child.

15 Children with disabilities need to use technology devices and services to increase and improve their ability to function independently in and out of school. Technology devices include dictation software, text readers, and computerized speaking devices. Parents, teachers, and other professionals will need training before they can teach the child to use technology.

(ii) who, by reason thereof needs special education and related services.[16]

(B) Child Aged 3 Through 9. The term 'child with a disability' for a child aged 3 through 9 (or any subset of that age range, including ages 3 through 5), [17] may, at the discretion of the State and the local educational agency, include a child–

(i) experiencing developmental delays, as defined by the State and as measured by appropriate diagnostic instruments and procedures, in 1 or more of the following areas: physical development; cognitive development; communication development; social or emotional development; or adaptive development; and

(ii) who, by reason thereof, needs special education and related services.[18, 19]

(4) Core Academic Subjects. The term 'core academic subjects' [20] has the meaning given the term in Section 9101 of the Elementary and Secondary Education Act of 1965.[21]

(5) Educational Service Agency. The term 'educational service agency' means a regional public multiservice agency-authorized by State law to develop, manage, and provide services or programs to local educational agencies; and recognized as an administrative agency for purposes of the provision of special education and related services provided within public elementary schools and secondary schools of the State; and includes any other public institution or agency having administrative control and direction over a public elementary school or secondary school.

(6) Elementary School. The term 'elementary school' means a nonprofit institutional day or residential school, including a public elementary charter school,[22] that provides elementary education, as determined under State law.

(7) Equipment. The term 'equipment' includes–

(A) machinery, utilities, and built-in equipment, and any necessary enclosures or structures to house such machinery, utilities, or equipment; and

(B) all other items necessary for the functioning of a particular facility as a facility for the provision of educational services, including items such as instructional equipment and necessary furniture; printed, published, and audio-visual instructional materials; telecommunications, sensory, and other technological aids and devices; and books, periodicals, documents, and other related materials.

(8) Excess Costs. The term 'excess costs' means those costs that are in excess of the average annual per-student expenditure in a local educational agency during the preceding school year for an elementary school or secondary school student, as may be appropriate, and which shall be computed after deducting-

(A) amounts received–

---

16 A child with a disability is not automatically eligible for special education and related services under IDEA. The key phrase is "who, by reason thereof, needs special education and related services." A child can advance steadily from grade to grade, without failing grades, and still be classified as a child with a disability. (See Regulation 300.101(c)) If the child only needs related services, the child is not eligible under IDEA 2004 per Regulation 300.8(a)(2). See also Commentary in the *Federal Register*, page 46549. If a child has a disability but does not need special education services, the child may be eligible for protections under Section 504 of the Rehabilitation Act.

17 Part C describes early intervention services for infants and toddlers with disabilities under three years of age and their families.

18 School districts may provide special education services to children with developmental delays, whether they do or do not have a specific disability label. If a child between the ages of 3 and 9 has a developmental delay but has not been found eligible for services under Section 1401(3)(A)(i), this section may open the door to special education services. The requirement that schools provide services to young children with developmental delays is intended to address their needs for early intervention services.

19 If a child only needs a related service, then depending on your state regulations, the child may or may not be eligible. (See Regulation 300.8)

20 Core academic subjects are defined as "English, reading or language arts, mathematics, science, foreign languages, civics and government, economics, arts, history, and geography." (20 U. S. C. § 7801)

21 All definitions in the No Child Left Behind Act are in *Wrightslaw: No Child Left Behind.*

22 For more information about charter schools, see Regulation 300.209.

(i) under part B;

(ii) under part A of title I of the Elementary and Secondary Education Act of 1965; and

(iii) under parts A and B of title III of that Act; and

(B) any State or local funds expended for programs that would qualify for assistance under any of those parts.

(9) Free Appropriate Public Education. The term 'free appropriate public education'[23] means special education and related services that–

(A) have been provided at public expense, under public supervision and direction, and without charge;

(B) meet the standards of the State educational agency;

(C) include an appropriate preschool, elementary school, or secondary school education in the State involved; and

(D) are provided in conformity with the individualized education program required under Section 1414(d) of this title.[24, 25]

(10) Highly Qualified.[26]

(A) In General. For any special education teacher, the term 'highly qualified' has the meaning given the term in Section 9101 of the Elementary and Secondary Education Act of 1965,[27] except that such term also-

(i) includes the requirements described in subparagraph (B); and

(ii) includes the option for teachers to meet the requirements of Section 9101 of such Act by meeting the requirements of subparagraph (C) or (D).[28]

(B) Requirements For Special Education Teachers. When used with respect to any public elementary school or secondary school special education teacher teaching in a State, such term means that–

(i) the teacher has obtained full State certification as a special education teacher (including certification obtained through alternative routes to certification), or passed the State special education teacher licensing examination, and holds a license to teach in the State as a special education teacher, except that when used with respect to any teacher teaching in a public charter school, the term means that the teacher meets the requirements set forth in the State's public charter school law;

(ii) the teacher has not had special education certification or licensure requirements waived on an emergency, temporary, or provisional basis; and

---

23 The term "free appropriate public education" (FAPE) is not clearly defined in IDEA but is defined in caselaw. In *Board of Education v. Rowley*, 458 U.S. 176 (1982), the U. S. Supreme Court concluded that FAPE is not the best program, nor is it a program designed to maximize a child's potential. When courts analyze the changes in IDEA 2004, they may require a higher standard.

24 In *Reexamining Rowley: A New Focus in Special Education Law*, attorney Scott Johnson argues that the "some educational benefit" standard in *Rowley* no longer reflects the present requirements of the Individuals with Disabilities Education Act. URL: www.harborhouselaw.com/articles/rowley.reexamine.johnson.htm (Retrieved on October 8, 2006)

25 Parents must never ask for what is "best" for a child nor that they want a program to maximize their child's potential. Evaluations from experts in the private sector should never recommend "the best program" for the child. Courts have held that children with disabilities are entitled to an "appropriate" education, not the "best" education. Use the terms "appropriate" or "minimally appropriate."

26 Parents of children who attend schools that receive Title I funds are entitled to information about the qualifications of their child's teachers and paraprofessionals, but must request this information in writing. If the child is taught for 4 weeks or more by a teacher who is not highly qualified, the school must notify the parent. (See Commentary in the *Federal Register*, page 46693.) Special education teachers should review Regulation 300.18.

27 The definition of a "highly qualified teacher" is in Title IX of No Child Left Behind at 20 U. S. C. § 7801(23). See also 20 U. S. C. § 6311(b)(1).

28 Special educators must meet the educational requirements for highly qualified teachers. The requirements are somewhat different for new and veteran teachers, for elementary, middle school, and high school teachers, for teachers of multiple subjects, and for teachers who teach to alternate standards.

(iii) the teacher holds at least a bachelor's degree.

(C) Special Education Teachers Teaching to Alternate Achievement Standards. When used with respect to a special education teacher who teaches core academic subjects exclusively to children who are assessed against alternate achievement standards established under the regulations promulgated under Section 1111(b)(1) of the Elementary and Secondary Education Act of 1965, such term means the teacher, whether new or not new to the profession, may either–

(i) meet the applicable requirements of Section 9101 of such Act for any elementary, middle, or secondary school teacher who is new or not new to the profession; or

(ii) meet the requirements of subparagraph (B) or (C) of Section 9101(23) of such Act as applied to an elementary school teacher, or, in the case of instruction above the elementary level, has subject matter knowledge appropriate to the level of instruction being provided, as determined by the State, needed to effectively teach to those standards.[29]

(D) Special Education Teachers Teaching Multiple Subjects. When used with respect to a special education teacher who teaches **2 or more core academic subjects exclusively to children with disabilities**, such term means that the teacher may either–

(i) meet the applicable requirements of Section 9101 of the Elementary and Secondary Education Act of 1965 for any elementary, middle, or secondary school teacher who is new or not new to the profession;

(ii) in the case of a teacher who is not new to the profession, **demonstrate competence in all the core academic subjects in which the teacher teaches** in the same manner as is required for an elementary, middle, or secondary school teacher who is not new to the profession under Section 9101(23)(C)(ii) of such Act, which may include a single, high objective uniform State standard of evaluation[30] covering multiple subjects; or

(iii) in the case of a **new special education teacher who teaches multiple subjects** and who is highly qualified in mathematics, language arts, or science, demonstrate competence in the other core academic subjects in which the teacher teaches in the same manner as is required for an elementary, middle, or secondary school teacher under Section 9101(23)(C)(ii) of such Act, which may include a single, **high objective uniform State standard of evaluation** covering multiple subjects, not later than 2 years after the date of employment.

(E) Rule of Construction. Notwithstanding any other individual right of action that a parent or student may maintain under this part, **nothing** in this section or part shall be construed to **create a right of action** on behalf of an individual student or class of students for the failure of a particular State educational agency or local educational agency employee to be highly qualified.[31]

(F) Definition For Purposes of the ESEA. A teacher who is highly qualified under this paragraph shall be considered highly qualified for purposes of the Elementary and Secondary Education Act of 1965.[32]

(11) Homeless Children. The term '**homeless children**' has the meaning given the term 'homeless children

29 For guidance about how No Child Left Behind applies to special educators and paraprofessionals, read Chapter 6 "NCLB for Teachers, Principals and Paraprofessionals," in *Wrightslaw: No Child Left Behind*. Dozens of NCLB resources are included in the **NCLB CD-ROM** in *Wrightslaw: No Child Left Behind*.

30 States have the option of developing a method by which teachers can demonstrate competence in the academic subjects they teach. This method must be based on a "high objective uniform state standard of evaluation" (HOUSSE) and must provide an objective way to determine if teachers have subject matter knowledge in the core academic subjects they teach. The multiple subject HOUSSE must not be based on a lesser standard.

31 There is no right of action (i.e., right to sue a state or school district) because a teacher is not highly qualified. However, parents may file complaints about inadequately trained teachers with the State department of education.

32 The timelines for highly qualified teachers are in No Child Left Behind, 20 U. S. C. § 6319(a)(2). Teachers hired after the law was enacted in 2002 (new hires) must be highly qualified. Teachers of core academic subjects must be highly qualified by the end of the 2005-2006 school year.

and youths' in Section 11434a of title 42.[33]

(12) Indian. The term 'Indian' means an individual who is a member of an Indian tribe.

(13) Indian Tribe. The term 'Indian tribe' means any Federal or State Indian tribe, band, rancheria, pueblo, colony, or community, including any Alaska Native village or regional village corporation (as defined in or established under the Alaska Native Claims Settlement Act (43 U. S. C. 1601 et seq.)).

(14) Individualized Education Program; IEP. The term 'individualized education program' or 'IEP' means a written statement for each child with a disability that is developed, reviewed, and revised in accordance with Section 1414(d) of this title.[34]

(15) Individualized Family Service Plan. The term 'individualized family service plan' has the meaning given the term in Section 1436 of this title.

(16) Infant or Toddler With A Disability. The term 'infant or toddler with a disability' has the meaning given the term in Section 1432 of this title.[35]

(17) Institution of Higher Education. The term 'institution of higher education'–

(A) has the meaning given the term in Section 1001 of this Title; and

(B) also includes any community college receiving funding from the Secretary of the Interior under the Tribally Controlled College or University Assistance Act of 1978.

(18) Limited English Proficient. The term 'limited English proficient' has the meaning given the term in Section 9101 of the Elementary and Secondary Education Act of 1965.[36]

(19) Local Educational Agency.

(A) In General. The term 'local educational agency' means a public board of education or other public authority legally constituted within a State for either administrative control or direction of, or to perform a service function for, public elementary schools or secondary schools in a city, county, township, school district, or other political subdivision of a State, or for such combination of school districts or counties as are recognized in a State as an administrative agency for its public elementary schools or secondary schools.

(B) Educational Service Agencies and Other Public Institutions or Agencies. The term includes –

(i) an educational service agency; and

(ii) any other public institution or agency having administrative control and direction of a public elementary school or secondary school.

(C) BIA Funded Schools. The term includes an elementary school or secondary school funded by the Bureau of Indian Affairs, but only to the extent that such inclusion makes the school eligible for programs for which specific eligibility is not provided to the school in another provision of law and the school does not have a student population that is smaller than the student population of the local educational agency receiving as-

---

33 Homeless children "lack a fixed, regular, and adequate nighttime residence . . . [are] sharing the housing of other persons . . . living in motels, hotels, trailer parks, or camping grounds . . . [or are] living in cars, parks, public spaces, abandoned buildings, substandard housing, bus or train stations, or similar settings." (42 U. S. C. § 11434a)

34 The legal requirements for IEPs, IEP teams, meeting attendance, when IEPs must be in effect, reviewing and revising IEPs, placements, and alternative ways to participate in IEP meetings are in Section 1414(d).

35 "An individual under 3 years of age who needs early intervention services because the individual (i) is experiencing developmental delays, as measured by appropriate diagnostic instruments and procedures in 1 or more of the areas of cognitive development, physical development, communication development, social or emotional development, and adaptive development; or (ii) has a diagnosed physical or mental condition that has a high probability of resulting in developmental delay; and . . ." (See 20 U. S. C. §1432 for the full text of this definition.)

36 "An individual between the ages of 3 and 21 who attends an elementary school or secondary school, who was not born in the United States or whose native language is not English, who may be a Native American, Alaska Native, or a resident of the outlying areas, or a migratory child whose native language is not English. The individual's difficulties in speaking, reading, writing, or understanding English may not permit the individual to be proficient on state assessments." (20 U. S. C. § 7801) For all NCLB definitions, see Appendix A in *Wrightslaw: No Child Left Behind.*

sistance under this title with the smallest student population, except that the school shall not be subject to the jurisdiction of any State educational agency other than the Bureau of Indian Affairs.

(20) Native Language. The term '**native language**', when used with respect to an individual who is limited English proficient, means the language normally used by the individual or, in the case of a child, the language normally used by the parents of the child.

(21) Nonprofit. The term '**nonprofit**', as applied to a school, agency, organization, or institution, means a school, agency, organization, or institution owned and operated by 1 or more nonprofit corporations or associations no part of the net earnings of which inures, or may lawfully inure, to the benefit of any private shareholder or individual.

(22) Outlying Area. The term '**outlying area**' means the United States Virgin Islands, Guam, American Samoa, and the Commonwealth of the Northern Mariana Islands.

(23) Parent. The term '**parent**' means–

(A) a natural, adoptive, or foster parent of a child (unless a foster parent is prohibited by State law from serving as a parent);

(B) a guardian (but not the State if the child is a ward of the State);

(C) an individual acting in the place of a natural or adoptive parent (including a grandparent, stepparent, or other relative) with whom the child lives, or an individual who is legally responsible for the child's welfare; or

(D) except as used in Sections 1415(b)(2) and 1439(a)(5), an individual assigned under either of those sections to be a surrogate parent.[37]

(24) Parent Organization. The term '**parent organization**' has the meaning given the term in Section 1471(g) of this title.

(25) Parent Training and Information Center. The term '**parent training and information center**' means a center assisted under Section 1471 or 1472 of this title.

(26) Related Services.[38]

(A) In General. The term '**related service**' means transportation, and such developmental, corrective, and other supportive services (including speech-language pathology and audiology services, interpreting services, psychological services, physical and occupational therapy, recreation, including therapeutic recreation, social work services, school nurse services[39] designed to enable a child with a disability to receive a free appropriate public education as described in the individualized education program of the child, counseling services, including rehabilitation counseling, orientation and mobility services, and medical services, except that such medical services shall be for diagnostic and evaluation purposes only) as may be required to assist a child with a disability to benefit from special education, and includes the early identification and assessment of disabling conditions in children.[40]

---

37 The definition of "parent" was expanded to include natural, adoptive, and foster parents, guardians, individuals who act in the place of a parent, individuals who are legally responsible for the child, and surrogate parents. See Regulation 300.519 for the definition of "surrogate parent."

38 Definitions of many related services are in Regulation 300.34(c).

39 "School nurse services" is a new and replaces "school health services" in IDEA 97.

40 Related services are services the child needs to benefit from special education. Compare the definitions of "related services" with "supplementary aids and services" (Section 1401(33)). Related services and supplementary services may include one-on-one tutoring or remediation of academic skills. The law does not require that a child be placed in a special education class in order to receive related services including tutoring or academic remediation.

(B) Exception. The term does not include a medical device that is surgically implanted, or the replacement of such device.[41]

(27) Secondary School. The term 'secondary school' means a nonprofit institutional day or residential school, including a public secondary charter school,[42] that provides secondary education, as determined under State law, except that it does not include any education beyond grade 12.

(28) Secretary. The term 'Secretary' means the Secretary of Education.

(29) Special Education. The term 'special education' means **specially designed instruction,**[43] at no cost to parents, to meet the **unique needs** of a child with a disability, including–

(A) instruction conducted in the classroom, in the home, in hospitals and institutions, and in other settings;[44] and

(B) instruction in physical education.

(30) Specific Learning Disability.

(A) In General. The term 'specific learning disability' means a disorder in 1 or more of the basic psychological processes involved in understanding or in using language, spoken or written, which disorder may manifest itself in the imperfect ability to listen, think, speak, read, write, spell, or do mathematical calculations.[45, 46]

(B) Disorders Included. Such term **includes** such conditions as **perceptual disabilities, brain injury, minimal brain dysfunction, dyslexia, and developmental aphasia.**[47]

(C) Disorders Not Included. Such term does not include a learning problem that is primarily the result of visual, hearing, or motor disabilities, of mental retardation, of emotional disturbance, or of environmental, cultural, or economic disadvantage.

(31) State. The term 'State' means each of the 50 States, the District of Columbia, the Commonwealth of Puerto Rico, and each of the outlying areas.

(32) State Educational Agency. The term 'State educational agency' means the State board of education or other agency or officer primarily responsible for the State supervision of public elementary schools and secondary schools, or, if there is no such officer or agency, an officer or agency designated by the Governor or by State law.

(33) Supplementary Aids and Services. The term 'supplementary aids and services' means aids, services, and other supports that are provided in **regular education classes** or other education-related settings to enable children with disabilities to be educated with nondisabled children to the maximum extent appropriate in accordance with Section 1412(a)(5) of this title.[48]

---

41 The exclusion of surgically implanted medical devices tracks the exception in the definitions of "Assistive Technology Device" and "Assistive Technology Service." While school districts are not responsible for surgically implanting devices, they may be responsible for corrective and supportive services. For example, schools may have to provide audiology services to operate, adjust and map cochlear implant devices.

42 For more information about charter schools, see Regulation 300.209.

43 The definition of "specially designed instruction" is in Regulation 300.39(b)(3).

44 Special education encompasses a range of services and may include one-on-one tutoring, intensive academic remediation, and 40-hour Applied Behavioral Analysis (ABA) programs. Special education is provided in a variety of settings, including the child's home.

45 The definition of "specific learning disability" did not change.

46 For more about specific learning disabilities and discrepancy models, read Section 1414(b)(6).

47 The terms used to describe disabilities are those used during the 1970's when Congress enacted Public Law 94-142. The term "minimal brain dysfunction" is "Attention Deficit Disorder." "Dyslexia" is a language learning disability in reading, writing, spelling, and/or math. From a legal perspective, dyslexia is a learning disability that adversely affects educational performance.

48 Supplementary aids and services are provided in general education classes so children with disabilities can be educated with their non-disabled peers and participate in extra curricular and non-academic settings. See Regulations 300.42, 300.107, and 300.117. Compare "supplementary aids and services" with "related services" in Section 1401(26).

(34) Transition Services. The term 'transition services'[49] means a coordinated set of activities for a child with a disability that–

(A) is designed to be within a results-oriented process, that is focused on improving the academic and functional achievement of the child with a disability to facilitate the child's movement from school to post-school activities, including post-secondary education, vocational education, integrated employment (including supported employment), continuing and adult education, adult services, independent living, or community participation;

(B) is based on the individual child's needs, taking into account the child's strengths, preferences, and interests; and

(C) includes instruction, related services, community experiences, the development of employment and other post-school adult living objectives, and, when appropriate, acquisition of daily living skills and functional vocational evaluation.[50]

(35) Universal Design. The term 'universal design' has the meaning given the term in Section 3002 in title 29.[51]

(36) Ward of the State.

(A) In General. The term 'ward of the State' means a child who, as determined by the State where the child resides, is a foster child, is a ward of the State, or is in the custody of a public child welfare agency.[52]

(B) Exception. The term **does not** include a foster child who has a foster parent who meets the definition of a parent in paragraph (23).

20 U. S. C. § 1402. Office of Special Education Programs

WRIGHTSLAW OVERVIEW: This section authorizes the Office of Special Education Programs as the principal agency to administer the IDEA. The Secretary selects the Director who reports directly to the Assistant Secretary for Special Education and Rehabilitative Services.

(a) Establishment. There shall be, within the Office of Special Education and Rehabilitative Services in the Department of Education, an Office of Special Education Programs, which shall be the principal agency in the Department for administering and carrying out this title and other programs and activities concerning the education of children with disabilities.

(b) Director. The Office established under subsection (a) shall be headed by a Director who shall be selected by the Secretary and shall report directly to the Assistant Secretary for Special Education and Rehabilitative Services.

(c) Voluntary and Uncompensated Services. Notwithstanding Section 1342 of title 31, United States Code, the Secretary is authorized to accept voluntary and uncompensated services in furtherance of the purposes of this title.

---

49 Remember the language in the "Purposes" about preparing disabled children for "further education." See also the new language about IEPs in Sections 1414(d)(1)(A)(i)(VIII)(aa) and (bb) about "measurable postsecondary goals" and "courses of study" to reach those goals and Section 1400(c)(14) that describes "effective transition services to promote successful post-school ... education."

50 The definition of transition services was changed to a "results-oriented process" that improves "the academic and functional achievement of the child with a disability" and facilitates the child's transition from school to employment and further education. Transition services are based on the individual child's needs and strengths.

51 The key concept in Universal Design, often called Universal Design for Learning, is that new curricular materials and learning technologies will be designed to be flexible to accommodate the unique learning styles of a wide range of individuals, including children with disabilities. Examples include accessible websites, electronic versions of textbooks and other materials; captioned and/or narrated videos; word processors with word prediction; and voice recognition. See www.nectac.org/topics/atech/udl.asp The definition of universal design is in the Assistive Technology Act at 29 U. S. C. § 3002(19).

52 "Ward of the State" is new in IDEA 2004. See also Section 1401(23) for the expanded definition of "parent" and Section 1414(a)(1)(D)(iii) about parental consent for children who are wards of the state.

20 U. S. C. § 1403. Abrogation of State Sovereign Immunity

WRIGHTSLAW OVERVIEW: States are not immune from suit in Federal court if they violate the IDEA.

(a) In General. A State shall not be immune under the 11th amendment to the Constitution of the United States from suit in Federal court for a violation of this title.

(b) Remedies. In a suit against a State for a violation of this title, remedies (including remedies both at law and in equity) are available for such a violation to the same extent as those remedies are available for such a violation in the suit against any public entity other than a State.

(c) Effective Date. Subsections (a) and (b) apply with respect to violations that occur in whole or part after October 30, 1990.

20 U. S. C. § 1404. Acquisition of Equipment; Construction or Alteration of Facilities

WRIGHTSLAW OVERVIEW: The U.S. Department of Education may authorize funds to acquire equipment, construct new facilities, or alter existing facilities.

(a) In General. If the Secretary determines that a program authorized under this title will be improved by permitting program funds to be used to acquire appropriate equipment, or to construct new facilities or alter existing facilities, the Secretary is authorized to allow the use of those funds for those purposes.

(b) Compliance With Certain Regulations. Any construction of new facilities or alteration of existing facilities under subsection (a) shall comply with the requirements of–

(1) appendix A of part 36 of title 28, Code of Federal Regulations (commonly known as the 'Americans with Disabilities Accessibility Guidelines for Buildings and Facilities'); or

(2) appendix A of subpart 101-19.6 of title 41, Code of Federal Regulations (commonly known as the 'Uniform Federal Accessibility Standards').

20 U. S. C. § 1405. Employment of Individuals with Disabilities

WRIGHTSLAW OVERVIEW: Recipients of funds must make positive efforts to employ individuals with disabilities.

The Secretary shall ensure that each recipient of assistance under this title makes positive efforts to employ and advance in employment qualified individuals with disabilities in programs assisted under this title.

20 U. S. C. § 1406. Requirements for Prescribing Regulations

WRIGHTSLAW OVERVIEW: The U.S. Department of Education is responsible for developing the federal special education regulations. After the Department publishes proposed regulations, there is a public comment period. Comments may be made in writing or at public meetings. After reviewing the comments, the Department publishes the Final Regulations. The federal special education regulations are published in the Federal Register (FR) and the Code of Federal Regulations (CFR) beginning at 34 CFR Part 300. New regulations may not lessen the protections in effect on July 20, 1983.

(a) In General. In carrying out the provisions of this title, the Secretary shall issue regulations under this title only to the extent that such regulations are necessary to ensure that there is compliance with the specific requirements of this title.

(b) Protections Provided to Children. The Secretary may not implement, or publish in final form, any regulation prescribed pursuant to this title that–

(1) violates or contradicts any provision of this title; or

(2) procedurally or substantively lessens the protections provided to children with disabilities under this title, as embodied in regulations in effect on July 20, 1983 (particularly as such protections related to parental

consent to initial evaluation or initial placement in special education, least restrictive environment, related services, timelines, attendance of evaluation personnel at individualized education program meetings, or qualifications of personnel), except to the extent that such regulation reflects the clear and unequivocal intent of Congress in legislation.[53]

(c) Public Comment Period. The Secretary shall provide a public comment period of not less than 75 days on any regulation proposed under part B or part C on which an opportunity for public comment is otherwise required by law.

(d) Policy Letters and Statements. The Secretary may not issue policy letters or other statements (including letters or statements regarding issues of national significance) that–

(1) violate or contradict any provision of this title; or

(2) establish a rule that is required for compliance with, and eligibility under, this title without following the requirements of Section 553 of title 5, United States Code.

(e) Explanation and Assurances. Any written response by the Secretary under subsection (d) regarding a policy, question, or interpretation under part B shall include an explanation in the written response that–

(1) such response is provided as informal guidance and is not legally binding;

(2) when required, such response is issued in compliance with the requirements of Section 553 of title 5, United States Code; and

(3) such response represents the interpretation by the Department of Education of the applicable statutory or regulatory requirements in the context of the specific facts presented.

(f) Correspondence From Department of Education Describing Interpretations of This Title.

(1) In General. The Secretary **shall**, on a **quarterly basis**, publish in the Federal Register, and **widely disseminate** to interested entities through various additional forms of communication, a **list of correspondence** from the Department of Education received by individuals during the previous quarter that describes the interpretations of the Department of Education of this title or the regulations implemented pursuant to this title.

(2) Additional Information. For each item of correspondence published in a list under paragraph (1), the Secretary shall–

(A) identify the topic addressed by the correspondence and shall include such other summary information as the Secretary determines to be appropriate; and

(B) ensure that all such correspondence is issued, where applicable, in compliance with the requirements of Section 553 of title 5, United States Code.

20 U. S. C. § 1407. State Administration

WRIGHTSLAW OVERVIEW: States must ensure that their rules, regulations, and policies conform to IDEA 2004.

(a) Rulemaking. Each State that receives funds under this title shall–

(1) ensure that any State rules, regulations, and policies relating to this title conform to the purposes of this title;

(2) identify in writing to local educational agencies located in the State and the Secretary **any such rule, regulation, or policy** as a State-imposed requirement that is **not required** by this title and Federal regulations; and

(3) minimize the number of rules, regulations, and policies to which the local educational agencies and schools located in the State are subject under this title.

---

53 The Department of Education may not publish regulations that lessen the protections provided in the 1983 regulations, unless this reflects the clear and unequivocal intent of Congress.

(b) Support and Facilitation. State rules, regulations, and policies under this title shall support and facilitate local educational agency and school-level system improvement designed to enable children with disabilities to meet the challenging State student academic achievement standards.

20 U. S. C. § 1408. Paperwork Reduction

WRIGHTSLAW OVERVIEW: This section about Paperwork Reduction is new in IDEA 2004. States may create pilot programs to reduce paperwork and other non-instructional burdens. The U. S. Department of Education may grant waivers to 15 States but may not waive procedural requirements under 20 U.S.C § 1415. Two years after IDEA is enacted, the Secretary must report to Congress on the effectiveness of these waivers.

(a) Pilot Program.

(1) Purpose. The purpose of this section is to provide an opportunity for States to identify ways to reduce paperwork burdens and other administrative duties that are directly associated with the requirements of this title, in order to increase the time and resources available for instruction and other activities aimed at improving educational and functional results for children with disabilities.

(2) Authorization.

(A) In General. In order to carry out the purpose of this section, the Secretary is authorized to grant waivers of statutory requirements of, or regulatory requirements relating to, part B for a period of time not to exceed 4 years with respect to not more than 15 States based on proposals submitted by States to reduce excessive paperwork and noninstructional time burdens that do not assist in improving educational and functional results for children with disabilities.

(B) Exception. The Secretary shall not waive under this section any statutory requirements of, or regulatory requirements relating to, applicable civil rights requirements.

(C) Rule of Construction. Nothing in this section shall be construed to–

(i) affect the right of a child with a disability to receive a free appropriate public education under part B; and

(ii) permit a State or local educational agency to waive procedural safeguards under Section 1415 of this title.

(3) Proposal.

(A) In General. A State desiring to participate in the program under this section shall submit a proposal to the Secretary at such time and in such manner as the Secretary may reasonably require.

(B) Content. The proposal shall include–

(i) a list of any statutory requirements of, or regulatory requirements relating to, part B that the State desires the Secretary to waive, in whole or in part; and

(ii) a list of any State requirements that the State proposes to waive or change, in whole or in part, to carry out a waiver granted to the State by the Secretary.

(4) Termination of Waiver. The Secretary shall terminate a State's waiver under this section if the Secretary determines that the State–

(A) needs assistance under Section 1416(d)(2)(A)(ii) of this title and that the waiver has contributed to or caused such need for assistance;

(B) needs intervention under Section 1416(d)(2)(A)(iii) of this title or needs substantial intervention under Section 1416(d)(2)(A)(iv) of this title; or

(C) failed to appropriately implement its waiver.

(b) Report. Beginning 2 years after the date of enactment of the Individuals with Disabilities Education Improvement Act of 2004, the Secretary shall include in the annual report to Congress submitted pursuant to Section 3486 of this title information related to the effectiveness of waivers granted under subsection (a), including any specific recommendations for broader implementation of such waivers, in—

    (1) reducing –

        (A) the paperwork burden on teachers, principals, administrators, and related service providers; and

        (B) noninstructional time spent by teachers in complying with part B;

    (2) enhancing longer-term educational planning;

    (3) improving positive outcomes for children with disabilities;

    (4) promoting collaboration between IEP Team members; and

    (5) ensuring satisfaction of family members.

20 U. S. C. § 1409. Freely Associated States

WRIGHTSLAW OVERVIEW: Grants are available to the "Freely Associated States."

The Republic of the Marshall Islands, the Federated States of Micronesia, and the Republic of Palau shall continue to be eligible for competitive grants administered by the Secretary under this title to the extent that such grants continue to be available to States and local educational agencies under this title.

End of Part A

Part B — Assistance for Education of All Children with Disabilities

WRIGHTSLAW OVERVIEW: Part B, Assistance for Education of All Children with Disabilities, governs special education for children between the ages of 3 and 21 and includes Sections 1411 through Section 1419 of Title 20 of the United States Code (U. S. C.).

20 U. S. C. § 1411. Authorization; allotment; use of funds; authorization of appropriations
20 U. S. C. § 1412. State eligibility
20 U. S. C. § 1413. Local educational agency eligibility
20 U. S. C. § 1414. Evaluations, eligibility determinations, IEPs, and educational placements
20 U. S. C. § 1415. Procedural safeguards
20 U. S. C. § 1416. Monitoring, technical assistance, and enforcement
20 U. S. C. § 1417. Administration
20 U. S. C. § 1418. Program information
20 U. S. C. § 1419. Preschool grants

For most readers, the key sections are Section 1412, Section 1414, and Section 1415. Section 1412 includes child find, least restrictive environment, unilateral placements, reimbursement, and state and district assessments. Section 1414 describes requirements for evaluations, reevaluations, consent, eligibility, IEPs, and placements. Section 1415 describes the rules of procedure designed to protect the rights of children with disabilities and their parents. These safeguards include the right to examine educational records and obtain an independent educational evaluation, and the legal requirements for prior written notice, procedural safeguards notice, due process complaint notice, due process hearings, resolution sessions, mediation, attorney's fees, and discipline.

20 U. S. C. § 1411. Authorization; Allotment; Use of Funds; Authorization of Appropriations.

WRIGHTSLAW OVERVIEW: Section 1411 provides funding formulas, ratios, definitions, and requirements. New in IDEA 2004 is the optional Local Educational Agency (LEA) Risk Pool in Section 1411(e)(3) that allows states to reserve up to 10% of funds for "risk pools" to address the "high need children" with disabilities. Funds in the risk pool may not be used for litigation expenses. The Regulations for Section 1411 begin at 300.700 through 300.717.

(a) **Grants to States.**

(1) **Purpose of Grants.** The Secretary shall make grants to States, outlying areas, and freely associated States, and provide funds to the Secretary of the Interior, to assist them to provide special education and related services to children with disabilities in accordance with this part.

(2) **Maximum amount.** The **maximum amount** of the grant **a State may receive** under this section–

(A) for fiscal years 2005 and 2006 is–

(i) **the number of children with disabilities** in the State who are receiving special education and related services–

(I) aged 3 through 5 if the State is eligible for a grant under Section 1419 of this title; and

(II) aged 6 through 21; multiplied by

(ii) 40 percent of the average per-pupil expenditure in public elementary schools and secondary schools in the United States; and

(B) for fiscal year 2007 and subsequent fiscal years is–

(i) the number of children with disabilities in the 2004-2005 school year in the State who received special education and related services–

(I) aged 3 through 5 if the State is eligible for a grant under Section 1419 of this title; and

(II) aged 6 through 21; multiplied by

(ii) 40 percent of the average per-pupil expenditure in public elementary schools and secondary schools in the United States; adjusted by

(iii) the rate of annual change in the sum of–

    (I) 85 percent of such State's population described in subsection (d)(3)(A)(i)(II); and

    (II) 15 percent of such State's population described in subsection (d)(3)(A)(i)(III).

(b) Outlying Areas and Freely Associated States, Secretary of the Interior.

  (1) Outlying Areas and Freely Associated States.

    (A) Funds Reserved. From the amount appropriated for any fiscal year under subsection (i), the Secretary shall reserve not more than 1 percent, which shall be used–

      (i) to provide assistance to the outlying areas in accordance with their respective populations of individuals aged 3 through 21; and

      (ii) to provide each freely associated State a grant in the amount that such freely associated State received for fiscal year 2003 under this part, but only if the freely associated State meets the applicable requirements of this part, as well as the requirements of Section 1411(b)(2)(C) of this title as such section was in effect on the day before the date of enactment of the Individuals with Disabilities Education Improvement Act of 2004.

    (B) Special Rule. The provisions of Public Law 95-134, permitting the consolidation of grants by the outlying areas, shall not apply to funds provided to the outlying areas or the freely associated States under this section.

    (C) Definition. In this paragraph, the term '**freely associated States**' means the Republic of the Marshall Islands, the Federated States of Micronesia, and the Republic of Palau.

  (2) Secretary of the Interior. From the amount appropriated for any fiscal year under subsection (i), the Secretary shall reserve 1.226 percent to provide assistance to the Secretary of the Interior in accordance with subsection (h).

(c) Technical Assistance.

  (1) In General. The Secretary may reserve not more than 1/2 of 1 percent of the amounts appropriated under this part for each fiscal year to provide technical assistance activities authorized under Section 1416(i) of this title.

  (2) Maximum amount. The maximum amount the Secretary may reserve under paragraph (1) for any fiscal year is $25,000,000, cumulatively adjusted by the rate of inflation as measured by the percentage increase, if any, from the preceding fiscal year in the Consumer Price Index For All Urban Consumers, published by the Bureau of Labor Statistics of the Department of Labor.

(d) Allocations to States.

  (1) In General. After reserving funds for technical assistance, and for payments to the outlying areas, the freely associated States, and the Secretary of the Interior under subsections (b) and (c) for a fiscal year, the Secretary shall allocate the remaining amount among the States in accordance with this subsection.

  (2) Special Rule for use of Fiscal Year 1999 Amount. If a State received any funds under this section for fiscal year 1999 on the basis of children aged 3 through 5, but does not make a free appropriate public education available to all children with disabilities aged 3 through 5 in the State in any subsequent fiscal year, the Secretary shall compute the State's amount for fiscal year 1999, solely for the purpose of calculating the State's allocation in that subsequent year under paragraph (3) or (4), by subtracting the amount allocated to the State for fiscal year 1999 on the basis of those children.

  (3) Increase in Funds. If the amount available for allocations to States under paragraph (1) for a fiscal year is equal to or greater than the amount allocated to the States under this paragraph for the preceding fiscal year, those allocations shall be calculated as follows:

(A) Allocation of Increase.

(i) In General. Except as provided in subparagraph (B), the Secretary shall allocate for the fiscal year-

(I) to each State the amount the State received under this section for fiscal year 1999;

(II) 85 percent of any remaining funds to States on the basis of the States' relative populations of children aged 3 through 21 who are of the same age as children with disabilities for whom the State ensures the availability of a free appropriate public education under this part; and

(III) 15 percent of those remaining funds to States on the basis of the States' relative populations of children described in subclause (II) who are living in poverty.

(ii) Data. For the purpose of making grants under this paragraph, the Secretary shall use the most recent population data, including data on children living in poverty, that are available and satisfactory to the Secretary.

(B) Limitations. Notwithstanding subparagraph (A), allocations under this paragraph shall be subject to the following:

(i) Preceding Year Allocation. No State's allocation shall be less than its allocation under this section for the preceding fiscal year.

(ii) Minimum. No State's allocation shall be less than the greatest of–

(I) the sum of–

(aa) the amount the State received under this section for fiscal year 1999; and

(bb) 1/3 of 1 percent of the amount by which the amount appropriated under subsection (i) for the fiscal year exceeds the amount appropriated for this section for fiscal year 1999;

(II) the sum of—

(aa) the amount the State received under this section for the preceding fiscal year; and

(bb) that amount multiplied by the percentage by which the increase in the funds appropriated for this section from the preceding fiscal year exceeds 1.5 percent; or

(III) the sum of—

(aa) the amount the State received under this section for the preceding fiscal year; and

(bb) that amount multiplied by 90 percent of the percentage increase in the amount appropriated for this section from the preceding fiscal year.

(iii) Maximum. Notwithstanding clause (ii), no State's allocation under this paragraph shall exceed the sum of–

(I) the amount the State received under this section for the preceding fiscal year; and

(II) that amount multiplied by the sum of 1.5 percent and the percentage increase in the amount appropriated under this section from the preceding fiscal year.

(C) Ratable Reduction. If the amount available for allocations under this paragraph is insufficient to pay those allocations in full, those allocations shall be ratably reduced, subject to subparagraph (B)(i).

(4) Decrease in Funds. If the amount available for allocations to States under paragraph (1) for a fiscal year is less than the amount allocated to the States under this section for the preceding fiscal year, those allocations shall be calculated as follows:

(A) Amounts Greater than Fiscal Year 1999 Allocations. If the amount available for allocations is greater than the amount allocated to the States for fiscal year 1999, each State shall be allocated the sum of–

(i) the amount the State received under this section for fiscal year 1999; and

(ii) an amount that bears the same relation to any remaining funds as the increase the State received under this section for the preceding fiscal year over fiscal year 1999 bears to the total of all such increases for all States.

(B) Amounts Equal to or Less than Fiscal Year 1999 Allocations.

(i) In General. If the amount available for allocations under this paragraph is equal to or less than the amount allocated to the States for fiscal year 1999, each State shall be allocated the amount the State received for fiscal year 1999.

(ii) Ratable Reduction. If the amount available for allocations under this paragraph is insufficient to make the allocations described in clause (i), those allocations shall be ratably reduced.

(e) State Level Activities.

(1) State Administration.

(A) In General. For the purpose of administering this part, including paragraph (3), Section 1419 of this title, and the coordination of activities under this part with, and providing technical assistance to, other programs that provide services to children with disabilities–

(i) each State may reserve for each fiscal year not more than the maximum amount the State was eligible to reserve for State administration under this section for fiscal year 2004 or $800,000 (adjusted in accordance with subparagraph (B)), whichever is greater; and

(ii) each outlying area may reserve for each fiscal year not more than 5 percent of the amount the outlying area receives under subsection (b)(1) for the fiscal year or $35,000, whichever is greater.

(B) Cumulative Annual Adjustments. For each fiscal year beginning with fiscal year 2005, the Secretary shall cumulatively adjust

(i) the maximum amount the State was eligible to reserve for State administration under this part for fiscal year 2004; and

(ii) $800,000, by the rate of inflation as measured by the percentage increase, if any, from the preceding fiscal year in the Consumer Price Index For All Urban Consumers, published by the Bureau of Labor Statistics of the Department of Labor.

(C) Certification. Prior to expenditure of funds under this paragraph, the State shall certify to the Secretary that the arrangements to establish responsibility for services pursuant to Section 1412(a)(12)(A) of this title are current.

(D) Part C. Funds reserved under subparagraph (A) may be used for the administration of part C, if the State educational agency is the lead agency for the State under such part.

(2) Other State Level Activities.

(A) State Level Activities.

(i) In General. Except as provided in clause (iii), for the purpose of carrying out State-level activities, each State may reserve for each of the fiscal years 2005 and 2006 not more than 10 percent from the amount of the State's allocation under subsection (d) for each of the fiscal years 2005 and 2006, respectively. For fiscal year 2007 and each subsequent fiscal year, the State may reserve the maximum amount the State was eligible to reserve under the preceding sentence for fiscal year 2006 (cumulatively adjusted by the rate of inflation as measured by the percentage increase, if any, from the preceding fiscal year in the Consumer Price Index For All Urban Consumers, published by the Bureau of Labor Statistics of the Department of Labor).

(ii) Small State Adjustment. Notwithstanding clause (i) and except as provided in clause (iii), in the case of a State for which the maximum amount reserved for State administration is not greater than $850,000, the State may reserve for the purpose of carrying out State-level activities for each of the fiscal years 2005 and 2006, not more than 10.5 percent from the amount of the State's allocation under subsection (d) for each of the fiscal years 2005 and 2006, respectively. For fiscal year 2007 and each subsequent fiscal year, such State may reserve the maximum amount the State was eligible to reserve under the preceding sentence for fiscal year 2006 (cumulatively adjusted by the rate of inflation as measured by the percentage increase, if any, from the preceding fiscal year in the Consumer Price Index For All Urban Consumers, published by the Bureau of Labor Statistics of the Department of Labor).

(iii) Exception. If a State does not reserve funds under paragraph (3) for a fiscal year, then–

(I) in the case of a State that is not described in clause (ii), for fiscal year 2005 or 2006, clause (i) shall be applied by substituting 9.0 percent for 10 percent; and

(II) in the case of a State that is described in clause (ii), for fiscal year 2005 or 2006, clause (ii) shall be applied by substituting 9.5 percent for 10.5 percent.

(B) Required Activities. Funds reserved under subparagraph (A) shall be used to carry out the following activities:

(i) For monitoring, enforcement, and complaint investigation.

(ii) To establish and implement the mediation process required by section 1415(e) of this title, including providing for the cost of mediators and support personnel.

(C) Authorized Activities. Funds reserved under subparagraph (A) may be used to carry out the following activities:

(i) For support and direct services, including technical assistance, personnel preparation, and professional development and training.

(ii) To support paperwork reduction activities, including expanding the use of technology in the IEP process.

(iii) To assist local educational agencies in providing positive behavioral interventions and supports and appropriate mental health services for children with disabilities.

(iv) To improve the use of technology in the classroom by children with disabilities to enhance learning.

(v) To support the use of technology, including technology with universal design principles and assistive technology devices, to maximize accessibility to the general education curriculum for children with disabilities.

(vi) Development and implementation of transition programs, including coordination of services with agencies involved in supporting the transition of children with disabilities to postsecondary activities.

(vii) To assist local educational agencies in meeting personnel shortages.

(viii) To support capacity building activities and improve the delivery of services by local educational agencies to improve results for children with disabilities.

(ix) Alternative programming for children with disabilities who have been expelled from school, and services for children with disabilities in correctional facilities, children enrolled in State-operated or State-supported schools, and children with disabilities in charter schools.

(x) To support the development and provision of appropriate accommodations for children with disabilities, or the development and provision of alternate assessments that are valid and reliable for assessing the performance of children with disabilities, in accordance with Sections 6311(b) and 7301 of this title.

(xi) To provide technical assistance to schools and local educational agencies, and direct services, including supplemental educational services as defined in 6316(e) of the this title to children with disabilities, in schools or local educational agencies identified for improvement under Section 6316 of this title on the sole basis of the assessment results of the disaggregated subgroup of children with disabilities, including providing professional development to special and regular education teachers, who teach children with disabilities, based on scientifically based research to improve educational instruction, in order to improve academic achievement to meet or exceed the objectives established by the State under Section 6311(b)(2)(G) of this title.

(3) Local Educational Agency Risk Pool.[1]

(A) In General.

(i) Reservation of Funds. For the purpose of assisting local educational agencies (including a charter school that is a local educational agency or a consortium of local educational agencies) in addressing the needs of high need children with disabilities, each State shall have the option to reserve for each fiscal year 10 percent of the amount of funds the State reserves for State-level activities under paragraph (2)(A)–

(I) to establish and make disbursements from the high cost fund to local educational agencies in accordance with this paragraph during the first and succeeding fiscal years of the high cost fund; and

(II) to support innovative and effective ways of cost sharing by the State, by a local educational agency, or among a consortium of local educational agencies, as determined by the State in coordination with representatives from local educational agencies, subject to subparagraph (B)(ii).

(ii) Definition of Local Educational Agency. In this paragraph the term 'local educational agency' **includes a charter school** that is a local educational agency, or a consortium of local educational agencies.

(B) Limitation on Uses of Funds.

(i) Establishment of High Cost Fund. A State shall not use any of the funds the State reserves pursuant to subparagraph (A)(i), but may use the funds the State reserves under paragraph (1), to establish and support the high cost fund.

(ii) Innovative and Effective Cost Sharing. A State shall not use more than 5 percent of the funds the State reserves pursuant to subparagraph (A)(i) for each fiscal year to support innovative and effective ways of cost sharing among consortia of local educational agencies.

(C) State Plan for High Cost Fund.

(i) Definition. The State educational agency **shall establish the State's definition of a high need child with a disability,** which definition shall be developed in consultation with local educational agencies.

(ii) State Plan. The State educational agency shall develop, not later than 90 days after the State reserves funds under this paragraph, annually review, and amend as necessary, a State plan for the high cost fund. Such State plan shall–

(I) establish, in coordination with representatives from local educational agencies, a definition of a high need child with a disability that, at a minimum—

(aa) addresses the financial impact a high need child with a disability has on the budget of the child's local educational agency; and

(bb) ensures that the cost of the high need child with a disability is greater than 3 times the average per pupil expenditure (as defined in Section 7801 of the this title) in that State;

(II) establish eligibility criteria for the participation of a local educational agency that, at a minimum, takes into account the number and percentage of high need children with disabilities served by a local educational agency;

(III) develop a funding mechanism that provides distributions each fiscal year to local educational agencies that meet the criteria developed by the State under subclause (II); and

---

1 The provision for risk pools to address the needs of "high need children with disabilities" is new. Funds in the risk pool may be disbursed for "innovative, effective ways of cost sharing" by districts and consortiums of districts. Funds in the risk pool may not be used to support litigation.

(IV) establish an annual schedule by which the State educational agency shall make its distributions from the high cost fund each fiscal year.

(iii) Public Availability. The State shall make its final **State plan publicly available not less than 30 days before the beginning of the school year**, including dissemination of such information on the State website.

(D) Disbursements from the High Cost Fund.

(i) In General. Each State educational agency shall make all annual disbursements from the high cost fund established under subparagraph (A)(i) in accordance with the State plan published pursuant to subparagraph (C).

(ii) Use of Disbursements. Each State educational agency shall make annual disbursements to eligible local educational agencies in accordance with its State plan under subparagraph (C)(ii).

(iii) Appropriate Costs. The costs associated with educating a high need child with a disability under subparagraph (C)(i) are only those costs associated with providing direct special education and related services to such child that are identified in such child's IEP.

(E) Legal Fees. The disbursements under subparagraph (D) **shall not support legal fees, court costs, or other costs associated with a cause of action** brought on behalf of a child with a disability to ensure a free appropriate public education for such child.

(F) Assurance of a Free Appropriate Public Education.- Nothing in this paragraph **shall be construed–**

(i) to limit or condition the right of a child with a disability who is assisted under this part to receive a free appropriate public education pursuant to Section 1412(a)(1) of this title in the least restrictive environment pursuant to Section 1412(a)(5) of this title; or

(ii) to authorize a State educational agency or local educational agency to establish a limit on what may be spent on the education of a child with a disability.

(G) Special Rule for Risk Pool and High Need Assistance Programs in Effect as of January 1, 2004. Notwithstanding the provisions of subparagraphs (A) through (F), a State may use funds reserved pursuant to this paragraph for implementing a placement neutral cost sharing and reimbursement program of high need, low incidence, catastrophic, or extraordinary aid to local educational agencies that provides services to high need students based on eligibility criteria for such programs that were created not later than January 1, 2004, and are currently in operation, if such program serves children that meet the requirement of the definition of a high need child with a disability as described in subparagraph (C)(ii)(I).

(H) Medicaid Services not Affected. Disbursements provided under this paragraph shall not be used to pay costs that otherwise would be reimbursed as medical assistance for a child with a disability under the State medicaid program under title XIX of the Social Security Act.

(I) Remaining Funds. Funds reserved under subparagraph (A) in any fiscal year but not expended in that fiscal year pursuant to subparagraph (D) shall be allocated to local educational agencies for the succeeding fiscal year in the same manner as funds are allocated to local educational agencies under subsection (f) for the succeeding fiscal year.

(4) Inapplicability of Certain Prohibitions. A State may use funds the State reserves under paragraphs (1) and (2) without regard to–

(A) the prohibition on commingling of funds in Section 1412(a)(17)(B) of this title; and

(B) the prohibition on supplanting other funds in Section 1412(a)(17)(C) of this title.

(5) Report on Use of Funds. As part of the information required to be submitted to the Secretary under Section 1412 of this title, each State shall annually describe how amounts under this section–

(A) will be used to meet the requirements of this title; and

(B) will be allocated among the activities described in this section to meet State priorities based on input from local educational agencies.

(6) Special Rule for Increased Funds. A State may use funds the State reserves under paragraph (1)(A) as a result of inflationary increases under paragraph (1)(B) to carry out activities authorized under clause (i), (iii), (vii), or (viii) of paragraph (2)(C).

(7) Flexibility in Using Funds for Part C. Any State eligible to receive a grant under Section 1419 of this title may use funds made available under paragraph (1)(A), subsection (f)(3), or Section 1419(f)(5) of this title to develop and implement a State policy jointly with the lead agency under part C and the State educational agency to provide early intervention services (which shall include an educational component that promotes school readiness and incorporates preliteracy, language, and numeracy skills) in accordance with part C to children with disabilities who are eligible for services under Section 1419 of this title and who previously received services under part C until such children enter, or are eligible under State law to enter, kindergarten, or elementary school as appropriate.

(f) Subgrants to Local Educational Agencies.

(1) Subgrants Required. Each State that receives a grant under this section for any fiscal year shall distribute any funds the State does not reserve under subsection (e) to local educational agencies (including public charter schools that operate as local educational agencies) in the State that have established their eligibility under Section 1413 of this title for use in accordance with this part.

(2) Procedure for Allocations to Local Educational Agencies. For each fiscal year for which funds are allocated to States under subsection (d), each State shall allocate funds under paragraph (1) as follows:

(A) Base Payments. The State shall first award each local educational agency described in paragraph (1) the amount the local educational agency would have received under this section for fiscal year 1999, if the State had distributed 75 percent of its grant for that year under Section 1411(d) of this title as Section 1411(d) of this title was then in effect.

(B) Allocation of Remaining Funds. After making allocations under subparagraph (A), the State shall—

(i) allocate 85 percent of any remaining funds to those local educational agencies on the basis of the relative numbers of children enrolled in public and private elementary schools and secondary schools within the local educational agency's jurisdiction; and

(ii) allocate 15 percent of those remaining funds to those local educational agencies in accordance with their relative numbers of children living in poverty, as determined by the State educational agency.

(3) Reallocation of Funds. If a State educational agency determines that a local educational agency is adequately providing a free appropriate public education to all children with disabilities residing in the area served by that local educational agency with State and local funds, the State educational agency may reallocate any portion of the funds under this part that are not needed by that local educational agency to provide a free appropriate public education to other local educational agencies in the State that are not adequately providing special education and related services to all children with disabilities residing in the areas served by those other local educational agencies.

(g) Definitions. In this section:

(1) Average per Pupil Expenditure in Public Elementary Schools and Secondary Schools in the United States. The term 'average per-pupil expenditure in public elementary schools and secondary schools in the United States' means—

(A) without regard to the source of funds—

(i) the aggregate current expenditures, during the second fiscal year preceding the fiscal year for which the determination is made (or, if satisfactory data for that year are not available, during the most recent preceding fiscal year for which satisfactory data are available) of all local educational agencies in the 50 States and the District of Columbia; plus

(ii) any direct expenditures by the State for the operation of those agencies; divided by

(B) the aggregate number of children in average daily attendance to whom those agencies provided free public education during that preceding year.

(2) State. The term 'State' means each of the 50 States, the District of Columbia, and the Commonwealth of Puerto Rico.

(h) Use of Amounts by Secretary of the Interior.

(1) Provision of Amounts for Assistance.

(A) In General. The Secretary of Education shall provide amounts to the Secretary of the Interior to meet the need for assistance for the education of children with disabilities on reservations aged 5 to 21, inclusive, enrolled in elementary schools and secondary schools for Indian children operated or funded by the Secretary of the Interior. The amount of such payment for any fiscal year shall be equal to 80 percent of the amount allotted under subsection (b)(2) for that fiscal year. Of the amount described in the preceding sentence–

(i) 80 percent shall be allocated to such schools by July 1 of that fiscal year; and

(ii) 20 percent shall be allocated to such schools by September 30 of that fiscal year.

(B) Calculation of Number of Children. In the case of Indian students aged 3 to 5, inclusive, who are enrolled in programs affiliated with the Bureau of Indian Affairs (referred to in this subsection as the BIA') schools and that are required by the States in which such schools are located to attain or maintain State accreditation, and which schools have such accreditation prior to the date of enactment of the Individuals with Disabilities Education Act Amendments of 1991, the school shall be allowed to count those children for the purpose of distribution of the funds provided under this paragraph to the Secretary of the Interior. The Secretary of the Interior shall be responsible for meeting all of the requirements of this part for those children, in accordance with paragraph (2).

(C) Additional Requirement. With respect to all other children aged 3 to 21, inclusive, on reservations, the State educational agency shall be responsible for ensuring that all of the requirements of this part are implemented.

(2) Submission of Information. The Secretary of Education may provide the Secretary of the Interior amounts under paragraph (1) for a fiscal year only if the Secretary of the Interior submits to the Secretary of Education information that–

(A) demonstrates that the Department of the Interior meets the appropriate requirements, as determined by the Secretary of Education, of Sections 1412 (including monitoring and evaluation activities) and 1413 of this title;

(B) includes a description of how the Secretary of the Interior will coordinate the provision of services under this part with local educational agencies, tribes and tribal organizations, and other private and Federal service providers;

(C) includes an assurance that there are public hearings, adequate notice of such hearings, and an opportunity for comment afforded to members of tribes, tribal governing bodies, and affected local school boards before the adoption of the policies, programs, and procedures related to the requirements described in subparagraph (A);

(D) includes an assurance that the Secretary of the Interior will provide such information as the Secretary of Education may require to comply with Section 1418 of this title;

(E) includes an assurance that the Secretary of the Interior and the Secretary of Health and Human Services have entered into a memorandum of agreement, to be provided to the Secretary of Education, for the coordination of services, resources, and personnel between their respective Federal, State, and local offices and with State and local educational agencies and other entities to facilitate the provision of services to Indian children with disabilities residing on or near reservations (such agreement shall provide for the apportionment of responsibilities and costs, including child find, evaluation, diagnosis, remediation or therapeutic measures, and (where appropriate) equipment and medical or personal supplies as needed for a child to remain in school or a program); and

(F) includes an assurance that the Department of the Interior will cooperate with the Department of Education in its exercise of monitoring and oversight of this application, and any agreements entered into between the Secretary of the Interior and other entities under this part, and will fulfill its duties under this part.

(3) Applicability. The Secretary shall withhold payments under this subsection with respect to the information described in paragraph (2) in the same manner as the Secretary withholds payments under Section 1416(e)(6) of this title.

(4) Payments for Education and Services for Indian Children with Disabilities Aged 3 Through 5.

(A) In General. With funds appropriated under subsection (i), the Secretary of Education shall make payments to the Secretary of the Interior to be distributed to tribes or tribal organizations (as defined under Section 450b of title 25) or consortia of tribes or tribal organizations to provide for the coordination of assistance for special education and related services for children with disabilities aged 3 through 5 on reservations served by elementary schools and secondary schools for Indian children operated or funded by the Department of the Interior. The amount of such payments under subparagraph (B) for any fiscal year shall be equal to 20 percent of the amount allotted under subsection (b)(2).

(B) Distribution of Funds. The Secretary of the Interior shall distribute the total amount of the payment under subparagraph (A) by allocating to each tribe, tribal organization, or consortium an amount based on the number of children with disabilities aged 3 through 5 residing on reservations as reported annually, divided by the total of those children served by all tribes or tribal organizations.

(C) Submission of Information. To receive a payment under this paragraph, the tribe or tribal organization shall submit such figures to the Secretary of the Interior as required to determine the amounts to be allocated under subparagraph (B). This information shall be compiled and submitted to the Secretary of Education.

(D) Use of Funds. The funds received by a tribe or tribal organization shall be used to assist in child find, screening, and other procedures for the early identification of children aged 3 through 5, parent training, and the provision of direct services. These activities may be carried out directly or through contracts or cooperative agreements with the BIA, local educational agencies, and other public or private nonprofit organizations. The tribe or tribal organization is encouraged to involve Indian parents in the development and implementation of these activities. The tribe or tribal organization shall, as appropriate, make referrals to local, State, or Federal entities for the provision of services or further diagnosis.

(E) Biennial Report. To be eligible to receive a grant pursuant to subparagraph (A), the tribe or tribal organization shall provide to the Secretary of the Interior a biennial report of activities undertaken under this paragraph, including the number of contracts and cooperative agreements entered into, the number of children contacted and receiving services for each year, and the estimated number of children needing services during the 2 years following the year in which the report is made. The Secretary of the Interior shall include a summary of this information on a biennial basis in the report to the Secretary of Education required under this subsection. The Secretary of Education may require any additional information from the Secretary of the Interior.

(F) Prohibitions. None of the funds allocated under this paragraph may be used by the Secretary of the Interior for administrative purposes, including child count and the provision of technical assistance.

(5) Plan for Coordination of Services. The Secretary of the Interior shall develop and implement a plan for the coordination of services for all Indian children with disabilities residing on reservations covered under this title. Such plan shall provide for the coordination of services benefiting those children from whatever source, including tribes, the Indian Health Service, other BIA divisions, and other Federal agencies. In developing the plan, the Secretary of the Interior shall consult with all interested and involved parties. The plan shall be based on the needs of the children and the system best suited for meeting those needs, and may involve the establishment of cooperative agreements between the BIA, other Federal agencies, and other entities. The plan shall also be distributed upon request to States, State educational agencies and local educational agencies, and other agencies providing services to infants, toddlers, and children with disabilities, to tribes, and to other interested parties.

(6) Establishment of Advisory Board. To meet the requirements of Section 1412(a)(21) of this title, the Secretary of the Interior shall establish, under the BIA, an advisory board composed of individuals involved in or concerned with the education and provision of services to Indian infants, toddlers, children, and youth with disabilities, including Indians with disabilities, Indian parents or guardians of such children, teachers, service providers, State and local educational officials, representatives of tribes or tribal organizations, representatives from State Interagency Coordinating Councils under Section 1441 of this title in States having reservations, and other members representing the various divisions and entities of the BIA. The chairperson shall be selected by the Secretary of the Interior. The advisory board shall–

(A) assist in the coordination of services within the BIA and with other local, State, and Federal agencies in the provision of education for infants, toddlers, and children with disabilities;

(B) advise and assist the Secretary of the Interior in the performance of the Secretary of the Interior's responsibilities described in this subsection;

(C) develop and recommend policies concerning effective inter– and intra-agency collaboration, including modifications to regulations, and the elimination of barriers to inter– and intra-agency programs and activities;

(D) provide assistance and disseminate information on best practices, effective program coordination strategies, and recommendations for improved early intervention services or educational programming for Indian infants, toddlers, and children with disabilities; and

(E) provide assistance in the preparation of information required under paragraph (2)(D).

(7) Annual Reports.

(A) In General. The advisory board established under paragraph (6) shall prepare and submit to the Secretary of the Interior and to Congress an annual report containing a description of the activities of the advisory board for the preceding year.

(B) Availability. The Secretary of the Interior shall make available to the Secretary of Education the report described in subparagraph (A).

(i) Authorizations of Appropriations. For the purpose of carrying out this part, other than Section 1419 of this title, there are authorized to be appropriated–

(1) $12,358,376,571 for fiscal year 2005;

(2) $14,648,647,143 for fiscal year 2006;

(3) $16,938,917,714 for fiscal year 2007;

(4) $19,229,188,286 for fiscal year 2008;

(5) $21,519,458,857 for fiscal year 2009;

(6) $23,809,729,429 for fiscal year 2010;

(7) $26,100,000,000 for fiscal year 2011; and

(8) such sums as may be necessary for fiscal year 2012 and each succeeding fiscal year.

20 U. S. C. § 1412. State Eligibility.

WRIGHTSLAW OVERVIEW: Section 1412 about State Eligibility is often called the "Catch-All" statute because it includes a variety of diverse topics including child find, least restrictive environment, transition to preschool programs, equitable services for children in private schools, unilateral placements, tuition reimbursement, and assessments. Section 1412(a)(3) describes requirements for child find. Section 1412(a)(5) describes requirements for educating children with disabilities in the least restrictive environment (LRE). Section 1412(a)(10) explains services that must be provided to children who attend private schools and includes new requirements about consultation with private schools and equitable services for children who attend private schools. It also contains the requirements for unilateral placements by parents and tuition reimbursement. Section 1412(a)(11) clarifies that the state is ultimately responsible for programs operated by local school districts and ensuring that children with disabilities receive a free appropriate education. Section 1412(a)(14) describes requirements for highly qualified special education teachers. Section 1412(a)(16) includes new requirements about participating in assessments, accommodations guidelines, and alternate assessments. Section 1412(a)(23) includes requirements about access to instructional materials. Section 1412(a)(25) describes the new prohibition on mandatory medication. The Regulations for Section 1412 begin at Section 300.100 and continue to Section 300.198.

(a) In General. A **State is eligible for assistance** under this part for a fiscal year **if the State submits a plan that provides assurances** to the Secretary **that the State has in effect policies and procedures** to ensure that the State meets **each of the following conditions:**

(1) Free Appropriate Public Education.

(A) In General. A **free appropriate public education is available to all children with disabilities** residing in the State between the **ages of 3 and 21, inclusive,** including children with disabilities **who have been**

suspended or expelled from school.[2]

(B) Limitation. The obligation to make a free appropriate public education available to all children with disabilities does not apply with respect to children–

(i) aged 3 through 5 and 18 through 21 in a State to the extent that its application to those children would be inconsistent with State law or practice, or the order of any court, respecting the provision of public education to children in those age ranges; and

(ii) aged 18 through 21 to the extent that State law does not require that special education and related services under this part be provided to children with disabilities who, in the educational placement **prior to their incarceration in an adult correctional facility–**

(I) **were not actually identified** as being a child with a disability under Section 1401 of this title; or

(II) **did not have an individualized education program** under this part.

(C) State Flexibility. A State that provides early intervention services in accordance with part C to a child who is eligible for services under Section 1419 of this title, is not required to provide such child with a free appropriate public education.[3]

(2) Full Educational Opportunity Goal. The State has established a goal of providing full educational opportunity to all children with disabilities and a detailed timetable for accomplishing that goal.

(3) Child Find.

(A) In General. All children with disabilities residing in the State, including children with disabilities who are **homeless children** or are **wards of the State** and children with disabilities **attending private schools**, regardless of the severity of their disabilities, **and who are in need of special education and related services, are identified, located, and evaluated** and a practical method is developed and implemented to determine which children with disabilities are currently receiving needed special education and related services.[4]

(B) Construction. Nothing in this title requires that children be classified by their disability so long as each child who has a disability listed in Section 1401 of this title and who, by reason of that disability, needs special education and related services is regarded as a child with a disability under this part.[5]

(4) Individualized Education Program. An individualized education program, or an individualized family service plan that meets the requirements of Section 1436(d) of this title, **is developed, reviewed, and revised for each child with a disability** in accordance with Section 1414(d) of this title.

(5) Least Restrictive Environment.

(A) In General. To the maximum extent appropriate, children with disabilities, including children in public or private institutions or other care facilities, **are educated with children who are not disabled,** and special classes, separate schooling, or other removal of children with disabilities from the regular educational

---

2   All children who are eligible for special education services under IDEA are entitled to a free appropriate public education (FAPE), including children who have been suspended or expelled from school. Before Congress enacted Public Law 94-142, millions of children with disabilities were not allowed to attend public schools. (See Findings in Section 1400(c) and Discipline in Section 1415(k)).

3   See Section 1432(4)(B) which describes early intervention services that "are provided at no cost except where a federal or State law provides for a system for payments by families, including a schedule of sliding fees . . . ."

4   Child find requires school districts to identify, locate, and evaluate all children with disabilities, including children who are home schooled, homeless, wards of the state, and children who attend private schools. See also Section 1412(a)(10) regarding the child find requirements that public schools have regarding students who attend private schools, including consultations with private school officials.

5   If the child has a disability that adversely affects educational performance (i.e., the child is eligible for special education services under Section 1401(3) of IDEA) the school is not required to determine the child's "label" or classification before it provides services. Schools often spend months performing evaluations before they provide any special education services. During this time, the child falls further behind. See also Section 1414(a)(1)(C)(i)(I) about the new 60 calendar day timeline between parental consent and completion of the evaluation process.

environment occurs only when the nature or severity of the disability of a child is such that education in regular classes with the use of supplementary aids and services cannot be achieved satisfactorily.[6]

(B) Additional Requirement.

(i) In General. A **State funding mechanism shall not result in placements that violate the requirements** of subparagraph (A), and a State shall not use a funding mechanism by which the State distributes funds on the basis of the type of setting in which a child is served that will result in the failure to provide a child with a disability a free appropriate public education according to the unique needs of the child as described in the child's IEP.

(ii) Assurance. If the State does not have policies and procedures to ensure compliance with clause (i), the State shall provide the Secretary an assurance that the State will revise the funding mechanism as soon as feasible to ensure that such mechanism does not result in such placements.

(6) Procedural Safeguards.

(A) In General. Children with disabilities and their parents are afforded the procedural safeguards required by Section 1415 of this title.

(B) Additional Procedural Safeguards. Procedures to ensure that **testing and evaluation materials and procedures** utilized for the purposes of evaluation and placement of children with disabilities for services under this title will be selected and administered so as **not** to be **racially or culturally discriminatory.** Such materials or procedures shall be provided and **administered in the child's native language or mode of communication**, unless it clearly is not feasible to do so, and **no single procedure shall be the sole criterion** for determining an appropriate educational program for a child.[7]

(7) Evaluation. Children with disabilities are evaluated in accordance with subsections (a) through (c) of Section 1414 of this title.

(8) Confidentiality. Agencies in the State comply with Section 1417(c) of this title (relating to the confidentiality of records and information).

(9) Transition from Part C to Preschool Programs. Children participating in early intervention programs assisted under part C, and who will participate in preschool programs assisted under this part, experience a **smooth and effective transition to those preschool programs** in a manner consistent with Section 1437(a)(9) of this title. By the third birthday of such a child, an individualized education program or, if consistent with Sections 1414(d)(2)(B) and 1436(d) of this title, an individualized family service plan, has been developed and is being implemented for the child. The local educational agency will participate in transition planning conferences arranged by the designated lead agency under Section 1435(a)(10) of this title.

(10) Children in Private Schools.

(A) Children Enrolled in Private Schools by Their Parents.

(i) In General. To the extent consistent with the number and location of **children with disabilities** in the State who are **enrolled by their parents in private elementary schools and secondary schools** in

---

6   The definition of "least restrictive environment" did not change. Judicial decisions about "mainstreaming," "least restrictive environment" (LRE) and "inclusion" vary, even within the same state. Some districts claim the law requires them to mainstream all children with disabilities, even children who need individualized instruction that cannot be delivered in general education classrooms. In other districts, parents must fight to have their disabled child "included" in general education classes. The law takes a commonsense approach to this issue: children with disabilities should be educated with children who are not disabled "to the maximum extent appropriate." However, children can receive one-to-one or small group instruction outside of regular classes if this is necessary for them to learn. The placement is to be as close to the child's home as possible, preferably in the school the child would attend if non-disabled. See Regulation 300.116.

7   In "Findings" at Section 1400(c), Congress described the over-representation of minority children and limited English proficient children in special education. These children often do not perform as well on traditional measures of intelligence and educational achievement. The requirements that evaluations shall be administered in the child's native language or mode of communication and that "no single procedure shall be the sole criterion" for determining an appropriate educational program, attempt to remedy evaluations that have caused minority children to be over-represented in special education.

the school district served by a local educational agency, **provision is made for the participation of those children in the program** assisted or carried out under this part by providing for such children special education and related services in accordance with the following requirements, unless the Secretary has arranged for services to those children under subsection (f):

(I) Amounts to be expended for the provision of those services (including **direct services to parentally placed private school children**) by the local educational agency shall be equal to a proportionate amount of Federal funds made available under this part.

(II) In calculating the proportionate amount of Federal funds, the local educational agency, after **timely and meaningful consultation with representatives of private schools** as described in clause (iii), **shall conduct a thorough and complete child find process** to determine the number of parentally placed children with disabilities attending private schools located in the local educational agency.

(III) Such **services to parentally placed private school children with disabilities may be provided to the children on the premises of private, including religious, schools,** to the extent consistent with law.

(IV) State and local funds may supplement and in no case shall supplant the proportionate amount of Federal funds required to be expended under this subparagraph.

(V) Each **local educational agency shall** maintain in its records and **provide to the State educational agency the number of children evaluated** under this subparagraph, the **number of children determined to be children with disabilities** under this paragraph, and the **number of children served** under this paragraph.

(ii) Child Find Requirement.

(I) **In General.** The requirements of paragraph (3) (relating to child find) **shall apply with respect to children with disabilities** in the State who are **enrolled in private, including religious, elementary schools and secondary schools.**

(II) **Equitable Participation.** The child find process shall be designed to **ensure the equitable participation of parentally placed private school children with disabilities** and an accurate count of such children.

(III) **Activities.** In carrying out this clause, the local educational agency, or where applicable, the State educational agency, shall undertake activities similar to those activities undertaken for the agency's public school children.

(IV) **Cost.** The **cost of carrying out this clause, including individual evaluations, may not be considered** in determining whether a local educational agency has met its obligations under clause (i).

(V) **Completion Period.** Such child find process shall be completed in a time period comparable to that for other students attending public schools in the local educational agency.

(iii) Consultation.

To ensure timely and meaningful consultation, a local educational agency, or where appropriate, a State educational agency, **shall consult with private school representatives and representatives of parents of parentally placed private school children with disabilities during the design and development of special education and related services for the children,**[8] including regarding—

---

8 IDEA includes new requirements about consultation between public school and private school officials and equitable participation of children who attend private schools. The consultation process in Section 1412(a)(10)(A) includes written affirmation, compliance, complaints to the state by private schools, and the provision of equitable services to children who attend private schools. The language about consultation with "private school representatives and representatives of parents of parentally placed private school children" brings IDEA 2004 into conformity with No Child Left Behind. (20 U. S. C. § 6320)

(I) the child find process and how **parentally placed private school children suspected of having a disability can participate equitably,**[9] including how parents, teachers, and private school officials will be informed of the process;

(II) the determination of the proportionate amount of Federal funds available to serve parentally placed private school children with disabilities under this subparagraph, including the determination of how the amount was calculated;

(III) the consultation process among the local educational agency, private school officials, and representatives of parents of parentally placed private school children with disabilities, including how such process will operate throughout the school year to ensure that parentally placed private school children with disabilities identified through the child find process can meaningfully participate in special education and related services;

(IV) how, where, and by whom special education and related services will be provided for parentally placed private school children with disabilities, including a discussion of types of services, including direct services and alternate service delivery mechanisms, how such services will be apportioned if funds are insufficient to serve all children, and how and when these decisions will be made; and

(V) how, **if the local educational agency disagrees with the views of the private school officials on the provision of services** or the types of services, whether provided directly or through a contract, the local educational agency **shall provide to the private school officials a written explanation of the reasons why the local educational agency chose not to provide services** directly or through a contract.

(iv) Written Affirmation. When timely and meaningful consultation as required by clause (iii) has occurred, the local educational agency **shall obtain a written affirmation signed by the representatives of participating private schools**, and if such representatives do not provide such affirmation within a reasonable period of time, the local educational agency shall forward the documentation of the consultation process to the State educational agency.

(v) Compliance.

(I) In General. A **private school official shall have the right to submit a complaint** to the State educational agency that the local educational agency did not engage in consultation that was meaningful and timely, or did not give due consideration to the views of the private school official.

(II) Procedure. If the private school official wishes to submit a complaint, the official **shall provide the basis of the noncompliance** with this subparagraph by the local educational agency to the State educational agency, and the local educational agency shall forward the appropriate documentation to the State educational agency. If the private school official is dissatisfied with the decision of the State educational agency, such **official may submit a complaint to the Secretary** by providing the basis of the noncompliance with this subparagraph by the local educational agency to the Secretary, and the State educational agency shall forward the appropriate documentation to the Secretary.

(vi) Provision of Equitable Services.

(I) Directly or Through Contracts. The provision of services pursuant to this subparagraph shall be provided

(aa) by employees of a public agency; or

(bb) through contract by the public agency with an individual, association, agency, organization, or other entity.

---

9 "No parentally-placed private school child with a disability has an individual right to receive some or all of the special education and related services that the child would receive if enrolled in a public school." See Regulation 300.137 and Commentary in the *Federal Register,* page 46595.

(II) Secular, Neutral, Nonideological. Special education and related services provided to parentally placed private school children with disabilities, including materials and equipment, shall be secular, neutral, and nonideological.[10]

(vii) Public Control of Funds. The control of funds used to provide special education and related services under this subparagraph, and title to materials, equipment, and property purchased with those funds, shall be in a public agency for the uses and purposes provided in this title, and a public agency shall administer the funds and property.

(B) Children Placed in, or Referred to, Private Schools by Public Agencies.

(i) In General. Children with disabilities in private schools and facilities are provided special education and related services, in accordance with an individualized education program, at no cost to their parents, if such children are placed in, or referred to, such schools or facilities by the State or appropriate local educational agency as the means of carrying out the requirements of this part or any other applicable law requiring the provision of special education and related services to all children with disabilities within such State.

(ii) Standards. In all cases described in clause (i), the State educational agency shall determine whether such schools and facilities meet standards that apply to State educational agencies and local educational agencies and that children so served **have all the rights** the children would have if served by such agencies.[11]

(C) Payment for Education of Children Enrolled in Private Schools Without Consent of or Referral by the Public Agency.

(i) In General. Subject to subparagraph (A), this part does not require a local educational agency to pay for the cost of education, including special education and related services, of a child with a disability at a private school or facility if that agency made a free appropriate public education available to the child and the parents elected to place the child in such private school or facility.

(ii) Reimbursement for Private School Placement. If the parents of a child with a disability, who previously received special education and related services under the authority of a public agency, **enroll the child in a private** elementary school or secondary **school without the consent of or referral** by the public agency, a **court or a hearing officer may require the agency to reimburse the parents** for the cost of that enrollment **if** the court or hearing officer finds that **the agency had not made a free appropriate public education available to the child in a timely manner prior to that enrollment.**[12]

(iii) Limitation on Reimbursement. The cost of **reimbursement** described in clause (ii) **may be reduced or denied–**

(I) **if–**

(aa) **at the most recent IEP meeting** that the parents attended prior to removal of the child from the public school, the **parents did not inform the IEP Team that they were rejecting the placement** proposed by the public agency to provide a free appropriate public education to their child, **including stating their concerns and their intent to enroll their child in a private school at public expense; or**

---

10 Court decisions about whether school districts must provide special education and related services at a child's private school differ around the country. Many courts have held that the public school must make these services available, but that services do not have to be provided at the private school.

11 If a public school places a child in a private school, the child has the same rights under IDEA as if the child attended a public school.

12 The law about reimbursement for unilateral parental placements in private schools did not change. If the parent removes the child from a public school program and places the child into a private program, the parent may be reimbursed for the costs of the private program if a hearing officer or court determines that the public school did not offer FAPE "in a timely manner."

(bb) **10 business days** (including any holidays that occur on a business day) **prior to the removal of the child** from the public school, the **parents did not give written notice** to the public agency of the information described in item (aa);[13]

(II) **if**, prior to the parents' removal of the child from the public school, the public agency **informed the parents**, through the notice requirements described in Section 1415(b)(3) of this title, **of its intent to evaluate the child** (including a statement of the purpose of the evaluation that was appropriate and reasonable), **but the parents did not make the child available for such evaluation**; or

(III) upon a **judicial finding of unreasonableness** with respect to actions taken **by the parents**.

(iv) **Exception**. Notwithstanding the notice requirement in clause (iii)(I), the cost of reimbursement

(I) **shall not be reduced or denied** for failure to provide such notice if–

(aa) the school prevented the parent from providing such notice;

(bb) the parents had not received notice, pursuant to Section 1415 of this title, of the notice requirement in clause (iii)(I); or

(cc) compliance with clause (iii)(I) would likely result in physical harm to the child; and

(II) **may**, in the discretion of a court or a hearing officer, **not be reduced or denied** for failure to provide such notice if–

(aa) the parent is illiterate or cannot write in English; or

(bb) compliance with clause (iii)(I) would likely result in serious emotional harm to the child.

(11) State Educational Agency Responsible for General Supervision.[14]

(A) In General. The State educational agency **is responsible for ensuring** that

(i) the requirements of this part are met;

(ii) all educational programs for children with disabilities in the State, including all such programs administered by any other State agency or local agency–

(I) are under the general supervision of individuals in the State who are responsible for educational programs for children with disabilities; and

(II) meet the educational standards of the State educational agency; and

(iii) in carrying out this part with respect to homeless children, the requirements of subtitle B of title VII of the McKinney-Vento Homeless Assistance Act (42 U. S. C. § 11431 *et seq.*) are met.[15]

(B) Limitation. Subparagraph (A) shall not limit the responsibility of agencies in the State other than the State educational agency to provide, or pay for some or all of the costs of, a free appropriate public education for any child with a disability in the State.

(C) Exception. Notwithstanding subparagraphs (A) and (B), the Governor (or another individual pursuant to State law), consistent with State law, may assign to any public agency in the State the responsibility of ensuring that the requirements of this part are met with respect to children with disabilities who are convicted as adults under State law and incarcerated in adult prisons.

(12) Obligations Related to and Methods of Ensuring Services–

(A) Establishing Responsibility for Services. The Chief Executive Officer of a State or designee of the officer shall ensure that an interagency agreement or other mechanism for interagency coordination is in ef-

---

13 Sample letters about the 10 business day notice of removal are in *Wrightslaw: From Emotions to Advocacy*.

14 State departments of education (SEAs) are responsible for supervising school districts (LEAs). State complaint procedures are described in Regulation 300.151 through 300.153. Many state departments of education view their role as a source of funding, technical assistance and training, not as an enforcement agency. In lawsuits, States often argue that they have sovereign immunity despite the clear opposite language in Section 1403, Abrogation of Sovereign Immunity.

15 See Chapter 10 for the full text of the McKinney-Vento Homeless Act.

fect between each public agency described in subparagraph (B) and the State educational agency, in order to ensure that all services described in subparagraph (B)(i) that are needed **to** ensure a free appropriate public education are provided, including the provision of such services during the pendency of any dispute under clause (iii). Such agreement or mechanism shall include the following:

(i) **Agency Financial Responsibility.** An identification of, or a method for defining, the financial responsibility of each agency for providing services described in subparagraph (B)(i) to ensure a free appropriate public education to children with disabilities, provided that the financial responsibility of each public agency described in subparagraph (B), including the State medicaid agency and other public insurers of children with disabilities, shall precede the financial responsibility of the local educational agency (or the State agency responsible for developing the child's IEP).

(ii) **Conditions and Terms of Reimbursement.** The conditions, terms, and procedures under which a local educational agency shall be reimbursed by other agencies.

(iii) **Interagency Disputes.** Procedures for resolving interagency disputes (including procedures under which local educational agencies may initiate proceedings) under the agreement or other mechanism to secure reimbursement from other agencies or otherwise implement the provisions of the agreement or mechanism.

(iv) **Coordination of Services Procedures.** Policies and procedures for agencies to determine and identify the interagency coordination responsibilities of each agency to promote the coordination and timely and appropriate delivery of services described in subparagraph (B)(i).

(B) Obligation of Public Agency.

(i) **In General.** If any public agency other than an educational agency is otherwise obligated under Federal or State law, or assigned responsibility under State policy pursuant to subparagraph (A), to provide or pay for any services that are also considered special education or related services (such as, but not limited to, services described in Section 1401(1) of this title relating to assistive technology devices, 1401(2) of this title relating to assistive technology services, 1401(26) of this title relating to related services, 1401(33) of this title relating to supplementary aids and services, and 1401(34) of this title relating to transition services) that are necessary for ensuring a free appropriate public education to children with disabilities within the State, such public agency shall fulfill that obligation or responsibility, either directly or through contract or other arrangement pursuant to subparagraph (A) or an agreement pursuant to subparagraph (C).

(ii) **Reimbursement for Services by Public Agency.** If a public agency other than an educational agency fails to provide or pay for the special education and related services described in clause (i), the local educational agency (or State agency responsible for developing the child's IEP) shall provide or pay for such services to the child.[16] Such local educational agency or State agency is authorized to claim reimbursement for the services from the public agency that failed to provide or pay for such services and such public agency shall reimburse the local educational agency or State agency pursuant to the terms of the interagency agreement or other mechanism described in subparagraph (A)(i) according to the procedures established in such agreement pursuant to subparagraph (A)(ii).

(C) **Special Rule.** The requirements of subparagraph (A) may be met through–

(i) State statute or regulation;

(ii) signed agreements between respective agency officials that clearly identify the responsibilities of each agency relating to the provision of services; or

(iii) other appropriate written methods as determined by the Chief Executive Officer of the State or designee of the officer and approved by the Secretary.

---

16 When other public agencies are responsible for providing services, they must comply with this section. Because IDEA focuses on the transition from school to work and further education, state Departments of Vocational Rehabilitation or other agencies may be responsible for providing services.

(13) Procedural Requirements Relating to Local Educational Agency Eligibility. The State educational agency will not make a final determination that a local educational agency is not eligible for assistance under this part without first affording that agency reasonable notice and an opportunity for a hearing.

(14) Personnel Qualifications.[17]

(A) In General. The State educational agency has established and maintains qualifications to ensure that personnel necessary to carry out this part are appropriately and adequately prepared and trained, including that those personnel have the content knowledge and skills to serve children with disabilities.[18]

(B) Related Services Personnel and Paraprofessionals. The qualifications under subparagraph (A) include qualifications for related services personnel and paraprofessionals that

(i) are consistent with any State-approved or State-recognized **certification, licensing, registration, or other comparable requirements** that apply to the professional discipline in which those personnel are providing special education or related services;

(ii) **ensure that related services personnel** who deliver services in their discipline or profession meet the requirements of clause (i) and **have not had certification or licensure requirements waived** on an emergency, temporary, or provisional basis; and

(iii) allow **paraprofessionals and assistants who are appropriately trained and supervised**, in accordance with State law, regulation, or written policy, in meeting the requirements of this part to be used to **assist in the provision of special education and related services** under this part to children with disabilities.

(C) Qualifications for Special Education Teachers. The qualifications described in subparagraph (A) shall ensure that each person employed as a **special education teacher** in the State who teaches elementary school, middle school, or secondary school **is highly qualified** by the deadline established in Section 6319(a)(2) of this title.[19]

(D) Policy. In implementing this Section, a State shall adopt a policy that includes a requirement that local educational agencies in the State **take measurable steps to recruit, hire, train, and retain highly qualified personnel** to provide special education and related services under this part to children with disabilities.

(E) Rule of Construction. Notwithstanding any other individual right of action that a parent or student may maintain under this part, **nothing** in this paragraph **shall be construed to create a right of action on behalf of an individual student** for the failure of a particular State educational agency or local educational agency staff person to be highly qualified, or to prevent a parent from filing a complaint about staff qualifications with the State educational agency as provided for under this part.[20]

(15) Performance Goals and Indicators. The State-

(A) has established **goals for the performance of children with disabilities** in the State that

(i) promote the purposes of this title, as stated in Section 1400(d) of this title;

(ii) are the same as the State's definition of **adequate yearly progress**, including the State's objectives

---

17 The requirements about the qualifications of special education teachers in Section 1412(a)(14) are new and track the highly qualified teacher requirements in No Child Left Behind. (20 U. S. C. § 6319) Teachers of core academic subjects must be highly qualified by the end of the 2005-2006 school year. (NCLB, 20 U. S. C. § 6319 (a)(2)) The requirements for related services personnel and paraprofessionals did not change in IDEA 2004.

18 The law requires states to take measurable steps "to recruit, hire, train, and retain highly qualified personnel to provide special education and related services." (Section 1412(a)(14)(D))

19 For more information about requirements for teachers and paraprofessionals, read Chapter 6, "NCLB for Teachers, Principals and Paraprofessionals" in *Wrightslaw: No Child Left Behind.*

20 There is no right of action (i.e., no right to sue a state or school district) because a teacher is not highly qualified, but this may be evidence that an IEP is not appropriate or that a teacher is not adequately trained to implement the IEP. Parents may file complaints about inadequately trained teachers with the State Department of Education.

for progress by children with disabilities, under Section 6311(b)(2)(C) of this title;

(iii) address **graduation rates and dropout rates**, as well as such other factors as the State may determine; and

(iv) are **consistent**, to the extent appropriate, **with any other goals and standards for children** established by the State;

(B) has established performance indicators the State will use to assess progress toward achieving the goals described in subparagraph (A), including **measurable annual objectives for progress** by children with disabilities under Section 6311(b)(2)(C)(v)(II)(cc) of this title;

(C) will annually report to the Secretary and the public on the progress of the State, and of children with disabilities in the State, toward meeting the goals established under subparagraph (A), which may include elements of the reports required under Section 6311(h) of this title.

(16) Participation in Assessments.[21]

(A) In General. All children with disabilities are included in **all** general State and districtwide **assessment programs**, including assessments described under Section 6311 of this title, with **appropriate accommodations and alternate assessments where necessary** and as indicated in their respective individualized education programs.[22]

(B) Accommodation Guidelines. The State (or, in the case of a districtwide assessment, the local educational agency) has developed guidelines for the provision of appropriate accommodations.

(C) Alternate Assessments.[23]

(i) In General. The State (or, in the case of a districtwide assessment, the local educational agency) has developed and implemented guidelines for the participation of children with disabilities in alternate assessments for those children who cannot participate in regular assessments under subparagraph (A) with accommodations as indicated in their respective individualized education programs.

(ii) Requirements for Alternate Assessments. The guidelines under clause (i) shall provide for alternate assessments that

(I) are **aligned** with the State's challenging **academic content standards and** challenging student **academic achievement standards**; and

(II) if the State has adopted alternate academic achievement standards permitted under the regulations promulgated to carry out Section 6311(b)(1) of this title, measure the achievement of children with disabilities against those standards.

(iii) Conduct of Alternate Assessments. The State conducts the alternate assessments described in this subparagraph.

(D) Reports. The State educational agency (or, in the case of a districtwide assessment, the local educational agency) makes available to the public, and **reports to the public** with the same frequency and in the same detail as it reports on the assessment of nondisabled children, the following:

(i) The number of children with disabilities participating in regular assessments, and the number of those children who were provided accommodations in order to participate in those assessments.

(ii) The number of children with disabilities participating in alternate assessments described in sub-

21 Section 1414(a)(16) was changed to: "**All** children with disabilities are included in **all** general State and districtwide assessment programs . . . **with appropriate accommodations** . . ." IDEA describes requirements for accommodation guidelines and alternate assessments.

22 The requirement that school districts include all children with disabilities in all State and district assessments may have a negative impact on schools that fail to use research-based methods to teach children with disabilities to read, write, and do arithmetic and who fail to assess progress frequently.

23 See the chapters about Alternate Assessments in the *Toolkit on Teaching and Assessing Students with Disabilities* (2006) from the U. S. Department of Education. URL: www.osepideasthatwork.org/toolkit/index.asp (Last visited on September 19, 2006)

paragraph (C)(ii)(I).

(iii) The number of children with disabilities participating in alternate assessments described in subparagraph (C)(ii)(II).

(iv) The **performance of children with disabilities on regular assessments and on alternate assessments** (if the number of children with disabilities participating in those assessments is sufficient to yield statistically reliable information and reporting that information will not reveal personally identifiable information about an individual student), compared with the achievement of all children, including children with disabilities, on those assessments.

(E) Universal Design. The State educational agency (or, in the case of a districtwide assessment, the local educational agency) shall, to the extent feasible, use universal design principles in developing and administering any assessments under this paragraph.[24]

(17) Supplementation of State, Local, and Other Federal Funds.

(A) Expenditures. Funds paid to a State under this part will be expended in accordance with all the provisions of this part.

(B) Prohibition Against Commingling. Funds paid to a State under this part will not be commingled with State funds.

(C) Prohibition Against Supplantation and Conditions for Waiver by Secretary. Except as provided in Section 1413 of this title, funds paid to a State under this part will be used to supplement the level of Federal, State, and local funds (including funds that are not under the direct control of State or local educational agencies) expended for special education and related services provided to children with disabilities under this part and in no case to supplant such Federal, State, and local funds, except that, where the State provides clear and convincing evidence that all children with disabilities have available to them a free appropriate public education, the Secretary may waive, in whole or in part, the requirements of this subparagraph if the Secretary concurs with the evidence provided by the State.

(18) Maintenance of State Financial Support.

(A) In General. The State does not reduce the amount of State financial support for special education and related services for children with disabilities, or otherwise made available because of the excess costs of educating those children, below the amount of that support for the preceding fiscal year.

(B) Reduction of Funds for Failure to Maintain Support. The Secretary shall reduce the allocation of funds under Section 1411 of this title for any fiscal year following the fiscal year in which the State fails to comply with the requirement of subparagraph (A) by the same amount by which the State fails to meet the requirement.

(C) Waivers for Exceptional or Uncontrollable Circumstances. The Secretary may waive the requirement of subparagraph (A) for a State, for 1 fiscal year at a time, if the Secretary determines that

(i) granting a waiver would be equitable due to exceptional or uncontrollable circumstances such as a natural disaster or a precipitous and unforeseen decline in the financial resources of the State; or

(ii) the State meets the standard in paragraph (17)(C) for a waiver of the requirement to supplement, and not to supplant, funds received under this part.

(D) Subsequent Years. If, for any year, a State fails to meet the requirement of subparagraph (A), including any year for which the State is granted a waiver under subparagraph (C), the financial support required of the State in future years under subparagraph (A) shall be the amount that would have been required in the absence of that failure and not the reduced level of the State's support.

---

24 The definition of Universal Design is in Section 1401(35). "The term 'universal design' is a philosophy for designing and delivering products and services that are usable by people with the widest range of functional capabilities. This includes products and services that are directly accessible (without requiring assistive technologies) and that are interoperable with assistive technologies." See Section 3(17) of Assistive Technology Act of 1998. (Retrieved from www.nectac.org/topics/atech/udl.asp)

(19) Public Participation. Prior to the adoption of any policies and procedures needed to comply with this Section (including any amendments to such policies and procedures), the State ensures that there are public hearings, adequate notice of the hearings, and an opportunity for comment available to the general public, including individuals with disabilities and parents of children with disabilities.

(20) Rule of Construction. In complying with paragraphs (17) and (18), a State may not use funds paid to it under this part to satisfy State-law mandated funding obligations to local educational agencies, including funding based on student attendance or enrollment, or inflation.

(21) State Advisory Panel.[25]

(A) In General. The State has established and maintains an advisory panel for the purpose of providing policy guidance with respect to special education and related services for children with disabilities in the State.

(B) Membership. Such advisory panel shall consist of members appointed by the Governor, or any other official authorized under State law to make such appointments, be representative of the State population, and be **composed of individuals involved in, or concerned with, the education of children with disabilities, including**–

(i) parents of children with disabilities (ages birth through 26);

(ii) individuals with disabilities;

(iii) teachers;

(iv) representatives of institutions of higher education that prepare special education and related services personnel;

(v) State and local education officials, including officials who carry out activities under subtitle B of title VII of the McKinney-Vento Homeless Assistance Act (42 U. S. C. 11431 et seq.);

(vi) administrators of programs for children with disabilities;

(vii) representatives of other State agencies involved in the financing or delivery of related services to children with disabilities;

(viii) representatives of private schools and public charter schools;

(ix) not less than 1 representative of a vocational, community, or business organization concerned with the provision of transition services to children with disabilities;

(x) a representative from the State child welfare agency responsible for foster care; and

(xi) representatives from the State juvenile and adult corrections agencies.

(C) Special Rule. A **majority** of the members of the panel **shall** be individuals with disabilities or parents of children with disabilities (ages birth through 26).

(D) Duties. The advisory panel shall–

(i) advise the State educational agency of unmet needs within the State in the education of children with disabilities;

(ii) comment publicly on any rules or regulations proposed by the State regarding the education of children with disabilities;

(iii) advise the State educational agency in developing evaluations and reporting on data to the Secretary under Section 1418 of this title;

(iv) advise the State educational agency in developing corrective action plans to address findings identified in Federal monitoring reports under this part; and

---

25 The majority of the members of state advisory panels shall be individuals with disabilities or parents of children with disabilities. Other members include representatives from private and charter schools, child welfare agencies, and corrections agencies.

(v) advise the State educational agency in developing and implementing policies relating to the coordination of services for children with disabilities.

(22) Suspension and Expulsion Rates.

(A) In General. The State educational agency **examines data**, including data disaggregated by race and ethnicity, to determine if **significant discrepancies are occurring in the rate of long-term suspensions and expulsions** of children with disabilities–

(i) among local educational agencies in the State; or

(ii) compared to such rates for nondisabled children within such agencies.

(B) Review and Revision of Policies. If such discrepancies are occurring, the State educational agency reviews and, if appropriate, revises (or requires the affected State or local educational agency to revise) its **policies, procedures, and practices relating to the development and implementation of IEPs, the use of positive behavioral interventions and supports, and procedural safeguards**, to ensure that such policies, procedures, and practices comply with this title.

(23) Access to Instructional Materials.[26]

(A) In General. The State adopts the National Instructional Materials Accessibility Standard (NIMAS) for the **purposes of providing instructional materials to blind persons** or other persons with print disabilities, in a timely manner after the publication of the National Instructional Materials Accessibility Standard in the Federal Register.

(B) Rights of State Educational Agency. Nothing in this paragraph shall be construed to require any State educational agency to coordinate with the National Instructional Materials Access Center. If a State educational agency chooses not to coordinate with the National Instructional Materials Access Center, such agency shall provide an assurance to the Secretary that the agency **will provide instructional materials to blind persons or other persons with print disabilities in a timely manner**.

(C) Preparation and Delivery of Files. If a State educational agency chooses to coordinate with the National Instructional Materials Access Center, not later than 2 years after the date of enactment of the Individuals with Disabilities Education Improvement Act of 2004, the agency, as part of any print instructional materials adoption process, procurement contract, or other practice or instrument used for purchase of print instructional materials, shall enter into a written contract with the publisher of the print instructional materials to–

(i) require the publisher to prepare and, on or before delivery of the print instructional materials, provide to the National Instructional Materials Access Center electronic files containing the contents of the print instructional materials using the National Instructional Materials Accessibility Standard; or

(ii) purchase instructional materials from the publisher that are produced in, or may be rendered in, specialized formats.

(D) Assistive Technology. In carrying out this paragraph, the State educational agency, to the maximum extent possible, shall work collaboratively with the State agency responsible for assistive technology programs.

(E) Definitions. In this paragraph:

(i) National Instructional Materials Access Center. The term 'National Instructional Materials Access Center' means the center established pursuant to Section 1474(e) of this title.

(ii) National Instructional Materials Accessibility Standard. The term 'National Instructional

---

26 The requirements about access to instructional materials and accessibility standards are new in IDEA 2004.

Materials Accessibility Standard' has the meaning given the term in Section 1474(e)(3)(A) of this title.[27]

(iii) Specialized Formats. The term 'specialized formats' has the meaning given the term in Section 1474(e)(3)(D) of this title.

(24) Overidentification and Disproportionality.[28] The State has in effect, consistent with the purposes of this title and with Section 1418(d) of this title, **policies and procedures designed to prevent the inappropriate overidentification or disproportionate representation by race and ethnicity** of children as children with disabilities, including children with disabilities with a particular impairment described in Section 1401 of this title.

(25) Prohibition on Mandatory Medication.[29]

(A) In General. The State educational agency **shall prohibit** State and local educational agency personnel from **requiring a child to obtain a prescription for a substance covered by the Controlled Substances Act** (21 U. S. C. 801 et seq.) **as a condition of attending school, receiving an evaluation** under subsection (a) or (c) of Section 1414 of this title, **or receiving services** under this title.

(B) Rule of Construction. Nothing in subparagraph (A) **shall be construed to create a Federal prohibition against** teachers and other **school personnel consulting or sharing classroom-based observations with parents or guardians** regarding a student's academic and functional performance, or behavior in the classroom or school, or regarding the need for evaluation for special education or related services under paragraph (3).

(b) State Educational Agency as Provider of Free Appropriate Public Education or Direct Services. If the State educational agency provides free appropriate public education to children with disabilities, or provides direct services to such children, such agency–

(1) shall comply with any additional requirements of Section 1413(a) of this title, as if such agency were a local educational agency; and

(2) may use amounts that are otherwise available to such agency under this part to serve those children without regard to Section 1413(a)(2)(A)(i) of this title (relating to excess costs).

(c) Exception for Prior State Plans.

(1) In General. If a State has on file with the Secretary policies and procedures that demonstrate that such State meets any requirement of subsection (a), including any policies and procedures filed under this part as in effect before the effective date of the Individuals with Disabilities Education Improvement Act of 2004, the Secretary shall consider such State to have met such requirement for purposes of receiving a grant under this part.

(2) Modifications Made by State. Subject to paragraph (3), an application submitted by a State in accordance with this section shall remain in effect until the State submits to the Secretary such modifications as the State determines necessary. This section shall apply to a modification to an application to the same extent and in the same manner as this section applies to the original plan.

(3) Modifications Required by the Secretary. If, after the effective date of the Individuals with Disabilities

---

27 The National Instructional Materials Accessibility Standard (NIMAS) provides a system to produce and distribute digital versions of textbooks and other instructional materials that can be converted to accessible formats. IDEA requires that all textbooks and supplemental curricular materials be provided as NIMAS files by mid-December 2006. The American Printing House for the Blind is the coordinating agency and the Center for Applied Special Technology (CAST) is providing technical support. See http://nimas.cast.org and www.ahead.org

28 This section about Overidentification and Disproportionality is new. In Findings, Congress found that "African-American children are identified as having mental retardation and emotional disturbance at rates greater than their White counterparts. Schools with predominately white students and teachers have placed disproportionately high numbers of their minority students into special education." (Section 1400(c)(12)(C)). States must develop policies and procedures to correct these problems.

29 The requirements that prohibit school personnel from requiring a child to obtain a prescription for a controlled substance (i.e., Ritalin, Adderal, etc.) in order to attend school, receive an evaluation, or receive special education services are new.

Education Improvement Act of 2004, the provisions of this title are amended (or the regulations developed to carry out this title are amended), there is a new interpretation of this title by a Federal court or a State's highest court, or there is an official finding of noncompliance with Federal law or regulations, then the Secretary may require a State to modify its application only to the extent necessary to ensure the State's compliance with this part.

(d) Approval by the Secretary.

(1) In General. If the Secretary determines that a State is eligible to receive a grant under this part, the Secretary shall notify the State of that determination.

(2) Notice and Hearing. The Secretary shall not make a final determination that a State is not eligible to receive a grant under this part until after providing the State–

(A) with reasonable notice; and

(B) with an opportunity for a hearing.

(e) Assistance Under Other Federal Programs. Nothing in this title permits a State to reduce medical and other assistance available, or to alter eligibility, under titles V and XIX of the Social Security Act with respect to the provision of a free appropriate public education for children with disabilities in the State.

(f) By-Pass for Children in Private Schools.

(1) In General. If, on the date of enactment of the Education of the Handicapped Act Amendments of 1983, a State educational agency was .prohibited by law from providing for the equitable participation in special programs of children with disabilities enrolled in private elementary schools and secondary schools as required by subsection (a)(10)(A), or if the Secretary determines that a State educational agency, local educational agency, or other entity has substantially failed or is unwilling to provide for such equitable participation, then the Secretary shall, notwithstanding such provision of law, arrange for the provision of services to such children through arrangements that shall be subject to the requirements of such subsection.

(2) Payments.

(A) Determination of Amounts. If the Secretary arranges for services pursuant to this subsection, the Secretary, after consultation with the appropriate public and private school officials, shall pay to the provider of such services for a fiscal year an amount per child that does not exceed the amount determined by dividing–

(i) the total amount received by the State under this part for such fiscal year; by

(ii) the number of children with disabilities served in the prior year, as reported to the Secretary by the State under Section 1418 of this title.

(B) Withholding of Certain Amounts. Pending final resolution of any investigation or complaint that may result in a determination under this subsection, the Secretary may withhold from the allocation of the affected State educational agency the amount the Secretary estimates will be necessary to pay the cost of services described in subparagraph (A).

(C) Period of Payments. The period under which payments are made under subparagraph (A) shall continue until the Secretary determines that there will no longer be any failure or inability on the part of the State educational agency to meet the requirements of subsection (a)(10)(A).

(3) Notice and Hearing.

(A) In General. The Secretary shall not take any final action under this subsection until the State educational agency affected by such action has had an opportunity, for not less than 45 days after receiving written notice thereof, to submit written objections and to appear before the Secretary or the Secretary's designee to show cause why such action should not be taken.

(B) Review of Action. If a State educational agency is dissatisfied with the Secretary's final action after a proceeding under subparagraph (A), such agency may, not later than 60 days after notice of such action, file with the United States court of appeals for the circuit in which such State is located a petition for review of that action. A copy of the petition shall be forthwith transmitted by the clerk of the court to the Secretary. The Secretary thereupon shall file in the court the record of the proceedings on which the Secretary based the Secretary's action, as provided in Section 2112 of title 28, United States Code.

(C) Review of Findings of Fact. The findings of fact by the Secretary, if supported by substantial evidence, shall be conclusive, but the court, for good cause shown, may remand the case to the Secretary to take further evidence, and the Secretary may thereupon make new or modified findings of fact and may modify the Secretary's previous action, and shall file in the court the record of the further proceedings. Such new or modified findings of fact shall likewise be conclusive if supported by substantial evidence.

(D) Jurisdiction of Court of Appeals; Review by United States Supreme Court. Upon the filing of a petition under subparagraph (B), the United States court of appeals shall have jurisdiction to affirm the action of the Secretary or to set it aside, in whole or in part. The judgment of the court shall be subject to review by the Supreme Court of the United States upon certiorari or certification as provided in Section 1254 of title 28, United States Code.

20 U. S. C. § 1413. Local Educational Agency Eligibility.

WRIGHTSLAW OVERVIEW: Section 1413 includes requirements for school district (LEA) and charter school eligibility. This section includes new requirements about purchasing instructional materials, records of migratory children, and early intervening services. School districts must provide services to children with disabilities who attend charter schools in the same manner as children who attend other public schools, and must provide supplementary services and related services on site at the charter school. Section 1413(a)(6) describes new requirements about access to instructional materials and the option of coordinating with the National Instructional Materials Access Center. Section 1413(f) describes new requirements for early intervening services. If a school district does not comply with the law, States can provide direct services.

(a) In General. A local educational agency is eligible for assistance under this part for a fiscal year if such agency submits a plan that provides assurances to the State educational agency that the local educational agency meets each of the following conditions:

(1) Consistency With State Policies. The local educational agency, in providing for the education of children with disabilities within its jurisdiction, has in effect policies, procedures, and programs that are consistent with the State policies and procedures established under Section 1412 of this title.

(2) Use of Amounts.

(A) In General. Amounts provided to the local educational agency under this part shall be expended in accordance with the applicable provisions of this part and–

(i) shall be used only to pay the excess costs of providing special education and related services to children with disabilities;

(ii) shall be used to supplement State, local, and other Federal funds and not to supplant such funds; and

(iii) shall not be used, except as provided in subparagraphs (B) and (C), to reduce the level of expenditures for the education of children with disabilities made by the local educational agency from local funds below the level of those expenditures for the preceding fiscal year.

(B) Exception. Notwithstanding the restriction in subparagraph (A)(iii), a local educational agency may reduce the level of expenditures where such reduction is attributable to–

(i) the voluntary departure, by retirement or otherwise, or departure for just cause, of special education personnel;

(ii) a decrease in the enrollment of children with disabilities;

(iii) the termination of the obligation of the agency, consistent with this part, to provide a program of special education to a particular child with a disability that is an exceptionally costly program, as determined by the State educational agency, because the child–

(I) has left the jurisdiction of the agency;

(II) has reached the age at which the obligation of the agency to provide a free appropriate public education to the child has terminated; or

(III) no longer needs such program of special education; or

(iv) the termination of costly expenditures for long-term purchases, such as the acquisition of equipment or the construction of school facilities.

(C) Adjustment to Local Fiscal Effort in Certain Fiscal Years.

(i) Amounts in Excess. Notwithstanding clauses (ii) and (iii) of subparagraph (A), for any fiscal year for which the allocation received by a local educational agency under Section 1411(f) of this title exceeds the amount the local educational agency received for the previous fiscal year, the local educational agency may reduce the level of expenditures otherwise required by subparagraph (A)(iii) by not more than 50 percent of the amount of such excess.

(ii) Use of Amounts to Carry Out Activities Under ESEA. If a local educational agency exercises the authority under clause (i), the agency shall use an amount of local funds equal to the reduction in expenditures under clause (i) to carry out activities authorized under the Elementary and Secondary Education Act of 1965. [20 U. S. C. § 6301 *et seq.*]

(iii) State Prohibition. Notwithstanding clause (i), if a State educational agency determines that a local educational agency is unable to establish and maintain programs of free appropriate public education that meet the requirements of subsection (a) or the State educational agency has taken action against the local educational agency under Section 1416 of this title, the State educational agency shall prohibit the local educational agency from reducing the level of expenditures under clause (i) for that fiscal year.

(iv) Special Rule. The amount of funds expended by a local educational agency under subsection (f) shall count toward the maximum amount of expenditures such local educational agency may reduce under clause (i).

(D) Schoolwide Programs Under Title I of the ESEA.[30] Notwithstanding subparagraph (A) or any other provision of this part, a local educational agency may use funds received under this part for any fiscal year to carry out a schoolwide program under Section 6314 of this title, except that the amount so used in any such program shall not exceed–

(i) the number of children with disabilities participating in the schoolwide program; multiplied by

(ii)

(I) the amount received by the local educational agency under this part for that fiscal year; divided by

(II) the number of children with disabilities in the jurisdiction of that agency.

(3) Personnel Development. The local educational agency **shall ensure that all personnel** necessary to carry out this part **are appropriately and adequately prepared**, subject to the requirements of Section 1412(a)(14) of this title and Section 6622 of this title.

(4) Permissive Use of Funds.

(A) Uses. Notwithstanding paragraph (2)(A) or Section 1412(a)(17)(B) of this title (relating to commingled funds), funds provided to the local educational agency under this part may be used for the following activities:

---

30 ESEA is also known as "No Child Left Behind." For the full text of 20 U. S. C. § 6314, see *Wrightslaw: No Child Left Behind*.

(i) Services and Aids That Also Benefit Nondisabled Children. For the costs of special education and related services, and supplementary aids and services, provided in a regular class or other education-related setting to a child with a disability in accordance with the individualized education program of the child, even if 1 or more nondisabled children benefit from such services.

(ii) Early Intervening Services. To develop and implement coordinated, early intervening educational services in accordance with subsection (f).

(iii) High Cost Education and Related Services. To establish and implement cost or risk sharing funds, consortia, or cooperatives for the local educational agency itself, or for local educational agencies working in a consortium of which the local educational agency is a part, **to pay for high cost special education and related services.**

(B) Administrative Case Management. A local educational agency may use funds received under this part to purchase appropriate technology for recordkeeping, data collection, and related case management activities of teachers and related services personnel providing services described in the individualized education program of children with disabilities, that is needed for the implementation of such case management activities.

(5) Treatment of Charter Schools[31] and Their Students. In carrying out this part with respect to charter schools that are public schools of the local educational agency, the local educational agency–

(A) **serves children with disabilities attending** those **charter schools in the same manner** as the local educational agency serves **children with disabilities in its other schools**, including providing supplementary and related services on site at the charter school to the same extent to which the local educational agency has a policy or practice of providing such services on the site to its other public schools; and

(B) provides funds under this part to those charter schools–

(i) on the same basis as the local educational agency provides funds to the local educational agency's other public schools, including proportional distribution based on relative enrollment of children with disabilities; and

(ii) at the same time as the agency distributes other Federal funds to the agency's other public schools, consistent with the State's charter school law.

(6) Purchase of Instructional Materials.

(A) In General. Not later than **2 years** after the date of enactment of the Individuals with Disabilities Education Improvement Act of 2004, a local educational agency that chooses to coordinate with the National Instructional Materials Access Center, when purchasing print instructional materials, shall acquire the print instructional materials in the same manner and subject to the same conditions as a State educational agency acquires print instructional materials under Section 1412(a)(23) of this title.

(B) Rights of Local Educational Agency. Nothing in this paragraph shall be construed to require a local educational agency to coordinate with the National Instructional Materials Access Center. If a local educational agency chooses not to coordinate with the National Instructional Materials Access Center, the local educational agency shall provide an assurance to the State educational agency that the local educational agency will provide instructional materials to blind persons or other persons with print disabilities in a timely manner.

(7) Information for State Educational Agency. The local educational agency shall provide the State educational agency with information necessary to enable the State educational agency to carry out its duties under this part, including, with respect to paragraphs (15) and (16) of Section 1412(a) of this title, information relating to the performance of children with disabilities participating in programs carried out under this part.

(8) Public Information. The local educational agency shall make available to parents of children with disabilities and to the general public all documents relating to the eligibility of such agency under this part.

---

31 For more information about charter schools, see Regulation 300.209.

(9) Records Regarding Migratory Children with Disabilities. The local educational agency shall cooperate in the Secretary's efforts under Section 6398 of this title to ensure the linkage of records pertaining to migratory children with a disability for the purpose of electronically exchanging, among the States, health and educational information regarding such children.

(b) Exception for Prior Local Plans.

(1) In General. If a local educational agency or State agency has on file with the State educational agency policies and procedures that demonstrate that such local educational agency, or such State agency, as the case may be, meets any requirement of subsection (a), including any policies and procedures filed under this part as in effect before the effective date of the Individuals with Disabilities Education Improvement Act of 2004, the State educational agency shall consider such local educational agency or State agency, as the case may be, to have met such requirement for purposes of receiving assistance under this part.

(2) Modification Made by Local Educational Agency. Subject to paragraph (3), an application submitted by a local educational agency in accordance with this section shall remain in effect until the local educational agency submits to the State educational agency such modifications as the local educational agency determines necessary.

(3) Modifications Required by State Educational Agency. If, after the effective date of the Individuals with Disabilities Education Improvement Act of 2004, the provisions of this title are amended (or the regulations developed to carry out this title are amended), there is a new interpretation of this title by Federal or State courts, or there is an official finding of noncompliance with Federal or State law or regulations, then the State educational agency may require a local educational agency to modify its application only to the extent necessary to ensure the local educational agency's compliance with this part or State law.

(c) Notification of Local Educational Agency or State Agency in Case of Ineligibility. If the State educational agency determines that a local educational agency or State agency is not eligible under this section, then the State educational agency shall notify the local educational agency or State agency, as the case may be, of that determination and shall provide such local educational agency or State agency with reasonable notice and an opportunity for a hearing.

(d) Local Educational Agency Compliance.[32]

(1) In General. If the State educational agency, after reasonable notice and an opportunity for a hearing, finds that a local educational agency or State agency that has been determined to be eligible under this section **is failing** to comply with any requirement described in subsection (a), the State educational agency **shall reduce or shall not provide any further payments** to the local educational agency or State agency until the State educational agency is satisfied that the local educational agency or State agency, as the case may be, is complying with that requirement.

(2) Additional Requirement. Any State agency or local educational agency in receipt of a notice described in paragraph (1) shall, by means of public notice, take such measures as may be necessary to bring the pendency of an action pursuant to this subsection to the attention of the public within the jurisdiction of such agency.

(3) Consideration. In carrying out its responsibilities under paragraph (1), the State educational agency **shall consider any decision made in a hearing held under Section 1415** of this title that is adverse to the local educational agency or State agency involved in that decision.[33]

(e) Joint Establishment of Eligibility.

(1) Joint Establishment.

(A) In General. A State educational agency may require a local educational agency to establish its eligibility jointly with another local educational agency if the State educational agency determines that the local educational agency will be ineligible under this section because the local educational agency will not be able

---

32 If a school district fails to comply with the requirements described in Section 1413(a), the State must eliminate payments until the district is in compliance. This requirement is not discretionary.

33 In determining compliance with the law and whether to withhold funds, the State **shall** consider due process decisions that are adverse to the LEA.

to establish and maintain programs of sufficient size and scope to effectively meet the needs of children with disabilities.

(B) Charter School Exception. A State educational agency may not require a charter school that is a local educational agency to jointly establish its eligibility under subparagraph (A) unless the charter school is explicitly permitted to do so under the State's charter school law.

(2) Amount of Payments. If a State educational agency requires the joint establishment of eligibility under paragraph (1), the total amount of funds made available to the affected local educational agencies shall be equal to the sum of the payments that each such local educational agency would have received under Section 1411(f) of this title if such agencies were eligible for such payments.

(3) Requirements. Local educational agencies that establish joint eligibility under this subsection shall–

(A) adopt policies and procedures that are consistent with the State's policies and procedures under Section 1412(a) of this title; and

(B) be jointly responsible for implementing programs that receive assistance under this part.

(4) Requirements for Educational Service Agencies.

(A) In General. If an educational service agency is required by State law to carry out programs under this part, the joint responsibilities given to local educational agencies under this subsection shall–

(i) not apply to the administration and disbursement of any payments received by that educational service agency; and

(ii) be carried out only by that educational service agency.

(B) Additional Requirement. Notwithstanding any other provision of this subsection, an educational service agency shall provide for the education of children with disabilities in the least restrictive environment, as required by Section 1412(a)(5) of this title.

(f) Early Intervening Services.[34]

(1) In General. A local educational agency **may not use more than 15 percent** of the amount such agency receives under this part for any fiscal year, less any amount reduced by the agency pursuant to subsection (a)(2)(C), if any, in combination with other amounts (which may include amounts other than education funds), to develop and implement coordinated, early intervening services, which may include interagency financing structures, for students in kindergarten through grade 12 (with a particular emphasis on students in kindergarten through grade 3) who have **not been identified as needing special education** or related services but **who need additional academic and behavioral support** to succeed in a general education environment.

(2) Activities. In implementing coordinated, early intervening services under this subsection, a local educational agency may carry out activities that include–

(A) **professional development** (which may be provided by entities other than local educational agencies) for teachers and other school staff to enable such personnel to deliver **scientifically based academic instruction and behavioral interventions**, including **scientifically based literacy instruction**,[35] and, where appropriate, instruction on the use of adaptive and instructional software; and

---

34 The new requirements for early intervening services reflect the requirement to use "proven methods of teaching and learning" based on "replicable research." (See Findings, Section 1400(c)(4)). School districts may use **up to 15 percent** of their funds from Part B to develop and implement early intervening services for students who need academic and behavioral assistance but have not been identified as needing special education services. Funds can be used for training so teachers have the knowledge and skills to deliver scientifically based academic instruction and literacy instruction. Funds can also be used to provide students with educational evaluations, services and supports, including scientifically based literacy instruction.

35 The definitions of reading, scientifically based reading research, the essential components of reading instruction, and screening, diagnostic, and classroom-based reading assessments are in No Child Left Behind at 20 U. S. C. Section 6368. (See *Wrightslaw: No Child Left Behind*)

(B) providing educational and behavioral evaluations, services, and supports, including **scientifically based literacy instruction.**

(3) Construction. Nothing in this subsection shall be construed to limit or create a right to a free appropriate public education under this part.

(4) Reporting. Each local educational agency that develops and maintains coordinated, early intervening services under this subsection shall annually report to the State educational agency on–

(A) the number of students served under this subsection; and

(B) the number of students served under this subsection who subsequently receive special education and related services under this title during the preceding 2-year period.

(5) Coordination with Elementary and Secondary Education Act of 1965. Funds made available to carry out this subsection may be used to carry out coordinated, early intervening services aligned with activities funded by, and carried out under, the Elementary and Secondary Education Act of 1965 if such funds are used to supplement, and not supplant, funds made available under the Elementary and Secondary Education Act of 1965 for the activities and services assisted under this subsection.

(g) Direct Services by the State Educational Agency.

(1) In General. A State educational agency shall use the payments that would otherwise have been available to a local educational agency or to a State agency to provide special education and related services directly to children with disabilities residing in the area served by that local educational agency, or for whom that State agency is responsible, if the State educational agency determines that the local educational agency or State agency, as the case may be–

(A) has not provided the information needed to establish the eligibility of such local educational agency or State agency under this section;

(B) is unable to establish and maintain programs of free appropriate public education that meet the requirements of subsection (a);

(C) is unable or unwilling to be consolidated with 1 or more local educational agencies in order to establish and maintain such programs; or

(D) has 1 or more children with disabilities who can best be served by a regional or State program or service delivery system designed to meet the needs of such children.

(2) Manner and Location of Education and Services. The State educational agency may provide special education and related services under paragraph (1) in such manner and at such locations (including regional or State centers) as the State educational agency considers appropriate. Such education and services shall be provided in accordance with this part.

(h) State Agency Eligibility. Any State agency that desires to receive a subgrant for any fiscal year under Section 1411(f) of this title shall demonstrate to the satisfaction of the State educational agency that –

(1) all children with disabilities who are participating in programs and projects funded under this part receive a free appropriate public education, and that those children and their parents are provided all the rights and procedural safeguards described in this part; and

(2) the agency meets such other conditions of this section as the Secretary determines to be appropriate.

(i) Disciplinary Information. The State may require that a local educational agency include in the records of a child with a disability a statement of **any current or previous disciplinary action** that has been taken against the child and transmit such statement to the same extent that such disciplinary information is included in, and transmitted with, the student records of nondisabled children. The statement may include a description of any behavior engaged in by the child that required disciplinary action, a description of the disciplinary action taken, and any other information that is relevant to the safety of the child and other individuals involved with the child. If the State adopts such a policy, and the child transfers from 1 school to another, the transmission of any of the child's records shall include both the child's current individualized education program and any such statement of current or previous disciplinary action that has been taken against the child.

(j) State Agency Flexibility.

(1) Adjustment to State Fiscal Effort in Certain Fiscal Years. For any fiscal year for which the allotment received by a State under Section 1411 of this title exceeds the amount the State received for the previous fiscal year and if the State in school year 2003-2004 or any subsequent school year pays or reimburses all local educational agencies within the State from State revenue 100 percent of the non-Federal share of the costs of special education and related services, the State educational agency, notwithstanding paragraphs (17) and (18) of Section 1412(a) of this title and Section 1412(b) of this title, may reduce the level of expenditures from State sources for the education of children with disabilities by not more than 50 percent of the amount of such excess.

(2) Prohibition. Notwithstanding paragraph (1), if the Secretary determines that a State educational agency is unable to establish, maintain, or oversee programs of free appropriate public education that meet the requirements of this part, or that the State needs assistance, intervention, or substantial intervention under Section 1416(d)(2)(A) of this title, the Secretary shall prohibit the State educational agency from exercising the authority in paragraph (1).

(3) Education Activities. If a State educational agency exercises the authority under paragraph (1), the agency shall use funds from State sources, in an amount equal to the amount of the reduction under paragraph (1), to support activities authorized under the Elementary and Secondary Education Act of 1965 or to support need based student or teacher higher education programs.

(4) Report. For each fiscal year for which a State educational agency exercises the authority under paragraph (1), the State educational agency shall report to the Secretary the amount of expenditures reduced pursuant to such paragraph and the activities that were funded pursuant to paragraph (3).

(5) Limitation. Notwithstanding paragraph (1), a State educational agency may not reduce the level of expenditures described in paragraph (1) if any local educational agency in the State would, as a result of such reduction, receive less than 100 percent of the amount necessary to ensure that all children with disabilities served by the local educational agency receive a free appropriate public education from the combination of Federal funds received under this title and State funds received from the State educational agency.

20 U. S. C. § 1414. Evaluations, Eligibility Determinations, Individualized Education Programs, and Educational Placements.

WRIGHTSLAW OVERVIEW: Section 1414 includes requirements for evaluations, reevaluations, eligibility, Individualized Education Programs, and educational placements. Section 1414(a) describes new requirements for initial evaluations, parental consent, the new 60-day timeline to complete evaluations, and new limits on reevaluations. Section 1414(b) describes evaluation procedures, new requirements about determining educational needs, and the movement away from using discrepancy models to identify children with specific learning disabilities. Section 1414(c) states that schools must review evaluations and information provided by parents and that schools must reevaluate a child before terminating eligibility, with two exceptions. IDEA 2004 made significant changes in Section 1414(d) about Individualized Education Programs (IEPs), IEP Team members, meeting attendance, consolidated meetings, and reviewing and revising IEPs. Section 1414(e) clarifies that the parent is a member of any group that makes decisions about a child's educational placement. Section 1414(f) is new and describes alternate means of participating in meetings. The Regulations about evaluations start at 300.300 and Commentary in the *Federal Register*, page 46629. The Regulations about IEPs start at 300.320 and Commentary in the *Federal Register*, page 46661.

(a) Evaluations, Parental Consent, and Reevaluations.

(1) Initial Evaluations.[36]

---

36 Section 1414(a)(1)(B) is new and states that the parents, the state department of education, other state agencies, and the school district may request an initial evaluation.

(A) In General. A State educational agency, other State agency, or local educational agency **shall conduct a full and individual initial evaluation** in accordance with this paragraph and subsection (b), before the initial provision of special education and related services to a child with a disability under this part.

(B) Request for Initial Evaluation.[37] Consistent with subparagraph (D), either a **parent** of a child,[38] or a State educational agency, other State agency, or local educational agency **may initiate a request for an initial evaluation** to determine if the child is a child with a disability.[39]

(C) Procedures.

(i) In General. Such initial evaluation shall consist of procedures–

(I) to determine whether a child is a child with a disability (as defined in Section 1401 of this title) **within 60 days of receiving parental consent** for the evaluation,[40] **or**, if the State establishes a timeframe within which the evaluation must be conducted, within such timeframe;[41] and

(II) to determine the **educational needs** of such child.

(ii) Exception. The relevant timeframe in clause (i)(I) shall not apply to a local educational agency if–

(I) a child enrolls in a school served by the local educational agency after the relevant timeframe in clause (i)(I) has begun and prior to a determination by the child's previous local educational agency as to whether the child is a child with a disability (as defined in Section 1401 of this title), but only if the subsequent local educational agency is making sufficient progress to ensure a prompt completion of the evaluation, and the parent and subsequent local educational agency agree to a specific time when the evaluation will be completed; or

(II) the parent of a child repeatedly fails or refuses to produce the child for the evaluation.

(D) Parental Consent.[42]

(i) In General.

(I) Consent for Initial Evaluation. The agency proposing to conduct an initial evaluation to determine if the child qualifies as a child with a disability as defined in Section 1401 of this title **shall obtain informed consent from the parent**[43] of such child before conducting the evaluation. Parental consent for evaluation **shall not** be construed as consent for placement for receipt of special education and related services.

(II) Consent for Services. An agency that is responsible for making a free appropriate public education available to a child with a disability under this part **shall** seek to obtain **informed consent** from the parent of such child before providing special education and related services to the child.

---

37 If a parent requests an evaluation and the LEA refuses, the LEA must provide Prior Written Notice (PWN). See Section 1415(c)(1) and the Commentary in the *Federal Register,* page 46636.

38 For sample letters, including a letter to request an evaluation for special education services, see ***Wrightslaw: From Emotions to Advocacy.***

39 A "child with a disability" is defined in Section 1401(3) in the statute and in Regulation 300.8.

40 IDEA 2004 includes a new requirement that initial evaluations and eligibility be completed within 60 days of receiving parental consent. When federal law and regulations create a timeline of "days," per Regulation 300.11, this means calendar days (not school days) unless the law or regulation specifies an alternative. Earlier reauthorizations of IDEA did not include a timeline, so some states adopted very long timelines, leading to delays that prevented children from receiving the services they needed. You need to check your State regulations for the timeline.

41 Some states have established timeframes beyond 60 calendar days. You need to check your state's regulations on this issue.

42 The school must obtain parental consent before conducting the initial evaluation. Parental consent for an evaluation is not consent for the child to receive special education services. For information about consent, see Regulation 300.9. For information about initial evaluations, see Regulation 300.301. The school must obtain informed parental consent before providing special education services.

43 The definitions of "parent" and "foster parent" are at Section 1401(23). The definition of "ward of the state" is at Section 1401(36).

(ii) Absence of Consent.[44]

(I) For Initial Evaluation. If the parent of such child **does not provide consent for an initial evaluation** under clause (i)(I), or the parent fails to respond to a request to provide the consent, the local educational agency **may pursue the initial evaluation of the child by utilizing the procedures described in Section 1415 of this title**, except to the extent inconsistent with State law relating to such parental consent.[45]

(II) For Services. If the parent of such child **refuses to consent to services** under clause (i)(II), the local educational agency **shall not provide special education and related services** to the child by utilizing the procedures described in Section 1415 of this title.

(III) Effect on Agency Obligations. If the parent of such child **refuses to consent to the receipt of special education and related services**, or the parent fails to respond to a request to provide such consent

(aa) the local educational agency **shall not** be considered to be in violation of the requirement to make available a free appropriate public education to the child for the failure to provide such child with the special education and related services for which the local educational agency requests such consent; and

(bb) the local educational agency **shall not** be required to convene an IEP meeting or develop an IEP under this section for the child for the special education and related services for which the local educational agency requests such consent.

(iii) Consent for Wards of the State.[46]

(I) In General. If the child is a ward of the State and is not residing with the child's parent, the agency shall make reasonable efforts to obtain the **informed consent from the parent** (as defined in Section 1401 of this title) of the child for an initial evaluation to determine whether the child is a child with a disability.

(II) Exception. The agency shall not be required to obtain informed consent from the parent of a child for an initial evaluation to determine whether the child is a child with a disability if–

(aa) despite reasonable efforts to do so, the agency cannot discover the whereabouts of the parent of the child;

(bb) the rights of the parents of the child have been terminated in accordance with State law; or

(cc) the rights of the parent to make educational decisions have been subrogated by a judge in accordance with State law and consent for an initial evaluation has been given by **an individual appointed by the judge to represent the child.**

---

44 "Absence of Consent" is new. If the parent does not consent to an evaluation, the district may request a due process hearing against the parent. However, if the parent does not consent to special education services, the district may not pursue a due process hearing against the parent. The "Effect on Agency Obligations" section is also new. If the parent refuses consent for services, the district has not violated the IDEA, and is not required to convene an IEP meeting or develop an IEP for the child.

45 Pursuant to Regulation 300.300(d)(4)(i), if the child is in a private school or home school, the LEA cannot use due process procedures to force the evaluation.

46 The consent requirements for children who are wards of the state are new. If the child is a ward of the state, the school must try to obtain parental consent for an initial evaluation. Exceptions to this requirement are listed in Section 1414(a)(1)(D)(iii)(II). If a judge terminates parental rights or takes educational decision-making rights from the parent, the judge may appoint another individual, such as a probation officer or social worker or other individual, who can make decisions for the child and give consent to an initial evaluation.

(E) Rule of Construction. The **screening of a student by a teacher or specialist** to determine appropriate instructional strategies for curriculum implementation **shall not be considered to be an evaluation for eligibility** for special education and related services.[47]

(2) Reevaluations.[48]

(A) In General. A local educational agency **shall ensure that a reevaluation** of each child with a disability is conducted in accordance with subsections (b) and (c)–

(i) **if** the local educational agency determines that the **educational or related services needs,** including improved academic achievement and functional performance, of the child **warrant a reevaluation**; or

(ii) **if** the child's **parents[49] or teacher requests a reevaluation.**

(B) Limitation. A reevaluation conducted under subparagraph (A) **shall occur**–

(i) not more frequently than **once a year,** unless the parent and the local educational agency agree otherwise; and

(ii) **at least once every 3 years**, unless the parent and the local educational agency agree that a reevaluation is unnecessary.[50]

(b) Evaluation Procedures.[51]

(1) Notice. The local educational agency **shall provide notice to the parents** of a child with a disability, in accordance with subsections (b)(3), (b)(4), and (c) of Section 1415 of this title, that describes any evaluation procedures such agency proposes to conduct.

(2) Conduct of Evaluation. In conducting the evaluation, the local educational agency **shall**–

(A) use a **variety of assessment tools and strategies to gather relevant functional, developmental, and academic information**, including **information provided by the parent**, that may assist in determining–

(i) **whether the child is a child with a disability**; and

(ii) the **content of the child's individualized education program**, including information related to enabling the child to be involved in and progress in the general education curriculum, or, for preschool children, to participate in appropriate activities;

(B) **not use any single measure or assessment as the sole criterion** for determining whether a child is a child with a disability or determining an appropriate educational program for the child; and

(C) **use technically sound instruments** that may assess the relative contribution of **cognitive and behavioral factors**, in addition to **physical or developmental factors.**

(3) Additional Requirements. Each local educational agency **shall ensure that**

---

47 A "screening" by a teacher or educational diagnostician to determine instructional strategies is not an "evaluation" subject to the parental consent requirements for evaluations in Section 1414.

48 The language about reevaluations changed. The school is not required to reevaluate a child more often than once a year, unless the parent and school agree otherwise. The school shall evaluate at least every three years, unless the parent and school agree that a reevaluation is unnecessary. The school must reevaluate if the child's educational needs change or if the child's parent or teacher request a reevaluation.

49 The right to an Independent Educational Evaluation (IEE) at public expense is in Section 1415(b)(1).

50 These limits on the frequency of reevaluations are likely to cause difficulties in developing IEPs. The law requires that the IEP include "a statement of the child's present levels of academic achievement and functional performance" (Section 1414(d)(1)(A)(i)). If the child has not been evaluated for a year or more, the IEP Team will not have accurate information about the child's present levels of academic achievement and functional performance. If a parent requests a reevaluation and the LEA refuses, as with initial evaluations, the LEA must provide Prior Written Notice (PWN). See Section 1415(c)(1) and Commentary in the *Federal Register,* page 46640.

51 The school "shall use a variety of assessment tools and strategies to gather relevant functional, developmental, and academic information" about the child. The school shall "not use any single measure or assessment as the sole criterion" for determining if a child is eligible. Information from the evaluation is to be used in determining the contents of the child's IEP and how to help the child make progress in the general education curriculum.

(A) **assessments and other evaluation materials** used to assess a child under this section—

(i) are selected and administered so as **not** to be **discriminatory on a racial or cultural basis**;

(ii) are provided and administered in the language and form most likely to **yield accurate information on what the child knows and can do academically, developmentally, and functionally**, unless it is not feasible to so provide or administer;

(iii) are used for purposes for which the assessments or measures are **valid and reliable**;

(iv) are administered by **trained and knowledgeable personnel**; and

(v) are administered in accordance with any instructions provided by the producer of such assessments;

(B) the child is assessed in **all areas of suspected disability**;[52]

(C) assessment tools and strategies that provide relevant information that directly assists persons in **determining the educational needs** of the child are provided; and

(D) assessments of children with disabilities **who transfer from 1 school district to another school district in the same academic year** are coordinated with such children's prior and subsequent schools, as necessary and as expeditiously as possible, to ensure prompt completion of full evaluations.[53]

(4) Determination of Eligibility and Educational Need.[54] Upon completion of the administration of assessments and other evaluation measures—

(A) the **determination of whether the child is a child with a disability** as defined in Section 1401(3) of this title and the **educational needs of the child** shall be made by a team of qualified professionals and the parent of the child in accordance with paragraph (5); and

(B) a copy of the **evaluation report** and the documentation of determination of eligibility **shall be given to the parent**.[55, 56]

(5) Special Rule for Eligibility Determination. In making a determination of eligibility under paragraph (4)(A), a child shall not be determined to be a child with a disability if the determinant factor for such determination is—

(A) **lack of appropriate instruction in reading, including in the essential components of reading instruction** (as defined in Section 6368(3) of this title);[57]

---

52 Be sure to inform the school **in writing** of all disabilities you suspect. It is more likely that you will get a useful evaluation if you provide each evaluator with a written copy of all your concerns and questions before beginning the evaluation.

53 IDEA 2004 includes additional requirements for assessments. When a child transfers to a new school, the receiving school must complete assessments "as expeditiously as possible to ensure prompt completion of full evaluations." The language that requires the school to assess children "in all areas of suspected disability" and that assessments shall provide relevant information to determine the child's educational needs did not change. Parents can help expedite the transfer of records by requesting in writing that the previous school forward records quickly.

54 "Determination of Eligibility" was changed to "Determination of Eligibility and Educational Need." A team of qualified professionals and the parent determine "whether the child is a child with a disability ... and the educational needs of the child..." The requirements about providing the parent with copies of the evaluation report and documentation of eligibility are unchanged.

55 If the parent disagrees with the school's decision regarding eligibility or classification of the child's disability, the parent should obtain a comprehensive psycho-educational evaluation from an expert in the private sector. For more on this topic, read Chapters 8, 10 and 11 in *Wrightslaw: From Emotions to Advocacy.*

56 The evaluation reports are to be provided "at no cost to the parent." Regulation 300.306(a)(2)

57 The language about "lack of appropriate instruction in reading, including the essential components of reading instruction" is new and brings IDEA into conformity with NCLB. The essential components of reading instruction are defined as explicit and systematic instruction in - (A) phonemic awareness; (B) phonics; (C) vocabulary development; (D) reading fluency, including oral reading skills; and (E) reading comprehension strategies. (See 20 U. S. C § 6368 in *Wrightslaw: No Child Left Behind* and the Commentary to the *Federal Register,* pages 46655 through 46657)

(B) lack of instruction in math;[58] or

(C) **limited English proficiency.**

(6) Specific Learning Disabilities.[59]

(A) In General. Notwithstanding Section 1407(b) of this title, when determining whether a child has a specific learning disability as defined in Section 1401 of this title, a local educational agency **shall not be required to take into consideration whether a child has a severe discrepancy between achievement and intellectual ability** in oral expression, listening comprehension, written expression, basic reading skill, reading comprehension,[60] mathematical calculation, or mathematical reasoning.[61]

(B) Additional Authority. In determining whether a child has a specific learning disability, a local educational agency **may** use a process that **determines if the child responds to scientific, research-based intervention**[62] **as a part of the evaluation procedures** described in paragraphs (2) and (3).[63, 64]

(c) Additional Requirements for Evaluation and Reevaluations.

(1) Review of Existing Evaluation Data. As part of an **initial evaluation** (if appropriate) and as part of **any reevaluation** under this section, the IEP Team and other qualified professionals, as appropriate, **shall** –

(A) **review existing evaluation data** on the child, **including**–

(i) **evaluations and information provided by the parents** of the child;

(ii) **current** classroom-based, local, or State **assessments, and** classroom-based **observations**; and

(iii) **observations** by teachers and related services providers; and

(B) on the basis of that review, and input from the child's parents, **identify what additional data**, if any, **are needed** to determine–

(i) whether the child is a child with a disability as defined in Section 1401(3) of this title, and the **educational needs of the child**,[65] or, in case of a reevaluation of a child, whether the child continues to have such a disability and such educational needs;

---

58 Regulation 300.306 explains that lack of "appropriate" instruction in math, as in reading, is the critical factor.

59 Schools are not required to determine if a child has a severe discrepancy between achievement and intellectual ability to determine that a child has a specific learning disability and needs special education services, nor are schools prohibited from using a discrepancy model. In lieu of a severe discrepancy, a child may be found to exhibit "a pattern of strengths and weaknesses in performance, achievement, or both, relative to age, state-approved grade level standards, or intellectual development . . ." See Regulation 300.309(a)(2)(ii) and 300.311(a)(5)(ii)(B).

60 Reading fluency is now included with reading comprehension, per Regulation 300.309(a)(1)(v).

61 Regulation 300.309 advises that a child may be eligible for services as a child with a specific learning disability "if the child does not achieve adequately for the child's age or to meet State-approved grade-level standards . . . " The eligibility requirements as a child with a specific learning disability are likely to vary from state to state. Check your state special education regulations for the requirements in your state.

62 The legal definition of "scientifically based research" is in No Child Left Behind, 20 U. S. C. § 9101(37) (see *Wrightslaw: No Child Left Behind*). Also, see Regulation 300.35 and the Glossary of Terms at the end of this book.

63 Response to scientific research-based intervention (RTI) is an educational issue, not a legal concept and thus is not given exhaustive analysis in this book. Schools may use Response to Intervention (RTI) to determine if the child responds to scientific, research-based intervention as part of the evaluation process, but RTI "does not replace the need for a comprehensive evaluation." See Commentary in the *Federal Register,* page 46648, which discusses Regulation 300.307(a)(2). For a comprehensive article about RTI from the Department of Education, see "Responsiveness to Intervention in the SLD Process" in the *Toolkit on Teaching and Assessing Students with Disabilities* at www.osepideasthatwork.org/toolkit/pdf/RTI_SLD.pdf (Retrieved on October 10, 2006).

64 The evaluation/eligibility timeline for a specific learning disability may be extended by mutual agreement. See Regulation 300.309(c). The child suspected of having a specific learning disability must be observed in the regular classroom after the child has been referred for an evaluation. See Regulation 300.310(b). The evaluation "may not use any single measure or assessment [such as RTI] as the sole criterion . . ." See Section 1414(b)(2)(B).

65 The language about using evaluations and reevaluations to determine the "educational needs of the child" and "present levels of academic achievement and related developmental needs of the child" are new in IDEA 2004. See Section 1414(c)(1)).

(ii) the **present levels of academic achievement and related developmental needs** of the child;

(iii) whether the child **needs** special education and related services, or in the case of a reevaluation of a child, whether the child continues to need special education and related services; and

(iv) **whether any additions or modifications to the special education and related services are needed** to enable the child **to meet the measurable annual goals** set out in the individualized education program of the child **and to participate**, as appropriate, **in the general education curriculum.**

(2) Source of Data. The local educational agency shall administer such assessments and other evaluation measures as may be needed to produce the data identified by the IEP Team under paragraph (1)(B).

(3) Parental Consent. Each local educational agency shall obtain informed parental consent, in accordance with subsection (a)(1)(D), prior to conducting any reevaluation of a child with a disability, except that such informed parental consent need not be obtained if the local educational agency can demonstrate that it had taken reasonable measures to obtain such consent and the child's parent has failed to respond.[66]

(4) Requirements If Additional Data Are Not Needed.[67] If the IEP Team and other qualified professionals, as appropriate, determine that no additional data are needed to determine whether the child continues to be a child with a disability and to determine the child's educational needs,[68] the local educational agency–

(A) shall notify the child's parents of–

(i) that determination and the reasons for the determination; and

(ii) the right of such parents to request an assessment to determine whether the child continues to be a child with a disability and to determine the child's educational needs; and

(B) shall not be required to conduct such an assessment unless requested to by the child's parents.[69]

(5) Evaluations Before Change in Eligibility.

(A) In General. Except as provided in subparagraph (B), a local educational agency **shall** evaluate a child with a disability in accordance with this section **before determining** that the child is no longer a child with a disability.[70]

(B) Exception.

(i) In General. The evaluation described in subparagraph (A) shall not be required before the termination of a child's eligibility under this part due to graduation from secondary school **with a regular diploma**, or due to exceeding the age eligibility for a free appropriate public education under State law.

(ii) Summary of Performance. For a child whose eligibility under this part terminates under circumstances described in clause (i), a local educational agency shall provide the child with a **summary of the child's academic achievement and functional performance**, which shall include recommendations on

---

66 Pursuant to Regulation 300.300(d)(4)(i), if the child is in a private school or home school, the LEA cannot use due process procedures to force a reevaluation.

67 The new language that allows school personnel to decide if "no additional data are needed" to determine educational needs or eligibility (Section 1414(c)(4)) appears to be at odds with the requirement that the school reevaluate "at least once every 3 years." (Section 1414 (a)(2)(B)(ii))

68 IEP Teams must determine the child's "educational needs" and "present levels of academic achievement and related developmental needs." If a child is not tested at regular intervals, the IEP Team will not have information about the child's educational needs, "present levels of academic achievement" and "related developmental needs." (Section 1414(d)(1)(A)(i)(I))

69 Parents have a right to request an assessment to determine their child's educational needs. (Section 1414(a)(4)(ii)). To ensure that your request is honored, make your request for an assessment of your child's educational needs in writing.

70 The school must evaluate a child before exiting the child from special education, unless the child meets one of the two exceptions in 1414(c)(5)(B)(i). A certificate of attendance, a special education diploma, or anything other than a "regular diploma" does not relieve the school of the requirement for a reevaluation.

how to assist the child in meeting the child's postsecondary goals.[71]

(d) Individualized Education Programs.[72, 73]

    (1) Definitions. In this title:

        (A) Individualized Education Program.

            (i) In General. The term 'individualized education program' or IEP' means a written statement for each child with a disability that is developed, reviewed, and revised in accordance with this section and that includes–

                (I) a statement of the child's present levels of academic achievement[74] and functional performance,[75] including–[76]

                    (aa) how the child's disability affects the child's involvement and progress in the general education curriculum;

                    (bb) for preschool children, as appropriate, how the disability affects the child's participation in appropriate activities; and

                    (cc) for children with disabilities who take alternate assessments aligned to alternate achievement standards, a description of benchmarks or short-term objectives;

                (II) a statement of measurable annual goal, including academic and functional goals,[77] designed to–

                    (aa) meet the child's needs that result from the child's disability to enable the child to be involved in and make progress in the general education curriculum; and

                    (bb) meet each of the child's other educational needs that result from the child's disability;

                (III) a description of how the child's progress toward meeting the annual goals described in subclause (II) will be measured[78] and when periodic reports on the progress the child is making toward

---

71 If parents or eligible students want the school to provide specific testing (e.g., the WAIS-III and W-J III) for college admissions, they should ensure that such testing is written into the child's transition plan, usually during the junior year. This requirement is new in IDEA 2004.

72 The IEP regulations begin at 300.320 through 300.328. Since the IEP regulations no longer include the comprehensive question and answer appendices, as in prior IDEA revisions, you need to obtain a copy of the *Federal Register* Commentary to the IEP regulations that begins on page 46661. The Commentary is on the Wrightslaw site at www.wrightslaw.com/idea/commentary.htm

73 The U. S. Department of Education does not "... encourage public agencies to prepare a draft IEP prior to the IEP Team meeting ... [however, the LEA] should provide the parent with a copy of its draft proposal, if the agency has developed one, **prior to the IEP Team meeting** so as to give the parent an opportunity to review the recommendations of the public agency prior to the IEP Team meeting, and be better able to engage in full discussion of the proposals for the IEP. It is not permissible for an agency to have the final IEP completed before an IEP Team meeting begins." See Commentary in the *Federal Register*, page 46678.

74 The term "academic achievement generally refers to the child's performance in academic areas (e.g., reading or language arts, math, science, and history.)" See Commentary in the *Federal Register*, pages 46661-46662. To learn about your child's standardized test scores in reading and math (i.e., standard scores, percentile ranks, age and grade equivalent scores), read Chapters 10 and 11 about "Tests and Measurements" in *Wrightslaw: From Emotions to Advocacy.*

75 The term "functional is a term that is generally understood to refer to skills or activities that are not considered academic or related to a child's academic achievement. Instead 'functional' is often used in the context of routine activities of everyday living." See Commentary in the *Federal Register*, page 46661.

76 The IEP must include "a statement of the child's present levels of academic achievement and functional performance ..." If the child takes an alternate assessment, the IEP must include "a description of benchmarks or short-term objectives."

77 To learn how to write IEPs that are Specific, Measurable, use Action words, are Realistic and Time specific, read Chapter 11, SMART IEPs, in *Wrightslaw: From Emotions to Advocacy.*

78 The IEP must include measurable annual goals that address the child's "present levels of academic achievement and functional performance." John Willis, evaluator and co-author of *Guide to the Identification of Learning Disabilities*, advised that "If the team is correctly using curriculum-based assessment as part of Response to Intervention in a Problem-Solving Model, progress on the short-term objectives and annual goals could be measured precisely. This may be something on which parents should insist."

meeting the annual goals (such as through the use of quarterly or other periodic reports, concurrent with the issuance of report cards) will be provided;

(IV) a statement of the special education and related services and supplementary aids and services, based on peer-reviewed research[79] to the extent practicable, to be provided to the child, or on behalf of the child, and a statement of the program modifications or supports for school personnel that will be provided for the child[80]

(aa) to advance appropriately toward attaining the annual goals;[81]

(bb) to be involved in and make progress in the general education curriculum in accordance with subclause (I) and to participate in **extracurricular and other nonacademic activities**; and

(cc) to be educated and participate with other children with disabilities and nondisabled children in the activities described in this subparagraph;

(V) an explanation of the extent, if any, to which the child **will not participate** with nondisabled children in the regular class and in the activities described in subclause (IV)(cc);

(VI)

(aa) a statement of any individual appropriate accommodations that are necessary to measure the academic achievement and functional performance of the child on State and districtwide assessments consistent with Section 1412(a)(16)(A) of this title; and

(bb) if the IEP Team determines that the child shall take an alternate assessment on a particular State or districtwide assessment of student achievement, a statement of why–

(AA) the child cannot participate in the regular assessment; and

(BB) the particular alternate assessment[82] selected is appropriate for the child;

(VII) the **projected date for the beginning of the services** and modifications described in subclause (IV), and the anticipated **frequency, location, and duration** of those services and modifications; and

(VIII) beginning not later than the first IEP to be in effect **when the child is 16**, and updated annually thereafter–

(aa) appropriate measurable postsecondary goals[83] based upon age appropriate transition assessments[84] related to training, education, employment, and, where appropriate, independent living skills;

---

79 Congress added new language about research-based instruction to IDEA 2004. "'Peer-reviewed research' . . . generally refers to research that is reviewed by qualified and independent reviewers to ensure that the quality of the information meets the standards of the field before the research is published. However, there is no single definition . . ." See Commentary in the *Federal Register*, page 46664.

80 IDEA contains new language about "individual appropriate accommodations" on state and district testing and new requirements for alternate assessments. The child's IEP must include "a statement of any individual appropriate accommodations that are necessary to measure the academic achievement and functional performance of the child on State and districtwide assessments..."

81 The U. S. Department of Education advised that instructional methodology may be written into an IEP. "The Department's longstanding position on including instructional methodology in a child's IEP is that it is an IEP Team's decision. Therefore, if an IEP Team determines that specific instructional methods are necessary for the child to receive FAPE, the instructional methods may be addressed in the IEP." See Commentary in the *Federal Register*, page 46665.

82 An alternate assessment might mean denial of a regular high school diploma. See Commentary in the *Federal Register*, page 46666.

83 "'Post secondary goals' . . . is generally understood to refer to those goals that a child hopes to achieve after leaving secondary school (i.e., high school)." See Commentary in the *Federal Register*, page 46668.

84 The requirements for transition in IEPs changed. The "first IEP to be in effect when the child is 16" means this IEP must be in effect by the child's 16th birthday.

(bb) the transition services (including **courses of study**)[85,86] needed to assist the child in reaching those goals; and

(cc) beginning **not later than 1 year** before the child reaches the age of majority under State law, a statement that the child has been informed of the child's rights under this title, if any, that will transfer to the child on reaching the age of majority under Section 1415(m) of this title.

(ii) Rule of Construction. Nothing in this section shall be construed to require –

(I) that additional information be included in a child's IEP beyond what is explicitly required in this section; and

(II) the IEP Team to include information under 1 component of a child's IEP that is already contained under another component of such IEP.

(B) Individualized Education Program Team. The term 'individualized education program team' or IEP Team' means a group of individuals composed of–

(i) the **parents** of a child with a disability;[87]

(ii) not less than 1 **regular education teacher** of such child (if the child is, or may be, participating in the regular education environment);

(iii) not less than 1 **special education teacher**, or where appropriate, not less than 1 special education provider[88] of such child;

(iv) a **representative of the local educational agency** who–

(I) is qualified to provide, or supervise the provision of, specially designed instruction to meet the unique needs of children with disabilities;

(II) is knowledgeable about the general education curriculum; and

(III) is knowledgeable about the availability of resources of the local educational agency;

(v) an individual who can **interpret** the instructional implications of **evaluation results**, who may be a member of the team described in clauses (ii) through (vi);

(vi) at the discretion of the parent or the agency, **other individuals** who have knowledge or special expertise regarding the child, including related services personnel as appropriate; and

(vii) whenever appropriate, **the child with a disability**.

(C) IEP Team Attendance.[89]

(i) Attendance Not Necessary.[90] A member of the IEP Team shall not be required to attend an IEP

---

85 Course of study can be "participation in advanced placement courses or a vocational education program." See Commentary in the *Federal Register*, page 46668.

86 Part B funds can be used for student "participation in transitional programs on college campuses or in community-based settings . . ." See Commentary in the *Federal Register*, page 46668.

87 The LEA "must take whatever action is necessary to ensure that the parent understands the proceedings of the IEP Team meeting, including arranging for an interpreter for parents with deafness or whose native language is other than English." See Regulation 300.322(e).

88 A special education provider is "responsible for implementing the IEP" and may be the child's speech pathologist, occupational therapist, or other person, dependent upon the child's disability and whether the child is receiving speech services, occupational therapy, or other services." See Commentary in the *Federal Register*, page 46675.

89 A member of the IEP Team may be excused from attending an IEP meeting if their area of curriculum or service will not be discussed or modified during the meeting. An IEP Team member may also be excused from an IEP meeting that involves their area of curriculum or service if they submit input in writing and if the parent and school consent. The parent's consent must be in writing.

90 "An LEA that routinely excuses IEP Team members from IEP Team meetings would not be in compliance with the requirements of the Act and therefore would be subject to the States' monitoring and enforcement provisions." See Commentary in the *Federal Register*, page 46674.

meeting,[91] in whole or in part, if the parent of a child with a disability and the local educational agency agree that the attendance of such member is not necessary because the member's area of the curriculum or related services is not being modified or discussed in the meeting.

(ii) Excusal. A member of the IEP Team **may be excused** from attending an IEP meeting, in whole or in part, when the meeting involves a modification to or discussion of the member's area of the curriculum or related services, **if–**

(I) the parent and the local educational agency consent to the excusal; and

(II) the member submits, in writing to the parent and the IEP Team, input into the development of the IEP prior to the meeting.

(iii) Written Agreement and Consent Required. A parent's agreement under clause (i) and consent under clause (ii) shall be in writing.

(D) IEP Team Transition. In the case of a child who was previously served under part C, an invitation to the initial IEP meeting **shall, at the request of the parent,** be sent to the part C service coordinator or other representatives of the part C system to assist with the smooth transition of services.

(2) Requirement That Program Be in Effect.

(A) In General. At the beginning of each school year, each local educational agency, State educational agency, or other State agency, as the case may be, **shall** have in effect, for each child with a disability in the agency's jurisdiction, an individualized education program,[92] as defined in paragraph (1)(A).[93]

(B) Program for Child Aged 3 Through 5. In the case of a child with a disability aged 3 through 5 (or, at the discretion of the State educational agency, a 2-year-old child with a disability who will turn age 3 during the school year), **the IEP Team shall consider the individualized family service plan** that contains the material described in Section 1436 of this title, and that is developed in accordance with this section, and the individualized family service plan may serve as the IEP of the child if using that plan as the IEP is–

(i) consistent with State policy; and

(ii) agreed to by the agency and the child's parents.[94]

(C) Program for Children Who Transfer School Districts.[95]

(i) In General.[96]

(I) Transfer within the Same State. In the case of a child with a disability who transfers school districts within the same academic year, who enrolls in a new school, and who had an IEP that was in effect in the same State, the local educational agency **shall** provide such child with a free appropriate

---

91 The Commentary to the IEP regulations states that "To ensure that all IEP Team members are aware of their responsibilities regarding the implementation of a child's IEP, Section 300.323(d) requires that the child's IEP be accessible to each regular education teacher, special education teacher, related services provider, and any other service provider who is responsible for its implementation." See Commentary in the *Federal Register*, page 46669.

92 IEPs must be in effect at the beginning of the school year for all children with disabilities, including children who are enrolled in private programs. Under IDEA 2004, public schools may be responsible for offering IEPs to students who attend private schools. (See Sections 1412(a)(3)+(10) about child find and private schools.) However, if the parent refuses to consent to an evaluation or to special education services, the school is not required to develop an IEP. (Section 1414(a)(1)(D)(ii)) If the parent refuses to permit the school to evaluate the child, any entitlement to reimbursement for a private school program may be reduced or barred. (Section 1412(a)(10))

93 See Regulation 300.323(c) for the 30-day IEP timeline.

94 "The IFSP may serve as the IEP of the child . . . [and the public agency] must provide to the child's parents a detailed explanation of the differences between an IFSP and an IEP . . ." See Regulation 300.323(b) and (c).

95 The subsection about programs for children who transfer is new. If the child transfers to a district in the same state or another state, the receiving school must provide comparable services to those in the sending district's IEP until they develop and implement a new IEP.

96 The Commentary to Regulation 300.323(f) explains that "the Department interprets 'comparable' to have the plain meaning of the word, which is 'similar' or 'equivalent.'" See Commentary in the *Federal Register*, page 46681.

public education, including services **comparable to** those described in the previously held IEP, in consultation with the parents **until such time** as the local educational agency **adopts** the previously held IEP or develops, adopts, and implements a new IEP that is consistent with Federal and State law.

(II) Transfer Outside State. In the case of a child with a disability who transfers school districts within the same academic year, who enrolls in a new school, and who had an IEP that was in effect in another State, the local educational agency shall provide such child with a free appropriate public education, including services **comparable to** those described in the previously held IEP, in consultation with the parents **until such time** as the local educational agency **conducts an evaluation** pursuant to subsection (a)(1), if determined to be necessary by such agency, and **develops a new IEP**, if appropriate, that is consistent with Federal and State law.[97]

(ii) Transmittal of Records. To facilitate the transition for a child described in clause (i)–

(I) the new school in which the child enrolls shall take reasonable steps to promptly obtain the child's records, including the IEP and supporting documents and any other records relating to the provision of special education or related services to the child, from the previous school in which the child was enrolled, pursuant to section 99.31(a)(2) of title 34, Code of Federal Regulations; and

(II) the previous school in which the child was enrolled shall take reasonable steps to promptly respond to such request from the new school.

(3) Development of IEP.

(A) In General. In developing each child's IEP, the IEP Team, subject to subparagraph (C), **shall consider**[98]

(i) the **strengths** of the child;

(ii) the **concerns of the parents** for enhancing the education of their child;[99]

(iii) the **results of** the initial evaluation or **most recent evaluation** of the child;[100] and

(iv) the **academic, developmental, and functional needs** of the child.[101]

(B) Consideration of Special Factors. The IEP Team shall–

(i) in the case of a child whose **behavior** impedes the child's learning or that of others, consider the use of **positive behavioral interventions** and supports, and other strategies, to address that behavior;

(ii) in the case of a child with **limited English proficiency**, consider the language needs of the child as such needs relate to the child's IEP;

(iii) in the case of a child who is **blind or visually impaired**, provide for instruction in Braille and the use of Braille unless the IEP Team determines, after an evaluation of the child's reading and writing skills, needs, and appropriate reading and writing media (including an evaluation of the child's future needs for instruction in Braille or the use of Braille), that instruction in Braille or the use of Braille is not appropriate for the child;

(iv) consider the **communication needs** of the child, and in the case of a child who is deaf or hard of hearing, consider the child's language and communication needs, opportunities for direct communica-

---

97 This is a new "initial" evaluation, not a reevaluation. See Commentary in the *Federal Register*, page 46682.

98 In developing the IEP, the IEP Team must consider the parents' concerns about the child's education, including concerns about inadequate progress. Some IEP Teams refuse to accept information from private sector evaluations of the child. The law clearly states that schools shall consider the most recent evaluation on the child.

99 A parent can consent to some services in an IEP and refuse to consent to other services. The agreed upon services must be implemented. See Regulation 300.300(d)(3) and 300.518(c).

100 Pursuant to regulation 300.613(a), upon request, the LEA must provide the parent with the child's education records prior to an IEP meeting.

101 The Department of Education published a model Individualized Education Program (IEP) form at the time the regulations were published. Links to the regulations and model forms are at www.wrightslaw.com/idea/law.htm

tions with peers and professional personnel in the child's language and communication mode, academic level, and full range of needs, including opportunities for direct instruction in the child's language and communication mode; and

(v) consider whether the child needs **assistive technology devices and services.**

(C) Requirement with Respect to Regular Education Teacher. A regular education teacher of the child, as a member of the IEP Team, shall, to the extent appropriate, participate in the development of the IEP of the child, including the determination of appropriate positive behavioral interventions and supports, and other strategies, and the determination of supplementary aids and services, program modifications, and support for school personnel consistent with paragraph (1)(A)(i)(IV).

(D) Agreement. In making changes to a child's IEP after the annual IEP meeting for a school year, the parent of a child with a disability and the local educational agency **may agree not to convene an IEP meeting** for the purposes of making such changes, and instead may develop a written document to amend or modify the child's current IEP.

(E) Consolidation of IEP Team Meetings. To the extent possible, the local educational agency shall encourage the consolidation of reevaluation meetings for the child and other IEP Team meetings for the child.

(F) Amendments. Changes to the IEP may be made either by the entire IEP Team or, as provided in subparagraph (D), by amending the IEP rather than by redrafting the entire IEP. **Upon request**, a parent shall be provided with a revised copy of the IEP with the amendments incorporated.

(4) Review and Revision of IEP. [102, 103]

(A) In General. The local educational agency **shall** ensure that, subject to subparagraph (B), the IEP Team—

(i) reviews the child's IEP periodically, but **not less frequently than annually,**[104] to determine whether the annual goals for the child are being achieved; and

(ii) **revises the IEP as appropriate** to address—

(I) any lack of expected progress toward the annual goals and in the general education curriculum, where appropriate;

(II) **the results of any reevaluation** conducted under this section;

(III) information about the child provided to, or by, the parents, as described in subsection (c)(1)(B);

(IV) the child's anticipated needs; or

(V) other matters.

(B) Requirement with Respect to Regular Education Teacher. A regular education teacher of the child, as a member of the IEP Team, shall, consistent with paragraph (1)(C), participate in the review and revision of the IEP of the child.

---

102   IDEA 2004 made significant changes to reviewing and revising IEPs. If the parent and school decide to amend or modify the IEP developed at the annual IEP meeting, and do not want to convene another IEP meeting, they may revise the IEP by agreement. The IEP Team must create a written document to amend or modify the IEP. This document should describe the changes or modifications in the IEP and note that, by agreement, an IEP meeting was not convened. The parent should request a copy of the revised IEP.

103   The Commentary to the regulations notes that: "The IEP Team is expected to act in the best interest of the child. As with any IEP Team meeting, if additional information is needed to finalize an appropriate IEP, there is nothing in the Act that prevents an IEP Team from reconvening after the needed information is obtained, as long as the IEP is developed in a timely manner." See Commentary in the *Federal Register,* page 46676.

104   "[A]n amendment to an IEP . . . [cannot] take the place of an annual IEP meeting." See Commentary in the *Federal Register,* page 46685.

(5) Multi-Year IEP Demonstration.[105]

   (A) Pilot Program.

   (i) Purpose. The purpose of this paragraph is to provide an opportunity for States to allow parents and local educational agencies the opportunity for long-term planning by offering the option of developing a comprehensive multi-year IEP, not to exceed 3 years, that is designed to coincide with the natural transition points[106] for the child.

   (ii) Authorization. In order to carry out the purpose of this paragraph, the Secretary is authorized to approve not more than 15 proposals from States to carry out the activity described in clause (i).

   (iii) Proposal.

   (I) In General. A State desiring to participate in the program under this paragraph shall submit a proposal to the Secretary at such time and in such manner as the Secretary may reasonably require.

   (II) Content. The proposal shall include–

   (aa) assurances that the development of a multi-year IEP under this paragraph is **optional for parents**;

   (bb) assurances that the parent is required to provide informed consent before a comprehensive multi-year IEP is developed;

   (cc) a list of required elements for each multi-year IEP, including–

   (AA) measurable goals pursuant to paragraph (1)(A)(i)(II), coinciding with natural transition points for the child, that will enable the child to be involved in and make progress in the general education curriculum and that will meet the child's other needs that result from the child's disability; and

   (BB) measurable annual goals for determining progress toward meeting the goals described in subitem (AA); and

   (dd) a description of the process for the review and revision of each multi-year IEP, including–

   (AA) a review by the IEP Team of the child's multi-year IEP at each of the child's **natural transition points**;

   (BB) in years other than a child's natural transition points, **an annual review of the child's IEP** to determine the child's current levels of progress and whether the annual goals for the child are being achieved, and a requirement to amend the IEP, as appropriate, to enable the child to continue to meet the measurable goals set out in the IEP;

   (CC) if the IEP Team determines on the basis of a review that the child is not making sufficient progress toward the goals described in the multi-year IEP, a requirement that the local educational agency shall ensure that the IEP Team carries out a more thorough review of the IEP in accordance with paragraph (4) within 30 calendar days; and

   (DD) at the request of the parent, a requirement that the IEP Team shall conduct a review of the child's multi-year IEP rather than or subsequent to an annual review.

   (B) Report. Beginning 2 years after the date of enactment of the Individuals with Disabilities Education Improvement Act of 2004, the Secretary shall submit an annual report to the Committee on Education and

---

105   IDEA 2004 authorizes a multi-year IEP pilot project. Fifteen states may apply for approval to use three-year IEPs. IEP review dates must be based on "natural transition points." Parents have the right to opt-out of this program. The parent of a child served under a multi-year IEP can have a review of the IEP without waiting for a natural transition point.

106   See Section 1414(d)(5)(C) for an explanation of "natural transition points."

the Workforce of the House of Representatives and the Committee on Health, Education, Labor, and Pensions of the Senate regarding the effectiveness of the program under this paragraph and any specific recommendations for broader implementation of such program, including

> (i) reducing–

>> (I) the paperwork burden on teachers, principals, administrators, and related service providers; and

>> (II) noninstructional time spent by teachers in complying with this part;

> (ii) enhancing longer-term educational planning;

> (iii) improving positive outcomes for children with disabilities;

> (iv) promoting collaboration between IEP Team members; and

> (v) ensuring satisfaction of family members.

(C) Definition. In this paragraph, the term '**natural transition points**' means those periods that are close in time to the transition of a child with a disability from preschool to elementary grades, from elementary grades to middle or junior high school grades, from middle or junior high school grades to secondary school grades, and from secondary school grades to post-secondary activities, **but in no case a period longer than 3 years.**

(6) Failure to Meet Transition Objectives. If a participating agency, other than the local educational agency, fails to provide the transition services described in the IEP in accordance with paragraph (1)(A)(i)(VIII), the local educational agency shall reconvene the IEP Team to identify alternative strategies to meet the transition objectives for the child set out in the IEP.

(7) Children with Disabilities in Adult Prisons.[107]

(A) In General. The following requirements shall not apply to children with disabilities who are **convicted as adults** under State law **and incarcerated in adult prisons**:

> (i) The requirements contained in Section 1412(a)(16) of this title and paragraph (1)(A)(i)(VI) (relating to participation of children with disabilities in general assessments).

> (ii) The requirements of items (aa) and (bb) of paragraph (1)(A)(i)(VIII) (relating to transition planning and transition services), do not apply with respect to such children whose eligibility under this part will end, because of such children's age, before such children will be released from prison.

(B) Additional Requirement. If a child with a disability is convicted as an adult under State law and incarcerated in an adult prison, the child's IEP Team may modify the child's IEP or placement notwithstanding the requirements of Sections 1412(a)(5)(A) of this title and paragraph (1)(A) if the State has demonstrated a bona fide security or compelling penological interest that cannot otherwise be accommodated.

(e) Educational Placements. Each local educational agency or State educational agency shall ensure that the **parents** of each child with a disability are **members of any group that makes decisions** on the educational placement of their child.[108]

---

107 A school district is not required to offer a free appropriate education to a child with a disability who was convicted as an adult and is incarcerated in an adult prison. A child who was convicted as an adult and is in prison (not jail) shall not be tested on the statewide assessments. The "appropriate measurable postsecondary goals," "transition services" and "courses of study" are not required. Sentences of less than one year are usually served in jails. Longer sentences are usually served in prisons. In general, individuals who are convicted of misdemeanors serve sentences in jails, while individuals convicted of felonies serve their sentences in prisons.

108 An educational placement "refers to the provision of special education and related services rather than a specific place, such as a specific classroom or specific school." See Commentary in the *Federal Register,* page 46687. Decisions about the child's placement cannot be made until after the IEP Team, which includes the child's parent(s), meets and reaches consensus about the IEP goals. Although the law on this issue is clear, school personnel sometimes decide on the child's placement before the IEP meeting.

(f) Alternative Means of Meeting Participation.[109] When conducting **IEP Team meetings** and placement meetings pursuant to this section, Section 1415(e) of this title, and Section 1415(f)(1)(B) of this title, and carrying out administrative matters under Section 1415 of this title (such as scheduling, exchange of witness lists, and status conferences), the parent of a child with a disability and a local educational agency may agree to use alternative means of meeting participation, such as **video conferences and conference calls.**

20 U. S. C. § 1415. Procedural Safeguards.

WRIGHTSLAW OVERVIEW: Section 1415 describes the procedural safeguards designed to protect the rights of children with disabilities and their parents. These safeguards include the right to participate in all meetings, to examine all educational records, and to obtain an independent educational evaluation (IEE) of the child. Parents have the right to written notice when the school proposes to change or refuses to change the identification, evaluation or placement of the child Section 1415(c). Section 1415(d) describes requirements for the Procedural Safeguards Notice that must be provided to parents.

Section 1415(e) describes requirements for using mediation to resolve disputes, legally binding written mediation agreements, and confidentiality. Section 1415(f) describes the requirements for due process hearings and the Resolution Session that may allow the parties to resolve their dispute before a due process hearing. Section 1415(f) includes new requirements for hearing officers and timelines, including a new two-year statute of limitations. Section 1415(i) describes the appeals process and the new 90-day deadline on appeals. Section 1415(j) is the "stay put" statute that allows the child to remain in the "current educational placement" during litigation.

Section 1415(k) is the discipline statute. This statute authorizes school personnel to place children in interim alternative educational settings. This statute includes manifestation determinations, placement as determined by the IEP Team, appeals, authority of the hearing officer, and transfer of rights at the age of majority.

The procedural safeguards regulations begin at 300.500 and the Commentary in the Federal Register begins at 46688.

(a) Establishment of Procedures. Any State educational agency, State agency, or local educational agency that receives assistance under this part shall establish and maintain procedures in accordance with this section to ensure that children with disabilities and their parents are guaranteed procedural safeguards with respect to the provision of a free appropriate public education by such agencies.

(b) Types of Procedures.[110] The procedures required by this section shall include the following:

(1) An opportunity for the parents of a child with a disability **to examine all records** relating to such child and **to participate in meetings** with respect to the **identification, evaluation, and educational placement** of the child, and the provision of a free appropriate public education to such child, and **to obtain an independent educational evaluation**[111, 112] of the child.

---

109 School meetings do not have to be face-to-face. IEP and placement meetings (Sections 1414(d)+(e)), mediation (Section 1415(e)), and due process (IEP) resolution sessions (Section 1415(f)(1)(B)) may be convened by conference calls or video conferences.

110 Parents have the right to examine all educational records, including test data. The right to examine records may include personal notes, if these notes have been shared with other staff. Parents should make their request for a complete copy of all files, including test data (i.e., standard scores, percentile ranks, age equivalent scores, and grade equivalent scores), in writing.

111 Parents have the right to obtain an Independent Educational Evaluation (IEE) of their child. Many school districts attempt to restrict the parent's choice of evaluators to a list of approved evaluators selected by the school. The Office of Special Education Programs issued a policy letter clarifying that parents have the right to choose their own independent evaluator. (See OSEP, Letter to Parker, 2004 on the Wrightslaw website at www.wrightslaw.com/info/test.eval.choice.osep.htm) See Regulation 300.502 regarding IEEs. See Commentary in the *Federal Register,* page 46690, regarding fees for an IEE.

112 At a minimum, the IEE should determine if the child has or continues to have a disability, and the educational needs of the child. "There is an affirmative obligation on a public agency to consider the results of a parent initiated evaluation at private expense in any decision regarding the provision of FAPE to the child." However, if an IEE is rejected or not given proper consideration by the LEA, it is "appropriate for the agency to explain to the parent why it believes that the parent-initiated evaluation does not meet agency criteria." See Commentary in the *Federal Register,* page 46690.

(2)

    (A) Procedures to protect the rights of the child whenever the parents of the child are not known, the agency cannot, after reasonable efforts, locate the parents, or the child is a ward of the State, including the assignment of an individual to act as a **surrogate for the parents**, which surrogate shall not be an employee of the State educational agency, the local educational agency, or any other agency that is involved in the education or care of the child. In the case of–

        (i) a child who is a **ward of the State**, such surrogate may alternatively be appointed by the judge overseeing the child's care provided that the surrogate meets the requirements of this paragraph; and

        (ii) an **unaccompanied homeless youth** as defined in Section 11434a(6) of title 42, the local educational agency shall appoint a surrogate in accordance with this paragraph.

    (B) The State shall make reasonable efforts to ensure the assignment of a surrogate **not more than 30 days after** there is a determination by the agency that the child needs a surrogate.

    (3) Written prior notice[113] to the parents of the child, in accordance with subsection (c)(1), whenever the local educational agency–

        (A) **proposes to initiate or change**; or

        (B) **refuses to initiate or change**, the identification, evaluation, or educational placement of the child, or the provision of a free appropriate public education to the child.

    (4) Procedures designed to ensure that the notice required by paragraph (3) is in the native language of the parents, unless it clearly is not feasible to do so.

    (5) An opportunity for mediation, in accordance with subsection (e).

    (6) An opportunity for any party to present a **complaint**

        (A) with respect to **any matter** relating to the identification, evaluation, or educational placement of the child, or the provision of a free appropriate public education to such child; and

        (B) which sets forth an alleged violation that occurred **not more than 2 years before** the date[114] the parent or public agency knew or should have known about the alleged action that forms the basis of the complaint, **or, if the State has an explicit time limitation** for presenting such a complaint under this part, in such time as the State law allows, except that the exceptions to the timeline described in subsection (f)(3)(D) shall apply to the timeline described in this subparagraph.

    (7)

    (A) Procedures that require either party, or the attorney representing a party, to provide **due process complaint notice**[115] in accordance with subsection (c)(2) (which shall remain confidential)–

        (i) to the other party, in the complaint filed under paragraph (6), and **forward a copy** of such notice to the State educational agency; and

        (ii) that shall include–

            (I) the name of the child, the address of the residence of the child (or available contact information in the case of a homeless child), and the name of the school the child is attending;

            (II) in the case of a homeless child or youth (within the meaning of Section 11434a(2) of title 42), available contact information for the child and the name of the school the child is attending;

            (III) a **description of the nature of the problem** of the child relating to such proposed initiation or change, including facts relating to such problem; and

---

113   The school district must provide, in writing, the reason for refusing to evaluate a child or change the educational program.

114   The two-year statute of limitations to present a complaint is new.

115   The party who requests a due process hearing must provide a detailed notice to the other party. This notice must include identifying information about the child, the nature of the problem, facts, and proposed resolution. The party who requests a due process hearing may not have the hearing until they provide this notice.

(IV) a **proposed resolution of the problem** to the extent known and available to the party at the time.[116]

(B) A requirement that a party **may not have a due process hearing until** the party, or the attorney representing the party, files a notice that meets the requirements of subparagraph (A)(ii).

(8) Procedures that require the State educational agency to develop a model form to assist parents in filing a complaint and due process complaint notice in accordance with paragraphs (6) and (7), respectively.

(c) Notification Requirements.

(1) Content of Prior Written Notice.[117] The notice required by subsection (b)(3) shall include–

(A) a description of the action **proposed or refused** by the agency;

(B) an **explanation** of why the agency proposes or refuses to take the action and a **description of each evaluation procedure, assessment, record, or report** the agency used as a basis for the proposed or refused action;

(C) a statement that the parents of a child with a disability have protection under the procedural safeguards of this part and, if this notice is not an initial referral for evaluation, the means by which a copy of a description of the procedural safeguards can be obtained;

(D) sources for parents to contact to obtain assistance in understanding the provisions of this part;

(E) a **description of other options** considered by the IEP Team and the reason why those options were rejected; and

(F) a **description of the factors** that are relevant to the agency's proposal or refusal.

(2) Due Process Complaint Notice.[118]

(A) Complaint. The **due process complaint notice** required under subsection (b)(7)(A) shall be deemed to be sufficient unless the party receiving the notice notifies the hearing officer and the other party in writing that the receiving party believes the notice has not met the requirements of subsection (b)(7)(A).

(B) Response to Complaint.

(i) Local Educational Agency Response.

(I) In General. If the local educational agency **has not sent a prior written notice** to the parent regarding the subject matter contained in the parent's due process complaint notice, such local educational agency **shall**, within 10 days of receiving the complaint, send to the parent a response that shall include–

---

116   A Due Process Complaint Notice can be a letter to request a due process hearing that includes the required components. To learn how to write persuasive letters that make readers want to help, read Chapter 24, "Letter to the Stranger," in **Wrightslaw: From Emotions to Advocacy.** Your state is required to develop a Model Form for requesting a due process hearing. See Regulation 300.509.

117   Prior Written Notice (PWN) is easier to understand if you eliminate the word "prior" from your analysis. Assume a parent requests that the school increase the child's speech language therapy from three 15-minute sessions per week (45 minutes per week) to three 30-minute sessions per week (90 minutes per week). If the school refuses, they must provide "written notice" about their refusal. This written notice must describe what they refused to do and their alternate proposal, if any. The notice must explain their rationale and must describe each evaluation procedure, assessment, record, or report used as the basis of their refusal. The notice must also provide a description of all other options the IEP Team considered and the reasons why the team rejected these options. Finally, the notice must describe any other factors that are relevant to their proposal or refusal. Schools often fail to provide Prior Written Notice when parents request more services or different services. IDEA 2004 strengthened prior written notice requirements and requires schools to provide this notice in the event of a due process hearing. (Section 1415(c)(2)(B)(i)(I))

118   Section 1415(c)(2) includes requirements and timelines for the Due Process Complaint Notice and the Amended Complaint Notice. If the school did not provide the parent with Prior Written Notice, the school must send this Notice within 10 days. The non-complaining party must respond to the complaint within 10 days. If the notice is insufficient, the receiving party must complain to the Hearing Officer within 15 days. (See Section 1415(c)(2)(C)) The Hearing Officer has 5 days to determine whether the complaint is sufficient. If it is not sufficient, an amended complaint may be filed.

(aa) an explanation of why the agency proposed or refused to take the action raised in the complaint;

(bb) a description of other options that the IEP Team considered and the reasons why those options were rejected;

(cc) a description of each evaluation procedure, assessment, record, or report the agency used as the basis for the proposed or refused action; and

(dd) a description of the factors that are relevant to the agency's proposal or refusal.

(II) Sufficiency. A response filed by a local educational agency pursuant to subclause (I) shall not be construed to preclude such local educational agency from asserting that the parent's due process complaint notice was insufficient where appropriate.

(ii) Other Party Response. Except as provided in clause (i), the non-complaining party **shall, within 10 days** of receiving the complaint, **send to the complainant a response** that specifically addresses the issues raised in the complaint.

(C) Timing. The party providing a hearing officer notification under subparagraph (A) shall provide the notification within 15 days of receiving the complaint.

(D) Determination. Within 5 days of receipt of the notification provided under subparagraph (C), the hearing officer shall make a determination on the face of the notice of whether the notification meets the requirements of subsection (b)(7)(A), and shall immediately notify the parties in writing of such determination.

(E) Amended Complaint Notice.

(i) In General. A party **may amend** its due process complaint notice **only if—**

(I) the other party **consents in writing** to such amendment and is given the opportunity to resolve the complaint through a meeting held pursuant to subsection (f)(1)(B); or

(II) the **hearing officer grants permission**, except that the hearing officer may only grant such permission at any time not later than 5 days before a due process hearing occurs.

(ii) Applicable Timeline. The applicable timeline for a due process hearing under this part shall recommence at the time the party files an amended notice, including the timeline under subsection (f)(1)(B).

(d) Procedural Safeguards Notice.[119]

(1) In General.

(A) Copy to Parents. A copy of the procedural safeguards available to the parents of a child with a disability **shall be given to the parents** only 1 time a year, **except** that a copy also shall be given to the parents—

(i) upon initial referral or parental request for evaluation;

(ii) upon the first occurrence of the filing of a complaint under subsection (b)(6); and

(iii) upon request by a parent.

(B) Internet Websites. A local educational agency may place a current copy of the procedural safeguards notice on its Internet website if such website exists.[120]

---

119   The purpose of the Procedural Safeguards Notice is to provide parents with information about their rights and protections under the law. Upon request for a due process hearing or at least once a year, parents must be provided with notice of the time period (statute of limitations) within which "to make a complaint." The Procedural Safeguards Notice also includes rights about mediation, "stay put," discipline, reimbursement for private placements, and attorneys' fees.

120   Simply referring the parent to the Procedural Safeguard Notice on the school website is not sufficient.

(2) Contents. The procedural safeguards notice[121] shall include a full explanation of the procedural safeguards, written **in the native language of the parents** (unless it clearly is not feasible to do so) and **written in an easily understandable manner,** available under this section and under regulations promulgated by the Secretary relating to–

(A) independent educational evaluation;

(B) prior written notice;

(C) parental consent;

(D) access to educational records;

(E) the opportunity to present and resolve complaints, including–

(i) the time period in which to make a complaint;

(ii) the opportunity for the agency to resolve the complaint; and

(iii) the availability of mediation;

(F) the child's placement during pendency of due process proceedings;

(G) procedures for students who are subject to placement in an interim alternative educational setting;

(H) requirements for unilateral placement by parents of children in private schools at public expense;

(I) due process hearings, including requirements for disclosure of evaluation results and recommendations;

(J) State-level appeals (if applicable in that State);

(K) civil actions, including the time period in which to file such actions; and

(L) attorneys' fees.

(e) Mediation.[122]

(1) In General. Any State educational agency or local educational agency that receives assistance under this part shall ensure that procedures are established and implemented to allow parties to disputes involving any matter, including matters arising **prior to the filing of a complaint** pursuant to subsection (b)(6), to resolve such disputes through a mediation process.

(2) Requirements. Such procedures **shall** meet the following requirements:

(A) The procedures shall ensure that the mediation process–

(i) **is voluntary** on the part of the parties;

(ii) is **not used to deny or delay a parent's right to a due process hearing** under subsection (f), or to deny any other rights afforded under this part; and

(iii) is conducted by a **qualified and impartial** mediator who is trained in effective mediation techniques.[123]

---

121   Many states have their own forms for Procedural Safeguards Notice. The Education Department published a model Procedural Safeguards Notice form. Links to the federal special education regulations and model forms are at www.wrightslaw.com/idea/law.htm and in the Resources section in Section Five of this book. Download and print the model "Procedural Safeguard Notice" from the Education Department of Education and keep it with this book.

122   Mediation is a confidential process that allows parties to resolve disputes without litigation. The mediator helps the parties express their views and positions and understand the views and positions of the other party. To be successful, both parties must discuss their views and differences frankly. Before entering into mediation, you need to understand your rights and the law. A due process hearing does not have to be pending to request mediation.

123   When you mediate or negotiate, your goals are to resolve the dispute and protect the parent-school relationship. The Bibliography includes recommended books that will help you learn to negotiate effectively. The terms of a mediated agreement can be incorporated into an IEP so that the IEP reflects the agreement. The mediator can act as a facilitator for an IEP meeting. See Commentary in the *Federal Register,* page 46695.

(B) Opportunity to Meet with a Disinterested Party. A local educational agency or a State agency may establish procedures to offer to parents and schools that choose not to use the mediation process, an opportunity to meet, at a time and location convenient to the parents, with a disinterested party who is under contract with–

(i) a parent training and information center or community parent resource center in the State established under Section 1471 of this title or 1472 of this title; or

(ii) an appropriate alternative dispute resolution entity, to encourage the use, and explain the benefits, of the mediation process to the parents.

(C) List of Qualified Mediators.[124] The State shall maintain a list of individuals who are qualified mediators[125] and knowledgeable in laws and regulations relating to the provision of special education and related services.

(D) Costs. The State **shall bear the cost** of the mediation process, including the costs of meetings described in subparagraph (B).

(E) Scheduling and Location. Each session in the mediation process shall be scheduled in a timely manner and shall be held in a location that is convenient to the parties to the dispute.[126]

(F) Written Agreement.[127] In the case that a resolution is reached to resolve the complaint through the mediation process, the parties shall execute **a legally binding agreement** that sets forth such resolution and that–

(i) states that **all discussions** that occurred during the mediation process **shall be confidential** and may not be used as evidence in any subsequent due process hearing or civil proceeding;

(ii) is signed by both the parent and a representative of the agency who has the authority to bind such agency; and

(iii) **is enforceable** in any State court of competent jurisdiction or in a district court of the United States.

(G) Mediation Discussions. Discussions that occur during the mediation process **shall be confidential** and may not be used as evidence in any subsequent due process hearing or civil proceeding.[128]

(f) Impartial Due Process Hearing. [129]

(1) In General.

(A) Hearing. Whenever a complaint has been received under subsection (b)(6) or (k), the parents or the local educational agency involved in such complaint shall have an opportunity for an impartial due process

---

124   The mediator's role is to facilitate the communication process. Mediators should not take positions or take sides. A good mediator does not have to be knowledgeable about special education law and practice but must know how to facilitate communication between parties. If mediators are not well trained in the process of mediation, their biases and opinions will have an adverse impact on the mediation process. Mediators are not arbitrators. Arbitrators issue rulings in favor of one party or the other.

125   Mediators are selected "on a random, rotational, or other impartial basis." See Regulation 300.506(b)(3)(ii).

126   Mediation sessions and resolution sessions do not have to be face-to-face, and per Section 1414(f), may be may be convened by conference calls or video conferences.

127   Legally binding written settlement agreements are new in IDEA 2004. Previously, when a party breached a mediation agreement, the other party had to enforce the agreement by filing suit under a breach of contract theory, usually in state court. Now a party can use the power of federal courts to ensure that settlement agreements are honored.

128   In mediation, discussions and admissions against interests by the parties are confidential. If the case is not settled, information from settlement discussions may not be used or disclosed in a subsequent trial. An attempt to use confidential disclosures from mediation or settlement discussions in court could cause the case to be dismissed or the judge to issue an adverse ruling.

129   IDEA 2004 includes many new pre-trial procedures and timelines for due process hearings.

hearing, which shall be conducted by the State educational agency or by the local educational agency, as determined by State law or by the State educational agency.[130]

(B) Resolution Session.[131]

(i) Preliminary Meeting. Prior to the opportunity for an impartial due process hearing under subparagraph (A), the local educational agency **shall convene a meeting with the parents and the relevant member or members of the IEP Team who have specific knowledge of the facts identified in the complaint**

(I) **within 15 days** of receiving notice of the parents' complaint;[132]

(II) which shall include a representative of the agency who has **decisionmaking authority** on behalf of such agency;

(III) which **may not include an attorney** of the local educational agency **unless the parent is accompanied by an attorney**; and

(IV) where the **parents of the child discuss their complaint, and the facts** that form the basis of the complaint, and the local educational agency is provided the opportunity to resolve the complaint, unless the parents and the local educational agency agree[133] in writing to waive such meeting, or agree to use the mediation process described in subsection (e)

(ii) Hearing. If the local educational agency has not resolved the complaint to the satisfaction of the parents **within 30 days** of the receipt of the complaint, the due process hearing may occur, and all of the applicable timelines for a due process hearing under this part shall commence.[134]

(iii) Written Settlement Agreement.[135] In the case that a resolution is reached to resolve the complaint at a meeting described in clause (i), the parties **shall** execute a **legally binding agreement** that is–

(I) signed by both the parent and a representative of the agency who has the authority to bind such agency; and

(II) enforceable in any State court of competent jurisdiction or in a district court of the United States.

(iv) Review Period. If the parties execute an agreement pursuant to clause (iii), a party **may void such agreement within 3 business days** of the agreement's execution.

---

130   States have "one-tier" or "two-tier" systems for due process hearings. In a one-tier system, the state department of education conducts the hearing and the losing party can appeal to state or federal court. In a two-tier system, the hearing is conducted by the school district. The losing party must appeal to the state department of education, which will appoint a review officer or review panel. After the review officer or panel issues a decision, the losing party can appeal to state or federal court.

131   The resolution session provides the parties with an opportunity to resolve their complaint before the due process hearing. The school district is required to convene the resolution session within 15 days of receiving the parent's due process complaint notice. The school district must send "the relevant member or members of the IEP Team" who have knowledge about the facts in the parent's complaint and a district representative who has decision-making authority (settlement authority). The school board attorney may not attend the resolution session, unless the parent is accompanied by an attorney. The parents and district may agree to waive the resolution session or use the mediation process. If the LEA initiates the due process hearing, a resolution session is not required. This meeting can be conducted by telephone or video conference call. See Commentary in the *Federal Register,* pages 46700-46701 and Regulation 300.328.

132   The "resolution session should not be postponed" even if the parent's complaint is insufficient. See Commentary in the *Federal Register,* page 46698.

133   Waiver of resolution session must be a joint written agreement. See Regulation 300.510.

134   The due process decision must be rendered within 45 days after the 30-day window. See Regulation 300.515(a).

135   The requirements for legally binding written settlement agreements are new. Previously, when a party breached a settlement agreement, the other party had to enforce the agreement by filing suit under a breach of contract theory. Now the power of the federal courts may be used to ensure that settlement agreements are honored. Either party may void a settlement agreement within 3 business days. Note: The three-day rule does not apply to settlement agreements created in mediation.

(2) Disclosure of Evaluations and Recommendations.[136]

(A) In General. Not less than **5 business days** prior to a hearing conducted pursuant to paragraph (1), each party **shall disclose** to all other parties all evaluations completed by that date, and recommendations based on the offering party's evaluations, that the party intends to use at the hearing.

(B) Failure to Disclose. A hearing officer may bar any party that fails to comply with subparagraph (A) from introducing the relevant evaluation or recommendation at the hearing without the consent of the other party.

(3) Limitations on Hearing.

(A) Person Conducting Hearing.[137] A hearing officer conducting a hearing pursuant to paragraph (1)(A) shall, at a minimum–

(i) not be–

(I) an employee of the State educational agency or the local educational agency involved in the education or care of the child; or

(II) a person having a personal or professional interest that conflicts with the person's objectivity in the hearing;

(ii) possess knowledge of, and the ability to understand, the provisions of this title, Federal and State regulations pertaining to this title, and legal interpretations of this title by Federal and State courts;

(iii) **possess the knowledge and ability to conduct hearings in accordance with appropriate, standard legal practice**; and

(iv) possess the knowledge and ability to render and write decisions in accordance with appropriate, standard legal practice.

(B) Subject Matter of Hearing. The party requesting the due process hearing **shall not be allowed** to raise issues at the due process hearing that were not raised in the notice filed under subsection (b)(7), unless the other party agrees otherwise.

(C) Timeline for Requesting Hearing.[138] A parent or agency shall request an impartial due process hearing within **2 years** of the date the parent or agency knew or should have known about the alleged action that forms the basis of the complaint, **or**, if the State has an explicit time limitation for requesting such a hearing under this part, in such time as the State law allows.

(D) Exceptions to the Timeline. The timeline described in subparagraph (C) shall not apply to a parent if the parent was prevented from requesting the hearing due to–

(i) specific misrepresentations by the local educational agency that it had resolved the problem forming the basis of the complaint; or

---

136 Evaluations and recommendations must be disclosed at least 5 business days before a due process hearing. Most state statutes and regulations, and standards of practice, require that all exhibits (including evaluations and recommendations), exhibit lists, and witness lists, be disclosed at least 5 days prior to a hearing. Failure to comply with requirements about disclosure often causes hearing officers to dismiss or postpone cases. For a sample document list that can be used as an exhibit list, see Chapter 9, "The File: Do It Right," in *Wrightslaw: From Emotions to Advocacy*. See also Regulation 300.512.

137 The law includes new standards for hearing officers. Hearing officers must be knowledgeable about the law, federal and state regulations, and caselaw. Hearing officers must also have the knowledge and ability to "conduct hearings and write decisions in accordance with appropriate standard legal practice." Hearing Officers may not be employees of the state department of education or the school district that is involved in the child's education, nor may they have a "personal or professional conflict of interest" that may affect their ability to be objective.

138 The two-year statute of limitations to present a complaint is new. If your state does not have a statute of limitations, you must request a due process hearing within two years. The two-year statute of limitations may not apply if the parent was prevented from requesting a hearing because of misrepresentations by the district or because the district withheld information it was required to provide.

(ii) the local educational agency's withholding of information from the parent that was required under this part to be provided to the parent.

(E) Decision of Hearing Officer.[139]

(i) In General. Subject to clause (ii), a decision made by a hearing officer **shall be made on substantive grounds** based on a determination of whether the child received a free appropriate public education.[140]

(ii) Procedural Issues.[141] In matters alleging a procedural violation, a hearing officer may find that a child did not receive a free appropriate public education **only if** the procedural inadequacies–

(I) impeded the child's right to a free appropriate public education;

(II) significantly impeded the parents' opportunity to participate in the decisionmaking process regarding the provision of a free appropriate public education to the parents' child; or

(III) **caused a deprivation of educational benefits.**

(iii) Rule of Construction. Nothing in this subparagraph shall be construed to preclude a hearing officer from ordering a local educational agency to comply with procedural requirements under this section.

(F) Rule of Construction. Nothing in this paragraph shall be construed to affect the right of a parent to file a complaint with the State educational agency.

(g) Appeal.[142]

(1) In General. If the hearing required by subsection (f) is conducted by a local educational agency, any party aggrieved by the findings and decision rendered in such a hearing may appeal such findings and decision to the State educational agency.

(2) Impartial Review and Independent Decision. The State educational agency shall conduct an impartial review of the findings and decision appealed under paragraph (1). The officer conducting such review shall make an independent decision upon completion of such review.

(h) Safeguards.[143] Any party to a hearing conducted pursuant to subsection (f) or (k), or an appeal conducted pursuant to subsection (g), shall be accorded –

(1) the right to be **accompanied and advised by counsel** and by individuals with special knowledge or training with respect to the problems of children with disabilities;

(2) the right to **present evidence and confront, cross-examine, and compel the attendance of witnesses**;

(3) the right to a written, or, at the option of the parents, electronic verbatim record of such hearing; and

(4) the right to written, or, at the option of the parents, electronic findings of fact and decisions, which findings and decisions–

---

139 Rulings by hearing officers should be based substantive issues, not procedural issues, unless the procedural violation impeded the child's right to a free appropriate public education, significantly impeded the parents' opportunity to participate in the decision-making, process or deprived the child of educational benefit. This language is new and incorporates existing caselaw about procedural and substantive issues.

140 Issues of substance include whether a child has a disability that adversely affects educational performance (eligibility), whether a child has received FAPE (a free appropriate public education), or whether a child needs extended school year (ESY) services.

141 Procedural issues include delays in scheduling evaluations, determining eligibility, convening IEP meetings, or the failure to include appropriate personnel in IEP meetings. The facts of a case will determine whether the procedural breach rises to the level identified in this subsection.

142 Most states have a single tier due process hearing system. In a single tier state, after the hearing, the losing party can appeal to state or federal court. This subsection (g) applies to two tier states in which an appeal is made to the State. After an adverse state level review decision, the losing party can appeal to court.

143 In a due process hearing, the parents or their attorney have the right to present evidence and cross-examine witnesses, and to issue subpoenas for witnesses. Parents have a right to a written verbatim record (transcript) of the hearing and to written findings of fact and decisions. In some states, parents may be represented by lay advocates.

(A) shall be made available to the public consistent with the requirements of Section 1417(b) of this title (relating to the confidentiality of data, information, and records); and

(B) shall be transmitted to the advisory panel established pursuant to Section 1412(a)(21) of this title.

(i) Administrative Procedures.

(1) In General.

(A) Decision Made in Hearing – A decision made in a hearing conducted pursuant to subsection (f) or (k) **shall be final**, except that any party involved in such hearing **may appeal** such decision under the provisions of subsection (g) and paragraph (2).

(B) Decision Made at Appeal. A decision made under subsection (g) **shall be final**, except that **any party may bring an action** under paragraph (2).[144]

(2) Right to Bring Civil Action.

(A) In General. Any party aggrieved by the findings and decision made under subsection (f) or (k) who does not have the right to an appeal under subsection (g), and **any party** aggrieved by the findings and decision made under this subsection, **shall have the right to bring a civil action** with respect to the complaint presented pursuant to this section, which action may be brought in any State court of competent jurisdiction or in a district court of the United States, without regard to the amount in controversy.[145]

(B) Limitation. The party bringing the action shall have **90 days** from the date of the decision of the hearing officer to bring such an action, **or**, if the State has an explicit time limitation for bringing such action under this part, in such time as the State law allows.[146]

(C) Additional Requirements. In any action brought under this paragraph, the court

(i) shall receive the records of the administrative proceedings;

(ii) shall hear additional evidence at the request of a party;[147] and

(iii) basing its decision on the preponderance of the evidence, shall grant such relief as the court determines is appropriate.

(3) Jurisdiction of District Courts; Attorneys' Fees.

(A) In General. The district courts of the United States shall have jurisdiction of actions brought under this section without regard to the amount in controversy.

(B) Award of Attorneys' Fees.

(i) In General. In any action or proceeding brought under this section, the court, in its discretion, **may award reasonable attorneys' fees** as part of the costs–

(I) to a prevailing party who is the parent of a child with a disability;

(II) to a prevailing party who is a State educational agency or local educational agency against the attorney of a parent who files a complaint or subsequent cause of action that is **frivolous, unreason-**

---

144   In two-tier states (discussed in Section 1415(f)(1)(A)), the losing party must first appeal to the state department of education (SEA). If the party does not appeal, the due process decision is the final decision.

145   In two-tier states, the losing party does not have a right to appeal to state or federal court until a decision is rendered by a Review Officer or Review Panel. After an adverse decision from the State, the losing party has a right to appeal to state or federal court.

146   The losing party has 90 days to appeal to state or federal court. This 90-day timeline is new. States may provide different or shorter timelines. You need to know your state's statute of limitations for filing appeals in Court. To be safe, it it is longer than 90 days, assume that the longer timeline does not apply.

147   Despite language in IDEA that the Court "shall hear additional evidence at the request of a party," many Courts will not hear evidence that could have been offered at the due process hearing. Parties should put all their evidence into the record during the due process hearing.

able, or without foundation, or against the attorney of a parent who continued to litigate after the litigation clearly became frivolous, unreasonable, or without foundation;[148] or

(III) to a prevailing State educational agency or local educational agency against the attorney of a parent, or against the parent, if the parent's complaint or subsequent cause of action was presented for any improper purpose, such as to **harass, to cause unnecessary delay, or to needlessly increase the cost of litigation.**[149]

(ii) Rule of Construction. Nothing in this subparagraph shall be construed to affect section 327 of the District of Columbia Appropriations Act, 2005.

(C) Determination of Amount of Attorneys' Fees. Fees awarded under this paragraph shall be based on rates prevailing in the community in which the action or proceeding arose for the kind and quality of services furnished. No bonus or multiplier may be used in calculating the fees awarded under this subsection.

(D) Prohibition of Attorneys' Fees and Related Costs for Certain Services.

(i) In General. Attorneys' fees may not be awarded and related costs may not be reimbursed in any action or proceeding under this section for services performed subsequent to the time of a written offer of settlement to a parent if–

(I) the offer is made within the time prescribed by Rule 68 of the Federal Rules of Civil Procedure or, in the case of an administrative proceeding, at any time more than 10 days before the proceeding begins;

(II) the offer is not accepted within 10 days; and

(III) the court or administrative hearing officer finds that the relief finally obtained by the parents is not more favorable to the parents than the offer of settlement.[150]

(ii) IEP Team Meetings. Attorneys' fees **may not be awarded** relating to any **meeting of the IEP Team** unless such meeting is convened as a result of an administrative proceeding or judicial action, **or**, at the discretion of the State, **for a mediation** described in subsection (e).

(iii) Opportunity to Resolve Complaints. A meeting conducted pursuant to subsection (f)(1)(B)(i)[151] shall not be considered–

(I) a meeting convened as a result of an administrative hearing or judicial action; or

(II) an administrative hearing or judicial action for purposes of this paragraph.

(E) Exception to Prohibition on Attorneys' Fees and Related Costs. Notwithstanding subparagraph (D), an award of attorneys' fees and related costs[152] may be made to a parent who is the prevailing party and who was substantially justified in rejecting the settlement offer.

---

148   Parents who prevail can recover attorneys' fees from school districts. Now, school districts may recover attorneys' fees from the parents' attorney under specific, limited circumstances. If the parent or the parent's attorney files a complaint that is frivolous, unreasonable, or for an improper purpose (i.e., to harass, cause unnecessary delay, or needlessly increase the cost of litigation), the Court may award attorneys' fees to the school district.

149   Some parents, driven by anger and frustration, request due process hearings although they have not prepared their case. They may be focused on perceived wrongs by the school, not on obtaining a program that will meet their child's needs. Unfortunately, many hearing officers and judges view parents of children with disabilities as emotional "loose cannons." These parents not only lose their cases, but they create ill will for other parents who use due process procedures to resolve disputes.

150   If the school district makes a written settlement offer 10 days before the due process hearing and the terms of the offer are the same or similar to the relief obtained through litigation, the parents may not be entitled to attorneys' fees. Attorneys' fees will not be awarded for IEP meetings. Some courts have held that only federal courts can award attorney's fees. Other courts have held that a state court or federal court can award attorneys' fees.

151   This refers to a resolution session meeting, thus no attorneys fees. See also *Federal Register* Commentary at 46708 regarding Regulation 300.517.

152   Pursuant to the U. S. Supreme Court decision in *Arlington v. Murphy* parents may not recover fees for expert witnesses even if the parents prevail (see U. S. Supreme Court decisions in Chapter 12).

(F) Reduction in Amount of Attorneys' Fees. Except as provided in subparagraph (G), whenever the court finds that

(i) the parent, or the parent's attorney, during the course of the action or proceeding, **unreasonably protracted** the final resolution of the controversy;

(ii) the amount of the attorneys' fees otherwise authorized to be awarded unreasonably exceeds the hourly rate prevailing in the community for similar services by attorneys of reasonably comparable skill, reputation, and experience;

(iii) the time spent and legal services furnished **were excessive** considering the nature of the action or proceeding; or

(iv) the attorney representing the parent did not provide to the local educational agency the appropriate information in the notice of the complaint described in subsection (b)(7)(A), the court shall reduce, accordingly, the amount of the attorneys' fees awarded under this section.

(G) Exception to Reduction in Amount of Attorneys' Fees. The provisions of subparagraph (F) shall not apply in any action or proceeding if the court finds that the State or local educational agency unreasonably protracted the final resolution of the action or proceeding or there was a violation of this section.

(j) Maintenance of Current Educational Placement.[153] Except as provided in **subsection (k)(4)**, during the pendency of any proceedings conducted pursuant to this section, unless the State or local educational agency and the parents otherwise agree, the **child shall remain in the then-current educational placement** of the child, or, if applying for initial admission to a public school, shall, with the consent of the parents, be placed in the public school program until all such proceedings have been completed.[154]

(k) Placement in Alternative Educational Setting.[155, 156]

(1) Authority of School Personnel.

(A) Case-by-Case Determination. School personnel may consider any unique circumstances on a **case-by-case** basis[157] when determining whether to order a change in placement for a child with a disability who violates a **code of student conduct**.

(B) Authority. School personnel under this subsection **may remove** a child with a disability who violates a code of student conduct[158] from their current placement to an appropriate interim alternative educational setting, another setting, or suspension, for **not more than 10 school days** (to the extent such alternatives are applied to children without disabilities).

---

153 The "Stay Put" statute holds that during the due process hearing and appeal, the child will remain (stay put) in the current educational placement. "Current educational placement" is not the physical location of services, but the nature of the educational program. This does not apply to transition from an early intervention program under Part C to an age 5-21 program under Part B. See Regulation 300.518(c) and Commentary in the *Federal Register,* page 46709.

154 Pursuant to the U. S. Supreme Court decisions in *Burlington* and *Carter,* the parent may remove a child from an inappropriate placement, place their child into a private program, and request reimbursement for the private placement, subject to the restrictions in Section 1412(a)(10). When the final decision at the State level awards reimbursement for a private placement, that private placement is the "current educational placement." If the school district appeals this decision, they must pay for the child's private placement while the case is being appealed. See the Regulation at 300.518(d).

155 This is the discipline statute. The Regulations begin at 300.530.

156 "A free appropriate public education is available to all children with disabilities residing in the State between the ages of 3 and 21, inclusive, including children with disabilities who have been suspended or expelled from school." (Section 1412(a)(1)(A))

157 Many school administrators and school boards refuse to exercise discretion in disciplinary matters. They claim "the law" does not allow them to evaluate the circumstances of a particular child's case. Congress added language that school personnel may "consider any unique circumstances on a case-by-case basis" in determining whether to order a change of placement. This clarifies that school officials may use discretion and consider each individual situation carefully, and rebuts arguments by administrators who refuse to exercise discretion.

158 If a child with a disability violates a code of student conduct, school officials may suspend the child for up to 10 days. Codes of Conduct are usually written policies adopted by the School Board.

(C) **Additional Authority.**[159] If school personnel seek to order a **change in placement that would exceed 10 school days** and the behavior that gave rise to the violation of the school code is **determined not to be a manifestation** of the child's disability pursuant to subparagraph (E), the relevant disciplinary procedures applicable to children without disabilities may be applied[160] to the child in the same manner and for the same duration in which the procedures would be applied to children without disabilities, except as provided in Section 1412(a)(1)[161] of this title although it may be provided in an interim alternative educational setting.

(D) **Services.** A child with a disability who is removed from the child's current placement under subparagraph (G) (irrespective of whether the behavior is determined to be a manifestation of the child's disability) or subparagraph (C) **shall** –

(i) **continue to receive educational services**, as provided in Section 1412(a)(1) of this title, so as to enable the child **to continue to participate in the general education curriculum**, although in another setting, **and to progress toward meeting the goals set out in the child's IEP**; and

(ii) receive, as appropriate, **a functional behavioral assessment, behavioral intervention services and modifications**, that are designed to address the behavior violation so that it does not recur.[162]

(E) **Manifestation Determination.**[163, 164]

(i) **In General.** Except as provided in subparagraph (B), **within 10 school days of any decision to change the placement** of a child with a disability **because of a violation of a code of student conduct**, the local educational agency, the parent, and relevant members of the IEP Team (as determined by the parent and the local educational agency) **shall review all relevant information** in the student's file, including the child's IEP, any teacher observations, and any relevant information provided by the parents to determine–

(I) **if the conduct** in question **was caused by, or had a direct and substantial relationship to, the child's disability**; or

(II) **if the conduct** in question **was the direct result of the local educational agency's failure to implement the IEP.**

---

159   Look at subsection (b)(c) and (d) of 300.530 for the distinctions between change of placement, a 10 day removal for one incident, a series of additional 10 day removals in one school year, and cumulative removals that exceed 10 days in one year. See Commentary in the *Federal Register*, pages 46714 to 46719.

160   If the school suspends the child with a disability for more than 10 days and determines that the child's behavior was not a manifestation of the disability, they may use the same procedures as with non-disabled children, but they must continue to provide the child with a free appropriate public education (FAPE). (Section 1412(a)(1)(A)) If the child has a Section 504 plan, and the behavior was not a manifestation of the disability, the school may suspend or expel the child. The child is not entitled to receive a free appropriate public education.

161   The school is obligated to provide a free, appropriate public education to the child, even if the child has been suspended or expelled.

162   If the school district suspends a child with a disability for more than 10 days, regardless of severity of the child's misconduct (i.e., violation of a code of conduct v. possession of a weapon), the child must continue to receive FAPE (see Section 1412(a)(1)(A)), so the child can participate in the general education curriculum, make progress on the IEP goals, and receive a functional behavioral assessment, behavioral intervention services and modifications to prevent the behavior from reoccurring.

163   The IEP Team must review all information about the child and determine if the negative behavior was caused by the child's disability, had a direct and substantial relationship to the disability, or was the result of the school's failure to implement the IEP.

164   If you are dealing with a discipline issue, you need to obtain a comprehensive psycho-educational evaluation of the child by an evaluator in the private sector who has expertise in the disability (i.e., autism, attention deficit, bipolar disorder, Asperger's syndrome, auditory processing deficits). The evaluator must analyze the relationship between the child's disability and behavior. If there is a causal relationship, the evaluator should write a detailed report that describes the child's disability, the basis for determining that the behavior was a manifestation of the disability, and recommendations for an appropriate program. If you are dealing with a manifestation review, ask the evaluator to attend the hearing to explain the findings and make recommendations about alternative plans. Your goal is to develop a win-win solution to the problem.

(ii) Manifestation. If the local educational agency, the parent, and relevant members of the IEP Team determine that either subclause (I) or (II) of clause (i) is applicable for the child, the conduct **shall be determined to be a manifestation of the child's disability.**

(F) Determination That Behavior Was a Manifestation. If the local educational agency, the parent, and relevant members of the IEP Team make the determination that the conduct was a manifestation of the child's disability, **the IEP Team shall—**

(i) **conduct a functional behavioral assessment, and implement a behavioral intervention plan**[165] for such child, provided that the local educational agency had not conducted such assessment prior to such determination before the behavior that resulted in a change in placement described in subparagraph (C) or (G);

(ii) in the situation where a behavioral intervention plan has been developed, **review** the behavioral intervention plan if the child already has such a behavioral intervention plan, and **modify** it, as necessary, **to address the behavior**; and

(iii) except as provided in subparagraph (G), return the child to the placement from which the child was removed, unless the parent and the local educational agency agree to a change of placement as part of the modification of the behavioral intervention plan.

(G) Special Circumstances. School personnel may remove a student to an interim alternative educational setting for **not more than 45 school days** without regard to whether the behavior is determined to be a manifestation of the child's disability, in cases where a child—

(i) **carries or possesses a weapon**[166] to or at school, on school premises, or to or at a school function under the jurisdiction of a State or local educational agency;

(ii) **knowingly possesses or uses illegal drugs**, or sells or solicits the sale of a controlled substance,[167] while at school, on school premises, or at a school function under the jurisdiction of a State or local educational agency; **or**

(iii) **has inflicted serious bodily injury** upon another person while at school, on school premises, or at a school function under the jurisdiction of a State or local educational agency.[168, 169]

(H) Notification. Not later than the date on which the decision to take disciplinary action is made, the local educational agency shall notify the parents of that decision, and of all procedural safeguards accorded under this section.

(2) Determination of Setting. The interim alternative educational setting in subparagraphs (C) and (G) of paragraph (1) **shall be determined by the IEP Team.**[170]

---

165 If the child's behavior did not involve weapons, drugs, or serious bodily injury (see Section 1415(k)(1)(G)), the child should return to the prior placement.

166 Section 1415(k)(7)(C) clarifies that the term "weapon" means a "dangerous weapon" capable of causing death or serious bodily injury.

167 If a doctor prescribes a controlled substance for the child, and the child has possession of the medication at school, this is not illegal possession or illegal use. The school may not expel or suspend the child for possessing prescribed medication. If the child attempts to sell or solicit the sale of the controlled substance, this "special circumstance" warrants a suspension for 45 school days and possible criminal prosecution.

168 See Section 1415(k)(7) for the statutory differences between "controlled drugs" (Schedule I - V) and "illegal drugs," and definitions of "weapon" and "serious bodily injury."

169 If the child's behavior involves a dangerous weapon, illegal drugs, or serious bodily injury, the child may be suspended for 45 school days even if the behavior was a manifestation of the disability. The child is still entitled to FAPE pursuant to Section 1412(a)(1)(A) and Section 1415(k)(1)(D).

170 The decision to place a child into an interim alternative educational setting shall be made by the IEP Team, not by an administrator or school board member. This is mandatory. The educational setting is an interim placement, not a permanent placement. Remember: parents are full members of the IEP Team.

(3) Appeal.

(A) In General. The parent of a child with a disability who disagrees with any decision regarding placement, or the manifestation determination under this subsection, or a local educational agency that believes that maintaining the current placement of the child is substantially likely to result in injury to the child or to others, may request a hearing.[171]

(B) Authority of Hearing Officer.[172]

(i) In General. A hearing officer shall hear, and make a determination regarding, an appeal requested under subparagraph (A).

(ii) Change of Placement Order. In making the determination under clause (i), the hearing officer may order a change in placement of a child with a disability. In such situations, the **hearing officer may**

(I) **return a child** with a disability to the placement from which the child was removed; or

(II) **order a change in placement** of a child with a disability to an appropriate interim alternative educational setting for not more than 45 school days if the hearing officer determines that maintaining the current placement of such child is substantially likely to result in injury to the child or to others.

(4) Placement During Appeals. When an appeal under paragraph (3) has been requested by either the parent or the local educational agency–

(A) the **child shall remain in the interim alternative educational setting** pending the decision of the hearing officer or until the expiration of the time period provided for in paragraph (1)(C), whichever occurs first, unless the parent and the State or local educational agency agree otherwise; and

(B) the State or local educational agency shall arrange for an **expedited hearing**, which shall occur within **20 school days** of the date the hearing is requested and shall result in a determination within **10 school days** after the hearing.[173]

(5) Protections for Children Not Yet Eligible for Special Education and Related Services.

(A) In General. A child who has not been determined to be eligible for special education and related services under this part and who has engaged in behavior that violates a code of student conduct, **may assert any of the protections** provided for in this part **if the local educational agency had knowledge** (as determined in accordance with this paragraph) that the child was a child with a disability before the behavior that precipitated the disciplinary action occurred.

(B) Basis of Knowledge. A local educational agency shall be deemed to have **knowledge**[174] that a child is a child with a disability if, **before** the behavior that precipitated the disciplinary action occurred–

(i) the parent of the child has **expressed concern in writing** to supervisory or administrative personnel of the appropriate educational agency, or a teacher of the child, that the child is in need of special education and related services;

---

171   The parent can request a hearing to appeal the manifestation determination or the decision to place the child in an interim alternative educational setting. The school can request a hearing to maintain the current educational placement if they think changing the placement is "substantially likely to result in injury." (See Section 1415(j) regarding "stay-put.") Appeal of a manifestation determination may be futile in a case that involves a dangerous weapon, illegal drugs, or serious bodily injury. The school can suspend a student for 45 school days for these behaviors even if the behavior was a manifestation of the child's disability.

172   A hearing officer has the authority to return the child to the original placement. If the hearing officer concludes that the child is likely to injure himself or others, the hearing officer may order the child to be placed in an interim alternative educational setting for not more than 45 school days.

173   Expedited hearings must be held within 20 school days and a decision rendered within 10 school days. While the decision is pending, the child shall remain in the alternative setting, unless the time limit for this placement expired.

174   If the school knew, or should have known, that the child is a child with a disability and entitled to an IEP, then the child is protected under IDEA. The factors affecting "knowledge" are listed. If the parent refused to permit an evaluation or special education services, the child loses these protections.

(ii) the parent of the child has **requested an evaluation** of the child pursuant to Section 1414(a)(1)(B) of this title; **or**

(iii) the teacher of the child, or other personnel of the local educational agency, **has expressed specific concerns** about a pattern of behavior demonstrated by the child, directly to the director of special education of such agency or to other supervisory personnel of the agency.[175]

(C) Exception. A local educational agency shall not be deemed to have knowledge that the child is a child with a disability if the **parent of the child has not allowed an evaluation** of the child pursuant to Section 1414 of this title **or has refused services** under this part or the child has been evaluated and it was determined that the child was not a child with a disability under this part.

(D) Conditions that Apply if No Basis of Knowledge.

(i) In General. If a local educational agency does not have knowledge that a child is a child with a disability (in accordance with subparagraph (B) or (C)) prior to taking disciplinary measures against the child, the child may be subjected to disciplinary measures applied to children without disabilities who engaged in comparable behaviors consistent with clause (ii).

(ii) Limitations. If a request is made for an evaluation of a child during the time period in which the child is subjected to disciplinary measures under this subsection, the evaluation **shall be conducted in an expedited manner**. If the child is determined to be a child with a disability, taking into consideration information from the evaluation conducted by the agency and information provided by the parents, the agency shall provide special education and related services[176] in accordance with this part, except that, pending the results of the evaluation, the child shall remain in the educational placement determined by school authorities.

(6) Referral to and Action by Law Enforcement and Judicial Authorities.[177]

(A) Rule of Construction. Nothing in this part shall be construed to prohibit an agency from reporting a crime committed by a child with a disability to appropriate authorities or to prevent State law enforcement and judicial authorities from exercising their responsibilities with regard to the application of Federal and State law to crimes committed by a child with a disability.

(B) Transmittal of Records. An agency reporting a crime committed by a child with a disability shall ensure that copies of the special education and disciplinary records of the child are transmitted for consideration by the appropriate authorities to whom the agency reports the crime.

(7) Definitions. In this subsection:

(A) Controlled Substance. The term 'controlled substance' means a drug or other substance identified under schedule I, II, III, IV, or V in Section 812(c) of title 21, United States Code.

(B) Illegal Drug. The term 'illegal drug' means a controlled substance but does **not** include a controlled substance that is legally possessed or used under the supervision of a licensed health-care professional or

---

175 If you are concerned that your child may have a disability, you must put your concerns in writing. You should document important conversations, meetings, and telephone calls with notes or letters that describe what happened, what you were told, and your concerns. To do less is unwise. Courts have little sympathy for individuals who know or should know they have rights, fail to safeguard their rights, then complain that their rights were violated. Courts believe that the party who complains that their rights were violated must prove that they took reasonable steps to protect themselves, yet their rights were still violated.

176 If the school did not have knowledge that the child had a disability and was entitled to an IEP, the child may be treated like a nondisabled child. If an evaluation is requested, it shall be expedited. Once it is determined that the child is eligible for special education and is entitled to an IEP, the child will receive all rights and protections under IDEA, including the detailed procedures provided in Section 1415(k).

177 The school is not prohibited or required to report crimes committed by children with disabilities. Discretion and common sense should prevail. The practice of reporting behavior caused by emotional disturbances as "crimes" puts law enforcement personnel into positions for which they have not been trained. Treating emotionally distraught or emotionally disturbed children as criminals may inflict permanent emotional damage on vulnerable children.

that is legally possessed[178] or used under any other authority under that Act or under any other provision of Federal law.

(C) Weapon. The term 'weapon'[179] has the meaning given the term 'dangerous weapon' under Section 930(g)(2) of title 18, United States Code.

(D) Serious Bodily Injury. The term 'serious bodily injury'[180] has the meaning given the term 'serious bodily injury' under paragraph (3) of subsection (h) of Section 1365 of title 18, United States Code.

(l) Rule of Construction. Nothing in this title shall be construed to restrict or limit the rights, procedures, and remedies available under the Constitution, the Americans with Disabilities Act of 1990, [42 USC § 12101] title V of the Rehabilitation Act of 1973, [29 USC § 790] or other Federal laws protecting the rights of children with disabilities, except that before the filing of a civil action under such laws seeking relief that is also available under this part, the procedures under subsections (f) and (g) shall be exhausted to the same extent as would be required had the action been brought under this part.[181]

(m) Transfer of Parental Rights at Age of Majority.[182]

(1) In General. A State that receives amounts from a grant under this part may provide that, **when a child with a disability reaches the age of majority** under State law (except for a child with a disability who has been determined to be incompetent under State law)–

(A) the agency shall provide any notice required by this section to both the individual and the parents;

(B) all other **rights accorded to parents** under this part **transfer to the child**;

(C) the agency shall notify the individual and the parents of the transfer of rights; and

(D) all rights accorded to parents under this part transfer to children who are incarcerated in an adult or juvenile Federal, State, or local correctional institution.

(2) Special Rule.[183] If, under State law, a child with a disability who has reached the age of majority under State law, who has not been determined to be incompetent, but **who is determined not to have the ability to provide informed consent** with respect to the educational program of the child, the State shall establish procedures **for appointing the parent of the child**, or if the parent is not available, another appropriate individual, to represent the educational interests of the child throughout the period of eligibility of the child under this part.

---

178   Many schools suspend and expel students who bring over-the-counter medications (i.e., aspirin, ibuprofen, Tums) to school, claiming that these medications are "drugs." This subsection clarifies that over-the-counter medications are not illegal drugs or controlled substances. A child with a disability who receives services under IDEA is protected from these abuses of power. A child who has a Section 504 Plan is not protected.

179   The term 'dangerous weapon' means a weapon, device, instrument, material, or substance, animate or inanimate, that is used for, or is readily capable of, causing death or serious bodily injury, except that such term does not include a pocket knife with a blade of less than 2 1/2 inches in length." (18 U. S. C. § 930(g)(2))

180   The term 'serious bodily injury' means bodily injury which involves (A) a substantial risk of death; (B) extreme physical pain; (C) protracted and obvious disfigurement; or (D) protracted loss or impairment of the function of a bodily member, organ, or mental faculty..." (18 U. S. C. § 1365(h)(3))

181   If a parent or child with a disability has a case against a school district or school employee for reasons, facts, and events that are not related to IDEA, they may file suit under that legal theory, but must usually initiate their case by a due process hearing. This often occurs when a lawsuit for dollar damages under Section 504 of the Rehabilitation Act is initiated. According to Section 1415(l): "before the filing of a civil action...the (due process) procedures under subsections (f) and (g) shall be exhausted . . ." This is called the "exhaustion of administrative remedies requirement." Case law in this area continues to evolve.

182   The district must provide notice to the parent and child that the parents' rights will transfer to the child when the child reaches the "age of majority," which is usually age eighteen. With a "grant of authority" or "power of attorney" a parent can continue to represent the educational interests of the child.

183   If possible, have your child write a statement that says, "I [child's name], pursuant to 20 U. S. C. Section 1415(m) and [your state's special education regulation section], hereby appoint my parent, [your name], to represent my educational interests." If the child is able, have this statement written out longhand, signed and dated. Use the language in your state's special education regulation verbatim. If possible, do not add to it, subtract from it, or rephrase it.

(n) Electronic Mail. A parent of a child with a disability may elect to receive notices required under this section by an electronic mail (**e-mail**) communication, if the agency makes such option available.[184]

(o) Separate Complaint. Nothing in this section shall be construed to preclude a parent from filing a separate due process complaint on an issue separate from a due process complaint already filed.[185]

20 U. S. C. § 1416. Monitoring, Technical Assistance, and Enforcement.

WRIGHTSLAW OVERVIEW: Section 1416 is the enforcement statute. Although the Department of Education is responsible for enforcing IDEA, the National Council on Disability found that the Department had never required states to enforce the law. As a result, no state was in compliance with the law, leaving parents who requested due process hearings to act as the main enforcers of the law.[186] After passing the No Child Left Behind Act in 2001, Congress looked at special education outcomes and added new language about Focused Monitoring. Previously, enforcement focused on procedural compliance. The Department of Education did not focus on whether schools and districts were teaching children with disabilities how to read, write, spell, do arithmetic or prepare the children for further education, employment, independent living. Section 1416 includes stronger language about accountability. If the Department of Education determines that a state department of education (SEA) "needs assistance" for two consecutive years, the Department shall take corrective action and impose special conditions. If the state remains in the "needs assistance" category for three consecutive years, the Department of Education may recover funds paid, withhold further funds, and refer the matter to the Department of Justice.

(a) Federal and State Monitoring.

(1) In General. The Secretary shall–

(A) monitor implementation of this part through–

(i) oversight of the exercise of general supervision by the States, as required in Section 1412(a)(11) of this title; and

(ii) the State performance plans, described in subsection (b);

(B) enforce this part in accordance with subsection (e); and

(C) require States to–

(i) monitor implementation of this part by local educational agencies; and

(ii) enforce this part in accordance with paragraph (3) and subsection (e).

(2) Focused Monitoring.[187] The primary focus of Federal and State monitoring activities described in paragraph (1) shall be on–

---

184   At the parent's option, the district can send notices by e-mail. Given the prevalence of email problems, this option is not recommended as the primary means of providing or receiving notice. You may want to receive notice by email as a supplement to the usual notification procedures.

185   If a due process hearing is pending on one issue, and a new issue arises, the parent may file a separate due process complaint notice. In the alternative, if the hearing officer and both sides agree, and the hearing has not been held, the parent may be able to file an Amended Complaint as described in Section 1415(c)(2)(E).

186   *Back to School on Civil Rights* is available from the National Council on Disability at: www.ncd.gov/newsroom/publications/2000/backtoschool_1.htm

187   In IDEA 2004, monitoring focuses on educational results and functional outcomes. This language is similar to No Child Left Behind and is a refreshing change from the focus on procedural compliance. When the special education law was passed in 1975 (Public Law 94-142), many children with disabilities were denied services without due process of law. As a result, the law focused on protecting the rights of children and their parents (Section 1400(d)(1)(B)) and providing remedies for violations. During the early years, educational outcomes took a back seat to procedural compliance. Before the IDEA was reauthorized in 1997, the word "measurable" (or any variation of the word) was rarely used to describe outcomes, goals, or objectives. When the law was reauthorized in 1997, the word "measurable" (or a variation of the word) appeared 16 times. In IDEA 2004, the word "measurable" appears 30 times. This measurable change in the frequency of the word "measurable" may bode well for the future.

(A) improving educational results[188] and functional outcomes for all children with disabilities; and

(B) ensuring that States meet the program requirements under this part, with a particular emphasis on those requirements that are most closely related to improving educational results for children with disabilities.

(3) Monitoring Priorities. The Secretary shall monitor the States, and **shall require each State to monitor the local educational agencies** located in the State (except the State exercise of general supervisory responsibility), using quantifiable indicators in each of the following priority areas, and using such qualitative indicators as are needed to adequately measure performance in the following priority areas:

(A) Provision of a free appropriate public education in the least restrictive environment.

(B) State exercise of general supervisory authority, including child find, effective monitoring, the use of resolution sessions, mediation, voluntary binding arbitration, and a system of transition services as defined in Sections 1401(34) and 1437(a)(9) of this title.

(C) Disproportionate representation of racial and ethnic groups in special education and related services, to the extent the representation is the result of inappropriate identification.

(4) Permissive Areas of Review. The Secretary shall consider other relevant information and data, including data provided by States under Section 1418 of this title.

(b) State Performance Plans.[189]

(1) Plan.

(A) In General. Not later than 1 year after the date of enactment of the Individuals with Disabilities Education Improvement Act of 2004, each State shall have in place a performance plan that evaluates that State's efforts to implement the requirements and purposes of this part and describes how the State will improve such implementation.

(B) Submission for Approval. Each State shall submit the State's performance plan to the Secretary for approval in accordance with the approval process described in subsection (c).

(C) Review. Each State shall review its State performance plan at least once every 6 years and submit any amendments to the Secretary.

(2) Targets.

(A) In General. As a part of the State performance plan described under paragraph (1), each State **shall establish measurable and rigorous targets** for the indicators established under the priority areas described in subsection (a)(3).

(B) Data Collection.

(i) In General. Each State shall collect valid and reliable information as needed to report annually to the Secretary on the priority areas described in subsection (a)(3).

(ii) Rule of Construction. Nothing in this title shall be construed to authorize the development of a nationwide database of personally identifiable information on individuals involved in studies or other collections of data under this part.

(C) Public Reporting and Privacy.

(i) In General. The State shall use the targets established in the plan and priority areas described in subsection (a)(3) to analyze the performance of each local educational agency in the State in implementing this part.

---

188   However, attempting to measure educational results from year to year appears to be a moving target. Why not take a child's initial standardized test data from eligibility and compare using the same tests to changes in one year, two years, and three years later.

189   Information on Monitoring and Enforcement activities of the U. S. Department of Education is at www.ed.gov/policy/speced/guid/idea/monitor/index.html (Last visited on September 22, 2006)

(ii) Report.

(I) Public Report. The State **shall report** annually **to the public** on **the performance of each local educational agency** located in the State on the targets in the State's performance plan. The State shall make the State's performance plan available through public means, including by posting on the website of the State educational agency, distribution to the media, and distribution through public agencies.

(II) State Performance Report. The State shall report annually to the Secretary on the performance of the State under the State's performance plan.

(iii) Privacy. The State shall not report to the public or the Secretary any information on performance that would result in the disclosure of personally identifiable information about individual children or where the available data is insufficient to yield statistically reliable information.

(c) Approval Process.

(1) Deemed Approval. The Secretary shall review (including the specific provisions described in subsection (b)) each performance plan submitted by a State pursuant to subsection (b)(1)(B) and the plan shall be deemed to be approved by the Secretary unless the Secretary makes a written determination, prior to the expiration of the 120-day period beginning on the date on which the Secretary received the plan, that the plan does not meet the requirements of this section, including the specific provisions described in subsection (b).

(2) Disapproval. The Secretary shall not finally disapprove a performance plan, except after giving the State notice and an opportunity for a hearing.

(3) Notification. If the Secretary finds that the plan does not meet the requirements, in whole or in part, of this section, the Secretary **shall** –

(A) give the State notice and an opportunity for a hearing; and

(B) notify the State of the finding, and in such notification shall–

(i) cite the specific provisions in the plan that do not meet the requirements; and

(ii) request additional information, only as to the provisions not meeting the requirements, needed for the plan to meet the requirements of this section.

(4) Response. If the State responds to the Secretary's notification described in paragraph (3)(B) during the 30-day period beginning on the date on which the State received the notification, and resubmits the plan with the requested information described in paragraph (3)(B)(ii), the Secretary shall approve or disapprove such plan prior to the later of –

(A) the expiration of the 30-day period beginning on the date on which the plan is resubmitted; or

(B) the expiration of the 120-day period described in paragraph (1).

(5) Failure to Respond. If the State does not respond to the Secretary's notification described in paragraph (3)(B) during the 30-day period beginning on the date on which the State received the notification, such plan shall be deemed to be disapproved.

(d) Secretary's Review and Determination.

(1) Review. The Secretary shall annually review the State performance report submitted pursuant to subsection (b)(2)(C)(ii)(II) in accordance with this section.

(2) Determination.

(A) In General. Based on the information provided by the State in the State performance report, information obtained through monitoring visits, and any other public information made available, the Secretary shall determine if the State–

(i) meets the requirements and purposes of this part;

(ii) needs assistance in implementing the requirements of this part;

(iii) needs intervention in implementing the requirements of this part; or

(iv) needs substantial intervention in implementing the requirements of this part.

(B) Notice and Opportunity for a Hearing. For determinations made under clause (iii) or (iv) of subparagraph (A), the Secretary shall provide reasonable notice and an opportunity for a hearing on such determination.

(e) Enforcement.

(1) Needs Assistance. If the Secretary determines, **for 2 consecutive years**, that a State needs assistance under subsection (d)(2)(A)(ii) in implementing the requirements of this part, the Secretary **shall take 1 or more of the following actions**:

(A) Advise the State of available sources of technical assistance that may help the State address the areas in which the State needs assistance, which may include assistance from the Office of Special Education Programs, other offices of the Department of Education, other Federal agencies, technical assistance providers approved by the Secretary, and other federally funded nonprofit agencies, and require the State to work with appropriate entities. Such technical assistance may include–

(i) the provision of advice by experts to address the areas in which the State needs assistance, including explicit plans for addressing the area for concern within a specified period of time;

(ii) assistance in identifying and implementing professional development, instructional strategies, and methods of instruction that are based on scientifically based research;

(iii) designating and using distinguished superintendents, principals, special education administrators, special education teachers, and other teachers to provide advice, technical assistance, and support; and

(iv) devising additional approaches to providing technical assistance, such as collaborating with institutions of higher education, educational service agencies, national centers of technical assistance supported under part D, and private providers of scientifically based technical assistance.

(B) Direct the use of State-level funds under Section 1411(e) of this title on the area or areas in which the State needs assistance.

(C) Identify the State as a **high-risk grantee and impose special conditions** on the State's grant under this part.

(2) Needs Intervention. If the Secretary determines, **for 3 or more consecutive years**, that a State needs intervention under subsection (d)(2)(A)(iii) in implementing the requirements of this part, the following shall apply:

(A) The Secretary may take any of the actions described in paragraph (1).

(B) The Secretary **shall take 1 or more of the following actions**:

(i) Require the State to prepare a corrective action plan or improvement plan if the Secretary determines that the State should be able to correct the problem within 1 year.

(ii) Require the State to enter into a compliance agreement under Section 1234f of this title, if the Secretary has reason to believe that the State cannot correct the problem within 1 year.

(iii) For each year of the determination, withhold not less than 20 percent and not more than 50 percent of the State's funds under Section 1411(e) of this title, until the Secretary determines the State has sufficiently addressed the areas in which the State needs intervention.

(iv) Seek to recover funds under Section 1234a this title.

(v) **Withhold**, in whole or in part, **any further payments** to the State under this part pursuant to paragraph (5).

(vi) Refer the matter for appropriate enforcement action, which may include referral to the Department of Justice.

(3) Needs Substantial Intervention. Notwithstanding paragraph (1) or (2), **at any time** that the Secretary determines that a State needs substantial intervention in implementing the requirements of this part or that there is a substantial failure to comply with any condition of a State educational agency's or local educational agency's eligibility under this part, the Secretary **shall take 1 or more of the following actions**:

(A) Recover funds under Section 1234a of this title.

(B) Withhold, in whole or in part, any further payments to the State under this part.

(C) Refer the case to the Office of the Inspector General at the Department of Education.

(D) Refer the matter for appropriate enforcement action, which may include **referral to the Department of Justice.**

(4) Opportunity for Hearing.

(A) Withholding Funds. Prior to withholding any funds under this section, the Secretary shall provide reasonable notice and an opportunity for a hearing to the State educational agency involved.

(B) Suspension. Pending the outcome of any hearing to withhold payments under subsection (b), the Secretary may suspend payments to a recipient, suspend the authority of the recipient to obligate funds under this part, or both, after such recipient has been given reasonable notice and an opportunity to show cause why future payments or authority to obligate funds under this part should not be suspended.

(5) Report to Congress. The Secretary shall report to the **Committee on Education and the Workforce of the House of Representatives and the Committee on Health, Education, Labor, and Pensions of the Senate** within 30 days of taking enforcement action pursuant to paragraph (1), (2), or (3), on the specific action taken and the reasons why enforcement action was taken.

(6) Nature of Withholding.

(A) Limitation. If the Secretary withholds further payments pursuant to paragraph (2) or (3), the Secretary may determine—

(i) that such withholding will be limited to programs or projects, or portions of programs or projects, that affected the Secretary's determination under subsection (d)(2); or

(ii) that the State educational agency shall not make further payments under this part to specified State agencies or local educational agencies that caused or were involved in the Secretary's determination under subsection (d)(2).

(B) Withholding Until Rectified. Until the Secretary is satisfied that the condition that caused the initial withholding has been substantially rectified—

(i) payments to the State under this part shall be withheld in whole or in part; and

(ii) payments by the State educational agency under this part shall be limited to State agencies and local educational agencies whose actions did not cause or were not involved in the Secretary's determination under subsection (d)(2), as the case may be.

(7) Public Attention. Any State that has received notice under subsection (d)(2) shall, by means of a public notice, take such measures as may be necessary to bring the pendency of an action pursuant to this subsection to the attention of the public within the State.

(8) Judicial Review.

(A) In General. If any State is dissatisfied with the Secretary's action with respect to the eligibility of the State under Section 1412 of this title, such State may, not later than 60 days after notice of such action, file with the United States court of appeals for the circuit in which such State is located a petition for review of that action. A copy of the petition shall be transmitted by the clerk of the court to the Secretary. The Secretary thereupon shall file in the court the record of the proceedings upon which the Secretary's action was based, as provided in Section 2112 of title 28, United States Code.

(B) Jurisdiction; Review by United States Supreme Court. Upon the filing of such petition, the court shall have jurisdiction to affirm the action of the Secretary or to set it aside, in whole or in part. The judgment of the court shall be subject to review by the Supreme Court of the United States upon certiorari or certification as provided in Section 1254 of title 28, United States Code.

(C) Standard of Review. The findings of fact by the Secretary, if supported by substantial evidence, shall be conclusive, but the court, for good cause shown, may remand the case to the Secretary to take further evidence, and the Secretary may thereupon make new or modified findings of fact and may modify the Secretary's previous action, and shall file in the court the record of the further proceedings. Such new or modified findings of fact shall be conclusive if supported by substantial evidence.

(f) State Enforcement. If a State educational agency determines that **a local educational agency is not meeting the requirements** of this part, including the targets in the State's performance plan, the State educational agency **shall prohibit** the local educational agency from reducing the local educational agency's maintenance of effort under Section 1413(a)(2)(C) of this title for any fiscal year.

(g) Rule of Construction. Nothing in this section shall be construed to restrict the Secretary from utilizing any authority under the General Education Provisions Act to monitor and enforce the requirements of this title.

(h) Divided State Agency Responsibility. For purposes of this section, where responsibility for ensuring that the requirements of this part are met with respect to children with disabilities who are convicted as adults under State law and incarcerated in adult prisons is assigned to a public agency other than the State educational agency pursuant to Section 1412(a)(11)(C) of this title, the Secretary, in instances where the Secretary finds that the failure to comply substantially with the provisions of this part are related to a failure by the public agency, shall take appropriate corrective action to ensure compliance with this part, except that

(1) any reduction or withholding of payments to the State shall be proportionate to the total funds allotted under Section 1411 of this title to the State as the number of eligible children with disabilities in adult prisons under the supervision of the other public agency is proportionate to the number of eligible individuals with disabilities in the State under the supervision of the State educational agency; and

(2) any withholding of funds under paragraph (1) shall be limited to the specific agency responsible for the failure to comply with this part.

(i) Data Capacity and Technical Assistance Review. The Secretary shall–

(1) review the data collection and analysis capacity of States to ensure that data and information determined necessary for implementation of this section is collected, analyzed, and accurately reported to the Secretary; and

(2) provide technical assistance (from funds reserved under Section 1411(c) of this title), where needed, to improve the capacity of States to meet the data collection requirements.

20 U. S. C. § 1417. Administration.

WRIGHTSLAW OVERVIEW: Section 1417 describes requirements for administering the law. The Department of Education may not mandate, direct, or control specific instructional content, curriculum or programs of instruction. When the special education regulations were published, the Department of Education published a model Individualized Education Program (IEP) form, an Individualized Family Service Plan (IFSP) form, procedural safeguards notice form, and prior written notice form.

(a) Responsibilities of Secretary. The Secretary shall–

(1) cooperate with, and (directly or by grant or contract) furnish technical assistance necessary to, a State in matters relating to–

(A) the education of children with disabilities; and

(B) carrying out this part; and

(2) provide short-term training programs and institutes.

(b) Prohibition Against Federal Mandates, Direction, or Control. Nothing in this title shall be construed to authorize an officer or employee of the Federal Government to mandate, direct, or control a State, local educational agency, or school's specific instructional content, academic achievement standards and assessments, curriculum, or program of instruction.

(c) Confidentiality. The Secretary shall take appropriate action, in accordance with Section 1232g of this title, to ensure the protection of the confidentiality of any personally identifiable data, information, and records collected or maintained by the Secretary and by State educational agencies and local educational agencies pursuant to this part.

(d) Personnel. The Secretary is authorized to hire qualified personnel necessary to carry out the Secretary's duties under subsection (a), under Section 1418 of this title, and under subpart 4 of part D, without regard to the provisions of title 5, United States Code, relating to appointments in the competitive service and without regard to chapter 51 and subchapter III of chapter 53 of such title relating to classification and general schedule pay rates, except that no more than 20 such personnel shall be employed at any time.

(e) Model Forms.[190] Not later than the date that the Secretary publishes final regulations under this title, to implement amendments made by the Individuals with Disabilities Education Improvement Act of 2004, the Secretary shall publish and disseminate widely to States, local educational agencies, and parent and community training and information centers–

(1) a model **IEP form**;

(2) a model **individualized family service plan (IFSP) form**;

(3) a model form of the **notice of procedural safeguards** described in Section 1415(d) of this title; and

(4) a model form of the **prior written notice** described in subsections (b)(3) and (c)(1) of Section 1415 of this title that is consistent with the requirements of this part and is sufficient to meet such requirements.

20 U. S. C. § 1418. Program Information.

WRIGHTSLAW OVERVIEW: IDEA 2004 requires States to provide detailed reports about the number and percentage of children with disabilities by race, ethnicity, English proficiency, gender, and disability category, including children removed from school. The state must report Information about litigation and due process hearings. To address issues of over-identification of minority children and the disproportionate number of minority children in special education, the Department of Education requires states to review and revise policies, procedures, and practices, and requires districts to publicly report on their revised policies, procedures and practices.

(a) In General. Each State that receives assistance under this part, and the Secretary of the Interior, **shall provide data each year to** the Secretary of Education and **the public** on the following:

(1)

(A) The number and percentage of children with disabilities, by race, ethnicity, limited English proficiency status, gender, and disability category, who are in each of the following separate categories:

(i) Receiving a free appropriate public education.

(ii) Participating in regular education.

(iii) In separate classes, separate schools or facilities, or public or private residential facilities.

(iv) For each year of age from age 14 through 21, stopped receiving special education and related services because of program completion (including graduation with a regular secondary school diploma), or other reasons, and the reasons why those children stopped receiving special education and related

---

190 Download the model forms from www.wrightslaw.com/idea/law.htm or check the Resources section at the end of this book for links to the model forms.

services.

    (v)

        (I) Removed to an interim alternative educational setting under Section 1415(k)(1) of this title.

        (II) The acts or items precipitating those removals.

        (III) The number of children with disabilities who are subject to long-term suspensions or expulsions.

    (B) The number and percentage of children with disabilities, by race, gender, and ethnicity, who are receiving early intervention services.

    (C) The number and percentage of children with disabilities, by race, gender, and ethnicity, who, from birth through age 2, stopped receiving early intervention services because of program completion or for other reasons.

    (D) The incidence and duration of disciplinary actions by race, ethnicity, limited English proficiency status, gender, and disability category, of children with disabilities, including suspensions of 1 day or more.

    (E) The number and percentage of children with disabilities who are removed to alternative educational settings or expelled as compared to children without disabilities who are removed to alternative educational settings or expelled.

    (F) The number of due process complaints filed under Section 1415 of this title and the number of hearings conducted.

    (G) The number of hearings requested under Section 1415(k) of this title and the number of changes in placements ordered as a result of those hearings.

    (H) The number of mediations held and the number of settlement agreements reached through such mediations.

    (2) The number and percentage of infants and toddlers, by race, and ethnicity, who are at risk of having substantial developmental delays (as defined in Section 1432 of this title), and who are receiving early intervention services under part C.

    (3) Any other information that may be required by the Secretary.

(b) Data Reporting.

    (1) Protection of Identifiable Data. The data described in subsection (a) shall be publicly reported by each State in a manner that does not result in the disclosure of data identifiable to individual children.

    (2) Sampling. The Secretary may permit States and the Secretary of the Interior to obtain the data described in subsection (a) through sampling.

(c) Technical Assistance. The Secretary may provide technical assistance to States to ensure compliance with the data collection and reporting requirements under this title.

(d) Disproportionality.[191]

    (1) In General. Each State that receives assistance under this part, and the Secretary of the Interior, shall provide for the collection and examination of data to determine if significant disproportionality based on race and ethnicity is occurring in the State and the local educational agencies of the State with respect to—

    (A) the identification of children as children with disabilities, including the identification of children as children with disabilities in accordance with a particular impairment described in Section 1401(3) of this title;

    (B) the placement in particular educational settings of such children; and

    (C) the incidence, duration, and type of disciplinary actions, including suspensions and expulsions.

---

191   See Section 1412(a)(24) about policies and practices regarding the over-identification or disproportionate representation by race and ethnicity.

(2) Review and Revision of Policies, Practices, and Procedures. In the case of a determination of significant disproportionality with respect to the identification of children as children with disabilities, or the placement in particular educational settings of such children, in accordance with paragraph (1), the State or the Secretary of the Interior, as the case may be, shall–

(A) provide for the review and, if appropriate, revision of the policies, procedures, and practices used in such identification or placement to ensure that such policies, procedures, and practices comply with the requirements of this title;

(B) require any local educational agency identified under paragraph (1) to reserve the maximum amount of funds under Section 1413(f) of this title to provide comprehensive coordinated early intervening services to serve children in the local educational agency, particularly children in those groups that were significantly overidentified under paragraph (1); and

(C) require the local educational agency to publicly report on the revision of policies, practices, and procedures described under subparagraph (A).

20 U. S. C. § 1419. Preschool Grants.

WRIGHTSLAW OVERVIEW: This section provides requirements for preschool grants.

(a) In General. The Secretary shall provide grants under this section to assist States to provide special education and related services, in accordance with this part

(1) to children with disabilities aged 3 through 5, inclusive; and

(2) at the State's discretion, to 2-year-old children with disabilities who will turn 3 during the school year.

(b) Eligibility. A State shall be eligible for a grant under this section if such State–

(1) is eligible under Section 1412 of this title to receive a grant under this part; and

(2) makes a free appropriate public education available to all children with disabilities, aged 3 through 5, residing in the State.

(c) Allocations to States.

(1) In General. The Secretary shall allocate the amount made available to carry out this section for a fiscal year among the States in accordance with paragraph (2) or (3), as the case may be.

(2) Increase in Funds. If the amount available for allocations to States under paragraph (1) for a fiscal year is equal to or greater than the amount allocated to the States under this section for the preceding fiscal year, those allocations shall be calculated as follows:

(A) Allocation.

(i) **In General.** Except as provided in subparagraph (B), the Secretary shall–

(I) allocate to each State the amount the State received under this section for fiscal year 1997;

(II) allocate 85 percent of any remaining funds to States on the basis of the States' relative populations of children aged 3 through 5; and

(III) allocate 15 percent of those remaining funds to States on the basis of the States' relative populations of all children aged 3 through 5 who are living in poverty.

(ii) **Data.** For the purpose of making grants under this paragraph, the Secretary shall use the most recent population data, including data on children living in poverty, that are available and satisfactory to the Secretary.

(B) Limitations. Notwithstanding subparagraph (A), allocations under this paragraph shall be subject to the following:

(i) **Preceding Years.** No State's allocation shall be less than its allocation under this section for the preceding fiscal year.

(ii) **Minimum**. No State's allocation shall be less than the greatest of–

(I) the sum of–

(aa) the amount the State received under this section for fiscal year 1997; and

(bb) 1/3 of 1 percent of the amount by which the amount appropriated under subsection (j) for the fiscal year exceeds the amount appropriated for this section for fiscal year 1997;

(II) the sum of–

(aa) the amount the State received under this section for the preceding fiscal year; and

(bb) that amount multiplied by the percentage by which the increase in the funds appropriated under this section from the preceding fiscal year exceeds 1.5 percent; or

(III) the sum of–

(aa) the amount the State received under this section for the preceding fiscal year; and

(bb) that amount multiplied by 90 percent of the percentage increase in the amount appropriated under this section from the preceding fiscal year.

(iii) **Maximum**. Notwithstanding clause (ii), no State's allocation under this paragraph shall exceed the sum of

(I) the amount the State received under this section for the preceding fiscal year; and

(II) that amount multiplied by the sum of 1.5 percent and the percentage increase in the amount appropriated under this section from the preceding fiscal year.

(C) **Ratable Reductions**. If the amount available for allocations under this paragraph is insufficient to pay those allocations in full, those allocations shall be ratably reduced, subject to subparagraph (B)(i).

(3) **Decrease in Funds**. If the amount available for allocations to States under paragraph (1) for a fiscal year is less than the amount allocated to the States under this section for the preceding fiscal year, those allocations shall be calculated as follows:

(A) **Allocations**. If the amount available for allocations is greater than the amount allocated to the States for fiscal year 1997, each State shall be allocated the sum of–

(i) the amount the State received under this section for fiscal year 1997; and

(ii) an amount that bears the same relation to any remaining funds as the increase the State received under this section for the preceding fiscal year over fiscal year 1997 bears to the total of all such increases for all States.

(B) **Ratable Reductions**. If the amount available for allocations is equal to or less than the amount allocated to the States for fiscal year 1997, each State shall be allocated the amount the State received for fiscal year 1997, ratably reduced, if necessary.

(d) **Reservation for State Activities**.

(1) **In General**. Each State may reserve not more than the amount described in paragraph (2) for administration and other State-level activities in accordance with subsections (e) and (f).

(2) **Amount Described**. For each fiscal year, the Secretary shall determine and report to the State educational agency an amount that is 25 percent of the amount the State received under this section for fiscal year 1997, cumulatively adjusted by the Secretary for each succeeding fiscal year by the lesser of –

(A) the percentage increase, if any, from the preceding fiscal year in the State's allocation under this section; or

(B) the percentage increase, if any, from the preceding fiscal year in the Consumer Price Index For All Urban Consumers published by the Bureau of Labor Statistics of the Department of Labor.

(e) State Administration.

(1) In General. For the purpose of administering this section (including the coordination of activities under this part with, and providing technical assistance to, other programs that provide services to children with disabilities) a State may use not more than 20 percent of the maximum amount the State may reserve under subsection (d) for any fiscal year.

(2) Administration of Part C. Funds described in paragraph (1) may be used for the administration of part C.

(f) Other State-Level Activities. Each State shall use any funds the State reserves under subsection (d) and does not use for administration under subsection (e)–

(1) for support services (including establishing and implementing the mediation process required by Section 1415(e) of this title), which may benefit children with disabilities younger than 3 or older than 5 as long as those services also benefit children with disabilities aged 3 through 5;

(2) for direct services for children eligible for services under this section;

(3) for activities at the State and local levels to meet the performance goals established by the State under Section 1412(a)(15) of this title;

(4) to supplement other funds used to develop and implement a statewide coordinated services system designed to improve results for children and families, including children with disabilities and their families, but not more than 1 percent of the amount received by the State under this section for a fiscal year;

(5) to provide early intervention services (which shall include an educational component that promotes school readiness and incorporates preliteracy, language, and numeracy skills) in accordance with part C to children with disabilities who are eligible for services under this section and who previously received services under part C until such children enter, or are eligible under State law to enter, kindergarten; or

(6) at the State's discretion, to continue service coordination or case management for families who receive services under part C.

(g) Subgrants to Local Educational Agencies.

(1) Subgrants Required. Each State that receives a grant under this section for any fiscal year shall distribute all of the grant funds that the State does not reserve under subsection (d) to local educational agencies in the State that have established their eligibility under Section 1413 of this title, as follows:

(A) Base Payments. The State shall first award each local educational agency described in paragraph (1) the amount that agency would have received under this section for fiscal year 1997 if the State had distributed 75 percent of its grant for that year under Section 1419(c)(3) of this title, as such section was then in effect.

(B) Allocation of Remaining Funds. After making allocations under subparagraph (A), the State shall

(i) allocate 85 percent of any remaining funds to those local educational agencies on the basis of the relative numbers of children enrolled in public and private elementary schools and secondary schools within the local educational agency's jurisdiction; and

(ii) allocate 15 percent of those remaining funds to those local educational agencies in accordance with their relative numbers of children living in poverty, as determined by the State educational agency.

(2) Reallocation of Funds. If a State educational agency determines that a local educational agency is adequately providing a free appropriate public education to all children with disabilities aged 3 through 5 residing in the area served by the local educational agency with State and local funds, the State educational agency may reallocate any portion of the funds under this section that are not needed by that local educational agency to provide a free appropriate public education to other local educational agencies in the State that are not adequately providing special education and related services to all children with disabilities aged 3 through 5 residing in the areas the other local educational agencies serve.

End of Part B

Part C – Infants and Toddlers with Disabilities

WRIGHTSLAW OVERVIEW: Part C governs early intervention services for infants and toddlers under age 3. Part C includes Sections 1431 through Section 1442 of Title 20 of the United States Code (U. S. C.): The regulations are not expected until 2008.[1]

20 U. S. C. § 1431. Findings and Policy
20 U. S. C. § 1432. Definitions
20 U. S. C. § 1433. General Authority
20 U. S. C. § 1434. Eligibility
20 U. S. C. § 1435. Requirements for Statewide System
20 U. S. C. § 1436. Individualized Family Service Plans
20 U. S. C. § 1437. State Application and Assurances
20 U. S. C. § 1438. Uses of Funds
20 U. S. C. § 1439. Procedural Safeguards
20 U. S. C. § 1440. Payor of Last Resort
20 U. S. C. § 1441. State Interagency Coordinating Council
20 U. S. C. § 1442. Federal Administration
20 U. S. C. § 1443. Allocation of Funds
20 U. S. C. § 1444. Authorization of Appropriations

20 U. S. C. § 1431. Findings and Policy.

WRIGHTSLAW OVERVIEW: Congress made significant changes to Findings and Policy in Part C by adding language about the need "to recognize the significant brain development that occurs during a child's first 3 years of life." The language about the need "to minimize the likelihood of institutionalization" was replaced by the need "to maximize the potential for individuals with disabilities to live independently in society."

(a) **Findings** - Congress finds that there is an urgent and substantial need –

(1) to enhance the development of infants and toddlers with disabilities, to **minimize their potential for developmental delay**, and to recognize the **significant brain development that occurs during a child's first 3 years of life**;

(2) to reduce the educational costs to our society, including our Nation's schools, **by minimizing the need for special education and related services** after infants and toddlers with disabilities reach school age;

(3) to **maximize the potential for individuals with disabilities to live independently in society**.

(4) to enhance the capacity of families to meet the special needs of their infants and toddlers with disabilities; and

(5) to enhance the capacity of State and local agencies and service providers to **identify, evaluate, and meet the needs of all children, particularly minority, low-income, inner city, and rural children,** and infants and toddlers in foster care.

(b) **Policy** - It is the policy of the United States to provide financial assistance to States –

(1) to develop and implement a **statewide, comprehensive, coordinated, multidisciplinary, interagency system that provides early intervention services** for infants and toddlers with disabilities and their families;

(2) to facilitate the coordination of payment for early intervention services from Federal, State, local, and private sources (including public and private insurance coverage);

---

1 According to the Office of Special Education Program (OSEP), "The Department intends to publish the NPRM in the Federal Register in early 2007, hold public meetings in the spring, and publish the final regulations in early 2008." This is a general timeline and is subject to change.

(3) to enhance State capacity to **provide quality early intervention services** and **expand and improve existing early intervention services** being provided to infants and toddlers with disabilities and their families; and

(4) to encourage States to **expand opportunities for children under 3 years of age who would be at risk of having substantial developmental delay** if they did not receive early intervention services.

20 U. S. C. § 1432. Definitions.

WRIGHTSLAW OVERVIEW: Section 1432 is similar to 20 U. S. C. § 1401 in Part A, and provides key definitions of early intervention services to infants and toddlers with disabilities in Part C of IDEA.

In this part:

(1) **At-Risk Infant or Toddler** - The term 'at-risk infant or toddler' means an individual under 3 years of age who would be at risk of experiencing a substantial developmental delay if early intervention services were not provided to the individual.

(2) **Council** - The term 'council' means a State interagency coordinating council established under Section 1441.

(3) **Developmental Delay** - The term 'developmental delay', when used with respect to an individual residing in a State, has the meaning given such term by the State under Section 1435(a)(1).

(4) **Early Intervention Services** - The term 'early intervention services'[2] means developmental services that

(A) are provided under public supervision;

(B) are provided at no cost except where Federal or State law provides for a system of payments by families, including a schedule of sliding fees;

(C) are designed to meet the developmental needs of an infant or toddler with a disability, as identified by the individualized family service plan team, in any 1 or more of the following areas:

(i) physical development;

(ii) cognitive development;

(iii) communication development;

(iv) social or emotional development; or

(v) adaptive development;

(D) meet the standards of the State in which the services are provided, including the requirements of this part;

(E) include -

(i) family training, counseling, and home visits;

(ii) special instruction;

(iii) speech-language pathology and audiology services, and sign language and cued language services;

(iv) occupational therapy;

(v) physical therapy;

(vi) psychological services;

(vii) service coordination services;

(viii) medical services only for diagnostic or evaluation purposes;

---

2   Early intervention services must be designed to meet the child's developmental needs, including needs in the physical, cognitive, communication, social and emotional, and adaptive areas. Many school districts offer one-size-fits-all school based programs that are not "designed to meet the developmental needs" of a particular infant or toddler.

(ix) early identification, screening, and assessment services;

(x) health services necessary to enable the infant or toddler to benefit from the other early intervention services;

(xi) social work services;

(xii) vision services;

(xiii) assistive technology devices and assistive technology services; and

(xiv) transportation and related costs that are necessary to enable an infant or toddler and the infant's or toddler's family to receive another service described in this paragraph;

(F) are **provided by qualified personnel**, including–

(i) special educators;

(ii) speech-language pathologists and audiologists;

(iii) occupational therapists;

(iv) physical therapists;

(v) psychologists;

(vi) social workers;

(vii) nurses;

(viii) registered dietitians;

(ix) family therapists;

(x) vision specialists, including ophthalmologists and optometrists;

(xi) orientation and mobility specialists; and

(xii) pediatricians and other physicians;[3]

(G) to the maximum extent appropriate, are **provided in natural environments, including the home,** and community settings in which children without disabilities participate; and

(H) are provided in conformity with an individualized family service plan[4] adopted in accordance with Section 1436.

(5) Infant or Toddler with a Disability - The term 'infant or toddler with a disability'-

(A) means an individual **under 3 years of age** who needs early intervention services because the individual

(i) is experiencing developmental delays, as measured by appropriate diagnostic instruments and procedures in one or more of the areas of cognitive development, physical development, communication development, social or emotional development, and adaptive development; or

(ii) has a diagnosed physical or mental condition that has a high probability of resulting in developmental delay; and

(B) **may** also include, at a State's discretion -

(i) at-risk infants and toddlers; and

(ii) children with disabilities who are eligible for services under Section 1419 and who previously received services under this part until such children enter, or are eligible under State law to enter, kindergarten or elementary school, as appropriate, provided that any programs under this part serving such

---

3 IDEA authorizes early intervention services from professional providers. An issue may arise as to whether service providers are "qualified" or whether services are provided by inadequately trained staff, including aides and paraprofessionals. Children may receive services from physicians for diagnostic and evaluation purposes, if necessary.

4 For the legal requirements for Individualized Family Service Plans, see 20 U. S. C. § 1436.

children shall include -

(I) an educational component that promotes school readiness and incorporates pre-literacy, language, and numeracy skills; and

(II) a written notification to parents of their rights and responsibilities in determining whether their child will continue to receive services under this part or participate in preschool programs under Section 1419.

20 U. S. C. § 1433. General Authority.

WRIGHTSLAW OVERVIEW: Section 1433 describes the authority of the U. S. Department of Education to make grants to States.

The Secretary shall, in accordance with this part, make grants to States (from their allotments under Section 1443) to assist each State to maintain and implement a statewide, comprehensive, coordinated, multidisciplinary, interagency system to provide early intervention services for infants and toddlers with disabilities and their families.

20 U. S. C. § 1434. Eligibility.

WRIGHTSLAW OVERVIEW: Section 1434 describes assurances States must provide in order to receive federal funds for early intervention programs.

In order to be eligible for a grant under Section 1433, a State shall provide assurances to the Secretary that the State –

(1) has adopted a policy that **appropriate early intervention services are available to all infants and toddlers with disabilities** in the State and their families, including Indian infants and toddlers with disabilities and their families residing on a reservation geographically located in the State, infants and toddlers with disabilities who are homeless children and their families, and infants and toddlers with disabilities who are wards of the State; and

(2) has in effect a statewide system that meets the requirements of Section 1435.

20 U. S. C. § 1435. Requirements for Statewide System.

WRIGHTSLAW OVERVIEW: This section describes the minimum requirements for early intervention programs. States must ensure that early intervention services are based on scientifically based research. Evaluations must be timely, comprehensive, multidisciplinary and must include a "family-directed identification of the needs of each family." The state must have a comprehensive child find system and public awareness programs and must maintain a central directory of information about early intervention services and resources. States must have personnel development systems that include training for paraprofessionals and primary referral sources, and procedures to ensure that personnel are adequately trained. States must ensure that early intervention services are provided in natural environments. Subsection (c) about "Flexibility to Serve Children 3 Years of Age Until Entrance into Elementary School" is new in IDEA 2004.

(a) In General - A statewide system described in Section 1433 shall include, at a minimum, the following components:

(1) A **rigorous definition of** the term 'developmental delay' that will be used by the State in carrying out programs under this part in order to appropriately identify infants and toddlers with disabilities that are in need of services under this part.

(2) A State policy that is in effect and that ensures that appropriate **early intervention services based on scientifically based research**, to the extent practicable, are available to all infants and toddlers with disabilities and their families, including Indian infants and toddlers with disabilities and their families residing on a reservation geographically located in the State and infants and toddlers with disabilities who are homeless children and their families.

(3) A **timely, comprehensive, multidisciplinary evaluation** of the functioning of each infant or toddler with a disability in the State, and a **family-directed identification of the needs of each family** of such an infant or

toddler, to assist appropriately in the development of the infant or toddler.

(4) For each infant or toddler with a disability in the State, an **individualized family service plan** in accordance with Section 1436, including service coordination services in accordance with such service plan.

(5) A **comprehensive child find system,** consistent with part B, including a system for making referrals to service providers that includes timelines and provides for participation by primary referral sources and that ensures **rigorous standards for appropriately identifying infants and toddlers with disabilities** for services under this part that will reduce the need for future services.

(6) A **public awareness program focusing on early identification** of infants and toddlers with disabilities, including the preparation and dissemination by the lead agency designated or established under paragraph (10) to all primary referral sources, especially hospitals and physicians, of information to be given to parents, especially to inform parents with premature infants, or infants with other physical risk factors associated with learning or developmental complications, on the availability of early intervention services under this part and of services under Section 1419, and procedures for assisting such sources in disseminating such information to parents of infants and toddlers with disabilities.

(7) A **central directory that includes information on early intervention services, resources, and experts** available in the State and research and demonstration projects being conducted in the State.

(8) A **comprehensive system of personnel development**, including the **training of paraprofessionals** and the **training of primary referral sources** with respect to the basic components of early intervention services available in the State that -

(A) **shall include -**

(i) implementing innovative strategies and activities for the recruitment and retention of early education service providers;

(ii) promoting the preparation of early intervention providers who are fully and appropriately qualified to provide early intervention services under this part; and

(iii) training personnel to coordinate transition services for infants and toddlers served under this part from a program providing early intervention services under this part and under part B (other than Section 1419), to a preschool program receiving funds under Section 1419, or another appropriate program; and

(B) **may include -**

(i) training personnel to work in rural and inner-city areas; and

(ii) training personnel in the emotional and social development of young children.

(9) Policies and procedures relating to the establishment and maintenance of **qualifications to ensure that personnel** necessary to carry out this part **are appropriately and adequately prepared and trained**, including the establishment and maintenance of qualifications that are consistent with any State-approved or recognized certification, licensing, registration, or other comparable requirements that apply to the area in which such personnel are providing early intervention services, except that nothing in this part (including this paragraph) shall be construed to prohibit the use of paraprofessionals and assistants who are appropriately trained and supervised in accordance with State law, regulation, or written policy, to assist in the provision of early intervention services under this part to infants and toddlers with disabilities.

(10) A **single line of responsibility in a lead agency** designated or established by the Governor for carrying out -

(A) the general administration and supervision of programs and activities receiving assistance under Section 1433, and the monitoring of programs and activities used by the State to carry out this part, whether or not such programs or activities are receiving assistance made available under Section 1433, to ensure that the State complies with this part;

(B) the identification and coordination of all available resources within the State from Federal, State, local, and private sources;

(C) the assignment of financial responsibility in accordance with Section 1437(a)(2) to the appropriate agencies;

(D) the development of procedures to ensure that services are provided to infants and toddlers with disabilities and their families under this part in a timely manner pending the resolution of any disputes among public agencies or service providers;

(E) the resolution of intra- and interagency disputes; and

(F) the entry into formal interagency agreements that define the financial responsibility of each agency for paying for early intervention services (consistent with State law) and procedures for resolving disputes and that include all additional components necessary to ensure meaningful cooperation and coordination.

(11) A policy pertaining to the contracting or making of other arrangements with service providers to provide early intervention services in the State, consistent with the provisions of this part, including the contents of the application used and the conditions of the contract or other arrangements.

(12) A procedure for securing timely reimbursements of funds used under this part in accordance with Section 1440(a).

(13) Procedural safeguards with respect to programs under this part, as required by Section 1439.

(14) A system for compiling data requested by the Secretary under Section 1418 that relates to this part.

(15) A State interagency coordinating council that meets the requirements of Section 1441.

(16) Policies and procedures to ensure that, consistent with Section 1436(d)(5) -

(A) to the maximum extent appropriate, early intervention services are **provided in natural environments**; and

(B) the provision of early intervention services for any infant or toddler with a disability occurs in a setting other than a natural environment that is most appropriate, as determined by the parent and the individualized family service plan team, only when early intervention cannot be achieved satisfactorily for the infant or toddler in a natural environment.

(b) Policy - In implementing subsection (a)(9), a State may adopt a policy that includes making ongoing good-faith efforts to recruit and hire appropriately and adequately trained personnel to provide early intervention services to infants and toddlers with disabilities, including, in a geographic area of the State where there is a shortage of such personnel, the most qualified individuals available who are making satisfactory progress toward completing applicable course work necessary to meet the standards described in subsection (a)(9).

(c) Flexibility To Serve Children 3 Years of Age Until Entrance Into Elementary School

(1) In General - A statewide system described in Section 1433 may include a State policy, developed and implemented jointly by the lead agency and the State educational agency, under which parents of children with disabilities who are eligible for services under Section 1419 and previously received services under this part, may choose the continuation of early intervention services (which shall include an educational component that promotes school readiness and incorporates preliteracy, language, and numeracy skills) for such children under this part until such children enter, or are eligible under State law to enter, kindergarten.

(2) Requirements - If a statewide system includes a State policy described in paragraph (1), the statewide system shall ensure that -

(A) parents of children with disabilities served pursuant to this subsection are provided annual notice that contains -

(i) a description of the rights of such parents to elect to receive services pursuant to this subsection or under part B; and

(ii) an explanation of the differences between services provided pursuant to this subsection and services provided under part B, including–

(I) types of services and the locations at which the services are provided;

(II) applicable procedural safeguards; and

(III) possible costs (including any fees to be charged to families as described in Section 1432(4)(B)), if any, to parents of infants or toddlers with disabilities;

(B) **services** provided pursuant to this subsection include an educational component that **promotes school readiness** and incorporates **preliteracy, language, and numeracy skills**;

(C) the State policy will not affect the right of any child served pursuant to this subsection to instead receive a free appropriate public education under part B;

(D) all early intervention services outlined in the child's individualized family service plan under Section 1436 are continued while any eligibility determination is being made for services under this subsection;

(E) the **parents** of infants or toddlers with disabilities (as defined in Section 1432(5)(A)) **provide informed written consent** to the State, before such infants or toddlers reach 3 years of age, as to **whether such parents intend to choose the continuation of early intervention services** pursuant to this subsection for such infants or toddlers;

(F) the requirements under Section 1437(a)(9) shall not apply with respect to a child who is receiving services in accordance with this subsection until not less than 90 days (and at the discretion of the parties to the conference, not more than 9 months) before the time the child will no longer receive those services; and

(G) there will be a **referral for evaluation** for early intervention services **of a child who experiences a substantiated case of trauma due to exposure to family violence** (as defined in Section 320 of the Family Violence Prevention and Services Act).

(3) Reporting Requirement - If a statewide system includes a State policy described in paragraph (1), the State shall submit to the Secretary, in the State's report under Section 1437(b)(4)(A), a report on the number and percentage of children with disabilities who are eligible for services under Section 1419 but whose parents choose for such children to continue to receive early intervention services under this part.

(4) Available Funds - If a statewide system includes a State policy described in paragraph (1), the policy shall describe the funds (including an identification as Federal, State, or local funds) that will be used to ensure that the option described in paragraph (1) is available to eligible children and families who provide the consent described in paragraph (2)(E), including fees (if any) to be charged to families as described in Section 1432(4)(B).

(5) Rules of Construction -

(A) Services Under Part B - If a statewide system includes a State policy described in paragraph (1), a State that provides services in accordance with this subsection to a child with a disability who is eligible for services under Section 1419 shall not be required to provide the child with a free appropriate public education under part B for the period of time in which the child is receiving services under this part.

(B) Services Under This Part - Nothing in this subsection **shall be construed** to require a provider of services under this part to provide a child served under this part with a **free appropriate public education**.

20 U. S. C. § 1436. Individualized Family Service Plan.

WRIGHTSLAW OVERVIEW: Section 1436 describes the legal requirements for Individualized Family Service Plans (IFSPs) which are similar to the requirements for Individualized Education Plans in Section 1414(d). Subsection (a) describes the assessment and program development process, including a "family-directed assessment" of the resources, priorities, and concerns of the family. Subsection (d) describes the required components of Individualized Family Service Plans. The requirements for "measurable results or outcomes expected to be achieved . . . including pre-literacy and language skills" and the "criteria, procedures, and timelines" that will be used to measure the child's progress are new, as are the requirements that early intervention services be "based on peer-reviewed research" in subsection (d)(4).

(a) Assessment and Program Development - A statewide system described in Section 1433 **shall provide, at a minimum,** for each infant or toddler with a disability, and the infant's or toddler's family, to receive -

(1) a **multidisciplinary assessment** of the **unique strengths and needs** of the infant or toddler and the identification of **services** appropriate to meet such needs;

(2) a **family-directed assessment** of the resources, priorities, and concerns of the family and the identification of the supports and services necessary to enhance the family's capacity to meet the developmental needs of the infant or toddler; and

(3) a **written individualized family service plan** developed by a multidisciplinary team, including the parents, as required by subsection (e), including a description of the appropriate transition services for the infant or toddler.

(b) Periodic Review - The individualized family service plan shall be evaluated once a year and the family shall be provided a review of the plan at 6-month intervals (or more often where appropriate based on infant or toddler and family needs).

(c) Promptness After Assessment - The individualized family service plan shall be developed within a reasonable time after the assessment required by subsection (a)(1) is completed. With the parents' consent, early intervention services may commence prior to the completion of the assessment.

(d) Content of Plan - The individualized family service plan shall be in writing and contain -

(1) a statement of the infant's or toddler's **present levels of physical development, cognitive development, communication development, social or emotional development, and adaptive development, based on objective criteria;**

(2) a statement of the **family's resources, priorities, and concerns** relating to enhancing the development of the family's infant or toddler with a disability;

(3) a statement of the **measurable results or outcomes** expected to be achieved for the infant or toddler and the family, including **pre-literacy and language skills**, as developmentally appropriate for the child, and the **criteria**, procedures, and timelines used **to determine** the degree to which **progress toward achieving the results or outcomes** is being made and whether modifications or revisions of the results or outcomes or services are necessary;

(4) a statement of specific **early intervention services based on peer-reviewed research**, to the extent practicable, necessary to meet the unique needs of the infant or toddler and the family, including the frequency, intensity, and method of delivering services;

(5) a statement of the **natural environments** in which early intervention services will appropriately be provided, including a justification of the extent, if any, to which the services will not be provided in a natural environment;

(6) the projected **dates for initiation of services** and the anticipated **length, duration, and frequency of the services;**

(7) the identification of the **service coordinator** from the profession most immediately relevant to the infant's or toddler's or family's needs (or who is otherwise qualified to carry out all applicable responsibilities under this part) who will be responsible for the implementation of the plan and coordination with other agencies and persons, including transition services; and

(8) the **steps to be taken to support the transition** of the toddler with a disability to preschool or other appropriate services.

(e) Parental Consent - The contents of the individualized family service plan shall be fully explained to the parents and **informed written consent from the parents shall be obtained prior to the provision of early intervention services** described in such plan. If the parents do not provide consent with respect to a particular early intervention service, then only the early intervention services to which consent is obtained shall be provided.

20 U. S. C. § 1437. State Application and Assurances.

WRIGHTSLAW OVERVIEW: This section describes the state grant application process, policies and procedures that must be used to ensure a smooth transition from early intervention, and assurances that States must provide about early intervention services for infants and toddlers with disabilities and their families.

(a) Application - A State desiring to receive a grant under Section 1433 shall submit an application to the Secretary at such time and in such manner as the Secretary may reasonably require. The application shall contain-

(1) a designation of the lead agency in the State that will be responsible for the administration of funds provided under Section 1433;

(2) a certification to the Secretary that the arrangements to establish financial responsibility for services provided under this part pursuant to Section 1440(b) are current as of the date of submission of the certification;

(3) information demonstrating eligibility of the State under Section 1434, including -

(A) information demonstrating to the Secretary's satisfaction that the State has in effect the statewide system required by Section 1433; and

(B) a description of services to be provided to infants and toddlers with disabilities and their families through the system;

(4) if the State provides services to at-risk infants and toddlers through the statewide system, a description of such services;

(5) a description of the uses for which funds will be expended in accordance with this part;

(6) a description of the State policies and procedures that require the referral for early intervention services under this part of a child under the age of 3 who -

(A) is involved in a substantiated case of child abuse or neglect; or

(B) is identified as affected by illegal substance abuse, or withdrawal symptoms resulting from prenatal drug exposure;

(7) a description of the procedure used to ensure that resources are made available under this part for all geographic areas within the State;

(8) a description of State policies and procedures that ensure that, prior to the adoption by the State of any other policy or procedure necessary to meet the requirements of this part, there are public hearings, adequate notice of the hearings, and an opportunity for comment available to the general public, including individuals with disabilities and parents of infants and toddlers with disabilities;

(9) a description of the **policies and procedures** to be used -

(A) to ensure a **smooth transition for toddlers receiving early intervention services** under this part (and children receiving those services under Section 1435(c)) **to preschool, school, other appropriate services, or exiting the program,** including a description of how -

(i) the families of such toddlers and children will be included in the transition plans required by subparagraph (c); and

(ii) the lead agency designated or established under Section 1435(a)(10) will -

(I) notify the local educational agency for the area in which such a child resides that the child will shortly reach the age of eligibility for preschool services under part B, as determined in accordance with State law;

(II) in the case of a child who may be eligible for such preschool services, with the approval of the family of the child, convene a conference among the lead agency, the family, and the local educational agency not less than 90 days (and at the discretion of all such parties, not more than 9 months) before the child is eligible for the preschool services, to discuss any such services that the child may receive; and

(III) in the case of a child who may not be eligible for such preschool services, with the approval of the family, make reasonable efforts to convene a conference among the lead agency, the family, and providers of other appropriate services for children who are not eligible for preschool services under part B, to discuss the appropriate services that the child may receive;

(B) to review the child's program options for the period from the child's third birthday through the remainder of the school year; and

(C) to establish a transition plan, including, as appropriate, steps to exit from the program;

(10) a description of State efforts to promote collaboration among Early Head Start programs under Section 1445A of the Head Start Act, early education and child care programs, and services under part C; and

(11) such other information and assurances as the Secretary may reasonably require.

(b) Assurances - The application described in subsection (a) -

(1) shall provide satisfactory assurance that Federal funds made available under Section 1443 to the State will be expended in accordance with this part;

(2) shall contain an assurance that the State will comply with the requirements of Section 1440;

(3) shall provide satisfactory assurance that the control of funds provided under Section 1443, and title to property derived from those funds, will be in a public agency for the uses and purposes provided in this part and that a public agency will administer such funds and property;

(4) shall provide for -

(A) making such reports in such form and containing such information as the Secretary may require to carry out the Secretary's functions under this part; and

(B) keeping such reports and affording such access to the reports as the Secretary may find necessary to ensure the correctness and verification of those reports and proper disbursement of Federal funds under this part;

(5) provide satisfactory assurance that Federal funds made available under Section 1443 to the State -

(A) will not be commingled with State funds; and

(B) will be used so as **to supplement** the level of **State and local funds** expended for infants and toddlers with disabilities and their families and **in no case to supplant those State and local funds**;

(6) shall provide satisfactory assurance that such fiscal control and fund accounting procedures will be adopted as may be necessary to ensure proper disbursement of, and accounting for, Federal funds paid under Section 1443 to the State;

(7) shall provide satisfactory **assurance that policies and procedures have been adopted to ensure meaningful involvement of underserved groups**, including minority, low-income, homeless, and rural families and children with disabilities who are wards of the State, in the planning and implementation of all the requirements of this part; and

(8) shall contain such other information and assurances as the Secretary may reasonably require by regulation.

(c) Standard for Disapproval of Application - The Secretary may not disapprove such an application unless the Secretary determines, after notice and opportunity for a hearing, that the application fails to comply with the requirements of this section.

(d) Subsequent State Application - If a State has on file with the Secretary a policy, procedure, or assurance that demonstrates that the State meets a requirement of this section, including any policy or procedure filed under this part (as in effect before the date of enactment of the Individuals with Disabilities Education Improvement Act of 2004), the Secretary shall consider the State to have met the requirement for purposes of receiving a grant under this part.

(e) Modification of Application - An application submitted by a State in accordance with this section shall remain in effect until the State submits to the Secretary such modifications as the State determines necessary. This section shall apply to a modification of an application to the same extent and in the same manner as this section applies to the original application.

(f) Modifications Required by the Secretary - The Secretary may require a State to modify its application under this section, but only to the extent necessary to ensure the State's compliance with this part, if–

(1) an amendment is made to this title, or a Federal regulation issued under this title;

(2) a new interpretation of this title is made by a Federal court or the State's highest court; or

(3) an official finding of noncompliance with Federal law or regulations is made with respect to the State.

20 U. S. C. § 1438. Uses of Funds.

WRIGHTSLAW OVERVIEW: This section describes how States may use funds, and includes direct early intervention services to infants and toddlers with disabilities.

In addition to using funds provided under Section 1433 to maintain and implement the statewide system required by such section, a State may use such funds–

(1) for d**irect early intervention services** for infants and toddlers with disabilities, and their families, under this part that are not otherwise funded through other public or private sources;

(2) to **expand and improve on services** for infants and toddlers and their families under this part that are otherwise available;

(3) to provide a free appropriate public education, in accordance with Part B, to **children with disabilities from their third birthday to the beginning of the following school year;**

(4) with the written consent of the parents, to continue to **provide early intervention services** under this part **to children with disabilities from their 3rd birthday until such children enter**, or are eligible under State law to enter, **kindergarten,** in lieu of a free appropriate public education provided in accordance with part B; and

(5) in any State that does not provide services for at-risk infants and toddlers under Section 1437(a)(4), to strengthen the statewide system by initiating, expanding, or improving collaborative efforts related to at-risk infants and toddlers, including establishing linkages with appropriate public or private community-based organizations, services, and personnel for the purposes of–

(A) identifying and evaluating at-risk infants and toddlers;

(B) making referrals of the infants and toddlers identified and evaluated under subparagraph (A); and

(C) conducting periodic follow-up on each such referral to determine if the status of the infant or toddler involved has changed with respect to the eligibility of the infant or toddler for services under this part.

20 U. S. C. § 1439. Procedural Safeguards.

WRIGHTSLAW OVERVIEW: Section 1439 describes the protections and safeguards for young children with disabilities and their parents. The wording in Section 1439 is similar to Section 1415 in Part B. Unlike Part B, parents have a right to accept or decline any early intervention service without jeopardizing their right to other early intervention services. Subsection (a)(5) describes procedures to protect the rights of the child when the parents are not known or cannot be found. Caselaw referencing Section 1415 will be used to resolve disputes about appropriate early intervention services.

(a) Minimum Procedures - The procedural safeguards required to be included in a statewide system under Section 1435(a)(13) shall provide, at a minimum, the following:

(1) The timely administrative resolution of complaints by parents. Any party aggrieved by the findings and decision regarding an administrative complaint shall have the right to bring a civil action with respect to the complaint in any State court of competent jurisdiction or in a district court of the United States without regard to the amount in controversy. In any action brought under this paragraph, the court shall receive the records of the administrative proceedings, shall hear additional evidence at the request of a party, and, basing its decision on the preponderance of the evidence, shall grant such relief as the court determines is appropriate.

(2) The **right to confidentiality of personally identifiable information**, including the right of parents to written notice of and written consent to the exchange of such information among agencies consistent with Federal and State law.

(3) The **right of the parents to** determine whether they, their infant or toddler, or other family members will **accept or decline any early intervention service** under this part in accordance with State law **without jeopardizing other early intervention services** under this part.

(4) The opportunity for parents **to examine records** relating to assessment, screening, eligibility determinations, and the development and implementation of the individualized family service plan.

(5) **Procedures to protect the rights of the infant or toddler whenever the parents** of the infant or toddler **are not known or cannot be found or** the infant or toddler is a ward of the State, including the assignment of an individual (who shall not be an employee of the State lead agency, or other State agency, and who shall not be any person, or any employee of a person, providing early intervention services to the infant or toddler or any family member of the infant or toddler) **to act as a surrogate for the parents.**

(6) **Written prior notice** to the parents of the infant or toddler with a disability whenever the State agency or service provider **proposes to initiate or change, or refuses to initiate or change, the identification, evaluation, or placement** of the infant or toddler with a disability, **or the provision of appropriate early intervention services** to the infant or toddler.

(7) Procedures designed to ensure that the notice required by paragraph (6) **fully informs the parents**, in the parents' native language, unless it clearly is not feasible to do so, of all procedures available pursuant to this section.

(8) The right of parents to **use mediation** in accordance with Section 1415, except that–

(A) any reference in the section to a State educational agency shall be considered to be a reference to a State's lead agency established or designated under Section 1435(a)(10);

(B) any reference in the section to a local educational agency shall be considered to be a reference to a local service provider or the State's lead agency under this part, as the case may be; and

(C) any reference in the section to the provision of a free appropriate public education to children with disabilities shall be considered to be a reference to the provision of appropriate early intervention services to infants and toddlers with disabilities.

(b) Services During Pendency of Proceedings - During the pendency of any proceeding or action involving a complaint by the parents of an infant or toddler with a disability, unless the State agency and the parents otherwise agree, the infant or toddler **shall continue to receive the appropriate early intervention services currently being provided or**, if applying for initial services, shall receive the **services not in dispute.**

20 U. S. C. § 1440. Payor of Last Resort.

WRIGHTSLAW OVERVIEW: This section clarifies that schools cannot require parents to use the child's health insurance benefits to pay for a free appropriate public education.

(a) Nonsubstitution - Funds provided under Section 1443 may not be used to satisfy a financial commitment for services that would have been paid for from another public or private source, including any medical program administered by the Secretary of Defense, but for the enactment of this part, except that whenever considered necessary to prevent a delay in the receipt of appropriate early intervention services by an infant, toddler, or family in a timely fashion, funds provided under Section 1443 may be used to pay the provider of services pending reimbursement from the agency that has ultimate responsibility for the payment.

(b) Obligations Related to and Methods of Ensuring Services -

(1) Establishing Financial Responsibility for Services -

(A) In General - The Chief Executive Officer of a State or designee of the officer shall ensure that an interagency agreement or other mechanism for interagency coordination is in effect between each public agency and the designated lead agency, in order to ensure–

(i) the provision of, and financial responsibility for, services provided under this part; and

(ii) such services are consistent with the requirements of Section 1435 and the State's application pursuant to Section 1437, including the provision of such services during the pendency of any such dispute.

(B) Consistency Between Agreements or Mechanisms Under Part B - The Chief Executive Officer of a State or designee of the officer shall ensure that the terms and conditions of such agreement or mechanism are consistent with the terms and conditions of the State's agreement or mechanism under Section 1412(a)(12), where appropriate.

(2) Reimbursement for Services by Public Agency -

(A) In General - If a public agency other than an educational agency fails to provide or pay for the services pursuant to an agreement required under paragraph (1), the local educational agency or State agency (as determined by the Chief Executive Officer or designee) shall provide or pay for the provision of such services to the child.

(B) Reimbursement - Such local educational agency or State agency is authorized to claim reimbursement for the services from the public agency that failed to provide or pay for such services and such public agency shall reimburse the local educational agency or State agency pursuant to the terms of the interagency agreement or other mechanism required under paragraph (1).

(3) Special Rule - The requirements of paragraph (1) may be met through–

(A) State statute or regulation;

(B) signed agreements between respective agency officials that clearly identify the responsibilities of each agency relating to the provision of services; or

(C) other appropriate written methods as determined by the Chief Executive Officer of the State or designee of the officer and approved by the Secretary through the review and approval of the State's application pursuant to Section 1437.

(c) Reduction of Other Benefits - Nothing in this part shall be construed to permit the State to reduce medical or other assistance available or to alter eligibility under title V of the Social Security Act (relating to maternal and child health) or title XIX of the Social Security Act (relating to Medicaid for infants or toddlers with disabilities) within the State.

20 U. S. C. § 1441. State Interagency Coordinating Council.

WRIGHTSLAW OVERVIEW: This section requires States to establish interagency coordinating councils to coordinate early intervention services, and is similar to 20 U. S. C. § 1412(21).

(a) Establishment -

(1) In General - A State that desires to receive financial assistance under this part shall establish a State interagency coordinating council.

(2) Appointment - The council shall be appointed by the Governor. In making appointments to the council, the Governor shall ensure that the membership of the council reasonably represents the population of the State.

(3) Chairperson - The Governor shall designate a member of the council to serve as the chairperson of the council, or shall require the council to so designate such a member. Any member of the council who is a representative of the lead agency designated under Section 1435(a)(10) may not serve as the chairperson of the council.

(b) Composition -

(1) In General - The council shall be composed as follows:

(A) Parents - Not less than 20 percent of the members shall be parents of infants or toddlers with disabilities or children with disabilities aged 12 or younger, with knowledge of, or experience with, programs for infants and toddlers with disabilities. Not less than 1 such member shall be a parent of an infant or toddler with a disability or a child with a disability aged 6 or younger.

(B) Service Providers - Not less than 20 percent of the members shall be public or private providers of early intervention services.

(C) State Legislature - Not less than 1 member shall be from the State legislature.

(D) Personnel Preparation - Not less than 1 member shall be involved in personnel preparation.

(E) Agency for Early Intervention Services - Not less than 1 member shall be from each of the State agencies involved in the provision of, or payment for, early intervention services to infants and toddlers with disabilities and their families and shall have sufficient authority to engage in policy planning and implementation on behalf of such agencies.

(F) Agency for Preschool Services - Not less than 1 member shall be from the State educational agency responsible for preschool services to children with disabilities and shall have sufficient authority to engage in policy planning and implementation on behalf of such agency.

(G) State Medicaid Agency - Not less than 1 member shall be from the agency responsible for the State Medicaid program.

(H) Head Start Agency - Not less than 1 member shall be a representative from a Head Start agency or program in the State.

(I) Child Care Agency - Not less than 1 member shall be a representative from a State agency responsible for child care.

(J) Agency for Health Insurance - Not less than 1 member shall be from the agency responsible for the State regulation of health insurance.

(K) Office of the Coordinator of Education of Homeless Children and Youth - Not less than 1 member shall be a representative designated by the Office of Coordinator for Education of Homeless Children and Youths.

(L) State Foster Care Representative - Not less than 1 member shall be a representative from the State child welfare agency responsible for foster care.

(M) Mental Health Agency - Not less than 1 member shall be a representative from the State agency responsible for children's mental health.

(2) Other Members - The council may include other members selected by the Governor, including a representative from the Bureau of Indian Affairs (BIA), or where there is no BIA-operated or BIA-funded school, from the Indian Health Service or the tribe or tribal council.

(c) Meetings - The council shall meet, at a minimum, on a quarterly basis, and in such places as the council determines necessary. The meetings shall be publicly announced, and, to the extent appropriate, open and accessible to the general public.

(d) Management Authority - Subject to the approval of the Governor, the council may prepare and approve a budget using funds under this part to conduct hearings and forums, to reimburse members of the council for reasonable and necessary expenses for attending council meetings and performing council duties (including child care for parent representatives), to pay compensation to a member of the council if the member is not employed or must forfeit wages from other employment when performing official council business, to hire staff, and to obtain the services of such professional, technical, and clerical personnel as may be necessary to carry out its functions under this part.

(e) Functions of Council -

(1) Duties - The council shall -

(A) advise and assist the lead agency designated or established under Section 1435(a)(10) in the performance of the responsibilities set forth in such section, particularly the identification of the sources of fiscal and other support for services for early intervention programs, assignment of financial responsibility to the appropriate agency, and the promotion of the interagency agreements;

(B) advise and assist the lead agency in the preparation of applications and amendments thereto;

(C) advise and assist the State educational agency regarding the transition of toddlers with disabilities to preschool and other appropriate services; and

(D) prepare and submit an annual report to the Governor and to the Secretary on the status of early intervention programs for infants and toddlers with disabilities and their families operated within the State.

(2) Authorized Activity - The council may advise and assist the lead agency and the State educational agency regarding the provision of appropriate services for children from birth through age 5. The council may advise appropriate agencies in the State with respect to the integration of services for infants and toddlers with disabilities and at-risk infants and toddlers and their families, regardless of whether at-risk infants and toddlers are eligible for early intervention services in the State.

(f) Conflict of Interest - No member of the council shall cast a vote on any matter that is likely to provide a direct financial benefit to that member or otherwise give the appearance of a conflict of interest under State law.

20 U. S. C. § 1442. Federal Administration.

WRIGHTSLAW OVERVIEW: Much of the language in Part B applies to this section. If the "lead agency" is not the State Education Agency (SEA), these requirements shall apply to the state and local mental health, social service, early intervention, health department, or other such agency that is appointed as the "lead agency."

Sections 1416, 1417, and 1418 shall, to the extent not inconsistent with this part, apply to the program authorized by this part, except that -

(1) any reference in such sections to a State educational agency shall be considered to be a reference to a State's lead agency established or designated under Section 1435(a)(10);

(2) any reference in such sections to a local educational agency, educational service agency, or a State agency shall be considered to be a reference to an early intervention service provider under this part; and

(3) any reference to the education of children with disabilities or the education of all children with disabilities shall be considered to be a reference to the provision of appropriate early intervention services to infants and toddlers with disabilities.

20 U. S. C. § 1443. Allocation of Funds.

WRIGHTSLAW OVERVIEW: This section describes the formulas and percentages related to the allocation and distribution of funds.

(a) Reservation of Funds for Outlying Areas -

(1) In General - From the sums appropriated to carry out this part for any fiscal year, the Secretary may reserve not more than 1 percent for payments to Guam, American Samoa, the United States Virgin Islands, and the Commonwealth of the Northern Mariana Islands in accordance with their respective needs for assistance under this part.

(2) Consolidation of Funds - The provisions of Public Law 95-134, permitting the consolidation of grants to the outlying areas, shall not apply to funds those areas receive under this part.

(b) Payments to Indians -

(1) In General - The Secretary shall, subject to this subsection, make payments to the Secretary of the Interior to be distributed to tribes, tribal organizations (as defined under Section 4 of the Indian Self-Determination and Education Assistance Act), or consortia of the above entities for the coordination of assistance in the provision of early intervention services by the States to infants and toddlers with disabilities and their families on reservations served by elementary schools and secondary schools for Indian children operated or funded by the Department of the Interior. The amount of such payment for any fiscal year shall be 1.25 percent of the aggregate of the amount available to all States under this part for such fiscal year.

(2) Allocation - For each fiscal year, the Secretary of the Interior shall distribute the entire payment received under paragraph (1) by providing to each tribe, tribal organization, or consortium an amount based on the number of infants and toddlers residing on the reservation, as determined annually, divided by the total of such children served by all tribes, tribal organizations, or consortia.

(3) Information - To receive a payment under this subsection, the tribe, tribal organization, or consortium shall submit such information to the Secretary of the Interior as is needed to determine the amounts to be distributed under paragraph (2).

(4) Use of Funds - The funds received by a tribe, tribal organization, or consortium shall be used to assist States in child find, screening, and other procedures for the early identification of Indian children under 3 years of age and for parent training. Such funds may also be used to provide early intervention services in accordance with this part. Such activities may be carried out directly or through contracts or cooperative agreements with the Bureau of Indian Affairs, local educational agencies, and other public or private nonprofit organizations. The tribe, tribal organization, or consortium is encouraged to involve Indian parents in the development and implementation of these activities. The above entities shall, as appropriate, make referrals to local, State, or Federal entities for the provision of services or further diagnosis.

(5) Reports - To be eligible to receive a payment under paragraph (2), a tribe, tribal organization, or consortium shall make a biennial report to the Secretary of the Interior of activities undertaken under this subsection, including the number of contracts and cooperative agreements entered into, the number of infants and toddlers contacted and receiving services for each year, and the estimated number of infants and toddlers needing services during the 2 years following the year in which the report is made. The Secretary of the Interior shall include a summary of this information on a biennial basis to the Secretary of Education along with such other information as required under Section 1411(h)(3)(E). The Secretary of Education may require any additional information from the Secretary of the Interior.

(6) Prohibited Uses of Funds - None of the funds under this subsection may be used by the Secretary of the Interior for administrative purposes, including child count, and the provision of technical assistance.

(c) State Allotments -

(1) In General - Except as provided in paragraphs (2) and (3), from the funds remaining for each fiscal year after the reservation and payments under subsections (a), (b), and (e), the Secretary shall first allot to each State an amount that bears the same ratio to the amount of such remainder as the number of infants and toddlers in the State bears to the number of infants and toddlers in all States.

(2) Minimum Allotments - Except as provided in paragraph (3), no State shall receive an amount under this section for any fiscal year that is less than the greater of –

(A) 1/2 of 1 percent of the remaining amount described in paragraph (1); or

(B) $500,000.

(3) Ratable Reduction -

(A) In General - If the sums made available under this part for any fiscal year are insufficient to pay the full amounts that all States are eligible to receive under this subsection for such year, the Secretary shall ratably reduce the allotments to such States for such year.

(B) **Additional Funds** - If additional funds become available for making payments under this subsection for a fiscal year, allotments that were reduced under subparagraph (A) shall be increased on the same basis the allotments were reduced.

(4) **Definitions** - In this subsection–

(A) the terms '**infants and toddlers**' mean children under 3 years of age; and

(B) the term 'State' means each of the 50 States, the District of Columbia, and the Commonwealth of Puerto Rico.

(d) **Reallotment of Funds** - If a State elects not to receive its allotment under subsection (c), the Secretary shall reallot, among the remaining States, amounts from such State in accordance with such subsection.

(e) **Reservation for State Incentive Grants** -

(1) **In General** - For any fiscal year for which the amount appropriated pursuant to the authorization of appropriations under Section 1444 exceeds $460,000,000, the Secretary shall reserve 15 percent of such appropriated amount to provide grants to States that are carrying out the policy described in Section 1435(c) in order to facilitate the implementation of such policy.

(2) **Amount of Grant** -

(A) **In General** - Notwithstanding paragraphs (2) and (3) of subsection (c), the Secretary shall provide a grant to each State under paragraph (1) in an amount that bears the same ratio to the amount reserved under such paragraph as the number of infants and toddlers in the State bears to the number of infants and toddlers in all States receiving grants under such paragraph.

(B) **Maximum Amount** - No State shall receive a grant under paragraph (1) for any fiscal year in an amount that is greater than 20 percent of the amount reserved under such paragraph for the fiscal year.

(3) **Carryover of Amounts** -

(A) **First Succeeding Fiscal Year** - Pursuant to Section 421(b) of the General Education Provisions Act, amounts under a grant provided under paragraph (1) that are not obligated and expended prior to the beginning of the first fiscal year succeeding the fiscal year for which such amounts were appropriated shall remain available for obligation and expenditure during such first succeeding fiscal year.

(B) **Second Succeeding Fiscal Year** - Amounts under a grant provided under paragraph (1) that are not obligated and expended prior to the beginning of the second fiscal year succeeding the fiscal year for which such amounts were appropriated shall be returned to the Secretary and used to make grants to States under Section 1433 (from their allotments under this section) during such second succeeding fiscal year.

20 U. S. C. § 1444. Authorization of Appropriations.

WRIGHTSLAW OVERVIEW: This section authorizes funds for fiscal years 2005 through 2010.

For the purpose of carrying out this part, there are authorized to be appropriated such sums as may be necessary for each of the fiscal years 2005 through 2010.

End of Part C

Part D — National Activities to Improve Education of Children with Disabilities

WRIGHTSLAW OVERVIEW: Part D was revised and reorganized into four subparts. This Part authorizes and provides funding for activities to improve the educational outcomes for children with disabilities. Findings is in Section 1450. Subpart 1 about State Personnel Development Grants includes purpose, definition of personnel, eligibility, applications, and how funds may be used. Subpart 2 about Personnel Preparation focuses improving educational outcomes and results by improving teacher training and professional development. Subpart 3 describes requirements for Parent Training and Information Centers and Community Resource Centers. Subpart 4 is General Provisions.

20 U. S. C. § 1450. Findings

Subpart 1 – State Personnel Development Grants

20 U. S. C. § 1451. Purpose; Definition of Personnel; Program Authority
20 U. S. C. § 1452. Eligibility and Collaborative Process
20 U. S. C. § 1453. Applications
20 U. S. C. § 1454. Use of Funds
20 U. S. C. § 1455. Authorization of Appropriations

Subpart 2 – Personnel Preparation, Technical Assistance, Model Demonstration Projects, and Dissemination of Information

20 U. S. C. § 1461. Purpose; Definition of Eligible Entity
20 U. S. C. § 1462. Personnel Development to Improve Services and Results for Children with Disabilities
20 U. S. C. § 1463. Technical Assistance, Demonstration Projects, Dissemination of Information, and Implementation of Scientifically Based Research
20 U. S. C. § 1464. Studies and Evaluations
20 U. S. C. § 1465. Interim Alternative Educational Settings, Behavioral Supports, and Systematic School Interventions
20 U. S. C. § 1466. Authorization of Appropriations

Subpart 3 – Supports to Improve Results for Children with Disabilities

20 U. S. C. § 1470. Purposes
20 U. S. C. § 1471. Parent Training and Information Centers
20 U. S. C. § 1472. Community Parent Resource Centers
20 U. S. C. § 1473. Technical Assistance for Parent Training and Information Centers
20 U. S. C. § 1474. Technology Development, Demonstration and Utilization; Media Services; and Instructional Materials
20 U. S. C. § 1475. Authorization of Appropriations

Subpart 4 – General Provisions

20 U. S. C. § 1481. Comprehensive Plan for Subparts 2 and 3
20 U. S. C. § 1482. Administrative Provisions

20 U. S. C. § 1450. Findings.

WRIGHTSLAW OVERVIEW: Congress made changes to "Findings." Section 1450 describes the critical need for adequately trained personnel and for "high quality, comprehensive professional development programs" so individuals who teach children with disabilities have the necessary knowledge and skills. Congress also emphasized the needs of parents for information and training to deal with the "multiple pressures of parenting," to build constructive working relationships with school personnel, and to be involved in planning and decision-making about early intervention, educational, and transition services for their children.

Congress finds the following:

(1) The Federal Government has an ongoing obligation to support activities that contribute to positive results for children with disabilities, enabling those children to lead productive and independent adult lives.

(2) Systemic change benefiting all students, including children with disabilities, requires the involvement of States, local educational agencies, parents, individuals with disabilities and their families, teachers and other service providers, and other interested individuals and organizations to develop and implement comprehensive strategies that improve educational results for children with disabilities.

(3) State educational agencies, in partnership with local educational agencies, parents of children with disabilities, and other individuals and organizations, are in the best position to improve education for children with disabilities and to address their special needs.

(4) **An effective educational system serving students with disabilities should -**

(A) **maintain high academic achievement standards** and clear performance goals for children with disabilities, consistent with the standards and expectations for all students in the educational system, and provide for appropriate and effective strategies and methods to ensure that all children with disabilities have the opportunity to achieve those standards and goals;

(B) clearly **define, in objective, measurable terms, the school and post-school results** that children with disabilities are expected to achieve; and

(C) **promote transition services** and coordinate State and local education, social, health, mental health, and other services, in addressing the full range of student needs, particularly the needs of children with disabilities who need significant levels of support to participate and learn in school and the community.

(5) The availability of an adequate number of qualified personnel is critical -

(A) to serve effectively children with disabilities;

(B) to assume leadership positions in administration and direct services;

(C) to provide teacher training; and

(D) to conduct high quality research to improve special education.

(6) High quality, comprehensive professional development programs are essential to ensure that the persons responsible for the education or transition of children with disabilities possess the skills and knowledge necessary to address the educational and related needs of those children.

(7) Models of professional development should be scientifically based and reflect successful practices, including strategies for recruiting, preparing, and retaining personnel.

(8) Continued support is essential for the development and maintenance of a coordinated and high quality program of research to inform successful teaching practices and model curricula for educating children with disabilities.

(9) Training, technical assistance, support, and dissemination activities are necessary to ensure that Parts B and C are fully implemented and achieve high quality early intervention, educational, and transitional results for children with disabilities and their families.

(10) Parents, teachers, administrators, and related services personnel need technical assistance and information in a timely, coordinated, and accessible manner in order to improve early intervention, educational, and

transitional services and results at the State and local levels for children with disabilities and their families.

(11) Parent training and information activities assist parents of a child with a disability in dealing with the multiple pressures of parenting such a child and are of particular importance in -

(A) playing a vital role in creating and preserving constructive relationships between parents of children with disabilities and schools by facilitating open communication between the parents and schools; encouraging dispute resolution at the earliest possible point in time; and discouraging the escalation of an adversarial process between the parents and schools;

(B) ensuring the involvement of parents in planning and decisionmaking with respect to early intervention, educational, and transitional services;

(C) achieving high quality early intervention, educational, and transitional results for children with disabilities;

(D) providing such parents information on their rights, protections, and responsibilities under this title to ensure improved early intervention, educational, and transitional results for children with disabilities;

(E) assisting such parents in the development of skills to participate effectively in the education and development of their children and in the transitions described in Section 1473(b)(6);

(F) supporting the roles of such parents as participants within partnerships seeking to improve early intervention, educational, and transitional services and results for children with disabilities and their families; and

(G) supporting such parents who may have limited access to services and supports, due to economic, cultural, or linguistic barriers.

(12) Support is needed to improve technological resources and integrate technology, including universally designed technologies, into the lives of children with disabilities, parents of children with disabilities, school personnel, and others through curricula, services, and assistive technologies.

Subpart 1 - State Personnel Development Grants

WRIGHTSLAW OVERVIEW: Subpart 1 about State Personnel Development Grants (Sections 1451 to 1455) includes purpose, definition of personnel, eligibility, applications, and how funds may be used.

20 U. S. C. § 1451. Purpose; Definition of Personnel; Program Authority.

WRIGHTSLAW OVERVIEW: Section 1451(a) describes the need to reform and improve personnel preparation and professional development programs to improve results for children with disabilities. The definition of "personnel" is in Section 1451(b). This section includes information about competitive grants, formula grants and continuation awards.

(a) **Purpose.** The purpose of this subpart is to assist State educational agencies in reforming and improving their systems for personnel preparation and professional development in early intervention, educational, and transition services in order to improve results for children with disabilities.

(b) **Definition of Personnel.** In this subpart the term 'personnel' means special education teachers, regular education teachers, principals, administrators, related services personnel, paraprofessionals, and early intervention personnel serving infants, toddlers, preschoolers, or children with disabilities, except where a particular category of personnel, such as related services personnel, is identified.

(c) **Competitive Grants.**

(1) **In General.** Except as provided in subsection (d), for any fiscal year for which the amount appropriated under Section 1455, that remains after the Secretary reserves funds under subsection (e) for the fiscal year, is less than $100,000,000, the Secretary shall award grants, on a competitive basis, to State educational agencies to carry out the activities described in the State plan submitted under Section 1453.

(2) Priority. In awarding grants under paragraph (1), the Secretary may give priority to State educational agencies that -

(A) are in States with the greatest personnel shortages; or

(B) demonstrate the greatest difficulty meeting the requirements of Section 1412(a)(14).

(3) Minimum Amount. The Secretary shall make a grant to each State educational agency selected under paragraph (1) in an amount for each fiscal year that is -

(A) not less than $500,000, nor more than $4,000,000, in the case of the 50 States, the District of Columbia, and the Commonwealth of Puerto Rico; and

(B) not less than $80,000 in the case of an outlying area.

(4) Increase in Amount. The Secretary may increase the amounts of grants under paragraph (4) to account for inflation.

(5) Factors. The Secretary shall determine the amount of a grant under paragraph (1) after considering -

(A) the amount of funds available for making the grants;

(B) the relative population of the State or outlying area;

(C) the types of activities proposed by the State or outlying area;

(D) the alignment of proposed activities with Section 1412(a)(14);

(E) the alignment of proposed activities with the State plans and applications submitted under Sections 1111 and 2112, respectively, of the Elementary and Secondary Education Act of 1965; and

(F) the use, as appropriate, of scientifically based research activities.

(d) Formula Grants.

(1) In General. Except as provided in paragraphs (2) and (3), for the first fiscal year for which the amount appropriated under Section 1455, that remains after the Secretary reserves funds under subsection (e) for the fiscal year, is equal to or greater than $100,000,000, and for each fiscal year thereafter, the Secretary shall allot to each State educational agency, whose application meets the requirements of this subpart, an amount that bears the same relation to the amount remaining as the amount the State received under Section 1411(d) for that fiscal year bears to the amount of funds received by all States (whose applications meet the requirements of this subpart) under Section 1411(d) for that fiscal year.

(2) Minimum Allotments for States That Received Competitive Grants.

(A) In General. The amount allotted under this subsection to any State educational agency that received a competitive multi-year grant under subsection (c) for which the grant period has not expired shall be not less than the amount specified for that fiscal year in the State educational agency's grant award document under that subsection.

(B) Special Rule. Each such State educational agency shall use the minimum amount described in subparagraph (A) for the activities described in the State educational agency's competitive grant award document for that year, unless the Secretary approves a request from the State educational agency to spend the funds on other activities.

(3) Minimum Allotment. The amount of any State educational agency's allotment under this subsection for any fiscal year shall not be less than -

(A) the greater of $500,000 or 1/2 of 1 percent of the total amount available under this subsection for that year, in the case of each of the 50 States, the District of Columbia, and the Commonwealth of Puerto Rico; and

(B) $80,000, in the case of an outlying area.

(4) Direct Benefit. In using grant funds allotted under paragraph (1), a State educational agency shall, through grants, contracts, or cooperative agreements, undertake activities that significantly and directly benefit the local educational agencies in the State.

(e) Continuation Awards.

(1) In General. Notwithstanding any other provision of this subpart, from funds appropriated under Section 1455 for each fiscal year, the Secretary shall reserve the amount that is necessary to make a continuation award to any State educational agency (at the request of the State educational agency) that received a multi-year award under this part (as this part was in effect on the day before the date of enactment of the Individuals with Disabilities Education Improvement Act of 2004), to enable the State educational agency to carry out activities in accordance with the terms of the multi-year award.

(2) Prohibition. A State educational agency that receives a continuation award under paragraph (1) for any fiscal year may not receive any other award under this Subpart for that fiscal year.

20 U. S. C. § 1452. Eligibility and Collaborative Process.

WRIGHTSLAW OVERVIEW: To receive grants under this section, state education agencies (SEAs) are required to develop partnerships with institutions of higher learning, state agencies that provide early intervention services, and other partners, including community-based and nonprofit organizations and organizations that represent the interests of individuals with disabilities and their parents.

(a) Eligible Applicants. A State educational agency may apply for a grant under this subpart for a grant period of not less than 1 year and not more than 5 years.

(b) Partners.

(1) In General. In order to be considered for a grant under this subpart, a State educational agency shall establish a partnership with local educational agencies and other State agencies involved in, or concerned with, the education of children with disabilities, including -

(A) not less than 1 institution of higher education; and

(B) the State agencies responsible for administering Part C, early education, child care, and vocational rehabilitation programs.

(2) Other Partners. In **order to be considered for a grant** under this subpart, a State educational agency shall work **in partnership with other persons and organizations** involved in, and concerned with, the education of children with disabilities, which may include -

(A) the Governor;

(B) parents of children with disabilities ages birth through 26;

(C) parents of nondisabled children ages birth through 26;

(D) individuals with disabilities;

(E) parent training and information centers or community parent resource centers funded under Sections 1471 and 1472, respectively;

(F) **community based and other nonprofit organizations** involved in the education and employment of individuals with disabilities;

(G) personnel as defined in Section 1451(b);

(H) the State advisory panel established under Part B;

(I) the State interagency coordinating council established under Part C;

(J) individuals knowledgeable about vocational education;

(K) the State agency for higher education;

(L) public agencies with jurisdiction in the areas of health, mental health, social services, and juvenile justice;

(M) other providers of professional development that work with infants, toddlers, preschoolers, and children with disabilities; and

(N) other individuals.

(3) **Required Partner.** If State law assigns responsibility for teacher preparation and certification to an individual, entity, or agency other than the State educational agency, the State educational agency shall -

(A) include that individual, entity, or agency as a partner in the partnership under this subsection; and

(B) ensure that any activities the State educational agency will carry out under this subpart that are within that partner's jurisdiction (which may include activities described in Section 1454(b)) are carried out by that partner.

20 U. S. C. § 1453. Applications.

WRIGHTSLAW OVERVIEW: Section 1453 describes the application process that state departments of education must complete before they can receive grants under Part D. The state plan shall include a plan that identifies and addresses state and local needs for personnel preparation and professional development. Section 1453(b) describes required elements of the state personnel development plan. Section 1453(c) describes requirements for using experts as peer reviewers of state plans.

(a) In General.

(1) **Submission.** A State educational agency that desires to receive a grant under this subpart shall submit to the Secretary an application at such time, in such manner, and including such information as the Secretary may require.

(2) **State Plan.** The application **shall include a plan** that identifies and addresses the State and local needs for the personnel preparation and professional development of personnel, as well as individuals who provide direct supplementary aids and services to children with disabilities, and that -

(A) is designed to enable the State to meet the requirements of Section 1412(a)(14) and Section 1435(a)(8) and (9);

(B) is based on an assessment of State and local needs that identifies critical aspects and areas in need of improvement related to the preparation, ongoing training, and professional development of personnel who serve infants, toddlers, preschoolers, and children with disabilities within the State, including -

(i) current and anticipated personnel vacancies and shortages; and

(ii) the number of preservice and inservice programs; and

(C) is integrated and aligned, to the maximum extent possible, with State plans and activities under the Elementary and Secondary Education Act of 1965, the Rehabilitation Act of 1973, and the Higher Education Act of 1965.

(3) **Requirement.** The State application shall contain an assurance that the State educational agency will carry out each of the strategies described in subsection (b)(4).

(b) Elements of State Personnel Development Plan. Each **State personnel development plan** under subsection (a)(2) shall-

(1) describe a partnership agreement that is in effect for the period of the grant, which agreement shall specify-

(A) the nature and extent of the partnership described in Section 1452(b) and the respective roles of each member of the partnership, including the partner described in Section 1452(b)(3) if applicable; and

(B) how the State educational agency will work with other persons and organizations involved in, and concerned with, the education of children with disabilities, including the respective roles of each of the persons and organizations;

(2) describe how the strategies and activities described in paragraph (4) will be coordinated with activities supported with other public resources (including Part B and Part C funds retained for use at the State level for personnel and professional development purposes) and private resources;

(3) describe how the State educational agency will align its personnel development plan under this subpart with the plan and application submitted under Sections 1111 and 2112, respectively, of the Elementary and Secondary Education Act of 1965;

(4) describe those strategies the State educational agency will use to address the professional development and personnel needs identified under subsection (a)(2) and how such strategies will be implemented, including

(A) a description of the programs and activities to be supported under this subpart that will provide personnel with the knowledge and skills to meet the needs of, and improve the performance and achievement of, infants, toddlers, preschoolers, and children with disabilities; and

(B) how such strategies will be integrated, to the maximum extent possible, with other activities supported by grants funded under Section 1462;

(5) provide an assurance that the State educational agency will provide technical assistance to local educational agencies to improve the quality of professional development available to meet the needs of personnel who serve children with disabilities;

(6) provide an assurance that the State educational agency will provide technical assistance to entities that provide services to infants and toddlers with disabilities to improve the quality of professional development available to meet the needs of personnel serving such children;

(7) describe how the State educational agency will recruit and retain highly qualified teachers and other qualified personnel in geographic areas of greatest need;

(8) describe the steps the State educational agency will take to ensure that poor and minority children are not taught at higher rates by teachers who are not highly qualified; and

(9) describe how the State educational agency will assess, on a regular basis, the extent to which the strategies implemented under this subpart have been effective in meeting the performance goals described in Section 1412(a)(15).

(c) Peer Review.

(1) In General. The Secretary shall use a **panel of experts** who are competent, by virtue of their training, expertise, or experience, to evaluate applications for grants under Section 1451(c)(1).

(2) Composition of Panel. A majority of a panel described in paragraph (1) shall be composed of individuals who are not employees of the Federal Government.

(3) Payment of Fees and Expenses of Certain Members. The Secretary may use available funds appropriated to carry out this subpart to pay the expenses and fees of panel members who are not employees of the Federal Government.

(d) Reporting Procedures. Each State educational agency that receives a grant under this subpart shall submit annual performance reports to the Secretary. The reports shall -

(1) describe the progress of the State educational agency in implementing its plan;

(2) analyze the effectiveness of the State educational agency's activities under this subpart and of the State educational agency's strategies for meeting its goals under Section 1412(a)(15); and

(3) identify changes in the strategies used by the State educational agency and described in subsection (b)(4), if any, to improve the State educational agency's performance.

20 U. S. C. § 1454. Use of Funds.

WRIGHTSLAW OVERVIEW: Section 1454 describes how states may use funds under Part D. Funds may be used for professional development to improve teaching practices by using effective instructional strategies, methods and skills. Funds may be used to train administrators and other school personnel to conduct effective IEP and IFSP meetings. Funds may be used to recruit and retain highly qualified special education teachers, reform tenure systems, test the subject matter knowledge of teachers, and reform certification and licensing requirements so teachers have subject matter knowledge and teaching skills.

(a) **Professional Development Activities.** A State educational agency that receives a grant under this subpart shall use the grant funds to support activities in accordance with the State's plan described in Section 1453, including 1 or more of the following:

(1) Carrying out programs that provide support to both special education and regular education teachers of children with disabilities and principals, such as programs that -

(A) provide teacher mentoring, team teaching, reduced class schedules and case loads, and intensive professional development;

(B) use standards or assessments for guiding beginning teachers that are consistent with challenging State student academic achievement and functional standards and with the requirements for professional development, as defined in Section 9101 of the Elementary and Secondary Education Act of 1965; and

(C) encourage collaborative and consultative models of providing early intervention, special education, and related services.

(2) Encouraging and supporting the training of special education and regular education teachers and administrators to effectively use and integrate technology -

(A) into curricula and instruction, including training to improve the ability to collect, manage, and analyze data to improve teaching, decision-making, school improvement efforts, and accountability;

(B) to enhance learning by children with disabilities; and

(C) to effectively communicate with parents.

(3) Providing professional development activities that -

(A) improve the knowledge of special education and regular education teachers concerning -

(i) the academic and developmental or functional needs of students with disabilities; or

(ii) effective instructional strategies, methods, and skills, and the use of State academic content standards and student academic achievement and functional standards, and State assessments, to improve teaching practices and student academic achievement;

(B) improve the **knowledge of special education and regular education teachers and principals** and, in appropriate cases, paraprofessionals, **concerning effective instructional practices**, and that -

(i) provide training in how to teach and address the needs of children with different learning styles and children who are limited English proficient;

(ii) involve collaborative groups of teachers, administrators, and, in appropriate cases, related services personnel;

(iii) provide **training in methods of** -

(I) **positive behavioral interventions** and supports to improve student behavior in the classroom;

(II) **scientifically based reading instruction**, including early literacy instruction;

(III) early and appropriate interventions to identify and help children with disabilities;

(IV) effective instruction for children with low incidence disabilities;

(V) successful transitioning to postsecondary opportunities; and

(VI) using classroom-based techniques to assist children prior to referral for special education;

(iv) provide training to enable personnel to work with and involve parents in their child's education, including parents of low income and limited English proficient children with disabilities;

(v) provide training for **special education personnel and regular education personnel** in planning, developing, and implementing effective and appropriate IEPs; and

(vi) provide training to meet the needs of students with significant health, mobility, or behavioral needs prior to serving such students;

(C) train administrators, principals, and other relevant school personnel in conducting effective IEP meetings; and

(D) train early intervention, preschool, and related services providers, and other relevant school personnel, in conducting effective individualized family service plan (IFSP) meetings.

(4) Developing and implementing initiatives to promote the recruitment and retention of highly qualified special education teachers, particularly initiatives that have been proven effective in recruiting and retaining highly qualified teachers, including programs that provide -

(A) teacher mentoring from exemplary special education teachers, principals, or superintendents;

(B) induction and support for special education teachers during their first 3 years of employment as teachers; or

(C) incentives, including financial incentives, to retain special education teachers who have a record of success in helping students with disabilities.

(5) Carrying out programs and activities that are designed to improve the quality of personnel who serve children with disabilities, such as -

(A) innovative professional development programs (which may be provided through partnerships that include institutions of higher education), including programs that train teachers and principals to integrate technology into curricula and instruction to improve teaching, learning, and technology literacy, which professional development shall be consistent with the definition of professional development in Section 9101 of the Elementary and Secondary Education Act of 1965; and

(B) the development and use of proven, cost effective strategies for the implementation of professional development activities, such as through the use of technology and distance learning.

(6) Carrying out programs and activities that are designed to improve the quality of early intervention personnel, including paraprofessionals and primary referral sources, such as -

(A) professional development programs to improve the delivery of early intervention services;

(B) initiatives to promote the recruitment and retention of early intervention personnel; and

(C) interagency activities to ensure that early intervention personnel are adequately prepared and trained.

(b) Other Activities. A State educational agency that receives a grant under this subpart shall use the grant funds to support activities in accordance with the State's plan described in Section 1453, including 1 or more of the following

(1) **Reforming special education and regular education teacher certification** (including recertification) or licensing requirements **to ensure that** -

(A) **special education and regular education teachers** have -

(i) the training and information necessary to address the full range of needs of children with disabilities across disability categories; and

(ii) the necessary subject matter knowledge and teaching skills in the academic subjects that the teachers teach;

(B) special education and regular education teacher certification (including recertification) or licensing requirements are aligned with challenging State academic content standards; and

(C) special education and regular education teachers have the **subject matter knowledge and teaching skills**, including technology literacy, necessary to help students with disabilities meet challenging State student academic achievement and functional standards.

(2) Programs that establish, expand, or improve alternative routes for State certification of special education teachers for highly qualified individuals with a baccalaureate or master's degree, including mid-career professionals from other occupations, paraprofessionals, and recent college or university graduates with records of academic distinction who demonstrate the potential to become highly effective special education teachers.

(3) Teacher advancement initiatives for special education teachers that promote professional growth and emphasize multiple career paths (such as paths to becoming a career teacher, mentor teacher, or exemplary teacher) and pay differentiation.

(4) Developing and implementing mechanisms to assist local educational agencies and schools in effectively recruiting and retaining highly qualified special education teachers.

(5) Reforming tenure systems, **implementing teacher testing for subject matter knowledge**, and implementing teacher testing for State certification or licensing, consistent with title II of the Higher Education Act of 1965.

(6) Funding projects to promote reciprocity of teacher certification or licensing between or among States for special education teachers, except that no reciprocity agreement developed under this paragraph or developed using funds provided under this subpart may lead to the weakening of any State teaching certification or licensing requirement.

(7) Assisting local educational agencies to serve children with disabilities through the development and use of proven, innovative strategies to deliver intensive professional development programs that are both cost effective and easily accessible, such as strategies that involve delivery through the use of technology, peer networks, and distance learning.

(8) Developing, or assisting local educational agencies in developing, merit based performance systems, and strategies that provide differential and bonus pay for special education teachers.

(9) Supporting activities that ensure that teachers are able to use challenging State academic content standards and student academic achievement and functional standards, and State assessments for all children with disabilities, to improve instructional practices and improve the academic achievement of children with disabilities.

(10) When applicable, coordinating with, and expanding centers established under, Section 2113(c)(18) of the Elementary and Secondary Education Act of 1965 to benefit special education teachers.

(c) **Contracts and Subgrants.** A State educational agency that receives a grant under this subpart -

(1) shall award contracts or subgrants to local educational agencies, institutions of higher education, parent training and information centers, or community parent resource centers, as appropriate, to carry out its State plan under this subpart; and

(2) may award contracts and subgrants to other public and private entities, including the lead agency under Part C, to carry out the State plan.

(d) **Use of Funds for Professional Development.** A State educational agency that receives a grant under this subpart shall use -

(1) not less than 90 percent of the funds the State educational agency receives under the grant for any fiscal

year for activities under subsection (a); and

(2) not more than 10 percent of the funds the State educational agency receives under the grant for any fiscal year for activities under subsection (b).

(e) Grants to Outlying Areas. Public Law 95-134, permitting the consolidation of grants to the outlying areas, shall not apply to funds received under this subpart.

20 U. S. C. § 1455. Authorization of Appropriations.

There are authorized to be appropriated to carry out this subpart such sums as may be necessary for each of the fiscal years 2005 through 2010.

Subpart 2 – Personnel Preparation, Technical Assistance, Model Demonstration Projects, and Dissemination of Information

WRIGHTSLAW OVERVIEW: Subpart 2 provides federal funds to improve early intervention, special education, and transition for children with disabilities by improving teacher training and professional development programs and helping States to improve their educational systems.

20 U. S. C. § 1461. Purpose; Definition of Eligible Entity.

WRIGHTSLAW OVERVIEW: Section 1461(a) describes the purpose of this statute – to improve early intervention, educational and transitional results for children with disabilities by helping states improve their educational systems.

(a) Purpose. The purpose of this subpart is -

(1) to provide **Federal funding for personnel preparation**, technical assistance, model demonstration projects, information dissemination, and studies and evaluations, in order to improve early intervention, educational, and transitional results for children with disabilities; and

(2) to assist State educational agencies and local educational agencies in improving their education systems for children with disabilities.

(b) Definition of Eligible Entity.

(1) In General. In this subpart, the term 'eligible entity' means -

(A) a State educational agency;

(B) a local educational agency;

(C) a public charter school that is a local educational agency under State law;

(D) an institution of higher education;

(E) a public agency not described in subparagraphs (A) through (D);

(F) a **private nonprofit organization**;

(G) an outlying area;

(H) an Indian tribe or a tribal organization (as defined under Section 4 of the Indian Self-Determination and Education Assistance Act); or

(I) a **for-profit organization**, if the Secretary finds it appropriate in light of the purposes of a particular competition for a grant, contract, or cooperative agreement under this subpart.

(2) Special Rule. The Secretary may limit which eligible entities described in paragraph (1) are eligible for a grant, contract, or cooperative agreement under this subpart to 1 or more of the categories of eligible entities described in paragraph (1).

20 U. S. C. § 1462. Personnel Development to Improve Services and Results for Children with Disabilities.

WRIGHTSLAW OVERVIEW: Section 1462 is new. This section addresses the need to ensure that all teachers have the necessary skills and knowledge of educational practices that have been determined, through scientifically based research, to be successful. To accomplish this goal, states need to shift the focus to academics in special education teacher preparation programs. Section 1462(a)(7) describes professional development for administrators in instructional leadership, behavior support, assessment, accountability, and positive relationships with parents. Section 1462(b) describes personnel development and support for beginning special educators, including an extended clinical learning opportunity or supervised practicum (5th year). Section 1462(c) describes preparation of individuals to work with students with low incidence disabilities. Section 1462(g) and (h) describe scholarships and service obligations.

(a) **In General.** The Secretary, on a competitive basis, shall award grants to, or enter into contracts or cooperative agreements with, eligible entities to carry out 1 or more of the following objectives:

(1) To help address the needs identified in the State plan described in Section 1453(a)(2) for highly qualified personnel, as defined in Section 1451(b), to work with infants or toddlers with disabilities, or children with disabilities, consistent with the qualifications described in Section 1412(a)(14).

(2) To ensure that those personnel have the necessary skills and knowledge, derived from practices that have been determined, through scientifically based research, to be successful in serving those children.

(3) To encourage **increased focus on academics and core content areas** in special education personnel preparation programs.

(4) To ensure that regular education teachers have the necessary skills and knowledge to provide instruction to students with disabilities in the regular education classroom.

(5) To ensure that all special education teachers are highly qualified.

(6) To ensure that preservice and in-service personnel preparation programs include training in -

(A) the use of new technologies;

(B) the area of early intervention, educational, and transition services;

(C) effectively involving parents; and

(D) positive behavioral supports.

(7) To provide high-quality professional development for principals, superintendents, and other administrators, including training in -

(A) instructional leadership;

(B) behavioral supports in the school and classroom;

(C) paperwork reduction;

(D) promoting improved collaboration between special education and general education teachers;

(E) assessment and accountability;

(F) ensuring effective learning environments; and

(G) fostering positive relationships with parents.

(b) **Personnel Development; Enhanced Support for Beginning Special Educators.**

(1) **In General.** In carrying out this section, the Secretary shall support activities -

(A) for personnel development, including activities for the preparation of personnel who will serve children with high incidence and low incidence disabilities, to prepare special education and general education teachers, principals, administrators, and related services personnel (and school board members, when appropriate) to meet the diverse and individualized instructional needs of children with disabilities and improve early intervention, educational, and transitional services and results for children with disabilities, consistent with the objectives described in subsection (a); and

(B) for enhanced support for beginning special educators, consistent with the objectives described in subsection (a).

(2) Personnel Development. In carrying out paragraph (1)(A), the Secretary shall support not less than 1 of the following activities:

(A) Assisting effective existing, improving existing, or developing new, collaborative personnel preparation activities undertaken by institutions of higher education, local educational agencies, and other local entities that incorporate best practices and scientifically based research, where applicable, in providing special education and general education teachers, principals, administrators, and related services personnel with the knowledge and skills to effectively support students with disabilities, including -

(i) working collaboratively in regular classroom settings;

(ii) using appropriate supports, accommodations, and curriculum modifications;

(iii) implementing effective teaching strategies, classroom-based techniques, and interventions to ensure appropriate identification of students who may be eligible for special education services, and to prevent the misidentification, inappropriate overidentification, or under-identification of children as having a disability, especially minority and limited English proficient children;

(iv) effectively working with and involving parents in the education of their children;

(v) utilizing strategies, including positive behavioral interventions, for addressing the conduct of children with disabilities that impedes their learning and that of others in the classroom;

(vi) effectively constructing IEPs, participating in IEP meetings, and implementing IEPs;

(vii) preparing children with disabilities to participate in statewide assessments (with or without accommodations) and alternate assessments, as appropriate, and to ensure that all children with disabilities are a part of all accountability systems under the Elementary and Secondary Education Act of 1965; and

(viii) working in high need elementary schools and secondary schools, including urban schools, rural schools, and schools operated by an entity described in Section 7113(d)(1)(A)(ii) of the Elementary and Secondary Education Act of 1965, and schools that serve high numbers or percentages of limited English proficient children.

(B) Developing, evaluating, and disseminating innovative models for the recruitment, induction, retention, and assessment of new, highly qualified teachers to reduce teacher shortages, especially from groups that are underrepresented in the teaching profession, including individuals with disabilities.

(C) Providing continuous personnel preparation, training, and professional development designed to provide support and ensure retention of special education and general education teachers and personnel who teach and provide related services to children with disabilities.

(D) Developing and improving programs for paraprofessionals to become special education teachers, related services personnel, and early intervention personnel, including interdisciplinary training to enable the paraprofessionals to improve early intervention, educational, and transitional results for children with disabilities.

(E) In the case of principals and superintendents, providing activities to promote instructional leadership and improved collaboration between general educators, special education teachers, and related services personnel.

(F) Supporting institutions of higher education with minority enrollments of not less than 25 percent for the purpose of preparing personnel to work with children with disabilities.

(G) Developing and improving programs to train special education teachers to develop an expertise in autism spectrum disorders.

(H) Providing continuous personnel preparation, training, and professional development designed to provide support and improve the qualifications of personnel who provide related services to children with disabilities, including to enable such personnel to obtain advanced degrees.

(3) Enhanced Support for Beginning Special Educators. In carrying out paragraph (1)(B), the Secretary shall support not less than 1 of the following activities:

(A) Enhancing and restructuring existing programs or developing preservice teacher education programs to prepare special education teachers, at colleges or departments of education within institutions of higher education, by incorporating an extended (such as an additional 5th year) clinical learning opportunity, field experience, or supervised practicum into such programs.

(B) Creating or supporting teacher-faculty partnerships (such as professional development schools) that

(i) consist of not less than -

(I) 1 or more institutions of higher education with special education personnel preparation programs;

(II) 1 or more local educational agencies that serve high numbers or percentages of low-income students; or

(III) 1 or more elementary schools or secondary schools, particularly schools that have failed to make adequate yearly progress on the basis, in whole and in part, of the assessment results of the disaggregated subgroup of students with disabilities;

(ii) may include other entities eligible for assistance under this part; and

(iii) provide -

(I) high-quality mentoring and induction opportunities with ongoing support for beginning special education teachers; or

(II) inservice professional development to beginning and veteran special education teachers through the ongoing exchange of information and instructional strategies with faculty.

(c) Low Incidence Disabilities; Authorized Activities.

(1) In General. In carrying out this section, the Secretary shall support activities, consistent with the objectives described in subsection (a) that benefit children with low incidence disabilities.

(2) Authorized Activities. Activities that may be carried out under this subsection include activities such as the following:

(A) Preparing persons who -

(i) have prior training in educational and other related service fields; and

(ii) are studying to obtain degrees, certificates, or licensure that will enable the persons to assist children with low incidence disabilities to achieve the objectives set out in their individualized education programs described in Section 1414(d), or to assist infants and toddlers with low incidence disabilities to achieve the outcomes described in their individualized family service plans described in Section 1436.

(B) Providing personnel from various disciplines with interdisciplinary training that will contribute to improvement in early intervention, educational, and transitional results for children with low incidence disabilities.

(C) Preparing personnel in the innovative uses and application of technology, including universally designed technologies, assistive technology devices, and assistive technology services -

(i) to enhance learning by children with low incidence disabilities through early intervention, educational, and transitional services; and

(ii) to improve communication with parents.

(D) Preparing personnel who provide services to visually impaired or blind children to teach and use Braille in the provision of services to such children.

(E) Preparing personnel to be qualified educational interpreters, to assist children with low incidence disabilities, particularly deaf and hard of hearing children in school and school related activities, and deaf and hard of hearing infants and toddlers and preschool children in early intervention and preschool programs.

(F) Preparing personnel who provide services to children with significant cognitive disabilities and children with multiple disabilities.

(G) Preparing personnel who provide services to children with low incidence disabilities and limited English proficient children.

(3) **Definition**. In this section, the term '**low incidence**' means -

(A) a visual or hearing impairment, or simultaneous visual and hearing impairments;

(B) a significant cognitive impairment; or

(C) any impairment for which a small number of personnel with highly specialized skills and knowledge are needed in order for children with that impairment to receive early intervention services or a free appropriate public education.

(4) **Selection of Recipients**. In selecting eligible entities for assistance under this subsection, the Secretary may give preference to eligible entities submitting applications that include 1 or more of the following:

(A) A proposal to prepare personnel in more than 1 low incidence disability, such as deafness and blindness.

(B) A demonstration of an effective collaboration between an eligible entity and a local educational agency that promotes recruitment and subsequent retention of highly qualified personnel to serve children with low incidence disabilities.

(5) **Preparation in Use of Braille**. The Secretary shall ensure that all recipients of awards under this subsection who will use that assistance to prepare personnel to provide services to visually impaired or blind children that can appropriately be provided in Braille, will prepare those individuals to provide those services in Braille.

(d) Leadership Preparation; Authorized Activities.

(1) **In General**. In carrying out this section, the Secretary shall support leadership preparation activities that are consistent with the objectives described in subsection (a).

(2) **Authorized Activities**. Activities that may be carried out under this subsection include activities such as the following:

(A) Preparing personnel at the graduate, doctoral, and postdoctoral levels of training to administer, enhance, or provide services to improve results for children with disabilities.

(B) Providing interdisciplinary training for various types of leadership personnel, including teacher preparation faculty, related services faculty, administrators, researchers, supervisors, principals, and other persons whose work affects early intervention, educational, and transitional services for children with disabilities, including children with disabilities who are limited English proficient children.

(e) Applications.

(1) **In General**. An eligible entity that wishes to receive a grant, or enter into a contract or cooperative agreement, under this section shall submit an application to the Secretary at such time, in such manner, and containing such information as the Secretary may require.

(2) **Identified State Needs.**

(A) **Requirement to Address Identified Needs.** An application for assistance under subsection (b), (c), or (d) shall include information demonstrating to the satisfaction of the Secretary that the activities described in the application will address needs identified by the State or States the eligible entity proposes to serve.

(B) **Cooperation with State Educational Agencies**. An eligible entity that is not a local educational agency or a State educational agency shall include in the eligible entity's application information demonstrating to the satisfaction of the Secretary that the eligible entity and 1 or more State educational agencies or local educational agencies will cooperate in carrying out and monitoring the proposed project.

(3) **Acceptance by States of Personnel Preparation Requirements**. The Secretary may require eligible entities to provide in the eligible entities' applications assurances from 1 or more States that such States intend to accept successful completion of the proposed personnel preparation program as meeting State personnel standards or other requirements in State law or regulation for serving children with disabilities or serving infants and toddlers with disabilities.

(f) Selection of Recipients.

(1) **Impact of Project**. In selecting eligible entities for assistance under this section, the Secretary shall consider the impact of the proposed project described in the application in meeting the need for personnel identified by the States.

(2) **Requirement for Eligible Entities to Meet State and Professional Qualifications**. The Secretary shall make grants and enter into contracts and cooperative agreements under this section only to eligible entities that meet State and professionally recognized qualifications for the preparation of special education and related services personnel, if the purpose of the project is to assist personnel in obtaining degrees.

(3) **Preferences**. In selecting eligible entities for assistance under this section, the Secretary may give preference to eligible entities that are institutions of higher education that are -

(A) educating regular education personnel to meet the needs of children with disabilities in integrated settings;

(B) educating special education personnel to work in collaboration with regular educators in integrated settings; and

(C) successfully recruiting and preparing individuals with disabilities and individuals from groups that are underrepresented in the profession for which the institution of higher education is preparing individuals.

(g) Scholarships. The Secretary may include funds for scholarships, with necessary stipends and allowances, in awards under subsections (b), (c), and (d).

(h) Service Obligation.

(1) **In General**. Each application for assistance under subsections (b), (c), and (d) shall include an assurance that the eligible entity will ensure that individuals who receive a scholarship under the proposed project agree to subsequently provide special education and related services to children with disabilities, or in the case of leadership personnel to subsequently work in the appropriate field, for a period of **2 years for every year** for which the scholarship was received or repay all or part of the amount of the scholarship, in accordance with regulations issued by the Secretary.

(2) **Special Rule**. Notwithstanding paragraph (1), the Secretary may reduce or waive the service obligation requirement under paragraph (1) if the Secretary determines that the service obligation is acting as a deterrent to the recruitment of students into special education or a related field.

(3) **Secretary's Responsibility**. The Secretary -

(A) shall ensure that individuals described in paragraph (1) comply with the requirements of that paragraph; and

(B) may use not more than 0.5 percent of the funds appropriated under subsection (i) for each fiscal year, to carry out subparagraph (A), in addition to any other funds that are available for that purpose.

(i) Authorization of Appropriations. There are authorized to be appropriated to carry out this section such sums as may be necessary for each of the fiscal years 2005 through 2010.

20 U. S. C. § 1463. Technical Assistance, Demonstration Projects, Dissemination of Information, and Implementation of Scientifically Based Research.

WRIGHTSLAW OVERVIEW: The federal government shall award grants and enter into contracts with entities to produce and disseminate research based knowledge that promotes academic achievement and improves results for children with disabilities.

(a) In General. The Secretary shall make competitive grants to, or enter into contracts or cooperative agreements with, eligible entities to provide technical assistance, support model demonstration projects, disseminate useful information, and implement activities that are supported by scientifically based research.

(b) Required Activities. Funds received under this section shall be used to support activities to improve services provided under this title, including the practices of professionals and others involved in providing such services to children with disabilities, that promote academic achievement and improve results for children with disabilities through -

(1) implementing effective strategies for addressing inappropriate behavior of students with disabilities in schools, including strategies to prevent children with emotional and behavioral problems from developing emotional disturbances that require the provision of special education and related services;

(2) improving the alignment, compatibility, and development of valid and reliable assessments and alternate assessments for assessing adequate yearly progress, as described under Section 1111(b)(2)(B) of the Elementary and Secondary Education Act of 1965;

(3) providing training for both regular education teachers and special education teachers to address the needs of students with different learning styles;

(4) disseminating information about innovative, effective, and efficient curricula designs, instructional approaches, and strategies, and identifying positive academic and social learning opportunities, that -

(A) provide effective transitions between educational settings or from school to post school settings; and

(B) improve educational and transitional results at all levels of the educational system in which the activities are carried out and, in particular, that improve the progress of children with disabilities, as measured by assessments within the general education curriculum involved; and

(5) applying scientifically based findings to facilitate systemic changes, related to the provision of services to children with disabilities, in policy, procedure, practice, and the training and use of personnel.

(c) Authorized Activities. Activities that may be carried out under this section include activities to improve services provided under this title, including the practices of professionals and others involved in providing such services to children with disabilities, that promote academic achievement and improve results for children with disabilities through -

(1) applying and testing research findings in typical settings where children with disabilities receive services to determine the usefulness, effectiveness, and general applicability of such research findings in such areas as improving instructional methods, curricula, and tools, such as textbooks and media;

(2) supporting and promoting the coordination of early intervention and educational services for children with disabilities with services provided by health, rehabilitation, and social service agencies;

(3) promoting improved alignment and compatibility of general and special education reforms concerned with curricular and instructional reform, and evaluation of such reforms;

(4) enabling professionals, parents of children with disabilities, and other persons to learn about, and implement, the findings of scientifically based research, and successful practices developed in model demonstration projects, relating to the provision of services to children with disabilities;

(5) conducting outreach, and disseminating information, relating to successful approaches to overcoming systemic barriers to the effective and efficient delivery of early intervention, educational, and transitional ser-

vices to personnel who provide services to children with disabilities;

(6) assisting States and local educational agencies with the process of planning systemic changes that will promote improved early intervention, educational, and transitional results for children with disabilities;

(7) promoting change through a multistate or regional framework that benefits States, local educational agencies, and other participants in partnerships that are in the process of achieving systemic-change outcomes;

(8) focusing on the needs and issues that are specific to a population of children with disabilities, such as providing single-State and multi-State technical assistance and in-service training -

(A) to schools and agencies serving deaf-blind children and their families;

(B) to programs and agencies serving other groups of children with low incidence disabilities and their families;

(C) addressing the postsecondary education needs of individuals who are deaf or hard-of-hearing; and

(D) to schools and personnel providing special education and related services for children with autism spectrum disorders;

(9) demonstrating models of personnel preparation to ensure appropriate placements and services for all students and to reduce disproportionality in eligibility, placement, and disciplinary actions for minority and limited English proficient children; and

(10) disseminating information on how to reduce inappropriate racial and ethnic disproportionalities identified under Section 1418.

(d) **Balance Among Activities and Age Ranges.** In carrying out this section, the Secretary shall ensure that there is an appropriate balance across all age ranges of children with disabilities.

(e) **Linking States to Information Sources.** In carrying out this section, the Secretary shall support projects that link States to technical assistance resources, including special education and general education resources, and shall make research and related products available through libraries, electronic networks, parent training projects, and other information sources, including through the activities of the National Center for Education Evaluation and Regional Assistance established under part D of the Education Sciences Reform Act of 2002.

(f) **Applications.**

(1) **In General.** An eligible entity that wishes to receive a grant, or enter into a contract or cooperative agreement, under this section shall submit an application to the Secretary at such time, in such manner, and containing such information as the Secretary may require.

(2) **Standards.** To the maximum extent feasible, each eligible entity shall demonstrate that the project described in the eligible entity's application is supported by scientifically valid research that has been carried out in accordance with the standards for the conduct and evaluation of all relevant research and development established by the National Center for Education Research.

(3) **Priority.** As appropriate, the Secretary shall give priority to applications that propose to serve teachers and school personnel directly in the school environment.

20 U. S. C. § 1464. Studies and Evaluations.

WRIGHTSLAW OVERVIEW: Section 1464 authorizes assessments, longitudinal studies, and a national assessment to determine if children with disabilities are benefiting from special education. The purpose of the national assessment is to determine if states and school districts are improving results, placing children in the least restrictive environment, reducing dropout rates, and addressing problem behaviors.

(a) **Studies and Evaluations.**

(1) **Delegation.** The Secretary shall delegate to the Director of the Institute of Education Sciences responsibility to carry out this section, other than subsections (d) and (f).

(2) Assessment. The Secretary shall, directly or through grants, contracts, or cooperative agreements awarded to eligible entities on a competitive basis, assess the progress in the implementation of this title, including the effectiveness of State and local efforts to provide -

(A) a free appropriate public education to children with disabilities; and

(B) early intervention services to infants and toddlers with disabilities, and infants and toddlers who would be at risk of having substantial developmental delays if early intervention services were not provided to the infants and toddlers.

(b) Assessment of National Activities.

(1) In General. The Secretary shall carry out a national assessment of activities carried out with Federal funds under this title in order -

(A) to determine the effectiveness of this title in achieving the purposes of this title;

(B) to provide timely information to the President, Congress, the States, local educational agencies, and the public on how to implement this title more effectively; and

(C) to provide the President and Congress with information that will be useful in developing legislation to achieve the purposes of this title more effectively.

(2) Scope of Assessment. The national assessment shall assess activities supported under this title, including

(A) the implementation of programs assisted under this title and the impact of such programs on addressing the developmental needs of, and improving the academic achievement of, children with disabilities to enable the children to reach challenging developmental goals and challenging State academic content standards based on State academic assessments;

(B) the types of programs and services that have demonstrated the greatest likelihood of helping students reach the challenging State academic content standards and developmental goals;

(C) the implementation of the professional development activities assisted under this title and the impact on instruction, student academic achievement, and teacher qualifications to enhance the ability of special education teachers and regular education teachers to improve results for children with disabilities; and

(D) the effectiveness of schools, local educational agencies, States, other recipients of assistance under this title, and the Secretary in achieving the purposes of this title by -

(i) improving the academic achievement of children with disabilities and their performance on regular statewide assessments as compared to nondisabled children, and the performance of children with disabilities on alternate assessments;

(ii) improving the participation of children with disabilities in the general education curriculum;

(iii) improving the transitions of children with disabilities at natural transition points;

(iv) placing and serving children with disabilities, including minority children, in the least restrictive environment appropriate;

(v) preventing children with disabilities, especially children with emotional disturbances and specific learning disabilities, from dropping out of school;

(vi) addressing the reading and literacy needs of children with disabilities;

(vii) reducing the inappropriate overidentification of children, especially minority and limited English proficient children, as having a disability;

(viii) improving the participation of parents of children with disabilities in the education of their children; and

(ix) resolving disagreements between education personnel and parents through alternate dispute resolution activities, including mediation.

(3) Interim and Final Reports. The Secretary shall submit to the President and Congress -

(A) an interim report that summarizes the preliminary findings of the assessment not later than 3 years after the date of enactment of the Individuals with Disabilities Education Improvement Act of 2004; and

(B) a final report of the findings of the assessment not later than 5 years after the date of enactment of such Act.

(c) Study on Ensuring Accountability for Students Who Are Held to Alternative Achievement Standards. The Secretary shall carry out a national study or studies to examine -

(1) the criteria that States use to determine -

(A) eligibility for alternate assessments; and

(B) the number and type of children who take those assessments and are held accountable to alternative achievement standards;

(2) the validity and reliability of alternate assessment instruments and procedures;

(3) the alignment of alternate assessments and alternative achievement standards to State academic content standards in reading, mathematics, and science; and

(4) the use and effectiveness of alternate assessments in appropriately measuring student progress and outcomes specific to individualized instructional need.

(d) Annual Report. The Secretary shall provide an annual report to Congress that -

(1) summarizes the research conducted under Part E of the Education Sciences Reform Act of 2002;

(2) analyzes and summarizes the data reported by the States and the Secretary of the Interior under Section 1418;

(3) summarizes the studies and evaluations conducted under this section and the timeline for their completion;

(4) describes the extent and progress of the assessment of national activities; and

(5) describes the findings and determinations resulting from reviews of State implementation of this title.

(e) Authorized Activities. In carrying out this section, the Secretary may support objective studies, evaluations, and assessments, including studies that -

(1) analyze measurable impact, outcomes, and results achieved by State educational agencies and local educational agencies through their activities to reform policies, procedures, and practices designed to improve educational and transitional services and results for children with disabilities;

(2) analyze State and local needs for professional development, parent training, and other appropriate activities that can reduce the need for disciplinary actions involving children with disabilities;

(3) assess educational and transitional services and results for children with disabilities from minority backgrounds, including -

(A) data on -

(i) the number of minority children who are referred for special education evaluation;

(ii) the number of minority children who are receiving special education and related services and their educational or other service placement;

(iii) the number of minority children who graduated from secondary programs with a regular diploma in the standard number of years; and

(iv) the number of minority children who drop out of the educational system; and

(B) the performance of children with disabilities from minority backgrounds on State assessments and other performance indicators established for all students;

(4) measure educational and transitional services and results for children with disabilities served under this title, including longitudinal studies that -

(A) examine educational and transitional services and results for children with disabilities who are 3 through 17 years of age and are receiving special education and related services under this title, using a national, representative sample of distinct age cohorts and disability categories; and

(B) examine educational results, transition services, postsecondary placement, and employment status for individuals with disabilities, 18 through 21 years of age, who are receiving or have received special education and related services under this title; and

(5) identify and report on the placement of children with disabilities by disability category.

(f) Study. The Secretary shall study, and report to Congress regarding, the extent to which States adopt policies described in Section 1435(c)(1) and on the effects of those policies.

20 U. S. C. § 1465. Interim Alternative Educational Settings, Behavioral Supports, and Systematic School Interventions.

WRIGHTSLAW OVERVIEW: Section 1465 is new. This section focuses on using effective, research based practices to improve behavioral supports and interim alternative educational settings. Strategies include improved training in behavioral supports and interventions, how to use research-based interventions, curriculum, ensuring that services are consistent with the IEP goals, and providing behavior specialists.

(a) Program Authorized. The Secretary may award grants, and enter into contracts and cooperative agreements, to support safe learning environments that support academic achievement for all students by -

(1) improving the quality of interim alternative educational settings; and

(2) providing increased behavioral supports and research-based, systemic interventions in schools.

(b) Authorized Activities. In carrying out this section, the Secretary may support activities to -

(1) establish, expand, or increase the scope of **behavioral supports and systemic interventions** by providing for **effective, research-based practices**, including -

(A) **training for school staff** on early identification, prereferral, and referral procedures;

(B) **training for** administrators, teachers, related services personnel, behavioral specialists, and other **school staff in positive behavioral interventions** and supports, **behavioral intervention planning**, and **classroom and student management techniques**;

(C) **joint training** for administrators, parents, teachers, related services personnel, behavioral specialists, and other school staff on effective strategies for positive behavioral interventions and behavior management strategies that focus on the **prevention of behavior problems**;

(D) developing or implementing specific curricula, programs, or interventions aimed at addressing behavioral problems;

(E) stronger linkages between school-based services and community-based resources, such as community mental health and primary care providers; or

(F) using behavioral specialists, related services personnel, and other staff necessary to implement behavioral supports; or

(2) **improve interim alternative educational settings** by -

(A) improving the training of administrators, teachers, related services personnel, behavioral specialists, and other school staff (including ongoing mentoring of new teachers) in behavioral supports and interventions;

(B) attracting and retaining a high quality, diverse staff;

(C) providing for referral to counseling services;

(D) utilizing research-based interventions, curriculum, and practices;

(E) allowing students to use instructional technology that provides individualized instruction;

(F) ensuring that the services are fully consistent with the goals of the individual student's IEP;

(G) promoting effective case management and collaboration among parents, teachers, physicians, related services personnel, behavioral specialists, principals, administrators, and other school staff;

(H) promoting interagency coordination and coordinated service delivery among schools, juvenile courts, child welfare agencies, community mental health providers, primary care providers, public recreation agencies, and community-based organizations; or

(I) providing for behavioral specialists to help students transitioning from interim alternative educational settings reintegrate into their regular classrooms.

(c) **Definition of Eligible Entity.** In this section, the term '**eligible entity**' means -

(1) a local educational agency; or

(2) a consortium consisting of a local educational agency and 1 or more of the following entities:

(A) Another local educational agency.

(B) A **community-based organization** with a demonstrated record of effectiveness in helping children with disabilities who have behavioral challenges succeed.

(C) An institution of higher education.

(D) A **community mental health provider**.

(E) An educational service agency.

(d) **Applications.** Any eligible entity that wishes to receive a grant, or enter into a contract or cooperative agreement, under this section shall -

(1) submit an application to the Secretary at such time, in such manner, and containing such information as the Secretary may require; and

(2) i**nvolve parents of participating students** in the design and implementation of the activities funded under this section.

(e) **Report and Evaluation.** Each eligible entity receiving a grant under this section shall prepare and submit annually to the Secretary a report on the outcomes of the activities assisted under the grant.

20 U. S. C. § 1466. Authorization of Appropriations.

(a) **In General.** There are authorized to be appropriated to carry out this subpart (other than Section 1462) such sums as may be necessary for each of the fiscal years 2005 through 2010.

(b) **Reservation.** From amounts appropriated under subsection (a) for fiscal year 2005, the Secretary shall reserve $1,000,000 to carry out the study authorized in Section 1464(c). From amounts appropriated under subsection (a) for a succeeding fiscal year, the Secretary may reserve an additional amount to carry out such study if the Secretary determines the additional amount is necessary.

Subpart 3 — Supports To Improve Results for Children with Disabilities

WRIGHTSLAW OVERVIEW: Subpart 3 focuses on the need to ensure that children with disabilities and their parents receive information and training. Section 1471 describes Parent Training and Information Centers; Section 1472 describes Community Parent Resource Centers. Section 1474 describes educational media services and the National Instructional Materials Access Center.

20 U. S. C. § 1470. Purposes.

WRIGHTSLAW OVERVIEW: Section 1470 describes the purposes for providing education and training to parents of children with disabilities.

The **purposes** of this subpart are to ensure that -

(1) children with disabilities and their **parents receive training and information** designed to assist the children in meeting **developmental and functional goals** and challenging **academic achievement goals,** and in preparing to **lead productive independent adult lives;**

(2) children with disabilities and their parents receive **training and information on their rights, responsibilities, and protections** under this title, in order to **develop the skills necessary to cooperatively and effectively participate in planning and decision making** relating to early intervention, educational, and transitional services;

(3) parents, teachers, administrators, early intervention personnel, related services personnel, and transition personnel receive coordinated and accessible technical assistance and information to assist such personnel in **improving early intervention, educational, and transitional services and results** for children with disabilities and their families; and

(4) appropriate technology and media are researched, developed, and demonstrated, to improve and implement early intervention, educational, and transitional services and results for children with disabilities and their families.

20 U. S. C. § 1471. Parent Training and Information Centers.

WRIGHTSLAW OVERVIEW: The Department of Education shall award grants to at least one parent organization in each state for a parent training and information center. Parent Training and Information Centers help parents learn about their children's disabilities, educational needs, how to communicate effectively with school personnel, how to participate in education decision-making and about their rights and how to use their rights.

(a) Program Authorized.

(1) In General. The Secretary may award grants to, and enter into contracts and cooperative agreements with, parent organizations to support **parent training and information centers** to carry out activities under this section.

(2) Definition of Parent Organization. In this section, the term **'parent organization' means a private nonprofit organization** (other than an institution of higher education) that -

(A) has a board of directors -

(i) the majority of whom are parents of children with disabilities ages birth through 26;

(ii) that includes -

(I) individuals working in the fields of special education, related services, and early intervention; and

(II) individuals with disabilities; and

(iii) the parent and professional members of which are broadly representative of the population to be served, including low-income parents and parents of limited English proficient children; and

(B) has as its mission serving families of children with disabilities who -

(i) are ages birth through 26; and

(ii) have the full range of disabilities described in Section 1402(3).

(b) Required Activities. Each **parent training and information center** that receives assistance under this section **shall -**

(1) **provide training and information that meets the needs of parents** of children with disabilities living in the area served by the center, particularly underserved parents and parents of children who may be inappropriately identified, to enable their children with disabilities to -

(A) meet developmental and functional goals, and challenging academic achievement goals that have been established for all children; and

(B) be prepared to lead productive independent adult lives, to the maximum extent possible;

(2) serve the parents of infants, toddlers, and children with the full range of disabilities described in Section 1402(3);

(3) ensure that the training and information provided meets the needs of low-income parents and parents of limited English proficient children;

(4) assist parents to -

(A) better understand the nature of their children's disabilities and their educational, developmental, and transitional needs;

(B) communicate effectively and work collaboratively with personnel responsible for providing special education, early intervention services, transition services, and related services;

(C) participate in decision-making processes and the development of individualized education programs under part B and individualized family service plans under part C;

(D) obtain appropriate information about the range, type, and quality of -

(i) options, programs, services, technologies, practices and interventions based on scientifically based research, to the extent practicable; and

(ii) resources available to assist children with disabilities and their families in school and at home;

(E) understand the provisions of this title for the education of, and the provision of early intervention services to, children with disabilities;

(F) participate in activities at the school level that benefit their children; and

(G) participate in school reform activities;

(5) in States where the State elects to contract with the parent training and information center, contract with State educational agencies to provide, consistent with subparagraphs (B) and (D) of Section 1415(e)(2), individuals who meet with parents to explain the mediation process to the parents;

(6) assist parents in resolving disputes in the most expeditious and effective way possible, including encouraging the use, and explaining the benefits, of alternative methods of dispute resolution, such as the mediation process described in Section 1415(e);

(7) assist parents and students with disabilities to **understand their rights and responsibilities** under this title, including those under Section 1415(m) upon the student's reaching the age of majority (as appropriate under State law);

(8) assist parents to understand the availability of, and how to effectively use, procedural safeguards under this title, including the resolution session described in Section 1415(e);

(9) assist parents in understanding, preparing for, and participating in, the process described in Section 1415(f)(1)(B);

(10) establish cooperative partnerships with community parent resource centers funded under Section 1472;

(11) network with appropriate clearinghouses, including organizations conducting national dissemination activities under Section 1463 and the Institute of Education Sciences, and with other national, State, and local organizations and agencies, such as protection and advocacy agencies, that serve parents and families of children

with the full range of disabilities described in Section 1402(3); and

(12) annually report to the Secretary on -

(A) the number and demographics of parents to whom the center provided information and training in the most recently concluded fiscal year;

(B) the effectiveness of strategies used to reach and serve parents, including underserved parents of children with disabilities; and

(C) the number of parents served who have resolved disputes through alternative methods of dispute resolution.

(c) **Optional Activities.** A parent training and information center that receives assistance under this section may provide information to teachers and other professionals to assist the teachers and professionals in improving results for children with disabilities.

(d) **Application Requirements.** Each application for assistance under this section shall identify with specificity the special efforts that the parent organization will undertake -

(1) to ensure that the needs for training and information of underserved parents of children with disabilities in the area to be served are effectively met; and

(2) to work with community based organizations, including community based organizations that work with low-income parents and parents of limited English proficient children.

(e) **Distribution of Funds.**

(1) **In General.** The Secretary shall -

(A) make not less than 1 award to a parent organization in each State for a parent training and information center that is designated as the statewide parent training and information center; or

(B) in the case of a large State, make awards to multiple parent training and information centers, but only if the centers demonstrate that coordinated services and supports will occur among the multiple centers.

(2) **Selection Requirement.** The Secretary shall select among applications submitted by parent organizations in a State in a manner that ensures the most effective assistance to parents, including parents in urban and rural areas, in the State.

(f) **Quarterly Review.**

(1) **Meetings.** The board of directors of each parent organization that receives an award under this section shall meet not less than once in each calendar quarter to review the activities for which the award was made.

(2) **Continuation Award.** When a parent organization requests a continuation award under this section, the board of directors shall submit to the Secretary a written review of the parent training and information program conducted by the parent organization during the preceding fiscal year.

20 U. S. C. § 1472. Community Parent Resource Centers.

WRIGHTSLAW OVERVIEW: The Department of Education may award grants to parents organizations that do not meet the criteria for a Parent Training and Information Center but focus on helping under-served parents. For example, centers may focus on helping low-income parents, parents of children with limited English proficiency, and parents with disabilities.

(a) **Program Authorized.**

(1) **In General.** The Secretary may award grants to, and enter into contracts and cooperative agreements with, local parent organizations to support **community parent resource centers** that will help ensure that underserved parents of children with disabilities, including low income parents, parents of limited English proficient children, and parents with disabilities, have the training and information the parents need to enable the parents to participate effectively in helping their children with disabilities -

(A) to meet developmental and functional goals, and challenging academic achievement goals that have been established for all children; and

(B) to be prepared to lead productive independent adult lives, to the maximum extent possible.

(2) Definition of Local Parent Organization. In this section, the term 'local parent organization' means a parent organization, as defined in Section 1471(a)(2), that -

(A) has a board of directors the majority of whom are parents of children with disabilities ages birth through 26 from the community to be served; and

(B) has as its mission serving parents of children with disabilities who -

(i) are ages birth through 26; and

(ii) have the full range of disabilities described in Section 1402(3).

(b) Required Activities. Each **community parent resource center** assisted under this section **shall** -

(1) **provide training and information that meets the training and information needs of parents** of children with disabilities proposed to be served by the grant, contract, or cooperative agreement;

(2) carry out the activities required of parent training and information centers under paragraphs (2) through (9) of Section 1471(b);

(3) establish cooperative partnerships with the parent training and information centers funded under Section 1471; and

(4) be designed to meet the specific needs of families who experience significant isolation from available sources of information and support.

20 U. S. C. § 1473. Technical Assistance for Parent Training and Information Centers.

WRIGHTSLAW OVERVIEW: The Department of Education may provide technical assistance to Parent Training and Information Centers and Community Parent Resource Centers.

(a) Program Authorized.

(1) In General. The Secretary may, directly or through awards to eligible entities, provide technical assistance for developing, assisting, and coordinating parent training and information programs carried out by parent training and information centers receiving assistance under Section 1471 and community parent resource centers receiving assistance under Section 1472.

(2) Definition of Eligible Entity. In this section, the term 'eligible entity' has the meaning given the term in Section 1461(b).

(b) Authorized Activities. The Secretary may provide technical assistance to a parent training and information center or a community parent resource center under this section in areas such as -

(1) effective coordination of parent training efforts;

(2) dissemination of scientifically based research and information;

(3) promotion of the use of technology, including assistive technology devices and assistive technology services;

(4) reaching underserved populations, including parents of low-income and limited English proficient children with disabilities;

(5) including children with disabilities in general education programs;

(6) facilitation of transitions from -

(A) early intervention services to preschool;

(B) preschool to elementary school;

(C) elementary school to secondary school; and

(D) secondary school to postsecondary environments; and

(7) promotion of alternative methods of dispute resolution, including mediation.

(c) Collaboration with Resource Centers. Each eligible entity receiving an award under subsection (a) **shall develop collaborative agreements** with the geographically appropriate regional resource center and, as appropriate, the regional educational laboratory supported under Section 174 of the Education Sciences Reform Act of 2002, to further parent and professional collaboration.

20 U. S. C. § 1474. Technology Development, Demonstration and Utilization; Media Services; and Instructional Materials.

WRIGHTSLAW OVERVIEW: Federal grants are available to promote the development of technology and educational media services. Section 1474(e) authorizes the National Instructional Materials Access Center that provides instructional materials to individuals who are blind or who have print disabilities.

(a) Program Authorized.

(1) In General. The Secretary, on a competitive basis, shall award grants to, and enter into contracts and cooperative agreements with, eligible entities to support activities described in subsections (b) and (c).

(2) Definition of Eligible Entity. In this section, the term 'eligible entity' has the meaning given the term in Section 1461(b).

(b) Technology Development, Demonstration, and Use.

(1) In General. In carrying out this section, the Secretary shall support activities to promote the development, demonstration, and use of technology.

(2) Authorized Activities. The following activities may be carried out under this subsection:

(A) Conducting research on and promoting the demonstration and use of innovative, emerging, and universally designed technologies for children with disabilities, by improving the transfer of technology from research and development to practice.

(B) Supporting research, development, and dissemination of technology with universal design features, so that the technology is accessible to the broadest range of individuals with disabilities without further modification or adaptation.

(C) Demonstrating the use of systems to provide parents and teachers with information and training concerning **early diagnosis of, intervention for, and effective teaching strategies for, young children with reading disabilities.**

(D) Supporting the use of **Internet-based communications** for students with cognitive disabilities in order to **maximize their academic and functional skills.**

(c) Educational Media Services.

(1) In General. In carrying out this section, the Secretary shall support -

(A) **educational media activities** that are designed to be of educational value in the classroom setting to children with disabilities;

(B) providing video description, open captioning, or closed captioning, that is appropriate for use in the classroom setting, of -

(i) television programs;

(ii) videos;

(iii) other materials, including programs and materials associated with new and emerging technologies, such as CDs, DVDs, video streaming, and other forms of multimedia; or

(iv) news (but only until September 30, 2006);

(C) distributing materials described in subparagraphs (A) and (B) through such mechanisms as a loan service; and

(D) providing free educational materials, including textbooks, in accessible media for visually impaired and print disabled students in elementary schools and secondary schools, postsecondary schools, and graduate schools.

(2) Limitation. The video description, open captioning, or closed captioning described in paragraph (1)(B) shall be provided only when the description or captioning has not been previously provided by the producer or distributor, or has not been fully funded by other sources.

(d) Applications.

(1) In General. Any eligible entity that wishes to receive a grant, or enter into a contract or cooperative agreement, under subsection (b) or (c) shall submit an application to the Secretary at such time, in such manner, and containing such information as the Secretary may require.

(2) Special Rule. For the purpose of an application for an award to carry out activities described in subsection (c)(1)(D), such eligible entity shall -

(A) be a national, nonprofit entity with a proven track record of meeting the needs of students with print disabilities through services described in subsection (c)(1)(D);

(B) have the capacity to produce, maintain, and distribute in a timely fashion, up-to-date textbooks in digital audio formats to qualified students; and

(C) have a demonstrated ability to significantly leverage Federal funds through other public and private contributions, as well as through the expansive use of volunteers.

(e) National Instructional Materials Access Center.

(1) In General. The Secretary shall establish and support, through the American Printing House for the Blind, a center to be known as the **National Instructional Materials Access Center** not later than 1 year after the date of enactment of the Individuals with Disabilities Education Improvement Act of 2004.

(2) Duties. The duties of the National Instructional Materials Access Center are the following:

(A) To receive and **maintain a catalog of print instructional materials** prepared in the National Instructional Materials Accessibility Standard, as established by the Secretary, made available to such center by the textbook publishing industry, State educational agencies, and local educational agencies.

(B) To provide **access to print instructional materials**, including textbooks, in accessible media, free of charge, **to blind or other persons with print disabilities in elementary schools and secondary schools**, in accordance with such terms and procedures as the National Instructional Materials Access Center may prescribe.

(C) To develop, adopt and publish procedures to protect against copyright infringement, with respect to the print instructional materials provided under Sections 1412(a)(23) and 1413(a)(6).

(3) Definitions. In this subsection:

(A) **Blind or Other Persons with Print Disabilities.** The term 'blind or other persons with print disabilities' means children served under this Act and who may qualify in accordance with the Act entitled 'An Act to provide books for the adult blind', approved March 3, 1931 (2 U. S. C. 135a; 46 Stat. 1487) to receive books and other publications produced in specialized formats.

(B) **National Instructional Materials Accessibility Standard.** The term 'National Instructional Materials Accessibility Standard' means the standard established by the Secretary to be used in the preparation of electronic files suitable and used solely for efficient conversion into specialized formats.[5]

---

[5] The National Instructional Materials Accessibility Standard (NIMAS) provides a system to produce and distribute digital versions of textbooks and other instructional materials that can be converted to accessible formats. IDEA requires that all textbooks and supplemental curricular materials be provided as NIMAS files by mid-December 2006. The American Printing House for the Blind is the coordinating agency and the Center for Applied Special Technology (CAST) is providing technical support. See also Section 1412(a)(23)

(C) Print Instructional Materials. The term 'print instructional materials' means printed textbooks and related printed core materials that are written and published primarily for use in elementary school and secondary school instruction and are required by a State educational agency or local educational agency for use by students in the classroom.

(D) Specialized Formats. The term 'specialized formats' has the meaning given the term in Section 121(d)(3) of Title 17, United States Code.

(4) Applicability. This subsection shall apply to print instructional materials published after the date on which the final rule establishing the National Instructional Materials Accessibility Standard was published in the Federal Register.

(5) Liability of the Secretary. Nothing in this subsection shall be construed to establish a private right of action against the Secretary for failure to provide instructional materials directly, or for failure by the National Instructional Materials Access Center to perform the duties of such center, or to otherwise authorize a private right of action related to the performance by such center, including through the application of the rights of children and parents established under this Act.

(6) Inapplicability. Subsections (a) through (d) shall not apply to this subsection.

20 U. S. C. § 1475. Authorization of Appropriations.

There are authorized to be appropriated to carry out this subpart such sums as may be necessary for each of the fiscal years 2005 through 2010.

Subpart 4 — General Provisions

20 U. S. C. § 1481. Comprehensive Plan for Subparts 2 and 3.

WRIGHTSLAW OVERVIEW: This section describes the requirements for a comprehensive plan to carry out the activities in Subparts 2 and 3, outreach to special populations, priorities, and eligibility for financial assistance.

(a) Comprehensive Plan.

(1) In General. After receiving input from interested individuals with relevant expertise, the Secretary shall develop and implement a comprehensive plan for activities carried out under Subparts 2 and 3 in order to enhance the provision of early intervention services, educational services, related services, and transitional services to children with disabilities under Parts B and C. To the extent practicable, the plan shall be coordinated with the plan developed pursuant to Section 178(c) of the Education Sciences Reform Act of 2002 and shall include mechanisms to address early intervention, educational, related service and transitional needs identified by State educational agencies in applications submitted for State personnel development grants under Subpart 1 and for grants under Subparts 2 and 3.

(2) Public Comment. The Secretary shall provide a public comment period of not less than 45 days on the plan.

(3) Distribution of Funds. In implementing the plan, the Secretary shall, to the extent appropriate, ensure that funds awarded under subparts 2 and 3 are used to carry out activities that benefit, directly or indirectly, children with the full range of disabilities and of all ages.

(4) Reports to Congress. The Secretary shall annually report to Congress on the Secretary's activities under Subparts 2 and 3, including an initial report not later than 12 months after the date of enactment of the Individuals with Disabilities Education Improvement Act of 2004.

(b) Assistance Authorized. The Secretary is authorized to award grants to, or enter into contracts or cooperative agreements with, eligible entities to enable the eligible entities to carry out the purposes of such subparts in accordance with the comprehensive plan described in subsection (a).

(c) Special Populations.

(1) Application Requirement. In making an award of a grant, contract, or cooperative agreement under Subpart 2 or 3, the Secretary shall, as appropriate, require an eligible entity to demonstrate how the eligible entity will address the needs of children with disabilities from minority backgrounds.

(2) Required Outreach and Technical Assistance. Notwithstanding any other provision of this title, the Secretary shall reserve not less than 2 percent of the total amount of funds appropriated to carry out Subparts 2 and 3 for either or both of the following activities:

(A) Providing outreach and technical assistance to historically Black colleges and universities, and to institutions of higher education with minority enrollments of not less than 25 percent, to promote the participation of such colleges, universities, and institutions in activities under this Subpart.

(B) Enabling historically Black colleges and universities, and the institutions described in subparagraph (A), to assist other colleges, universities, institutions, and agencies in improving educational and transitional results for children with disabilities, if the historically Black colleges and universities and the institutions of higher education described in subparagraph (A) meet the criteria established by the Secretary under this subpart.

(d) Priorities. The Secretary, in making an award of a grant, contract, or cooperative agreement under Subpart 2 or 3, may, without regard to the rulemaking procedures under Section 553 of Title 5, United States Code, limit competitions to, or otherwise give priority to -

(1) projects that address 1 or more -

(A) age ranges;

(B) disabilities;

(C) school grades;

(D) types of educational placements or early intervention environments;

(E) types of services;

(F) content areas, such as reading; or

(G) effective strategies for helping children with disabilities learn appropriate behavior in the school and other community based educational settings;

(2) projects that address the needs of children based on the severity or incidence of their disability;

(3) projects that address the needs of -

(A) low achieving students;

(B) underserved populations;

(C) children from low income families;

(D) limited English proficient children;

(E) unserved and underserved areas;

(F) rural or urban areas;

(G) children whose behavior interferes with their learning and socialization;

(H) children with reading difficulties;

(I) children in public charter schools;

(J) children who are gifted and talented; or

(K) children with disabilities served by local educational agencies that receive payments under Title VIII of the Elementary and Secondary Education Act of 1965;

(4) projects to reduce inappropriate identification of children as children with disabilities, particularly among

minority children;

(5) projects that are carried out in particular areas of the country, to ensure broad geographic coverage;

(6) projects that promote the development and use of technologies with universal design, assistive technology devices, and assistive technology services to maximize children with disabilities' access to and participation in the general education curriculum; and

(7) any activity that is authorized in Subpart 2 or 3.

(e) **Eligibility for Financial Assistance.** No State or local educational agency, or other public institution or agency, may receive a grant or enter into a contract or cooperative agreement under Subpart 2 or 3 that relates exclusively to programs, projects, and activities pertaining to children aged 3 through 5, inclusive, unless the State is eligible to receive a grant under Section 1419(b).

20 U. S. C. § 1482. Administrative Provisions.

(a) **Applicant and Recipient Responsibilities.**

(1) **Development and Assessment of Projects.** The Secretary shall require that an applicant for, and a recipient of, a grant, contract, or cooperative agreement for a project under Subpart 2 or 3 -

(A) involve individuals with disabilities or parents of individuals with disabilities ages birth through 26 in planning, implementing, and evaluating the project; and

(B) where appropriate, determine whether the project has any potential for replication and adoption by other entities.

(2) **Additional Responsibilities.** The Secretary may require a recipient of a grant, contract, or cooperative agreement under Subpart 2 or 3 to -

(A) share in the cost of the project;

(B) prepare any findings and products from the project in formats that are useful for specific audiences, including parents, administrators, teachers, early intervention personnel, related services personnel, and individuals with disabilities;

(C) disseminate such findings and products; and

(D) collaborate with other such recipients in carrying out subparagraphs (B) and (C).

(b) **Application Management.**

(1) **Standing Panel.**

(A) **In General.** The Secretary shall establish and use a **standing panel of experts** who are qualified, by virtue of their training, expertise, or experience, to evaluate each application under Subpart 2 or 3 that requests more than $75,000 per year in Federal financial assistance.

(B) **Membership.** The standing panel shall include, at a minimum -

(i) individuals who are representatives of institutions of higher education that plan, develop, and carry out high quality programs of personnel preparation;

(ii) individuals who design and carry out scientifically based research targeted to the improvement of special education programs and services;

(iii) individuals who have recognized experience and knowledge necessary to integrate and apply scientifically based research findings to improve educational and transitional results for children with disabilities;

(iv) individuals who administer programs at the State or local level in which children with disabilities participate;

(v) individuals who prepare parents of children with disabilities to participate in making decisions about the education of their children;

(vi) individuals who establish policies that affect the delivery of services to children with disabilities;

(vii) individuals who are parents of children with disabilities ages birth through 26 who are benefiting, or have benefited, from coordinated research, personnel preparation, and technical assistance; and

(viii) individuals with disabilities.

(C) Term. No individual shall serve on the standing panel for more than 3 consecutive years.

(2) Peer-Review Panels for Particular Competitions.

(A) Composition. The Secretary shall ensure that **each subpanel selected** from the standing panel that reviews an application under Subpart 2 or 3 includes -

(i) individuals with knowledge and expertise on the issues addressed by the activities described in the application; and

(ii) to the extent practicable, parents of children with disabilities ages birth through 26, individuals with disabilities, and persons from diverse backgrounds.

(B) Federal Employment Limitation. A majority of the individuals on each subpanel that reviews an application under Subpart 2 or 3 shall be individuals who are not employees of the Federal Government.

(3) Use of Discretionary Funds for Administrative Purposes.

(A) Expenses and Fees of Non-Federal Panel Members. The Secretary may use funds available under subpart 2 or 3 to pay the expenses and fees of the panel members who are not officers or employees of the Federal Government.

(B) Administrative Support. The Secretary may use not more than 1 percent of the funds appropriated to carry out Subpart 2 or 3 to pay non-Federal entities for administrative support related to management of applications submitted under Subpart 2 or 3, respectively.

(c) Program Evaluation. The Secretary may use funds made available to carry out Subpart 2 or 3 to evaluate activities carried out under Subpart 2 or 3, respectively.

(d) Minimum Funding Required.

(1) In General. Subject to paragraph (2), the Secretary shall ensure that, for each fiscal year, not less than the following amounts are provided under subparts 2 and 3 to address the following needs:

(A) $12,832,000 to address the educational, related services, transitional, and early intervention needs of children with deaf-blindness.

(B) $4,000,000 to address the postsecondary, vocational, technical, continuing, and adult education needs of individuals with deafness.

(C) $4,000,000 to address the educational, related services, and transitional needs of children with an emotional disturbance and those who are at risk of developing an emotional disturbance.

(2) Ratable Reduction. If the sum of the amount appropriated to carry out Subparts 2 and 3, and Part E of the Education Sciences Reform Act of 2002 for any fiscal year is less than $130,000,000, the amounts listed in paragraph (1) shall be ratably reduced for the fiscal year.

End of Part D

Part E – National Center for Special Education Research

WRIGHTSLAW OVERVIEW: Part E establishes the National Center for Special Education Research, referred to as The Special Education Research Center. The mission of the Research Center is to sponsor research to improve the developmental, educational and transitional results of special education, and to evaluate the effectiveness of the Individuals with Disabilities Education Act. Duties of the Research Center are to improve special education services, identify scientifically based educational practices that are effective, identify scientifically based related services that promote increased participation in general education settings, examine State standards and alternate assessments, improve reading and literacy skills of children with disabilities, and other issues.

20 U. S. C. § 9567. Establishment.

(a) **Establishment**. There is established in the Institute a **National Center for Special Education Research** (in this part referred to as the "**Special Education Research Center**").

(b) **Mission**. The **mission** of the Special Education Research Center is-

(1) to **sponsor research** to expand knowledge and understanding of the needs of infants, toddlers, and children with disabilities in order to improve the developmental, educational, and transitional results of such individuals;

(2) to sponsor research to improve services provided under, and support the implementation of, the Individuals with Disabilities Education Act (20 U. S. C. 1400 et seq.); and

(3) to evaluate the implementation and effectiveness of the Individuals with Disabilities Education Act in coordination with the National Center for Education Evaluation and Regional Assistance.

(c) **Applicability of Education Sciences Reform Act of 2002**. Parts A and F, and the standards for peer review of applications and for the conduct and evaluation of research under sections 133(a) and 134, respectively, shall apply to the Secretary, the Director, and the Commissioner in carrying out this part.

20 U. S. C. § 9567a. Commissioner for Special Education Research.

The Special Education Research Center shall be headed by a Commissioner for Special Education Research (in this part referred to as the Special Education Research Commissioner') who shall have substantial knowledge of the Special Education Research Center's activities, including a high level of expertise in the fields of research, research management, and the education of children with disabilities.

20 U. S. C. § 9567b. Duties.

(a) **General Duties**. The **Special Education Research Center shall** carry out research activities under this part consistent with the mission described in section 175(b), such as activities that -

(1) improve services provided under the Individuals with Disabilities Education Act in order to **improve--**

(A) **academic achievement, functional outcomes, and educational results** for children with disabilities; and

(B) developmental outcomes for infants or toddlers with disabilities;

(2) **identify scientifically based educational practices** that support learning and improve academic achievement, functional outcomes, and educational results for all students with disabilities;

(3) examine the special needs of preschool aged children, infants, and toddlers with disabilities, including factors that may result in developmental delays;

(4) identify scientifically based related services and interventions that promote participation and progress in the general education curriculum and general education settings;

(5) improve the alignment, compatibility, and development of valid and reliable assessments, including alternate assessments, as required by Section 6311(b) of this title;

(6) examine State content standards and alternate assessments for students with significant cognitive impairment in terms of academic achievement, individualized instructional need, appropriate education settings, and improved post-school results;

(7) examine the educational, developmental, and transitional needs of children with high incidence and low incidence disabilities;

(8) examine the extent to which overidentification and underidentification of children with disabilities occurs, and the causes thereof

(9) improve **reading and literacy skills** of children with disabilities;

(10) examine and improve secondary and postsecondary education and transitional outcomes and results for children with disabilities;

(11) examine methods of early intervention for children with disabilities, including children with multiple or complex developmental delays;

(12) examine and incorporate universal design concepts in the development of standards, assessments, curricula, and instructional methods to improve educational and transitional results for children with disabilities;

(13) improve the preparation of personnel, including early intervention personnel, who provide educational and related services to children with disabilities to increase the academic achievement and functional performance of students with disabilities;

(14) examine the excess costs of educating a child with a disability and expenses associated with high cost special education and related services;

(15) help parents improve educational results for their children, particularly related to transition issues;

(16) address the unique needs of children with significant cognitive disabilities; and

(17) examine the special needs of limited English proficient children with disabilities.

(b) Standards. The Special Education Research Commissioner shall ensure that activities assisted under this section-

(1) conform to high standards of quality, integrity, accuracy, validity, and reliability;

(2) are carried out in accordance with the standards for the conduct and evaluation of all research and development established by the National Center for Education Research; and

(3) are objective, secular, neutral, and nonideological, and are free of partisan political influence, and racial, cultural, gender, regional, or disability bias.

(c) Plan. The Special Education Research Commissioner shall propose to the Director a research plan, developed in collaboration with the Assistant Secretary for Special Education and Rehabilitative Services, that--

(1) is consistent with the priorities and mission of the Institute and the mission of the Special Education Research Center;

(2) is carried out, updated, and modified, as appropriate;

(3) is consistent with the purposes of the Individuals with Disabilities Education Act;

(4) contains an appropriate balance across all age ranges and types of children with disabilities;

(5) provides for research that is objective and uses measurable indicators to assess its progress and results; and

(6) is coordinated with the comprehensive plan developed under Section 1481 of the Individuals with Disabilities Education Act.

(d) Grants, Contracts, and Cooperative Agreements.

(1) In General. In carrying out the duties under this section, the Director may award grants to, or enter into contracts or cooperative agreements with, eligible applicants.

(2) Eligible Applicants. Activities carried out under this subsection through contracts, grants, or cooperative agreements shall be carried out only by recipients with the ability and capacity to conduct scientifically valid research.

(3) Applications. An eligible applicant that wishes to receive a grant, or enter into a contract or cooperative agreement, under this section shall submit an application to the Director at such time, in such manner, and containing such information as the Director may require.

(e) Dissemination. The Special Education Research Center shall--

(1) synthesize and disseminate, through the National Center for Education Evaluation and Regional Assistance, the findings and results of special education research conducted or supported by the Special Education Research Center; and

(2) assist the Director in the preparation of a biennial report, as described in Section 9519 of this title.

(f) Authorization of Appropriations. There are authorized to be appropriated to carry out this part such sums as may be necessary for each of fiscal years 2005 through 2010.

End of Part E

CHAPTER 6

Table of IDEA 2004 Regulations 34 CFR Part 300

Subpart A—General

Purposes and Applicability

300.1 Purposes.

300.2 Applicability of this part to State and local agencies.

Definitions Used in This Part

300.4 Act.

300.5 Assistive technology device.

300.6 Assistive technology service.

300.7 Charter school.

300.8 Child with a disability.

300.9 Consent.

300.10 Core academic subjects.

300.11 Day; business day; school day.

300.12 Educational service agency.

300.13 Elementary school.

300.14 Equipment.

300.15 Evaluation.

300.16 Excess costs.

300.17 Free appropriate public education.

300.18 Highly qualified special education teachers.

300.19 Homeless children.

300.20 Include.

300.21 Indian and Indian tribe.

300.22 Individualized education program.

300.23 Individualized education program team.

300.24 Individualized family service plan.

300.25 Infant or toddler with a disability.

300.26 Institution of higher education.

300.27 Limited English proficient.

300.28 Local educational agency.

300.29 Native language.

300.30 Parent.

300.31 Parent training and information center.

300.32 Personally identifiable.

300.33 Public agency.

300.34 Related services.

300.35 Scientifically based research.

300.36 Secondary school.

300.37 Services plan.

300.38 Secretary.

300.39 Special education.

300.40 State.

300.41 State educational agency.

300.42 Supplementary aids and services.

300.43 Transition services.

300.44 Universal design.

300.45 Ward of the State.

Subpart B—State Eligibility

General

300.100 Eligibility for assistance.

FAPE Requirements

300.101 Free appropriate public education (FAPE).

300.102 Limitation—exception to FAPE for certain ages.

Other FAPE Requirements

300.103 FAPE—methods and payments.

300.104 Residential placement.

300.105 Assistive technology.

300.106 Extended school year services.

300.107 Nonacademic services.

300.108 Physical education.

300.109 Full educational opportunity goal (FEOG).

Assistance to States for the Education of Children with Disabilities 34 CFR Part 300

Subpart A—General

Purposes and Applicability

§300.1 Purposes. The purposes of this part are—

(a) To ensure that all children with disabilities have available to them a free appropriate public education that emphasizes special education and related services designed to meet their **unique needs and prepare them for further education, employment, and independent living**;

(b) To ensure that the rights of children with disabilities and their parents are protected;

(c) To assist States, localities, educational service agencies, and Federal agencies to provide for the education of all children with disabilities; and

(d) To assess and ensure the effectiveness of efforts to educate children with disabilities. (Authority: 20 U. S. C. 1400(d))

§300.2 Applicability of this part to State and local agencies.

(a) **States**. This part applies to each State that receives payments under Part B of the Act, as defined in §300.4.

(b) **Public agencies within the State**. The provisions of this part—

(1) Apply to all political subdivisions of the State that are involved in the education of children with disabilities, including:

(i) The State educational agency (SEA).

(ii) Local educational agencies (LEAs), educational service agencies (ESAs), and public charter schools that are not otherwise included as LEAs or ESAs and are not a school of an LEA or ESA.

(iii) Other State agencies and schools (such as Departments of Mental Health and Welfare and State schools for children with deafness or children with blindness).

(iv) State and local juvenile and adult correctional facilities; and

(2) Are binding on each public agency in the State that provides special education and related services to children with disabilities, regardless of whether that agency is receiving funds under Part B of the Act.

(c) **Private schools and facilities**. Each public agency in the State is responsible for ensuring that the rights and protections under Part B of the Act are given to children with disabilities—

(1) Referred to or placed in private schools and facilities by that public agency; or

(2) Placed in private schools by their parents under the provisions of §300.148. (Authority: 20 U. S. C. 1412)

Definitions Used in This Part

§300.4 Act. Act means the **Individuals with Disabilities Education Act**, as amended. (Authority: 20 U. S. C. 1400(a))

§300.5 Assistive technology device. **Assistive technology device** means any item, piece of equipment, or product system, whether acquired commercially off the shelf, modified, or customized, that is used to increase, maintain, or improve the functional capabilities of a child with a disability. The term does not include a medical device that is surgically implanted, or the replacement of such device. (Authority: 20 U. S. C. 1401(1))

§300.6 Assistive technology service. **Assistive technology service** means any service that directly assists a child with a disability in the selection, acquisition, or use of an assistive technology device. The **term includes**—

(a) The evaluation of the needs of a child with a disability, including a functional evaluation of the child in the child's customary environment;

(b) Purchasing, leasing, or otherwise providing for the acquisition of assistive technology devices by children with disabilities;

(c) Selecting, designing, fitting, customizing, adapting, applying, maintaining, repairing, or replacing assistive technology devices;

(d) Coordinating and using other therapies, interventions, or services with assistive technology devices, such as those associated with existing education and rehabilitation plans and programs;

(e) Training or technical assistance for a child with a disability or, if appropriate, that child's family; and

(f) Training or technical assistance for professionals (including individuals providing education or rehabilitation services), employers, or other individuals who provide services to, employ, or are otherwise substantially involved in the major life functions of that child. (Authority: 20 U. S. C. 1401(2))

§300.7 Charter school. Charter school has the meaning given the term in section 5210(1) of the Elementary and Secondary Education Act of 1965, as amended, 20 U. S. C. 6301 *et seq.* (ESEA). (Authority: 20 U. S. C. 7221i(1))

§300.8 Child with a disability.

(a) General.

(1) **Child with a disability** means a child evaluated in accordance with §§300.304 through 300.311 as having mental retardation, a hearing impairment (including deafness), a speech or language impairment, a visual impairment (including blindness), a serious emotional disturbance (referred to in this part as "emotional disturbance"), an orthopedic impairment, autism, traumatic brain injury, an other health impairment, a Specific Learning Disability, deaf-blindness, or multiple disabilities, and who, by reason thereof, needs special education and related services.

(2)

(i) Subject to paragraph (a)(2)(ii) of this section, if it is determined, through an appropriate evaluation under §§300.304 through 300.311, that a child has one of the disabilities identified in paragraph (a)(1) of this section, **but only needs a related service and not special education, the child is not a child with a disability under this part**.

(ii) If, consistent with §300.39(a)(2), the related service required by the child is considered special education rather than a related service under State standards, the child would be determined to be a child with a disability under paragraph (a)(1) of this section.

(b) Children aged three through nine experiencing developmental delays. Child with a disability for children aged three through nine (or any subset of that age range, including ages three through five), may, subject to the conditions described in §300.111(b), include a child—

(1) Who is experiencing developmental delays, as defined by the State and as measured by appropriate diagnostic instruments and procedures, in one or more of the following areas: physical development, cognitive development, communication development, social or emotional development, or adaptive development; and

(2) Who, by reason thereof, needs special education and related services.

(c) Definitions of disability terms. The terms used in this definition of a child with a disability are defined as follows:

(1)

(i) **Autism** means a developmental disability significantly affecting verbal and nonverbal communication and social interaction, generally evident before age three, that adversely affects a child's educational performance. Other characteristics often associated with autism are engagement in repetitive activities and stereotyped movements, resistance to environmental change or change in daily routines, and unusual responses to sensory experiences.

(ii) Autism **does not apply** if a child's educational performance is adversely affected primarily because the child has an emotional disturbance, as defined in paragraph (c)(4) of this section.

(iii) A child who manifests the characteristics of autism after age three could be identified as having autism if the criteria in paragraph (c)(1)(i) of this section are satisfied.

(2) **Deaf-blindness** means concomitant hearing and visual impairments, the combination of which causes such severe communication and other developmental and educational needs that they cannot be accommodated in special education programs solely for children with deafness or children with blindness.

(3) **Deafness** means a hearing impairme nt that is so severe that the child is impaired in processing linguistic information through hearing, with or without amplification, that adversely affects a child's educational performance.

(4)

(i) Emotional disturbance means a condition exhibiting one or more of the following characteristics over a long period of time and to a marked degree that **adversely affects a child's educational performance**:

(A) An inability to learn that cannot be explained by intellectual, sensory, or health factors.

(B) An inability to build or maintain satisfactory interpersonal relationships with peers and teachers.

(C) Inappropriate types of behavior or feelings under normal circumstances.

(D) A general pervasive mood of unhappiness or depression.

(E) A tendency to develop physical symptoms or fears associated with personal or school problems.

(ii) Emotional disturbance includes schizophrenia. The term does not apply to children who are socially maladjusted, unless it is determined that they have an emotional disturbance under paragraph (c)(4)(i) of this section.

(5) Hearing impairment means an impairment in hearing, whether permanent or fluctuating, that adversely affects a child's educational performance but that is not included under the definition of deafness in this section.

(6) Mental retardation means significantly subaverage general intellectual functioning, existing concurrently with deficits in adaptive behavior and manifested during the developmental period, that adversely affects a child's educational performance.

(7) Multiple disabilities means concomitant impairments (such as mental retardation-blindness or mental retardation-orthopedic impairment), the combination of which causes such severe educational needs that they cannot be accommodated in special education programs solely for one of the impairments. Multiple disabilities does not include deaf-blindness.

(8) Orthopedic impairment means a severe orthopedic impairment that adversely affects a child's educational performance. The term includes impairments caused by a congenital anomaly, impairments caused by disease (e.g., poliomyelitis, bone tuberculosis), and impairments from other causes (e.g., cerebral palsy, amputations, and fractures or burns that cause contractures).

(9) Other health impairment means having limited strength, vitality, or alertness, including a heightened alertness to environmental stimuli, that results in limited alertness with respect to the educational environment, that—

(i) Is due to chronic or acute health problems such as **asthma, attention deficit disorder or attention deficit hyperactivity disorder, diabetes, epilepsy, a heart condition, hemophilia, lead poisoning, leukemia, nephritis, rheumatic fever, sickle cell anemia, and Tourette syndrome**; and

(ii) **Adversely affects a child's educational performance.**

(10) Specific learning disability.

(i) General. Specific learning disability means a disorder in one or more of the basic psychological processes involved in understanding or in using language, spoken or written, that may manifest itself in the imperfect ability to listen, think, speak, read, write, spell, or to do mathematical calculations, including conditions such as **perceptual disabilities**, brain injury, minimal brain dysfunction, **dyslexia**, and developmental aphasia.

(ii) Disorders not included. Specific learning disability does not include learning problems that are primarily the result of visual, hearing, or motor disabilities, of mental retardation, of emotional disturbance, or of environmental, cultural, or economic disadvantage.

(11) Speech or language impairment means a communication disorder, such as stuttering, impaired articulation, a language impairment, or a voice impairment, that adversely affects a child's educational performance.

(12) Traumatic brain injury means an acquired injury to the brain caused by an external physical force, resulting in total or partial functional disability or psychosocial impairment, or both, that adversely affects a child's educational performance. Traumatic brain injury applies to open or closed head injuries resulting in impairments in one or more areas, such as cognition; language; memory; attention; reasoning; abstract thinking; judgment; problem-solving; sensory, perceptual, and motor abilities; psychosocial behavior; physical functions; information processing; and speech. Traumatic brain injury does not apply to brain injuries that are congenital or degenerative, or to brain injuries induced by birth trauma.

(13) Visual impairment including blindness means an impairment in vision that, even with correction, adversely affects a child's educational performance. The term includes both partial sight and blindness. (Authority: 20 U. S. C. 1401(3); 1401(30))

§300.9 Consent. Consent means that—

(a) The parent has been **fully informed** of all information relevant to the activity for which consent is sought, in his or her native language, or through another mode of communication;

(b) The parent understands and agrees in writing to the carrying out of the activity for which his or her consent is sought, and the consent describes that activity and lists the records (if any) that will be released and to whom; and

(c)

(1) The parent understands that the granting of consent is voluntary on the part of the parent and may be revoked at any time.

(2) If a parent revokes consent, that revocation is not retroactive (i.e., it does not negate an action that has occurred after the consent was given and before the consent was revoked). (Authority: 20 U. S. C. 1414(a)(1)(D))

§300.10 Core academic subjects. Core academic subjects means **English, reading or language arts, mathematics, science, foreign languages, civics and government, economics, arts, history, and geography**. (Authority: 20 U. S. C. 1401(4))

§300.11 Day; business day; school day.

(a) Day means calendar day unless otherwise indicated as business day or school day.

(b) Business day means **Monday through Friday**, except for Federal and State holidays (unless holidays are specifically included in the designation of business day, as in §300.148(d)(1)(ii)).

(c)

(1) School day means any day, including a partial day that **children are in attendance at school** for instructional purposes.

(2) School day has the same meaning for all children in school, including children with and without disabilities. (Authority: 20 U. S. C. 1221e-3)

§300.12 Educational service agency. Educational service agency means—

(a) A regional public multiservice agency—

(1) Authorized by State law to develop, manage, and provide services or programs to LEAs;

(2) Recognized as an administrative agency for purposes of the provision of special education and related services provided within public elementary schools and secondary schools of the State;

(b) Includes any other public institution or agency having administrative control and direction over a public elementary school or secondary school; and

(c) Includes entities that meet the definition of intermediate educational unit in section 602(23) of the Act as in effect prior to June 4, 1997. (Authority: 20 U. S. C. 1401(5))

§300.13 Elementary school. Elementary school means a nonprofit institutional day or residential school, including a public elementary charter school, that provides elementary education, as determined under State law. (Authority: 20 U. S. C. 1401(6))

§300.14 Equipment. Equipment means —

(a) Machinery, utilities, and built-in equipment, and any necessary enclosures or structures to house the machinery, utilities, or equipment; and

(b) All other items necessary for the functioning of a particular facility as a facility for the provision of educational services, including items such as instructional equipment and necessary furniture; printed, published and audio-visual instructional materials; telecommunications, sensory, and other technological aids and devices; and books, periodicals, documents, and other related materials. (Authority: 20 U. S. C. 1401(7))

§300.15 Evaluation. Evaluation means procedures used in accordance with §§300.304 through 300.311 to determine whether a child has a disability and the nature and extent of the special education and related services that the child needs. (Authority: 20 U. S. C. 1414(a)-(c))

§300.16 Excess costs. Excess costs means those costs that are in excess of the average annual per-student expenditure in an LEA during the preceding school year for an elementary school or secondary school student, as may be appropriate, and that must be computed after deducting—

(a) Amounts received—

(1) Under Part B of the Act;

(2) Under Part A of title I of the ESEA; and

(3) Under Parts A and B of title III of the ESEA and;

(b) Any State or local funds expended for programs that would qualify for assistance under any of the parts described in paragraph (a) of this section, but excluding any amounts for capital outlay or debt service. (See Appendix A to part 300 for an example of how excess costs must be calculated.) (Authority: 20 U. S. C. 1401(8))

§300.17 Free appropriate public education. Free appropriate public education or FAPE means special education and related services that—

(a) Are provided at public expense, under public supervision and direction, and without charge;

(b) Meet the standards of the SEA, including the requirements of this part;

(c) Include an appropriate preschool, elementary school, or secondary school education in the State involved; and

(d) Are provided in conformity with an individualized education program (IEP) that meets the requirements of §§300.320 through 300.324. (Authority: 20 U. S. C. 1401(9))

§300.18 Highly qualified special education teachers.

(a) Requirements for special education teachers teaching core academic subjects. For any public elementary or secondary school special education teacher teaching core academic subjects, the term highly qualified has the meaning given the term in section 9101 of the ESEA and 34 CFR 200.56, except that the requirements for highly qualified also—

(1) Include the requirements described in paragraph (b) of this section; and

(2) Include the option for teachers to meet the requirements of section 9101 of the ESEA by meeting the requirements of paragraphs (c) and (d) of this section.

(b) Requirements for highly qualified special education teachers in general.

(1) When used with respect to any public elementary school or secondary school special education teacher teaching in a State, highly qualified requires that —

(i) The teacher has obtained full State certification as a special education teacher (including certification obtained through alternative routes to certification), or passed the State special education teacher licensing examination, and holds a license to teach in the State as a special education teacher, except that when used with respect to any teacher teaching in a public charter school, highly qualified means that the teacher meets the certification or licensing requirements, if any, set forth in the State's public charter school law;

(ii) The teacher has not had special education certification or licensure requirements waived on an emergency, temporary, or provisional basis; and

(iii) The teacher holds at least a bachelor's degree.

(2) A teacher will be considered to meet the standard in paragraph (b)(1)(i) of this section if that teacher is participating in an alternative route to special education certification program under which—

(i) The teacher—

(A) Receives high-quality professional development that is sustained, intensive, and classroom-focused in order to have a positive and lasting impact on classroom instruction, before and while teaching;

(B) Participates in a program of intensive supervision that consists of structured guidance and regular ongoing support for teachers or a teacher mentoring program;

(C) Assumes functions as a teacher only for a specified period of time not to exceed three years; and

(D) Demonstrates satisfactory progress toward full certification as prescribed by the State; and

(ii) The State ensures, through its certification and licensure process, that the provisions in paragraph (b)(2)(i) of this section are met.

(3) Any public elementary school or secondary school special education teacher teaching in a State, who is not teaching a core academic subject, is highly qualified if the teacher meets the requirements in paragraph (b)(1) or the requirements in (b)(1)(iii) and (b)(2) of this section.

(c) **Requirements for special education teachers teaching to alternate academic achievement standards.** When used with respect to a special education teacher who teaches core academic subjects exclusively to children who are assessed against alternate academic achievement standards established under 34 CFR 200.1(d), highly qualified means the teacher, whether new or not new to the profession, may either—

(1) Meet the applicable requirements of section 9101 of the ESEA and 34 CFR 200.56 for any elementary, middle, or secondary school teacher who is new or not new to the profession; or

(2) Meet the requirements of paragraph (B) or (C) of section 9101(23) of the ESEA as applied to an elementary school teacher, or, in the case of instruction above the elementary level, meet the requirements of paragraph (B) or (C) of section 9101(23) of the ESEA as applied to an elementary school teacher and have subject matter knowledge appropriate to the level of instruction being provided and needed to effectively teach to those alternate academic achievement standards, as determined by the State.

(d) **Requirements for special education teachers teaching multiple subjects.** Subject to paragraph (e) of this section, when used with respect to a special education teacher who teaches two or more core academic subjects exclusively to children with disabilities, highly qualified means that the teacher may either—

(1) Meet the applicable requirements of section 9101 of the ESEA and 34 CFR 200.56(b) or (c);

(2) In the case of a teacher who is not new to the profession, demonstrate competence in all the core academic subjects in which the teacher teaches in the same manner as is required for an elementary, middle, or secondary school teacher who is not new to the profession under 34 CFR 200.56(c) which may include a single, **high objective uniform State standard of evaluation** (HOUSSE) covering multiple subjects; or

(3) In the case of a new special education teacher who teaches multiple subjects and who is highly qualified in mathematics, language arts, or science, demonstrate, not later than two years after the date of employment, competence in the other core academic subjects in which the teacher teaches in the same manner as is required for an elementary, middle, or secondary school teacher under 34 CFR 200.56(c), which may include a single HOUSSE covering multiple subjects.

(e) **Separate HOUSSE standards for special education teachers.** Provided that any adaptations of the State's HOUSSE would not establish a lower standard for the content knowledge requirements for special education teachers and meet all the requirements for a HOUSSE for regular education teachers-–

(1) A State may develop a separate HOUSSE for special education teachers; and

(2) The standards described in paragraph (e)(1) of this section may include single HOUSSE evaluations that cover multiple subjects.

(f) **Rule of construction.** Notwithstanding any other individual right of action that a parent or student may maintain under this part, nothing in this part shall be construed to create a right of action on behalf of an individual student or class of students for the failure of a particular SEA or LEA employee to be highly qualified, or to prevent a parent from filing a complaint under §§300.151 through 300.153 about staff qualifications with the SEA as provided for under this part.

(g) **Applicability of definition to ESEA; and clarification of new special education teacher.**

(1) A teacher who is highly qualified under this section is considered highly qualified for purposes of the ESEA.

(2) For purposes of §300.18(d)(3), a fully certified regular education teacher who subsequently becomes fully certified or licensed as a special education teacher is a new special education teacher when first hired as a special education teacher.

(h) **Private school teachers not covered.** The requirements in this section do not apply to teachers hired by private elementary schools and secondary schools including private school teachers hired or contracted by LEAs to provide equitable services to parentally-placed private school children with disabilities under §300.138. (Authority: 20 U. S. C. 1401(10))

§300.19 Homeless children. Homeless children has the meaning given the term homeless children and youths in section 725 (42 U. S. C. 11434a) of the McKinney-Vento Homeless Assistance Act, as amended, 42 U. S. C. 11431 *et seq.* (Authority: 20 U. S. C. 1401(11))

§300.20 Include. Include means that the items named are not all of the possible items that are covered, whether like or unlike the ones named. (Authority: 20 U. S. C. 1221e-3)

§300.21 Indian and Indian tribe.

(a) **Indian** means an individual who is a member of an Indian tribe.

(b) **Indian tribe** means any Federal or State Indian tribe, band, rancheria, pueblo, colony, or community, including any Alaska Native village or regional village corporation (as defined in or established under the Alaska Native Claims Settlement Act, 43 U. S. C. 1601 *et seq.*).

(c) Nothing in this definition is intended to indicate that the Secretary of the Interior is required to provide services or funding to a State Indian tribe that is not listed in the *Federal Register* list of Indian entities recognized as eligible to receive services from the United States, published pursuant to Section 104 of the Federally Recognized Indian Tribe List Act of 1994, 25 U. S. C. 479a-1. (Authority: 20 U. S. C. 1401(12) and (13))

§300.22 Individualized education program. Individualized education program or IEP means a written statement for a child with a disability that is developed, reviewed, and revised in accordance with §§300.320 through 300.324. (Authority: 20 U. S. C. 1401(14))

§300.23 Individualized education program team. Individualized education program team or IEP Team means a group of individuals described in §300.321 that is responsible for developing, reviewing, or revising an IEP for a child with a disability. (Authority: 20 U. S. C. 1414(d)(1)(B))

§300.24 Individualized family service plan. Individualized family service plan or IFSP has the meaning given the term in section 636 of the Act. (Authority: 20 U. S. C. 1401(15))

§300.25 Infant or toddler with a disability. Infant or toddler with a disability—

(a) Means an individual **under three years of age who needs early intervention services** because the individual—

(1) Is experiencing developmental delays, as measured by appropriate diagnostic instruments and procedures in one or more of the areas of cognitive development, physical development, communication development, social or emotional development, and adaptive development; or

(2) Has a diagnosed physical or mental condition that has a high probability of resulting in developmental delay; and

(b) May also include, at a State's discretion—

(1) At-risk infants and toddlers; and

(2) Children with disabilities who are eligible for services under section 619 and who previously received services under Part C of the Act until such children enter, or are eligible under State law to enter, kindergarten or elementary school, as appropriate, provided that any programs under Part C of the Act serving such children shall include—

(i) An educational component that promotes school readiness and incorporates pre-literacy, language, and numeracy skills; and

(ii) A written notification to parents of their rights and responsibilities in determining whether their child will continue to receive services under Part C of the Act or participate in preschool programs under section 619. (Authority: 20 U. S. C. 1401(16) and 1432(5))

§300.26 Institution of higher education. Institution of higher education—

(a) Has the meaning given the term in section 101 of the Higher Education Act of 1965, as amended, 20 U. S. C. 1021 *et seq.* (HEA); and

(b) Also includes any community college receiving funds from the Secretary of the Interior under the Tribally Controlled Community College or University Assistance Act of 1978, 25 U. S. C. 1801, *et seq.* (Authority: 20 U. S. C. 1401(17))

§300.27 Limited English proficient. Limited English proficient has the meaning given the term in section 9101(25) of the ESEA. (Authority: 20 U. S. C. 1401(18))

§300.28 Local educational agency.

(a) General. Local educational agency or LEA means a public board of education or other public authority legally constituted within a State for either administrative control or direction of, or to perform a service function for, public elementary or secondary schools in a city, county, township, school district, or other political subdivision of a State, or for a combination of school districts or counties as are recognized in a State as an administrative agency for its public elementary schools or secondary schools.

(b) Educational service agencies and other public institutions or agencies. The term includes—

(1) An educational service agency, as defined in §300.12; and

(2) Any other public institution or agency having administrative control and direction of a public elementary school or secondary school, including a public nonprofit charter school that is established as an LEA under State law.

(c) BIA funded schools. The term includes an elementary school or secondary school funded by the Bureau of Indian Affairs, and not subject to the jurisdiction of any SEA other than the Bureau of Indian Affairs, but only to the extent that the inclusion makes the school eligible for programs for which specific eligibility is not provided to the school in another provision of law and the school does not have a student population that is smaller than the student population of the LEA receiving assistance under the Act with the smallest student population. (Authority: 20 U. S. C. 1401(19))

§300.29 Native language.

(a) Native language, when used **with respect to an individual who is limited English proficient**, means the following:

(1) The language normally used by that individual, or, in the case of a child, the language normally used by the parents of the child, except as provided in paragraph (a)(2) of this section.

(2) In all direct contact with a child (including evaluation of the child), the language normally used by the child in the home or learning environment.

(b) For an individual with deafness or blindness, or for an individual with no written language, **the mode of communication is that normally used** by the individual (such as sign language, Braille, or oral communication). (Authority: 20 U. S. C. 1401(20))

§300.30 Parent.

(a) **Parent** means—

(1) A **biological or adoptive parent** of a child;

(2) A **foster parent**, unless State law, regulations, or contractual obligations with a State or local entity prohibit a foster parent from acting as a parent;

(3) A **guardian** generally authorized to act as the child's parent, or authorized to make educational decisions for the child (but not the State if the child is a ward of the State);

(4) An individual acting in the place of a biological or adoptive parent (including a **grandparent, stepparent, or other relative**) with whom the child lives, or an individual who is legally responsible for the child's welfare; or

(5) A **surrogate parent** who has been appointed in accordance with ADD §300.519 or section 639(a)(5) of the Act.

(b)

(1) Except as provided in paragraph (b)(2) of this section, the biological or adoptive parent, when attempting to act as the parent under this part and when more than one party is qualified under paragraph (a) of this section to act as a parent, **must be presumed** to be the parent for purposes of this section **unless the biological or adoptive parent does not have legal authority** to make educational decisions for the child.

(2) If a judicial decree or order identifies a specific person or persons under paragraphs (a)(1) through (4) of this section to act as the "parent" of a child or to make educational decisions on behalf of a child, then such person or persons **shall** be determined to be the "parent" for purposes of this section. (Authority: 20 U. S. C. 1401(23))

§300.31 Parent training and information center.
Parent training and information center means a center assisted under sections 671 or 672 of the Act. (Authority: 20 U. S. C. 1401(25))

§300.32 Personally identifiable.
Personally identifiable means information that contains—

(a) The name of the child, the child's parent, or other family member;

(b) The address of the child;

(c) A personal identifier, such as the child's social security number or student number; or

(d) A list of personal characteristics or other information that would make it possible to identify the child with reasonable certainty. (Authority: 20 U. S. C. 1415(a))

§300.33 Public agency.
Public agency includes the **SEA, LEAs, ESAs, nonprofit public charter schools** that are not otherwise included as LEAs or ESAs and are not a school of an LEA or ESA, and any other political subdivisions of the State that are responsible for providing education to children with disabilities. (Authority: 20 U. S. C. 1412(a)(11))

§300.34 Related services.

(a) **General.** Related services means **transportation** and such developmental, corrective, and **other supportive services** as are required to assist a child with a disability to benefit from special education, and includes **speech-language pathology and audiology services**, interpreting services, psychological services, **physical and occupational therapy**, recreation, including therapeutic recreation, early identification and assessment of disabilities in children, counseling services, including rehabilitation counseling, orientation and mobility services, and medical services for diagnostic or evaluation purposes. Related services also include school health services and school nurse services, social work services in schools, and parent counseling and training.

(b) **Exception; services that apply to children with surgically implanted devices, including cochlear implants**.

(1) Related services **do not include a medical device that is surgically implanted**, the optimization of that device's functioning (e.g., mapping), maintenance of that device, or the replacement of that device.

(2) **Nothing** in paragraph (b)(1) of this section—

(i) **Limits** the right of a child with a surgically implanted device (e.g., cochlear implant) to receive related services (as listed in paragraph (a) of this section) that are determined by the IEP Team to be necessary for the child to receive FAPE.

(ii) **Limits** the responsibility of a public agency to appropriately monitor and maintain medical devices that are needed to maintain the health and safety of the child, including breathing, nutrition, or operation of other bodily functions, while the child is transported to and from school or is at school; **or**

(iii) **Prevents the routine checking** of an external component of a surgically-implanted device to make sure it is functioning properly, as required in §300.113(b).

(c) **Individual related services terms defined**. The terms used in this definition are defined as follows:

(1) **Audiology** includes—

(i) Identification of children with hearing loss;

(ii) Determination of the range, nature, and degree of hearing loss, including referral for medical or other professional attention for the habilitation of hearing;

(iii) Provision of habilitative activities, such as language habilitation, auditory training, speech reading (lip-reading), hearing evaluation, and speech conservation;

(iv) Creation and administration of programs for prevention of hearing loss;

(v) Counseling and guidance of children, parents, and teachers regarding hearing loss; and

(vi) Determination of children's needs for group and individual amplification, selecting and fitting an appropriate aid, and evaluating the effectiveness of amplification.

(2) **Counseling services** means services provided by qualified social workers, psychologists, guidance counselors, or other qualified personnel.

(3) **Early identification and assessment of disabilities in children** means the implementation of a formal plan for identifying a disability as early as possible in a child's life.

(4) **Interpreting services** includes—

(i) The following, when used with respect to children who are deaf or hard of hearing: Oral transliteration services, cued language transliteration services, sign language transliteration and interpreting services, and transcription services, such as communication access real-time translation (CART), C-Print, and TypeWell; and

(ii) Special interpreting services for children who are deaf-blind.

(5) **Medical services** means services provided by a licensed physician to determine a child's medically related disability that results in the child's need for special education and related services.

(6) **Occupational therapy** —

(i) Means services provided by a qualified occupational therapist; and

(ii) Includes—

(A) Improving, developing, or restoring functions impaired or lost through illness, injury, or deprivation;

(B) Improving ability to perform tasks for independent functioning if functions are impaired or lost; and

(C) Preventing, through early intervention, initial or further impairment or loss of function.

(7) **Orientation and mobility services**—

(i) Means services provided to blind or visually impaired children by qualified personnel to enable those students to attain systematic orientation to and safe movement within their environments in school, home, and community; and

(ii) Includes teaching children the following, as appropriate:

(A) Spatial and environmental concepts and use of information received by the senses (such as sound, temperature and vibrations) to establish, maintain, or regain orientation and line of travel (e.g., using sound at a traffic light to cross the street);

(B) To use the long cane or a service animal to supplement visual travel skills or as a tool for safely negotiating the environment for children with no available travel vision;

(C) To understand and use remaining vision and distance low vision aids; and

(D) Other concepts, techniques, and tools.

(8)

(i) **Parent counseling and training** means assisting parents in understanding the special needs of their child;

(ii) Providing parents with information about child development; and

(iii) Helping parents to acquire the necessary skills that will allow them to support the implementation of their child's IEP or IFSP.

(9) **Physical therapy** means services provided by a qualified physical therapist.

(10) **Psychological services** includes—

(i) Administering psychological and educational tests, and other assessment procedures;

(ii) Interpreting assessment results;

(iii) Obtaining, integrating, and interpreting information about child behavior and conditions relating to learning;

(iv) Consulting with other staff members in planning school programs to meet the special educational needs of children as indicated by psychological tests, interviews, direct observation, and behavioral evaluations;

(v) Planning and managing a program of psychological services, including psychological counseling for children and parents; and

(vi) Assisting in developing positive behavioral intervention strategies.

(11) **Recreation** includes—

(i) Assessment of leisure function;

(ii) Therapeutic recreation services;

(iii) Recreation programs in schools and community agencies; and

(iv) Leisure education.

(12) **Rehabilitation counseling services** means services provided by qualified personnel in individual or group sessions that focus specifically on career development, employment preparation, achieving independence, and integration in the workplace and community of a student with a disability. The term also includes vocational rehabilitation services provided to a student with a disability by vocational rehabilitation programs funded under the Rehabilitation Act of 1973, as amended, 29 U. S. C. 701 et seq.

(13) **School health services and school nurse services** means health services that are designed to enable a child with a disability to receive FAPE as described in the child's IEP. School nurse services are services provided by a qualified school nurse. School health services are services that may be provided by either a qualified school nurse or other qualified person.

(14) **Social work services in schools** includes—

(i) Preparing a social or developmental history on a child with a disability;

(ii) Group and individual counseling with the child and family;

(iii) Working in partnership with parents and others on those problems in a child's living situation (home, school, and community) that affect the child's adjustment in school;

(iv) Mobilizing school and community resources to enable the child to learn as effectively as possible in his or her educational program; and

(v) Assisting in developing positive behavioral intervention strategies.

(15) **Speech-language pathology services** includes—

(i) Identification of children with speech or language impairments;

(ii) Diagnosis and appraisal of specific speech or language impairments;

(iii) Referral for medical or other professional attention necessary for the habilitation of speech or language impairments;

(iv) Provision of speech and language services for the habilitation or prevention of communicative impairments; and

(v) Counseling and guidance of parents, children, and teachers regarding speech and language impairments.

(16) **Transportation** includes—

(i) Travel to and from school and between schools;

(ii) Travel in and around school buildings; and

(iii) Specialized equipment (such as special or adapted buses, lifts, and ramps), if required to provide special transportation for a child with a disability. (Authority: 20 U. S. C. 1401(26))

§300.35 Scientifically based research. Scientifically based research has the meaning given the term in section 9101(37) of the ESEA. (Authority: 20 U. S. C. 1411(e)(2)(C)(xi))

§300.36 Secondary school. Secondary school means a nonprofit institutional day or residential school, including a public secondary charter school that provides secondary education, as determined under State law, except that it does not include any education beyond grade 12. (Authority: 20 U. S. C. 1401(27))

§300.37 Services plan. Services plan means a written statement that describes the special education and related services the LEA will provide to a parentally-placed child with a disability enrolled in a private school who has been designated to receive services, including the location of the services and any transportation necessary, consistent with §300.132, and is developed and implemented in accordance with §§300.137 through 300.139. (Authority: 20 U. S. C. 1412(a)(10)(A))

§300.38 Secretary. Secretary means the Secretary of Education. (Authority: 20 U. S. C. 1401(28))

§300.39 Special education.

(a) **General**.

(1) Special education means **specially designed instruction**, at no cost to the parents, **to meet the unique needs of a child** with a disability, including—

(i) Instruction conducted in the classroom, in the home, in hospitals and institutions, and in other settings; and

(ii) Instruction in physical education.

(2) Special education **includes** each of the following, if the services otherwise meet the requirements of paragraph (a)(1) of this section—

(i) Speech-language pathology services, or any other related service, if the service is considered special education rather than a related service under State standards;

(ii) Travel training; and

(iii) Vocational education.

(b) **Individual special education terms defined**. The terms in this definition are defined as follows:

(1) **At no cost** means that all specially-designed instruction is provided without charge, **but does not preclude incidental fees that are normally charged to nondisabled students** or their parents as a part of the regular education program.

(2) **Physical education** means—

(i) The development of—

(A) Physical and motor fitness;
(B) Fundamental motor skills and patterns; and
(C) Skills in aquatics, dance, and individual and group games and sports (including intramural and lifetime sports); and

(ii) Includes special physical education, adapted physical education, movement education, and motor development.

(3) Specially designed instruction means **adapting, as appropriate to the needs of an eligible child** under this part, **the content, methodology, or delivery of instruction—**

(i) **To address the unique needs of the child** that result from the child's disability; and

(ii) **To ensure access of the child to the general curriculum,** so that the child can meet the educational standards within the jurisdiction of the public agency that apply to all children.

(4) Travel training means providing instruction, as appropriate, to children with **significant cognitive disabilities**, and any other children with disabilities who require this instruction, to enable them to—

(i) Develop **an awareness of the environment** in which they live; and

(ii) Learn the **skills necessary to move effectively and safely** from place to place within that environment (e.g., in school, in the home, at work, and in the community).

(5) Vocational education means organized educational programs that are directly related to the preparation of individuals for paid or unpaid employment, or for additional preparation for a career not requiring a baccalaureate or advanced degree. (Authority: 20 U. S. C. 1401(29))

§300.40 State. State means each of the 50 States, the District of Columbia, the Commonwealth of Puerto Rico, and each of the outlying areas. (Authority: 20 U. S. C. 1401(31))

§300.41 State educational agency. State educational agency or SEA means the State board of education or other agency or officer primarily responsible for the State supervision of public elementary schools and secondary schools, or, if there is no such officer or agency, an officer or agency designated by the Governor or by State law. (Authority: 20 U. S. C. 1401(32))

§300.42 Supplementary aids and services. Supplementary aids and services means aids, services, and other supports that are provided in regular education classes, other education-related settings, and in extracurricular and nonacademic settings, to enable children with disabilities to be educated with nondisabled children to the maximum extent appropriate in accordance with §§300.114 through 300.116. (Authority: 20 U. S. C. 1401(33))

§300.43 Transition services.

(a) Transition services means a **coordinated set of activities** for a child with a disability that—

(1) Is designed to be within a **results-oriented process**, that is focused on improving the academic and functional achievement of the child with a disability to facilitate the child's movement from **school to post school activities, including postsecondary education**, vocational education, integrated employment (including supported employment), continuing and adult education, adult services, independent living, or community participation;

(2) Is based on the individual child's needs, taking into account the child's strengths, preferences, and interests; and includes—

(i) Instruction;

(ii) Related services;

(iii) Community experiences;

(iv) The development of employment and other post-school adult living objectives; and

(v) If appropriate, acquisition of daily living skills and provision of a functional vocational evaluation.

(b) Transition services for children with disabilities may be special education, if provided as specially designed instruction, or a related service, if required to assist a child with a disability to benefit from special education. (Authority: 20 U. S. C. 1401(34))

§300.44 Universal design. Universal design has the meaning given the term in section 3 of the Assistive Technology Act of 1998, as amended, 29 U. S. C.3002. (Authority: 20 U. S. C. 1401(35))

§300.45 Ward of the State.

(a) General. Subject to paragraph (b) of this section, **ward of the State** means a child who, as determined by the State where the child resides, is—

(1) A foster child;

(2) A ward of the State; or

(3) In the custody of a public child welfare agency.

(b) Exception. Ward of the State **does not** include a foster child who has a foster parent who meets the definition of a parent in §300.30. (Authority: 20 U. S. C. 1401(36))

Subpart B—State Eligibility

General

§300.100 Eligibility for assistance. A State is eligible for assistance under Part B of the Act for a fiscal year if the State submits a plan that provides assurances to the Secretary that the State has in effect policies and procedures to ensure that the State meets the conditions in §§300.101 through 300.176. (Authority: 20 U. S. C. 1412(a))

FAPE Requirements

§300.101 Free appropriate public education (FAPE).

(a) General. A **free appropriate public education** must be available to all children residing in the State between the ages of **3 and 21**, inclusive, including children with disabilities who have been suspended or expelled from school, as provided for in §300.530(d).

(b) FAPE for children beginning at age 3.

(1) Each State must ensure that—

(i) The obligation to make FAPE available to each eligible child residing in the State begins no later than the child's third birthday; and

(ii) An IEP or an IFSP is in effect for the child by that date, in accordance with §300.323(b).

(2) If a child's third birthday occurs during the summer, the child's IEP Team shall determine the date when services under the IEP or IFSP will begin.

(c) Children advancing from grade to grade.

(1) Each State must ensure that FAPE is available to any individual child with a disability who needs special education and related services, **even though the child has not failed or been retained in a course or grade, and is advancing from grade to grade**.

(2) The determination that a child described in paragraph (a) of this section is eligible under this part, must be made on an individual basis by the group responsible within the child's LEA for making eligibility determinations. (Authority: 20 U. S. C. 1412(a)(1)(A))

§300.102 Limitation—exception to FAPE for certain ages.

(a) General. The obligation to make FAPE available to all children with disabilities does not apply with respect to the following:

(1) Children aged 3, 4, 5, 18, 19, 20, or 21 in a State to the extent that its application to those children would be inconsistent with State law or practice, or the order of any court, respecting the provision of public education to children of those ages.

(2)

(i) Children aged 18 through 21 to the extent that State law does not require that special education and related services under Part B of the Act be provided to students with disabilities who, in the last educational placement prior to their incarceration in an adult correctional facility—

(A) Were not actually identified as being a child with a disability under §300.8; and

(B) Did not have an IEP under Part B of the Act.

(ii) The exception in paragraph (a)(2)(i) of this section does not apply to children with disabilities, aged 18 through 21, who—

(A) Had been identified as a child with a disability under §300.8 and had received services in accordance with an IEP, but who left school prior to their incarceration; or

(B) Did not have an IEP in their last educational setting, but who had actually been identified as a child with a disability under §300.8.

(3)

(i) Children with disabilities who have **graduated** from high school with a **regular high school diploma**.

(ii) The exception in paragraph (a)(3)(i) of this section does not apply to children who have graduated from high school but have not been awarded a regular high school diploma.

(iii) Graduation from high school with a regular high school diploma constitutes a change in placement, requiring written prior notice in accordance with §300.503.

(iv) As used in paragraphs (a)(3)(i) through (a)(3) (iii) of this section, the term regular high school diploma does not include an alternative degree that is not fully aligned with the State's academic standards, such as a certificate or a general educational development credential (GED).

(4) Children with disabilities who are eligible under subpart H of this part, but who receive early intervention services under Part C of the Act.

(b) Documents relating to exceptions. The State must assure that the information it has provided to the Secretary regarding the exceptions in paragraph (a) of this section, as required by §300.700 (for purposes of making grants to States under this part), is current and accurate. (Authority: 20 U. S. C. 1412(a)(1)(B)-(C))

Other FAPE Requirements

§300.103 FAPE—methods and payments.

(a) Each State may use whatever State, local, Federal, and private sources of support that are available in the State to meet the requirements of this part. For example, if it is necessary to place a child with a disability in a residential facility, a State could use joint agreements between the agencies involved for sharing the cost of that placement.

(b) Nothing in this part relieves an insurer or similar third party from an otherwise valid obligation to provide or to pay for services provided to a child with a disability.

(c) Consistent with §300.323(c), the State must ensure that there is no delay in implementing a child's IEP, including any case in which the payment source for providing or paying for special education and related services to the child is being determined. (Authority: 20 U. S. C. 1401(8), 1412(a)(1))

§300.104 Residential placement. If placement in a public or private residential program is necessary to provide special education and related services to a child with a disability, **the program, including non-medical care and room and board, must be at no cost to the parents of the child**. (Authority: 20 U. S. C. 1412(a)(1), 1412(a)(10)(B))

§300.105 Assistive technology.

(a) Each public agency **must ensure that assistive technology devices** or **assistive technology services**, or both, as those terms are defined in §§300.5 and 300.6, respectively, are made available to a child with a disability if required as a part of the child's—

(1) Special education under §300.36;

(2) Related services under §300.34; **or**

(3) **Supplementary aids and services** under §§300.38 and 300.114(a)(2)(ii).

(b) On a case-by-case basis, the use of school-purchased assistive technology devices in a child's home or in other settings is required if the child's IEP Team determines that the child needs access to those devices in order to receive FAPE. (Authority: 20 U. S. C. 1412(a)(1), 1412(a)(12)(B)(i))

§300.106 Extended school year services.

(a) General.

(1) Each public agency must ensure that **extended school year services** are available as necessary to provide FAPE, consistent with paragraph (a)(2) of this section.

(2) Extended school year services must be provided only if a child's IEP Team determines, on an individual basis, in accordance with §§300.320 through 300.324, that the services are necessary for the provision of FAPE to the child.

(3) In implementing the requirements of this section, a public agency may not—

(i) Limit extended school year services to particular categories of disability; or

(ii) Unilaterally limit the type, amount, or duration of those services.

(b) Definition. As used in this section, the term extended school year services means special education and related services that—

(1) Are provided to a child with a disability—

(i) Beyond the normal school year of the public agency;

(ii) In accordance with the child's IEP; and

(iii) At no cost to the parents of the child; and

(2) Meet the standards of the SEA. (Authority: 20 U. S. C. 1412(a)(1))

§300.107 Nonacademic services. The State must ensure the following:

(a) Each public agency **must take steps**, including the provision of **supplementary aids and services** determined appropriate and necessary by the child's IEP Team, **to provide nonacademic and extracurricular services** and activities in the manner necessary to afford children with disabilities **an equal opportunity** for participation in those services and activities.

(b) Nonacademic and extracurricular services and activities **may include** counseling services, athletics, transportation, health services, recreational activities, special interest groups or clubs sponsored by the public agency, referrals to agencies that provide assistance to individuals with disabilities, and employment of students, including both employment by the public agency and assistance in making outside employment available. (Authority: 20 U. S. C. 1412(a)(1))

§300.108 Physical education. The State must ensure that public agencies in the State comply with the following:

(a) General. Physical education services, specially designed if necessary, must be made available to every child with a disability receiving FAPE, unless the public agency enrolls children without disabilities and does not provide physical education to children without disabilities in the same grades.

(b) Regular physical education. Each child with a disability must be afforded the opportunity to participate in the regular physical education program available to nondisabled children unless—

(1) The child is enrolled full time in a separate facility; or

(2) The child needs specially designed physical education, as prescribed in the child's IEP.

(c) Special physical education. If specially designed physical education is prescribed in a child's IEP, the public agency responsible for the education of that child must provide the services directly or make arrangements for those services to be provided through other public or private programs.

(d) Education in separate facilities. The public agency responsible for the education of a child with a disability who is enrolled in a separate facility must ensure that the child receives appropriate physical education services in compliance with this section. (Authority: 20 U. S. C. 1412(a)(5)(A))

§300.109 Full educational opportunity goal (FEOG). The State must have in effect policies and procedures to demonstrate that the State has established a goal of providing full educational opportunity to all children with disabilities, aged birth through 21, and a detailed timetable for accomplishing that goal. (Authority: 20 U. S. C. 1412(a)(2))

§300.110 Program options. The State must ensure that each public agency takes steps to ensure that its children with disabilities have available to them the variety of educational programs and services available to nondisabled children in the area served by the agency, including art, music, industrial arts, consumer and homemaking education, and vocational education. (Authority: 20 U. S. C. 1412(a)(2), 1413(a)(1))

§300.111 Child find.

(a) General.

(1) The State must have in effect policies and procedures to ensure that—

(i) **All children with disabilities residing in the State, including children with disabilities who are homeless children or are wards of the State, and children with disabilities attending private schools,** regardless of the severity of their disability, and who are in need of special education and related services, **are identified, located, and evaluated**; and

(ii) A practical method is developed and implemented to determine which children are currently receiving needed special education and related services.

(b) Use of term developmental delay. The following provisions apply with respect to implementing the child find requirements of this section:

(1) A State that adopts a definition of developmental delay under §300.8(b) determines whether the term applies to children aged three through nine, or to a subset of that age range (e.g., ages three through five).

(2) A State may not require an LEA to adopt and use the term developmental delay for any children within its jurisdiction.

(3) If an LEA uses the term developmental delay for children described in §300.8(b), the LEA must conform to both the State's definition of that term and to the age range that has been adopted by the State.

(4) If a State does not adopt the term developmental delay, an LEA may not independently use that term as a basis for establishing a child's eligibility under this part.

(c) Other children in child find. Child find **also must include**—

(1) Children who are suspected of being a child with a disability under §300.8 and in need of special education, even though they are advancing from grade to grade; and

(2) Highly mobile children, including migrant children.

(d) Construction. Nothing in the Act requires that children be classified by their disability so long as each child who has a disability that is listed in §300.8 and who, by reason of that disability, needs special education and related services is regarded as a child with a disability under Part B of the Act. (Authority: 20 U. S. C. 1401(3)); 1412(a)(3))

§300.112 Individualized education programs (IEP). The State must ensure that an IEP, or an IFSP that meets the requirements of section 636(d) of the Act, is developed, reviewed, and revised for each child with a disability in accordance with §§300.320 through 300.324, except as provided in §300.300(b)(3)(ii). (Authority: 20 U. S. C. 1412(a)(4))

§300.113 Routine checking of hearing aids and external components of surgically implanted medical devices.

(a) Hearing aids. Each public agency **must ensure that** hearing aids worn in school by children with hearing impairments, including deafness, are functioning properly.

(b) External components of surgically implanted medical devices.

(1) Subject to paragraph (b)(2) of this section, each public agency **must ensure** that the external components of surgically implanted medical devices **are functioning properly**.

(2) For a child with a surgically implanted medical device who is receiving special education and related services under this part, a public agency is not responsible for the **post-surgical maintenance, programming, or replacement** of the medical device that has been surgically implanted (or of an external component of the surgically implanted medical device). (Authority: 20 U. S. C. 1401(1), 1401(26)(B))

Least Restrictive Environment (LRE)

§300.114 LRE requirements.

(a) General.

(1) Except as provided in §300.324(d)(2) (regarding children with disabilities in adult prisons), the State must have in effect policies and procedures to ensure that public agencies in the State meet the LRE requirements of this section and §§300.115 through 300.120.

(2) Each public agency **must ensure that**—

(i) To the maximum extent appropriate, **children with disabilities**, including children in public or private institutions or other care facilities, **are educated with children who are nondisabled**; and

(ii) **Special classes, separate schooling, or other removal** of children with disabilities from the regular educational environment **occurs only if** the nature or severity of the disability is such that education in regular classes with the use of supplementary aids and services cannot be achieved satisfactorily.

(b) Additional requirement—State funding mechanism.

(1) **General.**

(i) A State funding mechanism must not result in placements that violate the requirements of paragraph (a) of this section; and

(ii) A State must not use a funding mechanism by which the State distributes funds on the basis of the type of setting in which a child is served that will result in the failure to provide a child with a disability FAPE according to the unique needs of the child, as described in the child's IEP.

(2) **Assurance.** If the State does not have policies and procedures to ensure compliance with paragraph (b)(1) of this section, the State must provide the Secretary an assurance that the State will revise the funding mechanism as soon as feasible to ensure that the mechanism does not result in placements that violate that paragraph. (Authority: 20 U. S. C. 1412(a)(5))

§300.115 Continuum of alternative placements.

(a) Each public agency must ensure that **a continuum of alternative placements** is available to meet the needs of children with disabilities for special education and related services.

(b) The continuum required in paragraph (a) of this section must—

(1) Include the alternative placements listed in the definition of special education under §300.39 (instruction in regular classes, special classes, special schools, home instruction, and instruction in hospitals and institutions); and

(2) Make provision for supplementary services (such as resource room or itinerant instruction) to be provided in conjunction with regular class placement. (Authority: 20 U. S. C. 1412(a)(5))

§300.116 Placements. In determining the educational placement of a child with a disability, including a preschool child with a disability, each public agency must ensure that—

(a) The placement decision—

(1) Is made by a group of persons, **including the parents**, and other persons knowledgeable about the child, the meaning of the evaluation data, and the placement options; and

(2) Is made in conformity with the LRE provisions of this subpart, including §§300.114 through 300.118;

(b) The child's **placement**—

(1) Is determined at least annually;

(2) Is based on the child's IEP; and

(3) Is **as close as possible to the child's home**;

(c) **Unless** the IEP of a child with a disability requires some other arrangement, the child is educated in the school that he or she would attend if nondisabled;

(d) In selecting the LRE, consideration is given to any **potential harmful effect on the child or on the quality of services** that he or she needs; and

(e) A child with a disability is **not removed from education in age-appropriate regular classrooms solely because of needed modifications** in the general education curriculum. (Authority: 20 U. S. C. 1412(a)(5))

§300.117 Nonacademic settings. In providing or arranging for the provision of nonacademic and extracurricular services and activities, including meals, recess periods, and the services and activities set forth in §300.107, each public agency must ensure that each child with a disability participates with nondisabled children in the extracurricular services and activities to the maximum extent appropriate to the needs of that child. The public agency must ensure that each child with a disability has the supplementary aids and services determined by the child's IEP Team to be appropriate and necessary for the child to participate in nonacademic settings. (Authority: 20 U. S. C. 1412(a)(5))

§300.118 Children in public or private institutions. Except as provided in §300.149(d) (regarding agency responsibility for general supervision of some individuals in adult prisons), an SEA must ensure that §300.114 is effectively implemented, including, if necessary, making arrangements with public and private institutions (such as a memorandum of agreement or special implementation procedures). (Authority: 20 U. S. C. 1412(a)(5))

§300.119 Technical assistance and training activities. Each SEA must carry out activities to ensure that teachers and administrators in all public agencies—

(a) Are fully informed about their responsibilities for implementing §300.114; and

(b) Are provided with technical assistance and training necessary to assist them in this effort. (Authority: 20 U. S. C. 1412(a)(5))

§300.120 Monitoring activities.

(a) The SEA must carry out activities to ensure that §300.114 is implemented by each public agency.

(b) If there is evidence that a public agency makes placements that are inconsistent with §300.114, the SEA must—

(1) Review the public agency's justification for its actions; and

(2) Assist in planning and implementing any necessary corrective action. (Authority: 20 U. S. C. 1412(a)(5))

Additional Eligibility Requirements

§300.121 Procedural safeguards.

(a) **General.** The State must have procedural safeguards in effect to ensure that each public agency in the State meets the requirements of §§300.500 through 300.536.

(b) **Procedural safeguards identified.** Children with disabilities and their parents must be afforded the procedural safeguards identified in paragraph (a) of this section. (Authority: 20 U. S. C. 1412(a)(6)(A))

§300.122 Evaluation. Children with disabilities must be evaluated in accordance with §§300.300 through 300.311 of subpart D of this part. (Authority: 20 U. S. C. 1412(a)(7))

§300.123 Confidentiality of personally identifiable information. The State must have policies and procedures in effect to ensure that public agencies in the State comply with §§300.610 through 300.626 related to protecting the confidentiality of any personally identifiable information collected, used, or maintained under Part B of the Act. (Authority: 20 U. S. C. 1412(a)(8); 1417(c))

§300.124 Transition of children from the Part C program to preschool programs. The State must have in effect policies and procedures to ensure that—

(a) Children participating in **early intervention programs** assisted under Part C of the Act, and who will participate in preschool programs assisted under Part B of the Act, **experience a smooth and effective transition** to those preschool programs in a manner consistent with section 637(a)(9) of the Act;

(b) By the **third birthday** of a child described in paragraph (a) of this section, **an IEP** or, if consistent with §300.323(b) and section 636(d) of the Act, an IFSP, **has been developed** and is being implemented for the child consistent with §300.101(b); and

(c) Each affected LEA will participate in transition planning conferences arranged by the designated lead agency under section 635(a)(10) of the Act. (Authority: 20 U. S. C. 1412(a)(9))

§§300.125-300.128 [Reserved]

Children in Private Schools

§300.129 State responsibility regarding children in private schools.

The State must have in effect policies and procedures that ensure that LEAs, and, if applicable, the SEA, meet the private school requirements in §§300.130 through 300.148. (Authority: 20 U. S. C. 1412(a)(10))

Children With Disabilities Enrolled by Their Parents in Private Schools

§300.130 Definition of parentally-placed private school children with disabilities.

Parentally-placed private school children with disabilities means children with disabilities enrolled by their parents in private, including religious, schools or facilities that meet the definition of elementary school in §300.13 or secondary school in §300.36, other than children with disabilities covered under §§300.145 through 300.147. (Authority: 20 U. S. C. 1412(a)(10)(A))

§300.131 Child find for parentally-placed private school children with disabilities.

(a) **General.** Each LEA must locate, identify, and evaluate all children with disabilities who are enrolled by their parents in private, including religious, elementary schools and secondary schools located in the school district served by the LEA, in accordance with paragraphs (b) through (e) of this section, and §§300.111 and 300.201.

(b) **Child find design.** The child find process must be designed to ensure—

(1) The **equitable participation** of parentally-placed private school children; and

(2) An accurate count of those children.

(c) **Activities.** In carrying out the requirements of this section, the LEA, or, if applicable, the SEA, must undertake activities similar to the activities undertaken for the agency's public school children.

(d) **Cost.** The cost of carrying out the child find requirements in this section, including individual evaluations, may not be considered in determining if an LEA has met its obligation under §300.133.

(e) **Completion period.** The child find process must be completed in a time period comparable to that for students attending public schools in the LEA consistent with §300.301.

(f) **Out-of-State children.** Each LEA in which private, including religious, elementary schools and secondary schools are located must, in carrying out the child find requirements in this section, include parentally-placed private school children who reside in a State other than the State in which the private schools that they attend are located. (Authority: 20 U. S. C. 1412(a)(10)(A)(ii))

§300.132 Provision of services for parentally-placed private school children with disabilities—basic requirement.

(a) **General.** To the extent consistent with the number and location of children with disabilities who are enrolled by their parents in private, including religious, elementary schools and secondary schools located in the school district served by the LEA, provision is made for the participation of those children in the program assisted or carried out under Part B of the Act by providing them with special education and related services, including direct services determined in accordance with §300.137, unless the Secretary has arranged for services to those children under the by-pass provisions in §§300.190 through 300.198.

(b) **Services plan for parentally-placed private school children with disabilities.** In accordance with paragraph (a) of this section and §§300.137 through 300.139, a services plan must be developed and implemented for each private school child with a disability who has been designated by the LEA in which the private school is located to receive special education and related services under this part.

(c) **Record keeping.** Each LEA must maintain in its records, and provide to the SEA, the following information related to parentally-placed private school children covered under §§300.130 through 300.144:

(1) The number of children evaluated;

(2) The number of children determined to be children with disabilities; and

(3) The number of children served. (Authority: 20 U. S. C. 1412(a)(10)(A)(i))

§300.133 Expenditures.

(a) **Formula.** To meet the requirement of §300.132(a), each LEA **must spend the following** on providing special education and related services (including direct services) **to parentally-placed private school children** with disabilities:

(1) For children **aged 3 through 21**, an amount that is the same proportion of the LEA's total subgrant under section 611(f) of the Act as the number of private school children with disabilities aged 3 through 21 who are enrolled by their parents in private, including religious, elementary schools and secondary schools located in the school district served by the LEA, is to the total number of children with disabilities in its jurisdiction aged 3 through 21.

(2)

(i) For children aged **three through five**, an amount that is the same proportion of the LEA's total subgrant under section 619(g) of the Act as the number of parentally-placed private school children with disabilities aged three through five who are enrolled by their parents in a private, including religious, elementary school located in the school district served by the LEA, is to the total number of children with disabilities in its jurisdiction aged three through five.

(ii) As described in paragraph (a)(2)(i) of this section, children aged three through five are considered to be parentally-placed private school children with disabilities enrolled by their parents in private, including religious, elementary schools, if they are enrolled in a private school that meets the definition of elementary school in §300.13.

(3) If an LEA has not expended for equitable services all of the funds described in paragraphs (a)(1) and (a)(2) of this section by the end of the fiscal year for which Congress appropriated the funds, the LEA must obligate the remaining funds for special education and related services (including direct services) to parentally-placed private school children with disabilities during a carry-over period of one additional year.

(b) **Calculating proportionate amount.** In calculating the proportionate amount of Federal funds to be provided for parentally-placed private school children with disabilities, the LEA, after timely and meaningful consultation with representatives of private schools under §300.134, must conduct a thorough and complete child find process to determine the number of parentally-placed children with disabilities attending private schools located in the LEA. (See Appendix B for an example of how proportionate share is calculated).

(c) Annual count of the number of parentally-placed private school children with disabilities.

(1) Each LEA must—

(i) After timely and meaningful consultation with representatives of parentally-placed private school children with disabilities (consistent with §300.134), determine the number of parentally-placed private school children with disabilities attending private schools located in the LEA; and

(ii) Ensure that the count is conducted on any date between October 1 and December 1, inclusive, of each year.

(2) The count must be used to determine the amount that the LEA must spend on providing special education and related services to parentally-placed private school children with disabilities in the next subsequent fiscal year.

(d) Supplement, not supplant. State and local funds may supplement and in no case supplant the proportionate amount of Federal funds required to be expended for parentally-placed private school children with disabilities under this part. (Authority: 20 U. S. C. 1412(a)(10)(A))

§300.134 Consultation. To ensure timely and meaningful consultation, **an LEA**, or, if appropriate, an SEA, **must consult with private school representatives** and representatives of parents of parentally-placed private school children with disabilities during the design and development of special education and related services for the children regarding the following:

(a) Child find. The child find process, including—

(1) How parentally-placed private school children suspected of having a disability can participate equitably; and

(2) How parents, teachers, and private school officials will be informed of the process.

(b) Proportionate share of funds. The determination of the proportionate share of Federal funds available to serve parentally-placed private school children with disabilities under §300.133(b), including the determination of how the proportionate share of those funds was calculated.

(c) Consultation process. The consultation process among the LEA, private school officials, and representatives of parents of parentally-placed private school children with disabilities, including how the process will operate throughout the school year to ensure that parentally-placed children with disabilities identified through the child find process can meaningfully participate in special education and related services.

(d) Provision of special education and related services. How, where, and by whom special education and related services will be provided for parentally-placed private school children with disabilities, including a discussion of—

(1) The types of services, including direct services and alternate service delivery mechanisms; and

(2) How special education and related services will be apportioned if funds are insufficient to serve all parentally-placed private school children; and

(3) How and when those decisions will be made;

(e) Written explanation by LEA regarding services. How, if the LEA disagrees with the views of the private school officials on the provision of services or the types of services (whether provided directly or through a contract), the LEA will provide to the private school officials a written explanation of the reasons why the LEA chose not to provide services directly or through a contract. (Authority: 20 U. S. C. 1412(a)(10)(A)(iii))

§300.135 Written affirmation.

(a) When timely and meaningful consultation, as required by §300.134, has occurred, the LEA must obtain a written affirmation signed by the representatives of participating private schools.

(b) If the representatives do not provide the affirmation within a reasonable period of time, the LEA must forward the documentation of the consultation process to the SEA. (Authority: 20 U. S. C. 1412(a)(10)(A)(iv))

§300.136 Compliance.

(a) General. A private school official has **the right to submit a complaint to the SEA** that the LEA—

(1) Did not engage in consultation that was meaningful and timely; or

(2) Did not give due consideration to the views of the private school official.

(b) Procedure.

(1) If the private school official wishes to submit a complaint, the official must provide to the SEA the basis of the noncompliance by the LEA with the applicable private school provisions in this part; and

(2) The LEA must forward the appropriate documentation to the SEA.

(3)

(i) If the private school official is dissatisfied with the decision of the SEA, the official may submit a complaint to the Secretary by providing the information on noncompliance described in paragraph (b)(1) of this section; and

(ii) The SEA must forward the appropriate documentation to the Secretary. (Authority: 20 U. S. C. 1412(a)(10)(A)(v))

§300.137 Equitable services determined.

(a) No individual right to special education and related services. No parentally-placed private school child with a disability **has an individual right to receive some or all of the special education and related services** that the child would receive if enrolled in a public school.

(b) Decisions.

(1) **Decisions** about the services that will be provided to parentally-placed private school children with disabilities under §§300.130 through 300.144 **must be made in accordance with paragraph (c) of this section** and §300.134(d).

(2) The LEA must make the final decisions with respect to the services to be provided to eligible parentally-placed private school children with disabilities.

(c) Services plan for each child served under §§300.130 through 300.144. If a child with a disability is enrolled in a religious or other private school by the child's parents and will receive special education or related services from an LEA, the LEA must—

(1) Initiate and conduct meetings to develop, review, and revise a services plan for the child, in accordance with §300.138(b); and

(2) Ensure that a representative of the religious or other private school attends each meeting. If the representative cannot attend, the LEA shall use other methods to ensure participation by the religious or other private school, including individual or conference telephone calls. (Authority: 20 U. S. C. 1412(a)(10)(A))

§300.138 Equitable services provided.

(a) General.

(1) The services provided to parentally-placed private school children with disabilities must be provided by personnel meeting the same standards as personnel providing services in the public schools, **except** that private elementary school and secondary school teachers who are providing equitable services to parentally-placed private school children with disabilities do not have to meet the highly qualified special education teacher requirements of §300.18.

(2) Parentally-placed private school children with disabilities **may receive a different amount of services** than children with disabilities in public schools.

(b) Services provided in accordance with a services plan.

(1) Each parentally-placed private school child with a disability who has been designated to receive services under §300.132 must have a **services plan** that describes the specific special education and related services that the LEA will provide to the child in light of the services that the LEA has determined, through the process described in §§300.134 and 300.137, it will make available to parentally-placed private school children with disabilities.

(2) The **services plan** must, to the extent appropriate—

(i) Meet the requirements of §300.320, or for a child ages three through five, meet the requirements of §300.323(b) with respect to the services provided; and

(ii) Be developed, reviewed, and revised consistent with §§300.321 through 300.324.

(c) Provision of equitable services.

(1) The provision of services pursuant to this section and §§300.139 through 300.143 must be provided:

(i) By employees of a public agency; or

(ii) Through contract by the public agency with an individual, association, agency, organization, or other entity.

(2) Special education and related services provided to parentally-placed private school children with disabilities, including materials and equipment, must be secular, neutral, and nonideological. (Authority: 20 U. S. C. 1412(a)(10)(A)(vi))

§300.139 Location of services and transportation.

(a) **Services on private school premises.** Services to parentally-placed private school children with disabilities may be provided on the premises of private, including religious, schools, to the extent consistent with law.

(b) **Transportation.**

(1) **General.**

(i) If necessary for the child to benefit from or participate in the services provided under this part, a parentally-placed private school child with a disability **must** be provided transportation—

(A) From the child's school or the child's home to a site other than the private school; and

(B) From the service site to the private school, or to the child's home, depending on the timing of the services.

(ii) LEAs are **not required** to provide transportation from the child's home to the private school.

(2) **Cost of transportation.** The cost of the transportation described in paragraph (b)(1)(i) of this section may be included in calculating whether the LEA has met the requirement of §300.133. (Authority: 20 U. S. C. 1412(a)(10)(A))

§300.140 Due process complaints and State complaints.

(a) **Due process not applicable, except for child find.**

(1) Except as provided in paragraph (b) of this section, the procedures in §§300.504 through 300.519 do not apply to complaints that an LEA has failed to meet the requirements of §§300.132 through 300.139, including the provision of services indicated on the child's services plan.

(b) **Child find complaints** - to be filed with the LEA in which the private school is located.

(1) The procedures in §§300.504 through 300.519 apply to complaints that an LEA has failed to meet the child find requirements in §300.131, including the requirements in §§300.300 through 300.311.

(2) Any due process complaint regarding the child find requirements (as described in paragraph (b)(1) of this section) must be filed with the LEA in which the private school is located and a copy must be forwarded to the SEA.

(c) **State complaints.**

(1) Any complaint that an SEA or LEA has failed to meet the requirements in §§300.132 through 300.135 and 300.137 through 300.144 must be filed in accordance with the procedures described in §§300.151 through 300.153.

(2) A complaint filed by a private school official under §300.136(a) must be filed with the SEA in accordance with the procedures in §300.136(b). (Authority: 20 U. S. C. 1412(a)(10)(A))

§300.141 Requirement that funds not benefit a private school.

(a) An LEA **may not** use funds provided under section 611 or 619 of the Act to finance the existing level of instruction in a private school or to otherwise benefit the private school.

(b) The LEA must use funds provided under Part B of the Act to meet the special education and related services needs of parentally-placed private school children with disabilities, but not for meeting—

(1) The needs of a private school; or

(2) The general needs of the students enrolled in the private school. (Authority: 20 U. S. C. 1412(a)(10)(A))

§300.142 Use of personnel.

(a) **Use of public school personnel.** An LEA may use funds available under sections 611 and 619 of the Act to make public school personnel available in other than public facilities—

(1) To the extent necessary to provide services under §§300.130 through 300.144 for parentally-placed private school children with disabilities; and

(2) If those services are not normally provided by the private school.

(b) Use of private school personnel. An LEA may use funds available under sections 611 and 619 of the Act to pay for the services of an employee of a private school to provide services under §§300.130 through 300.144 if—

(1) The employee performs the services outside of his or her regular hours of duty; and

(2) The employee performs the services under public supervision and control. (Authority: 20 U. S. C. 1412(a)(10)(A))

§300.143 Separate classes prohibited. An LEA may not use funds available under section 611 or 619 of the Act for classes that are organized **separately on the basis of school enrollment or religion** of the children if —

(a) The classes are at the same site; and

(b) The classes include children enrolled in public schools and children enrolled in private schools. (Authority: 20 U. S. C. 1412(a)(10)(A))

§300.144 Property, equipment, and supplies.

(a) A public agency must control and administer the funds used to provide special education and related services under §§300.137 through 300.139, and hold title to and administer materials, equipment, and property purchased with those funds for the uses and purposes provided in the Act.

(b) The public agency may place equipment and supplies in a private school for the period of time needed for the Part B program.

(c) The public agency must ensure that the equipment and supplies placed in a private school—

(1) Are used only for Part B purposes; and

(2) Can be removed from the private school without remodeling the private school facility.

(d) The public agency must remove equipment and supplies from a private school if—

(1) The equipment and supplies are no longer needed for Part B purposes; or

(2) Removal is necessary to avoid unauthorized use of the equipment and supplies for other than Part B purposes.

(e) No funds under Part B of the Act may be used for repairs, minor remodeling, or construction of private school facilities. (Authority: 20 U. S. C. 1412(a)(10)(A)(vii))

Children With Disabilities in Private Schools Placed or Referred by Public Agencies

§300.145 Applicability of §§300.146 through 300.147. Sections 300.146 through 300.147 apply only to children with disabilities who are or have been placed in or referred to a private school or facility by a public agency as a means of providing special education and related services. (Authority: 20 U. S. C. 1412(a)(10)(B))

§300.146 Responsibility of SEA. Each SEA must ensure that a child with a disability who is **placed in or referred** to a private school or facility **by a public agency** -

(a) Is provided special education and related services—

(1) In conformance with an IEP that meets the requirements of §§300.320 through 300.325; and

(2) At no cost to the parents;

(b) Is provided an education that meets the standards that apply to education provided by the SEA and LEAs including the requirements of this part, except for §300.18 and §300.156(c); and

(c) Has all of the rights of a child with a disability who is served by a public agency. (Authority: 20 U. S. C. 1412(a)(10)(B))

§300.147 Implementation by SEA. In implementing §300.146, the SEA must—

(a) Monitor compliance through procedures such as written reports, on-site visits, and parent questionnaires;

(b) Disseminate copies of applicable standards to each private school and facility to which a public agency has referred or placed a child with a disability; and

(c) Provide an opportunity for those private schools and facilities to participate in the development and revision of State standards that apply to them. (Authority: 20 U. S. C. 1412(a)(10)(B))

Children With Disabilities Enrolled by Their Parents in Private Schools When FAPE is at Issue

§300.148 Placement of children by parents when FAPE is at issue.

(a) **General.** This part **does not require an LEA to pay for the cost of education**, including special education and related services, of a child with a disability **at a private school** or facility **if that agency made FAPE available** to the child and the parents elected to place the child in a private school or facility. However, the public agency must include that child in the population whose needs are addressed consistent with §§300.131 through 300.144.

(b) **Disagreements about FAPE.** Disagreements between the parents and a public agency regarding the availability of a program appropriate for the child, and the question of financial reimbursement, are subject to the due process procedures in §§300.504 through 300.520.

(c) **Reimbursement for private school placement.** If the parents of a child with a disability, **who previously received special education and related services** under the authority of a public agency, enroll the child in a private preschool, elementary school, or secondary school without the consent of or referral by the public agency, a court or a hearing officer may require the agency to reimburse the parents for the cost of that enrollment if the court or hearing officer finds that the agency had not made FAPE available to the child in a timely manner prior to that enrollment and that the private placement is appropriate. A parental placement may be found to be appropriate by a hearing officer or a court even if it does not meet the State standards that apply to education provided by the SEA and LEAs.

(d) **Limitation on reimbursement.** The cost of reimbursement described in paragraph (c) of this section may be **reduced or denied**—

(1) If—

(i) At the most recent IEP Team meeting that the parents attended prior to removal of the child from the public school, the parents **did not inform the IEP Team that they were rejecting the placement** proposed by the public agency to provide FAPE to their child, including stating their concerns and their intent to enroll their child in a private school at public expense; or

(ii) At **least ten (10) business** days (including any holidays that occur on a business day) **prior to the removal** of the child from the public school, the parents **did not give written notice** to the public agency of the information described in paragraph (d)(1)(i) of this section;

(2) If, prior to the parents' removal of the child from the public school, the public agency informed the parents, through the notice requirements described in §300.503(a)(1), of its intent to evaluate the child (including a statement of the purpose of the evaluation that was appropriate and reasonable), but the **parents did not make the child available** for the evaluation; or

(3) Upon a judicial finding of unreasonableness with respect to actions taken by the parents.

(e) **Exception.** Notwithstanding the notice requirement in paragraph (d)(1) of this section, the cost of reimbursement—

(1) Must not be reduced or denied for failure to provide the notice if—

(i) The school prevented the parents from providing the notice;

(ii) The parents had not received notice, pursuant to §300.504, of the notice requirement in paragraph (d)(1) of this section; or

(iii) Compliance with paragraph (d)(1) of this section would likely result in physical harm to the child; and

(2) May, in the discretion of the court or a hearing officer, not be reduced or denied for failure to provide this notice if

(i) The parents are not literate or cannot write in English; or

(ii) Compliance with paragraph (d)(1) of this section would likely result in serious emotional harm to the child.

(Authority: 20 U. S. C. 1412(a)(10)(C))

SEA Responsibility for General Supervision and Implementation of Procedural Safeguards

§300.149 SEA responsibility for general supervision.

(a) The SEA is responsible for ensuring—

(1) That the requirements of this part are carried out; and

(2) That each educational program for children with disabilities administered within the State, including each program administered by any other State or local agency (but not including elementary schools and secondary schools for Indian children operated or funded by the Secretary of the Interior)—

(i) Is under the general supervision of the persons responsible for educational programs for children with disabilities in the SEA; and
(ii) Meets the educational standards of the SEA (including the requirements of this part).

(3) In carrying out this part with respect to homeless children, the requirements of subtitle B of title VII of the McKinney-Vento Homeless Assistance Act (42 U. S. C. 11431 et seq.) are met.

(b) The State must have in effect policies and procedures to ensure that it complies with the monitoring and enforcement requirements in §§300.600 through 300.602 and §§300.606 through 300.608.

(c) Part B of the Act does not limit the responsibility of agencies other than educational agencies for providing or paying some or all of the costs of FAPE to children with disabilities in the State.

(d) Notwithstanding paragraph (a) of this section, the Governor (or another individual pursuant to State law) may assign to any public agency in the State the responsibility of ensuring that the requirements of Part B of the Act are met with respect to students with disabilities who are convicted as adults under State law and incarcerated in adult prisons. (Authority: 20 U. S. C. 1412(a)(11); 1416)

§300.150 SEA implementation of procedural safeguards. The SEA (and any agency assigned responsibility pursuant to §300.149(d)) must have in effect procedures to inform each public agency of its responsibility for ensuring effective implementation of procedural safeguards for the children with disabilities served by that public agency. (Authority: 20 U. S. C. 1412(a)(11); 1415(a))

State Complaint Procedures

§300.151 Adoption of State complaint procedures.

(a) General. Each SEA must adopt written procedures for—

(1) Resolving any complaint, including a complaint filed by an organization or individual from another State, that meets the requirements of §300.153 by—

(i) Providing for the filing of a complaint with the SEA; and
(ii) At the SEA's discretion, providing for the filing of a complaint with a public agency and the right to have the SEA review the public agency's decision on the complaint; and
(2) Widely disseminating to parents and other interested individuals, including parent training and information centers, protection and advocacy agencies, independent living centers, and other appropriate entities, the State procedures under §§300.151 through 300.153.

(b) Remedies for denial of appropriate services. In resolving a complaint in which the SEA has found a failure to provide appropriate services, an SEA, pursuant to its general supervisory authority under Part B of the Act, must address—

(1) The failure to provide appropriate services, including corrective action appropriate to address the needs of the child (such as **compensatory services or monetary reimbursement**); and

(2) Appropriate future provision of services for all children with disabilities.(Authority: 20 U. S. C. 1221e-3)

§300.152 Minimum State complaint procedures.

(a) Time limit; minimum procedures. Each SEA must include in its complaint procedures a **time limit of 60 days** after a complaint is filed under §300.153 to—

(1) Carry out an independent on-site investigation, if the SEA determines that an investigation is necessary;

(2) Give the complainant the opportunity to submit additional information, either orally or in writing, about the allegations in the complaint;

(3) Provide the public agency with the opportunity to respond to the complaint, including, at a minimum—

(i) At the discretion of the public agency, a proposal to resolve the complaint; and
(ii) An opportunity for a parent who has filed a complaint and the public agency to voluntarily engage in mediation consistent with §300.506;
(4) Review all relevant information and make an independent determination as to whether the public agency is violating a requirement of Part B of the Act or of this part; and

(5) **Issue a written decision** to the complainant that addresses each allegation in the complaint and contains—

(i) **Findings of fact and conclusions**; and

(ii) The reasons for the SEA's final decision.

(b) Time extension; final decision; implementation. The SEA's procedures described in paragraph (a) of this section also must—

(1) Permit an extension of the time limit under paragraph (a) of this section only if—

(i) Exceptional circumstances exist with respect to a particular complaint; or

(ii) The parent (or individual or organization, if mediation or other alternative means of dispute resolution is available to the individual or organization under State procedures) and the public agency involved agree to extend the time to engage in mediation pursuant to paragraph (a)(3)(ii) of this section, or to engage in other alternative means of dispute resolution, if available in the State; and

(2) Include procedures for effective implementation of the SEA's final decision, if needed, including—

(i) Technical assistance activities;

(ii) Negotiations; and

(iii) Corrective actions to achieve compliance.

(c) Complaints filed under this section and due process hearings under §300.507 and §§300.530 through 300.532.

(1) If a written complaint is received that is **also** the subject of a due process hearing under §300.507 or §§300.530 through 300.532, or contains multiple issues of which one or more are part of that hearing, the State **must set aside** any part of the complaint that is being addressed in the due process hearing until the conclusion of the hearing. However, any issue in the complaint that is not a part of the due process action must be resolved using the time limit and procedures described in paragraphs (a) and (b) of this section.

(2) If an issue raised in a complaint filed under this section has previously been decided in a due process hearing involving the same parties—

(i) The due process hearing decision is binding on that issue; and

(ii) The SEA must inform the complainant to that effect.

(3) A complaint alleging a public agency's failure to implement a due process hearing decision **must be resolved by the SEA.** (Authority: 20 U. S. C. 1221e-3)

§300.153 Filing a complaint.

(a) An organization or individual may file a signed written complaint under the procedures described in §§300.151 through 300.152.

(b) The complaint **must include**—

(1) A statement that a public agency has violated a requirement of Part B of the Act or of this part;

(2) The facts on which the statement is based;

(3) The signature and contact information for the complainant; and

(4) If alleging violations with respect to a specific child—

(i) The name and address of the residence of the child;

(ii) The name of the school the child is attending;

(iii) In the case of a homeless child or youth (within the meaning of section 725(2) of the McKinney-Vento Homeless Assistance Act (42 U. S. C.11434a(2)), available contact information for the child, and the name of the school the child is attending;

(iv) A **description of the nature of the problem** of the child, including facts relating to the problem; and

(v) A **proposed resolution of the problem** to the extent known and available to the party at the time the complaint is filed.

(c) The complaint must allege a violation that occurred not more **than one year prior** to the date that the complaint is received in accordance with §300.151.

(d) The party filing the complaint must forward a copy of the complaint to the LEA or public agency serving the child at the same time the party files the complaint with the SEA. (Authority: 20 U. S. C. 1221e-3)

Methods of Ensuring Services

§300.154 Methods of ensuring services.

(a) **Establishing responsibility for services.** The Chief Executive Officer of a State or designee of that officer must ensure that an interagency agreement or other mechanism for interagency coordination is in effect between each noneducational public agency described in paragraph (b) of this section and the SEA, in order to ensure that all services described in paragraph (b)(1) of this section that are needed to ensure FAPE are provided, including the provision of these services during the pendency of any dispute under paragraph (a)(3) of this section. The agreement or mechanism must include the following:

(1) An identification of, or a method for defining, the financial responsibility of each agency for providing services described in paragraph (b)(1) of this section to ensure FAPE to children with disabilities. The financial responsibility of each noneducational public agency described in paragraph (b) of this section, including the State Medicaid agency and other public insurers of children with disabilities, must precede the financial responsibility of the LEA (or the State agency responsible for developing the child's IEP).

(2) The conditions, terms, and procedures under which an LEA must be reimbursed by other agencies.

(3) Procedures for resolving interagency disputes (including procedures under which LEAs may initiate proceedings) under the agreement or other mechanism to secure reimbursement from other agencies or otherwise implement the provisions of the agreement or mechanism.

(4) Policies and procedures for agencies to determine and identify the interagency coordination responsibilities of each agency to promote the coordination and timely and appropriate delivery of services described in paragraph (b)(1) of this section.

(b) **Obligation of noneducational public agencies.**

(1)

(i) If any public agency other than an educational agency is otherwise obligated under Federal or State law, or assigned responsibility under State policy or pursuant to paragraph (a) of this section, to provide or pay for any services that are also considered special education or related services (such as, but not limited to, services described in §300.5 relating to assistive technology devices, §300.6 relating to assistive technology services, §300.34 relating to related services, §300.41 relating to supplementary aids and services, and §300.42 relating to transition services) that are necessary for ensuring FAPE to children with disabilities within the State, the public agency must fulfill that obligation or responsibility, either directly or through contract or other arrangement pursuant to paragraph (a) of this section or an agreement pursuant to paragraph (c) of this section.

(ii) A noneducational public agency described in paragraph (b)(1)(i) of this section may not disqualify an eligible service for Medicaid reimbursement because that service is provided in a school context.

(2) If a public agency other than an educational agency fails to provide or pay for the special education and related services described in paragraph (b)(1) of this section, the LEA (or State agency responsible for developing the child's IEP) must provide or pay for these services to the child in a timely manner. The LEA or State agency is authorized to claim reimbursement for the services from the noneducational public agency that failed to provide or pay for these services and that agency must reimburse the LEA or State agency in accordance with the terms of the interagency agreement or other mechanism described in paragraph (a) of this section.

(c) **Special rule.** The requirements of paragraph (a) of this section may be met through—

(1) State statute or regulation;

(2) Signed agreements between respective agency officials that clearly identify the responsibilities of each agency relating to the provision of services; or

(3) Other appropriate written methods as determined by the Chief Executive Officer of the State or designee of that officer and approved by the Secretary.

(d) Children with disabilities who are covered by public benefits or insurance.

(1) A public agency may use the Medicaid or other public benefits or insurance programs in which a child participates to provide or pay for services required under this part, as permitted under the public benefits or insurance program, except as provided in paragraph (d)(2) of this section.

(2) With regard to services required to provide FAPE to an eligible child under this part, the public agency—

(i) **May not require parents to sign up for or enroll in public benefits or insurance programs in order for their child to receive FAPE under Part B of the Act;**

(ii) **May not require parents to incur an out-of-pocket expense such as the payment of a deductible or co-pay** amount incurred in filing a claim for services provided pursuant to this part, but pursuant to paragraph (g)(2) of this section, may pay the cost that the parents otherwise would be required to pay;

(iii) May not use a child's benefits under a public benefits or insurance program if that use would—

(A) **Decrease available lifetime coverage** or any other insured benefit;

(B) Result in the family paying for services that would otherwise be covered by the public benefits or insurance program and that are required for the child outside of the time the child is in school;

(C) Increase premiums or lead to the discontinuation of benefits or insurance; or

(D) Risk loss of eligibility for home and community-based waivers, based on aggregate health-related expenditures; and

(iv)

(A) Must obtain parental consent, consistent with §300.9, each time that access to public benefits or insurance is sought; and

(B) Notify parents that the parents' refusal to allow access to their public benefits or insurance does not relieve the public agency of its responsibility to ensure that all required services are provided at no cost to the parents.

(e) Children with disabilities who are covered by private insurance.

(1) With regard to services required to provide FAPE to an eligible child under this part, a public agency **may access the parents' private insurance proceeds only if** the parents provide consent consistent with §300.9.

(2) **Each time** the public agency proposes to access the parents' private insurance proceeds, the agency must—

(i) Obtain parental consent in accordance with paragraph (e)(1) of this section; and

(ii) Inform the parents that their refusal to permit the public agency to access their private insurance does not relieve the public agency of its responsibility to ensure that all required services are provided at no cost to the parents.

(f) Use of Part B funds.

(1) If a public agency is unable to obtain parental consent to use the parents' private insurance, or public benefits or insurance when the parents would incur a cost for a specified service required under this part, to ensure FAPE the public agency may use its Part B funds to pay for the service.

(2) To avoid financial cost to parents who otherwise would consent to use private insurance, or public benefits or insurance if the parents would incur a cost, the public agency may use its Part B funds to pay the cost that the parents otherwise would have to pay to use the parents' benefits or insurance (e.g., the deductible or co-pay amounts).

(g) Proceeds from public benefits or insurance or private insurance.

(1) Proceeds from public benefits or insurance or private insurance will not be treated as program income for purposes of 34 CFR 80.25.

(2) If a public agency spends reimbursements from Federal funds (e.g., Medicaid) for services under this part, those funds will not be considered "State or local" funds for purposes of the maintenance of effort provisions in §§300.163 and 300.203.

(h) Construction. Nothing in this part should be construed to alter the requirements imposed on a State Medicaid agency, or any other agency administering a public benefits or insurance program by Federal statute, regulations or policy under title XIX, or title XXI of the Social Security Act, 42 U. S. C. 1396 through 1396v and 42 U. S. C. 1397aa through 1397jj, or any other public benefits or insurance program. (Authority: 20 U. S. C. 1412(a)(12) and (e))

Additional Eligibility Requirements

§300.155 Hearings relating to LEA eligibility. The SEA must not make any final determination that an LEA is not eligible for assistance under Part B of the Act without first giving the LEA reasonable notice and an opportunity for a hearing under 34 CFR 76.401(d). (Authority: 20 U. S. C. 1412(a)(13))

§300.156 Personnel qualifications.

(a) **General.** The SEA must establish and **maintain qualifications** to ensure that personnel necessary to carry out the purposes of this part are appropriately and adequately prepared and trained, including that those personnel have the content knowledge and skills to serve children with disabilities.

(b) **Related services personnel and paraprofessionals.** The qualifications under paragraph (a) of this section must include **qualifications** for **related services personnel** and **paraprofessionals** that—

(1) Are consistent with any State-approved or State-recognized certification, licensing, registration, or other comparable requirements that apply to the professional discipline in which those personnel are providing special education or related services; and

(2) Ensure that related services personnel who deliver services in their discipline or profession—

(i) Meet the requirements of paragraph (b)(1) of this section; and

(ii) Have not had certification or licensure requirements waived on an emergency, temporary, or provisional basis; and

(iii) Allow paraprofessionals and assistants who are appropriately trained and supervised, in accordance with State law, regulation, or written policy, in meeting the requirements of this part to be used to assist in the provision of special education and related services under this part to children with disabilities.

(c) **Qualifications for special education teachers.** The qualifications described in paragraph (a) of this section **must ensure** that each person employed as a public school special education teacher in the State who teaches in an elementary school, middle school, or secondary school **is highly qualified** as a special education teacher by the deadline established in section 1119(a)(2) of the ESEA.

(d) **Policy.** In implementing this section, a State must adopt a policy that includes a requirement that LEAs in the State take measurable steps to recruit, hire, train, and retain highly qualified personnel to provide special education and related services under this part to children with disabilities.

(e) **Rule of construction.** Notwithstanding any other individual right of action that a parent or student may maintain under this part, **nothing in this part shall be construed to create a right of action on behalf of an individual** student or a class of students for the failure of a particular SEA or LEA employee to be highly qualified, or to prevent a parent from filing a complaint about staff qualifications with the SEA as provided for under this part. (Authority: 20 U. S. C. 1412(a)(14))

§300.157 Performance goals and indicators. The State must—

(a) Have in effect established goals for the performance of children with disabilities in the State that—

(1) Promote the purposes of this part, as stated in §300.1;

(2) Are the same as the State's objectives for progress by children in its definition of adequate yearly progress, including the State's objectives for progress by children with disabilities, under section 1111(b)(2)(C) of the ESEA, 20 U. S. C. 6311;

(3) Address graduation rates and dropout rates, as well as such other factors as the State may determine; and

(4) Are consistent, to the extent appropriate, with any other goals and academic standards for children established by the State;

(b) Have in effect established performance indicators the State will use to assess progress toward achieving the goals described in paragraph (a) of this section, including measurable annual objectives for progress by children with disabilities under section 1111(b)(2)(C)(v)(II)(cc) of the ESEA, 20 U. S. C. 6311; and

(c) Annually report to the Secretary and the public on the progress of the State, and of children with disabilities in the State, toward meeting the goals established under paragraph (a) of this section, which may include elements of the reports required under section 1111(h) of the ESEA. (Authority: 20 U. S. C. 1412(a)(15))

§§300.158-300.161 [Reserved] Note: For new §300.160, go to www.wrightslaw.com/bks/selaw2/supplement.htm

§300.162 Supplementation of State, local, and other Federal funds.

(a) **Expenditures.** Funds paid to a State under this part must be expended in accordance with all the provisions of this part.

(b) **Prohibition against commingling.**

(1) Funds paid to a State under this part must not be commingled with State funds.

(2) The requirement in paragraph (b)(1) of this section is satisfied by the use of a separate accounting system that includes an audit trail of the expenditure of funds paid to a State under this part. Separate bank accounts are not required. (See 34 CFR 76.702 (Fiscal control and fund accounting procedures).)

(c) **State-level nonsupplanting.**

(1) Except as provided in §300.203, funds paid to a State under Part B of the Act must be used to supplement the level of Federal, State, and local funds (including funds that are not under the direct control of the SEA or LEAs) expended for special education and related services provided to children with disabilities under Part B of the Act, and in no case to supplant those Federal, State, and local funds.

(2) If the State provides clear and convincing evidence that all children with disabilities have available to them FAPE, the Secretary may waive, in whole or in part, the requirements of paragraph (c)(1) of this section if the Secretary concurs with the evidence provided by the State under §300.164. (Authority: 20 U. S. C. 1412(a)(17))

§300.163 Maintenance of State financial support.

(a) **General.** A State must not reduce the amount of State financial support for special education and related services for children with disabilities, or otherwise made available because of the excess costs of educating those children, below the amount of that support for the preceding fiscal year.

(b) **Reduction of funds for failure to maintain support.** The Secretary reduces the allocation of funds under section 611 of the Act for any fiscal year following the fiscal year in which the State fails to comply with the requirement of paragraph (a) of this section by the same amount by which the State fails to meet the requirement.

(c) **Waivers for exceptional or uncontrollable circumstances.** The Secretary may waive the requirement of paragraph (a) of this section for a State, for one fiscal year at a time, if the Secretary determines that—

(1) Granting a waiver would be equitable due to exceptional or uncontrollable circumstances such as a natural disaster or a precipitous and unforeseen decline in the financial resources of the State; or

(2) The State meets the standard in §300.164 for a waiver of the requirement to supplement, and not to supplant, funds received under Part B of the Act.

(d) **Subsequent years.** If, for any fiscal year, a State fails to meet the requirement of paragraph (a) of this section, including any year for which the State is granted a waiver under paragraph (c) of this section, the financial support required of the State in future years under paragraph (a) of this section shall be the amount that would have been required in the absence of that failure and not the reduced level of the State's support. (Authority: 20 U. S. C. 1412(a)(18))

§300.164 Waiver of requirement regarding supplementing and not supplanting with Part B funds.

(a) Except as provided under §§300.202 through 300.205, funds paid to a State under Part B of the Act must be used to supplement and increase the level of Federal, State, and local funds (including funds that are not under the direct control of SEAs or LEAs) expended for special education and related services provided to children with disabilities under Part B of the Act and in no case to supplant those Federal, State, and local funds. A State may use funds it retains under §300.704(a) and (b) without regard to the prohibition on supplanting other funds.

(b) If a State provides clear and convincing evidence that all eligible children with disabilities throughout the State have FAPE available to them, the Secretary may waive for a period of one year in whole or in part the requirement under §300.162 (regarding State-level nonsupplanting) if the Secretary concurs with the evidence provided by the State.

(c) If a State wishes to request a waiver under this section, it must submit to the Secretary a written request that includes—

(1) An assurance that FAPE is currently available, and will remain available throughout the period that a waiver would be in effect, to all eligible children with disabilities throughout the State, regardless of the public agency that is responsible for providing FAPE to them. The assurance must be signed by an official who has the authority to provide that assurance as it applies to all eligible children with disabilities in the State;

(2) All evidence that the State wishes the Secretary to consider in determining whether all eligible children with dis-

abilities have FAPE available to them, setting forth in detail—

(i) The basis on which the State has concluded that FAPE is available to all eligible children in the State; and

(ii) The procedures that the State will implement to ensure that FAPE remains available to all eligible children in the State, which must include—

(A) The State's procedures under §300.111 for ensuring that all eligible children are identified, located and evaluated;

(B) The State's procedures for monitoring public agencies to ensure that they comply with all requirements of this part;

(C) The State's complaint procedures under §§300.151 through 300.153; and

(D) The State's hearing procedures under §§300.511 through 300.516 and §§300.530 through 300.536;

(3) A summary of all State and Federal monitoring reports, and State complaint decisions (see §§300.151 through 300.153) and hearing decisions (see §§300.511 through 300.516 and §§300.530 through 300.536), issued within three years prior to the date of the State's request for a waiver under this section, that includes any finding that FAPE has not been available to one or more eligible children, and evidence that FAPE is now available to all children addressed in those reports or decisions; and

(4) Evidence that the State, in determining that FAPE is currently available to all eligible children with disabilities in the State, has consulted with the State advisory panel under §300.167.

(d) If the Secretary determines that the request and supporting evidence submitted by the State makes a prima facie showing that FAPE is, and will remain, available to all eligible children with disabilities in the State, the Secretary, after notice to the public throughout the State, conducts a public hearing at which all interested persons and organizations may present evidence regarding the following issues:

(1) Whether FAPE is currently available to all eligible children with disabilities in the State.

(2) Whether the State will be able to ensure that FAPE remains available to all eligible children with disabilities in the State if the Secretary provides the requested waiver.

(e) Following the hearing, the Secretary, based on all submitted evidence, will provide a waiver, in whole or in part, for a period of one year if the Secretary finds that the State has provided clear and convincing evidence that FAPE is currently available to all eligible children with disabilities in the State, and the State will be able to ensure that FAPE remains available to all eligible children with disabilities in the State if the Secretary provides the requested waiver.

(f) A State may receive a waiver of the requirement of section 612(a)(18)(A) of the Act and §300.164 if it satisfies the requirements of paragraphs (b) through (e) of this section.

(g) The Secretary may grant subsequent waivers for a period of one year each, if the Secretary determines that the State has provided clear and convincing evidence that all eligible children with disabilities throughout the State have, and will continue to have throughout the one-year period of the waiver, FAPE available to them. (Authority: 20 U. S. C. 1412(a)(17)(C), (18)(C)(ii))

§300.165 Public participation.

(a) Prior to the adoption of any policies and procedures needed to comply with Part B of the Act (including any amendments to those policies and procedures), the State must ensure that there are public hearings, adequate notice of the hearings, and an opportunity for comment available to the general public, including individuals with disabilities and parents of children with disabilities.

(b) Before submitting a State plan under this part, a State must comply with the public participation requirements in paragraph (a) of this section and those in 20 U. S. C. 1232d(b)(7). (Authority: 20 U. S. C. 1412(a)(19); 20 U. S. C. 1232d(b)(7))

§300.166 Rule of construction. In complying with §§300.162 and 300.163, a State may not use funds paid to it under this part to satisfy State-law mandated funding obligations to LEAs, including funding based on student attendance or enrollment, or inflation. (Authority: 20 U. S. C. 1412(a)(20))

State Advisory Panel

§300.167 State advisory panel. The State must establish and maintain an advisory panel for the purpose of providing policy guidance with respect to special education and related services for children with disabilities in the State. (Authority: 20 U. S. C. 1412(a)(21)(A))

§300.168 Membership.

(a) **General.** The advisory panel must consist of members appointed by the Governor, or any other official authorized under State law to make such appointments, be representative of the State population and be composed of individuals involved in, or concerned with the education of children with disabilities, including—

(1) **Parents of children with disabilities** (ages birth through 26);

(2) **Individuals with disabilities;**

(3) **Teachers;**

(4) Representatives of institutions of higher education that prepare special education and related services personnel;

(5) State and local education officials, including officials who carry out activities under subtitle B of title VII of the McKinney-Vento Homeless Assistance Act, (42 U. S. C. 11431 et seq.);

(6) Administrators of programs for children with disabilities;

(7) Representatives of other State agencies involved in the financing or delivery of related services to children with disabilities;

(8) Representatives of private schools and public charter schools;

(9) Not less than one representative of a vocational, community, or business organization concerned with the provision of transition services to children with disabilities;

(10) A representative from the State child welfare agency responsible for foster care; and

(11) Representatives from the State juvenile and adult corrections agencies.

(b) **Special rule.** A **majority** of the members of the panel **must be individuals with disabilities or parents** of children with disabilities (ages birth through 26). (Authority: 20 U. S. C. 1412(a)(21)(B) and (C))

§300.169 Duties. The advisory panel must—

(a) Advise the SEA of unmet needs within the State in the education of children with disabilities;

(b) Comment publicly on any rules or regulations proposed by the State regarding the education of children with disabilities;

(c) Advise the SEA in developing evaluations and reporting on data to the Secretary under section 618 of the Act;

(d) Advise the SEA in developing corrective action plans to address findings identified in Federal monitoring reports under Part B of the Act; and

(e) Advise the SEA in developing and implementing policies relating to the coordination of services for children with disabilities. (Authority: 20 U. S. C. 1412(a)(21)(D))

Other Provisions Required for State Eligibility

§300.170 Suspension and expulsion rates.

(a) **General.** The SEA must examine data, including data disaggregated by race and ethnicity, to determine if significant discrepancies are occurring in the rate of long-term suspensions and expulsions of children with disabilities—

(1) Among LEAs in the State; or

(2) Compared to the rates for nondisabled children within those agencies.

(b) **Review and revision of policies.** If the discrepancies described in paragraph (a) of this section are occurring, the SEA must review and, if appropriate, revise (or require the affected State agency or LEA to revise) its policies, procedures, and practices relating to the development and implementation of IEPs, the use of positive behavioral interventions and supports, and procedural safeguards, to ensure that these policies, procedures, and practices comply with the Act. (Authority: 20 U. S. C. 1412(a)(22))

§300.171 Annual description of use of Part B funds.

(a) In order to receive a grant in any fiscal year a State must annually describe—

(1) How amounts retained for State administration and State-level activities under §300.704 will be used to meet the requirements of this part; and

(2) How those amounts will be allocated among the activities described in §300.704 to meet State priorities based on input from LEAs.

(b) If a State's plans for use of its funds under §300.704 for the forthcoming year do not change from the prior year, the State may submit a letter to that effect to meet the requirement in paragraph (a) of this section.

(c) The provisions of this section do not apply to the Virgin Islands, Guam, American Samoa, the Commonwealth of the Northern Mariana Islands, and the freely associated States. (Authority: 20 U. S. C. 1411(e)(5))

§300.172 Access to instructional materials.

(a) General. The State must—

(1) Adopt the National Instructional Materials Accessibility Standard (NIMAS), published as appendix C to part 300, for the purposes of providing instructional materials to)blind persons or other persons with print disabilities, in a timely manner after publication of the NIMAS in the Federal Register on July 19, 2006 (71 FR 41084); and

(2) Establish a State definition of "timely manner" for purposes of paragraphs (b)(2) and (b)(3) of this section if the State is not coordinating with the National Instructional Materials Access Center (NIMAC) or (b)(3) and (c)(2) of this section if the State is coordinating with the NIMAC.

(b) Rights and responsibilities of SEA.

(1) Nothing in this section shall be construed to require any SEA to coordinate with the NIMAC.

(2) If an SEA chooses not to coordinate with the NIMAC, the SEA must provide an assurance to the Secretary that it will provide instructional materials to blind persons or other persons with print disabilities in a timely manner.

(3) Nothing in this section relieves an SEA of its responsibility to ensure that children with disabilities who need instructional materials in accessible formats, but are not included under the definition of blind or other persons with print disabilities in §300.172(e)(1)(i) or who need materials that cannot be produced from NIMAS files, receive those instructional materials in a timely manner.

(4) In order to meet its responsibility under paragraphs (b)(2), (b)(3), and (c) of this section to ensure that children with disabilities who need instructional materials in accessible formats are provided those materials in a timely manner, the SEA must ensure that all public agencies take all reasonable steps to provide instructional materials in accessible formats to children with disabilities who need those instructional materials at the same time as other children receive instructional materials.

(c) Preparation and delivery of files. If an SEA chooses to coordinate with the NIMAC, as of December 3, 2006, the SEA must—

(1) As part of any print instructional materials adoption process, procurement contract, or other practice or instrument used for purchase of print instructional materials, enter into a written contract with the publisher of the print instructional materials to—

(i) Require the publisher to prepare and, on or before delivery of the print instructional materials, provide to NIMAC electronic files containing the contents of the print instructional materials using the NIMAS; or

(ii) Purchase instructional materials from the publisher that are produced in, or may be rendered in, specialized formats.

(2) Provide instructional materials to blind persons or other persons with print disabilities in a timely manner.

(d) Assistive technology. In carrying out this section, the SEA, to the maximum extent possible, must work collaboratively with the State agency responsible for assistive technology programs.

(e) Definitions.

(1) In this section and §300.210—

(i) Blind persons or other persons with print disabilities means children served under this part who may qualify to receive books and other publications produced in specialized formats in accordance with the Act entitled "An Act to provide books for adult blind," approved March 3, 1931, 2 U. S. C. 135a;

(ii) National Instructional Materials Access Center or NIMAC means the center established pursuant to section 674(e) of the Act;

(iii) National Instructional Materials Accessibility Standard or NIMAS has the meaning given the term in section 674(e)(3)(B) of the Act;

(iv) Specialized formats has the meaning given the term in section 674(e)(3)(D) of the Act.

(2) The definitions in paragraph (e)(1) of this section apply to each State and LEA, whether or not the State or LEA chooses to coordinate with the NIMAC. (Authority: 20 U. S. C. 1412(a)(23), 1474(e))

§300.173 Overidentification and disproportionality. The State must have in effect, consistent with the purposes of this part and with section 618(d) of the Act, policies and procedures designed to prevent the inappropriate overidentification or disproportionate representation by race and ethnicity of children as children with disabilities, including children with disabilities with a particular impairment described in §300.8. (Authority: 20 U. S. C. 1412(a)(24))

§300.174 Prohibition on mandatory medication.

(a) **General.** The SEA must **prohibit State and LEA personnel from requiring parents** to obtain a prescription for substances identified under schedules I, II, III, IV, or V in section 202(c) of the Controlled Substances Act (21 U. S. C.812(c)) for a child as a condition of attending school, receiving an evaluation under §§300.300 through 300.311, or receiving services under this part.

(b) **Rule of construction.** Nothing in paragraph (a) of this section shall be construed to create a Federal prohibition against teachers and other school personnel consulting or sharing classroom-based observations with parents or guardians regarding a student's academic and functional performance, or behavior in the classroom or school, or regarding the need for evaluation for special education or related services under §300.111 (related to child find).(Authority: 20 U. S. C. 1412(a)(25))

§300.175 SEA as provider of FAPE or direct services. If the SEA provides FAPE to children with disabilities, or provides direct services to these children, the agency—

(a) Must comply with any additional requirements of §§300.201 and 300.202 and §§300.206 through 300.226 as if the agency were an LEA; and

(b) May use amounts that are otherwise available to the agency under Part B of the Act to serve those children without regard to §300.202(b) (relating to excess costs). (Authority: 20 U. S. C. 1412(b))

§300.176 Exception for prior State plans.

(a) **General.** If a State has on file with the Secretary policies and procedures approved by the Secretary that demonstrate that the State meets any requirement of §300.100, including any policies and procedures filed under Part B of the Act as in effect before, December 3, 2004, the Secretary considers the State to have met the requirement for purposes of receiving a grant under Part B of the Act.

(b) **Modifications made by a State.**

(1) Subject to paragraph (b)(2) of this section, policies and procedures submitted by a State in accordance with this subpart remain in effect until the State submits to the Secretary the modifications that the State determines necessary.

(2) The provisions of this subpart apply to a modification to an application to the same extent and in the same manner that they apply to the original plan.

(c) **Modifications required by the Secretary.** The Secretary may require a State to modify its policies and procedures, but only to the extent necessary to ensure the State's compliance with this part, if—

(1) After December 3, 2004, the provisions of the Act or the regulations in this part are amended;

(2) There is a new interpretation of this Act by a Federal court or a State's highest court; or

(3) There is an official finding of noncompliance with Federal law or regulations. (Authority: 20 U. S. C. 1412(c)(2) and (3))

§300.177 States' sovereign immunity.

(a) **General.** A State that accepts funds under this part waives its immunity under the 11th amendment to the Constitution of the United States from suit in Federal court for a violation of this part.

(b) **Remedies.** In a suit against a State for a violation of this part, remedies (including remedies both at law and in equity) are available for such a violation in the suit against a public entity other than a State.

(c) **Effective date.** Paragraphs (a) and (b) of this section apply with respect to violations that occur in whole or part after the date of enactment of the Education of the Handicapped Act Amendments of 1990. (Authority: 20 U. S. C. 1404)

Department Procedures

§300.178 Determination by the Secretary that a State is eligible to receive a grant.

If the Secretary determines that a State is eligible to receive a grant under Part B of the Act, the Secretary notifies the State of that determination. (Authority: 20 U. S. C. 1412(d)(1))

§300.179 Notice and hearing before determining that a State is not eligible to receive a grant.

(a) General.

(1) The Secretary does not make a final determination that a State is not eligible to receive a grant under Part B of the Act until providing the State—

(i) With reasonable notice; and

(ii) With an opportunity for a hearing.

(2) In implementing paragraph (a)(1)(i) of this section, the Secretary sends a written notice to the SEA by certified mail with return receipt requested.

(b) Content of notice. In the written notice described in paragraph (a)(2) of this section, the Secretary—

(1) States the basis on which the Secretary proposes to make a final determination that the State is not eligible;

(2) May describe possible options for resolving the issues;

(3) Advises the SEA that it may request a hearing and that the request for a hearing must be made not later than 30 days after it receives the notice of the proposed final determination that the State is not eligible; and

(4) Provides the SEA with information about the hearing procedures that will be followed. (Authority: 20 U. S. C. 1412(d)(2))

§300.180 Hearing official or panel.

(a) If the SEA requests a hearing, the Secretary designates one or more individuals, either from the Department or elsewhere, not responsible for or connected with the administration of this program, to conduct a hearing.

(b) If more than one individual is designated, the Secretary designates one of those individuals as the Chief Hearing Official of the Hearing Panel. If one individual is designated, that individual is the Hearing Official. (Authority: 20 U. S. C. 1412(d)(2))

§300.181 Hearing procedures.

(a) As used in §§300.179 through 300.184 the term party or parties means the following:

(1) An SEA that requests a hearing regarding the proposed disapproval of the State's eligibility under this part.

(2) The Department official who administers the program of financial assistance under this part.

(3) A person, group or agency with an interest in and having relevant information about the case that has applied for and been granted leave to intervene by the Hearing Official or Hearing Panel.

(b) Within 15 days after receiving a request for a hearing, the Secretary designates a Hearing Official or Hearing Panel and notifies the parties.

(c) The Hearing Official or Hearing Panel may regulate the course of proceedings and the conduct of the parties during the proceedings. The Hearing Official or Hearing Panel takes all steps necessary to conduct a fair and impartial proceeding, to avoid delay, and to maintain order, including the following:

(1) The Hearing Official or Hearing Panel may hold conferences or other types of appropriate proceedings to clarify, simplify, or define the issues or to consider other matters that may aid in the disposition of the case.

(2) The Hearing Official or Hearing Panel may schedule a prehearing conference with the Hearing Official or Hearing Panel and the parties.

(3) Any party may request the Hearing Official or Hearing Panel to schedule a prehearing or other conference. The Hearing Official or Hearing Panel decides whether a conference is necessary and notifies all parties.

(4) At a prehearing or other conference, the Hearing Official or Hearing Panel and the parties may consider subjects such as—

(i) Narrowing and clarifying issues;

(ii) Assisting the parties in reaching agreements and stipulations;

(iii) Clarifying the positions of the parties;

(iv) Determining whether an evidentiary hearing or oral argument should be held; and

(v) Setting dates for—

(A) The exchange of written documents;

(B) The receipt of comments from the parties on the need for oral argument or evidentiary hearing;

(C) Further proceedings before the Hearing Official or Hearing Panel (including an evidentiary hearing or oral argument, if either is scheduled);

(D) Requesting the names of witnesses each party wishes to present at an evidentiary hearing and estimation of time for each presentation; or

(E) Completion of the review and the initial decision of the Hearing Official or Hearing Panel.

(5) A prehearing or other conference held under paragraph (c)(4) of this section may be conducted by telephone conference call.

(6) At a prehearing or other conference, the parties must be prepared to discuss the subjects listed in paragraph (b)(4) of this section.

(7) Following a prehearing or other conference the Hearing Official or Hearing Panel may issue a written statement describing the issues raised, the action taken, and the stipulations and agreements reached by the parties.

(d) The Hearing Official or Hearing Panel may require parties to state their positions and to provide all or part of the evidence in writing.

(e) The Hearing Official or Hearing Panel may require parties to present testimony through affidavits and to conduct cross-examination through interrogatories.

(f) The Hearing Official or Hearing Panel may direct the parties to exchange relevant documents or information and lists of witnesses, and to send copies to the Hearing Official or Panel.

(g) The Hearing Official or Hearing Panel may receive, rule on, exclude, or limit evidence at any stage of the proceedings.

(h) The Hearing Official or Hearing Panel may rule on motions and other issues at any stage of the proceedings.

(i) The Hearing Official or Hearing Panel may examine witnesses.

(j) The Hearing Official or Hearing Panel may set reasonable time limits for submission of written documents.

(k) The Hearing Official or Hearing Panel may refuse to consider documents or other submissions if they are not submitted in a timely manner unless good cause is shown.

(l) The Hearing Official or Hearing Panel may interpret applicable statutes and regulations but may not waive them or rule on their validity.

(m)

(1) The parties must present their positions through briefs and the submission of other documents and may request an oral argument or evidentiary hearing. The Hearing Official or Hearing Panel shall determine whether an oral argument or an evidentiary hearing is needed to clarify the positions of the parties.

(2) The Hearing Official or Hearing Panel gives each party an opportunity to be represented by counsel.

(n) If the Hearing Official or Hearing Panel determines that an evidentiary hearing would materially assist the resolution of the matter, the Hearing Official or Hearing Panel gives each party, in addition to the opportunity to be represented by counsel—

(1) An opportunity to present witnesses on the party's behalf; and

(2) An opportunity to cross-examine witnesses either orally or with written questions.

(o) The Hearing Official or Hearing Panel accepts any evidence that it finds is relevant and material to the proceedings and is not unduly repetitious.

(p)

(1) The Hearing Official or Hearing Panel—

(i) Arranges for the preparation of a transcript of each hearing;

(ii) Retains the original transcript as part of the record of the hearing; and

(iii) Provides one copy of the transcript to each party.

(2) Additional copies of the transcript are available on request and with payment of the reproduction fee.

(q) Each party must file with the Hearing Official or Hearing Panel all written motions, briefs, and other documents and must at the same time provide a copy to the other parties to the proceedings. (Authority: 20 U. S. C. 1412(d)(2))

§300.182 Initial decision; final decision.

(a) The Hearing Official or Hearing Panel prepares an initial written decision that addresses each of the points in the notice sent by the Secretary to the SEA under §300.179 including any amendments to or further clarifications of the issues, under §300.181(c)(7).

(b) The initial decision of a Hearing Panel is made by a majority of Panel members.

(c) The Hearing Official or Hearing Panel mails, by certified mail with return receipt requested, a copy of the initial decision to each party (or to the party's counsel) and to the Secretary, with a notice stating that each party has an opportunity to submit written comments regarding the decision to the Secretary.

(d) Each party may file comments and recommendations on the initial decision with the Hearing Official or Hearing Panel within 15 days of the date the party receives the Panel's decision.

(e) The Hearing Official or Hearing Panel sends a copy of a party's initial comments and recommendations to the other parties by certified mail with return receipt requested. Each party may file responsive comments and recommendations with the Hearing Official or Hearing Panel within seven days of the date the party receives the initial comments and recommendations.

(f) The Hearing Official or Hearing Panel forwards the parties' initial and responsive comments on the initial decision to the Secretary who reviews the initial decision and issues a final decision.

(g) The initial decision of the Hearing Official or Hearing Panel becomes the final decision of the Secretary unless, within 25 days after the end of the time for receipt of written comments and recommendations, the Secretary informs the Hearing Official or Hearing Panel and the parties to a hearing in writing that the decision is being further reviewed for possible modification.

(h) The Secretary rejects or modifies the initial decision of the Hearing Official or Hearing Panel if the Secretary finds that it is clearly erroneous.

(i) The Secretary conducts the review based on the initial decision, the written record, the transcript of the Hearing Official's or Hearing Panel's proceedings, and written comments.

(j) The Secretary may remand the matter to the Hearing Official or Hearing Panel for further proceedings.

(k) Unless the Secretary remands the matter as provided in paragraph (j) of this section, the Secretary issues the final decision, with any necessary modifications, within 30 days after notifying the Hearing Official or Hearing Panel that the initial decision is being further reviewed. (Authority: 20 U. S. C. 1412(d)(2))

§300.183 Filing requirements.

(a) Any written submission by a party under §§300.179 through 300.184 must be filed by hand delivery, by mail, or by facsimile transmission. The Secretary discourages the use of facsimile transmission for documents longer than five pages.

(b) The filing date under paragraph (a) of this section is the date the document is—

(1) Hand-delivered;

(2) Mailed; or

(3) Sent by facsimile transmission.

(c) A party filing by facsimile transmission is responsible for confirming that a complete and legible copy of the document was received by the Department.

(d) If a document is filed by facsimile transmission, the Secretary, the Hearing Official, or the Hearing Panel, as applicable, may require the filing of a follow-up hard copy by hand delivery or by mail within a reasonable period of time.

(e) If agreed upon by the parties, service of a document may be made upon the other party by facsimile transmission. (Authority: 20 U. S. C. 1412(d))

§300.184 Judicial review. If a State is dissatisfied with the Secretary's final decision with respect to the eligibility of the State under section 612 of the Act, the State may, not later than 60 days after notice of that decision, file with the United States Court of Appeals for the circuit in which that State is located a petition for review of that decision. A copy of the petition must be transmitted by the clerk of the court to the Secretary. The Secretary then files in the court the record of the proceedings upon which the Secretary's decision was based, as provided in 28 U. S. C. 2112. (Authority: 20 U. S. C. 1416(e)(8))

§300.185 [Reserved]

§300.186 Assistance under other Federal programs. Part B of the Act may not be construed to permit a State to reduce medical and other assistance available, or to alter eligibility, under titles V and XIX of the Social Security Act with respect to the provision of FAPE for children with disabilities in the State. (Authority: 20 U. S. C. 1412(e))

By-pass for Children in Private Schools

§300.190 By-pass—general.

(a) If, on December 2, 1983, the date of enactment of the Education of the Handicapped Act Amendments of 1983, an SEA was prohibited by law from providing for the equitable participation in special programs of children with disabilities enrolled in private elementary schools and secondary schools as required by section 612(a)(10)(A) of the Act, or if the Secretary determines that an SEA, LEA, or other public agency has substantially failed or is unwilling to provide for such equitable participation then the Secretary shall, notwithstanding such provision of law, arrange for the provision of services to these children through arrangements which shall be subject to the requirements of section 612(a)(10)(A) of the Act.

(b) The Secretary waives the requirement of section 612(a)(10)(A) of the Act and of §§300.131 through 300.144 if the Secretary implements a by-pass. (Authority: 20 U. S. C. 1412(f)(1))

§300.191 Provisions for services under a by-pass.

(a) Before implementing a by-pass, the Secretary consults with appropriate public and private school officials, including SEA officials, in the affected State, and as appropriate, LEA or other public agency officials to consider matters such as—

(1) Any prohibition imposed by State law that results in the need for a by-pass; and

(2) The scope and nature of the services required by private school children with disabilities in the State, and the number of children to be served under the by-pass.

(b) After determining that a by-pass is required, the Secretary arranges for the provision of services to private school children with disabilities in the State, LEA or other public agency in a manner consistent with the requirements of section 612(a)(10)(A) of the Act and §§300.131 through 300.144 by providing services through one or more agreements with appropriate parties.

(c) For any fiscal year that a by-pass is implemented, the Secretary determines the maximum amount to be paid to the providers of services by multiplying—

(1) A per child amount determined by dividing the total amount received by the State under Part B of the Act for the fiscal year by the number of children with disabilities served in the prior year as reported to the Secretary under section 618 of the Act; by

(2) The number of private school children with disabilities (as defined in §§300.8(a) and 300.130) in the State, LEA or other public agency, as determined by the Secretary on the basis of the most recent satisfactory data available, which may include an estimate of the number of those children with disabilities.

(d) The Secretary deducts from the State's allocation under Part B of the Act the amount the Secretary determines is necessary to implement a by-pass and pays that amount to the provider of services. The Secretary may withhold this amount from the State's allocation pending final resolution of any investigation or complaint that could result in a determination that a by-pass must be implemented. (Authority: 20 U. S. C. 1412(f)(2))

§300.192 Notice of intent to implement a by-pass.

(a) Before taking any final action to implement a by-pass, the Secretary provides the SEA and, as appropriate, LEA or other public agency with written notice.

(b) In the written notice, the Secretary—

(1) States the reasons for the proposed by-pass in sufficient detail to allow the SEA and, as appropriate, LEA or other public agency to respond; and

(2) Advises the SEA and, as appropriate, LEA or other public agency that it has a specific period of time (at least 45 days) from receipt of the written notice to submit written objections to the proposed by-pass and that it may request in writing the opportunity for a hearing to show cause why a by-pass should not be implemented.

(c) The Secretary sends the notice to the SEA and, as appropriate, LEA or other public agency by certified mail with return receipt requested. (Authority: 20 U. S. C. 1412(f)(3)(A))

§300.193 Request to show cause. An SEA, LEA or other public agency in receipt of a notice under §300.192 that seeks an opportunity to show cause why a by-pass should not be implemented must submit a written request for a show cause hearing to the Secretary, within the specified time period in the written notice in §300.192(b)(2). (Authority: 20 U. S. C. 1412(f)(3))

§300.194 Show cause hearing.

(a) If a show cause hearing is requested, the Secretary—

(1) Notifies the SEA and affected LEA or other public agency, and other appropriate public and private school officials of the time and place for the hearing;

(2) Designates a person to conduct the show cause hearing. The designee must not have had any responsibility for the matter brought for a hearing; and

(3) Notifies the SEA, LEA or other public agency, and representatives of private schools that they may be represented by legal counsel and submit oral or written evidence and arguments at the hearing.

(b) At the show cause hearing, the designee considers matters such as—

(1) The necessity for implementing a by-pass;

(2) Possible factual errors in the written notice of intent to implement a by-pass; and

(3) The objections raised by public and private school representatives.

(c) The designee may regulate the course of the proceedings and the conduct of parties during the pendency of the proceedings. The designee takes all steps necessary to conduct a fair and impartial proceeding, to avoid delay, and to maintain order.

(d) The designee has no authority to require or conduct discovery.

(e) The designee may interpret applicable statutes and regulations, but may not waive them or rule on their validity.

(f) The designee arranges for the preparation, retention, and, if appropriate, dissemination of the record of the hearing.

(g) Within 10 days after the hearing, the designee—

(1) Indicates that a decision will be issued on the basis of the existing record; or

(2) Requests further information from the SEA, LEA, other public agency, representatives of private schools or Department officials. (Authority: 20 U. S. C. 1412(f)(3))

§300.195 Decision.

(a) The designee who conducts the show cause hearing—

(1) Within 120 days after the record of a show cause hearing is closed, issues a written decision that includes a statement of findings; and

(2) Submits a copy of the decision to the Secretary and sends a copy to each party by certified mail with return receipt requested.

(b) Each party may submit comments and recommendations on the designee's decision to the Secretary within 30 days of the date the party receives the designee's decision.

(c) The Secretary adopts, reverses, or modifies the designee's decision and notifies all parties to the show cause hearing of the Secretary's final action. That notice is sent by certified mail with return receipt requested. (Authority: 20 U. S. C. 1412(f)(3))

§300.196 Filing requirements.

(a) Any written submission under §300.194 must be filed by hand-delivery, by mail, or by facsimile transmission. The Secretary discourages the use of facsimile transmission for documents longer than five pages.

(b) The filing date under paragraph (a) of this section is the date the document is—

(1) Hand-delivered;

(2) Mailed; or

(3) Sent by facsimile transmission.

(c) A party filing by facsimile transmission is responsible for confirming that a complete and legible copy of the document was received by the Department.

(d) If a document is filed by facsimile transmission, the Secretary or the hearing officer, as applicable, may require the filing of a follow-up hard copy by hand-delivery or by mail within a reasonable period of time.

(e) If agreed upon by the parties, service of a document may be made upon the other party by facsimile transmission.

(f) A party must show a proof of mailing to establish the filing date under paragraph (b)(2) of this section as provided in 34 CFR 75.102(d). (Authority: 20 U. S. C. 1412(f)(3))

§300.197 Judicial review. If dissatisfied with the Secretary's final action, the SEA may, within 60 days after notice of that action, file a petition for review with the United States Court of Appeals for the circuit in which the State is located. The procedures for judicial review are described in section 612(f)(3)(B) through (D) of the Act. (Authority: 20 U. S. C. 1412(f)(3)(B)-(D))

§300.198 Continuation of a by-pass. The Secretary continues a by-pass until the Secretary determines that the SEA, LEA or other public agency will meet the requirements for providing services to private school children. (Authority: 20 U. S. C. 1412(f)(2)(C))

State Administration

§300.199 State administration.

(a) Rulemaking. Each State that receives funds under Part B of the Act must—

(1) Ensure that any State rules, regulations, and policies relating to this part conform to the purposes of this part;

(2) Identify in writing to LEAs located in the State and the Secretary any such rule, regulation, or policy as a State-imposed requirement that is not required by Part B of the Act and Federal regulations; and

(3) Minimize the number of rules, regulations, and policies to which the LEAs and schools located in the State are subject under Part B of the Act.

(b) Support and facilitation. State rules, regulations, and policies under Part B of the Act must support and facilitate LEA and school-level system improvement designed to enable children with disabilities to meet the challenging State student academic achievement standards. (Authority: 20 U. S. C. 1407)

Subpart C—Local Educational Agency Eligibility

§300.200 Condition of assistance. An LEA is eligible for assistance under Part B of the Act for a fiscal year if the agency submits a plan that provides assurances to the SEA that the LEA meets each of the conditions in §§300.201 through 300.213. (Authority: 20 U. S. C. 1413(a))

§300.201 Consistency with State policies. The LEA, in providing for the education of children with disabilities within its jurisdiction, must have in effect policies, procedures, and programs that are consistent with the State policies and procedures established under §§300.101 through 300.163, and §§300.165 through 300.174. (Authority: 20 U. S. C. 1413(a)(1))

§300.202 Use of amounts.

(a) General. Amounts provided to the LEA under Part B of the Act—

(1) Must be expended in accordance with the applicable provisions of this part;

(2) Must be used only to pay the excess costs of providing special education and related services to children with disabilities, consistent with paragraph (b) of this section; and

(3) Must be used to supplement State, local, and other Federal funds and not to supplant those funds.

(b) Excess cost requirement.

(1) General.

(i) The excess cost requirement prevents an LEA from using funds provided under Part B of the Act to pay for all of the costs directly attributable to the education of a child with a disability, subject to paragraph (b)(1)(ii) of this section.

(ii) The excess cost requirement does not prevent an LEA from using Part B funds to pay for all of the costs directly attributable to the education of a child with a disability in any of the ages 3, 4, 5, 18, 19, 20, or 21, if no local or State funds are available for nondisabled children of these ages. However, the LEA must comply with the nonsupplanting and other requirements of this part in providing the education and services for these children.

(2)

(i) An LEA meets the excess cost requirement if it has spent at least a minimum average amount for the education of its children with disabilities before funds under Part B of the Act are used.

(ii) The amount described in paragraph (b)(2)(i) of this section is determined in accordance with the definition of excess costs in §300.16. That amount may not include capital outlay or debt service.

(3) If two or more LEAs jointly establish eligibility in accordance with §300.223, the minimum average amount is the average of the combined minimum average amounts determined in accordance with the definition of excess costs in §300.16 in those agencies for elementary or secondary school students, as the case may be. (Authority: 20 U. S. C. 1413(a)(2)(A))

§300.203 Maintenance of effort.

(a) General. Except as provided in §§300.204 and 300.205, funds provided to an LEA under Part B of the Act must not be used to reduce the level of expenditures for the education of children with disabilities made by the LEA from local funds below the level of those expenditures for the preceding fiscal year.

(b) Standard.

(1) Except as provided in paragraph (b)(2) of this section, the SEA must determine that an LEA complies with paragraph (a) of this section for purposes of establishing the LEA's eligibility for an award for a fiscal year if the LEA budgets, for the education of children with disabilities, at least the same total or per capita amount from either of the following sources as the LEA spent for that purpose from the same source for the most recent prior year for which information is available:

(i) Local funds only.

(ii) The combination of State and local funds.

(2) An LEA that relies on paragraph (b)(1)(i) of this section for any fiscal year must ensure that the amount of local funds it budgets for the education of children with disabilities in that year is at least the same, either in total or per capita, as the amount it spent for that purpose in the most recent fiscal year for which information is available and the standard in paragraph (b)(1)(i) of this section was used to establish its compliance with this section.

(3) The SEA may not consider any expenditures made from funds provided by the Federal Government for which the SEA is required to account to the Federal Government or for which the LEA is required to account to the Federal Government directly or through the SEA in determining an LEA's compliance with the requirement in paragraph (a) of this section. (Authority: 20 U. S. C. 1413(a)(2)(A))

§300.204 Exception to maintenance of effort.
Notwithstanding the restriction in §300.203(a), an LEA may reduce the level of expenditures by the LEA under Part B of the Act below the level of those expenditures for the preceding fiscal year if the reduction is attributable to any of the following:

(a) The voluntary departure, by retirement or otherwise, or departure for just cause, of special education or related services personnel.

(b) A decrease in the enrollment of children with disabilities.

(c) The termination of the obligation of the agency, consistent with this part, to provide a program of special education to a particular child with a disability that is an exceptionally costly program, as determined by the SEA, because the child—

(1) Has left the jurisdiction of the agency;

(2) Has reached the age at which the obligation of the agency to provide FAPE to the child has terminated; or

(3) No longer needs the program of special education.

(d) The termination of costly expenditures for long-term purchases, such as the acquisition of equipment or the construction of school facilities.

(e) The assumption of cost by the high cost fund operated by the SEA under §300.704(c). (Authority: 20 U. S. C. 1413(a)(2)(B))

§300.205 Adjustment to local fiscal efforts in certain fiscal years.

(a) Amounts in excess. Notwithstanding §300.202(a)(2) and (b) and §300.203(a), and except as provided in paragraph

(d) of this section and §300.230(e)(2), for any fiscal year for which the allocation received by an LEA under §300.705 exceeds the amount the LEA received for the previous fiscal year, the LEA may reduce the level of expenditures otherwise required by §300.203(a) by not more than 50 percent of the amount of that excess.

(b) Use of amounts to carry out activities under ESEA. If an LEA exercises the authority under paragraph (a) of this section, the LEA must use an amount of local funds equal to the reduction in expenditures under paragraph (a) of this section to carry out activities that could be supported with funds under the ESEA regardless of whether the LEA is using funds under the ESEA for those activities.

(c) State prohibition. Notwithstanding paragraph (a) of this section, if an SEA determines that an LEA is unable to establish and maintain programs of FAPE that meet the requirements of section 613(a) of the Act and this part or the SEA has taken action against the LEA under section 616 of the Act and subpart F of these regulations, the SEA must prohibit the LEA from reducing the level of expenditures under paragraph (a) of this section for that fiscal year.

(d) Special rule. The amount of funds expended by an LEA for early intervening services under §300.226 shall count toward the maximum amount of expenditures that the LEA may reduce under paragraph (a) of this section. (Authority: 20 U. S. C. 1413(a)(2)(C))

§300.206 Schoolwide programs under title I of the ESEA.

(a) General. Notwithstanding the provisions of §§300.202 and 300.203 or any other provision of Part B of the Act, an LEA may use funds received under Part B of the Act for any fiscal year to carry out a schoolwide program under section 1114 of the ESEA, except that the amount used in any schoolwide program may not exceed—

(1)

(i) The amount received by the LEA under Part B of the Act for that fiscal year; divided by

(ii) The number of children with disabilities in the jurisdiction of the LEA; and multiplied by

(2) The number of children with disabilities participating in the schoolwide program.

(b) Funding conditions. The funds described in paragraph (a) of this section are subject to the following conditions:

(1) The funds must be considered as Federal Part B funds for purposes of the calculations required by §300.202(a)(2) and (a)(3).

(2) The funds may be used without regard to the requirements of §300.202(a)(1).

(c) Meeting other Part B requirements. Except as provided in paragraph (b) of this section, all other requirements of Part B of the Act must be met by an LEA using Part B funds in accordance with paragraph (a) of this section, including ensuring that children with disabilities in schoolwide program schools—

(1) Receive services in accordance with a properly developed IEP; and

(2) Are afforded all of the rights and services guaranteed to children with disabilities under the Act. (Authority: 20 U. S. C. 1413(a)(2)(D))

§300.207 Personnel development. The LEA must ensure that all personnel necessary to carry out Part B of the Act are appropriately and adequately prepared, subject to the requirements of §300.156 (related to personnel qualifications) and section 2122 of the ESEA. (Authority: 20 U. S. C. 1413(a)(3))

§300.208 Permissive use of funds.

(a) Uses. Notwithstanding §§300.202, 300.203(a), and 300.162(b), funds provided to an LEA under Part B of the Act may be used for the following activities:

(1) Services and aids that also benefit nondisabled children. For the costs of special education and related services, and supplementary aids and services, provided in a regular class or other education-related setting to a child with a disability in accordance with the IEP of the child, even if one or more nondisabled children benefit from these services.

(2) Early intervening services. To develop and implement coordinated, early intervening educational services in accordance with §300.226.

(3) High cost special education and related services. To establish and implement cost or risk sharing funds, consortia, or cooperatives for the LEA itself, or for LEAs working in a consortium of which the LEA is a part, to pay for high cost special education and related services.

(b) Administrative case management. An LEA may use funds received under Part B of the Act to purchase appropriate technology for recordkeeping, data collection, and related case management activities of teachers and related services personnel providing services described in the IEP of children with disabilities, that is needed for the implementation of those case management activities. (Authority: 20 U. S. C. 1413(a)(4))

§300.209 Treatment of charter schools and their students.

(a) Rights of children with disabilities. Children with disabilities who attend public charter schools and their parents **retain all rights under this part.**

(b) Charter schools that are public schools of the LEA.

(1) In carrying out Part B of the Act and these regulations with respect to charter schools that are public schools of the LEA, the LEA must—

(i) Serve children with disabilities attending those charter schools in the same manner as the LEA serves children with disabilities in its other schools, including providing supplementary and related services on site at the charter school to the same extent to which the LEA has a policy or practice of providing such services on the site to its other public schools; and

(ii) Provide funds under Part B of the Act to those charter schools—

(A) On the same basis as the LEA provides funds to the LEA's other public schools, including proportional distribution based on relative enrollment of children with disabilities; and

(B) At the same time as the LEA distributes other Federal funds to the LEA's other public schools, consistent with the State's charter school law.

(2) If the public charter school is a school of an LEA that receives funding under §300.705 and includes other public schools—

(i) The LEA is responsible for ensuring that the requirements of this part are met, unless State law assigns that responsibility to some other entity; and

(ii) The LEA must meet the requirements of paragraph (b)(1) of this section.

(c) Public charter schools that are LEAs. If the public charter school is an LEA, consistent with §300.28, that receives funding under §300.705, that charter school is responsible for ensuring that the requirements of this part are met, unless State law assigns that responsibility to some other entity.

(d) Public charter schools that are not an LEA or a school that is part of an LEA.

(1) If the public charter school is not an LEA receiving funding under §300.705, or a school that is part of an LEA receiving funding under §300.705, the SEA is responsible for ensuring that the requirements of this part are met.

(2) Paragraph (d)(1) of this section does not preclude a State from assigning initial responsibility for ensuring the requirements of this part are met to another entity. However, the SEA must maintain the ultimate responsibility for ensuring compliance with this part, consistent with §300.149. (Authority: 20 U. S. C. 1413(a)(5))

§300.210 Purchase of instructional materials.

(a) General. Not later than December 3, 2006, an LEA that chooses to coordinate with the National Instructional Materials Access Center (NIMAC), when purchasing print instructional materials, must acquire those instructional materials in the same manner, and subject to the same conditions as an SEA under §300.172.

(b) Rights of LEA.

(1) Nothing in this section shall be construed to require an LEA to coordinate with the NIMAC.

(2) If an LEA chooses not to coordinate with the NIMAC, the LEA must provide an assurance to the SEA that the LEA will provide instructional materials to blind persons or other persons with print disabilities in a timely manner.

(3) Nothing in this section relieves an LEA of its responsibility to ensure that children with disabilities who need instructional materials in accessible formats but are not included under the definition of blind or other persons with print disabilities in §300.172(e)(1)(i) or who need materials that cannot be produced from NIMAS files, receive those instructional materials in a timely manner. (Authority: 20 U. S. C. 1413(a)(6))

§300.211 Information for SEA. The LEA must provide the SEA with information necessary to enable the SEA to carry out its duties under Part B of the Act, including, with respect to §§300.157 and 300.160, information relating to the performance of children with disabilities participating in programs carried out under Part B of the Act. (Authority: 20 U. S. C. 1413(a)(7))

§300.212 Public information. The LEA must make available to parents of children with disabilities and to the general public all documents relating to the eligibility of the agency under Part B of the Act. (Authority: 20 U. S. C. 1413(a)(8))

§300.213 Records regarding migratory children with disabilities. The LEA must cooperate in the Secretary's efforts under section 1308 of the ESEA to ensure the linkage of records pertaining to migratory children with disabilities for the purpose of electronically exchanging, among the States, health and educational information regarding those children. (Authority: 20 U. S. C. 1413(a)(9))

§§300.214-300.219 [Reserved]

§300.220 Exception for prior local plans.

(a) **General.** If an LEA or a State agency described in §300.228 has on file with the SEA policies and procedures that demonstrate that the LEA or State agency meets any requirement of §300.200, including any policies and procedures filed under Part B of the Act as in effect before December 3, 2004, the SEA must consider the LEA or State agency to have met that requirement for purposes of receiving assistance under Part B of the Act.

(b) **Modification made by an LEA or State agency.** Subject to paragraph (c) of this section, policies and procedures submitted by an LEA or a State agency in accordance with this subpart remain in effect until the LEA or State agency submits to the SEA the modifications that the LEA or State agency determines are necessary.

(c) **Modifications required by the SEA.** The SEA may require an LEA or a State agency to modify its policies and procedures, but only to the extent necessary to ensure the LEA's or State agency's compliance with Part B of the Act or State law, if—

(1) After December 3, 2004, the effective date of the Individuals with Disabilities Education Improvement Act of 2004, the applicable provisions of the Act (or the regulations developed to carry out the Act) are amended;

(2) There is a new interpretation of an applicable provision of the Act by Federal or State courts; or

(3) There is an official finding of noncompliance with Federal or State law or regulations. (Authority: 20 U. S. C. 1413(b))

§300.221 Notification of LEA or State agency in case of ineligibility. If the SEA determines that an LEA or State agency is not eligible under Part B of the Act, then the SEA must—

(a) Notify the LEA or State agency of that determination; and

(b) Provide the LEA or State agency with reasonable notice and an opportunity for a hearing. (Authority: 20 U. S. C. 1413(c))

§300.222 LEA and State agency compliance.

(a) **General.** If the SEA, after reasonable notice and an opportunity for a hearing, finds that an LEA or State agency that has been determined to be eligible under this subpart is failing to comply with any requirement described in §§300.201 through 300.213, the SEA must reduce or must not provide any further payments to the LEA or State agency until the SEA is satisfied that the LEA or State agency is complying with that requirement.

(b) **Notice requirement.** Any State agency or LEA in receipt of a notice described in paragraph (a) of this section must, by means of public notice, take the measures necessary to bring the pendency of an action pursuant to this section to the attention of the public within the jurisdiction of the agency.

(c) **Consideration.** In carrying out its responsibilities under this section, each SEA must consider any decision resulting from a hearing held under §§300.511 through 300.533 that is adverse to the LEA or State agency involved in the decision. (Authority: 20 U. S. C. 1413(d))

§300.223 Joint establishment of eligibility.

(a) **General.** An SEA may require an LEA to establish its eligibility jointly with another LEA if the SEA determines that the LEA will be ineligible under this subpart because the agency will not be able to establish and maintain programs of sufficient size and scope to effectively meet the needs of children with disabilities.

(b) **Charter school exception.** An SEA may not require a charter school that is an LEA to jointly establish its eligibility under paragraph (a) of this section unless the charter school is explicitly permitted to do so under the State's charter school statute.

(c) **Amount of payments.** If an SEA requires the joint establishment of eligibility under paragraph (a) of this section, the total amount of funds made available to the affected LEAs must be equal to the sum of the payments that each LEA would have received under §300.705 if the agencies were eligible for those payments. (Authority: 20 U. S. C. 1413(e)(1) and (2))

§300.224 Requirements for establishing eligibility.

(a) **Requirements for LEAs in general.** LEAs that establish joint eligibility under this section must—

(1) Adopt policies and procedures that are consistent with the State's policies and procedures under §§300.101 through 300.163, and §§300.165 through 300.174; and

(2) Be jointly responsible for implementing programs that receive assistance under Part B of the Act.

(b) **Requirements for educational service agencies in general.** If an educational service agency is required by State law to carry out programs under Part B of the Act, the joint responsibilities given to LEAs under Part B of the Act—

(1) Do not apply to the administration and disbursement of any payments received by that educational service agency; and

(2) Must be carried out only by that educational service agency.

(c) **Additional requirement.** Notwithstanding any other provision of §§300.223 through 300.224, an educational service agency must provide for the education of children with disabilities in the least restrictive environment, as required by §300.112. (Authority: 20 U. S. C. 1413(e)(3) and (4))

§300.225 [Reserved]

§300.226 Early intervening services.

(a) **General.** An LEA **may not use more than 15 percent** of the amount the LEA receives under Part B of the Act for any fiscal year, less any amount reduced by the LEA pursuant to §300.205, if any, in combination with other amounts (which may include amounts other than education funds), to develop and implement coordinated, early intervening services, which may include interagency financing structures, **for students in kindergarten through grade 12** (with a particular emphasis on students in kindergarten through grade three) who are not currently identified as needing special education or related services, but **who need additional academic and behavioral support** to succeed in a general education environment. (See Appendix D for examples of how §300.205(d), regarding local maintenance of effort, and §300.226(a) affect one another.)

(b) **Activities.** In implementing coordinated, early intervening services under this section, an LEA may carry out activities that include—

(1) Professional development (which may be provided by entities other than LEAs) for teachers and other school staff to enable such personnel to deliver scientifically based academic and behavioral interventions, including scientifically based literacy instruction, and, where appropriate, instruction on the use of adaptive and instructional software; and

(2) Providing educational and behavioral evaluations, services, and supports, including scientifically based literacy instruction.

(c) **Construction.** Nothing in this section shall be construed to either limit or create a right to FAPE under Part B of the Act or to delay appropriate evaluation of a child suspected of having a disability.

(d) **Reporting.** Each LEA that develops and maintains coordinated, early intervening services under this section must annually report to the SEA on—

(1) The number of children served under this section who received early intervening services; and

(2) The number of children served under this section who received early intervening services and subsequently receive special education and related services under Part B of the Act during the preceding two year period.

(e) **Coordination with ESEA.** Funds made available to carry out this section may be used to carry out coordinated, early intervening services aligned with activities funded by, and carried out under the ESEA if those funds are used to supplement, and not supplant, funds made available under the ESEA for the activities and services assisted under this section. (Authority: 20 U. S. C. 1413(f))

§300.227 Direct services by the SEA.

(a) **General.**

(1) An SEA must use the payments that would otherwise have been available to an LEA or to a State agency to provide special education and related services directly to children with disabilities residing in the area served by that LEA, or for whom that State agency is responsible, if the SEA determines that the LEA or State agency—

(i) Has not provided the information needed to establish the eligibility of the LEA or State agency, or elected not to apply for its Part B allotment, under Part B of the Act;

(ii) Is unable to establish and maintain programs of FAPE that meet the requirements of this part;

(iii) Is unable or unwilling to be consolidated with one or more LEAs in order to establish and maintain the programs; or

(iv) Has one or more children with disabilities who can best be served by a regional or State program or service delivery system designed to meet the needs of these children.

(2) SEA administrative procedures.

(i) In meeting the requirements in paragraph (a)(1) of this section, the SEA may provide special education and related services directly, by contract, or through other arrangements.

(ii) The excess cost requirements of §300.202(b) do not apply to the SEA.

(b) **Manner and location of education and services**. The SEA may provide special education and related services under paragraph (a) of this section in the manner and at the locations (including regional or State centers) as the SEA considers appropriate. The education and services must be provided in accordance with this part. (Authority: 20 U. S. C. 1413(g))

§300.228 State agency eligibility. Any State agency that desires to receive a subgrant for any fiscal year under §300.705 must demonstrate to the satisfaction of the SEA that—

(a) All children with disabilities who are participating in programs and projects funded under Part B of the Act receive FAPE, and that those children and their parents are provided all the rights and procedural safeguards described in this part; and

(b) The agency meets the other conditions of this subpart that apply to LEAs. (Authority: 20 U. S. C. 1413(h))

§300.229 Disciplinary information.

(a) The State may require that a public agency include in the records of a child with a disability a statement of any current or previous disciplinary action that has been taken against the child and transmit the statement to the same extent that the disciplinary information is included in, and transmitted with, the student records of nondisabled children.

(b) The statement may include a description of any behavior engaged in by the child that required disciplinary action, a description of the disciplinary action taken, and any other information that is relevant to the safety of the child and other individuals involved with the child.

(c) If the State adopts such a policy, and the child transfers from one school to another, the transmission of any of the child's records must include both the child's current IEP and any statement of current or previous disciplinary action that has been taken against the child. (Authority: 20 U. S. C. 1413(i))

§300.230 SEA flexibility.

(a) **Adjustment to State fiscal effort in certain fiscal years**. For any fiscal year for which the allotment received by a State under §300.703 exceeds the amount the State received for the previous fiscal year and if the State in school year 2003-2004 or any subsequent school year pays or reimburses all LEAs within the State from State revenue 100 percent of the non-Federal share of the costs of special education and related services, the SEA, notwithstanding §§300.162 through 300.163 (related to State-level nonsupplanting and maintenance of effort), and §300.175 (related to direct services by the SEA) may reduce the level of expenditures from State sources for the education of children with disabilities by not more than 50 percent of the amount of such excess.

(b) **Prohibition**. Notwithstanding paragraph (a) of this section, if the Secretary determines that an SEA is unable to establish, maintain, or oversee programs of FAPE that meet the requirements of this part, or that the State needs assistance, intervention, or substantial intervention under §300.603, the Secretary prohibits the SEA from exercising the authority in paragraph (a) of this section.

(c) **Education activities**. If an SEA exercises the authority under paragraph (a) of this section, the agency must use funds from State sources, in an amount equal to the amount of the reduction under paragraph (a) of this section, to support activities authorized under the ESEA, or to support need-based student or teacher higher education programs.

(d) **Report**. For each fiscal year for which an SEA exercises the authority under paragraph (a) of this section, the SEA must report to the Secretary—

(1) The amount of expenditures reduced pursuant to that paragraph; and

(2) The activities that were funded pursuant to paragraph (c) of this section.

(e) Limitation.

(1) Notwithstanding paragraph (a) of this section, an SEA may not reduce the level of expenditures described in paragraph (a) of this section if any LEA in the State would, as a result of such reduction, receive less than 100 percent of the amount necessary to ensure that all children with disabilities served by the LEA receive FAPE from the combination of Federal funds received under Part B of the Act and State funds received from the SEA.

(2) If an SEA exercises the authority under paragraph (a) of this section, LEAs in the State may not reduce local effort under §300.205 by more than the reduction in the State funds they receive. (Authority: 20 U. S. C. 1413(j))

Subpart D—Evaluations, Eligibility Determinations, Individualized Education Programs, and Educational Placements

Parental Consent

§300.300 Parental consent.

(a) Parental consent for initial evaluation.

(1)

(i) The public agency proposing to conduct an **initial evaluation** to determine if a child qualifies as a child with a disability under §300.8 **must**, after providing notice consistent with §§300.503 and 300.504, **obtain informed consent**, consistent with §300.9, from the parent of the child before conducting the evaluation.

(ii) Parental consent for initial evaluation **must not be construed as consent for** initial provision of special education and related **services**.

(iii) The public agency must make reasonable efforts to obtain the informed consent from the parent for an initial evaluation to determine whether the child is a child with a disability.

(2) For initial evaluations only, if the child is a ward of the State and is not residing with the child's parent, the public agency is not required to obtain informed consent from the parent for an initial evaluation to determine whether the child is a child with a disability if—

(i) Despite reasonable efforts to do so, the public agency cannot discover the whereabouts of the parent of the child;

(ii) The rights of the parents of the child have been terminated in accordance with State law; or

(iii) The rights of the parent to make educational decisions have been subrogated by a judge in accordance with State law and consent for an initial evaluation has been given by an individual appointed by the judge to represent the child.

(3)

(i) If the parent of a child **enrolled in public school** or seeking to be enrolled in public school **does not provide consent for initial evaluation** under paragraph (a)(1) of this section, or the parent fails to respond to a request to provide consent, the public agency **may**, but is not required to, pursue the initial evaluation of the child by utilizing the **procedural safeguards** in subpart E of this part (including the mediation procedures under §300.506 or the **due process procedures** under §§300.507 through 300.516), if appropriate, except to the extent inconsistent with State law relating to such parental consent.

(ii) The public agency does not violate its obligation under §300.111 and §§300.301 through 300.311 if it declines to pursue the evaluation.

(b) Parental consent for services.

(1) A public agency that is responsible for making FAPE available to a child with a disability **must obtain informed consent from the parent of the child before the initial provision of special education and related services** to the child.

(2) The public agency must make reasonable efforts to obtain informed consent from the parent for the initial provision of special education and related services to the child.

(3) If the parent of a child **fails to respond or refuses to consent to services** under paragraph (b)(1) of this section, the public agency **may not** use the procedures in subpart E of this part (including the mediation procedures under §300.506 or the **due process procedures** under §§300.507 through 300.516) in order to obtain agreement or a ruling that the services may be provided to the child.

(4) If the parent of the child refuses to consent to the initial provision of special education and related services, or the parent fails to respond to a request to provide consent for the initial provision of special education and related services, the public agency—

(i) Will not be considered to be in violation of the requirement to make available FAPE to the child for the failure to provide the child with the special education and related services for which the public agency requests consent; and

(ii) **Is not required to convene an IEP Team** meeting or develop an IEP under §§300.320 and 300.324 for the child for the special education and related services for which the public agency requests such consent.

(c) Parental consent for reevaluations.

(1) Subject to paragraph (c)(2) of this section, each public agency—

(i) **Must obtain informed parental consent**, in accordance with §300.300(a)(1), **prior to conducting any reevaluation** of a child with a disability.

(ii) If the parent refuses to consent to the reevaluation, the public agency may, but is not required to, pursue the reevaluation by using the consent override procedures described in paragraph (a)(3) of this section.

(iii) The public agency does not violate its obligation under §300.111 and §§300.301 through 300.311 if it declines to pursue the evaluation or reevaluation.

(2) The informed parental consent described in paragraph (c)(1) of this section need not be obtained if the public agency can demonstrate that—

(i) It made reasonable efforts to obtain such consent; and

(ii) The child's parent has failed to respond.

(d) Other consent requirements.

(1) Parental consent is not required before—-

(i) Reviewing existing data as part of an evaluation or a reevaluation; or

(ii) Administering a test or other evaluation that is administered to all children unless, before administration of that test or evaluation, consent is required of parents of all children.

(2) In addition to the parental consent requirements described in paragraph (a) of this section, a State may require parental consent for other services and activities under this part if it ensures that each public agency in the State establishes and implements effective procedures to ensure that a parent's refusal to consent does not result in a failure to provide the child with FAPE.

(3) **A public agency may not use a parent's refusal to consent to one service or activity under paragraphs (a) or (d)(2) of this section to deny the parent or child any other service, benefit, or activity of the public agency,** except as required by this part.

(4)

(i) If a parent of a child who is home schooled or placed in a private school by the parents at their own expense does not provide consent for the initial evaluation or the reevaluation, or the parent fails to respond to a request to provide consent, the public agency **may not** use the consent override procedures (described in paragraphs (a)(3) and (c)(1) of this section); and

(ii) The public agency is not required to consider the child as eligible for services under §§300.132 through 300.144.

(5) To meet the reasonable efforts requirement in paragraphs (a)(1)(iii), (a)(2)(i), (b)(2), and (c)(2)(i) of this section, the public agency must document its attempts to obtain parental consent using the procedures in §300.322(d) (Authority: 20 U. S. C. 1414(a)(1)(D) and 1414(c))

Evaluations and Reevaluations

§300.301 Initial evaluations.

(a) **General.** Each public agency must conduct a full and individual initial evaluation, in accordance with §§300.304 through 300.306, before the initial provision of special education and related services to a child with a disability under this part.

(b) **Request for initial evaluation.** Consistent with the consent requirements in §300.300, either a parent of a child or a public agency may initiate a request for an initial evaluation to determine if the child is a child with a disability.

(c) **Procedures for initial evaluation.** The initial evaluation—

(1)

(i) Must be conducted **within 60 days** of receiving parental consent for the evaluation; **or**

(ii) If the State establishes a timeframe within which the evaluation must be conducted, within that timeframe; and

(2) Must consist of procedures—

(i) To determine if the child is **a child with a disability** under §300.8; and

(ii) To determine the **educational needs** of the child.

(d) **Exception.** The timeframe described in paragraph (c)(1) of this section does not apply to a public agency if—

(1) The parent of a child repeatedly fails or refuses to produce the child for the evaluation; or

(2) A child enrolls in a school of another public agency after the relevant timeframe in paragraph (c)(1) of this section has begun, and prior to a determination by the child's previous public agency as to whether the child is a child with a disability under §300.8.

(e) The exception in paragraph (d)(2) of this section applies only if the subsequent public agency is making sufficient progress to ensure a prompt completion of the evaluation, and the parent and subsequent public agency agree to a specific time when the evaluation will be completed. (Authority: 20 U. S. C. 1414(a))

§300.302 Screening for instructional purposes is not evaluation.
The screening of a student by a teacher or specialist to determine appropriate instructional strategies for curriculum implementation shall not be considered to be an evaluation for eligibility for special education and related services. (Authority: 20 U. S. C. 1414(a)(1)(E))

§300.303 Reevaluations.

(a) **General.** A public agency must ensure that a reevaluation of each child with a disability is conducted in accordance with §§300.304 through 300.311—

(1) If the public agency determines that the **educational or related services needs, including improved academic achievement and functional performance**, of the child warrant a reevaluation; or

(2) If the child's parent or teacher requests a reevaluation.

(b) **Limitation.** A reevaluation conducted under paragraph (a) of this section—

(1) May occur not more than once a year, unless the parent and the public agency agree otherwise; and

(2) Must occur at least once every 3 years, unless the parent and the public agency agree that a reevaluation is unnecessary. (Authority: 20 U. S. C. 1414(a)(2))

§300.304 Evaluation procedures.

(a) **Notice.** The public agency must provide notice to the parents of a child with a disability, in accordance with §300.503, that describes any evaluation procedures the agency proposes to conduct.

(b) **Conduct of evaluation.** In conducting the evaluation, the public agency must—

(1) Use a variety of assessment tools and strategies to gather relevant functional, developmental, and academic information about the child, including information provided by the parent, that may assist in determining—

(i) Whether the child is a child with a disability under §300.8; and

(ii) **The content of the child's IEP**, including information related to enabling the child to be involved in and progress in the general education curriculum (or for a preschool child, to participate in appropriate activities);

(2) **Not use any single measure or assessment** as the sole criterion for determining whether a child is a child with a disability and for determining an appropriate educational program for the child; and

(3) Use technically sound instruments that may assess the relative contribution of cognitive and behavioral factors, in addition to physical or developmental factors.

(c) **Other evaluation procedures**. Each public agency must ensure that—

(1) Assessments and other evaluation materials used to assess a child under this part—

(i) Are selected and administered so as **not to be discriminatory** on a racial or cultural basis;

(ii) Are provided and administered in the child's native language or other mode of communication and in the form most likely to yield accurate information on what the child knows and can do academically, developmentally, and functionally, unless it is clearly not feasible to so provide or administer;

(iii) Are used for the purposes for which the assessments or measures are valid and reliable;

(iv) Are administered by trained and knowledgeable personnel; and

(v) Are administered in accordance with any instructions provided by the producer of the assessments.

(2) Assessments and other evaluation materials include those tailored to assess specific areas of educational need and not merely those that are designed to provide a single general intelligence quotient.

(3) Assessments are selected and administered so as best to ensure that if an assessment is administered to a child with impaired sensory, manual, or speaking skills, **the assessment results accurately reflect the child's aptitude or achievement level** or whatever other factors the test purports to measure, rather than reflecting the child's impaired sensory, manual, or speaking skills (unless those skills are the factors that the test purports to measure).

(4) The child is **assessed in all areas related to the suspected disability**, including, if appropriate, health, vision, hearing, social and emotional status, general intelligence, academic performance, communicative status, and motor abilities;

(5) Assessments of children with disabilities who transfer from one public agency to another public agency in the same school year are coordinated with those children's prior and subsequent schools, as necessary and as expeditiously as possible, consistent with §300.301(d)(2) and (e), to ensure prompt completion of full evaluations.

(6) In evaluating each child with a disability under §§300.304 through 300.306, the **evaluation is sufficiently comprehensive to identify all of the child's special education and related services needs**, whether or not commonly linked to the disability category in which the child has been classified.

(7) Assessment tools and strategies that provide relevant information that directly assists persons in determining the educational needs of the child are provided. (Authority: 20 U. S. C. 1414(b)(1)-(3), 1412(a)(6)(B))

§300.305 Additional requirements for evaluations and reevaluations.

(a) **Review of existing evaluation data**. As part of an initial evaluation (if appropriate) and as part of any reevaluation under this part, the IEP Team and other qualified professionals, as appropriate, must—

(1) Review existing evaluation data on the child, including—

(i) **Evaluations and information provided by the parents of the child;**

(ii) Current classroom-based, local, or State assessments, and classroom-based observations; and

(iii) Observations by teachers and related services providers; and

(2) On the basis of that review, and input from the child's parents, identify what additional data, if any, are needed to determine—

(i)

(A) Whether the child is a child with a disability, as defined in §300.8, and the educational needs of the child; or

(B) In case of a reevaluation of a child, whether the child continues to have such a disability, and the educational needs of the child;

(ii) The present levels of **academic achievement and related developmental needs of the child;**

(iii)

(A) **Whether the child needs special education and related services**; or

(B) In the case of a reevaluation of a child, whether the child **continues to need** special education and related services; and

(iv) Whether any additions or modifications to the special education and related services are needed to enable the child to meet the measurable annual goals set out in the IEP of the child and to participate, as appropriate, in the general education curriculum.

(b) Conduct of review. The group described in paragraph (a) of this section **may conduct its review without a meeting**.

(c) Source of data. The public agency must administer such assessments and other evaluation measures as may be needed to produce the data identified under paragraph (a) of this section.

(d) Requirements if additional data are not needed.

(1) If the IEP Team and other qualified professionals, as appropriate, determine that no additional data are needed to determine whether the child continues to be a child with a disability, and to determine the child's educational needs, the public agency must notify the child's parents of—-

(i) That determination and the reasons for the determination; and

(ii) The right of the parents to request an assessment to determine whether the child continues to be a child with a disability, and to determine the child's educational needs.

(2) The public agency is not required to conduct the assessment described in paragraph (d)(1)(ii) of this section unless requested to do so by the child's parents.

(e) Evaluations before change in eligibility.

(1) Except as provided in paragraph (e)(2) of this section, a public agency **must evaluate a child with a disability** in accordance with §§300.304 through 300.311 **before determining that the child is no longer a child with a disability**.

(2) The evaluation described in paragraph (e)(1) of this section is not required before the termination of a child's eligibility under this part due to graduation from secondary school with a regular diploma, or due to exceeding the age eligibility for FAPE under State law.

(3) For a child whose eligibility terminates under circumstances described in paragraph (e)(2) of this section, a public agency **must provide the child with a summary of the child's academic achievement and functional performance**, which shall include recommendations on how to assist the child in meeting the child's postsecondary goals. (Authority: 20 U. S. C. 1414(c))

§300.306 Determination of eligibility.

(a) General. Upon completion of the administration of assessments and other evaluation measures—

(1) A group of qualified professionals and the parent of the child determines whether the child **is a child with a disability**, as defined in §300.8, in accordance with paragraph (c) of this section **and the educational needs of the child**; and

(2) The public agency **provides a copy of the evaluation report and the documentation of determination of eligibility at no cost to the parent.**

(b) Special rule for eligibility determination. A child **must not be determined to be a child with a disability** under this part—

(1) **If** the determinant factor for that determination is—

(i) **Lack of appropriate instruction** in reading, including the **essential components of reading instruction** (as defined in section 1208(3) of the ESEA);

(ii) Lack of **appropriate instruction in math**; or

(iii) Limited English proficiency; and

(2) If the child does not otherwise meet the eligibility criteria under §300.8(a).

(c) Procedures for determining eligibility and educational need.

(1) In interpreting evaluation data for the purpose of determining if a child is a child with a disability under §300.8, and the educational needs of the child, each public agency must—

(i) Draw upon information from a variety of sources, including aptitude and achievement tests, parent input, and teacher recommendations, as well as information about the child's physical condition, social or cultural background, and adaptive behavior; and

(ii) Ensure that information obtained from all of these sources is documented and carefully considered.

(2) **If a determination is made that a child has a disability and needs special education and related services, an IEP must be developed for the child** in accordance with §§300.320 through 300.324. (Authority: 20 U. S. C. 1414(b)(4) and (5))

Additional Procedures for Identifying Children With Specific Learning Disabilities

§300.307 Specific learning disabilities.

(a) **General**. A State must adopt, consistent with §300.309, criteria for determining whether a child has a **specific learning disability** as defined in §300.8(c)(10). In addition, the criteria adopted by the State—

(1) Must **not require the use of a severe discrepancy** between intellectual ability and achievement for determining whether a child has a specific learning disability, as defined in §300.8(c)(10);

(2) Must permit the use of a process based on the child's response to scientific, research-based intervention; and

(3) May permit the use of other alternative research-based procedures for determining whether a child has a specific learning disability, as defined in §300.8(c)(10).

(b) **Consistency with State criteria**. A public agency must use the State criteria adopted pursuant to paragraph (a) of this section in determining whether a child has a specific learning disability. (Authority: 20 U. S. C. 1221e-3; 1401(30); 1414(b)(6))

§300.308 Additional group members. The determination of whether a child suspected of having a specific learning disability is a child with a disability as defined in §300.8, must be made by the child's parents and a team of qualified professionals, which must include—

(a)

(1) The child's regular teacher; or

(2) If the child does not have a regular teacher, a regular classroom teacher qualified to teach a child of his or her age; or

(3) For a child of less than school age, an individual qualified by the SEA to teach a child of his or her age; and

(b) At least one person qualified to conduct individual diagnostic examinations of children, such as a school psychologist, speech-language pathologist, or remedial reading teacher. (Authority: 20 U. S. C. 1221e-3; 1401(30); 1414(b)(6))

§300.309 Determining the existence of a specific learning disability.

(a) The group described in §300.306 may determine that a child has a specific learning disability, as defined in §300.8(c)(10), if—

(1) The child does not achieve **adequately for the child's age or to meet State-approved grade-level standards in one or more** of the following areas, when provided with learning experiences and instruction appropriate for the child's age or State-approved grade–level standards:

(i) Oral expression.

(ii) Listening comprehension.

(iii) Written expression.

(iv) Basic reading skill.

(v) Reading fluency skills.

(vi) Reading comprehension.

(vii) Mathematics calculation.

(viii) Mathematics problem solving.

(2)

(i) The child does not make **sufficient progress to meet age or State-approved grade-level standards in one or more**

of the areas identified in paragraph (a)(1) of this section when using a process based on the child's **response to scientific, research-based intervention**; or

(ii) The child exhibits a **pattern of strengths and weaknesses** in performance, achievement, or both, relative to age, State-approved grade-level standards, or intellectual development, that is determined by the group to be relevant to the identification of a specific learning disability, using appropriate assessments, consistent with §§300.304 and 300.305; and

(3) The group determines that its findings under paragraphs (a)(1) and (2) of this section are not primarily the result of—

(i) A visual, hearing, or motor disability;

(ii) Mental retardation;

(iii) Emotional disturbance;

(iv) Cultural factors;

(v) Environmental or economic disadvantage; or

(vi) Limited English proficiency.

(b) To ensure that underachievement in a child suspected of having a specific learning disability **is not due to lack of appropriate instruction** in reading or math, the group **must consider**, as part of the evaluation described in §§300.304 through 300.306—

(1) Data that demonstrate that prior to, or as a part of, the referral process, the child was provided appropriate instruction in regular education settings, delivered by qualified personnel; and

(2) Data-based documentation of **repeated assessments of achievement at reasonable intervals, reflecting formal assessment** of student progress during instruction, which was provided to the child's parents.

(c) The public agency must promptly request parental consent to evaluate the child to determine if the child needs special education and related services, and **must adhere to the timeframes** described in §§300.301 and 300.303, **unless extended by mutual written agreement** of the child's parents and a group of qualified professionals, as described in §300.306(a)(1)—

(1) If, prior to a referral, a child has not made adequate progress after an appropriate period of time when provided instruction, as described in paragraphs (b)(1) and (b)(2) of this section; and

(2) Whenever a child is referred for an evaluation. (Authority: 20 U. S. C. 1221e-3; 1401(30); 1414(b)(6))

§300.310 Observation.

(a) The public agency must ensure that the **child is observed in the child's learning environment** (including the regular classroom setting) to document the child's academic performance and behavior in the areas of difficulty.

(b) The group described in §300.306(a)(1), in determining whether a child has a specific learning disability, must decide to—

(1) Use information from an observation in routine classroom instruction and monitoring of the child's performance that was done before the child was referred for an evaluation; or

(2) Have at least one member of the group described in §300.306(a)(1) conduct an **observation** of the child's academic performance **in the regular classroom** after the child has been referred for an evaluation and parental consent, consistent with §300.300(a), is obtained.

(c) In the case of a child of less than school age or out of school, a group member must observe the child in an environment appropriate for a child of that age. (Authority: 20 U. S. C. 1221e-3; 1401(30); 1414(b)(6))

§300.311 Specific documentation for the eligibility determination.

(a) For a child suspected of having a specific learning disability, the documentation of the determination of eligibility, as required in §300.306(a)(2), **must contain a statement** of—

(1) Whether the child has a specific learning disability;

(2) The basis for making the determination, including an assurance that the determination has been made in accordance with §300.306(c)(1);

(3) The relevant behavior, if any, noted during the observation of the child and the relationship of that behavior to the child's academic functioning;

(4) The educationally relevant medical findings, if any;

(5) Whether—

(i) The child does not achieve adequately for the child's age or to meet State-approved grade-level standards consistent with §300.309(a)(1); and

(ii)

(A) The child **does not make sufficient progress to meet age or State-approved grade-level standards** consistent with §300.309(a)(2)(i); or

(B) The child exhibits a **pattern of strengths and weaknesses in performance, achievement, or both**, relative to age, State-approved grade level standards or intellectual development consistent with §300.309(a)(2)(ii);

(6) The determination of the group concerning the effects of a visual, hearing, or motor disability; mental retardation; emotional disturbance; cultural factors; environmental or economic disadvantage; or limited English proficiency on the child's achievement level; and

(7) If the child has participated in a process that assesses the child's **response to scientific, research-based intervention**--

(i) The instructional strategies used and **the student-centered data collected**; and

(ii) The documentation that the child's parents were notified about—

(A) The State's policies regarding the amount and nature of student performance data that would be collected and the general education services that would be provided;

(B) Strategies for increasing the child's rate of learning; and

(C) The parents' right to request an evaluation.

(b) Each group member **must certify in writing** whether the report reflects the member's conclusion. If it does not reflect the member's conclusion, the group member must submit a separate statement presenting the member's conclusions. (Authority: 20 U. S. C. 1221e-3; 1401(30); 1414(b)(6))

Individualized Education Programs

§300.320 Definition of individualized education program.

(a) General. As used in this part, the term individualized education program or IEP means a written statement for each child with a disability that is developed, reviewed, and revised in a meeting in accordance with §§300.320 through 300.324, and that must include—

(1) A statement of the child's **present levels of academic achievement and functional performance**, including—

(i) How the child's disability affects the child's involvement and progress in the general education curriculum (i.e., the same curriculum as for nondisabled children); or

(ii) For preschool children, as appropriate, how the disability affects the child's participation in appropriate activities;

(2)

(i) A statement of **measurable annual goals**, including academic and functional goals designed to—

(A) Meet the child's needs that result from the child's disability to enable the child to be involved in and make progress in the general education curriculum; and

(B) Meet each of the child's other educational needs that result from the child's disability;

(ii) For children with disabilities who take a**lternate assessments** aligned to alternate academic achievement standards, **a description of benchmarks or short-term objectives**;

(3) A description of—

(i) How the child's progress toward meeting the annual goals described in paragraph (2) of this section will be measured; and

(ii) When periodic reports on the progress the child is making toward meeting the annual goals (such as through the use of quarterly or other periodic reports, concurrent with the issuance of report cards) will be provided;

(4) A **statement of the special education and related services and supplementary aids and services, based on peer-reviewed research** to the extent practicable, to be provided to the child, or on behalf of the child, and a statement of the program **modifications or supports for school personnel** that will be provided to enable the child—

(i) To advance appropriately toward attaining the annual goals;

(ii) To be involved in and make progress in the general education curriculum in accordance with paragraph (a)(1) of this section, and to participate in extracurricular and other nonacademic activities; and

(iii) To be educated and participate with other children with disabilities and nondisabled children in the activities described in this section;

(5) An explanation of the extent, if any, to which the child will not participate with nondisabled children in the regular class and in the activities described in paragraph (a)(4) of this section;

(6)

(i) A statement of **any individual appropriate accommodations** that are necessary to measure the academic achievement and functional performance of the child **on State and districtwide assessments** consistent with section 612(a)(16) of the Act; and

(ii) If the IEP Team determines that the child must take an alternate assessment instead of a particular regular State or districtwide assessment of student achievement, a statement of **why**—

(A) The child cannot participate in the regular assessment; and

(B) The particular alternate assessment selected is appropriate for the child; and

(7) The **projected date for the beginning of the services** and modifications described in paragraph (a)(4) of this section, and the anticipated **frequency, location, and duration** of those services and modifications.

(b) Transition services. Beginning **not later than the first IEP to be in effect when the child turns 16**, or younger if determined appropriate by the IEP Team, and updated annually, thereafter, the **IEP must include**—

(1) Appropriate measurable postsecondary goals based upon age appropriate transition assessments related to training, education, employment, and, where appropriate, independent living skills; and

(2) The **transition services (including courses of study)** needed to assist the child in reaching those goals.

(c) Transfer of rights at age of majority. Beginning not later than one year before the child reaches the age of majority under State law, the IEP must include a statement that the child has been informed of the child's rights under Part B of the Act, if any, that will transfer to the child on reaching the age of majority under §300.520.

(d) Construction. Nothing in this section shall be construed to require—

(1) That additional information be included in a child's IEP beyond what is explicitly required in section 614 of the Act; or

(2) The IEP Team to **include information under one component** of a child's IEP **that is already contained** under another component of the child's IEP. (Authority: 20 U. S. C. 1414(d)(1)(A) and (d)(6))

§300.321 IEP Team.

(a) General. The public agency must ensure that the IEP Team for each child with a disability includes—

(1) The **parents** of the child;

(2) Not less than one **regular education teacher** of the child (if the child is, or may be, participating in the regular education environment);

(3) Not less than **one special education teacher** of the child, or where appropriate, not less than one special education provider of the child;

(4) A **representative** of the public agency who—

(i) Is qualified to provide, or supervise the provision of, specially designed instruction to meet the unique needs of children with disabilities;

(ii) Is knowledgeable about the general education curriculum; and

(iii) Is knowledgeable about the availability of resources of the public agency.

(5) An individual who can interpret **the instructional implications** of evaluation results, who may be a member of the team described in paragraphs (a)(2) through (a)(6) of this section;

(6) At the discretion of the parent or the agency, **other individuals** who have knowledge or special expertise regarding the child, including related services personnel as appropriate; and

(7) Whenever appropriate, **the child with a disability.**

(b) Transition services participants.

(1) In accordance with paragraph (a)(7) of this section, the public agency **must invite a child with a disability** to attend the child's IEP Team meeting **if a purpose of the meeting will be the consideration of the postsecondary goals for the child and the transition services** needed to assist the child in reaching those goals under §300.320(b).

(2) If the child does not attend the IEP Team meeting, the public agency must take other steps to ensure that the child's preferences and interests are considered.

(3) To the extent appropriate, with the consent of the parents or a child who has reached the age of majority, in implementing the requirements of paragraph (b)(1) of this section, the public agency must invite a representative of any participating agency that is likely to be responsible for providing or paying for transition services.

(c) Determination of knowledge and special expertise. The determination of the knowledge or special expertise of any individual described in paragraph (a)(6) of this section **must be made by the party** (parents or public agency) **who invited the individual** to be a member of the IEP Team.

(d) Designating a public agency representative. A public agency may designate a public agency member of the IEP Team to also serve as the agency representative, if the criteria in paragraph (a)(4) of this section are satisfied.

(e) IEP Team attendance.

(1) A member of the IEP Team described in paragraphs (a)(2) through (a)(5) of this section **is not required to attend** an IEP Team meeting, in whole or in part, **if** the parent of a child with a disability and the public agency agree, in writing, that the attendance of the member is not necessary because the member's area of the curriculum or related services is not being modified or discussed in the meeting.

(2) A member of the IEP Team described in paragraph (e)(1) of this section **may be excused** from attending an IEP Team meeting, in whole or in part, when the meeting involves a modification to or discussion of the member's area of the curriculum or related services, if—

(i) The parent, in writing, and the public agency consent to the excusal; and

(ii) The member **submits, in writing** to the parent and the IEP Team, **input** into the development of the IEP prior to the meeting.

(f) Initial IEP Team meeting for child under Part C. In the case of a child who was previously served under Part C of the Act, **an invitation** to the initial IEP Team meeting **must, at the request of the parent, be sent** to the Part C service coordinator or other representatives of the Part C system to assist with the smooth transition of services. (Authority: 20 U. S. C. 1414(d)(1)(B)-(d)(1)(D))

§300.322 Parent participation.

(a) Public agency responsibility - general. Each public agency must take steps to **ensure that one or both of the parents of a child with a disability are present at each IEP Team** meeting or are afforded the opportunity to participate, including-

(1) Notifying parents of the meeting early enough to ensure that they will have an opportunity to attend; and

(2) Scheduling the meeting at a mutually agreed on time and place.

(b) Information provided to parents.

(1) The **notice** required under paragraph (a)(1) of this section must—

(i) Indicate the **purpose, time, and location of the meeting and who will be in attendance;** and

(ii) Inform the parents of the provisions in §300.321(a)(6) and (c) (relating to the participation of other individuals on the IEP Team who have knowledge or special expertise about the child), and §300.321(f) (relating to the participation of the Part C service coordinator or other representatives of the Part C system at the initial IEP Team meeting for a child previously served under Part C of the Act).

(2) For a child with a disability beginning not later than **the first IEP to be in effect when the child turns 16**, or younger if determined appropriate by the IEP Team, the **notice also must—**

(i) Indicate—

(A) That a purpose of the meeting will be **the consideration of the postsecondary goals and transition services** for the child, in accordance with §300.320(b); and

(B) **That the agency will invite the student**; and

(ii) Identify any other agency that will be invited to send a representative.

(c) Other methods to ensure parent participation. If neither parent can attend an IEP Team meeting, the public agency must use other methods to ensure **parent participation**, including **individual or conference telephone calls**, consistent with §300.328 (related to alternative means of meeting participation).

(d) Conducting an IEP Team meeting without a parent in attendance. A meeting may be conducted without a parent in attendance if the public agency is unable to convince the parents that they should attend. In this case, the public agency must keep a record of its attempts to arrange a mutually agreed on time and place, such as—

(1) Detailed records of telephone calls made or attempted and the results of those calls;

(2) Copies of correspondence sent to the parents and any responses received; and

(3) Detailed records of visits made to the parent's home or place of employment and the results of those visits.

(e) Use of interpreters or other action, as appropriate. The public agency **must take whatever action is necessary** to ensure that the parent understands the proceedings of the IEP Team meeting, including arranging for an **interpreter** for parents with deafness or whose native language is other than English.

(f) Parent copy of child's IEP. The public agency must give the parent a copy of the child's IEP at no cost to the parent. (Authority: 20 U. S. C. 1414(d)(1)(B)(i))

§300.323 When IEPs must be in effect.

(a) General. At the **beginning of each school year**, each public agency **must have in effect**, for each child with a disability within its jurisdiction, an IEP, as defined in §300.320.

(b) IEP or IFSP for children aged three through five.

(1) In the case of a child with a disability aged three through five (or, at the discretion of the SEA, a two-year-old child with a disability who will turn age three during the school year), the **IEP Team must consider an IFSP** that contains the IFSP content (including the natural environments statement) described in section 636(d) of the Act and its implementing regulations (including an educational component that promotes school readiness and incorporates pre-literacy, language, and numeracy skills for children with IFSPs under this section who are at least three years of age), and that is developed in accordance with the IEP procedures under this part. The IFSP may serve as the IEP of the child, if using the IFSP as the IEP is—

(i) Consistent with State policy; and

(ii) Agreed to by the agency and the child's parents.

(2) In implementing the requirements of paragraph (b)(1) of this section, the public agency must—

(i) Provide to the child's parents a detailed explanation of the differences between an IFSP and an IEP; and

(ii) If the parents choose an IFSP, obtain written informed consent from the parents.

(c) Initial IEPs; provision of services. Each public agency must ensure that—

(1) A meeting to develop an IEP for a child is conducted **within 30 days** of a determination that the child needs special education and related services; **and**

(2) **As soon as possible** following development of the IEP, special education and related services are made available to the child in accordance with the child's IEP.

(d) Accessibility of child's IEP to teachers and others. Each public agency must ensure that—

(1) The child's **IEP is accessible to each regular education teacher**, special education teacher, related services provider, and any other service provider who is responsible for its implementation; **and**

(2) Each teacher and provider described in paragraph (d)(1) of this section is **informed of—**

(i) His or her **specific responsibilities** related to implementing the child's IEP; **and**

(ii) **The specific accommodations, modifications**, and supports that must be provided for the child in accordance with the IEP.

(e) IEPs for children who transfer public agencies in the same State. If a child with a disability (who had an IEP that was in effect in a previous public agency in the same State) **transfers to a new public agency in the same State**, and enrolls in a new school within the same school year, the new public agency (in consultation with the parents) must provide FAPE to the child (**including services comparable to** those described in the child's IEP from the previous public agency), **until** the new public agency **either—**

(1) **Adopts the child's IEP** from the previous public agency; **or**

(2) **Develops, adopts, and implements a new IEP** that meets the applicable requirements in §§300.320 through 300.324.

(f) IEPs for children who transfer from another State. If a child with a disability (who had an IEP that was in effect in a previous public agency in another State) **transfers to a public agency in a new State**, and enrolls in a new school within the same school year, the new public agency (in consultation with the parents) must provide the child with FAPE (**including services comparable to** those described in the child's IEP from the previous public agency), **until** the new public agency—

(1) **Conducts an evaluation** pursuant to §§300.304 through 300.306 (if determined to be necessary by the new public agency); **and**

(2) **Develops, adopts, and implements a new IEP**, if appropriate, that meets the applicable requirements in §§300.320 through 300.324.

(g) Transmittal of records. To facilitate the transition for a child described in paragraphs (e) and (f) of this section—

(1) The **new public agency** in which the child enrolls **must take reasonable steps to promptly obtain the child's records**, including the IEP and supporting documents and any other records relating to the provision of special education or related services to the child, from the previous public agency in which the child was enrolled, pursuant to 34 CFR 99.31(a)(2); and

(2) The previous public agency in which the child was enrolled must take **reasonable steps to promptly respond** to the request from the new public agency. (Authority: 20 U. S. C. 1414(d)(2)(A)-(C))

Development of IEP

§300.324 Development, review, and revision of IEP.

(a) Development of IEP.

(1) **General. In** developing each child's IEP, **the IEP Team must consider—**

(i) The **strengths** of the child;

(ii) The **concerns of the parents** for enhancing the education of their child;

(iii) The **results of the initial or most recent evaluation** of the child; and

(iv) The **academic, developmental, and functional needs** of the child.

(2) **Consideration of special factors.** The IEP Team must—

(i) In the case of a child whose behavior impedes the child's learning or that of others, consider the use of **positive behavioral interventions** and supports, and other strategies, to address that behavior;

(ii) In the case of a child with **limited English proficiency**, consider the language needs of the child as those needs relate to the child's IEP;

(iii) In the case of a child who is **blind or visually impaired**, provide for instruction in **Braille** and the use of Braille unless the IEP Team determines, after an evaluation of the child's reading and writing skills, needs, and appropriate reading and writing media (including an evaluation of the child's future needs for instruction in Braille or the use of Braille), that instruction in Braille or the use of Braille is not appropriate for the child;

(iv) Consider the **communication needs** of the child, and in the case of a child who is deaf or hard of hearing, consider the child's language and communication needs, opportunities for direct communications with peers and professional personnel in the child's language and communication mode, academic level, and full range of needs, including opportunities for direct instruction in the child's language and communication mode; and

(v) Consider whether the child needs assistive technology devices and services.

(3) Requirement with respect to regular education teacher. A regular education teacher of a child with a disability, as a member of the IEP Team, **must**, to the extent appropriate, **participate** in the development of the IEP of the child, including the determination of—

(i) Appropriate positive behavioral interventions and supports and other strategies for the child; and

(ii) Supplementary aids and services, program modifications, and support for school personnel consistent with §300.320(a)(4).

(4) Agreement.

(i) In **making changes to a child's IEP** after the annual IEP Team meeting for a school year, the parent of a child with a disability and the public agency **may agree not to convene an IEP Team** meeting for the purposes of making those changes, and instead may develop a **written document to amend or modify** the child's current IEP.

(ii) If changes are made to the child's IEP in accordance with paragraph (a)(4)(i) of this section, the public agency must ensure that the child's IEP Team is informed of those changes.

(5) Consolidation of IEP Team meetings. To the extent possible, the public agency **must encourage the consolidation of reevaluation meetings for the child and other IEP Team meetings** for the child.

(6) Amendments. Changes to the IEP may be made either by the entire IEP Team at an IEP Team meeting, or as provided in paragraph (a)(4) of this section, **by amending the IEP** rather than by redrafting the entire IEP. Upon request, a parent must be provided with a revised copy of the IEP with the amendments incorporated.

(b) Review and revision of IEPs.

(1) General. Each public agency **must** ensure that, subject to paragraphs (b)(2) and (b)(3) of this section, the IEP Team—

(i) **Reviews the child's IEP periodically, but not less than annually**, to determine whether the annual goals for the child are being achieved; and

(ii) **Revises the IEP, as appropriate**, to address—

(A) Any lack of expected progress toward the annual goals described in §300.320(a)(2), and in the general education curriculum, if appropriate;

(B) **The results of any reevaluation** conducted under §300.303;

(C) **Information about the child provided** to, or **by, the parents**, as described under §300.305(a)(2);

(D) The child's anticipated needs; or

(E) Other matters.

(2) Consideration of special factors. In conducting a review of the child's IEP, the IEP Team must consider the special factors described in paragraph (a)(2) of this section.

(3) Requirement with respect to regular education teacher. A regular education teacher of the child, as a member of the IEP Team, must, consistent with paragraph (a)(3) of this section, participate in the review and revision of the IEP of the child.

(c) Failure to meet transition objectives.

(1) Participating agency failure. If a participating agency, other than the public agency, fails to provide the transition services described in the IEP in accordance with §300.320(b), the public agency must reconvene the IEP Team to identify alternative strategies to meet the transition objectives for the child set out in the IEP.

(2) Construction. Nothing in this part relieves any participating agency, including a State vocational rehabilitation agency, of the responsibility to provide or pay for any transition service that the agency would otherwise provide to children with disabilities who meet the eligibility criteria of that agency.

(d) Children with disabilities in adult prisons.

(1) Requirements that do not apply. The following requirements do not apply to children with disabilities who are **convicted as adults under State law and incarcerated in adult prisons**:

(i) The requirements contained in section 612(a)(16) of the Act and §300.320(a)(6) (relating to participation of children with disabilities in **general assessments**).

(ii) The requirements in §300.320(b) (relating to **transition planning and transition services**) do not apply with respect to the children whose eligibility under Part B of the Act will end, because of their age, before they will be eligible to be released from prison based on consideration of their sentence and eligibility for early release.

(2) Modifications of IEP or placement.

(i) Subject to paragraph (d)(2)(ii) of this section, the IEP Team of a child with a disability who is **convicted as an adult under State law and incarcerated in an adult prison** may modify the child's IEP or placement if the State has demonstrated a bona fide security or compelling penological interest that cannot otherwise be accommodated.

(ii) The requirements of §§300.320 (relating to IEPs), and 300.112 (relating to LRE), do not apply with respect to the modifications described in paragraph (d)(2)(i) of this section. (Authority: 20 U. S. C. 1412(a)(1), 1412(a)(12)(A)(i), 1414(d)(3), (4)(B), and (7); and 1414(e))

§300.325 Private school placements by public agencies.

(a) Developing IEPs.

(1) **Before a public agency places a child** with a disability **in**, or refers a child to, **a private school** or facility, the agency must initiate and conduct a meeting to develop an IEP for the child in accordance with §§300.320 and 300.324.

(2) The agency must ensure that **a representative of the private school or facility attends the meeting.** If the representative cannot attend, the agency must use other methods to ensure participation by the private school or facility, including individual or conference telephone calls.

(b) Reviewing and revising IEPs.

(1) After a child with a disability enters a private school or facility, **any meetings** to review and revise the child's IEP **may be** initiated and **conducted by the private school** or facility at the discretion of the public agency.

(2) If the private school or facility initiates and conducts these meetings, the public agency must ensure that the parents and an agency representative—

(i) Are involved in any decision about the child's IEP; and

(ii) Agree to any proposed changes in the IEP before those changes are implemented.

(c) Responsibility. Even if a private school or facility implements a child's IEP, responsibility for compliance with this part remains with the public agency and the SEA. (Authority: 20 U. S. C. 1412(a)(10)(B))

§300.326 [Reserved]

§300.327 Educational placements. Consistent with §300.501(c), each public agency must ensure that the **parents** of each child with a disability **are members of any group** that makes decisions on the educational placement of their child. (Authority: 20 U. S. C. 1414(e))

§300.328 Alternative means of meeting participation. When conducting IEP Team meetings and placement meetings pursuant to this subpart, and subpart E of this part, and carrying out administrative matters under section 615 of the Act (such as scheduling, exchange of witness lists, and status conferences), the parent of a child with a disability and a public agency may agree to use alternative means of meeting participation, such as **video conferences and conference calls**. (Authority: 20 U. S. C. 1414(f))

Subpart E—Procedural Safeguards

Due Process Procedures for Parents and Children

§300.500 Responsibility of SEA and other public agencies. Each SEA must ensure that each public agency establishes, maintains, and implements procedural safeguards that meet the requirements of §§300.500 through 300.536. (Authority: 20 U. S. C. 1415(a))

§300.501 Opportunity to examine records; parent participation in meetings.

(a) **Opportunity to examine records**. The parents of a child with a disability must be afforded, in accordance with the procedures of §§300.613 through 300.621, an opportunity to inspect and review all education records with respect to—

(1) The identification, evaluation, and educational placement of the child; and

(2) The provision of FAPE to the child.

(b) **Parent participation in meetings**.

(1) The parents of a child with a disability must be afforded an opportunity **to participate in meetings with respect to**—

(i) The **identification, evaluation, and educational placement** of the child; and

(ii) The provision of FAPE to the child.

(2) Each public agency must provide notice consistent with §300.322(a)(1) and (b)(1) to ensure that parents of children with disabilities have the opportunity to participate in meetings described in paragraph (b)(1) of this section.

(3) A **meeting does not include** informal or unscheduled conversations involving public agency personnel and conversations on issues such as teaching methodology, lesson plans, or coordination of service provision. A meeting also does not include preparatory activities that public agency personnel engage in to develop a proposal or response to a parent proposal that will be discussed at a later meeting.

(c) **Parent involvement in placement decisions**.

(1) Each public agency must ensure that a parent of **each child with a disability is a member of any group that makes decisions on the educational placement** of the parent's child.

(2) In implementing the requirements of paragraph (c)(1) of this section, the public agency must use procedures consistent with the procedures described in §300.322(a) through (b)(1).

(3) If neither parent can participate in a meeting in which a decision is to be made relating to the educational placement of their child, the public agency must use other methods to ensure their participation, including individual or conference telephone calls, or video conferencing.

(4) A placement decision may be made by a group without the involvement of a parent, if the public agency is unable to obtain the parent's participation in the decision. In this case, the public agency must have a record of its attempt to ensure their involvement. (Authority: 20 U. S. C. 1414(e), 1415(b)(1))

§300.502 Independent educational evaluation.

(a) **General**.

(1) The parents of a child with a disability **have the right under this part to obtain an independent educational evaluation** of the child, subject to paragraphs (b) through (e) of this section.

(2) Each public agency must provide to parents, upon request for an independent educational evaluation, information about where an independent educational evaluation may be obtained, and the agency criteria applicable for independent educational evaluations as set forth in paragraph (e) of this section.

(3) For the purposes of this subpart—

(i) **Independent educational evaluation** means an evaluation conducted by a qualified examiner who is not employed by the public agency responsible for the education of the child in question; and

(ii) Public expense means that the public agency either pays for the full cost of the evaluation or ensures that the evaluation is otherwise provided at no cost to the parent, consistent with §300.103.

(b) **Parent right to evaluation at public expense**.

(1) A parent has the **right to an independent educational evaluation** at public expense if the parent disagrees with an evaluation obtained by the public agency, subject to the conditions in paragraphs (b)(2) through (4) of this section.

(2) If a parent requests an independent educational evaluation at public expense, **the public agency must**, without unnecessary delay, **either**—

(i) **File a due process complaint** to request a hearing to show that its evaluation is appropriate; **or**

(ii) **Ensure that an independent educational evaluation is provided at public expense**, unless the agency demonstrates in a hearing pursuant to §§300.507 through 300.513 that the evaluation obtained by the parent did not meet agency criteria.

(3) If the public agency files a **due process complaint notice** to request a hearing and the final decision is that the agency's evaluation is appropriate, the parent still has the right to an independent educational evaluation, but not at public expense.

(4) If a parent requests an independent educational evaluation, the public agency may ask for the parent's reason why he or she objects to the public evaluation. However, the public agency **may not require the parent to provide an explanation and may not unreasonably delay** either providing the independent educational evaluation at public expense or filing a due process complaint to request a due process hearing to defend the public evaluation.

(5) A parent is entitled to only one independent educational evaluation at public expense each time the public agency conducts an evaluation with which the parent disagrees.

(c) Parent-initiated evaluations. If the parent obtains an independent educational evaluation at public expense **or shares with the public agency an evaluation obtained at private expense**, the results of the evaluation—

(1) **Must be considered by the public agency**, if it meets agency criteria, in any decision made with respect to the provision of FAPE to the child; and

(2) May be presented by any party as evidence at a hearing on a due process complaint under subpart E of this part regarding that child.

(d) Requests for evaluations by hearing officers. If a hearing officer requests an independent educational evaluation as part of a hearing on a due process complaint, the cost of the evaluation must be at public expense.

(e) Agency criteria.

(1) If an independent educational evaluation is at public expense, the criteria under which the evaluation is obtained, including the location of the evaluation and the qualifications of the examiner, must be the same as the criteria that the public agency uses when it initiates an evaluation, to the extent those criteria are consistent with the parent's right to an independent educational evaluation.

(2) **Except** for the criteria described in paragraph (e)(1) of this section, **a public agency may not impose conditions or timelines** related to obtaining an independent educational evaluation at public expense. (Authority: 20 U. S. C. 1415(b)(1) and (d)(2)(A))

§300.503 Prior notice by the public agency; content of notice.

(a) Notice. Written notice that meets the requirements of paragraph (b) of this section must be given to the parents of a child with a disability a reasonable time before the public agency—

(1) Proposes to initiate or change the identification, evaluation, or educational placement of the child or the provision of FAPE to the child; or

(2) Refuses to initiate or change the identification, evaluation, or educational placement of the child or the provision of FAPE to the child.

(b) Content of notice. The notice required under paragraph (a) of this section must include—

(1) A **description of the action proposed or refused** by the agency;

(2) An **explanation of why** the agency proposes or refuses to take the action;

(3) A **description of each evaluation procedure, assessment, record, or report** the agency used as a basis for the proposed or refused action;

(4) A statement that the parents of a child with a disability have protection under the procedural safeguards of this part and, if this notice is not an initial referral for evaluation, the means by which a copy of a description of the procedural safeguards can be obtained;

(5) Sources for parents to contact to obtain assistance in understanding the provisions of this part;

(6) A **description of other options** that the IEP Team considered and the reasons why those options were rejected; and

(7) A **description of other factors** that are relevant to the agency's proposal or refusal.

(c) Notice in understandable language.

(1) The notice required under paragraph (a) of this section must be—

(i) Written in **language understandable** to the general public; and

(ii) Provided in the **native language of the parent** or other mode of communication used by the parent, unless it is clearly not feasible to do so.

(2) If the native language or other mode of communication of the parent is not a written language, the public agency must take steps to ensure—

(i) That the notice is **translated orally or by other means** to the parent in his or her native language or other mode of communication;

(ii) That **the parent understands the content** of the notice; and

(iii) That there is **written evidence that the requirements** in paragraphs (c)(2)(i) and (ii) of this section **have been met.** (Authority: 20 U. S. C. 1415(b)(3) and (4), 1415(c)(1), 1414(b)(1))

§300.504 Procedural safeguards notice.

(a) General. A copy of the procedural safeguards available to the parents of a child with a disability must be given to the parents only **one time a school year, except** that a copy also must be given to the parents—

(1) **Upon initial referral or parent request for evaluation;**

(2) Upon receipt of the first State complaint under §§300.151 through 300.153 and upon receipt of the first due process complaint under §300.507 in a school year;

(3) In accordance with the **discipline procedures** in §300.530(h); and

(4) **Upon request** by a parent.

(b) Internet Web site. A public agency may place a current copy of the procedural safeguards notice on its Internet Web site if a Web site exists.

(c) Contents. The procedural safeguards notice **must include a full explanation of all of the procedural safeguards** available under §300.148, §§300.151 through 300.153, §300.300, §§300.502 through 300.503, §§300.505 through 300.518, §§300.530 through 300.536 and §§300.610 through 300.625 relating to—

(1) **Independent educational evaluations;**

(2) **Prior written notice;**

(3) **Parental consent;**

(4) **Access to education records;**

(5) Opportunity to present and resolve complaints through the **due process complaint** and **State complaint** procedures, including—

(i) The **time period in which to file a complaint;**

(ii) The opportunity for the agency to resolve the complaint; and

(iii) The **difference between the due process complaint and the State complaint procedures**, including the jurisdiction of each procedure, what issues may be raised, filing and decisional timelines, and relevant procedures;

(6) The availability of mediation;

(7) The child's placement during the pendency of any due process complaint;

(8) Procedures for students who are subject to placement in an interim alternative educational setting;

(9) Requirements for **unilateral placement by parents** of children in private schools at public expense;

(10) Hearings on due process complaints, including requirements for disclosure of evaluation results and recommendations;

(11) State-level appeals (if applicable in the State);

(12) Civil actions, including the time period in which to file those actions; and

(13) Attorneys' fees.

(d) Notice in understandable language. The notice required under paragraph (a) of this section must meet the requirements of §300.503(c). (Authority: 20 U. S. C. 1415(d))

§300.505 Electronic mail. A parent of a child with a disability may elect to receive notices required by §§300.503, 300.504, and 300.508 by an electronic mail communication, if the public agency makes that option available. (Authority: 20 U. S. C. 1415(n))

§300.506 Mediation.

(a) General. Each public agency must ensure that procedures are established and implemented to allow parties to disputes involving any matter under this part, including matters arising prior to the filing of a due process complaint, **to resolve disputes through a mediation** process.

(b) Requirements. The procedures **must meet the following requirements**:

(1) The procedures must ensure that the mediation process—

(i) Is **voluntary** on the part of the parties;

(ii) Is **not used to deny or delay a parent's right** to a hearing on the parent's due process complaint, or to deny any other rights afforded under Part B of the Act; and

(iii) Is conducted by a **qualified and impartial mediator** who is trained in effective mediation techniques.

(2) A public agency may establish procedures to offer to parents and schools that choose not to use the mediation process, an opportunity to meet, at a time and location convenient to the parents, with a disinterested party—

(i) Who is under contract with an appropriate alternative dispute resolution entity, or a parent training and information center or community parent resource center in the State established under section 671 or 672 of the Act; and

(ii) Who would explain the benefits of, and encourage the use of, the mediation process to the parents.

(3)

(i) The State must maintain a **list of individuals** who are qualified mediators and knowledgeable in laws and regulations relating to the provision of special education and related services.

(ii) The SEA must select mediators on a **random, rotational, or other impartial** basis.

(4) The **State must bear the cost of the mediation process**, including the costs of meetings described in paragraph (b)(2) of this section.

(5) Each session in the mediation process must be scheduled in a timely manner and must be held in a **location that is convenient** to the parties to the dispute.

(6) If the parties resolve a dispute through the mediation process, the parties must execute a **legally binding agreement** that sets forth that resolution and that—

(i) States that all discussions that occurred during the mediation process will remain **confidential and may not be used as evidence** in any subsequent due process hearing or civil proceeding; and

(ii) Is signed by both the **parent** and a **representative of the agency who has the authority to bind** such agency.

(7) A written, signed mediation agreement under this paragraph is **enforceable in any State court** of competent jurisdiction **or in a district court of the United States**.

(8) Discussions that occur during the mediation process must be **confidential** and may not be used as evidence in any subsequent due process hearing or civil proceeding of any Federal court or State court of a State receiving assistance under this part.

(c) Impartiality of mediator.

(1) An individual who serves as a mediator under this part—

(i) May not be an employee of the SEA or the LEA that is involved in the education or care of the child; and

(ii) Must not have a personal or professional interest that conflicts with the person's objectivity.

(2) A person who otherwise qualifies as a mediator is not an employee of an LEA or State agency described under §300.228 solely because he or she is paid by the agency to serve as a mediator. (Authority: 20 U. S. C. 1415(e))

§300.507 Filing a due process complaint.

  (a) General.

    (1) A **parent or a public agency may file a due process complaint** on **any of the matters** described in §300.503(a)(1) and (2) (relating to the identification, evaluation or educational placement of a child with a disability, or the provision of FAPE to the child).

    (2) The **due process complaint must allege a violation that occurred not more than two years** before the date the parent or public agency knew or should have known about the alleged action that forms the basis of the due process complaint, **or, if the State has an explicit time limitation** for filing a due process complaint under this part, in the time allowed by that State law, except that the exceptions to the timeline described in §300.511(f) apply to the timeline in this section.

  (b) Information for parents. The public agency must inform the parent of any free or low-cost legal and other relevant services available in the area if—

    (1) The parent requests the information; or

    (2) The parent or the agency files a due process complaint under this section. (Authority: 20 U. S. C. 1415(b)(6))

§300.508 Due process complaint.

  (a) General.

    (1) The public agency must have procedures that require either party, or the attorney representing a party, to provide to the other party a **due process complaint** (which must remain **confidential**).

    (2) The party filing a due process complaint **must forward a copy of the due process complaint to the SEA.**

  (b) Content of complaint. The due process complaint required in paragraph (a)(1) of this section **must include—**

    (1) The name of the child;

    (2) The address of the residence of the child;

    (3) The name of the school the child is attending;

    (4) In the case of a homeless child or youth (within the meaning of section 725(2) of the McKinney-Vento Homeless Assistance Act (42 U. S. C. 11434a(2)), available contact information for the child, and the name of the school the child is attending;

    (5) A **description of the nature of the problem** of the child relating to the proposed or refused initiation or change, including **facts relating to the problem**; and

    (6) A **proposed resolution** of the problem to the extent known and available to the party at the time.

  (c) Notice required before a hearing on a due process complaint. A party **may not have a hearing** on a due process complaint **until the party, or the attorney** representing the party, **files a due process complaint that meets the requirements** of paragraph (b) of this section.

  (d) Sufficiency of complaint.

    (1) The due process complaint required by this section **must be deemed sufficient unless** the party receiving the due process complaint notifies the hearing officer and the other party in writing, within 15 days of receipt of the due process complaint, that the receiving party believes the due process complaint does not meet the requirements in paragraph (b) of this section.

    (2) **Within five days** of receipt of notification under paragraph (d)(1) of this section, the hearing officer must make a determination on the face of the due process complaint of whether the due process complaint meets the requirements of paragraph (b) of this section, and must immediately notify the parties in writing of that determination.

    (3) A party may **amend** its due process complaint **only if—**

      (i) The other party **consents** in writing to the amendment and **is given the opportunity to resolve** the due process complaint through a meeting held pursuant to §300.510; **or**

      (ii) The **hearing officer grants permission**, except that the hearing officer may only grant permission to amend at any time not later than five days before the due process hearing begins.

    (4) If a party files an **amended due process complaint, the timelines** for the resolution meeting in §300.510(a) and the time period to resolve in §300.510(b) **begin again** with the filing of the amended due process complaint.

(e) LEA response to a due process complaint.

(1) If the LEA has not sent a **prior written notice** under §300.503 to the parent regarding the subject matter contained in the parent's due process complaint, the LEA must, within 10 days of receiving the due process complaint, send to the parent a response that includes—

(i) An explanation of why the agency proposed or refused to take the action raised in the due process complaint;

(ii) A description of other options that the IEP Team considered and the reasons why those options were rejected;

(iii) A description of each evaluation procedure, assessment, record, or report the agency used as the basis for the proposed or refused action; and

(iv) A description of the other factors that are relevant to the agency's proposed or refused action.

(2) A response by an LEA under paragraph (e)(1) of this section shall not be construed to preclude the LEA from asserting that the parent's due process complaint was insufficient, where appropriate.

(f) Other party response to a due process complaint. Except as provided in paragraph (e) of this section, the party receiving a due process complaint **must, within 10 days** of receiving the due process complaint, **send to the other party a response** that specifically addresses the issues raised in the due process complaint. (Authority: 20 U. S. C. 1415(b)(7), 1415(c)(2))

§300.509 Model forms.

(a) Each SEA must develop model forms to assist parents and public agencies in filing a due process complaint in accordance with §§300.507(a) and 300.508(a) through (c) and to assist parents and other parties in filing a State complaint under §§300.151 through 300.153. However, the SEA or LEA may not require the use of the model forms.

(b) Parents, public agencies, and other parties may use the appropriate model form described in paragraph (a) of this section, or another form or other document, so long as the form or document that is used meets, as appropriate, the content requirements in §300.508(b) for filing a due process complaint, or the requirements in §300.153(b) for filing a State complaint. (Authority: 20 U. S. C. 1415(b)(8))

§300.510 Resolution process.

(a) **Resolution meeting.**

(1) **Within 15 days** of receiving notice of the parent's due process complaint, and prior to the initiation of a due process hearing under §300.511, **the LEA must convene a meeting** with the parent and the **relevant member** or members **of the IEP** Team who have specific knowledge of the facts identified in the due process complaint that—

(i) Includes a representative of the public agency who has **decision-making authority** on behalf of that agency; and

(ii) **May not include an attorney of the LEA unless** the parent is accompanied by an attorney.

(2) The **purpose of the meeting is for the parent of the child to discuss the due process complaint, and the facts** that form the basis of the due process complaint, so that the LEA has the opportunity to resolve the dispute that is the basis for the due process complaint.

(3) The meeting described in paragraph (a)(1) and (2) of this section **need not be held if—**

(i) The **parent and the LEA agree in writing to waive** the meeting; or

(ii) The **parent and the LEA agree to use the mediation** process described in §300.506.

(4) The parent and the LEA determine the relevant members of the IEP Team to attend the meeting.

(b) **Resolution period.**

(1) If the LEA has not resolved the due process complaint to the satisfaction of the parent **within 30 days** of the receipt of the due process complaint, the due process hearing may occur.

(2) Except as provided in paragraph (c) of this section, the timeline for issuing a final decision under §300.515 begins at the expiration of this 30-day period.

(3) **Except where the parties have jointly agreed to waive the resolution process or to use mediation**, notwithstanding paragraphs (b)(1) and (2) of this section, the **failure of the parent** filing a due process complaint **to participate in the resolution meeting will delay** the timelines for the resolution process and due process hearing until the meeting is held.

(4) If the LEA is **unable to obtain the participation of the parent** in the resolution meeting after reasonable efforts have been made (and documented using the procedures in §300.322(d)), the LEA may, at the conclusion of the 30-day period, request that a hearing officer **dismiss the parent's due process complaint.**

(5) If the **LEA fails to hold the resolution meeting** specified in paragraph (a) of this section **within 15 days** of receiving notice of a parent's due process complaint or fails to participate in the resolution meeting, the parent may seek the intervention of a hearing officer to **begin the due process hearing timeline.**

(c) **Adjustments to 30-day resolution period.** The **45-day timeline** for the due process hearing in §300.515(a) starts the day **after one** of the following events:

(1) Both parties agree in writing to **waive** the resolution meeting;

(2) After either the mediation or resolution meeting starts but before the end of the 30-day period, the parties **agree** in writing that **no agreement is possible**;

(3) If both parties agree in writing to continue the mediation at the end of the 30-day resolution period, but later, the parent or public agency **withdraws** from the mediation process.

(d) **Written settlement agreement.** If a resolution to the dispute is reached at the meeting described in paragraphs (a)(1) and (2) of this section, the parties must execute a legally binding agreement that is—

(1) Signed by both the parent and a representative of the agency who has the authority to bind the agency; and

(2) Enforceable in any State court of competent jurisdiction or in a district court of the United States, or, by the SEA, if the State has other mechanisms or procedures that permit parties to seek enforcement of resolution agreements, pursuant to §300.537.

(e) **Agreement review period.** If the parties execute an agreement pursuant to paragraph (d) of this section, a party may void the agreement within 3 business days of the agreement's execution. (Authority: 20 U. S. C. 1415(f)(1)(B))

§300.511 Impartial due process hearing.

(a) **General.** Whenever a due process complaint is received under §300.507 or §300.532, the parents or the LEA involved in the dispute must have an opportunity for an impartial due process hearing, consistent with the procedures in §§300.507, 300.508, and 300.510.

(b) **Agency responsible for conducting the due process hearing**. The hearing described in paragraph (a) of this section must be conducted by the SEA or the public agency directly responsible for the education of the child, as determined under State statute, State regulation, or a written policy of the SEA.

(c) **Impartial hearing officer.**

(1) At a minimum, a **hearing officer—**

(i) **Must not be—**

(A) An employee of the SEA or the LEA that is involved in the education or care of the child; or

(B) A person having a personal or professional interest that conflicts with the person's objectivity in the hearing;

(ii) Must possess knowledge of, and the ability to understand, the provisions of the Act, Federal and State regulations pertaining to the Act, and legal interpretations of the Act by Federal and State courts;

(iii) Must possess the knowledge and ability to conduct hearings in accordance with appropriate, **standard legal practice**; and

(iv) Must possess the knowledge and ability to render and write decisions in accordance with appropriate, standard legal practice.

(2) A person who otherwise qualifies to conduct a hearing under paragraph (c)(1) of this section is not an employee of the agency solely because he or she is paid by the agency to serve as a hearing officer.

(3) Each public agency must keep a **list of the persons** who serve as hearing officers. The list must include a statement of the qualifications of each of those persons.

(d) **Subject matter of due process hearings**. The party requesting the due process hearing **may not raise issues at the due process hearing** that were not raised in the due process complaint filed under §300.508(b), unless the other party agrees otherwise.

(e) **Timeline for requesting a hearing.** A parent or agency **must request an impartial hearing on their due process complaint within two years** of the date the parent or agency knew or should have known about the alleged action that forms the basis of the due process complaint, **or if the State** has an explicit time limitation for requesting such a due process hearing under this part, in the time allowed by that State law.

(f) Exceptions to the timeline. The timeline described in paragraph (e) of this section does not apply to a parent if the parent was prevented from filing a due process complaint due to—

(1) **Specific misrepresentations** by the LEA that it had resolved the problem forming the basis of the due process complaint; or

(2) The LEA's **withholding of information** from the parent that was required under this part to be provided to the parent. (Authority: 20 U. S. C. 1415(f)(1)(A), 1415(f)(3)(A)–(D))

§300.512 Hearing rights.

(a) General. Any party to a hearing conducted pursuant to §§300.507 through 300.513 or §§300.530 through 300.534, or an appeal conducted pursuant to §300.514, has the right to—

(1) Be accompanied and advised by counsel and by individuals with special knowledge or training with respect to the problems of children with disabilities;

(2) **Present evidence and confront, cross-examine, and compel the attendance of witnesses;**

(3) **Prohibit the introduction of any evidence** at the hearing that has **not been disclosed** to that party **at least five business days** before the hearing;

(4) Obtain a written, or, at the option of the parents, electronic, verbatim record of the hearing; and

(5) Obtain written, or, at the option of the parents, electronic findings of fact and decisions.

(b) Additional disclosure of information.

(1) At least five business days prior to a hearing conducted pursuant to §300.511(a), each party must disclose to all other parties all evaluations completed by that date and recommendations based on the offering party's evaluations that the party intends to use at the hearing.

(2) A hearing officer may bar any party that fails to comply with paragraph (b)(1) of this section from introducing the relevant evaluation or recommendation at the hearing without the consent of the other party.

(c) Parental rights at hearings. Parents involved in hearings must be given the right to—

(1) Have the child who is the subject of the hearing present;

(2) Open the hearing to the public; and

(3) Have the record of the hearing and the findings of fact and decisions described in paragraphs (a)(4) and (a)(5) of this section provided at no cost to parents. (Authority: 20 U. S. C. 1415(f)(2), 1415(h))

§300.513 Hearing decisions.

(a) Decision of hearing officer on the provision of FAPE.

(1) Subject to paragraph (a)(2) of this section, a hearing officer's determination of whether a child received FAPE must be based on **substantive grounds.**

(2) In matters alleging a **procedural violation**, a hearing officer may find that a child did not receive a FAPE **only if** the procedural inadequacies—

(i) Impeded the child's right to a FAPE;

(ii) Significantly impeded the parent's opportunity to participate in the decision-making process regarding the provision of a FAPE to the parent's child; or

(iii) **Caused a deprivation of educational benefit.**

(3) Nothing in paragraph (a) of this section shall be construed to preclude a hearing officer from ordering an LEA to comply with procedural requirements under §§300.500 through 300.536.

(b) Construction clause. Nothing in §§300.507 through 300.513 shall be construed to affect the right of a parent to file an appeal of the due process hearing decision with the SEA under §300.514(b), if a State level appeal is available.

(c) Separate request for a due process hearing. Nothing in §§300.500 through 300.536 shall be construed to preclude a parent from filing a separate due process complaint on an issue separate from a due process complaint already filed.

(d) Findings and decision to advisory panel and general public. The public agency, after deleting any personally identifiable information, must—

(1) Transmit the findings and decisions referred to in §300.512(a)(5) to the State advisory panel established under §300.167; and

(2) Make those findings and decisions available to the public. (Authority: 20 U. S. C. 1415(f)(3)(E) and (F), 1415(h)(4), 1415(o))

§300.514 Finality of decision; appeal; impartial review.

(a) **Finality of hearing decision**. A decision made in a hearing conducted pursuant to §§300.507 through 300.513 or §§300.530 through 300.534 is final, except that any party involved in the hearing may appeal the decision under the provisions of paragraph (b) of this section and §300.516.

(b) **Appeal of decisions; impartial review.**

(1) If the hearing required by §300.511 is conducted by a public agency other than the SEA, any party aggrieved by the findings and decision in the hearing may appeal to the SEA.

(2) If there is an appeal, the SEA must conduct an impartial review of the findings and decision appealed. The official conducting the review must—

(i) Examine the entire hearing record;

(ii) Ensure that the procedures at the hearing were consistent with the requirements of due process;

(iii) Seek additional evidence if necessary. If a hearing is held to receive additional evidence, the rights in §300.512 apply;

(iv) Afford the parties an opportunity for oral or written argument, or both, at the discretion of the reviewing official;

(v) Make an independent decision on completion of the review; and

(vi) Give a copy of the written, or, at the option of the parents, electronic findings of fact and decisions to the parties.

(c) **Findings and decision to advisory panel and general public**. The SEA, after deleting any personally identifiable information, must—

(1) Transmit the findings and decisions referred to in paragraph (b)(2)(vi) of this section to the State advisory panel established under §300.167; and

(2) Make those findings and decisions available to the public.

(d) **Finality of review decision**. The decision made by the reviewing official is final unless a party brings a civil action under §300.516. (Authority: 20 U. S. C. 1415(g) and (h)(4), 1415(i)(1)(A), 1415(i)(2))

§300.515 Timelines and convenience of hearings and reviews.

(a) The public agency must ensure that **not later than 45 days** after the expiration of the 30 day period under §300.510(b), or the adjusted time periods described in §300.510(c)—

(1) A final decision is reached in the hearing; and

(2) A copy of the decision is mailed to each of the parties.

(b) The SEA must ensure that not later than 30 days after the receipt of a request for a review—

(1) A final decision is reached in the review; and

(2) A copy of the decision is mailed to each of the parties.

(c) A hearing or reviewing officer may grant specific extensions of time beyond the periods set out in paragraphs (a) and (b) of this section at the request of either party.

(d) Each hearing and each review involving oral arguments must be conducted at a time and place that is reasonably convenient to the parents and child involved. (Authority: 20 U. S. C. 1415(f)(1)(B)(ii), 1415(g), 1415(i)(1))

§300.516 Civil action.

(a) **General**. Any party **aggrieved by the findings and decision** made under §§300.507 through 300.513 or §§300.530 through 300.534 who does not have the **right to an appeal** under §300.514(b), and any party aggrieved by the findings and decision under §300.514(b), has the **right to bring a civil action** with respect to the due process complaint notice requesting a due process hearing under §300.507 or §§300.530 through 300.532. The action may be brought in any State court of competent jurisdiction or in a district court of the United States without regard to the amount in controversy.

(b) Time limitation. The party bringing the action shall **have 90 days from the date of the decision** of the hearing officer or, if applicable, the decision of the State review official, to file a civil action, **or, if the State** has an explicit time limitation for bringing civil actions under Part B of the Act, in the time allowed by that State law.

(c) Additional requirements. In any action brought under paragraph (a) of this section, the court—

(1) Receives the records of the administrative proceedings;

(2) Hears additional evidence at the request of a party; and

(3) Basing its decision on the preponderance of the evidence, grants the relief that the court determines to be appropriate.

(d) Jurisdiction of district courts. The district courts of the United States have jurisdiction of actions brought under section 615 of the Act without regard to the amount in controversy.

(e) Rule of construction. Nothing in this part restricts or limits the rights, procedures, and remedies available under the Constitution, the Americans with Disabilities Act of 1990, title V of the Rehabilitation Act of 1973, or other Federal laws protecting the rights of children with disabilities, except that before the filing of a civil action under these laws seeking relief that is also available under section 615 of the Act, **the procedures under §§300.507 and 300.514 must be exhausted** to the same extent as would be required had the action been brought under section 615 of the Act. (Authority: 20 U. S. C. 1415(i)(2) and (3)(A), 1415(l))

§300.517 Attorneys' fees.

(a) In general.

(1) In any action or proceeding brought under section 615 of the Act, the court, in its discretion, **may award reasonable attorneys' fees** as part of the costs to—

(i) The prevailing party who is the parent of a child with a disability;

(ii) To a **prevailing party who is an SEA or LEA against the attorney of a parent** who files a complaint or subsequent cause of action that is **frivolous, unreasonable, or without foundation,** or against the attorney of a parent who **continued to litigate** after the litigation clearly became frivolous, unreasonable, or without foundation; **or**

(iii) To a **prevailing SEA or LEA against the attorney of a parent, or against the parent,** if the parent's **request** for a due process hearing or subsequent cause of action was presented for any **improper purpose, such as to harass, to cause unnecessary delay,** or to needlessly increase the cost of litigation.

(2) Nothing in this subsection shall be construed to affect section 327 of the District of Columbia Appropriations Act, 2005.

(b) Prohibition on use of funds.

(1) **Funds under Part B of the Act may not be used to pay attorneys' fees** or costs of a party related to any action or proceeding under section 615 of the Act and subpart E of this part.

(2) Paragraph (b)(1) of this section does not preclude a public agency from using funds under Part B of the Act for conducting an action or proceeding under section 615 of the Act.

(c) Award of fees. A court awards **reasonable attorneys' fees** under section 615(i)(3) of the Act consistent with the following:

(1) Fees awarded under section 615(i)(3) of the Act must be based on **rates prevailing in the community** in which the action or proceeding arose for the kind and quality of services furnished. No bonus or multiplier may be used in calculating the fees awarded under this paragraph.

(2)

(i) Attorneys' fees may not be awarded and related costs may not be reimbursed in any action or proceeding under section 615 of the Act for services performed subsequent to the time of a written offer of settlement to a parent if—

(A) The offer is made within the time prescribed by Rule 68 of the Federal Rules of Civil Procedure or, in the case of an administrative proceeding, at any time more than 10 days before the proceeding begins;

(B) The offer is not accepted within 10 days; and

(C) The court or administrative hearing officer finds that the relief finally obtained by the parents is not more favorable to the parents than the offer of settlement.

(ii) Attorneys' fees may not be awarded relating to any meeting of the IEP Team unless the meeting is convened as a result of an administrative proceeding or judicial action, or at the discretion of the State, for a mediation described in §300.506.

(iii) A meeting conducted pursuant to §300.510 shall not be considered—

(A) A meeting convened as a result of an administrative hearing or judicial action; or

(B) An administrative hearing or judicial action for purposes of this section.

(3) Notwithstanding paragraph (c)(2) of this section, an award of attorneys' fees and related costs may be made **to a parent who is the prevailing party** and who was substantially justified in rejecting the settlement offer.

(4) Except as provided in paragraph (c)(5) of this section, the court reduces, accordingly, the amount of the attorneys' fees awarded under section 615 of the Act, if the court finds that—

(i) The parent, or the parent's attorney, during the course of the action or proceeding, **unreasonably protracted the final resolution** of the controversy;

(ii) The amount of the attorneys' fees otherwise authorized to be awarded unreasonably exceeds the hourly rate prevailing in the community for similar services by attorneys of reasonably comparable skill, reputation, and experience;

(iii) The time spent and legal services furnished were excessive considering the nature of the action or proceeding; or

(iv) The attorney representing the parent did not provide to the LEA the appropriate information in the due process request notice in accordance with §300.508.

(5) The provisions of paragraph (c)(4) of this section **do not apply** in any action or proceeding if the court finds that the State or local agency unreasonably protracted the final resolution of the action or proceeding or there was a violation of section 615 of the Act. (Authority: 20 U. S. C. 1415(i)(3)(B)–(G))

§300.518 Child's status during proceedings.

(a) **Except** as provided in §300.533, **during the pendency of any administrative or judicial proceeding regarding a due process complaint notice** requesting a due process hearing under §300.507, unless the State or local agency and the parents of the child agree otherwise, **the child** involved in the complaint must remain in his or her **current educational placement.**

(b) If the complaint involves an application for **initial admission** to public school, the child, with the consent of the parents, must be placed in the public school until the completion of all the proceedings.

(c) If the complaint involves an **application for initial services** under this part **from a child who is transitioning from Part C of the Act to Part B** and is no longer eligible for Part C services because the child has turned three, **the public agency is not required** to provide the Part C services that the child had been receiving. If the child is found eligible for special education and related services under Part B and the parent consents to the initial provision of special education and related services under §300.300(b), **then the public agency must provide those special education and related services that are not in dispute between the parent and the public agency.**

(d) If the hearing officer in a due process hearing conducted by the SEA or a State review official in an administrative appeal agrees with the child's parents that a change of placement is appropriate, **that placement must be treated as an agreement** between the State and the parents for purposes of paragraph (a) of this section. (Authority: 20 U. S. C. 1415(j))

§300.519 Surrogate parents.

(a) **General.** Each public agency must ensure that the rights of a child are protected when—

(1) No parent (as defined in §300.30) can be identified;

(2) The public agency, after reasonable efforts, cannot locate a parent;

(3) The child is a ward of the State under the laws of that State; or

(4) The child is an unaccompanied homeless youth as defined in section 725(6) of the McKinney-Vento Homeless Assistance Act (42 U. S. C. 11434a(6)).

(b) Duties of public agency. The duties of a public agency under paragraph (a) of this section include the assignment of an individual to act as a surrogate for the parents. This must include a method—

(1) For determining whether a child needs a surrogate parent; and

(2) For assigning a surrogate parent to the child.

(c) Wards of the State. In the case of a child who is a ward of the State, the surrogate parent alternatively may be appointed by the judge overseeing the child's case, provided that the surrogate meets the requirements in paragraphs (d)(2)(i) and (e) of this section.

(d) Criteria for selection of surrogate parents.

(1) The public agency may select a surrogate parent in any way permitted under State law.

(2) Public agencies must ensure that a person selected as a surrogate parent—

(i) Is not an employee of the SEA, the LEA, or any other agency that is involved in the education or care of the child;

(ii) Has no personal or professional interest that conflicts with the interest of the child the surrogate parent represents; and

(iii) Has knowledge and skills that ensure adequate representation of the child.

(e) Non-employee requirement; compensation. A person otherwise qualified to be a surrogate parent under paragraph (d) of this section is not an employee of the agency solely because he or she is paid by the agency to serve as a surrogate parent.

(f) Unaccompanied homeless youth. In the case of a child who is an unaccompanied **homeless youth**, appropriate staff of emergency shelters, transitional shelters, independent living programs, and street outreach programs may be appointed as temporary surrogate parents without regard to paragraph (d)(2)(i) of this section, until a surrogate parent can be appointed that meets all of the requirements of paragraph (d) of this section.

(g) Surrogate parent responsibilities. The **surrogate parent may represent the child in all** matters relating to—

(1) The identification, evaluation, and educational placement of the child; and

(2) The provision of FAPE to the child.

(h) SEA responsibility. The SEA must make reasonable efforts to ensure the assignment of a surrogate parent not more than **30 days** after a public agency determines that the child needs a surrogate parent. (Authority: 20 U. S. C. 1415(b)(2))

§300.520 Transfer of parental rights at age of majority.

(a) General. A State may provide that, when **a child with a disability reaches the age of majority** under State law that applies to all children (except for a child with a disability who has been determined to be incompetent under State law)—

(1)

(i) The public agency must provide any notice required by this part to both the child and the parents; and

(ii) All rights accorded to parents under Part B of the Act transfer to the child;

(2) All rights accorded to parents under Part B of the Act transfer to children who are incarcerated in an adult or juvenile, State or local correctional institution; and

(3) Whenever a State provides for the transfer of rights under this part pursuant to paragraph (a)(1) or (a)(2) of this section, the agency must notify the child and the parents of the transfer of rights.

(b) Special rule. A State **must establish procedures for appointing the parent of a child with a disability,** or, if the parent is not available, another appropriate individual, to represent the educational interests of the child throughout the period of the child's eligibility under Part B of the Act if, under State law, **a child who has reached the age of majority, but has not been determined to be incompetent,** can be determined not to have the ability to provide informed consent with respect to the child's educational program. (Authority: 20 U. S. C. 1415(m))

§§300.521-300.529 [Reserved]

Discipline Procedures

§300.530 Authority of school personnel.

(a) **Case-by-case determination.** School personnel may consider any unique circumstances on a case-by-case basis when determining whether a change in placement, consistent with the other requirements of this section, is appropriate for a child with a disability who violates a code of student conduct.

(b) **General.**

(1) School personnel under this section **may remove** a child with a disability who violates a code of student conduct from his or her current placement to an appropriate interim alternative educational setting, another setting, or suspension, for **not more than 10 consecutive school days** (to the extent those alternatives are applied to children without disabilities), and **for additional removals of not more than 10 consecutive school days** in that same school year for separate incidents of misconduct (**as long** as those removals do not constitute a change of placement under §300.536).

(2) **After a child with a disability has been removed from his or her current placement for 10 school days in the same school year, during any subsequent days of removal the public agency must provide services to the extent required under paragraph (d) of this section.**

(c) **Additional authority.** For disciplinary changes in placement that **would exceed 10 consecutive school days**, if the behavior that gave rise to the violation of the school code is **determined not to be a manifestation of the child's disability** pursuant to paragraph (e) of this section, school personnel may apply the relevant disciplinary procedures to children with disabilities in the same manner and for the same duration as the procedures would be applied to children without disabilities, except as provided in paragraph (d) of this section.

(d) **Services.**

(1) A child with a disability **who is removed from the child's current placement** pursuant to paragraphs (c), or (g) of this section must—

(i) **Continue to receive educational services**, as provided in §300.101(a), so as to enable the child to continue to participate in the **general education curriculum**, although in another setting, and to **progress toward meeting the goals set out in the child's IEP**; and

(ii) Receive, as appropriate, a **functional behavioral assessment, and behavioral intervention services and modifications**, that are designed to address the behavior violation **so that it does not recur.**

(2) The services required by paragraph (d)(1), (d)(3), (d)(4), and (d)(5) of this section **may be provided in an interim alternative educational setting.**

(3) A public agency is **only required to provide services during periods of removal** to a child with a disability who has been removed from his or her current placement for **10 school days or less in that school year, if it provides services to a child without disabilities** who is similarly removed.

(4) After a child with a disability has been removed from his or her current placement **for 10 school days in the same school year**, if the current removal is for not more than 10 consecutive school days and is not a change of placement under §300.536, school personnel, in consultation with at least one of the child's teachers, determine the extent to which services are needed, as provided in §300.101(a), so as **to enable the child to continue to participate in the general education curriculum,** although in another setting, and to progress toward meeting the goals set out in the child's IEP.

(5) If the removal is a change of placement under §300.536, the child's IEP Team determines appropriate services under paragraph (d)(1) of this section.

(e) **Manifestation determination.**

(1) **Within 10 school days** of any decision to change the placement of a child with a disability because of a violation of a code of student conduct, **the LEA, the parent, and relevant members of the child's IEP Team** (as determined by the parent and the LEA) must review all relevant information in the student's file, including the child's IEP, any teacher observations, and any relevant information provided by the parents to determine—

(i) If the **conduct in question was caused by, or had a direct and substantial relationship to**, the child's disability; or

(ii) If the conduct in question was the direct result of the **LEA's failure to implement the IEP.**

(2) The conduct **must be determined to be a manifestation** of the child's disability if the LEA, the parent, and relevant members of the child's IEP Team determine that **a condition in either** paragraph (e)(1)(i) or (1)(ii) of this section was met.

(3) If the LEA, the parent, and relevant members of the child's IEP Team determine the condition described in paragraph **(e)(1)(ii) of this section was met, the LEA must take immediate steps** to remedy those deficiencies.

(f) Determination that behavior was a manifestation. If the LEA, the parent, and relevant members of the IEP Team make the determination that the conduct was a manifestation of the child's disability, the IEP Team must—

(1) **Either-–**

(i) Conduct a **functional behavioral assessment**, unless the LEA had conducted a functional behavioral assessment before the behavior that resulted in the change of placement occurred, and implement a behavioral intervention plan for the child; or

(ii) If a **behavioral intervention plan** already has been developed, **review** the behavioral intervention plan, **and modify it**, as necessary, to address the behavior; and

(2) Except as provided in paragraph (g) of this section, return the child to the placement from which the child was removed, **unless the parent and the LEA agree to a change of placement** as part of the modification of the behavioral intervention plan.

(g) Special circumstances. School personnel may remove a student to an interim alternative educational setting for not more than 45 school days **without regard to whether the behavior is determined to be a manifestation** of the child's disability, if the child—

(1) Carries a **weapon** to or possesses a weapon at school, on school premises, or to or at a school function under the jurisdiction of an SEA or an LEA;

(2) Knowingly possesses or uses **illegal drugs**, or sells or solicits the sale of a controlled substance, while at school, on school premises, or at a school function under the jurisdiction of an SEA or an LEA; or

(3) Has inflicted **serious bodily injury** upon another person while at school, on school premises, or at a school function under the jurisdiction of an SEA or an LEA.

(h) Notification. On the date on which the decision is made to make a removal that constitutes a change of placement of a child with a disability because of a violation of a code of student conduct, the LEA must notify the parents of that decision, and provide the parents the procedural safeguards notice described in §300.504.

(i) Definitions. For purposes of this section, the following definitions apply:

(1) **Controlled substance** means a drug or other substance identified under schedules I, II, III, IV, or V in section 202(c) of the Controlled Substances Act (21 U. S. C. 812(c)).

(2) **Illegal drug** means a controlled substance; but does not include a controlled substance that is legally possessed or used under the supervision of a licensed health-care professional or that is legally possessed or used under any other authority under that Act or under any other provision of Federal law.

(3) **Serious bodily injury** has the meaning given the term "serious bodily injury" under paragraph (3) of subsection (h) of section 1365 of title 18, United States Code.

(4) **Weapon** has the meaning given the term "dangerous weapon" under paragraph (2) of the first subsection (g) of section 930 of title 18, United States Code. (Authority: 20 U. S. C. 1415(k)(1) and (7))

§300.531 Determination of setting. The child's IEP Team determines the interim alternative educational setting for services under §300.530(c), (d)(5), and (g). (Authority: 20 U. S. C. 1415(k)(2))

§300.532 Appeal.

(a) General. The parent of a child with a disability who **disagrees with any decision** regarding placement under §§300.530 and 300.531, **or the manifestation determination** under §300.530(e), **or an LEA that believes that maintaining the current placement of the child is substantially likely to result in injury** to the child or others, **may appeal** the decision by requesting a hearing. The hearing is requested by **filing a complaint** pursuant to §§300.507 and 300.508(a) and (b).

(b) Authority of hearing officer.

(1) A hearing officer under §300.511 hears, and makes a determination regarding an appeal under paragraph (a) of this section.

(2) In making the determination under paragraph (b)(1) of this section, the hearing officer **may**—

(i) **Return the child** with a disability to the placement from which the child was removed if the hearing officer determines that the removal was a violation of §300.530 or that the child's behavior was a manifestation of the child's disability; or

(ii) **Order a change of placement** of the child with a disability to an appropriate interim alternative educational setting for **not more than 45 school days** if the hearing officer determines that maintaining the current placement of the child is substantially likely to result in injury to the child or to others.

(3) The procedures under paragraphs (a) and (b)(1) and (2) of this section may be repeated, if the LEA believes that returning the child to the original placement is substantially likely to result in injury to the child or to others.

(c) Expedited due process hearing.

(1) Whenever a hearing is requested under paragraph (a) of this section, the parents or the LEA involved in the dispute must have an opportunity for an impartial due process hearing consistent with the requirements of §§300.507 and 300.508(a) through (c) and §§300.510 through 300.514, except as provided in paragraph (c)(2) through (4) of this section.

(2) The SEA or LEA is responsible for arranging the **expedited due process hearing, which must occur within 20 school days** of the date the complaint requesting the hearing is filed. The hearing officer must make a determination within 10 school days after the hearing.

(3) Unless the parents and LEA agree in writing to waive the resolution meeting described in paragraph (c)(3)(i) of this section, or agree to use the mediation process described in §300.506--

(i) A **resolution meeting must occur within seven days** of receiving notice of the due process complaint; and

(ii) The due process hearing may proceed unless the matter has been resolved to the satisfaction of both parties **within 15 days** of the receipt of the due process complaint.

(4) A State may establish different State-imposed procedural rules for expedited due process hearings conducted under this section than it has established for other due process hearings, but, except for the timelines as modified in paragraph (c)(3) of this section, the State must ensure that the requirements in §§300.510 through 300.514 are met.

(5) The decisions on expedited due process hearings are appealable consistent with §300.514. (Authority: 20 U. S. C. 1415(k)(3) and (4)(B), 1415(f)(1)(A))

§300.533 Placement during appeals. When an appeal under §300.532 has been made by either the parent or the LEA, the child must remain in the interim alternative educational setting pending the decision of the hearing officer or until the expiration of the time period specified in §300.530(c) or (g), whichever occurs first, unless the parent and the SEA or LEA agree otherwise. (Authority: 20 U. S. C. 1415(k)(4)(A))

§300.534 Protections for children not determined eligible for special education and related services.

(a) General. A child who has not been determined to be eligible for special education and related services under this part and who has engaged in behavior that violated a code of student conduct, **may assert any of the protections** provided for in this part **if the public agency had knowledge** (as determined in accordance with paragraph (b) of this section) that the child was a child with a disability before the behavior that precipitated the disciplinary action occurred.

(b) Basis of knowledge. A public agency must be deemed to have knowledge that a child is a child with a disability if before the behavior that precipitated the disciplinary action occurred—

(1) The parent of the child **expressed concern in writing** to supervisory or administrative personnel of the appropriate educational agency, or a teacher of the child, that the child is in need of special education and related services;

(2) The parent of the child **requested an evaluation** of the child pursuant to §§300.300 through 300.311; or

(3) The teacher of the child, or other personnel of the LEA, **expressed specific concerns** about a pattern of behavior demonstrated by the child directly to the director of special education of the agency or to other supervisory personnel of the agency.

(c) Exception. A public agency would not be deemed to have knowledge under paragraph (b) of this section if—

(1) The parent of the child—

(i) **Has not allowed an evaluation** of the child pursuant to §§300.300 through 300.311; or

(ii) **Has refused services** under this part; or

(2) The child has been evaluated in accordance with §§300.300 through 300.311 and determined to not be a child with a disability under this part.

(d) Conditions that apply if no basis of knowledge.

(1) If a public agency does not have knowledge that a child is a child with a disability (in accordance with paragraphs (b) and (c) of this section) prior to taking disciplinary measures against the child, the child may be subjected to the disciplinary measures applied to children without disabilities who engage in comparable behaviors consistent with paragraph (d)(2) of this section.

(2)

(i) If a **request is made for an evaluation** of a child during the time period in which the child is subjected to disciplinary measures under §300.530, the evaluation must be conducted in an **expedited manner**.

(ii) Until the evaluation is completed, the child remains in the educational placement determined by school authorities, which can include suspension or expulsion without educational services.

(iii) If the child is determined to be a child with a disability, taking into consideration information from the evaluation conducted by the agency and information provided by the parents, the agency must provide special education and related services in accordance with this part, including the requirements of §§300.530 through 300.536 and section 612(a)(1)(A) of the Act. (Authority: 20 U. S. C. 1415(k)(5))

§300.535 Referral to and action by law enforcement and judicial authorities.

(a) Rule of construction. Nothing in this part prohibits an agency from reporting a crime committed by a child with a disability to appropriate authorities or prevents State law enforcement and judicial authorities from exercising their responsibilities with regard to the application of Federal and State law to crimes committed by a child with a disability.

(b) Transmittal of records.

(1) An agency reporting a crime committed by a child with a disability **must** ensure that copies of the special education and disciplinary records of the child are transmitted for consideration by the appropriate authorities to whom the agency reports the crime.

(2) An agency reporting a crime under this section **may** transmit copies of the child's special education and disciplinary records only to the extent that the transmission is permitted by the Family Educational Rights and Privacy Act. (Authority: 20 U. S. C. 1415(k)(6))

§300.536 Change of placement because of disciplinary removals.

(a) For purposes of removals of a child with a disability from the child's current educational placement under §§300.530 through 300.535, a change of placement occurs if—

(1) The removal is for more than 10 consecutive school days; or

(2) The child has been subjected to a series of removals that constitute a pattern—

(i) Because the series of removals total more than 10 school days in a school year;

(ii) Because the child's behavior is substantially similar to the child's behavior in previous incidents that resulted in the series of removals; and

(iii) Because of such additional factors as the length of each removal, the total amount of time the child has been removed, and the proximity of the removals to one another.

(b)

(1) The public agency determines on a case-by-case basis whether a pattern of removals constitutes a change of placement.

(2) This determination is subject to review through due process and judicial proceedings. (Authority: 20 U. S. C. 1415(k))

§300.537 State enforcement mechanisms. Notwithstanding §§300.506(b)(7) and 300.510(d)(2), which provide for judicial enforcement of a written agreement reached as a result of mediation or a resolution meeting, there is nothing in this part that would prevent the SEA from using other mechanisms to seek enforcement of that agreement, provided that use of those mechanisms is not mandatory and does not delay or deny a party the right to seek enforcement of the written agreement in a State court of competent jurisdiction or in a district court of the United States. (Authority: 20 U. S. C. 1415(e)(2)(F), 1415(f)(1)(B))

§§300.538–300.599 [Reserved]

Subpart F—Monitoring, Enforcement, Confidentiality, and Program Information

Monitoring, Technical Assistance, and Enforcement

§300.600 State monitoring and enforcement.

(a) The State must monitor the implementation of this part, enforce this part in accordance with §300.604(a)(1) and (a)(3), (b)(2)(i) and (b)(2)(v), and (c)(2), and annually report on performance under this part.

(b) The primary focus of the State's monitoring activities must be on—

(1) Improving educational results and functional outcomes for all children with disabilities; and

(2) Ensuring that public agencies meet the program requirements under Part B of the Act, with a particular emphasis on those requirements that are most closely related to improving educational results for children with disabilities.

(c) As a part of its responsibilities under paragraph (a) of this section, the State must use quantifiable indicators and such qualitative indicators as are needed to adequately measure performance in the priority areas identified in paragraph (d) of this section, and the indicators established by the Secretary for the State performance plans.

(d) The State must monitor the LEAs located in the State, using quantifiable indicators in each of the following priority areas, and using such qualitative indicators as are needed to adequately measure performance in those areas:

(1) Provision of FAPE in the least restrictive environment.

(2) State exercise of general supervision, including child find, effective monitoring, the use of resolution meetings, mediation, and a system of transition services as defined in §300.43 and in 20 U. S. C. 1437(a)(9).

(3) Disproportionate representation of racial and ethnic groups in special education and related services, to the extent the representation is the result of inappropriate identification. (Authority: 20 U. S. C. 1416(a))

§300.601 State performance plans and data collection.

(a) **General.** Not later than December 3, 2005, each State must have in place a performance plan that evaluates the State's efforts to implement the requirements and purposes of Part B of the Act, and describes how the State will improve such implementation.

(1) Each State must submit the State's performance plan to the Secretary for approval in accordance with the approval process described in section 616(c) of the Act.

(2) Each State must review its State performance plan at least once every six years, and submit any amendments to the Secretary.

(3) As part of the State performance plan, each State must establish measurable and rigorous targets for the indicators established by the Secretary under the priority areas described in §300.600(d).

(b) **Data collection.**

(1) Each State must collect valid and reliable information as needed to report annually to the Secretary on the indicators established by the Secretary for the State performance plans.

(2) If the Secretary permits States to collect data on specific indicators through State monitoring or sampling, and the State collects the data through State monitoring or sampling, the State must collect data on those indicators for each LEA at least once during the period of the State performance plan.

(3) Nothing in Part B of the Act shall be construed to authorize the development of a nationwide database of personally identifiable information on individuals involved in studies or other collections of data under Part B of the Act. (Authority: 20 U. S. C. 1416(b))

§300.602 State use of targets and reporting.

(a) **General.** Each State must use the targets established in the State's performance plan under §300.601 and the priority areas described in §300.600(d) to analyze the performance of each LEA.

(b) Public reporting and privacy.

(1) Public report.

(i) Subject to paragraph (b)(1)(ii) of this section, the State must—

(A) Report annually to the public on the performance of each LEA located in the State on the targets in the State's performance plan; and

(B) Make the State's performance plan available through public means, including by posting on the Web site of the SEA, distribution to the media, and distribution through public agencies.

(ii) If the State, in meeting the requirements of paragraph (b)(1)(i) of this section, collects performance data through State monitoring or sampling, the State must include in its report under paragraph (b)(1)(i)(A) of this section the most recently available performance data on each LEA, and the date the data were obtained.

(2) State performance report. The State must report annually to the Secretary on the performance of the State under the State's performance plan.

(3) **Privacy.** The State must not report to the public or the Secretary any information on performance that would result in the disclosure of **personally identifiable information about individual children,** or where the available data are insufficient to yield statistically reliable information. (Authority: 20 U. S. C. 1416(b)(2)(C))

§300.603 Secretary's review and determination regarding State performance.

(a) Review. The **Secretary annually reviews the State's performance report** submitted pursuant to §300.602(b)(2).

(b) Determination.

(1) General. Based on the information provided by the State in the State's annual performance report, information obtained through monitoring visits, and any other public information made available, the Secretary determines if the State—

(i) Meets the requirements and purposes of Part B of the Act;

(ii) Needs assistance in implementing the requirements of Part B of the Act;

(iii) Needs intervention in implementing the requirements of Part B of the Act; or

(iv) Needs substantial intervention in implementing the requirements of Part B of the Act.

(2) Notice and opportunity for a hearing.

(i) For determinations made under paragraphs (b)(1)(iii) and (b)(1)(iv) of this section, the Secretary provides reasonable notice and an opportunity for a hearing on those determinations.

(ii) The hearing described in paragraph (b)(2) of this section consists of an opportunity to meet with the Assistant Secretary for Special Education and Rehabilitative Services to demonstrate why the Department should not make the determination described in paragraph (b)(1) of this section. (Authority: 20 U. S. C. 1416(d))

§300.604 Enforcement.

(a) Needs assistance. If the Secretary determines, **for two consecutive years,** that a State needs assistance under §300.603(b)(1)(ii) in implementing the requirements of Part B of the Act, the Secretary takes one or more of the following actions:

(1) Advises the State of available sources of technical assistance that may help the State address the areas in which the State needs assistance, which may include assistance from the Office of Special Education Programs, other offices of the Department of Education, other Federal agencies, technical assistance providers approved by the Secretary, and other federally funded nonprofit agencies, and requires the State to work with appropriate entities. Such technical assistance may include—

(i) The provision of advice by experts to address the areas in which the State needs assistance, including explicit plans for addressing the area for concern within a specified period of time;

(ii) Assistance in identifying and implementing professional development, instructional strategies, and methods of instruction that are based on scientifically based research;

(iii) Designating and using distinguished superintendents, principals, special education administrators, special education teachers, and other teachers to provide advice, technical assistance, and support; and

(iv) Devising additional approaches to providing technical assistance, such as collaborating with institutions of higher education, educational service agencies, national centers of technical assistance supported under Part D of the Act, and private providers of scientifically based technical assistance.

(2) Directs the use of State-level funds under section 611(e) of the Act on the area or areas in which the State needs assistance.

(3) Identifies the State as a high-risk grantee and impose special conditions on the State's grant under Part B of the Act.

(b) Needs intervention. If the Secretary determines, for three or more consecutive years, that a State needs intervention under §300.603(b)(1)(iii) in implementing the requirements of Part B of the Act, the following shall apply:

(1) The Secretary may take any of the actions described in paragraph (a) of this section.

(2) The Secretary takes one or more of the following actions:

(i) Requires the State to prepare **a corrective action plan** or improvement plan if the Secretary determines that the State should be able to correct the problem within one year.

(ii) Requires the State to enter into a compliance agreement under section 457 of the General Education Provisions Act, as amended, 20 U. S. C. 1221 et seq. (GEPA), if the Secretary has reason to believe that the State cannot correct the problem within one year.

(iii) For each year of the determination, withholds not less than 20 percent and not more than 50 percent of the State's funds under section 611(e) of the Act, until the Secretary determines the State has sufficiently addressed the areas in which the State needs intervention.

(iv) Seeks to recover funds under section 452 of GEPA.

(v) Withholds, in whole or in part, any further payments to the State under Part B of the Act.

(vi) Refers the matter for appropriate enforcement action, which may include referral to the Department of Justice.

(c) Needs substantial intervention. Notwithstanding paragraph (a) or (b) of this section, at any time that the Secretary determines that a State **needs substantial intervention** in implementing the requirements of Part B of the Act or that there **is a substantial failure to comply** with any condition of an SEA's or LEA's eligibility under Part B of the Act, the Secretary takes one or more of the following actions:

(1) Recovers funds under section 452 of GEPA.

(2) Withholds, in whole or in part, any further payments to the State under Part B of the Act.

(3) Refers the case to the Office of the Inspector General at the Department of Education.

(4) Refers the matter for appropriate enforcement action, which may include referral to the **Department of Justice**.

(d) Report to Congress. The Secretary reports to the Committee on Education and the Workforce of the House of Representatives and the Committee on Health, Education, Labor, and Pensions of the Senate within 30 days of taking enforcement action pursuant to paragraph (a), (b), or (c) of this section, on the specific action taken and the reasons why enforcement action was taken. (Authority: 20 U. S. C. 1416(e)(1)-(e)(3), (e)(5))

§300.605 Withholding funds.

(a) Opportunity for hearing. Prior to withholding any funds under Part B of the Act, the Secretary provides reasonable notice and an opportunity for a hearing to the SEA involved, pursuant to the procedures in §§300.180 through 300.183.

(b) Suspension. Pending the outcome of any hearing to withhold payments under paragraph (a) of this section, the Secretary may suspend payments to a recipient, suspend the authority of the recipient to obligate funds under Part B of the Act, or both, after the recipient has been given reasonable notice and an opportunity to show cause why future payments or authority to obligate funds under Part B of the Act should not be suspended.

(c) Nature of withholding.

(1) If the Secretary determines that it is appropriate to withhold further payments under §300.604(b)(2) or (c)(2), the Secretary may determine—

(i) That the withholding will be limited to programs or projects, or portions of programs or projects, that affected the Secretary's determination under §300.603(b)(1); or

(ii) That the SEA must not make further payments under Part B of the Act to specified State agencies or LEAs that caused or were involved in the Secretary's determination under §300.603(b)(1).

(2) Until the Secretary is satisfied that the condition that caused the initial withholding has been substantially rectified—

(i) Payments to the State under Part B of the Act must be withheld in whole or in part; and

(ii) Payments by the SEA under Part B of the Act must be limited to State agencies and LEAs whose actions did not cause or were not involved in the Secretary's determination under §300.603(b)(1), as the case may be. (Authority: 20 U. S. C. 1416(e)(4), (e)(6))

§300.606 Public attention. Any State that has received notice under §§300.603(b)(1)(ii) through (iv) must, by means of a public notice, take such measures as may be necessary to notify the public within the State of the pendency of an action taken pursuant to §300.604. (Authority: 20 U. S. C. 1416(e)(7))

§300.607 Divided State agency responsibility. For purposes of this subpart, if responsibility for ensuring that the requirements of Part B of the Act are met with respect to children with disabilities who are convicted as adults under State law and incarcerated in adult prisons is assigned to a public agency other than the SEA pursuant to §300.149(d), and if the Secretary finds that the failure to comply substantially with the provisions of Part B of the Act are related to a failure by the public agency, the Secretary takes appropriate corrective action to ensure compliance with Part B of the Act, except that—

(a) Any reduction or withholding of payments to the State under §300.604 must be proportionate to the total funds allotted under section 611 of the Act to the State as the number of eligible children with disabilities in adult prisons under the supervision of the other public agency is proportionate to the number of eligible individuals with disabilities in the State under the supervision of the SEA; and

(b) Any withholding of funds under §300.604 must be limited to the specific agency responsible for the failure to comply with Part B of the Act. (Authority: 20 U. S. C. 1416(h))

§300.608 State enforcement.

(a) If an SEA determines that an LEA is not meeting the requirements of Part B of the Act, including the targets in the State's performance plan, **the SEA must prohibit the LEA from reducing the LEA's maintenance of effort** under §300.203 for any fiscal year.

(b) Nothing in this subpart shall be construed to restrict a State from utilizing any other authority available to it to monitor and enforce the requirements of Part B of the Act. (Authority: 20 U. S. C. 1416(f); 20 U. S. C. 1412(a)(11))

§300.609 Rule of construction. Nothing in this subpart shall be construed to restrict the Secretary from utilizing any authority under GEPA, including the provisions in 34 CFR parts 76, 77, 80, and 81 to monitor and enforce the requirements of the Act, including the imposition of special conditions under 34 CFR 80.12. (Authority: 20 U. S. C. 1416(g))

Confidentiality of Information

§300.610 Confidentiality. The Secretary takes appropriate action, in accordance with section 444 of GEPA, to ensure the protection of the confidentiality of any personally identifiable data, information, and records collected or maintained by the Secretary and by SEAs and LEAs pursuant to Part B of the Act, and consistent with §§300.611 through 300.627. (Authority: 20 U. S. C. 1417(c))

§300.611 Definitions.

As used in §§300.611 through 300.625—

(a) **Destruction** means physical destruction or removal of personal identifiers from information so that the information is no longer personally identifiable.

(b) **Education records** means the type of records covered under the definition of "education records" in 34 CFR part 99 (the regulations implementing the Family Educational Rights and Privacy Act of 1974, 20 U. S. C. 1232g (FERPA)).

(c) **Participating agency** means any agency or institution that collects, maintains, or uses personally identifiable information, or from which information is obtained, under Part B of the Act. (Authority: 20 U. S. C. 1221e-3, 1412(a)(8), 1417(c))

§300.612 Notice to parents.

(a) The SEA must give notice that is adequate to fully inform parents about the requirements of §300.123, including—

(1) A description of the extent that the notice is given in the native languages of the various population groups in the State;

(2) A description of the children on whom personally identifiable information is maintained, the types of information sought, the methods the State intends to use in gathering the information (including the sources from whom information is gathered), and the uses to be made of the information;

(3) A summary of the policies and procedures that participating agencies must follow regarding storage, disclosure to third parties, retention, and **destruction of personally identifiable information**; and

(4) A description of all of the rights of parents and children regarding this information, including the rights under FERPA and implementing regulations in 34 CFR part 99.

(b) Before any major identification, location, or evaluation activity, the notice must be published or announced in newspapers or other media, or both, with circulation adequate to notify parents throughout the State of the activity. (Authority: 20 U. S. C. 1412(a)(8); 1417(c))

§300.613 Access rights.

(a) Each participating agency **must permit parents to inspect and review any education records relating to their children** that are collected, maintained, or used by the agency under this part. The agency must comply with a request without unnecessary delay **and before any meeting regarding an IEP**, or any hearing pursuant to §300.507 or §§300.530 through 300.532, or resolution session pursuant to §300.510, and in no case more than 45 days after the request has been made.

(b) The right to **inspect and review education records** under this section **includes—**

(1) The right to a response from the participating agency to reasonable **requests for explanations and interpretations** of the records;

(2) The right to request that the **agency provide copies** of the records containing the information if failure to provide those copies would effectively prevent the parent from exercising the right to inspect and review the records; and

(3) The **right to have a representative of the parent inspect** and review the records.

(c) An agency may **presume that the parent has authority to inspect and review records relating to his or her child unless** the agency has been advised that the parent does not have the authority under applicable State law governing such matters as guardianship, separation, and divorce. (Authority: 20 U. S. C. 1412(a)(8); 1417(c))

§300.614 Record of access.
Each participating agency **must keep a record of parties obtaining access to education records** collected, maintained, or used under Part B of the Act (except access by parents and authorized employees of the participating agency), including the name of the party, the date access was given, and the purpose for which the party is authorized to use the records. (Authority: 20 U. S. C. 1412(a)(8); 1417(c))

§300.615 Records on more than one child.
If any education record includes information on more than one child, the parents of those children have the right to inspect and review only the information relating to their child or to be informed of that specific information. (Authority: 20 U. S. C. 1412(a)(8); 1417(c))

§300.616 List of types and locations of information.
Each participating agency must provide parents on request a list of the types and locations of education records collected, maintained, or used by the agency. (Authority: 20 U. S. C. 1412(a)(8); 1417(c))

§300.617 Fees.

(a) Each participating agency may charge **a fee for copies of records** that are made for parents under this part if the fee does not effectively prevent the parents from exercising their right to inspect and review those records.

(b) A participating agency **may not charge a fee to search** for or to retrieve information under this part. (Authority: 20 U. S. C. 1412(a)(8); 1417(c))

§300.618 Amendment of records at parent's request.

(a) A parent who believes that information in the education records collected, maintained, or used under this part **is inaccurate or misleading or violates the privacy or other rights** of the child may request the participating agency that maintains the information to amend the information.

(b) The agency must decide whether to amend the information in accordance with the request within a reasonable period of time of receipt of the request.

(c) If the agency decides to refuse to amend the information in accordance with the request, it must inform the parent of the refusal and advise the parent of the **right to a hearing** under §300.619. (Authority: 20 U. S. C. 1412(a)(8); 1417(c))

§300.619 Opportunity for a hearing. The agency must, on request, **provide an opportunity for a hearing to challenge information in education records** to ensure that it is not inaccurate, misleading, or otherwise in violation of the privacy or other rights of the child. (Authority: 20 U. S. C. 1412(a)(8); 1417(c))

§300.620 Result of hearing.

(a) If, as a result of the hearing, the agency decides that the information is inaccurate, misleading or otherwise in violation of the privacy or other rights of the child, **it must amend the information** accordingly and so inform the parent in writing.

(b) If, as a result of the hearing, the agency decides that the information is not inaccurate, misleading, or otherwise in violation of the privacy or other rights of the child, it must inform the parent of the parent's right to place in the records the agency maintains on the child a statement commenting on the information or setting forth any reasons for disagreeing with the decision of the agency.

(c) Any explanation placed in the records of the child under this section must—

(1) Be maintained by the agency as part of the records of the child as long as the record or contested portion is maintained by the agency; and

(2) If the records of the child or the contested portion is disclosed by the agency to any party, the explanation must also be disclosed to the party. (Authority: 20 U. S. C. 1412(a)(8); 1417(c))

§300.621 Hearing procedures. A hearing held under §300.619 must be conducted according to the procedures in 34 CFR 99.22. (Authority: 20 U. S. C. 1412(a)(8); 1417(c))

§300.622 Consent.

(a) Parental consent must be obtained before personally identifiable information is disclosed to parties, other than officials of participating agencies in accordance with paragraph (b)(1) of this section, unless the information is contained in education records, and the disclosure is authorized without parental consent under 34 CFR part 99.

(b)

(1) Except as provided in paragraphs (b)(2) and (b)(3) of this section, **parental consent is not required** before personally identifiable information is released to officials of participating agencies for purposes of meeting a requirement of this part.

(2) Parental consent, or the consent of an eligible child who has reached the age of majority under State law, must be obtained before personally identifiable information is released to officials of participating agencies providing or paying for transition services in accordance with §300.321(b)(3).

(3) If a child is enrolled, or is going to enroll in a private school that is **not located in the LEA of the parent's residence,** parental consent must be obtained before any personally identifiable information about the child is released between officials in the LEA where the private school is located and officials in the LEA of the parent's residence. (Authority: 20 U. S. C. 1412(a)(8); 1417(c))

§300.623 Safeguards.

(a) Each participating agency must protect the confidentiality of personally identifiable information at collection, storage, disclosure, and destruction stages.

(b) One official at each participating agency must assume responsibility for ensuring the confidentiality of any personally identifiable information.

(c) All persons collecting or using personally identifiable information must receive training or instruction regarding the State's policies and procedures under §300.123 and 34 CFR part 99.

(d) Each participating agency must maintain, for public inspection, a current listing of the names and positions of those employees within the agency who may have access to personally identifiable information. (Authority: 20 U. S. C. 1412(a)(8); 1417(c))

§300.624 Destruction of information.

(a) The public agency must inform parents when personally identifiable information collected, maintained, or used under this part is no longer needed to provide educational services to the child.

(b) The information must be destroyed at the request of the parents. However, a permanent record of a student's name, address, and phone number, his or her grades, attendance record, classes attended, grade level completed, and year completed may be maintained without time limitation. (Authority: 20 U. S. C. 1412(a)(8); 1417(c))

§300.625 Children's rights.

(a) The SEA must have in effect policies and procedures regarding the extent to which children are afforded rights of privacy similar to those afforded to parents, taking into consideration the age of the child and type or severity of disability.

(b) Under the regulations for FERPA in 34 CFR 99.5(a), the rights of parents regarding education records are transferred to the student at age 18.

(c) If the rights accorded to parents under Part B of the Act are transferred to a student who reaches the age of majority, consistent with §300.520, the rights regarding educational records in §§300.613 through 300.624 must also be transferred to the student. However, the public agency must provide any notice required under section 615 of the Act to the student and the parents. (Authority: 20 U. S. C. 1412(a)(8); 1417(c))

§300.626 Enforcement. The SEA must have in effect the policies and procedures, including sanctions that the State uses, to ensure that its policies and procedures consistent with §§300.611 through 300.625 are followed and that the requirements of the Act and the regulations in this part are met. (Authority: 20 U. S. C. 1412(a)(8); 1417(c))

§300.627 Department use of personally identifiable information. If the Department or its authorized representatives collect any personally identifiable information regarding children with disabilities that is not subject to the Privacy Act of 1974, 5 U. S. C. 552a, the Secretary applies the requirements of 5 U. S. C. 552a(b)(1) and (b)(2), 552a(b)(4) through (b)(11); 552a(c) through 552a(e)(3)(B); 552a(e)(3)(D); 552a(e)(5) through (e)(10); 552a(h); 552a(m); and 552a(n); and the regulations implementing those provisions in 34 CFR part 5b. (Authority: 20 U. S. C. 1412(a)(8); 1417(c))

Reports - Program Information

§300.640 Annual report of children served—report requirement.

(a) The SEA must annually report to the Secretary on the information required by section 618 of the Act at the times specified by the Secretary.

(b) The SEA must submit the report on forms provided by the Secretary. (Authority: 20 U. S. C. 1418(a))

§300.641 Annual report of children served—information required in the report.

(a) For purposes of the annual report required by section 618 of the Act and §300.640, the State and the Secretary of the Interior must count and report the number of children with disabilities receiving special education and related services on any date between October 1 and December 1 of each year.

(b) For the purpose of this reporting provision, a child's age is the child's actual age on the date of the child count.

(c) The SEA may not report a child under more than one disability category.

(d) If a child with a disability has more than one disability, the SEA must report that child in accordance with the following procedure:

(1) If a child has only two disabilities and those disabilities are deafness and blindness, and the child is not reported as having a developmental delay, that child must be reported under the category "deaf-blindness."

(2) A child who has more than one disability and is not reported as having deaf-blindness or as having a developmental delay must be reported under the category "multiple disabilities." (Authority: 20 U. S. C. 1418(a), (b))

§300.642 Data reporting.

(a) **Protection of personally identifiable data.** The data described in section 618(a) of the Act and in §300.641 must be publicly reported by each State in a manner that does not result in disclosure of data identifiable to individual children.

(b) **Sampling.** The Secretary may permit States and the Secretary of the Interior to obtain data in section 618(a) of the Act through sampling. (Authority: 20 U. S. C. 1418(b))

§300.643 Annual report of children served—certification. The SEA must include in its report a certification signed by an authorized official of the agency that the information provided under §300.640 is an accurate and unduplicated count of children with disabilities receiving special education and related services on the dates in question. (Authority: 20 U. S. C. 1418(a)(3))

§300.644 Annual report of children served—criteria for counting children. The SEA may include in its report children with disabilities who are enrolled in a school or program that is operated or supported by a public agency, and that—

(a) Provides them with both special education and related services that meet State standards;

(b) Provides them only with special education, if a related service is not required, that meets State standards; or

(c) In the case of children with disabilities enrolled by their parents in private schools, counts those children who are eligible under the Act and receive special education or related services or both that meet State standards under §§300.132 through 300.144. (Authority: 20 U. S. C. 1418(a))

§300.645 Annual report of children served—other responsibilities of the SEA. In addition to meeting the other requirements of §§300.640 through 300.644, the SEA must—

(a) Establish procedures to be used by LEAs and other educational institutions in counting the number of children with disabilities receiving special education and related services;

(b) Set dates by which those agencies and institutions must report to the SEA to ensure that the State complies with §300.640(a);

(c) Obtain certification from each agency and institution that an unduplicated and accurate count has been made;

(d) Aggregate the data from the count obtained from each agency and institution, and prepare the reports required under §§300.640 through 300.644; and

(e) Ensure that documentation is maintained that enables the State and the Secretary to audit the accuracy of the count. (Authority: 20 U. S. C. 1418(a))

§300.646 Disproportionality.

(a) General. Each State that receives assistance under Part B of the Act, and the Secretary of the Interior, must provide for the collection and examination of data to determine if significant disproportionality based on race and ethnicity is occurring in the State and the LEAs of the State with respect to—

(1) The identification of children as children with disabilities, including the identification of children as children with disabilities in accordance with a particular impairment described in section 602(3) of the Act;

(2) The placement in particular educational settings of these children; and

(3) The incidence, duration, and type of disciplinary actions, including suspensions and expulsions.

(b) Review and revision of policies, practices, and procedures. In the case of a determination of significant disproportionality with respect to the identification of children as children with disabilities, or the placement in particular educational settings of these children, in accordance with paragraph (a) of this section, the State or the Secretary of the Interior must—

(1) Provide for the review and, if appropriate revision of the policies, procedures, and practices used in the identification or placement to ensure that the policies, procedures, and practices comply with the requirements of the Act.

(2) Require any LEA identified under paragraph (a) of this section to reserve the maximum amount of funds under section 613(f) of the Act to provide comprehensive coordinated early intervening services to serve children in the LEA, particularly, but not exclusively, children in those groups that were significantly overidentified under paragraph (a) of this section; and

(3) Require the LEA to publicly report on the revision of policies, practices, and procedures described under paragraph (b)(1) of this section. (Authority: 20 U. S. C. 1418(d))

Subpart G—Authorization, Allotment, Use of Funds, and Authorization of Appropriations

Allotments, Grants, and Use of Funds

§300.700 Grants to States.

(a) Purpose of grants. The Secretary makes grants to States, outlying areas, and freely associated States (as defined in §300.717), and provides funds to the Secretary of the Interior, to assist them to provide special education and related services to children with disabilities in accordance with Part B of the Act.

(b) Maximum amount. The maximum amount of the grant a State may receive under section 611 of the Act is—

(1) For fiscal years 2005 and 2006—

(i) The number of children with disabilities in the State who are receiving special education and related services—

(A) Aged three through five, if the State is eligible for a grant under section 619 of the Act; and

(B) Aged 6 through 21; multiplied by—

(ii) Forty (40) percent of the average per-pupil expenditure in public elementary schools and secondary schools in the United States (as defined in §300.717); and

(2) For fiscal year 2007 and subsequent fiscal years—

(i) The number of children with disabilities in the 2004–2005 school year in the State who received special education and related services—

(A) Aged three through five if the State is eligible for a grant under section 619 of the Act; and

(B) Aged 6 through 21; multiplied by

(ii) Forty (40) percent of the average per-pupil expenditure in public elementary schools and secondary schools in the United States (as defined in §300.717);

(iii) Adjusted by the rate of annual change in the sum of—

(A) Eighty-five (85) percent of the State's population of children aged 3 through 21 who are of the same age as children with disabilities for whom the State ensures the availability of FAPE under Part B of the Act; and

(B) Fifteen (15) percent of the State's population of children described in paragraph (b)(2)(iii)(A) of this section who are living in poverty. (Authority: 20 U. S. C. 1411(a) and (d))

§300.701 Outlying areas, freely associated States, and the Secretary of the Interior.

(a) Outlying areas and freely associated States.

(1) Funds reserved. From the amount appropriated for any fiscal year under section 611(i) of the Act, the Secretary reserves not more than one percent, which must be used—

(i) To provide assistance to the outlying areas in accordance with their respective populations of individuals aged 3 through 21; and

(ii) To provide each freely associated State a grant in the amount that the freely associated State received for fiscal year 2003 under Part B of the Act, but only if the freely associated State—

(A) Meets the applicable requirements of Part B of the Act that apply to States.

(B) Meets the requirements in paragraph (a)(2) of this section.

(2) Application. Any freely associated State that wishes to receive funds under Part B of the Act must include, in its application for assistance—

(i) Information demonstrating that it will meet all conditions that apply to States under Part B of the Act.

(ii) An assurance that, notwithstanding any other provision of Part B of the Act, it will use those funds only for the direct provision of special education and related services to children with disabilities and to enhance its capacity to make FAPE available to all children with disabilities;

(iii) The identity of the source and amount of funds, in addition to funds under Part B of the Act, that it will make available to ensure that FAPE is available to all children with disabilities within its jurisdiction; and

(iv) Such other information and assurances as the Secretary may require.

(3) Special rule. The provisions of Public Law 95-134, permitting the consolidation of grants by the outlying areas, do not apply to funds provided to the outlying areas or to the freely associated States under Part B of the Act.

(b) Secretary of the Interior. From the amount appropriated for any fiscal year under section 611(i) of the Act, the Secretary reserves 1.226 percent to provide assistance to the Secretary of the Interior in accordance with §§300.707 through 300.716. (Authority: 20 U. S. C. 1411(b))

§300.702 Technical assistance.

(a) In general. The Secretary may reserve not more than one-half of one percent of the amounts appropriated under Part B of the Act for each fiscal year to support technical assistance activities authorized under section 616(i) of the Act.

(b) Maximum amount. The maximum amount the Secretary may reserve under paragraph (a) of this section for any fiscal year is $25,000,000, cumulatively adjusted by the rate of inflation as measured by the percentage increase, if any, from the preceding fiscal year in the Consumer Price Index For All Urban Consumers, published by the Bureau of Labor Statistics of the Department of Labor. (Authority: 20 U. S. C. 1411(c))

§300.703 Allocations to States.

(a) General. After reserving funds for technical assistance under §300.702, and for payments to the outlying areas, the freely associated States, and the Secretary of the Interior under §300.701 (a) and (b) for a fiscal year, the Secretary allocates the remaining amount among the States in accordance with paragraphs (b), (c), and (d) of this section.

(b) Special rule for use of fiscal year 1999 amount. If a State received any funds under section 611 of the Act for fiscal year 1999 on the basis of children aged three through five, but does not make FAPE available to all children with disabilities aged three through five in the State in any subsequent fiscal year, the Secretary computes the State's amount for fiscal year 1999, solely for the purpose of calculating the State's allocation in that subsequent year under paragraph (c) or (d) of this section, by subtracting the amount allocated to the State for fiscal year 1999 on the basis of those children.

(c) Increase in funds. If the amount available for allocations to States under paragraph (a) of this section for a fiscal year is equal to or greater than the amount allocated to the States under section 611 of the Act for the preceding fiscal year, those allocations are calculated as follows:

(1) Allocation of increase.

(i) General. Except as provided in paragraph (c)(2) of this section, the Secretary allocates for the fiscal year—

(A) To each State the amount the State received under this section for fiscal year 1999;

(B) Eighty-five (85) percent of any remaining funds to States on the basis of the States' relative populations of children aged 3 through 21 who are of the same age as children with disabilities for whom the State ensures the availability of FAPE under Part B of the Act; and

(C) Fifteen (15) percent of those remaining funds to States on the basis of the States' relative populations of children described in paragraph (c)(1)(i)(B) of this section who are living in poverty.

(ii) Data. For the purpose of making grants under this section, the Secretary uses the most recent population data, including data on children living in poverty, that are available and satisfactory to the Secretary.

(2) Limitations. Notwithstanding paragraph (c)(1) of this section, allocations under this section are subject to the following:

(i) Preceding year allocation. No State's allocation may be less than its allocation under section 611 of the Act for the preceding fiscal year.

(ii) Minimum. No State's allocation may be less than the greatest of—

(A) The sum of—

(1) The amount the State received under section 611 of the Act for fiscal year 1999; and

(2) One third of one percent of the amount by which the amount appropriated under section 611(i) of the Act for the fiscal year exceeds the amount appropriated for section 611 of the Act for fiscal year 1999;

(B) The sum of—

(1) The amount the State received under section 611 of the Act for the preceding fiscal year; and

(2) That amount multiplied by the percentage by which the increase in the funds appropriated for section 611 of the Act from the preceding fiscal year exceeds 1.5 percent; or

(C) The sum of—

(1) The amount the State received under section 611 of the Act for the preceding fiscal year; and

(2) That amount multiplied by 90 percent of the percentage increase in the amount appropriated for section 611 of the Act from the preceding fiscal year.

(iii) Maximum. Notwithstanding paragraph (c)(2)(ii) of this section, no State's allocation under paragraph (a) of this section may exceed the sum of—

(A) The amount the State received under section 611 of the Act for the preceding fiscal year; and

(B) That amount multiplied by the sum of 1.5 percent and the percentage increase in the amount appropriated under section 611 of the Act from the preceding fiscal year.

(3) Ratable reduction. If the amount available for allocations to States under paragraph (c) of this section is insufficient to pay those allocations in full, those allocations are ratably reduced, subject to paragraph (c)(2)(i) of this section.

(d) Decrease in funds. If the amount available for allocations to States under paragraph (a) of this section for a fiscal year is less than the amount allocated to the States under section 611 of the Act for the preceding fiscal year, those allocations are calculated as follows:

(1) Amounts greater than fiscal year 1999 allocations. If the amount available for allocations under paragraph (a) of this section is greater than the amount allocated to the States for fiscal year 1999, each State is allocated the sum of—

(i) 1999 amount. The amount the State received under section 611 of the Act for fiscal year 1999; and

(ii) Remaining funds. An amount that bears the same relation to any remaining funds as the increase the State received under section 611 of the Act for the preceding fiscal year over fiscal year 1999 bears to the total of all such increases for all States.

(2) Amounts equal to or less than fiscal year 1999 allocations.

(i) General. If the amount available for allocations under paragraph (a) of this section is equal to or less than the amount allocated to the States for fiscal year 1999, each State is allocated the amount it received for fiscal year 1999.

(ii) Ratable reduction. If the amount available for allocations under paragraph (d) of this section is insufficient to make the allocations described in paragraph (d)(2)(i) of this section, those allocations are ratably reduced. (Authority: 20 U. S. C. 1411(d))

§300.704 State-level activities.

(a) State administration.

(1) For the purpose of administering Part B of the Act, including paragraph (c) of this section, section 619 of the Act, and the coordination of activities under Part B of the Act with, and providing technical assistance to, other programs that provide services to children with disabilities—

(i) Each State may reserve for each fiscal year not more than the maximum amount the State was eligible to reserve for State administration under section 611 of the Act for fiscal year 2004 or $800,000 (adjusted in accordance with paragraph (a)(2) of this section), whichever is greater; and

(ii) Each outlying area may reserve for each fiscal year not more than five percent of the amount the outlying area receives under §300.701(a) for the fiscal year or $35,000, whichever is greater.

(2) For each fiscal year, beginning with fiscal year 2005, the Secretary cumulatively adjusts—

(i) The maximum amount the State was eligible to reserve for State administration under section 611 of the Act for fiscal year 2004; and

(ii) $800,000, by the rate of inflation as measured by the percentage increase, if any, from the preceding fiscal year in the Consumer Price Index for All Urban Consumers, published by the Bureau of Labor Statistics of the Department of Labor.

(3) Prior to expenditure of funds under paragraph (a) of this section, the State must certify to the Secretary that the arrangements to establish responsibility for services pursuant to section 612(a)(12)(A) of the Act are current.

(4) Funds reserved under paragraph (a)(1) of this section may be used for the administration of Part C of the Act, if the SEA is the lead agency for the State under that Part.

(b) Other State-level activities.

(1) States may reserve a portion of their allocations for other State-level activities. The maximum amount that a State may reserve for other State-level activities is as follows:

(i) If the amount that the State sets aside for State administration under paragraph (a) of this section is greater than $850,000 and the State opts to finance a high cost fund under paragraph (c) of this section:

(A) For fiscal years 2005 and 2006, 10 percent of the State's allocation under §300.703.

(B) For fiscal year 2007 and subsequent fiscal years, an amount equal to 10 percent of the State's allocation for fiscal year 2006 under §300.703 adjusted cumulatively for inflation.

(ii) If the amount that the State sets aside for State administration under paragraph (a) of this section is greater than $850,000 and the State opts not to finance a high cost fund under paragraph (c) of this section—

(A) For fiscal years 2005 and 2006, nine percent of the State's allocation under §300.703.

(B) For fiscal year 2007 and subsequent fiscal years, an amount equal to nine percent of the State's allocation for fiscal year 2006 adjusted cumulatively for inflation.

(iii) If the amount that the State sets aside for State administration under paragraph (a) of this section is less than or equal to $850,000 and the State opts to finance a high cost fund under paragraph (c) of this section:

(A) For fiscal years 2005 and 2006, 10.5 percent of the State's allocation under §300.703.

(B) For fiscal year 2007 and subsequent fiscal years, an amount equal to 10.5 percent of the State's allocation for fiscal year 2006 under §300.703 adjusted cumulatively for inflation.

(iv) If the amount that the State sets aside for State administration under paragraph (a) of this section is equal to or less than $850,000 and the State opts not to finance a high cost fund under paragraph (c) of this section:

(A) For fiscal years 2005 and 2006, nine and one-half percent of the State's allocation under §300.703.

(B) For fiscal year 2007 and subsequent fiscal years, an amount equal to nine and one-half percent of the State's allocation for fiscal year 2006 under §300.703 adjusted cumulatively for inflation.

(2) The adjustment for inflation is the rate of inflation as measured by the percentage of increase, if any, from the preceding fiscal year in the Consumer Price Index for All Urban Consumers, published by the Bureau of Labor Statistics of the Department of Labor.

(3) Some portion of the funds reserved under paragraph (b)(1) of this section must be used to carry out the following activities:

(i) For monitoring, enforcement, and complaint investigation; and

(ii) To establish and implement the mediation process required by section 615(e) of the Act, including providing for the costs of mediators and support personnel;

(4) Funds reserved under paragraph (b)(1) of this section also may be used to carry out the following activities:

(i) For support and direct services, including technical assistance, personnel preparation, and professional development and training;

(ii) To support paperwork reduction activities, including expanding the use of technology in the IEP process;

(iii) To assist LEAs in providing positive behavioral interventions and supports and mental health services for children with disabilities;

(iv) To improve the use of technology in the classroom by children with disabilities to enhance learning;

(v) To support the use of technology, including technology with universal design principles and assistive technology devices, to maximize accessibility to the general education curriculum for children with disabilities;

(vi) Development and implementation of transition programs, including coordination of services with agencies involved in supporting the transition of students with disabilities to postsecondary activities;

(vii) To assist LEAs in meeting personnel shortages;

(viii) To support capacity building activities and improve the delivery of services by LEAs to improve results for children with disabilities;

(ix) Alternative programming for children with disabilities who have been expelled from school, and services for children with disabilities in correctional facilities, children enrolled in State-operated or State-supported schools, and children with disabilities in charter schools;

(x) To support the development and provision of appropriate accommodations for children with disabilities, or the development and provision of alternate assessments that are valid and reliable for assessing the performance of children with disabilities, in accordance with sections 1111(b) and 6111 of the ESEA; and

(xi) To provide technical assistance to schools and LEAs, and direct services, including supplemental educational services as defined in section 1116(e) of the ESEA to children with disabilities, in schools or LEAs identified for improvement under section 1116 of the ESEA on the sole basis of the assessment results of the disaggregated subgroup of children with disabilities, including providing professional development to special and regular education teachers, who teach children with disabilities, based on scientifically based research to improve educational instruction, in order to improve academic achievement to meet or exceed the objectives established by the State under section 1111(b)(2)(G) of the ESEA.

(c) Local educational agency high cost fund.

(1) In general—

(i) For the purpose of assisting LEAs (including a charter school that is an LEA or a consortium of LEAs) in addressing the needs of high need children with disabilities, each State has the option to reserve for each fiscal year 10 percent of the amount of funds the State reserves for other State-level activities under paragraph (b)(1) of this section—

(A) To finance and make disbursements from the high cost fund to LEAs in accordance with paragraph (c) of this section during the first and succeeding fiscal years of the high cost fund; and

(B) To support innovative and effective ways of cost sharing by the State, by an LEA, or among a consortium of LEAs, as determined by the State in coordination with representatives from LEAs, subject to paragraph (c)(2)(ii) of this section.

(ii) For purposes of paragraph (c) of this section, local educational agency includes a charter school that is an LEA, or a consortium of LEAs.

(2)

(i) A State must not use any of the funds the State reserves pursuant to paragraph (c)(1)(i) of this section, which are solely for disbursement to LEAs, for costs associated with establishing, supporting, and otherwise administering the fund. The State may use funds the State reserves under paragraph (a) of this section for those administrative costs.

(ii) A State must not use more than 5 percent of the funds the State reserves pursuant to paragraph (c)(1)(i) of this section for each fiscal year to support innovative and effective ways of cost sharing among consortia of LEAs.

(3)

(i) The SEA must develop, not later than 90 days after the State reserves funds under paragraph (c)(1)(i) of this section, annually review, and amend as necessary, a State plan for the high cost fund. Such State plan must—

(A) Establish, in consultation and coordination with representatives from LEAs, a definition of a high need child with a disability that, at a minimum—

(1) Addresses the financial impact a high need child with a disability has on the budget of the child's LEA; and

(2) Ensures that the cost of the high need child with a disability is greater than 3 times the average per pupil expenditure (as defined in section 9101 of the ESEA) in that State;

(B) Establish eligibility criteria for the participation of an LEA that, at a minimum, take into account the number and percentage of high need children with disabilities served by an LEA;

(C) Establish criteria to ensure that placements supported by the fund are consistent with the requirements of §§300.114 through 300.118;

(D) Develop a funding mechanism that provides distributions each fiscal year to LEAs that meet the criteria developed by the State under paragraph(c)(3)(i)(B) of this section;

(E) Establish an annual schedule by which the SEA must make its distributions from the high cost fund each fiscal year; and

(F) If the State elects to reserve funds for supporting innovative and effective ways of cost sharing under paragraph (c)(1)(i)(B) of this section, describe how these funds will be used.

(ii) The State must make its final State plan available to the public not less than 30 days before the beginning of the school year, including dissemination of such information on the State Web site.

(4)

(i) Each SEA must make all annual disbursements from the high cost fund established under paragraph (c)(1)(i) of this section in accordance with the State plan published pursuant to paragraph (c)(3) of this section.

(ii) The costs associated with educating a high need child with a disability, as defined under paragraph (c)(3)(i)(A) of this section, are only those costs associated with providing direct special education and related services to the child that are identified in that child's IEP, including the cost of room and board for a residential placement determined necessary, consistent with §300.114, to implement a child's IEP.

(iii) The funds in the high cost fund remain under the control of the State until disbursed to an LEA to support a specific child who qualifies under the State plan for the high cost funds or distributed to LEAs, consistent with paragraph (c)(9) of this section.

(5) The disbursements under paragraph (c)(4) of this section must not be used to support legal fees, court costs, or other costs associated with a cause of action brought on behalf of a child with a disability to ensure FAPE for such child.

(6) Nothing in paragraph (c) of this section—

(i) Limits or conditions the right of a child with a disability who is assisted under Part B of the Act to receive FAPE pursuant to section 612(a)(1) of the Act in the least restrictive environment pursuant to section 612(a)(5) of the Act; or

(ii) Authorizes an SEA or LEA to establish a limit on what may be spent on the education of a child with a disability.

(7) Notwithstanding the provisions of paragraphs (c)(1) through (6) of this section, a State may use funds reserved pursuant to paragraph (c)(1)(i) of this section for implementing a placement neutral cost sharing and reimbursement program of high need, low incidence, catastrophic, or extraordinary aid to LEAs that provides services to high need children based on eligibility criteria for such programs that were created not later than January 1, 2004, and are currently in operation, if such program serves children that meet the requirement of the definition of a high need child with a disability as described in paragraph (c)(3)(i)(A) of this section.

(8) Disbursements provided under paragraph (c) of this section must not be used to pay costs that otherwise would be reimbursed as medical assistance for a child with a disability under the State Medicaid program under Title XIX of the Social Security Act.

(9) Funds reserved under paragraph (c)(1)(i) of this section from the appropriation for any fiscal year, but not expended pursuant to paragraph (c)(4) of this section before the beginning of their last year of availability for obligation, must be allocated to LEAs in the same manner as other funds from the appropriation for that fiscal year are allocated to LEAs under §300.705 during their final year of availability.

(d) **Inapplicability of certain prohibitions**. A State may use funds the State reserves under paragraphs (a) and (b) of this section without regard to—

(1) The prohibition on commingling of funds in §300.162(b).

(2) The prohibition on supplanting other funds in §300.162(c).

(e) **Special rule for increasing funds**. A State may use funds the State reserves under paragraph (a)(1) of this section as a result of inflationary increases under paragraph (a)(2) of this section to carry out activities authorized under paragraph(b)(4)(i), (iii), (vii), or (viii) of this section.

(f) **Flexibility in using funds for Part C**. Any State eligible to receive a grant under section 619 of the Act may use funds made available under paragraph (a)(1) of this section, §300.705(c), or §300.814(e) to develop and implement a State policy jointly with the lead agency under Part C of the Act and the SEA to provide early intervention services (which must include an educational component that promotes school readiness and incorporates preliteracy, language, and numeracy skills) in accordance with Part C of the Act to children with disabilities who are eligible for services under section 619 of the Act and who previously received services under Part C of the Act until the children enter, or are eligible under State law to enter, kindergarten, or elementary school as appropriate. (Authority: 20 U. S. C. 1411(e))

§300.705 Subgrants to LEAs.

(a) **Subgrants required**. Each State that receives a grant under section 611 of the Act for any fiscal year must distribute any funds the State does not reserve under §300.704 to LEAs (including public charter schools that operate as LEAs) in the State that have established their eligibility under section 613 of the Act for use in accordance with Part B of the Act.

(b) **Allocations to LEAs**. For each fiscal year for which funds are allocated to States under §300.703, each State shall allocate funds as follows:

(1) Base payments. The State first must award each LEA described in paragraph (a) of this section the amount the LEA would have received under section 611 of the Act for fiscal year 1999, if the State had distributed 75 percent of its grant for

that year under section 611(d) of the Act, as that section was then in effect.

(2) Base payment adjustments. For any fiscal year after 1999—

(i) If a new LEA is created, the State must divide the base allocation determined under paragraph (b)(1) of this section for the LEAs that would have been responsible for serving children with disabilities now being served by the new LEA, among the new LEA and affected LEAs based on the relative numbers of children with disabilities ages 3 through 21, or ages 6 through 21 if a State has had its payment reduced under §300.703(b), currently provided special education by each of the LEAs;

(ii) If one or more LEAs are combined into a single new LEA, the State must combine the base allocations of the merged LEAs; and

(iii) If, for two or more LEAs, geographic boundaries or administrative responsibility for providing services to children with disabilities ages 3 through 21 change, the base allocations of affected LEAs must be redistributed among affected LEAs based on the relative numbers of children with disabilities ages 3 through 21, or ages 6 through 21 if a State has had its payment reduced under §300.703(b), currently provided special education by each affected LEA.

(3) Allocation of remaining funds. After making allocations under paragraph (b)(1) of this section, as adjusted by paragraph (b)(2) of this section, the State must—

(i) Allocate 85 percent of any remaining funds to those LEAs on the basis of the relative numbers of children enrolled in public and private elementary schools and secondary schools within the LEA's jurisdiction; and

(ii) Allocate 15 percent of those remaining funds to those LEAs in accordance with their relative numbers of children living in poverty, as determined by the SEA.

(c) **Reallocation of funds.** If an SEA determines that an LEA is adequately providing FAPE to all children with disabilities residing in the area served by that agency with State and local funds, the SEA may reallocate any portion of the funds under this part that are not needed by that LEA to provide FAPE to other LEAs in the State that are not adequately providing special education and related services to all children with disabilities residing in the areas served by those other LEAs. (Authority: 20 U. S. C. 1411(f))

§300.706 [Reserved]

Secretary of the Interior

§300.707 Use of amounts by Secretary of the Interior.

(a) **Definitions.** For purposes of §§300.707 through 300.716, the following definitions apply:

(1) Reservation means Indian Country as defined in 18 U. S. C. 1151.

(2) Tribal governing body has the definition given that term in 25 U. S. C. 2021(19).

(b) **Provision of amounts for assistance.** The Secretary provides amounts to the Secretary of the Interior to meet the need for assistance for the education of children with disabilities on reservations aged 5 to 21, inclusive, enrolled in elementary schools and secondary schools for Indian children operated or funded by the Secretary of the Interior. The amount of the payment for any fiscal year is equal to 80 percent of the amount allotted under section 611(b)(2) of the Act for that fiscal year. Of the amount described in the preceding sentence, after the Secretary of the Interior reserves funds for administration under §300.710, 80 percent must be allocated to such schools by July 1 of that fiscal year and 20 percent must be allocated to such schools by September 30 of that fiscal year.

(c) **Additional requirement.** With respect to all other children aged 3 to 21, inclusive, on reservations, the SEA of the State in which the reservation is located must ensure that all of the requirements of Part B of the Act are implemented. (Authority: 20 U. S. C. 1411(h)(1))

§300.708 Submission of information. The Secretary may provide the Secretary of the Interior amounts under §300.707 for a fiscal year only if the Secretary of the Interior submits to the Secretary information that—

(a) Meets the requirements of section 612(a)(1), (3) through (9), (10)(B) through (C), (11) through (12), (14) through (16), (19), and (21) through (25) of the Act (including monitoring and evaluation activities);

(b) Meets the requirements of section 612(b) and (e) of the Act;

(c) Meets the requirements of section 613(a)(1), (2)(A)(i), (7) through (9) and section 613(i) of the Act (references to LEAs in these sections must be read as references to elementary schools and secondary schools for Indian children operated or funded by the Secretary of the Interior);

(d) Meets the requirements of section 616 of the Act that apply to States (references to LEAs in section 616 of the Act must be read as references to elementary schools and secondary schools for Indian children operated or funded by the Secretary of the Interior).

(e) Meets the requirements of this part that implement the sections of the Act listed in paragraphs (a) through (d) of this section;

(f) Includes a description of how the Secretary of the Interior will coordinate the provision of services under Part B of the Act with LEAs, tribes and tribal organizations, and other private and Federal service providers;

(g) Includes an assurance that there are public hearings, adequate notice of the hearings, and an opportunity for comment afforded to members of tribes, tribal governing bodies, and affected local school boards before the adoption of the policies, programs, and procedures related to the requirements described in paragraphs (a) through (d) of this section;

(h) Includes an assurance that the Secretary of the Interior provides the information that the Secretary may require to comply with section 618 of the Act;

(i)

(1) Includes an assurance that the Secretary of the Interior and the Secretary of Health and Human Services have entered into a memorandum of agreement, to be provided to the Secretary, for the coordination of services, resources, and personnel between their respective Federal, State, and local offices and with the SEAs and LEAs and other entities to facilitate the provision of services to Indian children with disabilities residing on or near reservations.

(2) The agreement must provide for the apportionment of responsibilities and costs, including child find, evaluation, diagnosis, remediation or therapeutic measures, and (where appropriate) equipment and medical or personal supplies, as needed for a child with a disability to remain in a school or program; and

(j) Includes an assurance that the Department of the Interior will cooperate with the Department in its exercise of monitoring and oversight of the requirements in this section and §§300.709 through 300.711 and §§300.713 through 300.716, and any agreements entered into between the Secretary of the Interior and other entities under Part B of the Act, and will fulfill its duties under Part B of the Act. The Secretary withholds payments under §300.707 with respect to the requirements described in this section in the same manner as the Secretary withholds payments under section 616(e)(6) of the Act. (Authority: 20 U. S. C. 1411(h)(2) and (3))

§300.709 Public participation. In fulfilling the requirements of §300.708 the Secretary of the Interior must provide for public participation consistent with §300.165. (Authority: 20 U. S. C. 1411(h))

§300.710 Use of funds under Part B of the Act.

(a) The Secretary of the Interior may reserve five percent of its payment under §300.707(b) in any fiscal year, or $500,000, whichever is greater, for administrative costs in carrying out the provisions of §§300.707 through 300.709, 300.711, and 300.713 through 300.716.

(b) Payments to the Secretary of the Interior under §300.712 must be used in accordance with that section. (Authority: 20 U. S. C. 1411(h)(1)(A))

§300.711 Early intervening services.

(a) The Secretary of the Interior may allow each elementary school and secondary school for Indian children operated or funded by the Secretary of the Interior to use not more than 15 percent of the amount the school receives under §300.707(b) for any fiscal year, in combination with other amounts (which may include amounts other than education funds), to develop and implement coordinated, early intervening services, which may include interagency financing structures, for children in kindergarten through grade 12 (with a particular emphasis on children in kindergarten through grade three) who have not been identified as needing special education or related services but who need additional academic and behavioral support to succeed in a general education environment, in accordance with section 613(f) of the Act.

(b) Each elementary school and secondary school for Indian children operated or funded by the Secretary of the Interior that develops and maintains coordinated early intervening services in accordance with section 613(f) of the Act and §300.226 must annually report to the Secretary of the Interior in accordance with section 613(f) of the Act. (Authority: 20 U. S. C. 1411(h) and 1413(f))

§300.712 Payments for education and services for Indian children with disabilities aged three through five.

(a) **General**. With funds appropriated under section 611(i) of the Act, the Secretary makes payments to the Secretary of the Interior to be distributed to tribes or tribal organizations (as defined under section 4 of the Indian Self-Determination and Education Assistance Act) or consortia of tribes or tribal organizations to provide for the coordination of assistance for special education and related services for children with disabilities aged three through five on reservations served by elementary schools and secondary schools for Indian children operated or funded by the Department of the Interior. The amount of the payments under paragraph (b) of this section for any fiscal year is equal to 20 percent of the amount allotted under §300.701(b).

(b) **Distribution of funds**. The Secretary of the Interior must distribute the total amount of the payment under paragraph (a) of this section by allocating to each tribe, tribal organization, or consortium an amount based on the number of children with disabilities aged three through five residing on reservations as reported annually, divided by the total of those children served by all tribes or tribal organizations.

(c) **Submission of information**. To receive a payment under this section, the tribe or tribal organization must submit the figures to the Secretary of the Interior as required to determine the amounts to be allocated under paragraph (b) of this section. This information must be compiled and submitted to the Secretary.

(d) **Use of funds.**

(1) The funds received by a tribe or tribal organization must be used to assist in child find, screening, and other procedures for the early identification of children aged three through five, parent training, and the provision of direct services. These activities may be carried out directly or through contracts or cooperative agreements with the BIA, LEAs, and other public or private nonprofit organizations. The tribe or tribal organization is encouraged to involve Indian parents in the development and implementation of these activities.

(2) The tribe or tribal organization, as appropriate, must make referrals to local, State, or Federal entities for the provision of services or further diagnosis.

(e) **Biennial report**. To be eligible to receive a grant pursuant to paragraph (a) of this section, the tribe or tribal organization must provide to the Secretary of the Interior a biennial report of activities undertaken under this section, including the number of contracts and cooperative agreements entered into, the number of children contacted and receiving services for each year, and the estimated number of children needing services during the two years following the year in which the report is made. The Secretary of the Interior must include a summary of this information on a biennial basis in the report to the Secretary required under section 611(h) of the Act. The Secretary may require any additional information from the Secretary of the Interior.

(f) **Prohibitions**. None of the funds allocated under this section may be used by the Secretary of the Interior for administrative purposes, including child count and the provision of technical assistance. (Authority: 20 U. S. C. 1411(h)(4))

§300.713 Plan for coordination of services.

(a) The Secretary of the Interior must develop and implement a plan for the coordination of services for all Indian children with disabilities residing on reservations served by elementary schools and secondary schools for Indian children operated or funded by the Secretary of the Interior.

(b) The plan must provide for the coordination of services benefiting those children from whatever source, including tribes, the Indian Health Service, other BIA divisions, other Federal agencies, State educational agencies, and State, local, and tribal juvenile and adult correctional facilities.

(c) In developing the plan, the Secretary of the Interior must consult with all interested and involved parties.

(d) The plan must be based on the needs of the children and the system best suited for meeting those needs, and may involve the establishment of cooperative agreements between the BIA, other Federal agencies, and other entities.

(e) The plan also must be distributed upon request to States; to SEAs, LEAs, and other agencies providing services to infants, toddlers, and children with disabilities; to tribes; and to other interested parties. (Authority: 20 U. S. C. 1411(h)(5))

§300.714 Establishment of advisory board.

(a) To meet the requirements of section 612(a)(21) of the Act, the Secretary of the Interior must establish, under the BIA, an advisory board composed of individuals involved in or concerned with the education and provision of services to Indian infants, toddlers, children, and youth with disabilities, including Indians with disabilities, Indian parents or guardians of such children, teachers, service providers, State and local educational officials, representatives of tribes or tribal organizations, representatives from State Interagency Coordinating Councils under section 641 of the Act in States having reservations, and other members representing the various divisions and entities of the BIA. The chairperson must be selected by the Secretary of the Interior.

(b) The advisory board must—

(1) Assist in the coordination of services within the BIA and with other local, State, and Federal agencies in the provision of education for infants, toddlers, and children with disabilities;

(2) Advise and assist the Secretary of the Interior in the performance of the Secretary of the Interior's responsibilities described in section 611(h) of the Act;

(3) Develop and recommend policies concerning effective inter- and intra-agency collaboration, including modifications to regulations, and the elimination of barriers to inter- and intra-agency programs and activities;

(4) Provide assistance and disseminate information on best practices, effective program coordination strategies, and recommendations for improved early intervention services or educational programming for Indian infants, toddlers, and children with disabilities; and

(5) Provide assistance in the preparation of information required under §300.708(h). (Authority: 20 U. S. C. 1411(h)(6))

§300.715 Annual reports.

(a) **In general**. The advisory board established under §300.714 must prepare and submit to the Secretary of the Interior and to Congress an annual report containing a description of the activities of the advisory board for the preceding year.

(b) **Availability**. The Secretary of the Interior must make available to the Secretary the report described in paragraph (a) of this section. (Authority: 20 U. S. C. 1411(h)(7))

§300.716 Applicable regulations. The Secretary of the Interior must comply with the requirements of §§300.103 through 300.108, 300.110 through 300.124, 300.145 through 300.154, 300.156 through 300.160, 300.165, 300.170 through 300.186, 300.226, 300.300 through 300.606, 300.610 through 300.646, and 300.707 through 300.716. (Authority: 20 U. S. C. 1411(h)(2)(A))

Definitions that Apply to this Subpart

§300.717 Definitions applicable to allotments, grants, and use of funds. As used in this subpart—

(a) **Freely associated States** means the Republic of the Marshall Islands, the Federated States of Micronesia, and the Republic of Palau;

(b) **Outlying areas** means the United States Virgin Islands, Guam, American Samoa, and the Commonwealth of the Northern Mariana Islands;

(c) **State** means each of the 50 States, the District of Columbia, and the Commonwealth of Puerto Rico; and

(d) **Average per-pupil expenditure in public elementary schools and secondary schools in the United States** means—

(1) Without regard to the source of funds—

(i) The aggregate current expenditures, during the second fiscal year preceding the fiscal year for which the determination is made (or, if satisfactory data for that year are not available, during the most recent preceding fiscal year for which satisfactory data are available) of all LEAs in the 50 States and the District of Columbia); plus

(ii) Any direct expenditures by the State for the operation of those agencies; divided by

(2) The aggregate number of children in average daily attendance to whom those agencies provided free public education during that preceding year. (Authority: 20 U. S. C. 1401(22), 1411(b)(1)(C) and (g))

Acquisition of Equipment and Construction or Alteration of Facilities

§300.718 Acquisition of equipment and construction or alteration of facilities.

(a) **General**. If the Secretary determines that a program authorized under Part B of the Act will be improved by permitting program funds to be used to acquire appropriate equipment, or to construct new facilities or alter existing facilities, the Secretary may allow the use of those funds for those purposes.

(b) **Compliance with certain regulations**. Any construction of new facilities or alteration of existing facilities under paragraph (a) of this section must comply with the requirements of—

(1) Appendix A of part 36 of title 28, Code of Federal Regulations (commonly known as the "Americans with Disabilities Accessibility Standards for Buildings and Facilities"); or

(2) Appendix A of subpart 101-19.6 of title 41, Code of Federal Regulations (commonly known as the "Uniform Federal Accessibility Standards"). (Authority: 20 U. S. C. 1404)

Subpart H—Preschool Grants for Children with Disabilities

§300.800 In general. The Secretary provides grants under section 619 of the Act to assist States to provide special education and related services in accordance with Part B of the Act—

(a) To children with disabilities aged three through five years; and

(b) At a State's discretion, to two-year-old children with disabilities who will turn three during the school year. (Authority: 20 U. S. C. 1419(a))

§§300.801-300.802 [Reserved]

§300.803 Definition of State. As used in this subpart, State means each of the 50 States, the District of Columbia, and the Commonwealth of Puerto Rico. (Authority: 20 U. S. C. 1419(i))

§300.804 Eligibility. A State is eligible for a grant under section 619 of the Act if the State—

(a) Is eligible under section 612 of the Act to receive a grant under Part B of the Act; and

(b) Makes FAPE available to all children with disabilities, aged three through five, residing in the State. (Authority: 20 U. S. C. 1419(b))

§300.805 [Reserved]

§300.806 Eligibility for financial assistance. No State or LEA, or other public institution or agency, may receive a grant or enter into a contract or cooperative agreement under subpart 2 or 3 of Part D of the Act that relates exclusively to programs, projects, and activities pertaining to children aged three through five years, unless the State is eligible to receive a grant under section 619(b) of the Act. (Authority: 20 U. S. C. 1481(e))

§300.807 Allocations to States. The Secretary allocates the amount made available to carry out section 619 of the Act for a fiscal year among the States in accordance with §§300.808 through 300.810. (Authority: 20 U. S. C. 1419(c)(1))

§300.808 Increase in funds. If the amount available for allocation to States under §300.807 for a fiscal year is equal to or greater than the amount allocated to the States under section 619 of the Act for the preceding fiscal year, those allocations are calculated as follows:

(a) Except as provided in §300.809, the Secretary—

(1) Allocates to each State the amount the State received under section 619 of the Act for fiscal year 1997;

(2) Allocates 85 percent of any remaining funds to States on the basis of the States' relative populations of children aged three through five; and

(3) Allocates 15 percent of those remaining funds to States on the basis of the States' relative populations of all children aged three through five who are living in poverty.

(b) For the purpose of making grants under this section, the Secretary uses the most recent population data, including data on children living in poverty, that are available and satisfactory to the Secretary. (Authority: 20 U. S. C. 1419(c)(2)(A))

§300.809 Limitations.

(a) Notwithstanding §300.808, allocations under that section are subject to the following:

(1) No State's allocation may be less than its allocation under section 619 of the Act for the preceding fiscal year.

(2) No State's allocation may be less than the greatest of—

(i) The sum of—

(A) The amount the State received under section 619 of the Act for fiscal year 1997; and

(B) One-third of one percent of the amount by which the amount appropriated under section 619(j) of the Act for the fiscal year exceeds the amount appropriated for section 619 of the Act for fiscal year 1997;

(ii) The sum of—

(A) The amount the State received under section 619 of the Act for the preceding fiscal year; and

(B) That amount multiplied by the percentage by which the increase in the funds appropriated under section 619 of the Act from the preceding fiscal year exceeds 1.5 percent; or

(iii) The sum of—

(A) The amount the State received under section 619 of the Act for the preceding fiscal year; and

(B) That amount multiplied by 90 percent of the percentage increase in the amount appropriated under section 619 of the Act from the preceding fiscal year.

(b) Notwithstanding paragraph (a)(2) of this section, no State's allocation under §300.808 may exceed the sum of—

(1) The amount the State received under section 619 of the Act for the preceding fiscal year; and

(2) That amount multiplied by the sum of 1.5 percent and the percentage increase in the amount appropriated under section 619 of the Act from the preceding fiscal year.

(c) If the amount available for allocation to States under §300.808 and paragraphs (a) and (b) of this section is insufficient to pay those allocations in full, those allocations are ratably reduced, subject to paragraph (a)(1) of this section. (Authority: 20 U. S. C. 1419(c)(2)(B) and (c)(2)(C))

§300.810 Decrease in funds. If the amount available for allocations to States under §300.807 for a fiscal year is less than the amount allocated to the States under section 619 of the Act for the preceding fiscal year, those allocations are calculated as follows:

(a) If the amount available for allocations is greater than the amount allocated to the States for fiscal year 1997, each State is allocated the sum of—

(1) The amount the State received under section 619 of the Act for fiscal year 1997; and

(2) An amount that bears the same relation to any remaining funds as the increase the State received under section 619 of the Act for the preceding fiscal year over fiscal year 1997 bears to the total of all such increases for all States.

(b) If the amount available for allocations is equal to or less than the amount allocated to the States for fiscal year 1997, each State is allocated the amount the State received for fiscal year 1997, ratably reduced, if necessary. (Authority: 20 U. S. C. 1419(c)(3))

§300.811 [Reserved]

§300.812 Reservation for State activities.

(a) Each State may reserve not more than the amount described in paragraph (b) of this section for administration and other State-level activities in accordance with §§300.813 and 300.814.

(b) For each fiscal year, the Secretary determines and reports to the SEA an amount that is 25 percent of the amount the State received under section 619 of the Act for fiscal year 1997, cumulatively adjusted by the Secretary for each succeeding fiscal year by the lesser of—

(1) The percentage increase, if any, from the preceding fiscal year in the State's allocation under section 619 of the Act; or

(2) The rate of inflation, as measured by the percentage increase, if any, from the preceding fiscal year in the Consumer Price Index for All Urban Consumers, published by the Bureau of Labor Statistics of the Department of Labor. (Authority: 20 U. S. C. 1419(d))

§300.813 State administration.

(a) For the purpose of administering section 619 of the Act (including the coordination of activities under Part B of the Act with, and providing technical assistance to, other programs that provide services to children with disabilities), a State may use not more than 20 percent of the maximum amount the State may reserve under §300.812 for any fiscal year.

(b) Funds described in paragraph (a) of this section may also be used for the administration of Part C of the Act. (Authority: 20 U. S. C. 1419(e))

§300.814 Other State-level activities. Each State must use any funds the State reserves under §300.812 and does not use for administration under §300.813—

(a) For support services (including establishing and implementing the mediation process required by section 615(e) of the Act), which may benefit children with disabilities younger than three or older than five as long as those services also benefit children with disabilities aged three through five;

(b) For direct services for children eligible for services under section 619 of the Act;

(c) For activities at the State and local levels to meet the performance goals established by the State under section 612(a)(15) of the Act;

(d) To supplement other funds used to develop and implement a statewide coordinated services system designed to improve results for children and families, including children with disabilities and their families, but not more than one percent of the amount received by the State under section 619 of the Act for a fiscal year;

(e) To provide early intervention services (which must include an educational component that promotes school readiness and incorporates preliteracy, language, and numeracy skills) in accordance with Part C of the Act to children with disabilities who are eligible for services under section 619 of the Act and who previously received services under Part C of the Act until such children enter, or are eligible under State law to enter, kindergarten; or

(f) At the State's discretion, to continue service coordination or case management for families who receive services under Part C of the Act, consistent with §300.814(e). (Authority: 20 U. S. C. 1419(f))

§300.815 Subgrants to LEAs. Each State that receives a grant under section 619 of the Act for any fiscal year must distribute all of the grant funds that the State does not reserve under §300.812 to LEAs in the State that have established their eligibility under section 613 of the Act. (Authority: 20 U. S. C. 1419(g)(1))

§300.816 Allocations to LEAs.

(a) **Base payments**. The State must first award each LEA described in §300.815 the amount that agency would have received under section 619 of the Act for fiscal year 1997 if the State had distributed 75 percent of its grant for that year under section 619(c)(3), as such section was then in effect.

(b) **Base payment adjustments**. For fiscal year 1998 and beyond—

(1) If a new LEA is created, the State must divide the base allocation determined under paragraph (a) of this section for the LEAs that would have been responsible for serving children with disabilities now being served by the new LEA, among the new LEA and affected LEAs based on the relative numbers of children with disabilities ages three through five currently provided special education by each of the LEAs;

(2) If one or more LEAs are combined into a single new LEA, the State must combine the base allocations of the merged LEAs; and

(3) If for two or more LEAs, geographic boundaries or administrative responsibility for providing services to children with disabilities ages three through five changes, the base allocations of affected LEAs must be redistributed among affected LEAs based on the relative numbers of children with disabilities ages three through five currently provided special education by each affected LEA.

(c) **Allocation of remaining funds**. After making allocations under paragraph (a) of this section, the State must—

(1) Allocate 85 percent of any remaining funds to those LEAs on the basis of the relative numbers of children enrolled in public and private elementary schools and secondary schools within the LEA's jurisdiction; and

(2) Allocate 15 percent of those remaining funds to those LEAs in accordance with their relative numbers of children living in poverty, as determined by the SEA.

(d) **Use of best data**. For the purpose of making grants under this section, States must apply on a uniform basis across all LEAs the best data that are available to them on the numbers of children enrolled in public and private elementary and secondary schools and the numbers of children living in poverty. (Authority: 20 U. S. C. 1419(g)(1))

§300.817 Reallocation of LEA funds. If an SEA determines that an LEA is adequately providing FAPE to all children with disabilities aged three through five residing in the area served by the LEA with State and local funds, the SEA may reallocate any portion of the funds under section 619 of the Act that are not needed by that LEA to provide FAPE to other LEAs in the State that are not adequately providing special education and related services to all children with disabilities aged three through five residing in the areas the other LEAs serve. (Authority: 20 U. S. C. 1419(g)(2))

§300.818 Part C of the Act inapplicable. Part C of the Act does not apply to any child with a disability receiving FAPE, in accordance with Part B of the Act, with funds received under section 619 of the Act. (Authority: 20 U. S. C. 1419(h))

End of IDEA 2004 Regulations

Section Three

Other Federal Statutes

CHAPTER 7

Section 504 of the
Rehabilitation Act of 1973

In this chapter, you will learn about the rights under Section 504 of the Rehabilitation Act, as contrasted with the rights under the Individuals with Disabilities Education Act (IDEA). You will learn that Section 504 does not require public schools to provide a special education program that is individualized to meet the needs of a child with a disability, with the goal of enabling the child to become independent and self-sufficient. You will also learn that the child with a Section 504 Plan[1] does not have the legal protections available to the child who has an IEP under the IDEA.

Except for accessibility of buildings, and modifications and accommodations in testing, Section 504 provides fewer protections and benefits to children with disabilities than IDEA. You will find selected portions of Section 504 at the end of this chapter.

The key portion of **Section 504 of the Rehabilitation Act** states:

> No otherwise qualified individual with a disability in the United States, as defined in Sec. 705(20) of this title, shall, solely **by reason of her or his disability, be excluded from the participation in, be denied the benefits of, or be subjected to discrimination** under any program or activity receiving Federal financial assistance or under any program or activity conducted by any Executive agency or by the United States Postal Service . . .[2]

One important benefit of Section 504 relates to legal remedies if a school district discriminates, excludes, or retaliates against a parent, child or school district employee for exercising their rights.[3] In addition, a complaint to the Office of Civil Rights under Section 504 can be more effective than a complaint to the state department of education under IDEA.

Purpose

Section 504 is a broad *civil rights* law. The law applies to students and other individuals with disabilities, parents, and also to school district employees. A Section 504 case is often known as 1983 action.[4]

---

1 A "Section 504" Plan does not have to be written and does not require parental agreement. See the 504 Regulations at 34 CFR 104.31-104.39 at www.wrightslaw.com/law/504/sec504.regs.pdf. See the sample 504 Plan at www.dredf.org/section504.html (Retrieved October 9, 2006)

2 29 U. S. C. § 794(a)

3 For cases filed against school districts by teachers and other school personnel, go to www.wrightslaw.com/info/sec504.index. htm

4 Civil action for deprivation of rights. Every person who, under color of any statute, ordinance, regulation, custom, or usage, of any State or Territory or the District of Columbia, subjects, or causes to be subjected, any citizen of the United States or other person within the jurisdiction thereof to the deprivation of any rights, privileges, or immunities secured by the Constitution and laws, shall be liable to the party injured in an action at law, suit in equity, or other proper proceeding for redress, except that in any action brought against a judicial officer for an act or omission taken in such officer's judicial capacity, injunctive relief shall not be granted unless a declaratory decree was violated or declaratory relief was unavailable. . . . (42 U. S. C. § 1983)

The purpose of Section 504 is to protect individuals with disabilities from discrimination for reasons related to their disabilities. Prohibited discrimination includes exclusion from school activities, the unnecessary provision of unequal or separate services, and disability harassment. Examples include not allowing children with disabilities to participate in school field trips, sending children with disabilities home from school earlier than nondisabled children, and retaliating against parents and school employees who advocate for children with disabilities.

The purpose of the Individuals with Disabilities Education Act is "to ensure that all children with disabilities have available to them a free, appropriate education that emphasizes special education and related services designed to meet their unique needs and prepare them for further education, employment, and independent living . . ."[5] Section 504 does not ensure that the child with a disability will receive an individualized educational program designed to meet the child's unique needs and provide the child with educational benefit, with the goal of preparing the child for "further education, employment and independent living."

Protection from Discrimination

Section 504 protects individuals with disabilities from discrimination. Children who receive special education services under IDEA are automatically protected by Section 504. The child with a disability who has a 504 Plan does not have the same procedural protections available to children with disabilities and their parents under IDEA.

Accommodations, Modifications and Services

Under Section 504, the child with a disability may receive accommodations and modifications that are not available to nondisabled children. All children with disabilities who receive special education and related services under IDEA are entitled to these accommodations, modifications and services.

Eligibility

To be eligible for protections under Section 504, an individual must have a physical or mental impairment that substantially limits at least one major life activity. Examples of major life activities are walking, seeing, hearing, speaking, breathing, reading, writing, performing math calculations, working, caring for oneself, performing manual tasks, and other activities.

If the child has an "impairment" that "substantially limits" one or more major life activities (like reading, writing, performing math calculations, walking, hearing, or self care), but does not *need* special education services, the child is eligible for protections under Section 504.

Section 504 requires the school to perform an evaluation that draws information from a variety of sources. The school may develop a 504 Plan but the plan does not have to be written. Section 504 does not require a meeting before a change in placement.

Confusion about Rights and Benefits

Some parents and educators believe that a child who is eligible for special education and related services under IDEA must be placed in special education classes, while a child with a 504 Plan may remain in regular education classes. Relying upon this inaccurate information, school personnel often advise parents that their children will be better served with a 504 Plan, not an IEP.

Do you remember what IDEA says about educating children with disabilities in the "least restrictive environment?" Children with disabilities are to be educated with children who are not disabled "to the maximum extent

5   See Purposes of IDEA in Section 1400(d).

appropriate." Educating children in special classes, separate schools, or removing children with disabilities from the regular education environment should only occur when the school cannot educate the child in regular classes with supplementary aids and services.

Remember: Special education is a service, not a place or placement.[6]

Access v. Educational Benefit

To clarify the differences between the laws, change the facts. Assume that your special needs child uses a wheelchair. Under Section 504, your child shall be provided with **access to an education.** Reasonable modifications may be made to the school building. Your child may receive "reasonable" accommodations when taking tests. The child may have the services of an aide to assist in the bathroom. The purpose of these modifications, accommodations and services is to provide the child with access to an education.

Under Section 504 regulations, a "free appropriate public education" is "the provision of regular or special education and related aids and services that . . . are designed to meet individual educational needs of persons with disabilities **as adequately as the needs of persons without disabilities are met** . . ." (34 C.F.R.§ 104.33(b)(1))

Now assume that your child who uses a wheelchair also has neurological problems that adversely affect the child's ability to learn. Under the IDEA, in addition to access, your child is entitled to an education that is designed to meet the child's unique needs and from which the child receives educational benefit. Under Section 504, the child has access to the same free appropriate public education that is available to children who are not disabled.

Discipline

Children with Section 504 Plans and those with IEPs have some protections in school discipline incidents. If the child with a Section 504 Plan misbehaves and the school decides the child's behavior is not a manifestation of the disability, the school can expel the child, just as they can expel a nondisabled child. Under IDEA, the school must continue to provide the child with a free, appropriate education, even if the child is suspended or expelled from school.

Procedural Safeguards

Section 504 does not include a clearly established "Prior Written Notice" requirement.[7] In contrast, IDEA includes an elaborate system of procedural safeguards designed to protect the child and parents. These safeguards include written notice before any change of placement and the right to an independent educational evaluation[8] at public expense. Section 504 does not include these protections.

Impartial Hearings

Section 504 and IDEA require school districts to conduct impartial hearings when parents disagree with their child's identification, evaluation, or placement. Section 504 also permits a hearing to review alleged discrimination. Under Section 504, the parent has an opportunity to participate and obtain representation by counsel. The details are left to the discretion of the school district and hearing officer. Contrast this with the detailed procedural safeguards in Section 1415 of the Individuals with Disabilities Education Act.

---

6   See Regulation 300.39.
7   See Regulation 300.503.
8   See Regulation 300.502.

In Summation

In this chapter, you learned about Section 504 of the Rehabilitation Act and how it differs from the Individuals with Disabilities Education Act.[9] You learned that Section 504 focuses on accommodations, modifications, services, and improved building accessibility to provide access to education.

You learned that Section 504 does not require public schools to provide an educational program that is individualized to meet the needs of a disabled child with the goal of enabling the child to become independent and self-sufficient. You learned that the child with a Section 504 Plan does not have the protections that are available to the child who has an IEP under the IDEA.[10] To learn more about Section 504, go to www.wrightslaw.com/info/sec504.index.htm or enter the term into the search box at www.wrightslaw.com

You will find key portions of Section 504 of the Rehabilitation Act below.

In the next chapter, you will learn about important features in the No Child Left Behind Act and how Congress aligned the Individuals with Disabilities Act with the No Child Left Behind Act.

<h1 style="text-align:center">Section 504 of the Rehabilitation Act of 1973
29 U. S. C. 701 et seq.</h1>

29 U. S. C. § 701. Findings; purpose; policy

(a) Findings. Congress finds that--

(1) millions of Americans have one or more physical or mental disabilities and the number of Americans with such disabilities is increasing;

(2) individuals with disabilities constitute **one of the most disadvantaged groups in society**;

(3) **disability is a natural part of the human experience** and in no way diminishes the **right of individuals** to

(A) live independently;

(B) enjoy self-determination;

(C) make choices;

(D) contribute to society;

(E) pursue meaningful careers; and

(F) enjoy full inclusion and integration in the economic, political, social, cultural, and educational mainstream of American society;

(4) increased employment of individuals with disabilities can be achieved through implementation of statewide workforce investment systems under title I of the Workforce Investment Act of 1998 [29 U. S. C. 2801 et seq.] that provide meaningful and effective participation for individuals with disabilities in workforce investment activities and activities carried out under the vocational rehabilitation program established under title I, and through the provision of independent living services, support services, and meaningful opportunities for employment in integrated work settings through the provision of reasonable accommodations;

(5) individuals with disabilities continually encounter various forms of discrimination in such critical areas as employment, housing, public accommodations, education, transportation, communication, recreation, institutionalization, health services, voting, and public services; and

(6) the goals of the Nation properly include the goal of providing individuals with disabilities with the tools necessary to-

---

9 See "Comparison of IDEA, Section 504 and ADA" at www.cde.state.co.us/cdesped/download/pdf/504Comparison.pdf and "An Overview of ADA, IDEA and Section 504" at http://ericec.org/digests/e606.html (Retrieved on October 9, 2006)

10 To learn more about Section 504 and discrimination, go to www.wrightslaw.com/info/sec504.index.htm or enter the terms into the search box at www.wrightslaw.com

(A) make informed choices and decisions; and

(B) achieve **equality of opportunity, full inclusion and integration** in society, employment, independent living, and economic and social self-sufficiency, for such individuals.

(b) **Purpose.** The purposes of this chapter are--

(1) to empower individuals with disabilities to **maximize employment, economic self-sufficiency, independence, and inclusion and integration into society**, through--

(A) statewide workforce investment systems implemented in accordance with title I of the Workforce Investment Act of 1998 (29 U. S. C. 2801 et seq.) that include, as integral components, comprehensive and coordinated state-of-the-art programs of vocational rehabilitation;

(B) independent living centers and services;

(C) research;

(D) training;

(E) demonstration projects; and

(F) the guarantee of equal opportunity; and

(2) to ensure that the Federal Government plays a leadership role in **promoting the employment of individuals with disabilities**, especially individuals with significant disabilities, and in assisting States and providers of services in fulfilling the aspirations of such individuals with disabilities for meaningful and gainful employment and independent living.

(c) **Policy.** It is the policy of the United States that all programs, projects, and activities receiving assistance under this chapter shall be carried out in a manner consistent with the principles of--

(1) respect for individual dignity, personal responsibility, self-determination, and pursuit of meaningful careers, based on informed choice, of individuals with disabilities;

(2) respect for the privacy, rights, and equal access (including the use of accessible formats), of the individuals;

(3) inclusion, integration, and full participation of the individuals;

(4) support for the involvement of an individual's representative if an individual with a disability requests, desires, or needs such support; and

(5) support for individual and systemic advocacy and community involvement.

29 U. S. C.§ 705. Definitions

For the purposes of this chapter:

. . .

(20) **Individual with a disability**

(A) **In general.** Except as otherwise provided in subparagraph (B), the term "individual with a disability" means any individual who -

(i) has a physical or mental impairment which for such individual constitutes or results in a substantial impediment to employment; and

(ii) can benefit in terms of an employment outcome from vocational rehabilitation services provided pursuant to subchapter I, III, or VI of this chapter.

(B) **Certain programs; limitations on major life activities.** Subject to subparagraphs (C), (D), (E), and (F), the term "individual with a disability" means, for purposes of sections 701, 711, and 712 of this title, and subchapters II, IV, V, and VII of this chapter, any person who -

(i) has a physical or mental impairment which substantially limits one or more of such person's major life activities;

(ii) has a record of such an impairment; or

(iii) is regarded as having such an impairment.

(C) Rights and advocacy provisions

(i) In general; exclusion of individuals engaging in drug use. For purposes of subchapter V of this chapter, the term "individual with a disability" does not include an individual who is currently engaging in the illegal use of drugs, when a covered entity acts on the basis of such use.

(ii) Exception for individuals no longer engaging in drug use. Nothing in clause (i) shall be construed to exclude as an individual with a disability an individual who -

(I) has successfully completed a supervised drug rehabilitation program and is no longer engaging in the illegal use of drugs, or has otherwise been rehabilitated successfully and is no longer engaging in such use;

(II) is participating in a supervised rehabilitation program and is no longer engaging in such use; or

(III) is erroneously regarded as engaging in such use, but is not engaging in such use; except that it shall not be a violation of this chapter for a covered entity to adopt or administer reasonable policies or procedures, including but not limited to drug testing, designed to ensure that an individual described in subclause (I) or (II) is no longer engaging in the illegal use of drugs.

(iii) Exclusion for certain services. Notwithstanding clause (i), for purposes of programs and activities providing health services and services provided under subchapters I, II, and III of this chapter, an individual shall not be excluded from the benefits of such programs or activities on the basis of his or her current illegal use of drugs if he or she is otherwise entitled to such services.

(iv) Disciplinary action. For purposes of programs and activities providing educational services, local educational agencies may take disciplinary action pertaining to the use or possession of illegal drugs or alcohol against any student who is an individual with a disability and who currently is engaging in the illegal use of drugs or in the use of alcohol to the same extent that such disciplinary action is taken against students who are not individuals with disabilities.

Furthermore, the due process procedures at section 104.36 of title 34, Code of Federal Regulations (or any corresponding similar regulation or ruling) shall not apply to such disciplinary actions.

(v) Employment; exclusion of alcoholics. For purposes of sections 793 and 794 of this title as such sections relate to employment, the term "individual with a disability" does not include any individual who is an alcoholic whose current use of alcohol prevents such individual from performing the duties of the job in question or whose employment, by reason of such current alcohol abuse, would constitute a direct threat to property or the safety of others.

(D) Employment; exclusion of individuals with certain diseases or infections. For the purposes of sections 793 and 794 of this title, as such sections relate to employment, such term does not include an individual who has a currently contagious disease or infection and who, by reason of such disease or infection, would constitute a direct threat to the health or safety of other individuals or who, by reason of the currently contagious disease or infection, is unable to perform the duties of the job.

(E) Rights provisions; exclusion of individuals on basis of homosexuality or bisexuality. For the purposes of sections 791, 793, and 794 of this title -

(i) for purposes of the application of subparagraph (B) to such sections, the term "impairment" does not include homosexuality or bisexuality; and

(ii) therefore the term "individual with a disability" does not include an individual on the basis of homosexuality or bisexuality.

(F) Rights provisions; exclusion of individuals on basis of certain disorders. For the purposes of sections 791, 793, and 794 of this title, the term "individual with a disability" does not include an individual on the basis of-

(i) transvestism, transsexualism, pedophilia, exhibitionism, voyeurism, gender identity disorders not resulting from physical impairments, or other sexual behavior disorders;

(ii) compulsive gambling, kleptomania, or pyromania; or

(iii) psychoactive substance use disorders resulting from current illegal use of drugs.

(G) Individuals with disabilities. The term "individuals with disabilities" means more than one individual with a disability.

. . .

(37) Transition services. The term "transition services" means a coordinated set of activities for a student, designed within an outcome-oriented process, that promotes movement from school to post school activities, including postsecondary education, vocational training, integrated employment (including supported employment), continuing and adult education, adult services, independent living, or community participation. The coordinated set of activities shall be based upon the individual student's needs, taking into account the student's preferences and interests, and shall include instruction, community experiences, the development of employment and other post school adult living objectives, and, when appropriate, acquisition of daily living skills and functional vocational evaluation.

. . .

29 U. S. C. § 794. Nondiscrimination under Federal grants and programs

(a) Promulgation of rules and regulations. No otherwise qualified individual with a disability in the United States, as defined in section 705(20) of this title, **shall, solely by reason of her or his disability, be excluded** from the participation in, be denied the benefits of, or be subjected to discrimination under any program or activity **receiving** Federal financial assistance or under any program or activity conducted by any Executive agency or by the United States Postal Service. The head of each such agency shall promulgate such regulations as may be necessary to carry out the amendments to this section made by the Rehabilitation, Comprehensive Services, and Developmental Disabilities Act of 1978. Copies of any proposed regulation shall be submitted to appropriate authorizing committees of the Congress, and such regulation may take effect no earlier than the thirtieth day after the date on which such regulation is so submitted to such committees.

(b) "Program or activity" defined. For the purposes of this section, the term "program or activity" means all of the operations of-

(1)

(A) a department, agency, special purpose district, or other instrumentality of a State or of a local government; or

(B) the entity of such State or local government that distributes such assistance and each such department or agency (and each other State or local government entity) to which the assistance is extended, in the case of assistance to a State or local government;

(2)

(A) a college, university, or other postsecondary institution, or a public system of higher education; or

(B) a local educational agency (as defined in section 7801 of title 20), system of vocational education, or other school system;

(3)

(A) an entire corporation, partnership, or other private organization, or an entire sole proprietorship

(i) if assistance is extended to such corporation, partnership, private organization, or sole proprietorship as a whole; or

(ii) which is principally engaged in the business of providing education, health care, housing, social services, or parks and recreation; or

(B) the entire plant or other comparable, geographically separate facility to which Federal financial assistance is extended, in the case of any other corporation, partnership, private organization, or sole proprietorship; or

(4) any other entity which is established by two or more of the entities described in paragraph (1), (2), or (3); any part of which is extended Federal financial assistance.

(c) Significant structural alterations by small providers. Small providers are not required by subsection (a) of this section to make significant structural alterations to their existing facilities for the purpose of assuring program accessibility, if alternative means of providing the services are available. The terms used in this subsection shall be construed with reference to the regulations existing on March 22, 1988.

(d) Standards used in determining violation of section. The standards used to determine whether this section has been violated in a complaint alleging employment discrimination under this section shall be the standards applied under title I of the Americans with Disabilities Act of 1990 (42 U. S. C. 12111 et seq.) and the provisions of sections 501 through 504, and 510, of the Americans with Disabilities Act of 1990 (42 U.S.C. 12201-12204 and 12210), as such sections relate to employment.

29 U.S.C. § 794a. Remedies and attorney fees

(a)

(1) The remedies, procedures, and rights set forth in section 717 of the Civil Rights Act of 1964 (42 U.S.C. 2000e-16), including the application of sections 706(f) through 706(k) (42 U.S.C. 2000e-5(f) through (k)), shall be available, with respect to any complaint under section 791 of this title, to any employee or applicant for employment aggrieved by the final disposition of such complaint, or by the failure to take final action on such complaint. In fashioning an equitable or affirmative action remedy under such section, a court may take into account the reasonableness of the cost of any necessary work place accommodation, and the availability of alternatives therefor or other appropriate relief in order to achieve an equitable and appropriate remedy.

(2) The remedies, procedures, and rights set forth in title VI of the Civil Rights Act of 1964 [42 U.S.C. 2000d et seq.] shall be available to any person aggrieved by any act or failure to act by any recipient of Federal assistance or Federal provider of such assistance under section 794 of this title.

(b) In any action or proceeding to enforce or charge a violation of a provision of this subchapter, the court, in its discretion, may allow the prevailing party, other than the United States, a reasonable attorney's fee as part of the costs.

CHAPTER 8

No Child Left Behind Act of 2001

When Congress reauthorized the Individuals with Disabilities Education Act, they made changes to bring IDEA 2004 into conformity with the No Child Left Behind Act of 2001 (Elementary and Secondary Education Act).

Congress added new definitions[1] to IDEA. Special education teachers who teach core academic subjects must meet the highly qualified teacher requirements of No Child Left Behind. To bring IDEA into conformity with NCLB, IDEA 2004 requires states to establish performance goals for children with disabilities that are consistent with the goals and standards for non-disabled children. States are required to report their progress in educating children with disabilities, and their graduation and dropout rates.

In determining if a child is eligible for special education services under IDEA, a child is not eligible if the child's problems are due to "lack of appropriate instruction in reading, including in the *essential components of reading instruction*[2] as defined in Section 1208(3) of ESEA."[3]

Purpose

When you read the Findings and Purposes of the Individuals with Disabilities Education Act, you learned that the Purpose is the most important statute in a law. Read the Purpose of the No Child Left Behind Act:

> The purpose of this title is to ensure that **all children** have a fair, equal, and significant opportunity to obtain a **high-quality education and reach**, at a minimum, **proficiency** on challenging State academic achievement standards and state academic assessments.[4]

No Child Left Behind requires schools and school districts to meet the educational needs of *all* children, including children with disabilities, English language learners, minority and migratory children, and other neglected groups of children, and to publicly report their progress in educating these children every year.

Key requirements of the law include annual proficiency tests in grades 3-8, a highly qualified teacher in every classroom, research-based instruction, increased parental rights, school choice, and public reporting of progress by schools, school districts and states. These requirements are strategies to accomplish the purpose of the law.

No Child Left Behind is not a new law. When Congress reauthorized the Elementary and Secondary Education Act (ESEA) of 1965, they gave that law a new name — the No Child Left Behind Act of 2001.[5]

Background

When the No Child Left Behind was enacted, millions of children were leaving school without the basic skills they need to make it in the real world.

---

1   Core academic subjects, limited English proficient, "highly qualified" teachers, and homeless children.
2   See "Four Great Definitions of Reading" at www.wrightslaw.com/nclb/4defs.reading.htm
3   20 U. S. C. § 1414(b)(5)
4   20 U. S. C. § 6301
5   For the full text of the No Child Left Behind Act, see *Wrightslaw: No Child Left Behind* by Peter Wright, Pamela Wright, and Suzanne Heath, published by Harbor House Law Press, Inc.

According to the Nation's Report Card:[6]

- Only 36 percent of 12th graders are proficient in reading
- Only 18 percent of 12th graders are proficient in science
- Only 17 percent of 12th graders are proficient in math
- Only 11 percent of 12th graders are proficientg in U. S. history

Closing the Gap

Nationally, there is a significant gap between the achievement test scores of children from low-income families, racial minorities, children with disabilities, English language learners, and the test scores of other children. Children with disabilities are one of the groups that have often been left behind.

No Child Left Behind seeks to close that achievement gap by holding states, local school districts, and schools accountable for improving the academic achievement of all children. The provisions in No Child Left Behind that affect children and their parents include:

- Annual proficiency testing
- Research based reading programs
- Highly qualified teachers
- Parents' right to know the qualifications of their child's teachers
- Supplemental educational services and public school choice
- Parent involvement and empowerment[7]

Annual Proficiency Testing

By 2005, schools were required to test all children in math and reading every year in grades 3 through 8. By 2007, schools must begin to test children in science.

Annual assessments or proficiency tests provide you with information about the school's progress in teaching your child and other groups of children.[8] This information will help you ensure that your child is not left behind or trapped in a failing school. Annual testing also provides valuable information to your child's teachers. Teachers will know the strengths and weaknesses of their students. This information will help teachers develop lessons and ensure that all students meet or exceed state standards.

Research Based Reading Programs

No Child Left Behind focuses on teaching young children, including children with disabilities, to read. One goal of NCLB is that all children will read at grade level by the end of grade three. According to the Nation's Report Card:

- 32 percent of 4th graders are proficient readers
- 33 percent of 8th graders are proficient readers
- 36 percent of 12th graders are proficient readers

---

6 http://nces.ed.gov/nationsreportcard/about/national.asp

7 These rights vary slightly from school to school, based on the source of funding. For full details, see *Wrightslaw: No Child Left Behind*.

8 According to the implementing regulations for No Child Left Behind, "one percent of all students is approximately 9.0 percent of students with disabilities" have "significant cognitive disabilities." Thus, 91 percent of students with disabilities do not have "significant cognitive disabilities" that prevent them from learning grade level material. See *Federal Register*, Volume 68, page 68699, published December 9, 2003,

The reading skills of most children with disabilities lag behind the skills of their peers, regardless of the child's disability. Many schools use reading programs that are not effective in teaching children to read. NCLB provides funds for states and districts to use "in establishing reading programs for students in kindergarten through grade 3 that are based on scientifically based reading research, *to ensure that every student can read at grade level or above not later than the end of grade 3*."[9] (emphasis added) NCLB includes the legal definitions of reading, the essential components of reading instruction, diagnostic reading assessments, and reading research.

Key Definitions

Reading

No Child Left Behind includes the legal definition of reading:

"Reading is a complex system of deriving meaning from print that requires all of the following:

(A) The skills and knowledge to understand how phonemes, or speech sounds, are connected to print,

(B) The ability to decode unfamiliar words,

(C) The ability to read fluently,

(D) Sufficient background information and vocabulary to foster reading comprehension,

(E) The development of appropriate active strategies to construct meaning from print,

(F) The development and maintenance of a motivation to read."[10]

Essential Components of Reading Instruction

No Child Left Behind defines the five essential components of reading instruction.

"The term 'essential components of reading instruction' means explicit and systematic instruction in-

(A) phonemic awareness,

(B) phonics,

(C) vocabulary development,

(D) reading fluency, including oral reading skills, and

(E) reading comprehension strategies."[11]

Diagnostic Reading Assessments

No Child Left Behind defines diagnostic reading assessments.

"The term 'diagnostic reading assessment' means an assessment that is-

(i) valid, reliable, and based on scientifically based reading research; and

(ii) used for the purpose of-

(I) identifying a child's specific areas of strengths and weaknesses so that the child has learned to read by the end of grade 3;

(II) determining any difficulties that a child may have in learning to read and the potential cause of such difficulties; and

(III) helping to determine possible reading intervention strategies and related special needs."[12]

---

9   20 U. S. C. § 6361
10   20 U. S. C. § 6368(5)
11   20 U. S. C. § 6368(3)
12   20 U. S. C. § 6368(7)

Scientifically Based Reading Research

No Child Left Behind defines scientifically based reading research.

"The term 'scientifically based reading research' means research that–

(A) applies rigorous, systematic, and objective procedures to obtain valid knowledge relevant to reading development, reading instruction, and reading difficulties; and

(B) includes research that–

(i) employs systematic, empirical methods that draw on observation or experiment;

(ii) involves rigorous data analyses that are adequate to test the stated hypotheses and justify the general conclusions drawn;

(iii) relies on measurements or observational methods that provide valid data across evaluators and observers and across multiple measurements and observations; and

(iv) has been accepted by a peer-reviewed journal or approved by a panel of independent experts through a comparably rigorous, objective, and scientific review."[13]

Teacher Qualifications

Highly Qualified Requirements

The requirements about qualifications of special education teachers are new and track the highly qualified teacher requirements in No Child Left Behind.[14] A "highly qualified teacher" has full State certification (no waivers), holds a license to teach, and meets State requirements. The requirements are somewhat different for elementary, middle school, and high school teachers, for teachers of multiple subjects, and for teachers who teach to alternate standards.[15]

Special educators who teach core academic subjects must be highly qualified by the end of the 2005-2006 school year. Special educators who do not provide instruction in core academic subjects are not required to meet the highly qualified teacher requirements. IDEA 2004 requires States to take measurable steps "to recruit, train, and retain highly qualified personnel to provide special education and related services."[16]

Parents' Right to Know Qualifications of Their Child's Teachers

At the beginning of each school year, school districts that receive Title I funds must notify parents that they may request specific information about the qualifications of their children's teachers. At a minimum, parents have a right to know–

- if the teacher is certified or licensed to teach the grade levels and subjects she is teaching
- if the teacher's certification or licensure was waived under an emergency or provisional status
- the teacher's college major and any graduate degree or certification
- if the child received services from a paraprofessional, the qualifications of that paraprofessional[17]

See the sample letter to request information about the qualifications of your child's teachers at the end of this chapter.

---

13 20 U. S. C. § 6368(6)
14 20 U. S. C. § 1412(a)(14)
15 20 U. S. C. § 1401(10)(B)
16 20 U. S. C. § 1412(c)(14)
17 20 U. S. C. § 6311

Choices and Options

Public School Choice

If your child attends a Title I School that fails to meet its Adequate Yearly Progress goal for *two consecutive years*, your child may transfer to a non-failing school within the district. If all schools in your district fail to meet their AYP goals for two consecutive years, your child may attend a better-performing school in another school district. If your child transfers to a better-performing school, the child may remain there until he or she completes the highest grade in that school.

Supplemental Educational Services

If your child attends a Title I school that fails to meet its Adequate Yearly Progress goal for *three consecutive years*, the school must provide supplemental educational services to the students from low-income families who remain in the school. Supplemental educational services include tutoring, after-school programs, and summer programs. Supplemental services must be free to parents.

Parents may choose a tutor or other supplemental service provider from a list of approved providers maintained by the state. The state must ensure that all providers on the list have a history of success. The district may give preference to the lowest-achieving children from low-income families who request supplemental services.

Supplemental services providers must provide parents and the school with information about student progress. Providers must ensure that instruction meets state and local standards, including state student academic achievement standards. Providers must also comply with health, safety, and civil rights laws.

Your Child's IEP

As you develop your child's IEP, you need to be familiar with the essential components of reading instruction. The definitions of reading and research based reading programs apply to all programs, all schools, all children, all the time. These terms define and describe the minimum requirements for your child's reading program at school.

Don't forget that the timeline for teaching a child to read fluently is by the end of *grade three*.[18]

Participation in Assessments

In IDEA 2004, the language about who will participate in assessments was changed to "*All* children with disabilities are included in *all* general State and districtwide assessment programs . . . with *appropriate accommodations, where necessary* and as indicated in their respective individualized education programs."[19] (emphasis added) Some parents are afraid that including their children with disabilities in these assessments will cause the child to be retained or denied a diploma. The purpose of these tests is to determine how well schools are performing their job of educating children, not to punish children when schools don't do their job.

Adaptations and Accommodations

For children with disabilities who receive services under IDEA and have Individualized Education Programs (IEPs), NCLB mandates that the child will receive "the reasonable adaptations and accommodations for students with disabilities . . . necessary to measure the academic achievement of such students relative to State academic content and State student academic achievement standards."

IDEA 2004 requires the child's IEP to include:

a statement of any individual appropriate accommodations that are necessary to measure the academic achievement and functional performance of the child on State and districtwide assessments . .

---

18 20 U. S. C. § 6361
19 20 U. S. C. § 1412(c)(16)(A)

. [and] if the IEP Team determines that the child shall take an alternate assessment on a particular State or districtwide assessment of student achievement, a statement of why...the child cannot participate in the regular assessment; and . . . [why] the particular alternate assessment selected is appropriate for the child . . . .[20]

In Summation

In this chapter, you learned about key provisions of the No Child Left Behind Act and how these provisions were incorporated into the Individuals with Disabilities Education Act of 2004. You learned the legal definitions of reading, the essential components of reading programs, reading assessments, and scientifically based research. You learned that No Child Left Behind and IDEA 2004 require schools to provide children with disabilities with appropriate accommodations on all state and district tests.

To learn how NCLB will affect your child's education, parents should read Chapter 5 in *Wrightslaw: No Child Left Behind*. Educators will be interested in Chapter 6, "No Child Left Behind for Teachers, Principals and Paraprofessionals." Attorneys and advocates who represent the interests of children with disabilities will be interested in the questions in Chapter 7, "No Child Left Behind for Attorneys and Advocates."

On the next page is a sample letter to request information about the qualifications of your child's teachers that you can adapt to your circumstances. In the next chapter, you will learn about the Family Educational Rights and Privacy Act.

---

20 20 U. S. C. § 1414(d)(1)(A)(i)(VI)

Sample Letter to Request Information about Teachers' Qualifications

Debra Pratt
17456 General Puller Highway
Deltaville, Virginia 23043
804-758-8400

May 1, 2007

Dr. Deborah Harrison, Principal
Deltaville Middle School
1000 Main Street
Deltaville, Virginia 23043

Re: Kelsey Pratt (DOB: 01/01/93)
School: Deltaville Middle School

Dear Dr. Harrison:

My daughter Kelsey is a seventh grade student at Deltaville Middle School. She has four teachers: Ms. Adams, Mr. Brown, Ms. Canady, and Ms. Davis, a substitute math teacher. Kelsey also receives tutoring from Ms. Evans, a paraprofessional.

When I read an article about No Child Left Behind on the U. S. Department of Education website, I learned that I am entitled to information about my child's teachers, including:

(1) Whether the teacher has met State qualification and licensing criteria for the grade levels and subject areas in which the teacher provides instruction;

(2) Whether the teacher is teaching under emergency or other provisional status through which State qualification or licensing criteria have been waived.

(3) The baccalaureate degree major of the teacher and any other graduate certification or degree held by the teacher, and the field of discipline of the certification or degree.

(4) Whether the child is provided services by paraprofessionals and, if so, their qualifications.

I am requesting this information about the qualifications of Kelsey's teachers and paraprofessional. I believe the information will help me work more effectively with her teachers.

If you have questions about my request, please call me at work (899-555-9876) or at home (899-555-1234) after 6 p.m., or you may email me at debrapratt@deltavilleva.com. Thanks in advance for your help.

Sincerely,

Debra Pratt
Debra Pratt

CHAPTER 9

Family Educational Rights and Privacy Act

This chapter begins with an overview of the Family Educational Rights and Privacy Act. Following the overview is the text of the statute.

The Family Educational Rights and Privacy Act (FERPA) deals with educational records, privacy and confidentiality, parent access to educational records, parent amendment of records, and destruction of records. The purpose of this statute is to protect the privacy of parents and students. FERPA applies to all agencies and institutions that receive federal funds, including elementary and secondary schools, colleges, and universities.

The statute is in the United States Code at 20 U. S. C. 1232g and 1232h. The regulations are in the Code of Federal Regulations at 34 C.F.R Part 99.

Educational Records

Education records means, "those records, files, documents, and other materials which (i) contain information directly related to a student; and (ii) are maintained by an educational agency or institution or by a person acting for such agency or institution."

Personal notes and memory aids that are used only by the person who made them are not educational records. However, if the notes are shared with or disclosed to another individual, they become educational records.

Instructional materials shall be made available to parents and include "teacher's manuals, films, tapes, or other supplementary material which will be used in connection with any survey, analysis, or evaluation as part of any applicable program shall be available for inspection by the parents or guardians of the children."[1] Test materials, including test protocols and answer sheets are educational records and must be disclosed. The Office for Civil Rights has determined that the test protocols used by a psychologist to prepare a report are educational records and must be produced to the parents. Destruction of records violates the parent's right of access.

The Office for Civil Rights found that the transcript of a hearing is an educational record for purposes of Section 504. Due process decisions are educational records. Tapes of IEP meetings are educational records as are IEPs.

Right to Inspect and Review Educational Records

Parents have a right to inspect and review all educational records relating to their child. This right to includes the right to have copies of records and to receive explanations and interpretations from school officials. Agencies must comply with requests to inspect and review records within forty-five days.[2]

Copies of records must be provided to the parent if failure to do so would prevent the parent from exercising the right to view records. Schools may charge reasonable copying fees unless the fee would "effectively prevent" the parent or student from exercising the right to inspect and review the records. Fees may not be charged for searching and retrieving records.

According to the FERPA regulations "If circumstances effectively prevent the parent or eligible student from

---

1   20 U. S. C. 1232h(a)
2   Some states have education records laws that provide stronger rights than FERPA. Check your state statute.

exercising the right to inspect and review the student's education records, the educational agency or institution, or SEA or its component, shall (1) Provide the parent or eligible student with a copy of the records requested; or (2) Make other arrangements for the parent or eligible student to inspect and review the requested records."

If the parent believes that the educational record contains inaccurate or misleading information, the parent may ask the agency to amend the record. The parent may also request a hearing to correct or challenge misleading or inaccurate information.

Confidentiality and Personally Identifiable Information

Personally identifiable information may not be disclosed without written consent of the parent. "Personally identifiable information" includes, but is not limited to:

(a) The student's name;

(b) The name of the student's parent or other family member;

(c) The address of the student or student's family;

(d) A personal identifier, such as the student's social security number or student number;

(e) A list of personal characteristics that would make the student's identity easily traceable; or

(f) Other information that would make the student's identity easily traceable.

Disclosure and Destruction of Records

Records may be released without consent to "other school officials, including teachers within the educational institution or local educational agency, who have been determined by such agency or institution to have legitimate educational interests." Records may be released to "officials of other schools or school systems in which the student seeks or intends to enroll, upon condition that the student's parents be notified of the transfer, receive a copy of the record if desired, and have an opportunity for a hearing to challenge the content of the record . . . ." Directory information may be released without consent.[3] Disclosures may be made without consent in health and safety emergencies. Law enforcement agencies and monitoring agencies have access to confidential records. The agency must maintain a log of all disclosures without parental consent. Consent for disclosure must be signed and dated and include information about the recipients of information.

In non-special education matters, the right to sue for a violation of confidentiality may be limited by *Gonzaga University v. Doe*, 536 U.S. 273 (2002). See also *Owasso Ind. Sch. Dist. v. Falvo*, 534 U.S. 426 (2002). Recent cases protect the right of Protection and Advocacy agencies to access education records in investigations of abuse.[4]

Pursuant to the General Educational Provisions Act, schools must retain records for at least five years. The school may not destroy any education records if there is an outstanding request to inspect and review the records under this section.

In Summation

In this chapter, you learned about education records, privacy, confidentiality of personal information, notice, disclosures and destruction of records. In the next chapter, you will learn about the McKinney-Vento Homeless Assistance Act, including the requirement that decisions must be made "in the child's best interests."

---

3   The Family Educational Rights and Privacy Act (FERPA) requires that the school district, with some exceptions, obtain your written consent prior to the disclosure of personally identifiable information from your child's education records. The school district may disclose appropriately designated "directory information" without your written consent, unless you advise the district to the contrary in accordance with district procedures. See "Family Educational Rights and Privacy Act (FERPA) Model Notice for Directory Information" at www.ed.gov/policy/gen/guid/fpco/pdf/ht100902a.pdf (Retrieved on October 9, 2006)

4   See www.ndrn.org for more information about these cases.

Family Educational Rights and Privacy Act
20 U. S. C. 1232g et seq.

(a) Conditions for availability of funds to educational agencies or institutions; inspection and review of education records; specific information to be made available; procedure for access to education records; reasonableness of time for such access; hearings; written explanations by parents; definitions

(1)

(A) **No funds** shall be made available under any applicable program to any educational agency or institution which has **a policy of denying, or** which **effectively prevents, the parents** of students who are or have been in attendance at a school of such agency or at such institution, as the case may be, the **right to inspect and review the education records** of their children. If any material or document in the education record of a student includes information on more than one student, the parents of one of such students shall have the right to inspect and review only such part of such material or document as relates to such student or to be informed of the specific information contained in such part of such material. Each educational agency or institution shall establish appropriate procedures for the granting of a **request by parents for access to the education records** of their children **within a reasonable period of time**, but **in no case more than forty-five days after the request** has been made.

(B) No funds under any applicable program shall be made available to any State educational agency (whether or not that agency is an educational agency or institution under this section) that has a policy of denying, or effectively prevents, the parents of students the right to inspect and review the education records maintained by the State educational agency on their children who are or have been in attendance at any school of an educational agency or institution that is subject to the provisions of this section.

(C) The first sentence of subparagraph (A) shall not operate to make available to students in institutions of postsecondary education the following materials:

(i) financial records of the parents of the student or any information contained therein;

(ii) confidential letters and statements of recommendation, which were placed in the education records prior to January 1, 1975, if such letters or statements are not used for purposes other than those for which they were specifically intended;

(iii) if the student has signed a waiver of the student's right of access under this subsection in accordance with subparagraph (D), confidential recommendations—

(I) respecting admission to any educational agency or institution,

(II) respecting an application for employment, and

(III) respecting the receipt of an honor or honorary recognition.

(D) A student or a person applying for admission may waive his right of access to confidential statements described in clause (iii) of subparagraph (C), except that such waiver shall apply to recommendations only if

(i) the student is, upon request, notified of the names of all persons making confidential recommendations and

(ii) such recommendations are used solely for the purpose for which they were specifically intended. Such waivers may not be required as a condition for admission to, receipt of financial aid from, or receipt of any other services or benefits from such agency or institution.

(2) No funds shall be made available under any applicable program to any educational agency or institution unless the parents of students who are or have been in attendance at a school of such agency or at such institution are provided an opportunity for a hearing by such agency or institution, in accordance with regu-

lations of the Secretary, to challenge the content of such student's education records, in order to insure that the records are not inaccurate, misleading, or otherwise in violation of the privacy rights of students, and to provide an opportunity for the correction or deletion of any such inaccurate, misleading or otherwise inappropriate data contained therein and to insert into such records a written explanation of the parents respecting the content of such records.

(3) For the purposes of this section the term **"educational agency or institution"** means any public or private agency or institution which is the recipient of funds under any applicable program.

(4)

(A) For the purposes of this section, the term **"education records"** means, except as may be provided otherwise in subparagraph (B), those records, files, documents, and other materials which -

(i) contain information directly related to a student; and

(ii) are maintained by an educational agency or institution or by a person acting for such agency or institution.

(B) The term **"education records" does not include** -

(i) records of instructional, supervisory, and administrative personnel and educational personnel ancillary thereto which are in the sole possession of the maker thereof and which are not accessible or revealed to any other person except a substitute;

(ii) records maintained by a law enforcement unit of the educational agency or institution that were created by that law enforcement unit for the purpose of law enforcement;

(iii) in the case of persons who are employed by an educational agency or institution but who are not in attendance at such agency or institution, records made and maintained in the normal course of business which relate exclusively to such person in that person's capacity as an employee and are not available for use for any other purpose; or

(iv) records on a student who is eighteen years of age or older, or is attending an institution of postsecondary education, which are made or maintained by a physician, psychiatrist, psychologist, or other recognized professional or paraprofessional acting in his professional or paraprofessional capacity, or assisting in that capacity, and which are made, maintained, or used only in connection with the provision of treatment to the student, and are not available to anyone other than persons providing such treatment, except that such records can be personally reviewed by a physician or other appropriate professional of the student's choice.

(5)

(A) For the purposes of this section the term **"directory information"** relating to a student includes the following: the student's name, address, telephone listing, date and place of birth, major field of study, participation in officially recognized activities and sports, weight and height of members of athletic teams, dates of attendance, degrees and awards received, and the most recent previous educational agency or institution attended by the student.

(B) Any educational agency or institution making public directory information **shall give public notice** of the categories of information which it has designated as such information with respect to each student attending the institution or agency and shall allow a reasonable period of time after such notice has been given for a parent to inform the institution or agency that any or all of the information designated should not be released without the parent's prior consent.

(6) For the purposes of this section, the term **"student"** includes any person with respect to whom an educational agency or institution maintains education records or personally identifiable information, but does not include a person who has not been in attendance at such agency or institution.

(b) Release of education records; parental consent requirement; exceptions; compliance with judicial orders and subpoenas; audit and evaluation of federally-supported education programs; recordkeeping

(1) No funds shall be made available under any applicable program to any educational agency or institution which has a policy or practice of permitting the release of education records (or personally identifiable information contained therein other than directory information, as defined in paragraph (5) of subsection (a) of this section) of students without the written consent of their parents to any individual, agency, or organization, other than to the following—

(A) other school officials, including teachers within the educational institution or local educational agency, who have been determined by such agency or institution to have legitimate educational interests, including the educational interests of the child for whom consent would otherwise be required;

(B) officials of other schools or school systems in which the student seeks or intends to enroll, upon condition that the student's parents be notified of the transfer, receive a copy of the record if desired, and have an opportunity for a hearing to challenge the content of the record;

(C)

(i) authorized representatives of

(I) the Comptroller General of the United States,

(II) the Secretary, or

(III) State educational authorities, under the conditions set forth in paragraph (3), or

(ii) authorized representatives of the Attorney General for law enforcement purposes under the same conditions as apply to the Secretary under paragraph (3);

(D) in connection with a student's application for, or receipt of, financial aid;

(E) State and local officials or authorities to whom such information is specifically allowed to be reported or disclosed pursuant to State statute adopted -

(i) before November 19, 1974, if the allowed reporting or disclosure concerns the juvenile justice system and such system's ability to effectively serve the student whose records are released, or

(ii) after November 19, 1974, if -

(I) the allowed reporting or disclosure concerns the juvenile justice system and such system's ability to effectively serve, prior to adjudication, the student whose records are released; and

(II) the officials and authorities to whom such information is disclosed certify in writing to the educational agency or institution that the information will not be disclosed to any other party except as provided under State law without the prior written consent of the parent of the student.[1]

(F) organizations conducting studies for, or on behalf of, educational agencies or institutions for the purpose of developing, validating, or administering predictive tests, administering student aid programs, and improving instruction, if such studies are conducted in such a manner as will not permit the personal identification of students and their parents by persons other than representatives of such organizations and such information will be destroyed when no longer needed for the purpose for which it is conducted;

(G) accrediting organizations in order to carry out their accrediting functions;

(H) parents of a dependent student of such parents, as defined in section 152 of title 26;

(I) subject to regulations of the Secretary, in connection with an emergency, appropriate persons if the knowledge of such information is necessary to protect the health or safety of the student or other persons; and

(J)

(i) the entity or persons designated in a Federal grand jury subpoena, in which case the court shall order, for good cause shown, the educational agency or institution (and any officer, director, employee, agent, or attorney for such agency or institution) on which the subpoena is served, to not disclose to any person the existence or contents of the subpoena or any information furnished to the grand jury in response to the subpoena; and

(ii) the entity or persons designated in any other subpoena issued for a law enforcement purpose, in which case the court or other issuing agency may order, for good cause shown, the educational agency or institution (and any officer, director, employee, agent, or attorney for such agency or institution) on which the subpoena is served, to not disclose to any person the existence or contents of the subpoena or any information furnished in response to the subpoena. Nothing in subparagraph (E) of this paragraph shall prevent a State from further limiting the number or type of State or local officials who will continue to have access thereunder.

(2) No funds shall be made available under any applicable program to any educational agency or institution which has a policy or practice of releasing, or providing access to, any personally identifiable information in education records other than directory information, or as is permitted under paragraph (1) of this subsection, unless-

(A) there is written consent from the student's parents specifying records to be released, the reasons for such release, and to whom, and with a copy of the records to be released to the student's parents and the student if desired by the parents, or

(B) except as provided in paragraph (1)(J), such information is furnished in compliance with judicial order, or pursuant to any lawfully issued subpoena, upon condition that parents and the students are notified of all such orders or subpoenas in advance of the compliance therewith by the educational institution or agency.

(3) Nothing contained in this section shall preclude authorized representatives of

(A) the Comptroller General of the United States,

(B) the Secretary, or

(C) State educational authorities from having access to student or other records which may be necessary in connection with the audit and evaluation of Federally-supported education programs, or in connection with the enforcement of the Federal legal requirements which relate to such programs: Provided, That except when collection of personally identifiable information is specifically authorized by Federal law, any data collected by such officials shall be protected in a manner which will not permit the personal identification of students and their parents by other than those officials, and such personally identifiable data shall be destroyed when no longer needed for such audit, evaluation, and enforcement of Federal legal requirements.

(4)

(A) Each educational agency or institution **shall maintain a record**, kept with the education records of each student, which will indicate **all individuals** (other than those specified in paragraph (1)(A) of this subsection), **agencies, or organizations which have requested or obtained access to a student's education records** maintained by such educational agency or institution, and which will indicate specifically the legitimate interest that each such person, agency, or organization has in obtaining this information. Such record of access shall be available only to parents, to the school official and his assistants who are responsible for the custody of such records, and to persons or organizations authorized in, and under the conditions of, clauses (A) and (C) of paragraph (1) as a means of auditing the operation of the system.

(B) With respect to this subsection, personal information shall only be transferred to a third party on the condition that such party will not permit any other party to have access to such information without the written consent of the parents of the student. If a third party outside the educational agency or institution permits access to information in violation of paragraph (2)(A), or fails to destroy information in violation of paragraph (1)(F), the educational agency or institution shall be prohibited from permitting access to information from education records to that third party for a period of not less than five years.

(5) Nothing in this section shall be construed to prohibit State and local educational officials from having access to student or other records which may be necessary in connection with the audit and evaluation of any federally or State supported education program or in connection with the enforcement of the Federal legal

requirements which relate to any such program, subject to the conditions specified in the proviso in paragraph (3).

(6)

(A) Nothing in this section shall be construed to prohibit an institution of postsecondary education from disclosing, to an alleged victim of any crime of violence (as that term is defined in section 16 of title 18), or a nonforcible sex offense, the final results of any disciplinary proceeding conducted by such institution against the alleged perpetrator of such crime or offense with respect to such crime or offense.

(B) Nothing in this section shall be construed to prohibit an institution of postsecondary education from disclosing the final results of any disciplinary proceeding conducted by such institution against a student who is an alleged perpetrator of any crime of violence (as that term is defined in section 16 of title 18), or a nonforcible sex offense, if the institution determines as a result of that disciplinary proceeding that the student committed a violation of the institution's rules or policies with respect to such crime or offense.

(C) For the purpose of this paragraph, the final results of any disciplinary proceeding—

(i) shall include only the name of the student, the violation committed, and any sanction imposed by the institution on that student; and

(ii) may include the name of any other student, such as a victim or witness, only with the written consent of that other student.

(7)

(A) Nothing in this section may be construed to prohibit an educational institution from disclosing information provided to the institution under section 14071 of title 42 concerning registered sex offenders who are required to register under such section.

(B) The Secretary shall take appropriate steps to notify educational institutions that disclosure of information described in subparagraph (A) is permitted.

(c) **Surveys or data-gathering activities; regulations**. Not later than 240 days after October 20, 1994, the Secretary shall adopt appropriate regulations or procedures, or identify existing regulations or procedures, which protect the rights of privacy of students and their families in connection with any surveys or data-gathering activities conducted, assisted, or authorized by the Secretary or an administrative head of an education agency. Regulations established under this subsection shall include provisions controlling the use, dissemination, and protection of such data. No survey or data-gathering activities shall be conducted by the Secretary, or an administrative head of an education agency under an applicable program, unless such activities are authorized by law.

(d) **Students' rather than parents' permission or consent**. For the purposes of this section, whenever a student has attained eighteen years of age, or is attending an institution of postsecondary education, the permission or consent required of and the rights accorded to the parents of the student shall thereafter only be required of and accorded to the student.

(e) **Informing parents or students of rights under this section**. No funds shall be made available under any applicable program to any educational agency or institution unless such agency or institution effectively informs the parents of students, or the students, if they are eighteen years of age or older, or are attending an institution of postsecondary education, of the rights accorded them by this section.

(f) **Enforcement; termination of assistance**. The Secretary shall take appropriate actions to enforce this section and to deal with violations of this section, in accordance with this chapter, except that action to terminate assistance may be taken only if the Secretary finds there has been a failure to comply with this section, and he has determined that compliance cannot be secured by voluntary means.

(g) **Office and review board; creation; functions**. The Secretary shall establish or designate an office and review board within the Department for the purpose of investigating, processing, reviewing, and adjudicating violations of this section and complaints which may be filed concerning alleged violations of this section. Except for the conduct of hearings, none of the functions of the Secretary under this section shall be carried out in any of the regional offices of such Department.

(h) Disciplinary records; disclosure. Nothing in this section shall prohibit an educational agency or institution from-

(1) including appropriate information in the education record of any student concerning disciplinary action taken against such student for conduct that posed a significant risk to the safety or well-being of that student, other students, or other members of the school community; or

(2) disclosing such information to teachers and school officials, including teachers and school officials in other schools, who have legitimate educational interests in the behavior of the student.

(i) Drug and alcohol violation disclosures

(1) In general. Nothing in this Act or the Higher Education Act of 1965 [20 U. S. C. 1001 et seq.] shall be construed to prohibit an institution of higher education from disclosing, to a parent or legal guardian of a student, information regarding any violation of any Federal, State, or local law, or of any rule or policy of the institution, governing the use or possession of alcohol or a controlled substance, regardless of whether that information is contained in the student's education records, if-

(A) the student is under the age of 21; and

(B) the institution determines that the student has committed a disciplinary violation with respect to such use or possession.

(2) State law regarding disclosure. Nothing in paragraph (1) shall be construed to supersede any provision of State law that prohibits an institution of higher education from making the disclosure described in subsection (a) of this section.

(j) Investigation and prosecution of terrorism

(1) In general. Notwithstanding subsections (a) through (i) of this section or any provision of State law, the Attorney General (or any Federal officer or employee, in a position not lower than an Assistant Attorney General, designated by the Attorney General) may submit a written application to a court of competent jurisdiction for an ex parte order requiring an educational agency or institution to permit the Attorney General (or his designee) to-

(A) collect education records in the possession of the educational agency or institution that are relevant to an authorized investigation or prosecution of an offense listed in section 2332b (g)(5)(B) of title 18, or an act of domestic or international terrorism as defined in section 2331 of that title; and

(B) for official purposes related to the investigation or prosecution of an offense described in paragraph (1)(A), retain, disseminate, and use (including as evidence at trial or in other administrative or judicial proceedings) such records, consistent with such guidelines as the Attorney General, after consultation with the Secretary, shall issue to protect confidentiality.

(2) Application and approval.

(A) In general. An application under paragraph (1) shall certify that there are specific and articulable facts giving reason to believe that the education records are likely to contain information described in paragraph (1)(A).

(B) The court shall issue an order described in paragraph (1) if the court finds that the application for the order includes the certification described in subparagraph (A).

(3) Protection of educational agency or institution. An educational agency or institution that, in good faith, produces education records in accordance with an order issued under this subsection shall not be liable to any person for that production.

(4) Record-keeping. Subsection (b)(4) of this section does not apply to education records subject to a court order under this subsection.

20 U. S. C. 1232h. Protection of pupil rights

(a) **Inspection of instructional materials by parents or guardians**. All instructional materials, including teacher's manuals, films, tapes, or other supplementary material which will be used in connection with any survey, analysis, or evaluation as part of any applicable program **shall be available** for inspection by the parents or guardians of the children.

(b) **Limits on survey, analysis, or evaluations. No student shall be required**, as part of any applicable program, **to submit to a survey, analysis, or evaluation that reveals information** concerning—

(1) political affiliations or beliefs of the student or the student's parent;

(2) mental or psychological problems of the student or the student's family;

(3) sex behavior or attitudes;

(4) illegal, anti-social, self-incriminating, or demeaning behavior;

(5) critical appraisals of other individuals with whom respondents have close family relationships;

(6) legally recognized privileged or analogous relationships, such as those of lawyers, physicians, and ministers;

(7) religious practices, affiliations, or beliefs of the student or student's parent; or

(8) income (other than that required by law to determine eligibility for participation in a program or for receiving financial assistance under such program), without the prior consent of the student (if the student is an adult or emancipated minor), or in the case of an unemancipated minor, without the prior written consent of the parent.

(c) **Development of local policies concerning student privacy, parental access to information, and administration of certain physical examinations to minors.**

(1) **Development and adoption of local policies.** Except as provided in subsections (a) and (b) of this section, a local educational agency that receives funds under any applicable program shall develop and adopt policies, in consultation with parents, regarding the following:

(A)

(i) The **right of a parent of a student to inspect**, upon the request of the parent, a survey created by a third party before the survey is administered or distributed by a school to a student; and

(ii) any applicable procedures for granting a request by a parent for reasonable access to such survey within a reasonable period of time after the request is received.

(B) **Arrangements to protect student privacy** that are provided by the agency in the event of the administration or distribution of a survey to a student containing one or more of the following items (including the right of a parent of a student to inspect, upon the request of the parent, **any survey** containing one or more of such items):

(i) Political affiliations or beliefs of the student or the student's parent.

(ii) Mental or psychological problems of the student or the student's family.

(iii) Sex behavior or attitudes.

(iv) Illegal, anti-social, self-incriminating, or demeaning behavior.

(v) Critical appraisals of other individuals with whom respondents have close family relationships.

(vi) Legally recognized privileged or analogous relationships, such as those of lawyers, physicians, and ministers.

(vii) Religious practices, affiliations, or beliefs of the student or the student's parent.

(viii) Income (other than that required by law to determine eligibility for participation in a program or for receiving financial assistance under such program).

(C)

(i) The **right of a parent** of a student **to inspect**, upon the request of the parent, **any instructional material used as part of the educational curriculum** for the student; and

(ii) any applicable procedures for granting a request by a parent for reasonable access to instructional material within a reasonable period of time after the request is received.

(D) The administration of physical examinations or screenings that the school or agency may administer to a student.

(E) The **collection**, disclosure, or use of personal information collected from students for the purpose of **marketing or for selling** that information (or otherwise providing that information to others for that purpose), including arrangements to protect student privacy that are provided by the agency in the event of such collection, disclosure, or use.

(F)

(i) The right of a parent of a student to inspect, upon the request of the parent, any instrument used in the collection of personal information under subparagraph (E) before the instrument is administered or distributed to a student; and

(ii) any applicable procedures for granting a request by a parent for reasonable access to such instrument within a reasonable period of time after the request is received.

(2) Parental notification.

(A) Notification of policies. The policies developed by a local educational agency under paragraph (1) shall provide for reasonable notice of the adoption or continued use of such policies directly to the parents of students enrolled in schools served by that agency. At a minimum, the agency shall—

(i) provide such notice at least annually, at the beginning of the school year, and within a reasonable period of time after any substantive change in such policies; and

(ii) offer an opportunity for the parent (and for purposes of an activity described in subparagraph (C)(i), in the case of a student of an appropriate age, the student) to opt the student out of participation in an activity described in subparagraph (C).

(B) Notification of specific events. The local educational agency shall directly notify the parent of a student, at least annually at the beginning of the school year, of the specific or approximate dates during the school year when activities described in subparagraph (C) are scheduled, or expected to be scheduled.

(C) Activities requiring notification. The following activities require notification under this paragraph:

(i) Activities involving the collection, disclosure, or use of personal information collected from students for the purpose of marketing or for selling that information (or otherwise providing that information to others for that purpose).

(ii) The administration of any survey containing one or more items described in clauses (i) through (viii) of paragraph (1)(B).

(iii) Any nonemergency, invasive physical examination or screening that is-

(I) required as a condition of attendance;

(II) administered by the school and scheduled by the school in advance; and

(III) not necessary to protect the immediate health and safety of the student, or of other students.

(3) Existing policies. A local educational agency need not develop and adopt new policies if the State educational agency or local educational agency has in place, on January 8, 2002, policies covering the requirements of paragraph (1). The agency shall provide reasonable notice of such existing policies to parents and guardians of students, in accordance with paragraph (2).

(4) Exceptions.

(A) Educational products or services. Paragraph (1)(E) does not apply to the collection, disclosure, or use of personal information collected from students for the exclusive purpose of developing, evaluating, or providing educational products or services for, or to, students or educational institutions, such as the following:

(i) College or other postsecondary education recruitment, or military recruitment.

(ii) Book clubs, magazines, and programs providing access to low-cost literary products.

(iii) Curriculum and instructional materials used by elementary schools and secondary schools.

(iv) Tests and assessments used by elementary schools and secondary schools to provide cognitive, evaluative, diagnostic, clinical, aptitude, or achievement information about students (or to generate other statistically useful data for the purpose of securing such tests and assessments) and the subsequent analysis and public release of the aggregate data from such tests and assessments.

(v) The sale by students of products or services to raise funds for school-related or education-related activities.

(vi) Student recognition programs.

(B) State law exception. The provisions of this subsection—

(i) shall not be construed to preempt applicable provisions of State law that require parental notification; and

(ii) do not apply to any physical examination or screening that is permitted or required by an applicable State law, including physical examinations or screenings that are permitted without parental notification.

(5) General provisions.

(A) Rules of construction.

(i) This section does not supersede section 1232g of this title.

(ii) Paragraph (1)(D) **does not apply** to a survey administered to a student in accordance with the Individuals with Disabilities Education Act (20 U. S. C. 1400 et seq.).

(B) Student rights. The rights provided to parents under this section transfer to the student when the student turns 18 years old, or is an emancipated minor (under an applicable State law) at any age.

(C) Information activities. The Secretary shall annually inform each State educational agency and each local educational agency of the educational agency's obligations under this section and section 1232g of this title.

(D) Funding. A State educational agency or local educational agency may use funds provided under part A of title V of the Elementary and Secondary Education Act of 1965 [20 U. S. C. 7201 et seq.] to enhance parental involvement in areas affecting the in-school privacy of students.

(6) Definitions. As used in this subsection

(A) Instructional material. The term "**instructional material**" means instructional content that is provided to a student, regardless of its format, including printed or representational materials, audio-visual materials, and materials in electronic or digital formats (such as materials accessible through the Internet). The term does not include academic tests or academic assessments.

(B) Invasive physical examination. The term "**invasive physical examination**" means any medical examination that involves the exposure of private body parts, or any act during such examination that includes incision, insertion, or injection into the body, but does not include a hearing, vision, or scoliosis screening.

(C) Local educational agency. The term "**local educational agency**" means an elementary school, secondary school, school district, or local board of education that is the recipient of funds under an applicable program, but does not include a postsecondary institution.

(D) Parent. The term "**parent**" includes a legal guardian or other person standing in *loco parentis* (such as a grandparent or stepparent with whom the child lives, or a person who is legally responsible for the welfare of the child).

(E) Personal information. The term "personal information" means individually identifiable information including-

(i) a student or parent's first and last name;

(ii) a home or other physical address (including street name and the name of the city or town);

(iii) a telephone number; or

(iv) a Social Security identification number.

(F) Student. The term "**student**" means any elementary school or secondary school student.

(G) Survey. The term "**survey**" includes an evaluation.

(d) Notice. Educational agencies and institutions shall give parents and students effective notice of their rights under this section.

(e) Enforcement. The Secretary shall take such action as the Secretary determines appropriate to enforce this section, except that action to terminate assistance provided under an applicable program shall be taken only if the Secretary determines that-

(1) there has been a failure to comply with such section; and

(2) compliance with such section cannot be secured by voluntary means.

(f) Office and review board. The Secretary shall establish or designate an office and review board within the Department of Education to investigate, process, review, and adjudicate violations of the rights established under this section.

End of FERPA

CHAPTER 10

McKinney-Vento Homeless Assistance Act

For children who have been traumatized by the loss of home, friends, and perhaps death or injury of family members, returning to school is not only important for educational purposes; attendance at a school becomes an oasis of normalcy for them – Michael O'Connor, Esq.[1]

Education for Homeless Children and Youth

The McKinney-Vento Homeless Assistance Act requires that all school districts ensure that children whose families are homeless have access to school. This chapter begins with an overview of the McKinney-Vento Homeless Act, followed by the text of the statute. The statute is cited as 42 U. S. C. § 11431, *et seq.*

Policy Statement

The McKinney-Vento Homeless Assistance Act includes this Statement of Policy:

Each state shall ensure that each child of a homeless individual and each homeless youth has equal access to the same free, appropriate public education, including a public preschool education, as provided to other children and youths . . . to ensure that homeless children and youths are afforded the same free, appropriate public education as provided to other children and youths.[2]

States are prohibited from segregating ". . . homeless children in separate schools or separate programs within a school, based on the child's status as homeless."[3]

Definition of "Homeless Children and Youth"

Homeless children and youth means "individuals who lack a fixed, regular, and adequate nighttime residence . . . and includes children and youth who are sharing the housing of other persons due to loss of housing, economic hardship . . . are living in motels, hotels, trailer parks, or camping grounds . . . in emergency or transitional shelters; are abandoned in hospitals; or are awaiting foster care placement . . . are living in cars, parks, public spaces, abandoned buildings, substandard housing, bus or train stations, or similar settings; and migratory children."[4]

"In Best Interest of the Child"

School districts *shall* make decisions in the best interest of the child. In determining the best interest of the child, schools *shall*:

- Keep a homeless child or youth in the school of origin except when doing so is contrary to the wishes of the child's parent or guardian . . .
- Provide a written explanation, including a statement regarding the right to appeal to the parent or guard-

---

1   *Education Rights of Homeless Children* by Michael O'Connor, Esq. at www.wrightslaw.com/info/homeless.educate.htm, see also www.advocatesforchildren.org

2   42 U. S. C. §11431

3   42 U. S. C. § 11432(e)(3)

4   42 U. S. C. § 11434a(2)

ian if the school district sends a child to a school other than the school of origin or a school requested by the parent or guardian

- Ensure that the homeless liaison helps to make placement and enrollment decisions for an unaccompanied youth.[5]

Immediate Enrollment Required

School districts are required to **immediately enroll** homeless children, even if medical, academic and residency **records are not available.** The school shall immediately contact the last school attended to obtain relevant records. If the child needs immunizations or medical records, the school shall immediately refer the parent or guardian to the school district liaison who shall assist in obtaining the necessary immunizations or medical records.[6]

If there is a dispute about enrollment, the child "shall be **immediately admitted** to the school in which enrollment is sought, pending resolution of the dispute."[7]

Notice of Educational Rights

The law requires that a "**notice of the educational rights** of homeless children and youths is disseminated where such children and youths receive services . . . such as schools, family shelters, and soup kitchens . . . and that the parent or guardian . . . is fully informed of all transportation services . . . ."[8]

Child Find and Surrogate Parents

In IDEA 2004, the "Child Find" requirements that school districts identify, evaluate and provide services to all children with disabilities were specifically extended to homeless children.[9] The law also requires that "unaccompanied youth" (i.e., a homeless adolescent who is not accompanied by a parent or guardian) have a surrogate parent appointed. If the child is living in a homeless shelter, an employee of the shelter may serve as a temporary surrogate. [10]

Children with Disabilities Who Are Homeless

Children with disabilities who are homeless were expressly recognized when IDEA was reauthorized. IDEA incorporated the definition of "homeless children"[11] from the McKinney-Vento Act.

In Summation

In this chapter, you learned about powerful rights in the McKinney-Vento Homeless Assistance Act. States are responsible for ensuring that homeless children receive a free, appropriate public education. School districts are required to make decisions in the "best interests of the child," to ensure that homeless children are not segregated or stigmatized, and to provide notice of the rights of homeless children. The full text of the McKinney-Vento Homeless Assistance Act begins on the following page.

In the next section of *Wrightslaw: Special Education Law, 2nd Edition*, you learn about special education caselaw. Chapter 11 includes an overview of eight special education cases decided by the U. S. Supreme Court. Chapter 12 includes the full text of these decisions.

---

5   42 U. S. C. § 11432(g)(3)(B)
6   42 U. S. C. § 11432(g)(3)(C)
7   42 U. S. C. § 11432(g)(3)(E)
8   42 U. S. C. § 11432(g)(6)(A)
9   20 U. S. C. § 1412(a)(3)(A)
10 See Regulation 300.519
11 20 U. S. C. § 1401(11)

McKinney-Vento Homeless Assistance Act
42 U. S. C. § 11431 et seq.

42 U. S. C. §11431.Statement of policy

The following is the policy of the Congress:

(1) Each State educational agency shall ensure that **each child of a homeless individual and each homeless youth has equal access to the same free, appropriate public education, including a public preschool education**, as provided to other children and youths.

(2) In any State that has a compulsory residency requirement as a component of the State's compulsory school attendance laws or other laws, regulations, practices, or policies that may act as a barrier to the enrollment, attendance, or success in school of homeless children and youths, the State will review and undertake steps to revise such laws, regulations, practices, or policies **to ensure that homeless children and youths are afforded the same free, appropriate public education as provided to other children and youths.**

(3) Homelessness alone is not sufficient reason to separate students from the mainstream school environment.

(4) **Homeless children and youths should have access to the education and other services that such children and youths need** to ensure that such children and youths have an opportunity to meet the same challenging State student academic achievement standards to which all students are held.

42 U. S. C. §11432. Grants for State and local activities for the education of homeless children and youth

(a) General Authority. The Secretary is **authorized to make grants to States** in accordance with the provisions of this section to enable such States to carry out the activities described in subsections (d) through (g) of this section.

(b) Application. No State may receive a grant under this section unless the State educational agency submits an application to the Secretary at such time, in such manner, and containing or accompanied by such information as the Secretary may reasonably require.

(c) Allocation and reservations

(1) Allocation.

(A) Subject to subparagraph (B), the Secretary is authorized to allot to each State an amount that bears the same ratio to the amount appropriated for such year under section 11435 of this title that remains after the Secretary reserves funds under paragraph (2) and uses funds to carry out section 11434(d) and (h) of this title, as the amount allocated under section 1122 of the Elementary and Secondary Education Act of 1965 [20 U. S. C. 6332] to the State for that year bears to the total amount allocated under section 1122 of such Act to all States for that year, except that no State shall receive less than the greater of—

(i) $150,000;

(ii) one-fourth of 1 percent of the amount appropriated under section 11435 of this title for that year; or

(iii) the amount such State received under this section for fiscal year 2001.

(B) If there are insufficient funds in a fiscal year to allot to each State the minimum amount under subparagraph (A), the Secretary shall ratably reduce the allotments to all States based on the proportionate share that each State received under this subsection for the preceding fiscal year.

(2) Reservations.

(A) The Secretary is authorized to reserve 0.1 percent of the amount appropriated for each fiscal year under section 11435 of this title to be allocated by the Secretary among the United States Virgin Islands, Guam, American Samoa, and the Commonwealth of the Northern Mariana Islands, according to their respective need for assistance under this part, as determined by the Secretary.

(B)

(i) The Secretary shall transfer 1 percent of the amount appropriated for each fiscal year under section 11435 of this title to the Department of the Interior for programs for Indian students served by schools funded by the Secretary of the Interior, as determined under the Indian Self-Determination and Education Assistance Act (25 U. S. C. 450 et seq.), that are consistent with the purposes of the programs described in this part.

(ii) The Secretary and the Secretary of the Interior shall enter into an agreement, consistent with the requirements of this part, for the distribution and use of the funds described in clause (i) under terms that the Secretary determines best meet the purposes of the programs described in this part. Such agreement shall set forth the plans of the Secretary of the Interior for the use of the amounts transferred, including appropriate goals, objectives, and milestones.

(3) State defined. For purposes of this subsection, the term "State" does not include the United States Virgin Islands, Guam, American Samoa, or the Commonwealth of the Northern Mariana Islands.

(d) Activities. Grants under this section **shall be used for the following**:

(1) To carry out the policies set forth in section 11431 of this title in the State.

(2) To **provide activities for, and services to, homeless children**, including preschool-aged homeless children, and youths that **enable such children and youths to enroll in, attend, and succeed in school**, or, if appropriate, in preschool programs.

(3) To **establish or designate** an **Office of Coordinator for Education of Homeless Children and Youths** in the State educational agency in accordance with subsection (f) of this section.

(4) To prepare and carry out the State plan described in subsection (g) of this section.

(5) To develop and implement **professional development programs for school personnel** to heighten their awareness of, and capacity to respond to, specific problems in the education of homeless children and youths.

(e) State and local subgrants.

(1) Minimum disbursements by states. From the sums made available each year to carry out this part, the State educational agency shall distribute not less than 75 percent in subgrants to local educational agencies for the purposes of carrying out section 11433 of this title, except that States funded at the minimum level set forth in subsection (c)(1) of this section shall distribute not less than 50 percent in subgrants to local educational agencies for the purposes of carrying out section 11433 of this title.

(2) Use by State educational agency. A State educational agency may use funds made available for State use under this part to conduct activities under subsection (f) of this section directly or through grants or contracts.

(3) Prohibition on segregating homeless students.

(A) In general. Except as provided in subparagraph (B) and section 11433(a)(2)(B)(ii) of this title, in providing a free public education to a homeless child or youth, **no State** receiving funds under this part **shall segregate such child or youth in a separate school, or in a separate program within a school, based on such child's or youth's status as homeless.**

(B) Exception[12]

. . .

(f) **Functions of the Office of Coordinator.** The Coordinator for Education of Homeless Children and Youths established in each State **shall–**

(1) **gather reliable, valid, and comprehensive information on the nature and extent of the problems homeless children and youths** have in gaining access to public preschool programs and to public elementary schools and secondary schools, the **difficulties in identifying the special needs** of such children and youths, any progress made by the State educational agency and local educational agencies in the State in addressing such problems and difficulties, and the **success of the programs** under this part in allowing homeless children and youths to enroll in, attend, and succeed in, school;

(2) develop and carry out the State plan described in subsection (g) of this section;

(3) collect and transmit to the Secretary, at such time and in such manner as the Secretary may require, a report containing such information as the Secretary determines is necessary to assess the educational needs of homeless children and youths within the State;

(4) **facilitate coordination between the State educational agency, the State social services agency, and other agencies** (including agencies providing mental health services) **to provide services to homeless children,** including preschool-aged homeless children, and youths, and to families of such children and youths;

(5) in order to improve the provision of comprehensive education and related services to homeless children and youths and their families, coordinate and collaborate with–

(A) **educators,** including child development and preschool program personnel;

(B) **providers of services** to homeless and runaway children and youths and homeless families (including domestic violence agencies, shelter operators, transitional housing facilities, runaway and homeless youth centers, and transitional living programs for homeless youths);

(C) **local educational agency liaisons** designated under subsection (g)(1)(J)(ii) of this section for homeless children and youths; and

(D) **community organizations and groups** representing homeless children and youths and their families; and

(6) provide technical assistance to local educational agencies in coordination with local educational agency liaisons designated under subsection (g)(1)(J)(ii) of this section, to ensure that local educational agencies comply with the requirements of subsection (e)(3) of this section and paragraphs (3) through (7) of subsection (g) of this section.

(g) **State Plan.**

(1) **In General.** Each State **shall submit to the Secretary a plan to provide for the education of homeless children and youths** within the State. Such plan shall include the following:

(A) A description of how such children and youths are (or will be) given the opportunity to meet the **same challenging State academic achievement standards** all students are expected to meet.

(B) A description of the procedures the State educational agency will use **to identify such children and youths** in the State and to assess their special needs.

(C) A **description of procedures for the prompt resolution of disputes regarding the educational placement** of homeless children and youths.

(D) A description of programs for school personnel (including principals, attendance officers, teachers, enrollment personnel, and pupil services personnel) to heighten the awareness of such personnel of the

---

12 The exception to 3(A) continued for several pages with numerous procedural safeguard requirements and was limited to San Joaquin County, Orange County, and San Diego County, in California, and Maricopa County, in Arizona. For that reason, it is not included in this document.

specific needs of runaway and homeless youths.

(E) A **description of procedures that ensure** that homeless children and youths who meet the relevant eligibility criteria are able to participate in Federal, State, or local food programs.

(F) A description of procedures that ensure that–

(i) homeless children have **equal access to the same public preschool programs**, administered by the State agency, as provided to other children in the State;

(ii) homeless youths and youths separated from the public schools are identified and accorded **equal access to appropriate secondary education and support services**; and

(iii) homeless children and youths who meet the relevant eligibility criteria are able to participate in Federal, State, or local **before- and after-school care programs**.

(G) Strategies to address problems identified in the report provided to the Secretary under subsection (f)(3) of this section.

(H) Strategies to address other problems with respect to the education of homeless children and youths, including **problems resulting from enrollment delays** that are caused by–

(i) immunization and medical records requirements;

(ii) residency requirements;

(iii) lack of birth certificates, school records, or other documentation;

(iv) guardianship issues; or

(v) uniform or dress code requirements.

(I) A demonstration that the State educational agency and local educational agencies in the State have developed, and shall review and revise, **policies to remove barriers to the enrollment and retention of homeless children and youths in schools** in the State.

(J) Assurances that–

(i) the State educational agency and local educational agencies in the State will adopt policies and practices to **ensure that homeless children and youths are not stigmatized or segregated** on the basis of their status as homeless;

(ii) local educational agencies will designate an appropriate staff person, who may also be a co-ordinator for other Federal programs, as a local educational agency liaison for homeless children and youths, to carry out the duties described in paragraph (6)(A); and

(iii) the State and its local educational agencies will adopt policies and practices to ensure that transportation is provided, at the request of the parent or guardian (or in the case of an unaccompanied youth, the liaison), to and from the school of origin, as determined in paragraph (3)(A), in accordance with the following, as applicable:

(I) If the homeless child or youth continues to live in the area served by the local educational agency in which the school of origin is located, the child's or youth's **transportation to and from the school** of origin **shall be provided or arranged** by the local educational agency in which the school of origin is located.

(II) If the homeless child's or youth's living arrangements in the area served by the local educational agency of origin terminate and the child or youth, though continuing his or her education in the school of origin, begins living in an area served by another local educational agency, the local educational agency of origin and the local educational agency in which the homeless child or youth is living shall agree upon a method to apportion the responsibility and costs for providing the child with transportation to and from the school of origin. If the local educational agencies are unable to agree upon such method, the responsibility and costs for transportation shall be shared equally.

(2) Compliance.

    (A) In general. Each plan adopted under this subsection shall also describe how the State will ensure that local educational agencies in the State will comply with the requirements of paragraphs (3) through (7).

    (B) Coordination. Such plan shall indicate what technical assistance the State will furnish to local educational agencies and how compliance efforts will be coordinated with the local educational agency liaisons designated under paragraph (1)(J)(ii).

(3) Local educational agency requirements.

    (A) In general. The **local educational agency serving each child or youth** to be assisted under this part **shall, according to the child's or youth's best interest–**

        (i) **continue the child's or youth's education** in the school of origin for the duration of homelessness–

            (I) in any case in which a **family becomes homeless between academic years or during an academic year**; or

            (II) for the **remainder of the academic year**, if the child or youth becomes permanently housed during an academic year; or

        (ii) enroll the child or youth in any public school that non-homeless students who live in the attendance area in which the child or youth is actually living are eligible to attend.

    (B) Best interest. In determining **the best interest of the child or youth** under subparagraph (A), the local educational agency **shall–**

        (i) to the extent feasible, **keep a homeless child or youth in the school of origin**, except when doing so is contrary to the wishes of the child's or youth's parent or guardian;

        (ii) **provide a written explanation, including a statement regarding the right to appeal** under subparagraph (E), to the homeless child's or youth's parent or guardian, if the local educational agency sends such child or youth to a school other than the school of origin or a school requested by the parent or guardian; and

        (iii) in the case of **an unaccompanied youth**, ensure that **the homeless liaison** designated under paragraph (1)(J)(ii) **assists in placement or enrollment decisions** under this subparagraph, considers the views of such unaccompanied youth, and provides notice to such youth of the right to appeal under subparagraph (E).

    (C) Enrollment.

        (i) The school selected in accordance with this paragraph **shall immediately enroll the homeless child or youth, even if the child or youth is unable to produce records normally required for enrollment,** such as previous academic records, medical records, proof of residency, or other documentation.

        (ii) The enrolling school **shall immediately contact the school last attended** by the child or youth to obtain relevant academic and other records.

        (iii) If the child or youth **needs to obtain immunizations, or immunization or medical records,** the enrolling school **shall immediately refer the parent or guardian** of the child or youth **to the local educational agency liaison** designated under paragraph (1)(J)(ii), **who shall assist** in obtaining necessary immunizations, or immunization or medical records, in accordance with subparagraph (D).

    (D) Records. Any record ordinarily kept by the school, including immunization or medical records, academic records, birth certificates, guardianship records, and evaluations for special services or programs, regarding each homeless child or youth shall be maintained–

(i) so that the records are available, in a timely fashion, when a child or youth enters a new school or school district; and

(ii) in a manner consistent with section 1232g of title 20.

(E) **Enrollment disputes. If a dispute arises over school selection or enrollment** in a school–

(i) the **child or youth shall be immediately admitted to the school in which enrollment is sought, pending resolution of the dispute;**

(ii) the **parent or guardian** of the child or youth **shall be provided with a written explanation of the school's decision regarding school selection or enrollment, including the rights of the parent, guardian, or youth to appeal the decision;**

(iii) the child, youth, parent, or guardian **shall be referred to the local educational agency liaison** designated under paragraph (1)(J)(ii), who shall **carry out the dispute resolution process** as described in paragraph (1)(C) **as expeditiously as possible** after receiving notice of the dispute; and

(iv) in the case of **an unaccompanied youth,** the homeless liaison shall ensure that the youth **is immediately enrolled in school pending resolution of the dispute.**

(F) **Placement choice.** The **choice regarding placement** shall be made regardless of whether the **child or youth lives with the homeless parents or has been temporarily placed elsewhere.**

(G) **School of origin defined.** In this paragraph, the term "school of origin" means the school that the child or youth attended when permanently housed or the school in which the child or youth was last enrolled.

(H) **Contact information.** Nothing in this part shall prohibit a local educational agency from requiring a parent or guardian of a homeless child to submit contact information.

(4) **Comparable services.** Each homeless child or youth to be assisted under this part **shall be provided services comparable to services offered to other students in the school** selected under paragraph (3), including the following:

(A) **Transportation services.**

(B) **Educational services for which the child or youth meets the eligibility criteria,** such as services provided under title I of the Elementary and Secondary Education Act of 1965 [20 U. S. C. 6301 et seq.] or similar State or local programs, educational programs for children with disabilities, and educational programs for students with limited English proficiency.

(C) Programs in **vocational and technical education.**

(D) Programs for **gifted and talented students.**

(E) **School nutrition programs.**

(5) **Coordination.**

(A) **In general.** Each local educational agency serving homeless children and youths that receives assistance under this part **shall coordinate–**

(i) the **provision of services** under this part with local social services agencies and **other agencies or programs providing services** to homeless children and youths and their families, including services and programs funded under the Runaway and Homeless Youth Act (42 U. S. C. 5701 *et. seq.*); and

(ii) with other local educational agencies on inter-district issues, such as transportation or transfer of school records.

(B) **Housing assistance.** If applicable, each State educational agency and local educational agency that receives assistance under this part shall coordinate with State and local housing agencies responsible for developing the **comprehensive housing affordability strategy** described in section 12705 of this title **to minimize educational disruption for children and youths who become homeless.**

(C) Coordination purpose. The coordination required under subparagraphs (A) and (B) shall be designed to–

(i) ensure that homeless children and youths have access and reasonable proximity to available education and related support services; and

(ii) raise the awareness of school personnel and service providers of the effects of short-term stays in a shelter and other challenges associated with homelessness.

(6) Local educational agency liaison.

(A) Duties. Each local educational agency liaison for homeless children and youths, designated under paragraph (1)(J)(ii), **shall ensure** that–

(i) **homeless children and youths are identified by school personnel** and through coordination activities with other entities and agencies;

(ii) **homeless children and youths enroll in, and have a full and equal opportunity to succeed in, schools of that local educational agency;**

(iii) homeless families, children, and youths **receive educational services** for which such families, children, and youths are eligible, including Head Start and Even Start programs and preschool programs administered by the local educational agency, **and referrals** to health care services, dental services, mental health services, and other appropriate services;

(iv) the **parents or guardians** of homeless children and youths **are informed of the educational and related opportunities available** to their children and are provided with meaningful opportunities to participate in the education of their children;

(v) **public notice of the educational rights of homeless children and youths is disseminated where such children and youths receive services under this chapter, such as schools, family shelters, and soup kitchens;**

(vi) enrollment disputes are mediated in accordance with paragraph (3)(E); and

(vii) the **parent or guardian** of a homeless child or youth, and any unaccompanied youth, **is fully informed of all transportation services**, including transportation to the school of origin, as described in paragraph (1)(J)(iii), and is assisted in accessing transportation to the school that is selected under paragraph (3)(A).

(B) Notice. State coordinators established under subsection (d)(3) of this section and local educational agencies shall inform school personnel, service providers, and advocates working with homeless families of the duties of the local educational agency liaisons.

(C) Local and State coordination. Local educational agency liaisons for homeless children and youths shall, as a part of their duties, coordinate and collaborate with State coordinators and community and school personnel responsible for the provision of education and related services to homeless children and youths.

(7) Review and revisions.

(A) In general. Each State educational agency and local educational agency that receives assistance under this part shall review and revise any policies that may act as barriers to the enrollment of homeless children and youths in schools that are selected under paragraph (3).

(B) Consideration. In reviewing and revising such policies, consideration shall be given to issues concerning transportation, immunization, residency, birth certificates, school records and other documentation, and guardianship.

(C) Special attention. Special attention shall be given to ensuring the enrollment and attendance of homeless children and youths who are not currently attending school.

42 U. S. C. §11433 - Local educational agency subgrants for education of homeless children and youth

(a) **General authority.**

(1) **In general.** The State educational agency shall, in accordance with section 11432(e) of this title, and from amounts made available to such agency under section 11435 of this title, make subgrants to local educational agencies for the purpose of facilitating the enrollment, attendance, and success in school of homeless children and youths.

(2) **Services.**

(A) **In general.** Services under paragraph (1)–

(i) may be provided through programs on school grounds or at other facilities;

(ii) shall, to the maximum extent practicable, be provided through existing programs and mechanisms that integrate homeless children and youths with non-homeless children and youths; and

(iii) shall be designed to expand or improve services provided as part of a school's regular academic program, but not to replace such services provided under such program.

(B) **Services on school grounds.** If services under paragraph (1) are provided on school grounds, schools–

(i) may use funds under this part to provide the same services to other children and youths who are determined by the local educational agency to be at risk of failing in, or dropping out of, school, subject to the requirements of clause (ii); and

(ii) except as otherwise provided in section 11432(e)(3)(B) of this title, shall not provide services in settings within a school that segregate homeless children and youths from other children and youths, except as necessary for short periods of time–

(I) for health and safety emergencies; or

(II) to provide temporary, special, and supplementary services to meet the unique needs of homeless children and youths.

(3) **Requirement.** Services provided under this section shall not replace the regular academic program and shall be designed to expand upon or improve services provided as part of the school's regular academic program.

(b) **Application.** A local educational agency that desires to receive a subgrant under this section **shall submit an application** to the State educational agency at such time, in such manner, and containing or accompanied by such information as the State educational agency may reasonably require. Such application shall include the following:

(1) An **assessment of the educational and related needs of homeless children and youths** in the area served by such agency (which may be undertaken as part of needs assessments for other disadvantaged groups).

(2) A **description of the services and programs** for which assistance is sought to address the needs identified in paragraph (1).

(3) An assurance that the local educational agency's combined fiscal effort per student, or the aggregate expenditures of that agency and the State with respect to the provision of free public education by such agency for the fiscal year preceding the fiscal year for which the determination is made, was not less than 90 percent of such combined fiscal effort or aggregate expenditures for the second fiscal year preceding the fiscal year for which the determination is made.

(4) An assurance that the applicant complies with, or will use requested funds to comply with, paragraphs (3) through (7) of section 11432(g) of this title.

(5) A description of policies and procedures, consistent with section 11432(e)(3) of this title, that the agency will implement to ensure that activities carried out by the agency will not isolate or stigmatize homeless children and youths.

(c) Awards.

(1) In general. The State educational agency shall, in accordance with the requirements of this part and from amounts made available to it under section 11435 of this title, make competitive subgrants to local educational agencies that submit applications under subsection (b) of this section. Such **subgrants shall be awarded on the basis of the need** of such agencies for assistance under this part and the quality of the applications submitted.

(2) Need. In determining need under paragraph (1), the State educational agency may consider the number of homeless children and youths enrolled in preschool, elementary, and secondary schools within the area served by the local educational agency, and **shall consider the needs of such children and youths and the ability of the local educational agency to meet such needs.** The State educational agency may also consider the following:

(A) The extent to which the proposed use of funds will **facilitate the enrollment, retention, and educational success** of homeless children and youths.

(B) The extent to which the application–

(i) reflects coordination with other local and State agencies that serve homeless children and youths; and

(ii) describes how the applicant will meet the requirements of section 11432(g)(3) of this title.

(C) The extent to which the applicant exhibits in the application and in current practice a commitment to education for all homeless children and youths.

(D) Such other criteria as the State agency determines appropriate.

(3) Quality. In determining the quality of applications under paragraph (1), the State educational agency shall consider the following:

(A) The applicant's needs assessment under subsection (b)(1) of this section and the likelihood that the program presented in the application will meet such needs.

(B) The types, intensity, and coordination of the services to be provided under the program.

(C) The involvement of parents or guardians of homeless children or youths in the education of their children.

(D) The extent to which homeless children and youths will be integrated within the regular education program.

(E) The quality of the applicant's evaluation plan for the program.

(F) The extent to which services provided under this part will be coordinated with other services available to homeless children and youths and their families.

(G) Such other measures as the State educational agency considers indicative of a high-quality program, such as the extent to which the local educational agency will provide case management or related services to unaccompanied youths.

(4) Duration of grants. Grants awarded under this section shall be for terms not to exceed 3 years.

(d) Authorized activities. A **local educational agency may use funds** awarded under this section for activities that carry out the purpose of this part, including the following:

(1) The provision of **tutoring, supplemental instruction, and enriched educational services** that are linked to the achievement of the same challenging State academic content standards and challenging State student academic achievement standards the State establishes for other children and youths.

(2) The provision of **expedited evaluations of the strengths and needs of homeless children** and youths, including **needs and eligibility for programs and services** (such as educational programs for gifted and talented students, **children with disabilities**, and students with limited English proficiency, services provided under title I of the Elementary and Secondary Education Act of 1965 [20 U. S. C. 6301 *et seq.*] or similar State or local programs, programs in vocational and technical education, and school nutrition programs).

(3) **Professional development** and other activities **for educators and pupil services personnel** that are designed to **heighten the understanding and sensitivity** of such personnel **to the needs of homeless children and youths, the rights of such children and youths** under this part, and the **specific educational needs of runaway and homeless youths.**

(4) The provision of **referral services** to homeless children and youths for medical, dental, mental, and other health services.

(5) The provision of assistance to defray the **excess cost of transportation** for students under section 11432(g)(4)(A) of this title, not otherwise provided through Federal, State, or local funding, where necessary to enable students to attend the school selected under section 11432(g)(3) of this title.

(6) The provision of **developmentally appropriate early childhood education programs**, not otherwise provided through Federal, State, or local funding, for preschool-aged homeless children.

(7) The provision of services and assistance **to attract, engage, and retain homeless children and youths, and unaccompanied youths**, in public school programs and services provided to non-homeless children and youths.

(8) The provision for homeless children and youths of **before- and after-school, mentoring, and summer programs** in which a teacher or other qualified individual provides **tutoring, homework assistance, and supervision of educational activities.**

(9) If necessary, the payment of fees and other costs associated with tracking, obtaining, and transferring records necessary to enroll homeless children and youths in school, including birth certificates, immunization or medical records, academic records, guardianship records, and evaluations for special programs or services.

(10) The **provision of education and training to the parents** of homeless children and youths about the rights of, and resources available to, such children and youths.

(11) The development of coordination between schools and agencies providing services to homeless children and youths, as described in section 11432(g)(5) of this title.

(12) The **provision of pupil services (including violence prevention counseling)** and referrals for such services.

(13) Activities to address the particular **needs** of homeless children and youths **that may arise from domestic violence.**

(14) The adaptation of space and **purchase of supplies for any non-school facilities** made available under subsection (a)(2) of this section to provide services under this subsection.

(15) The **provision of school supplies, including those supplies to be distributed at shelters or temporary housing facilities,** or other appropriate locations.

(16) The **provision of other extraordinary or emergency assistance needed to enable homeless children and youths to attend school.**

42 U. S. C. §11434. Secretarial responsibilities.

(a) **Review of State plans.** In reviewing the State plan submitted by a State educational agency under section 11432(g) of this title, the Secretary shall use a peer review process and shall evaluate whether State laws, policies,

and practices described in such plan adequately address the problems of homeless children and youths relating to access to education and placement as described in such plan.

(b) Technical assistance. The Secretary shall provide support and technical assistance to a State educational agency to assist such agency in carrying out its responsibilities under this part, if requested by the State educational agency.

(c) Notice. The Secretary shall, before the next school year that begins after January 8, 2002, create and disseminate nationwide a public notice of the educational rights of homeless children and youths and disseminate such notice to other Federal agencies, programs, and grantees, including Head Start grantees, Health Care for the Homeless grantees, Emergency Food and Shelter grantees, and homeless assistance programs administered by the Department of Housing and Urban Development.

(d) Evaluation and dissemination. The Secretary shall conduct evaluation and dissemination activities of programs designed to meet the educational needs of homeless elementary and secondary school students, and may use funds appropriated under section 11435 of this title to conduct such activities.

(e) Submission and distribution. The Secretary shall require applications for grants under this part to be submitted to the Secretary not later than the expiration of the 60-day period beginning on the date that funds are available for purposes of making such grants and shall make such grants not later than the expiration of the 120-day period beginning on such date.

(f) Determination by Secretary. The Secretary, based on the information received from the States and information gathered by the Secretary under subsection (h) of this section, shall determine the extent to which State educational agencies are ensuring that each homeless child and homeless youth has access to a free appropriate public education, as described in section 11431(1) of this title.

(g) Guidelines. The Secretary shall develop, issue, and publish in the Federal Register, not later than 60 days after January 8, 2002, school enrollment guidelines for States with respect to homeless children and youths. The guidelines shall describe-

(1) successful ways in which a State may assist local educational agencies to immediately enroll homeless children and youths in school; and

(2) how a State can review the State's requirements regarding immunization and medical or school records and make such revisions to the requirements as are appropriate and necessary in order to enroll homeless children and youths in school immediately.

(h) Information.

(1) In general. From funds appropriated under section 11435 of this title, the Secretary shall, directly or through grants, contracts, or cooperative agreements, periodically collect and disseminate data and information regarding-

(A) the number and location of homeless children and youths;

(B) the education and related services such children and youths receive;

(C) the extent to which the needs of homeless children and youths are being met; and

(D) such other data and information as the Secretary determines to be necessary and relevant to carry out this part.

(2) Coordination. The Secretary shall coordinate such collection and dissemination with other agencies and entities that receive assistance and administer programs under this part.

(i) Report. Not later than 4 years after January 8, 2002, the Secretary shall prepare and submit to the President and the Committee on Education and the Workforce of the House of Representatives and the Committee on Health, Education, Labor, and Pensions of the Senate a report on the status of education of homeless children and youths, which shall include information on--

(1) the education of homeless children and youths; and

(2) the actions of the Secretary and the effectiveness of the programs supported under this part.

42 U. S. C. §11434a - Definitions

For purposes of this part:

(1) The terms "**enroll**" and "**enrollment**" include attending classes and participating fully in school activities.

(2) The term "**homeless children and youths**"–

(A) **means individuals who lack a fixed, regular, and adequate nighttime residence** (within the meaning of section 11302(a)(1) of this title); and

(B) **includes -**

(i) **children and youths who are sharing the housing of other persons due to loss of housing, economic hardship,** or a similar reason; are **living in motels, hotels, trailer parks, or camping grounds** due to the lack of alternative adequate accommodations; are **living in emergency or transitional shelters**; are abandoned in hospitals; or are awaiting foster care placement;

(ii) **children and youths who have a primary nighttime residence** that is a public or private place **not designed for or ordinarily used as a regular sleeping accommodation** for human beings (within the meaning of section 11302(a)(2)(C) of this title);

(iii) children and youths who are **living in cars, parks, public spaces, abandoned buildings, substandard housing, bus or train stations, or similar settings**; and

(iv) **migratory children** (as such term is defined in section 6399 of title 20 who qualify as homeless for the purposes of this part because the children are living in circumstances described in clauses (i) through (iii).

(3) The terms "**local educational agency**" and "**State educational agency**" have the meanings given such terms in section 7801 of title 20.

(4) The term "**Secretary**" means the Secretary of Education.

(5) The term "**State**" means each of the 50 States, the District of Columbia, and the Commonwealth of Puerto Rico.

(6) The term "**unaccompanied youth**" includes a youth not in the physical custody of a parent or guardian.

42 U. S. C. §11435. Authorization of Appropriations

For the purpose of carrying out this part, there are authorized to be appropriated $70,000,000 for fiscal year 2002 and such sums as may be necessary for each of fiscal years 2003 through 2007.

End of McKinney-Vento Homeless Assistance Act

Section Four

U. S. Supreme Court Cases

CHAPTER 11

Overview
U. S. Supreme Court Cases

In this chapter, you will learn about decisions in eight special education cases decided by the United States Supreme Court.[1] You will also learn about a case that will be decided during the 2006-2007 term. The full text of the decisions is in Chapter 12. As you read, you will see how the issues have changed since the first Supreme Court decision in 1982.

Congress enacted Public Law 94-142 in 1975. The law, originally known as the Education of All Handicapped Children Act, is now the Individuals with Disabilities Education Act of 2004. The law requires public schools to provide a free, appropriate public education (FAPE) to children with disabilities at no cost to the child's parent.

After the law was enacted, courts began to issue different rulings about this term. As more cases were litigated, some courts decided that a "free appropriate public education" meant that the handicapped child was entitled to an education that would help the child become self-sufficient. Other courts decided that school districts were required "to maximize the potential of each handicapped child commensurate with the opportunity provided non-handicapped children."

When a parent or school appeals a case to the U. S. Supreme Court, they file a Petition for Certiorari. Out of several thousand of Petitions received each year, the Supreme Court grants cert in fewer than 100 cases. When the Supreme Court agrees to hear a case, the Court also determines the issue or "Question Presented."

In 1982, the U. S. Supreme Court agreed to hear its first special education case.

Free Appropriate Public Education (FAPE): *Bd. of Education v. Rowley* (1982)

Amy Rowley was a deaf child who attended school in the Hendrick Hudson Central School District in New York. When Amy entered first grade, her parents requested that the school provide a qualified sign-language interpreter in her academic classes. After consulting with various experts, the school refused to provide an interpreter because "Amy was achieving educationally, academically, and socially" without this assistance.

After losing at the due process and review levels, Amy's parents appealed to the U. S. District Court. The Court found that Amy "is a remarkably well adjusted child who . . . performs better than the average child in her class and is advancing easily from grade to grade."[2]

However, the Court also found that Amy "understands considerably less of what is going on in class than she would if she were not deaf" and "is not learning as much, or performing as well academically, as she would without her handicap." *Id.* The Court concluded that this disparity between Amy's achievement and her potential indicated that she was not receiving a "free appropriate public education" which was defined by that district court as "an opportunity to achieve her full potential commensurate with the opportunity provided to other children."

---

[1] The cases included in this book are the most critical decisions issued by the U. S. Supreme Court. The Court has published other decisions. See *Smith v. Robinson*, 468 U.S. 992 (1984), *Dellmuth v. Muth*, 491 U.S. 223 (1989), *Zobrest v. Catalina Foothills Sch. District*, 509 U.S. 1 (1993), and *Bd. of Educ. Kiryas Joel Village School v. Grumet*, 512 U.S. 687 (1994). In some instances, Congress changed the statute after a decision. Other cases have had less impact on parents and schools.

[2] *Rowley v. Bd. of Education*, 483 F. Supp. 528, 531 (SD NY 1980)

Id.

The school district appealed. The U. S. Court of Appeals for the Second Circuit affirmed the District Court's decision. The school district appealed to the U. S. Supreme Court.

Questions Presented by the Case

What is meant by the Act's requirement of a free appropriate public education?

What is the role of state and federal courts in exercising the review granted by Section 1415?

In *Rowley*, the Supreme Court described the requirements of a free appropriate public education as:

providing personalized instruction with sufficient support services to permit the child to benefit educationally from that instruction. Such instruction and services must be provided at public expense, must meet the State's educational standards, must approximate the grade levels used in the State's regular education, and must comport with the child's IEP . . . if the child is being educated in the regular classrooms of the public education system, should be reasonably calculated to enable the child to achieve passing marks and advance from grade to grade.

After reviewing the legislative history of Education of All Handicapped Children Act (now IDEA), the Court held:

the intent of the Act was more to open the door of public education to handicapped children on appropriate terms than to guarantee any particular level of education once inside . . . We conclude that the "basic floor of opportunity" provided by the Act consists of access to specialized instruction and related services which are individually designed to provide educational benefit to the child.

The decision in *Rowley* clarified that children with disabilities were entitled to *access* to an education that provided *educational benefit*. They were not entitled to the "best" education, nor were they entitled to an education that would "maximize" their potential. Parents and school districts continue to disagree about what constitutes an appropriate special education program for a particular child.

When Health Services Are Necessary for FAPE: *Irving School District v. Tatro* (1984)

Amber Tatro was born with spina bifida. She had orthopedic and speech impairments and a neurogenic bladder. To prevent injury to her kidneys, Amber had to be catheterized every three or four hours by a procedure called "clean intermittent catheterization" (CIC). The procedure was described as "a simple one that may be performed in a few minutes by a layperson with less than an hour's training." Although the school agreed to provide special education for Amber, they refused to administer CIC because they viewed it as a medical service, not a "related service."

Initially, the U. S. District Court found that CIC was not a "related service" under the Education of All Handicapped Children Act (now IDEA) and that Section 504 of the Rehabilitation Act did not require "the setting up of government health care for people seeking to participate in federally funded programs."

The U. S. Court of Appeals reversed. It held that CIC was a "related service" because Amber could not attend school or benefit from special education without it. The case was remanded back to the District Court. The District Court held that because a nurse or other qualified person could administer CIC without engaging in the unauthorized practice of medicine, the procedure was not a "medical service" but was a "related service."

In 1984, Amber's case was appealed to the Supreme Court.

Questions Presented by the Case

Is 'medical treatment,' such as clean intermittent catheterization, a 'related service' required under the Education for All Handicapped Children Act and required to be provided to the minor Respondent?

Is a public school required to provide and perform medical treatment prescribed by the physician of a handicapped child by the Education of All Handicapped Children Act or the Rehabilitation Act of 1973?

The Court held that CIC is a "related service" under the Education of the Handicapped Act:

CIC is a supportive service . . . required to assist a handicapped child to benefit from special education . . . without having CIC services available during the school day, Amber cannot attend school and benefit from special education.

Quoting their decision in *Rowley*, the Court held:

As we have stated before, Congress sought primarily to make public education available to handicapped children and to make such access meaningful . . . .A service that enables a handicapped child to remain at school during the day is an important means of providing the child with the meaningful access to education that Congress envisioned.

Tuition Reimbursement: *Burlington School Comm. v. Dept. of Ed* (1985)

Dissatisfied about their children's lack of progress in public school programs, parents began to remove their children from these programs and place their children into private special education programs. Some parents requested that their school districts reimburse them for the costs of the child's special education in private programs.

If the public school provides an appropriate educational program, parents are not entitled to reimbursement for a private placement. If the school district does not provide the child with an appropriate education, and the parent places the child into a private special education program where the child does receive an appropriate education, should the parent be reimbursed?

Some courts held that the date for reimbursement did not begin until after the case was litigated and won by the parents, a process that often took years and led to delaying tactics by school districts. Other courts held that reimbursement was retroactive to the date of placement, or the date of denial of an appropriate education. A split among Circuits emerged on this issue.

To resolve this split, the U.S. Supreme Court agreed to hear the case of Michael Panico.

Questions Presented by the Case

Does the potential relief available under § 1415(e)(2) include reimbursement to parents for private school tuition and related expenses?

Does § 1415(e)(3) bar such reimbursement to parents who reject a proposed IEP and place a child in a private school without the consent of local school authorities?

In *Burlington*, the legal issue was whether Michael Panico's parents could be reimbursed for his education at a private special education school on the state's list of approved schools from the initial date of placement. The Panico family and the Massachusetts Department of Education brought the suit against the Town of Burlington, Massachusetts.

In the unanimous decision, Justice Rehnquist held that the special education statutes were enacted to benefit handicapped children. He described the issues that parents face in deciding whether to remove their child from an inadequate public school program:

parents who disagree with the proposed IEP are faced with a choice: go along with the IEP to the detriment of their child if it turns out to be inappropriate or pay for what they consider to be the appropriate placement. If they choose the latter course, which conscientious parents who have adequate means and who are reasonably confident of their assessment normally would, it would be an empty victory several years later that they were right but that these expenditures could not in a proper case be reimbursed by the school officials.

In a case where a court determines that a private placement desired by the parents was proper under the Act and that an IEP calling for placement in a public school was inappropriate, it seems clear beyond cavil that 'appropriate' relief would include a prospective injunction directing the school officials to develop and implement at public expense an IEP placing the child in a private school.

Discipline and Long-Term Expulsions: *Honig v. Doe* (1985)

In *Honig v. Doe*, the Supreme Court issued its first and only decision in a school discipline case, which was described as follows:

The present dispute grows out of efforts of certain officials of the San Francisco Unified School District to expel two emotionally disturbed children from school indefinitely for violent and disruptive conduct related to their disabilities.

The Court described Respondent John Doe as:

a socially and physically awkward 17 year old who experienced considerable difficulty controlling his impulses and anger . . . . Frustrating situations were an unfortunately prominent feature of Doe's school career: physical abnormalities, speech difficulties, and poor grooming habits made him the target of teasing and ridicule as early as the first grade . . . [his] social skills had deteriorated and he could tolerate only minor frustration before exploding.

Respondent Jack Smith was identified as an emotionally disturbed child by the time he entered second grade . . . he had been physically and emotionally abused as an infant and young child . . . despite above average intelligence, he experienced academic and social problems . . . extreme hyperactivity and low self-esteem.

Questions Presented by the Case

Do expulsions and indefinite suspensions of children for conduct related to their disabilities deprive them of their right to a free appropriate public education?

Can a 'dangerousness exception' be made to the "stay-put" requirements in Section 1415?

Citing *Mills v. Board of Education of District of Columbia*,[3] and the legislative history of the law, the Supreme Court held:

One of the evils Congress sought to remedy was the unilateral exclusion of disabled children by schools . . . one of the purposes of 1415(e)(3) was 'to prevent school officials from removing a child from the regular public school classroom over the parents' objection pending completion of the review proceedings.'

[The law] . . . demonstrates a congressional intent to strip schools of the unilateral authority they had traditionally employed to exclude disabled students, particularly emotionally disturbed students, from school. This Court will not rewrite the statute to infer a 'dangerousness' exception on the basis of obviousness or congressional inadvertence, since, in drafting the statute, Congress devoted close attention to *Mills* . . . thereby establishing that the omission of an emergency exception for dangerous students was intentional.

Although the Supreme Court issued a powerful pro-child decision in *Honig*, school officials continue to remove handicapped children from school for behaviors related to their disabilities.

Parental Choice and Educational Benefit: *Florence Co. School District IV v. Shannon Carter* (1993)

The Supreme Court agreed to review the Fourth Circuit's decision in *Florence County School District Four v.*

---

3   348 F. Supp. 866 (DC 1972)

Shannon Carter,[4] after a Court of Appeals ruling in a similar case created a split among circuits.

The Supreme Court found that:

> Shannon Carter was classified as learning disabled in 1985, while a ninth grade student . . . . School officials met with Shannon's parents to formulate an individualized education program (IEP) for Shannon . . . and established specific goals in reading and mathematics of four months progress for the entire school year. Shannon's parents were dissatisfied and requested a hearing to challenge the appropriateness of the IEP . . . . In the meantime, Shannon's parents placed her in Trident Academy, a private school specializing in educating children with disabilities . . . . Shannon graduated in the spring of 1988.

After a hearing officer and state review officer ruled against them, Shannon's parents filed suit in federal court, seeking reimbursement for her tuition and other costs incurred at Trident. The District Court ruled in the parents' favor and held that the school district's proposed educational program and achievement goals of the IEP were "wholly inadequate" and ordered Florence County to reimburse Shannon's parents for her education at Trident Academy.

Florence County appealed to the U. S. Court of Appeals for the Fourth Circuit, arguing that because Trident was a "self-contained school," it was not the least restrictive environment (LRE), and they should not have to pay for Shannon's education. Citing *Rowley*, the Court of Appeals held that since the school district had defaulted on its obligation to provide Shannon with a free, appropriate public education (FAPE), "the private school placement is 'proper under the Act' if the education provided by the private school is 'reasonably calculated to enable the child to receive educational benefits." This ruling was in direct conflict with the Second Circuit's decision in *Tucker v. Bay Shore Union Free School District*[5] and created a "split among circuits." The Supreme Court agreed to hear the case and resolve the split.

Question Presented by the Case

> May a court order reimbursement for parents who withdrew their child from a public school that did not provide an appropriate education under the Individuals with Disabilities Education Act and put the child in a private school that is in substantial – but not complete – compliance with the Act?

In a unanimous opinion written by Justice Sandra Day O'Connor, the Supreme Court held that parents who withdraw their child from a public school that does not provide an appropriate education and enroll their child in a private school are entitled to reimbursement if the child receives an appropriate education at the private school. The Court also held that the requirement that public schools meet state standards does not apply when parents place their child in a private program because these requirements were not intended to apply to parental placements. Citing the Court of Appeals decision, Justice O'Connor wrote:

> Indeed the school district's emphasis on state standards is somewhat ironic . . . to forbid parents from educating their child at a school that provides an appropriate education simply because that school lacks the stamp of approval of the same public school system that failed to meet the child's needs in the first place.

Justice O'Connor responded to Florence County's "unreasonable burden on financially strapped schools" argument with this advice:

> Public educational authorities who want to avoid reimbursing parents for the private education of a disabled child can do one of two things: give the child a free appropriate public education in a public setting, or place the child in an appropriate private setting of the State's choice. This is IDEA's mandate, and school officials who conform to it need not worry about reimbursement claims.

The decision in *Florence County School District IV v. Shannon Carter* opened the door to reimbursement for parents who developed special education programs tailored to the unique needs of their children, especially home-based Applied Behavioral Analysis (ABA) programs for young children with autism.

---

4   950 F. 2d 156 (4th Cir. 1991)
5   873 F. 2d 563 (2nd Cir. 1989)

When Nursing Services Are Necessary for FAPE: *Cedar Rapids v. Garret F.* (1999)

In *Cedar Rapids v. Garret F.*, the Supreme Court revisited the *"Tatro"* issue of related services.

Respondent Garret F. is a friendly, creative, and intelligent young man. When Garret was four years old, his spinal column was severed in a motorcycle accident. Though paralyzed from the neck down, his mental capacities were unaffected. He is able to speak, to control his motorized wheelchair through use of a puff and suck straw, and to operate a computer with a device that responds to head movements.

Garret is currently a student in the Cedar Rapids Community School District (District), he attends regular classes in a typical school program, and his academic performance has been a success. Garret is, however, ventilator dependent, and therefore requires a responsible individual nearby to attend to certain physical needs while he is in school.

Question Presented by the Case

Do schools that receive federal funding under the Individuals with Disabilities Education Act have to pay for one-on-one nursing assistance for certain of their disabled students?

In a 7-to-2 decision, the Court held that if the services are "related" to keeping a disabled child in school and able to access educational opportunities available to other children, school districts that receive IDEA funds must provide these services. Justice Stevens wrote the majority opinion:

This case is about whether meaningful access to the public schools will be assured, not the level of education that a school must finance once access is attained. It is undisputed that the services at issue must be provided if Garret is to remain in school.

Under the statute, our precedent and the purposes of the IDEA, the district must fund such related services to help guarantee that students like Garret are integrated into the public school . . . Congress intended to open the door of public education to all qualified children and required participating states to educate handicapped children with non-handicapped children whenever possible.

Burden of Proof in Due Process Hearings: *Schaffer v. Weast* (2005)

The next two cases decided by the U. S. Supreme Court dealt with procedural issues at special education due process hearings. The first case focused on who had the burden of proof in due process hearings – the parents or the school.

Brian Schaffer had learning disabilities and speech-language impairments. From kindergarten through seventh grade, he attended a private school. When school officials advised Brian's parents that he needed a different school to meet his needs, his parents contacted their local public school system. When the school district offered a program that was not sufficiently intensive, the parents enrolled Brian in a private special education school and requested a due process hearing.

After a due process hearing, the Administrative Law Judge held that the parents bore the burden of persuasion and ruled for the school district. The parents appealed to the U. S. District Court. The Court reversed and remanded, concluding that the burden of persuasion is on the school district.

During this time, the public school offered Brian a placement in a high school that had a special learning center. The parents accepted, and Brian attended this program until he graduated from high school.

The case bounced between the U. S. District Court, the U. S. Court of Appeals for the Fourth Circuit, and the Administrative Law Judge on the burden of proof issue. Finally, the Supreme Court agreed to hear the case.

Question Presented by the Case

At an administrative hearing assessing the appropriateness of an IEP, which party bears the burden of persuasion – the parents or the school district?

In a 6-2 ruling, the Supreme Court held that the party that seeks relief (i.e., that wants to change the status quo by changing the IEP) bears the burden of proof. In the majority opinion, Justice O'Connor wrote:

> If parents believe their child's IEP is inappropriate, they may request an impartial due process hearing. 1415(f) The Act is silent, however, as to which party bears the burden of persuasion at such a hearing. We hold that the burden lies, it is typically does, on the party seeking relief.

The case does not adversely affect States that already place the burden of proof on one party or the other. Justice O'Connor emphasized the limited nature of this decision:

> We hold no more than we must to resolve the case at hand: The burden of proof in an administrative hearing challenging an IEP is properly placed upon the party seeking relief. In this case, the party is Brian, as represented by his parents. But the rule applies with equal effect to school districts: If they seek to challenge an IEP, they will in turn bear the burden of persuasion before an ALJ.

Two Justices dissented from the majority. Justice Breyer believed that the case should be remanded back to Maryland to determine the issue.

Justice Ginsburg dissented because she was persuaded that "policy considerations, convenience, and fairness" call for assigning the burden of proof to the school district in this case. Citing the infamous *Deal v. Hamilton County Bd. of Ed.* case, in which a Tennessee school district spent over 2 million dollars on attorneys fees[6] in an effort to avoid providing services to a child with autism, she wrote:

> Understandably, school districts striving to balance their budgets, if "[left] to [their] own devices" will favor educational options that enable them to conserve resources. *Deal v. Hamilton County Bd. of Ed.*, 392 F. 3d 840, 864-865 (6th Cir. 2004)

Reimbursement for Expert Witness Fees: *Arlington v. Murphy* (2006)

The next case about procedural issues at due process hearings focused on reimbursement for costs incurred during litigation.

Pearl and Theodore Murphy requested that Arlington Central School District pay for their son Joseph's tuition at a private school that specialized in educating children with learning disabilities. A lay advocate represented the parents at a special education due process hearing. At other times, the lay advocate acted as an educational consultant.

The parents prevailed in the District Court and the U. S. Court of Appeals for the Second Circuit.

After the parents prevailed, they requested reimbursement for their attorneys' fees and costs. Their "costs" included $29,350 in fees for the lay advocate. The District Court reduced the award to $8,650 for the advocate's services, in part because she was not an attorney so the parents were not entitled to recover some of her expenses.

The school district appealed the award of costs to the lay advocate.

Question Presented by the Case

> Does the attorneys' fee-shifting provision authorize a court to award "expert" fees to the parents of a child with a disability who is a prevailing party under the IDEA?

In a 6-3 ruling, the majority held that parents who prevail in due process hearings are not entitled to recover fees paid to expert witnesses as part of their costs. The majority opinion by Justice Alito acknowledged that the legislative history of the Individuals with Disabilities Education Act supports the interpretation that "costs" includes reimbursement for expert witness fees. According to the Conference Committee Report issued when the IDEA was reauthorized:

---

6   "Henry Says County Schools Spent $2,280,000 On One Lawsuit" in *The Chattanoogan* (March 3, 2005) www.chattanoogan.com/articles/article_63389.asp (Retrieved October 8, 2006)

The conferees intend that the term 'attorneys' fees as part of the costs include reasonable expenses and fees of expert witnesses and the reasonable costs of any test or evaluation which is found necessary for the preparation of the . . . case. H.R. Conf. Rep. No. 99-687 at 5.

Despite this clear, unambiguous language, the majority held:

Whatever weight this legislative history would merit in another context, it is not sufficient here. Putting the legislative history aside, we see virtually no support for respondents' position.

Justice Breyer wrote a vigorous dissent:

Members of Congress did make clear their intent by . . . approving a Conference Report that specified that "the term 'attorneys' fees as part of the costs" includes reasonable expenses of expert witnesses and reasonable costs of any test or evaluation . . . necessary for the preparation of the parent or guardian's case . . .

There are two strong reasons for interpreting the statutory phrase to include the award of expert fees. First, that is what Congress said it intended by the phrase. Second, that interpretation furthers the IDEA's statutorily defined purposes.

In this dissent, Justice Breyer expressed concerns that this ruling "will leave many parents and guardians 'without an expert with the firepower to match the opposition' . . . a far cry from the level playing field that Congress envisioned."

Parental Representation in Federal Court: *Jacob Winkelman, et. al. v. Parma City Sch. Bd.* (2007)

In 2005, the U. S. Court of Appeals for the Sixth Circuit held that IDEA does not grant parents the right to represent their child in federal court. Unless parents retain an attorney, the child's case will be dismissed. This decision caused a split among Circuits on the issue of parental representation.

The parents appealed to the U. S. Supreme Court. On October 27, 2006, the Supreme Court agreed to hear *Jacob Winkelman, et. al. v. Parma City School Board* and resolve this split among circuits.

Question Presented by the Case

To what extent, if any, may a non-lawyer parent of a minor child with a disability proceed *pro se* in a federal court action brought pursuant to the Individuals with Disabilities Education Act, 20 U.S.C. 1400 *et seq.*?

At the time ***Wrightslaw: Special Education Law, 2nd Edition*** went to press, briefs had not been filed and a date had not been set for oral argument. A decision is expected during the 2006-2007 term. The outcome of this case and the decision will be published on the Wrightslaw website.[7]

In Summation

In this chapter, you read the questions presented in eight special education cases decided by the U. S. Supreme Court and the question presented in a case that will be decided by the Court during the 2006-2007 term. The next chapter includes the full text of these decisions.

---

7 Updates on *Winkelman v. Parma* and other cases that will be appealed to the U. S. Supreme Court are available at www.wrightslaw.com/news.htm

CHAPTER 12

U.S. Supreme Court Cases

The Supreme Court of the United States

458 U. S. 176

BOARD OF EDUCATION OF THE HENDRICK HUDSON CENTRAL SCHOOL DISTRICT, WESTCHESTER COUNTY, et al.,

Petitioners

v.

AMY ROWLEY, by her parents, ROWLEY et al.,

Respondent

No. 80-1002

On a Writ of Certiorari to the United States Court of Appeals for The Second Circuit. 632 F. 2d 945, reversed and remanded.

June 28, 1982

Before Burger, C.J., and Brennan, White, Marshall, Blackmun, Powell, Rehnquist, Stevens, O'Connor, JJ.

REHNQUIST, J., delivered the opinion of the Court, in which BURGER, C. J., and POWELL, STEVENS, and O'CONNOR, JJ., joined. BLACKMUN, J., filed an opinion, concurring in the judgment.

WHITE, J., filed a dissenting opinion, in which BRENNAN and MARSHALL, JJ., joined.

JUSTICE REHNQUIST delivered the opinion of the Court.

This case presents a question of statutory interpretation Petitioners contend that the Court of Appeals and the District Court misconstrued the requirements imposed by the Congress upon States which receive federal funds under the Education for All Handicapped Children Act. We agree and reverse the judgment of the Court of Appeals.

I

The Education for All Handicapped Children Act of 1975 (Act), 20 U.S.C. 1401 *et seq.*, provides federal money to assist state and local agencies in educating handicapped children, and conditions such funding upon a States com-

pliance with extensive goals and procedures. The Act represents an ambitious federal effort to promote the education of handicapped children, and was passed in response to Congress' perception that a majority of handicapped in the United States "were either totally excluded from schools or [were] sitting idly in regular classrooms awaiting the time when they were old enough to 'drop out.'" H.R. Rep. No. 94-332. P. 2 (1975). The Acts evolution and major provisions shed light on the question of statutory interpretation which is at he heart of this case.

Congress first addressed the problem of education the handicapped in 1966 when it amended the Elementary and Secondary Education Act of 1965 to establish a grant program "for the purpose of assisting the States in the initiation, expansion, and improvement of programs and projects . . . for the education of handicapped children." Pub. L. No. 89-750, 161, 80 Stat. 1204 (1966). That program was repealed in 1970 by the Education for the Handicapped Act, Pub. L. No. 91-230, 84 Star, 175, Part B of which established a grant program similar in purpose to the repealed legislation. Neither the 1966 nor 1970 legislation contained specific guidelines for state use of the grant money; both were aimed primarily at stimulating the States to develop educational resources and to train personnel for educating the handicapped.[1]

Dissatisfied with the progress being made under these earlier enactments, and spurred by two district court decisions holding that handicapped children should be given access to a public education,[2] Congress in 1974 greatly increased federal funding for education of the handicapped and for the first time required recipient States to adopt "a goal of providing full educational opportunities to all handicapped children." Pub. L. 93-380, 88 Stat. 579, 583 (1974) (the 1974 statute). The 1974 statute was recognized as an interim measure only, adopted "in order to give the Congress an additional year in which to study what if any additional Federal assistance [was] required to enable the States to meet the needs of handicapped children." H.R. Rep. No. 94-332, *supra*, p. 4. The ensuing year of study produced the Education for All Handicapped Children Act of 1975.

344 • Chapter 12 • U. S. Supreme Court Cases

In order to qualify for federal financial assistance under the Act, a State must demonstrate that it "has in effect a policy that assures all handicapped children the right to a free appropriate public education." 20 U. S. C. 1412(1). That policy must be reflected in a state plan submitted to and approved by the Secretary of Education 1413[3], which describes in detail the goals, programs, and timetables under which the State intends to educate handicapped children within its borders. 1412. 1413. States receiving money under the Act must provide education to the handicapped by priority, first "to handicapped children who are not receiving an education" and second "to handicapped children . . . with the most severe handicaps who are receiving an inadequate education," 1413(3), and to the maximum extent appropriate" must educate handicapped children "with children who are not handicapped." 1412(5)[4]. The Act broadly defines "handicapped children" to include "mentally retarded, hard of hearing, deaf, speech impaired, visually handicapped, seriously emotionally disturbed, orthopedically impaired, [and] other health impaired children, [and] children with specific learning disabilities." 1401(1)[5]

The "free appropriate public education" required by the Act is tailored to the unique needs of the handicapped child by means of an "individualized educational program" (IEP). 1401(18). The IEP, which is prepared at a meeting between a qualified representative of the local educational agency, the child's teacher, the child parents or guardian, and, where appropriate, the child, consists of a written document containing

(A) a student of the present levels of educational performance of the child,

(B) a statement of annual goals, including short-term instructional objectives,

(C) a statement of the specific educational services to be provided to such child, and the extent to which such child will be able to participate in regular educational programs,

(D) the projected date for initiation and anticipated duration of such service, and

(E) appropriate objective criteria and evaluation procedures and schedules for determining, on at least an annual basis, whether instructional objectives are being achieved." 1401(19).

Local or regional educational agencies must review, and where appropriate revise, each child's IEP at least annually. 1404(a)(5). See also 1413(a)(11), 1414(a)(5).

In addition to the state plan and the IEP already described, the Act imposes extensive procedural requirements upon State receiving federal funds under its provisions. Parents or guardians of handicapped children must be notified of any proposed change in "the identification, evaluation, or educational placement of the child or the provision of a free appropriate public education to the child," and must be permitted to being a complaint about "any matter relating to" such evaluation and education. 1415(b)(1)(D) and (E).[6] Complaints brought by parents or guardians must be resolved at "an impartial due process hearing," and appeal to the State educational agency must be provided if the initial hearing is held at the local or regional level. 1415(B)(2) and (c)[7] Thereafter, "any party aggrieved by the findings and decisions" of the state administrative hearing has "the right to bring a civil action with respect to the complaint . . . in any State court of competent jurisdiction or in a district court of the United Stated without regard to the amount in controversy." 1415(e)(2).

Thus, although the Act leaves to the States the primary responsibility for developing and executing educational programs for handicapped children, it imposes significant requirements to be followed in the discharge of that responsibility. Compliance is assured by provisions permitting the withholding of federal funds upon determination that a participating state or local agency has failed to satisfy the requirements of the Act, 1414(b)(A), 1416, and by the provision for judicial review. At present, all States except New Mexico receive federal funds under the portions of the Act at issue today. Brief for the United States as Amicus Curiae 2, n. 2.

II

This case arose in connection with the education of Amy Rowley, a deaf student at the Furnace Woods School in the Hendrick Hudson Central School District, Peekskill, New York. Amy has minimal residual hearing and is an excellent lip reader. During the year before she began attending furnace Woods, a meeting between her parents and school administrators resulted in a decision to place in a regular kindergarten class in order to determine what supplement services would be necessary to her education. Several members of the school administration prepared for Amy's arrival by attending a course in sign-language interpretation, and a teletype machine was installed in the principal's office to facilitate communication with her parents who are also deaf.

At the end of the trial period it was determined that Amy should remain in the kindergarten class, but that she should be provided with an FM hearing aid which would amplify words spoken into a wireless receiver by the teacher or fellow students during certain classroom activities. Amy successfully completed her kindergarten year.

As required by the Act, an IEP was prepared for Amy during the fall of her first-grade year. The IEP provided that Amy should be educated in a regular classroom at Furnace Woods, should continue to use the FM hearing aid, and should receive instruction from a tutor for the deaf for one hour each day and from a speech therapist for three hours each week. The Rowleys agreed with the IEP but insisted that Amy also be provided a qualified sign-language interpreter in all of her academic classes. Such an interpreter had been placed in Amy's kindergarten class for a two-week experimental period, but the interpreter had reported that Amy did not need his services at that time. The school administrators likewise concluded that Amy did not need such an interpreter in her first-grade classroom. They reached this conclusion after consulting the school district's Committee on the Handicapped, which had received expert evidence from Amy's parents on the importance of a sign-language interpreter, received testimony from Amy's teacher and other persons familiar with her academic and social progress, and visited a class for the deaf.

When their request for an interpreter was denied, the Rowleys demanded and received a hearing before an independent examiner. After receiving evidence from both sides, the examiner agreed with the administrators' determination that an interpreter was not necessary because "Amy was achieving educationally, academically, and socially" without such assistance. App. to Pet. for Cert. F-22. The examiner's decision was affirmed on appeal by the New York Commissioner of Education on the basis of substantial evidence in the record. *Id.*, at E-4. Pursuant to the Act's provision for judicial review, the Rowleys then brought an action in the United States District Court for the Southern District of New York, claiming that the administrators' denial of the sign-language interpreter constituted a denial of the "free appropriate public education" guaranteed by the Act.

The District Court found that Amy "is a remarkably well adjusted child" who interacts and communicates well with her classmates and has "developed an extraordinary rapport" with her teachers. 483 F. Supp, 528, 531. It also found that "she performs better than the average child in her class and is advancing easily from grade to grade," *id.*, at 534, but "that she understands considerably less of what goes on in class than she would if she were not deaf" and thus "is not learning as much, or performing as well academically, as she would without her handicap," *id.*, at 532. This disparity between Amy's achievement and her potential led the court to decide that she was not receiving a "free appropriate public education" which the court defined as "an opportunity to achieve [her] full potential commensurate with the opportunity provided to other children." *id.*, at 534. According to the District Court, such a standard "requires that the potential of the handicapped child be measured and compared to his or her performance, and that the remaining differential or 'shortfall' be compared to the shortfall experienced by nonhandicapped children.' *Ibid.* The District Court's definition arose from its assumption that the responsibility for "giving content to the requirement of an 'appropriate education'" had 'been left entirely

to the federal courts and the hearing officers.' *Id.*, at 533.[8]

A divided panel of the United States Court of Appeals for the Second Circuit affirmed. The Court of Appeals "agree[d] with the [D]istrict [C]ourt's conclusions of law," and held that its 'findings of fact [were] not clearly erroneous." 632 F. 2d 945, 947 (1980).

We granted certiorari to review the lower courts' interpretation of the Act. Such review requires us to consider two questions: What is meant by the Act's requirement of a "free appropriate public education"? And what is the role of state and federal courts in exercising the review granted by 1415 of the Act? We consider these questions separately.[9]

III

A

This is the first case in which this Court has been called upon to interpreter any provision of the Act. As noted previously, the District Court and Court of Appeals concluded that "the Act itself does nor define 'appropriate education,'" 483 F. Supp., at 533, but leaves "to the courts and the hearing officers" the responsibility of "giv[ing] content to the requirement of an appropriate education." *Ibid.* see also 632 F. 2d, at 947.

Petitioners contend that the definition of the phrase "free appropriate public education" used by the courts below overlooks the definition of the phrase actually found in the Act. Respondents agree that the Act defines "free appropriate public education," but contend that the statutory definition is not "functional" and thus "offers judges no guidance in their consideration of controversies involving the 'identification, evaluation, or educational placement of the child or the provision of a free appropriate public education," Brief for Respondents 28. The United States, appearing as amicus curiae on behalf of respondents, states that "[a]lthough the Act includes definitions of 'free appropriate public education' and other related terms, the statutory definitions do not adequately explain what is meant by 'appropriate,'" Brief for United States as Amicus Curiae.

We are loath to conclude that Congress failed to offer any assistance in defining the meaning of the principal substantive phrase used in the Act. It is beyond dispute that, contrary to the conclusions of the courts below, the Act does expressly define "free appropriate public education":

The term ' free appropriate public education' means special education and related services which

(A) have been provided at public expenses, under public supervision and direction, and without charge,

(B) meet the standards of the State educational agency,

(C) include an appropriate preschool, elementary, or secondary school education in the State involved, and

> (D) are provided in conformity with the individualized education program required under section 1414(a)(5) of this title." 1401(18) (emphasis added).

"Special education," as referred to in this definition, means "specially designed instruction, at no cost to parents or guardians, to meet the unique needs of a handicapped child, including classroom instruction, instruction in physical education, home instruction, and instruction in hospitals and institutions." 1401(16). "Related services" are defined as "transportation, and such developmental, corrective, and other supportive services . . . as may be required to assist a handicapped child to benefit from special education." 1401(17).[10]

Like many statutory definitions, this one tends toward the cryptic rather than the comprehensive, but that is scarcely a reason for abandoning the quest for legislative intent. Whether or not the definition is a "functional" one, as respondents contend it is not, it is the principal tool which Congress has given us for parsing the critical phrase of the Act, we think more must be made of it than either respondents or the United States seems willing to admit.

According to the definitions contained in the Act, a "free appropriate public education" consists of educational instruction specially designed to meet the unique needs of the handicapped child, supported by such services as are necessary to permit the child "to benefit" from the instruction. Almost as a checklist for adequacy under the Act, the definition also requires that such instruction and services be provided at public expense and under public supervision, meet the State's educational standards, approximate the grade levels used in the State's regular education, and comport with the child's IEP. Thus, if personalized instruction is being provided with sufficient supportive services to permit the child to benefit from the instruction, and the other items on the definitional checklist are satisfied, the child is receiving a "free appropriate public education" as defined by the Act.

Other portions of the statute also shed light on congressional intent. Congress found that of the roughly eight million handicapped children in the United States at the time of enactment, one million were "excluded entirely form the public school system" and more than half were receiving an inappropriate education. Note to 1401. In addition, as mentioned in Part I, the Act requires States to extend educational services first to those children who are receiving no education and second to those children who are receiving an "inadequate education." 1412(3). When these express statutory findings and priorities are read together with the Act's extensive procedural requirements and its definition of "free appropriate public education," the face of the statute evinces a congressional intent to bring previously excluded handicapped children into public education systems of the States and to require the States to adopt procedures which would result in individualized consideration of and instruction for each child.

Noticeably absent from the language of the statue is any substantive standard prescribing the level of education to be accorded handicapped children. Certainly the language of the statute contains no requirement like the one imposed by the lower courts-that States maximize the potential of handicapped children "commensurate with the opportunity provided to other children." 483 F. Supp., at 534. That standard was expounded by the District court without reference to the statutory definitions or even to the legislative history of the Act. Although we find the statutory definition of "free appropriates public education" to be helpful in our interpretation of the Act, there remains the question of whether the legislative history indicates a congressional intent that such education meet some additional substantive standard. For an answer, we turn to that history.[11]

B
(i)

As suggested in Part I, federal support for education of the handicapped is a fairly recent development. Before passage of the Act some States has passed laws to improve the educational services afford handicapped children,[12] but many of these children were excluded completely form any form of public education or were left to fend for themselves in classrooms designed for the education of their nonhandicapped peers. The House Report begins by emphasizing this exclusion and misplacement, noting that millions of handicapped children "were either totally excluded form schools or [were] sitting idly in regular classrooms awaiting the time when they were old enough to 'drop out.'" H.R. Rep, No. 94-332, supra, at 2. See also S. Rep. No. 94-168, p. 8 (1975). One of the Act's two principal sponsors in the Senate urged its passage in similar terms:

> "While much progress has been made in the last few years, we can take no solace in that progress until all handicapped children are, in fact, receiving an education. The most recent statistics provided by the Bureau of Education for the Handicapped estimate that . . . 1.75 million handicapped children do not receive any educational services, and 2.5 million handicapped children are not receiving an appropriate education." 121 Cong. Rec. 1946 (1975) (remarks of Sen. Williams).

This concern, stressed repeatedly throughout the legislative history,[13] confirms the impression conveyed by the language of statute: By passing the Act, Congress sought primarily to make public education available to handicapped children. But in seeking to provide such access to public education, Congress did not impose upon the states any greater substantive educational standard than would be necessary to make such access meaningful. Indeed, Congress expressly "recognized that in many instances the process of providing special education and related services to handicapped children is not guaranteed to produce any particular outcome." S. Rep. No. 94-168, *supra*, at 11. Thus, the intent of the Act was more to open the door of public education to handicapped children on appropriate terms than to guarantee any particular level of education once inside.

Both the House and the Senate reports attribute the impetus for the Act and its predecessors to two federal court judgments rendered in 1971 and 1972. As the Senate Report states, passage of the act "followed a series of landmark court cases establishing in law the right to education for all handicapped children." S. Rep. No. 94-168, *supra*, at 6.[14] The first case, *Pennsylvania Association for Retarded Children v. Commonwealth of Pennsylvania (PARC)*, 334 F. Supp. 1257 (1971) 343 F. Supp. 279 (ED PA 1972), was a suit on behalf of retarded children challenging the constitutionality of a Pennsylvania statue which acted to exclude them from public education and training. The case ended in a consent decree which enjoined the State from "den[ying] to any mentally retarded child **access** to a free public program of education and training." 334 F. Supp. at 1258 (emphasis added).

PARC was followed by *Mills v. Board of Education of the District of Columbia*, 343 F. Supp. 866 (DC 1972), a case in which the plaintiff handicapped children had been excluded from the District of Columbia public schools. The court judgment, quoted at page 6 of the Senate Report on the Act, provided:

> "that no handicapped child eligible for publicly supported education in the District of Columbia public schools shall be **excluded** from a regular school assignment by a Rule, policy, or practice of the Board of Education of the District of Columbia or its agents unless such child is provided
>
> (a) **adequate** alternative educational services suited to the child's needs, which may include special education or tuition grants, and
>
> (b) a constitutionally adequate prior hearing and periodic review of the child's status, progress, and the **adequacy** of any educational alternative." 348 F. Supp., at 878 (emphasis added).

Mills and *PARC* both held that handicapped children must be given access to an adequate, publicly supported education. Neither case purports to require any particular substantive level of education.[15] Rather, like the language of the Act, the cases set forth extensive procedures to be followed in formulating personalized educational programs for handicapped children. See 348 F. Supp., at 878-883; 334 F. Supp., at 1258-1267.[16] The fact that both *PARC* and *Mills*

are discussed at length in the legislative reports[17] suggest that the principles which they established are the principles which, to a significant extent, guided the drafters of the Act. Indeed, immediately after discussing these cases the Senate Report describes the 1974 statute as having "incorporated the major principles of the right to education cases." S. Rep. No 94-168, *supra*, at 8. Those principles in turn became the basis of the Act, which itself was designed to effectuate the purposes of the 1974 statute. H.R. Rep. No. 94-332, *supra*, at 5.[18]

That the Act imposes no clear obligation upon recipient States beyond the requirement that handicapped children receive some form of specialized education is perhaps best demonstrated by the fact that Congress, in explaining the need for the Act, equated an "appropriate education" to the receipt of some specialized educational services.

The Senate report states: 'The most recent statistics provided by the Bureau of education for the Handicapped estimate that of the more than 8 million children...with handicapping conditions requiring special education and related services, only 3.9 million such children are receiving an appropriate education." S. Rep. No. 94-332, *supra*, at 8.[19] This statement, which reveals Congress' view that 3.9 million handicapped children were "receiving an appropriate education" in 1975, is followed immediately in the Senate Report by a table showing that 3.9 million handicapped children were "served " in 1975 and a slightly larger numbers were "unserved." A similar statement and table appear in the House report. H.R. Rep. No. 94-332, *supra*, at 11-12.

It is evident from the legislative history that the characterization of handicapped children as "served" referred to children who were receiving some form of specialized educational services from the States, and that the characterization of children as "unserved" referred to those who were receiving no specialized educational services. For example, a letter sent to the United States Commissioner of Education by the House Committee on Education and Labor, signed by two key sponsors of the Act in the House, asked the commissioner to identify the number of handicapped " children served" in each State. The letter asked for statistics on the number of children "being served" in various types of "special education programs" and the number of children who were not "receiving educational services." Hearing on S. 6 before the Subcommittee on the Handicapped of the Senate Committee on Labor and Public Welfare, 94th Cong. 1st Sess., 205-207 (1975). Similarly, Senator Randolph, one of the Act 's principal sponsors in the Senate, noted that roughly one-half of the handicapped children in the United States "are receiving special educational services." *Id*., at 1.[20] By characterizing the 3.9 million handicapped children who were "served" as children who were receiving an appropriate education," the Senate and House reports unmistakably disclose Congress' perception of the type of education required by the Act: an "appropriate education" is provided when personalized educational services are provided.[21]

(ii)

Respondents contend that "the goal of the Act is to provide each handicapped child with an equal educational opportunity." Brief for Respondents 35. We think, however, that the requirement that a State provides specialized educational services to handicapped children generates no additional requirement that the services so provided be sufficient to maximize each child's potential "commensurate with the opportunity provided other children."

Respondents and the United States correctly note that Congress sought "to provide assistance to the States carrying out their responsibilities under the Constitution of the United States to provide equal protection of the laws." S. Rep. No. 94-168, *supra*, at 13.[22] But we do not think that such statements imply a congressional intent to achieve: strict equality of opportunity or services.

The educational opportunities provided by our public school systems undoubtedly differ from student to student, depending upon a myriad of factors that might affect a particular student's ability to assimilate information presented in the classroom. The requirement that States provide "equal" educational opportunities would thus seem to present an entirely unworkable standard requiring impossible measurements and comparisons. Similarly, furnishing handicapped children with only such services as are available to nonhandicapped children would in all probability fall short of the statutory requirement of "free appropriate public education." To require, on the other hand, the furnishing of every special service necessary to maximize each handicapped child's potential is, we think, further than Congress intended to go. Thus to speak in terms of "equal" services in one instance give less than what is required by the Act and in another instance more. The theme of the Act is "free appropriate public education," a phrase which is too complex to be captured by the word "equal" whether on is speaking of opportunities or services.

The legislative conception of the requirements of equal protection was undoubtedly informed by the two district court decisions referred to above. But cases such as *Mills* and *PARC* held simply that handicapped children may not be excluded from entirely public education. In *Mills*, the District Court said:

> If sufficient funds are not available to finance all of the services and programs that are needed and desirable in the system, then the available funds must be expended equitably in such a manner that no child is entirely excluded from a publicly supported education consistent with his needs and ability to benefit therefrom." 348 F Supp., at 876.

The *PARC* Court used similar language, saying "[i]t is the commonwealth's obligation to place each mentally retarded child in a free, public program of education and training appropriate to the child's capacity. . ." 334 F. Supp., at 1260. The right of access to free public education enunciated by these cases is significantly different from any notion of absolute equality of opportunity regardless of capacity. To the extent the Congress might have looked further than these cases which are mentioned in the legislative history at the time of enactment of the Act, this Court has held at least twice that the Equal Protection Clause of the Fourteenth Amendment does not require States to expend equal financial resources on the education of each child. *San Antonio School District v. Rodriguez*, 411 U.S. 1(1975); *Mcinnis v. Shapiro*, 238 F.Supp. 327 (ND Ill. 1968), aff'd sub nom, *Mcinnis v. Ogilvie*, 394 U.S. 322 (1969).

In explaining the need for federal legislation, the House Report noted that "no congressional legislation has required a precise guarantee for handicapped children, i.e., a basic floor of opportunity that would bring into compliance all school districts with the constitutional right of equal protection with respect to handicapped children." H.R. Rep. No. 94-332, *supra*, at 14. Assuming that the Act was designed to fill the need identified in the House Report-that is, to provide a "basic floor of opportunity' consistent with equal protection-neither the Act nor its history persuasively demonstrate that Congress thought that equal protection required anything more than equal access. Therefore, Congress' desire to provide specialized educational services, even in furtherance of "equality," cannot be read as imposing any particular substantive educational standard upon the States.

The District Court and the Court of Appeals thus erred when they held that the Act requires New York to maximize the potential of each handicapped child commensurate with the opportunity provided nonhandicapped children. Desirable though that goal might be, it is not the standard that Congress imposed upon States which receive funding under the Act. Rather, Congress sought primarily to identify and evaluate handicapped children, and to provide them with access to a free public education.

(iii)

Implicit in the congressional purpose of providing access to a "free appropriate public education" is the requirement that the education to which access is provided be sufficient to confer some educational benefit upon the handicapped child. It would do little good for Congress to spend millions of dollars in providing access to public education only to have the handicapped child receive no benefit from that education. The statutory definition of "free appropriate public education," in addition to requiring that States provide each child with "specially designed instruction," expressly requires the provision of "such . . .

supportive services . . . as may be required to assist a handi-capped child to benefit from special education." 1401(17) (emphasis added). We therefore conclude that the "basic floor of opportunity" provided by the Act consists of access to specialized instruction and related services which are individually designed to provide educational benefit to the handicapped child.[23]

The determination of when handicapped children are receiving sufficient educational benefits to satisfy the requirements of the Act presents a more difficult problem. The Act requires participating States to educate a wide spectrum of handicapped children, from the marginally hearing-impaired to the profoundly retarded palsied. It is clear that the benefits obtainable by children at one end of the spectrum will differ dramatically form those obtainable by children at the other end, with infinite variations in between. One child may have little difficulty competing successfully in an academic setting with nonhandicapped children while another child may encounter great difficulty in acquiring even the most basic of self-maintenance skills. We do not attempt today to establish any one test for determining the adequacy of educational benefits conferred upon all children covered by the Act. Because in this case we are presented with a handicapped child who is receiving substantial specialized instruction and related services, and who is performing above average in the regular classrooms of a public school system, we confine our analysis to the situation.

The Act requires participating States to educate handicapped children with nonhandicapped children whenever possible.[24] When the "mainstreaming" preference of the Act has been met and a child is being educated in the regular classrooms of a public school system, the system itself monitors the educational progress of the child. Regular examinations are administered, grades are awarded, and yearly advancement to higher grade levels is permitted for those children who attain an adequate knowledge of the course material. The grading and advancement system thus constitutes an important factor in determining educational benefit. Children who graduate from our public school systems are considered by our society to have been "educated" at least to the grade level they have completed, and access to an "education" for handicapped children is precisely what Congress sought to provide in the Act.[25]

C

When the language of the Act and its legislative history are considered together, the requirements imposed by Congress become tolerably clear. Insofar as a State is required to provide a handicapped child with a "free appropriate public education," we hold that it satisfies this requirement by providing personalized instruction with sufficient support services to permit the child to benefit educationally from that instruction. Such instruction and

services must be provided at public expense, must meet the State's educational standards, must approximate the grade levels used in the State's regular education, and must comport with the child's IEP. In addition, the IEP, and therefore the personalized instruction, should be formulated in accordance with the requirements of the Act, and if the child is being educated in the regular classrooms of the public education system, should be reasonably calculated to enable the child to achieve passing marks and advance from grade to grade.[26]

IV
A

As mentioned in Part I, the Act permits "any party aggrieved by the findings and decision" of the state administrative hearings "to bring a civil action "in" any State Court of competent jurisdiction or in a district court of the United States without regard to the amount in controversy." 1415(e)(2). The complaint, and therefore the civil action, may concern "any matter relating to the identification, evaluation, or educational placement of the child, or the provision of a free appropriate public education to such child." 1415(b)(1)(E). In reviewing the complaint, the Act provides that a court "shall receive the record of the state administrative proceedings, shall hear additional evidence at the request of a party, and, basing its decision on the preponderance of the evidence, shall grant such relief as the court determines is appropriate." 1415(e)(2).

The parties disagree sharply over the meaning of these provisions, petitioners contending that courts are given only limited authority to review for state compliance with the Act's procedural requirements and no power to review the substance of the state program, and respondents contending that the Act requires courts to exercise *de novo* review over state educational decisions and policies. We find petitioners' contention unpersuasive, for Congress expressly rejected provisions that would have so severely restricted the role of reviewing courts. In substituting the current language of the statue for language that would have made state administrative findings conclusive if supported by substantial evidence, the Conference Committee explained that courts were to make "independent decisions based on a preponderance of the evidence." S. Conf. Rep.No. 94-455, *supra*, at 50. (See also 121 Cong. Rec. 37416 (1975), remarks of Senator Williams).

But although we find that this grant of authority is broader than claimed by petitioners, we think the fact that it is found in 1415 of the Act, which is entitled "Procedural Safeguards," is not without significance when the elaborate and highly specific procedural safeguards embodied in 1415 are contrasted with the general and somewhat imprecise substantive admonitions contained in the Act, we think that the importance Congress attached to these procedural safeguards cannot be gainsaid. It seems to us no exaggeration to say that Congress placed every bit as much emphasis upon compliance with procedures giving parents and guardians a large measure of participation at every stage of the administrative process, see, e.g. 1415(a)-(d), as it did upon the measurement of the resulting IEP against a substantive standard. We think that the congressional emphasis upon full participation of concerned parties throughout the development of the IEP, as well as the requirements that state and local plans be submitted to the Commissioner for approval, demonstrate the legislative conviction that adequate compliance with the procedures prescribed would in most cases assure much if not all of what Congress wished in the way of substantive content in an IEP.

Thus, the provision that a reviewing court base its decision on the "preponderance of the evidence" is by no means an invitation to the court to substitute their own notions of sound educational policy for those of the school authorities which they review. The very importance which Congress has attached to compliance with certain procedures in the preparation of an IEP would be frustrated if a court were permitted simply to set state decisions aside. The fact that 1415(e) requires that the reviewing court "receive the records of the [state] administrative proceedings" carries with it the implied requirement that due weight shall be given to these proceedings. And we find nothing in the Act to suggest that merely because Congress was rather sketchy in establishing substantive requirements, as opposed to procedural requirements for the preparation of an IEP, it intended that reviewing courts should have a free hand to impose substantive standards of review which cannot be derived from the Act itself. In short, the statutory authorization to grant "such relief as the court determines is appropriate' cannot be read without reference to the obligations, largely procedural in nature, which are imposed upon recipient States by Congress.

Therefore, a court's inquiry in suits brought under 1415(e)(2) is twofold. First, has the State complied with the procedures set forth in the Act?[27] And second, is the individualized educational program developed through the Act's procedures reasonably calculated to enable the child to receive educational benefits?[28] If these requirements are met, the State has complied with the obligations imposed by Congress and the courts can require no more.

B

In assuring that the requirements of the Act have been met, courts must be careful to avoid imposing their view of preferable educational methods upon the States.[29] The primary responsibility for formulating the education to be accorded a handicapped child, and for choosing the educational method most suitable to the child's needs, was left by the Act to state and local educational agencies in cooperation with the parents or guardian of the child. The Act expressly charges States with the responsibility of "acquir-

ing and disseminating to teachers and administrators of programs for handicapped children significant information derived form educational research, demonstration, and similar projects, and of adopting, where appropriate, promising educational practices and materials." 1413(a)(3). In the face of such a clear statutory directive, it seems highly unlikely that congress intended courts to overturn a State's choice of appropriate educational theories in a proceeding conducted pursuant to 1415(e)(2).[30]

We previously have cautioned that courts lack the "specialized knowledge and experience" necessary to resolve "persistent and difficult questions of educational policy." *San Antonio School District v. Rodriguez*, 411 U.S. 1, 42 (1973). We think that Congress shared that view when it passed the Act. As already demonstrated, Congress' intention was not that the Act displace the primacy of States in the field of education, but that the states receive funds to assist them in extending their educational systems to handicapped. Therefore, once a court determines that the requirements of the Act have been met, questions of methodology are for resolution by the States.

V

Entrusting a child's education to state and local agencies does not leave the child without protection. Congress sought to protect individual children by providing for parental involvement in the development of State plans and policies, *supra*, at 4-5 and n. 6, and in the formulation of the child's individual educational program. As the Senate Report states:

> The Committee recognizes that in may instances the process of providing special education and related services to handicapped children is not guaranteed to produce any particular outcome. By changing the language of the provision relating to individualized educational programs to emphasize the process of parent and child involvement, and to provide a written record of reasonable expectations, the Committee intends to clarify that such individualized planning conferences are a way to provide parent involvement and protection to assure that appropriate services are provided to a handicapped child. S. Rep. No. 94-168, *supra*, at 11-12. See also S. Conf. Rep. No. 94-445, p. 30 (1975); 45 CFR 121a.345 (1980).

As this very case demonstrates, parents and guardians will not lack ardor in seeking to ensure that handicapped children receive all the benefits to which they are entitled by the Act.[31]

VI

Applying these principles to the facts of this case, we conclude that the court of Appeals erred in affirming the decision of the District Court. Neither the District Court nor the Court of Appeals found that petitioners had failed to comply with the procedures of the Act, and the findings of neither court would support a conclusion that Amy's educational program failed to comply with the substantive requirements of the Act. On the contrary, the District Court found that the "evidence firmly establishes that Amy is receiving an 'adequate' education, since she performs better than the average child in her class and is advancing easily from grade to grade." 483 F Supp., at 534.

In light of this finding, and of the fact that Amy was receiving personalized instruction and related services calculated by the Furnace Woods school administrators to meet her educational needs, the lower courts should not have concluded that the Act requires the provision of a sign-language interpreter. Accordingly, the decision of the Court of appeals is reversed and the case is remanded for further proceedings consistent with this opinion.[32]

SO ORDERED.

JUSTICE BLACKBMUN, concurring in the judgment.

Although I reach the same result as the Court of the Education for All Handicapped Children Act differently. Congress unambiguously stated that it intended to "to take a more active role under its responsibility for equal protection of the laws to guarantee that handicapped children are provided **equal educational opportunity**." S. Rep. No. 94-168, p. 9 (1975) (emphasis added). See also 20 U.S.C. 1412(2)(A)(i) (requiring States to establish plans with the 'goal of providing full educational opportunity to all handicapped children").

As I have observed before, "[i]t seems plain to me that Congress, in enacting [this statue], intended to do more than merely set out politically self-serving but essentially meaningless language about what the [handicapped] deserve at the hands of state . . . authorities." *Pennhurst State School v. Halderman*, 451 U.S. 1, 32 (1981) (opinion concurring in part and concurring in judgment).

The clarity of the legislative intent convinces me that the relevant question here is not, as the court says, whether Amy Rowley's individualized education program was "reasonably calculated to enable [her] to receive educational benefits," measured in part by whether or not she "achieves passing marks and advances from grade to grade." Rather, the question is whether Amy's program, viewed as a whole, offered her an opportunity to understand and participate in the classroom that was substantially equal to that given her nonhandicapped classmates. This is a standard predicated on equal educational opportunity and equal access to the educational process, rather than upon Amy's achievement of any particular educational outcome.

In answering this question, I believe that the District Court and the court of Appeals should have given greater deference than they did to the findings of the School District's

impartial hearing officer and the State's Commissioner of Education, both of whom sustained petitioner's refusal to add sign-language interpreter to Amy's individualized education program. 20 U.S.C. 1415(e)(2) (requiring reviewing court to "receive the records of the administrative proceeding" before granting relief). I would suggest further that those courts focused too narrowly on the presence or absence of a particular service-a sign-language interpreter-rather than on the total package of services furnished to Amy by the School Board.

As the Court demonstrates, petitioner Board has provided Amy Rowley considerably more than "a teacher with a loud voice." See post, at 4 (dissenting opinion). By concentrating on whether Amy was "learning as much, or performing as well academically, as she would without her handicap," 483 F. Supp. 528, 532 (SDNY 1980), the District Court and the Court of Appeals paid too little attention to whether, on the entire record, respondent's individualized education program offered her an educational equal to that provided her nonhandicapped classmates. Because I believe that standard has been satisfied here, I agree that the judgment of the Court of Appeals should be reversed.

Endnotes

1 See S. Rep. No. 94-168, p. 5 (1975; H.R. Rep. No. 94-332, pp. 2-3 (1975).

2 Two cases, *Mills v. Board of Education of District of Columbia*, 348 F.Supp. 866 (DC 1972), and *Pennsylvania Assn. for Retarded Children v. Commonwealth*, 334 F.Supp. 1257 (ED Pa. 1971) and 343 F.Supp. 279 (1972), were later identified as the most prominent of the cases contributing to Congress' enactment of the Act and the statutes which preceded it. H. R. Rep., at 3-4. Both decisions are discussed in Part III of this opinion.

3 All functions of the Commissioner of Education, formerly an officer in the Department of Health, Education, and Welfare, were transferred to the Secretary of Education in 1979 when Congress passed the Department of Education Organization Act, 20 U. S. C. § 3401 *et seq.* (1976 ed., Supp. IV). See 20 U. S. C. § 3441(a)(1) (1976 ed., Supp. IV).

4 Despite this preference for "mainstreaming" handicapped children -- educating them with nonhandicapped children -- Congress recognized that regular classrooms simply would not be a suitable setting for the education of many handicapped children. The Act expressly acknowledges that "the nature or severity of the handicap [may be] such that education in regular classes with the use of supplementary aids and services cannot be achieved satisfactorily." § 1412(5). The Act thus provides for the education of some handicapped children in separate classes or institutional settings. See *ibid.*; § 1413(a)(4).

5 In addition to covering a wide variety of handicapping conditions, the Act requires special educational services for children "regardless of the severity of their handicap." §§ 1412(2)(C), 1414(a)(1)(A).

6   The requirements that parents be permitted to file complaints regarding their child's education, and be present when the child's IEP is formulated, represent only two examples of Congress' effort to maximize parental involvement in the education of each handicapped child. In addition, the Act requires that parents be permitted "to examine all relevant records with respect to the identification, evaluation, and educational placement of the child, and . . . to obtain an independent educational evaluation of the child." § 1415(b)(1)(A). See also §§ 1412(4), 1414(a)(4). State educational policies and the state plan submitted to the Secretary of Education must be formulated in "consultation with individuals involved in or concerned with the education of handicapped children, including handicapped individuals and parents or guardians of handicapped children." § 1412(7). See also § 1412(2)(E). Local agencies, which receive funds under the Act by applying to the state agency, must submit applications which assure that they have developed procedures for "the participation and consultation of the parents or [guardians] of [handicapped] children" in local educational programs, § 1414(a)(1)(C)(iii), and the application itself, along with "all pertinent documents related to such application," must be made "available to parents, guardians, and other members of the general public." § 1414(a)(4).

7   "Any party" to a state or local administrative hearing must "be accorded (1) the right to be accompanied and advised by counsel and by individuals with special knowledge or training with respect to the problems of handicapped children, (2) the right to present evidence and confront, cross examine, and compel the attendance of witnesses, (3) the right to a written or electronic verbatim record of such hearing, and (4) the right to written findings of fact and decisions." § 1415(d).

8   For reasons that are not revealed in the record, the District Court concluded that "[the] Act itself does not define 'appropriate education.'" 483 F.Supp., at 533. In fact, the Act expressly defines the phrase "free appropriate public education," see § 1401(18), to which the District Court was referring. See 483 F.Supp., at 533. After overlooking the statutory definition, the District Court sought guidance not from regulations interpreting the Act, but from regulations promulgated under § 504 of the Rehabilitation Act. See 483 F.Supp., at 533, citing 45 CFR § 84.33(b)

9   The IEP which respondents challenged in the District Court was created for the 1978- 1979 school year. Petitioners contend that the District Court erred in reviewing that IEP after the school year had ended and before the school administrators were able to develop another IEP for subsequent years. We disagree. Judicial review invariably takes more than nine months to complete, not to mention the time consumed during the preceding state administrative hearings. The District Court thus correctly ruled that it retained jurisdiction to grant relief because the alleged deficiencies in the IEP were capable of repetition as to the parties before it yet evading review. 483 F.Supp. 536, 538 (1980). See *Murphy v. Hunt*, 455 U.S. 478, 482 (1982); *Weinstein v. Bradford*, 423 U.S. 147, 149 (1975).

10   Examples of "related services" identified in the Act are "speech pathology and audiology, psychological services, physical and occupational therapy, recreation, and medical and counseling services, except that such medical services shall be for diagnostic and evaluation purposes only." § 1401(17).

11   The dissent, finding that "the standard of the courts below seems . . . to reflect the congressional purpose" of the Act, post, at 218, concludes that our answer to this question "is not a satisfactory one." Post, at 216. Presumably, the dissent also agrees with the District Court's conclusion that "it has been left entirely to the courts and the hearing officers to give content to the requirement of an 'appropriate education.'" 483 F. Supp., at 533. It thus seems that the dissent would give the courts carte blanche to impose upon the States whatever burden their various judgments indicate should be imposed. Indeed, the dissent clearly characterizes the requirement of an "appropriate education" as open-ended, noting that "if there are limits not evident from the face of the statute on what may be considered an 'appropriate education,' they must be found in the purpose of the statute or its legislative history." Post, at 213. Not only are we unable to find any suggestion from the face of the statute that the requirement of an "appropriate education" was to be limitless, but we also view the dissent's approach as contrary to the fundamental proposition that Congress, when exercising its spending power, can impose no burden upon the States unless it does so unambiguously. See *infra*, at 204, n. 26. No one can doubt that this would have been an easier case if Congress had seen fit to provide a more comprehensive statutory definition of the phrase "free appropriate public education." But Congress did not do so, and "our problem is to construe what Congress has written. After all, Congress expresses its purpose by words. It is for us to ascertain -- neither to add nor to subtract, neither to delete nor to distort." 62 Cases of *Jam v. United States*, 340 U.S. 593, 596 (1951). We would be less than faithful to our obligation to construe what Congress has written if in this case we were to disregard the statutory language and legislative history of the Act by concluding that Congress had imposed upon the States a burden of unspecified proportions and weight, to be revealed only through case-by-case adjudication in the courts.

12   See H. R. Rep., at 10; Note, The Education of All Handicapped Children Act of 1975, 10 U. Mich. J. L. Ref. 110, 119 (1976).

13   See, e. g., 121 Cong. Rec. 19494 (1975) (remarks of Sen. Javits) ("all too often, our handicapped citizens have been denied the opportunity to receive an adequate education"); id., at 19502 (remarks of Sen. Cranston) (millions of handicapped "children . . . are largely excluded from the educational opportunities that we give to our other children"); id., at 23708 (remarks of Rep. Mink) ("handicapped children . . . are denied access to public schools because of a lack of trained personnel").

14   Similarly, the Senate Report states that it was an "[increased] awareness of the educational needs of handicapped children and landmark court decisions establishing the right to education for handicapped children [that] pointed to the necessity of an expanded federal fiscal role." S. Rep., at 5. See also H. R. Rep., at 2-3.

15 The only substantive standard which can be implied from these cases comports with the standard implicit in the Act. *PARC* states that each child must receive "access to a free public program of education and training appropriate to his learning capacities," 334 F.Supp., at 1258 (emphasis added), and that further state action is required when it appears that "the needs of the mentally retarded child are not being adequately served," *id.*, at 1266. (Emphasis added.) *Mills* also speaks in terms of "adequate" educational services, 348 F.Supp., at 878, and sets a realistic standard of providing some educational services to each child when every need cannot be met. "If sufficient funds are not available to finance all of the services and programs that are needed and desirable in the system then the available funds must be expended equitably in such a manner that no child is entirely excluded from a publicly supported education consistent with his needs and ability to benefit therefrom. The inadequacies of the District of Columbia Public School System whether occasioned by insufficient funding or administrative inefficiency, certainly cannot be permitted to bear more heavily on the 'exceptional' or handicapped child than on the normal child." *Id.*, at 876.

16 Like the Act, *PARC* required the State to "identify, locate, [and] evaluate" handicapped children, 334 F.Supp., at 1267, to create for each child an individual educational program, id., at 1265, and to hold a hearing "on any change in educational assignment," id., at 1266. *Mills* also required the preparation of an individual educational program for each child. In addition, *Mills* permitted the child's parents to inspect records relevant to the child's education, to obtain an independent educational evaluation of the child, to object to the IEP and receive a hearing before an independent hearing officer, to be represented by counsel at the hearing, and to have the right to confront and cross-examine adverse witnesses, all of which are also permitted by the Act. 348 F.Supp., at 879-881. Like the Act, *Mills* also required that the education of handicapped children be conducted pursuant to an overall plan prepared by the District of Columbia, and established a policy of educating handicapped children with nonhandicapped children whenever possible. *Ibid.*

17 See S. Rep., at 6-7; H. R. Rep., at 3-4.

18 The 1974 statute "incorporated the major principles of the right to education cases," by "[adding] important new provisions to the Education of the Handicapped Act which require the States to: establish a goal of providing full educational opportunities to all handicapped children; provide procedures for insuring that handicapped children and their parents or guardians are guaranteed procedural safeguards in decisions regarding identification, evaluation, and educational placement of handicapped children; establish procedures to insure that, to the maximum extent appropriate, handicapped children . . . are educated with children who are not handicapped; . . . and, establish procedures to insure that testing and evaluation materials and procedures utilized for the purposes of classification and placement of handicapped children will be selected and administered so as not to be racially or culturally discriminatory." S. Rep., at 8.

The House Report explains that the Act simply incorporated these purposes of the 1974 statute: the Act was intended "primarily to amend . . . the Education of the Handicapped Act in order to provide permanent authorization and a comprehensive mechanism which will insure that those provisions enacted during the 93rd Congress [the 1974 statute] will result in maximum benefits for handicapped children and their families." H. R. Rep., at 5. Thus, the 1974 statute's purpose of providing handicapped children access to a public education became the purpose of the Act.

19 These statistics appear repeatedly throughout the legislative history of the Act, demonstrating a virtual consensus among legislators that 3.9 million handicapped children were receiving an appropriate education in 1975. See, e. g., 121 Cong. Rec. 19486 (1975) (remarks of Sen. Williams); *id.*, at 19504 (remarks of Sen. Schweicker); *id.*, at 23702 (remarks of Rep. Madden); *ibid.* (remarks of Rep. Brademas); *id.*, at 23709 (remarks of Rep. Minish); *id.*, at 37024 (remarks of Rep. Brademas); *id.*, at 37027 (remarks of Rep. Gude); *id.*, at 37417 (remarks of Sen. Javits); *id.*, at 37420 (remarks of Sen. Hathaway).

20 Senator Randolph stated: "[Only] 55 percent of the school-aged handicapped children and 22 percent of the pre-school-aged handicapped children are receiving special educational services." Hearings on S. 6 before the Subcommittee on the Handicapped of the Senate Committee on Labor and Public Welfare, 94th Cong., 1st Sess., 1 (1975). Although the figures differ slightly in various parts of the legislative history, the general thrust of congressional calculations was that roughly one-half of the handicapped children in the United States were not receiving specialized educational services, and thus were not "served." See, e. g., 121 Cong. Rec. 19494 (1975) (remarks of Sen. Javits) ("only 50 percent of the Nation's handicapped children received proper education services"); *id.*, at 19504 (remarks of Sen. Humphrey) ("[almost] 3 million handicapped children, while in school, receive none of the special services that they require in order to make education a meaningful experience"); *id.*, at 23706 (remarks of Rep. Quie) ("only 55 percent [of handicapped children] were receiving a public education"); *id.*, at 23709 (remarks of Rep. Biaggi) ("[over] 3 million [handicapped] children in this country are receiving either below par education or none at all").

Statements similar to those appearing in the text, which equate "served" as it appears in the Senate Report to "receiving special educational services," appear throughout the legislative history. See, e. g., *id.*, at 19492 (remarks of Sen. Williams); *id.*, at 19494 (remarks of Sen. Javits); *id.*, at 19496 (remarks of Sen. Stone); id., at 19504-19505 (remarks of Sen. Humphrey); *id.*, at 23703 (remarks of Rep. Brademas); Hearings on H. R. 7217 before the Subcommittee on Select Education of the House Committee on Education and Labor, 94th Cong., 1st Sess., 91, 150, 153 (1975); Hearings on H. R. 4199 before the Select Subcommittee on Education of the House Committee on Education and Labor, 93d Cong., 1st Sess., 130, 139 (1973). See also 34 CFR § 300.343 (1981).

21 In seeking to read more into the Act than its language or legislative history will permit, the United States focuses upon

the word "appropriate," arguing that "the statutory definitions do not adequately explain what [it means]." Brief for United States as Amicus Curiae 13. Whatever Congress meant by an "appropriate" education, it is clear that it did not mean a potential-maximizing education.

The term as used in reference to educating the handicapped appears to have originated in the *PARC* decision, where the District Court required that handicapped children be provided with "education and training appropriate to [their] learning capacities." 334 F.Supp., at 1258. The word appears again in the *Mills* decision, the District Court at one point referring to the need for "an appropriate educational program," 348 F.Supp., at 879, and at another point speaking of a "suitable publicly-supported education," *id.*, at 878. Both cases also refer to the need for an "adequate" education. See 334 F.Supp., at 1266; 348 F.Supp., at 878.

The use of "appropriate" in the language of the Act, although by no means definitive, suggests that Congress used the word as much to describe the settings in which handicapped children should be educated as to prescribe the substantive content or supportive services of their education. For example, § 1412(5) requires that handicapped children be educated in classrooms with nonhandicapped children "to the maximum extent appropriate." Similarly, § 1401(19) provides that, "whenever appropriate," handicapped children should attend and participate in the meeting at which their IEP is drafted. In addition, the definition of "free appropriate public education" itself states that instruction given handicapped children should be at an "appropriate preschool, elementary, or secondary school" level. § 1401(18)(C). The Act's use of the word "appropriate" thus seems to reflect Congress' recognition that some settings simply are not suitable environments for the participation of some handicapped children. At the very least, these statutory uses of the word refute the contention that Congress used "appropriate" as a term of art which concisely expresses the standard found by the lower courts.

22 See also 121 Cong. Rec. 19492 (1975) (remarks of Sen. Williams); *id.*, at 19504 (remarks of Sen. Humphrey).

23 This view is supported by the congressional intention, frequently expressed in the legislative history, that handicapped children be enabled to achieve a reasonable degree of self-sufficiency. After referring to statistics showing that many handicapped children were excluded from public education, the Senate Report states:

"The long range implications of these statistics are that public agencies and taxpayers will spend billions of dollars over the lifetimes of these individuals to maintain such persons as dependents and in a minimally acceptable lifestyle. With proper education services, many would be able to become productive citizens, contributing to society instead of being forced to remain burdens. Others, through such services, would increase their independence, thus reducing their dependence on society." S. Rep., at 9. See also H. R. Rep., at 11.

Similarly, one of the principal Senate sponsors of the Act stated that "providing appropriate educational services now means that many of these individuals will be able to become a contributing part of our society, and they will not have to depend on subsistence payments from public funds." 121 Cong. Rec. 19492 (1975) (remarks of Sen. Williams). See also *id.*, at 25541 (remarks of Rep. Harkin); *id.*, at 37024-37025 (remarks of Rep. Brademas); *id.*, at 37027 (remarks of Rep. Gude); *id.*, at 37410 (remarks of Sen. Randolph); *id.*, at 37416 (remarks of Sen. Williams).

The desire to provide handicapped children with an attainable degree of personal independence obviously anticipated that state educational programs would confer educational benefits upon such children. But at the same time, the goal of achieving some degree of self-sufficiency in most cases is a good deal more modest than the potential-maximizing goal adopted by the lower courts.

Despite its frequent mention, we cannot conclude, as did the dissent in the Court of Appeals, that self-sufficiency was itself the substantive standard which Congress imposed upon the States. Because many mildly handicapped children will achieve self-sufficiency without state assistance while personal independence for the severely handicapped may be an unreachable goal, "self-sufficiency" as a substantive standard is at once an inadequate protection and an overly demanding requirement. We thus view these references in the legislative history as evidence of Congress' intention that the services provided handicapped children be educationally beneficial, whatever the nature or severity of their handicap.

24 Title 20 U. S. C. § 1412(5) requires that participating States establish "procedures to assure that, to the maximum extent appropriate, handicapped children, including children in public or private institutions or other care facilities, are educated with children who are not handicapped, and that special classes, separate schooling, or other removal of handicapped children from the regular educational environment occurs only when the nature or severity of the handicap is such that education in regular classes with the use of supplementary aids and services cannot be achieved satisfactorily."

25 We do not hold today that every handicapped child who is advancing from grade to grade in a regular public school system is automatically receiving a "free appropriate public education." In this case, however, we find Amy's academic progress, when considered with the special services and professional consideration accorded by the Furnace Woods school administrators, to be dispositive.

26 In defending the decisions of the District Court and the Court of Appeals, respondents and the United States rely upon isolated statements in the legislative history concerning the achievement of maximum potential, see H. R. Rep., at 13, as support for their contention that Congress intended to impose greater substantive requirements than we have found. These statements, however, are too thin a reed on which to base an interpretation of the Act which disregards both its language and the balance of its legislative history. "Passing references and isolated phrases are not controlling

when analyzing a legislative history." *Department of State v. Washington Post Co.*, 456 U.S. 595, 600 (1982). Moreover, even were we to agree that these statements evince a congressional intent to maximize each child's potential, we could not hold that Congress had successfully imposed that burden upon the States. "[Legislation] enacted pursuant to the spending power is much in the nature of a contract: in return for federal funds, the States agree to comply with federally imposed conditions. The legitimacy of Congress' power to legislate under the spending power thus rests on whether the State voluntarily and knowingly accepts the terms of the 'contract.' . . . Accordingly, if Congress intends to impose a condition on the grant of federal moneys, it must do so unambiguously." *Pennhurst State School v. Halderman*, 451 U.S. 1, 17 (1981) (footnote omitted). As already demonstrated, the Act and its history impose no requirements on the States like those imposed by the District Court and the Court of Appeals. A fortiori Congress has not done so unambiguously, as required in the valid exercise of its spending power.

27 This inquiry will require a court not only to satisfy itself that the State has adopted the state plan, policies, and assurances required by the Act, but also to determine that the State has created an IEP for the child in question which conforms with the requirements of § 1401(19).

28 When the handicapped child is being educated in the regular classrooms of a public school system, the achievement of passing marks and advancement from grade to grade will be one important factor in determining educational benefit. See Part III, *supra*.

29 In this case, for example, both the state hearing officer and the District Court were presented with evidence as to the best method for educating the deaf, a question long debated among scholars. See Large, *Special Problems of the Deaf Under the Education for All Handicapped Children Act of 1975*, 58 Wash. U. L. Q. 213, 229 (1980). The District Court accepted the testimony of respondents' experts that there was "a trend supported by studies showing the greater degree of success of students brought up in deaf households using [the method of communication used by the Rowleys]." 483 F.Supp., at 535.

30 It is clear that Congress was aware of the States' traditional role in the formulation and execution of educational policy. "Historically, the States have had the primary responsibility for the education of children at the elementary and secondary level." 121 Cong. Rec. 19498 (1975) (remarks of Sen. Dole). See also *Epperson v. Arkansas*, 393 U.S. 97, 104 (1968) ("By and large, public education in our Nation is committed to the control of state and local authorities").

31 In addition to providing for extensive parental involvement in the formulation of state and local policies, as well as the preparation of individual educational programs, the Act ensures that States will receive the advice of experts in the field of educating handicapped children. As a condition for receiving federal funds under the Act, States must create "an advisory panel, appointed by the Governor or any other official authorized under State law to make such appointments, composed of individuals involved in or concerned with the education of handicapped children, including handicapped individuals, teachers, parents or guardians of handicapped children, State and local education officials, and administrators of programs for handicapped children, which (A) advises the State educational agency of unmet needs within the State in the education of handicapped children, [and] (B) comments publicly on any rules or regulations proposed for issuance by the State regarding the education of handicapped children." § 1413(a)(12).

32 Because the District Court declined to reach respondents' contention that petitioners had failed to comply with the Act's procedural requirements in developing Amy's IEP, 483 F.Supp., at 533, n. 8, the case must be remanded for further proceedings consistent with this opinion.

JUSTICE WHITE, with whom JUSTICE BRENNAN and JUSTICE MARSHALL join, **dissenting**.

In order to reach its result in this case, the majority opinion contradicts itself, the language of the statute, and the legislative history. Both the majority's standard for a "free appropriate education" and its standard for judicial review disregard congressional intent.[1]

I

The majority first turns its attention to the meaning of a "free appropriate public education." the Act provides:

The term "free appropriate public education" means special education and related services which (A) have been provided at public expense, under public supervision and direction, and without charge, (B) meet the standard of the State educational agency, (c) include an appropriate preschool, elementary agency, (D) are provided in conformity with the individualized education program required under section 1414(a)(5) of this title." 20 U.S.C. 1401(18).

The majority reads this statutory language as establishing a congressional intent limited to bringing "previously excluded handicapped children into the public education systems of the States and requiring the States to adopt procedures which would result in individualized consideration of and instruction for each child." *Ante*, at 12. In its attempt to constrict the definition of "appropriate" and the thrust of the Act, the majority opinion states, "Noticeably absent from the language of the statute is any substantive standard prescribing the level of education to be accorded handicapped children. Certainly the language of the statute contains no requirements like the one imposed by the lower courts-that States commensurate with the opportunity provided to other children." quoting 483, F. Supp. at 534.

I agree that the language of the Act does not contain a substantive standard beyond requiring that the education offered must be "appropriate." However, if there are limits not evident from the face of the statute on what may be considered an "appropriate education," they must be found in the purpose of the statute or its legislative history. The Act itself announces it will provide a "full educational opportunity to all handicapped children." 20 U.S.C. 1412(2)(A) (emphasis added). This goal is repeated throughout the legislative history, in statements too frequent to be "passing references and isolated phrases." Ante, at 27, n. 26, quoting Department of State v. Washington Post Co., __ U.S.__ (1982). These statements elucidate the meaning of "appropriate." According to the Senate Report, for example, the Act does "guarantee that handicapped children are provided equal educational opportunity." S. Rep. No. 94-168, at 9 (1975) (emphasis added). This promise appears throughout the legislative history. See 121 Cong. Rec. 19482-19483 (1975) (remarks of Sen. Randolph); *id.*, at 19504 (Sen. Humphrey); *id.*, at 19505 (Sen. Beall); *id.*, at 23704 (Rep Brademas); *id.*, at 25538 (Rep. Cornell); *id.*, at 25540 (Rep. Grassley); *id.*, at 37025 (Rep. Perkins); *id.*, at 37030 (Rep. Mink); *id.*, at 37412 (Sen. Taft); *id.*, at 37413 (Sen. Williams); *id.*, at 37418-37419 (Sen. Cranston); *id.*, at 37419-37420 (Sen. Beall).

Indeed, at times the purpose of the Act was described as tailoring each handicapped child's educational plan to enable the child "to achieve his or her maximum potential." H.R. Rep. No. 94-332, 94th Cong., 1st Sess. 13 19 (1975), See 121 Cong. Rec. 23709 (1975). Sen. Stafford, one of the sponsors of the Act, declared "We can all agree that the education given a handicapped child should be equivalent, at least, to the one those children who are not handicapped receive." 121 Cong. Rec. 19483 (1975). The legislative history thus directly supports the conclusion that the Act intends to give handicapped children an educational opportunity commensurate with that given other children.

The majority opinion announces a different substantive standard, that "Congress did not impose upon the States any greater substantive standard than would be necessary to make such access meaningful." While "meaningful" is no more enlightening than "appropriate," the Court purports to clarify itself. Because Amy was provided with some specialized instruction from which she obtained some benefit and because she passed from grade to grade, she was receiving a meaningful and therefore appropriate education. [2]

This falls far short of what the Act intended. The Act details as specifically as possible the kind of specialized education each handicapped child must receive. It would apparently satisfy the Court's standard of "access to specialized instruction and related services which are individually designed to provide educational benefit to the handicapped child," for a deaf child such as Amy to be given a teacher with a loud voice, for she would benefit from that service. The Act requires more. It defines "special educa-

tion" to mean "specifically designed instruction, at no cost to parents or guardians, to meet the unique needs of a handicapped child." 1401(16) (emphasis added).[3] Providing a teacher with a loud voice would not meet Amy's needs and would not satisfy the Act. The basic floor of opportunity is instead, as the courts below recognized, intended to eliminate the effects of the handicap, at least to the extent that the child will be given an equal opportunity to learn if that is reasonably possible. Amy Rowley, without a sign language interpreter, comprehends less than half of what is said in the classroom-less than half of what normal children comprehend. This is hardly an equal opportunity to learn, even if Amy makes passing grades.

Despite its reliance on the use of "appropriate" in the definition of the Act, the majority opinion speculates that "Congress used the word as much described the settings in which the children should be educated as to prescribe the substantive content or supportive services of their education." Of course, the word "appropriate" can be applied in many ways; at times in the Act, Congress used it to recommend mainstreaming handicapped children; at other points, it used the word to refer to the content of the individualized education. The issue before us is what standard the word "appropriate" incorporates when it is used to modify "education." The answer given by the Court is not a satisfactory one.

II

The Court's discussion of the standard for judicial review is as flawed as its discussion of a "free appropriate public education." According to the Court, a court can ask only whether the State has "complied with the procedures set forth in the Act" and whether the individualized education program is "reasonably calculated to enable the child to receive educational benefit." Both the language of the Act and legislative history, however, demonstrate that Congress intended the courts to conduct a far more searching inquiry.

The majority assigns major significance to the review provision's being found in a section entitled "Procedural Safeguards." But where else would a provision for judicial review belong? The majority does acknowledge that the current language, specifying that a court "shall receive the record of the administrative proceedings, shall hear additional evidence at the request of a party, and basing its decision on the preponderance of the evidence, shall grant such relief as the court determines is appropriate," 1415(e)(2), was substituted at Conference for language that would have restricted the role of the reviewing court much more sharply. It is clear enough to me that Congress decided to reduce substantially judicial deference to state administrative decisions.

The legislative history shows that judicial review is not

limited to procedural matters and that the state educational agencies are given first, but not final, responsibility for the content of a handicapped child's education. The Conference committee directs courts to make an "independent decision." S. Conf. Rep. No. 94-455, at 50. The deliberate change in the review provision is an unusually clear indication that Congress intended courts to undertake substantive review instead of relying on the conclusions of the state agency.

On the floor of the Senate, Senator Williams, the chief sponsor of the bill, committee chairman, and floor manager responsible for the legislation in the Senate, emphasized the breath of the review provisions at both the administrative and judicial levels:

> Any parent or guardian may present a complaint concerning **any matter** regarding the identification, evaluation, or educational placement of the child or the provision of a free appropriate public education to such a child.

> In this regard, Mr. President, I would like to stress that the language referring to "free appropriate education" has been adopted to make clear that a complaint may involve matters such a questions respecting a child's individualized education program, questions of whether special education and related services are being provided without charge to the parents or guardians, questions relating to whether to the services provided a child meet the standards of the State education agency, **or any other question** within the scope of the definition of "free appropriate public education." In addition, it should be clear that a parent or guardian may present a complaint alleging that a State or local education agency has refused to provide services to which a child may be entitled or alleging that the State or local educational agency has erroneously classified a child as as handicapped child when, in fact, that child is not a handicapped child. 121 Cong. Rec. 37415 (emphasis added).

There is no doubt that the state agency itself must make substantive decisions. The legislative history reveals that the courts are to consider, de novo, the same issues. Senator Williams explicitly stated that the civil action permitted under the Act encompasses all matters related to the original complaint. *Id.*, at 37416.

Thus, the Court's limitations on judicial review have no support in either the language of the Act or the legislative history. Congress did not envision that inquiry would end if a showing is made that the child is receiving passing marks and is advancing from grade to grade. Instead, it intended to permit a full and searching inquiry into any aspect of a handicapped child's education. The court's standard, for example, would not permit a challenge to part of the IEP; the legislative history demonstrate beyond doubt that Congress intended such challenge to be possible, even if the plan as developed is reasonably calculated to give the child some benefits.

Parents can challenge the IEP for failing to supply the special education and related services needed by the individual handicapped child. That is what the Rowleys did. As the Government observes,

> "Courts called upon to review the content of an IEP, in accordance with 20 U.S.C. 1415(e) inevitably are required to make a judgment on the basis of the evidence presented, concerning whether the educational methods proposed by the local school district are 'appropriate' for the handicapped child involved." Brief for United States as Amicus Curiae 13.

The courts below, as they were required by the Act, did precisely that.

Under the judicial review provisions of the Act, neither the District Court nor the Court of Appeals was bound by the state's construction of what an "appropriate" education means in general or by what the state authorities considered to be an appropriate education for Amy Rowley. Because the standard of the courts below seems to me to reflect the congressional purpose and because their factual findings are not clearly erroneous, I respectfully dissent.

Endnotes

1 The Court's opinion relies heavily on the statement, which occurs throughout the legislative history, that, at the time of enactment, one million of the roughly eight million handicapped children in the United States were excluded entirely from the public school system and more than half were receiving an inappropriate education. See, e.g. *ante*, at pp. 11, 18-19. But this statement was often linked to statements urging equal educational opportunity. See, e.g. *121 Cong. Rec.* 19502 (remarks of Sen. Cranston); *id.* at 23702 (remarks of Rep. Brademas). That is, Congress wanted not only to bring handicapped children into schoolhouse, but wanted also to benefit them once they had entered.

2 As further support of its conclusion, the majority opinion turns to *Pennsylvania Association for Retarded Children v. Commonwalth of Pennsylvania (PARC)*, 334 F. Supp. 1257 (1971), 343 F. Supp. 279 (ED Pa. 1972) and *Mills v. Board of Education of the District of Columbia*, 348 F. Supp. 866 (DDC 1972). That these decisions served as an impetus for the Act does not, however, establish them as the limit of the Act. In any case, the very language that the majority quotes from Mills sets a standard not of some education, but of educational opportunity equal to that of non-handicapped children.

Indeed, *Mills*, relying on decisions since called into question by this Court's opinion in *San Antonio School District v. Rodriquez*, 411 U.S. 1 (1973), states:

In *Hobson v. Hansen* [269 F. Supp. 401 (DD,) Judge Wright found that denying poor public school children educational opportunity equal to that available to more affluent public school children was violative of the Due Process Clause of the Fifth Amendment. *A fortiori*, the defendants' conduct here, denying plaintiffs and their class not just an equal publicly supported education while providing such education to other children, is violative of the Due Process Clause." 348 F.Supp., at 875. Whatever the effect of *Rodriquez* on the validity of this reasoning, the statement exposes the majority's mischaracterization of the opinion and thus of the assumptions of the legislature that passed the Act.

3 "Related services' are "transportation, and such developmental, corrective, and other supportive services . . . as may be required to assist a handicapped child to benefit from special education." 1401(17).

The Supreme Court of the United States

468 U. S. 883 (1984)

IRVING INDEPENDENT SCHOOL DISTRICT,

Petitioners

v.

TATRO, et. Ex., Individually and as Next Friends of TATRO, a Minor,

Respondent

No. 83-558.

Decided July 5, 1984

BURGER, C. J., delivered the opinion of the Court, in which WHITE, BLACKMUN, POWELL, REHNQUIST, and O'CONNOR, JJ., joined, and in all but Part III of which BRENNAN, MARSHALL, and STEVENS, JJ., joined.

BRENNAN, J., filed an opinion concurring in part and dissenting in part, in which MARSHALL, J., joined, post, p. 896. STEVENS, J., filed an opinion concurring in part and dissenting in part, post, p. 896.

CHIEF JUSTICE BURGER delivered the opinion of the Court.

We granted certiorari to determine whether the Education of the Handicapped Act or the Rehabilitation Act of 1973 requires a school district to provide a handicapped child with clean intermittent catheterization during school hours.

I

Amber Tatro is an 8-year-old girl born with a defect known as spina bifida. As a result, she suffers from orthopedic and speech impairments and a neurogenic bladder, which prevents her from emptying her bladder voluntarily. Consequently, she must be catheterized every three or four hours to avoid injury to her kidneys. In accordance with accepted medical practice, clean intermittent catheterization (CIC), a procedure involving the insertion of a catheter into the urethra to drain the bladder, has been prescribed. The procedure is a simple one that may be performed in a few minutes by a layperson with less than an hour's training. Amber's parents, babysitter, and teenage brother are all qualified to administer CIC, and Amber soon will be able to perform this procedure herself.

In 1979 petitioner Irving Independent School District agreed to provide special education for Amber, who was then three and one-half years old. In consultation with her parents, who are respondents here, petitioner developed an individualized education program for Amber under the [468 U.S. 883, 886] requirements of the Education of the Handicapped Act, 84 Stat. 175, as amended significantly by the Education for All Handicapped Children Act of 1975, 89 Stat. 773, 20 U.S.C. 1401(19), 1414(a)(5). The individualized education program provided that Amber would attend early childhood development classes and receive special services such as physical and occupational therapy. That program, however, made no provision for school personnel to administer CIC.

Respondents unsuccessfully pursued administrative remedies to secure CIC services for Amber during school hours.[1] In October 1979 respondents brought the present action in District Court against petitioner, the State Board of Education, and others. See 1415(e)(2). They sought an injunction ordering petitioner to provide Amber with CIC and sought damages and attorney's fees. First, respondents invoked the Education of the Handicapped Act. Because Texas received funding under that statute, petitioner was required to provide Amber with a "free appropriate public education," 1412(1), 1414(a)(1)(C)(ii), which is defined to include "related services," 1401(18). Respondents argued that CIC is one such "related service."[2] Second, respondents invoked 504 of the Rehabilitation Act of 1973, 87 Stat. 394, as amended, 29 U.S.C. 794, which forbids an individual, by reason of a handicap, to be "excluded from the [468 U.S. 883, 887] "participation in, be denied the benefits of, or be subjected to discrimination under" any program receiving federal aid.

The District Court denied respondents' request for a preliminary injunction. *Tatro v. Texas*, 481 F. Supp. 1224 (N. D. Tex. 1979). That court concluded that CIC was not a "related service" under the Education of the Handicapped Act because it did not serve a need arising from the effort to educate. It also held that 504 of the Rehabilitation Act did not require "the setting up of governmental health care for people seeking to participate" in federally funded programs. *Id.*, at 1229.

The Court of Appeals reversed. *Tatro v. Texas*, 625 F.2d 557 (CA5 1980) (*Tatro I*). First, it held that CIC was a "related service" under the Education of the Handicapped Act, 20 U.S.C. 1401(17), because without the procedure Amber could not attend classes and benefit from special education. Second, it held that petitioner's refusal to provide CIC effectively excluded her from a federally funded educational program in violation of 504 of the Rehabilitation Act. The Court of Appeals remanded for the District Court to develop a factual record and apply these legal principles.

On remand petitioner stressed the Education of the Handicapped Act's explicit provision that "medical services" could qualify as "related services" only when they served the purpose of diagnosis or evaluation. See n. 2, *supra*. The District Court held that under Texas law a nurse or other qualified person may administer CIC without engaging in the unauthorized practice of medicine, provided that a doctor prescribes and supervises the procedure. The District Court then held that, because a doctor was not needed to administer CIC, provision of the procedure was not a "medical service" for purposes of the Education of the Handicapped Act. Finding CIC to be a "related service" under that Act, the District Court ordered petitioner and the State Board of Education to modify Amber's individualized education program [468 U.S. 883, 888] to include provision of CIC during school hours. It also awarded compensatory damages against petitioner. *Tatro v. Texas*, 516 F. Supp. 968 (ND Tex. 1981).[3]

On the authority of *Tatro I*, the District Court then held that respondents had proved a violation of 504 of the Rehabilitation Act. Although the District Court did not rely on this holding to authorize any greater injunctive or compensatory relief, it did invoke the holding to award attorney's fees against petitioner and the State Board of Education[4] 516 F. Supp., at 968; App. to Pet. for Cert. 55a-63a. The Rehabilitation Act, unlike the Education of the Handicapped Act, authorizes prevailing parties to recover attorney's fees. See 29 U.S.C. 794a.

The Court of Appeals affirmed. *Tatro v. Texas*, 703 F.2d 823 (CA5 1983) (*Tatro II*). That court accepted the District Court's conclusion that state law permitted qualified persons to administer CIC without the physical presence of a doctor, and it affirmed the award of relief under the Education of the Handicapped Act. In affirming the award of attorney's fees based on a finding of liability under the Rehabilitation Act, the Court of Appeals held that no change of circumstances since *Tatro I* justified a different result.

We granted certiorari, 464 U.S. 1007 (1983), and we affirm in part and reverse in part.

II.

This case poses two separate issues. The first is whether the Education of the Handicapped Act requires petitioner to [468 U.S. 883, 889] provide CIC services to Amber. The second is whether 504 of the Rehabilitation Act creates such an obligation. We first turn to the claim presented under the Education of the Handicapped Act.

States receiving funds under the Act are obliged to satisfy certain conditions. A primary condition is that the state implement a policy "that assures all handicapped children the right to a free appropriate public education." 20 U.S.C. 1412(1). Each educational agency applying to a state for funding must provide assurances in turn that its program aims to provide "a free appropriate public education to all handicapped children." 1414(a)(1)(C)(ii).

A "free appropriate public education" is explicitly defined as "special education and related services." 1401(18).[5] The term "special education" means

"specially designed instruction, at no cost to parents or guardians, to meet the unique needs of a handicapped child, including classroom instruction, instruction in physical education, home instruction, and instruction in hospitals and institutions." 1401(16).

"Related services" are defined as

"transportation, and such developmental, corrective, and other supportive services (including speech pathology and audiology, psychological services, physical and occupational therapy, recreation, and medical and counseling services, except that such medical services shall be for diagnostic and evaluation purposes only) as may be required to assist a handicapped child to benefit from [468 U.S. 883, 890] special education, and includes the early identification and assessment of handicapping conditions in children." 1401(17) (emphasis added).

The issue in this case is whether CIC is a "related service" that petitioner is obliged to provide to Amber. We must answer two questions: first, whether CIC is a "supportive servic[e] . . . required to assist a handicapped child to benefit from special education"; and second, whether CIC is excluded from this definition as a "medical servic[e]" serving purposes other than diagnosis or evaluation.

A.

The Court of Appeals was clearly correct in holding that CIC is a "supportive servic[e] . . . required to assist a handicapped child to benefit from special education."[6] It is clear on this record that, without having CIC services available during the school day, Amber cannot attend school and thereby "benefit from special education." CIC services therefore fall squarely within the definition of a "supportive service."[7] [468 U.S. 883, 891]

As we have stated before, "Congress sought primarily to make public education available to handicapped children" and "to make such access meaningful." *Board of Education of Hendrick Hudson Central School District v. Rowley*, 458 U.S. 176, 192 (1982). A service that enables a handicapped child to remain at school during the day is an important means of providing the child with the meaningful access to education that Congress envisioned. The Act makes specific provision for services, like transportation, for example, that do no more than enable a child to be physically present in class, see 20 U.S.C. 1401(17); and the Act specifically authorizes grants for schools to alter buildings and equipment to make them accessible to the handicapped, 1406; see S. Rep. No. 94-168, p. 38 (1975); 121 Cong. Rec. 19483-19484 (1975) (remarks of Sen. Stafford). Services like CIC that permit a child to remain at school during the day are no less related to the effort to educate than are services that enable the child to reach, enter, or exit the school.

We hold that CIC services in this case qualify as a "supportive servic[e] . . . required to assist a handicapped child to benefit from special education."[8]

B.

We also agree with the Court of Appeals that provision of CIC is not a "medical servic[e]," which a school is required to provide only for purposes of diagnosis or evaluation. See 20 U.S.C. 1401(17). We begin with the regulations of the [468 U.S. 883, 892] Department of Education, which are entitled to deference.[9] See, e. g., *Blum v. Bacon*, 457 U.S. 132, 141 (1982). The regulations define "related services" for handicapped children to include "school health services," 34 CFR 300.13(a) (1983), which are defined in turn as "services provided by a qualified school nurse or other qualified person," 300.13(b) (10). "Medical services" are defined as "services provided by a licensed physician." 300.13(b)(4).[10] Thus, the Secretary has determined that the services of a school nurse otherwise qualifying as a "related service" are not subject to exclusion as a "medical service," but that the services of a physician are excludable as such.

This definition of "medical services" is a reasonable interpretation of congressional intent. Although Congress devoted little discussion to the "medical services" exclusion, the Secretary could reasonably have concluded that it was designed to spare schools from an obligation to provide a service that might well prove unduly expensive and beyond the range of their competence.[11] From this understanding of [468 U.S. 883, 893] congressional purpose, the Secretary could reasonably have concluded that Congress intended to impose the obligation to provide school nursing services.

Congress plainly required schools to hire various specially trained personnel to help handicapped children, such as "trained occupational therapists, speech therapists, psychologists, social workers and other appropriately trained personnel." S. Rep. No. 94-168, *supra*, at 33. School nurses have long been a part of the educational system, and the Secretary could therefore reasonably conclude that school nursing services are not the sort of burden that Congress intended to exclude as a "medical service." By limiting the "medical services" exclusion to the services of a physician or hospital, both far more expensive, the Secretary has given a permissible construction to the provision.

Petitioner's contrary interpretation of the "medical services" exclusion is unconvincing. In petitioner's view, CIC is a "medical service," even though it may be provided by a nurse or trained layperson; that conclusion rests on its reading of Texas law that confines CIC to uses in accordance with a physician's prescription and under a physician's ultimate supervision. Aside from conflicting with the Secretary's reasonable interpretation of congressional intent, however, such a rule would be anomalous. Nurses in petitioner School District are authorized to dispense oral medications and administer emergency injections in accordance with a physician's prescription. This kind of service for nonhandicapped children is difficult to distinguish from the provision of CIC to the handicapped.[12] It would be strange indeed if Congress, [468 U.S. 883, 894] in attempting to extend special services to handicapped children, were unwilling to guarantee them services of a kind that are routinely provided to the nonhandicapped.

To keep in perspective the obligation to provide services that relate to both the health and educational needs of handicapped students, we note several limitations that should minimize the burden petitioner fears. First, to be entitled to related services, a child must be handicapped so as to require special education. See 20 U.S.C. 1401(1); 34 CFR 300.5 (1983). In the absence of a handicap that requires special education, the need for what otherwise might qualify as a related service does not create an obligation under the Act. See 34 CFR 300.14, Comment (1) (1983).

Second, only those services necessary to aid a handicapped child to benefit from special education must be provided, regardless how easily a school nurse or layperson could furnish them. For example, if a particular medication or treatment may appropriately be administered to a handicapped child other than during the school day, a school is not required to provide nursing services to administer it.

Third, the regulations state that school nursing services must be provided only if they can be performed by a nurse or other qualified person, not if they must be performed by a physician. See 34 CFR 300.13(a), (b)(4), (b)(10) (1983). It bears mentioning that here not even the services of a nurse are required; as is conceded, a layperson with minimal training is qualified to provide CIC. See also, e. g., *Department of Education of Hawaii v. Katherine D.*, 727 F.2d 809 (CA9 1983). [468 U.S. 883, 895]

Finally, we note that respondents are not asking petitioner to provide equipment that Amber needs for CIC. Tr. of Oral Arg. 18-19. They seek only the services of a qualified person at the school.

We conclude that provision of CIC to Amber is not subject to exclusion as a "medical service," and we affirm the Court of Appeals' holding that CIC is a "related service" under the Education of the Handicapped Act.[13] [13]

III.

Respondents sought relief not only under the Education of the Handicapped Act but under 504 of the Rehabilitation Act as well. After finding petitioner liable to provide CIC under the former, the District Court proceeded to hold that petitioner was similarly liable under 504 and that respondents were therefore entitled to attorney's fees under 505 of the Rehabilitation Act, 29 U.S.C. 794a. We hold today, in

Smith v. Robinson, post, p. 992, that 504 is inapplicable when relief is available under the Education of the Handicapped Act to remedy a denial of educational services. Respondents are therefore not entitled to relief under 504, and we reverse the Court of Appeals' holding that respondents [468 U.S. 883, 896] are entitled to recover attorney's fees. In all other respects, the judgment of the Court of Appeals is affirmed.

It is so ordered.

Endnotes

1 The Education of the Handicapped Act's procedures for administrative hearings are set out in 20 U.S.C. 1415. In this case a hearing officer ruled that the Education of the Handicapped Act did require the school to provide CIC, and the Texas Commissioner of Education adopted the hearing officer's decision. The State Board of Education reversed, holding that the Act did not require petitioner to provide CIC.

2 As discussed more fully later, the Education of the Handicapped Act defines "related services" to include "supportive services (including . . . medical and counseling services, except that such medical services shall be for diagnostic and evaluation purposes only) as may be required to assist a handicapped child to benefit from special education." 20 U.S.C. 1401(17).

3 The District Court dismissed the claims against all defendants other than petitioner and the State Board, though it retained the members of the State Board "in their official capacities for the purpose of injunctive relief." 516 F. Supp., at 972-974.

4 The District Court held that 505 of the Rehabilitation Act, 29 U.S.C. 794a, which authorizes attorney's fees as a part of a prevailing party's costs, abrogated the State Board's immunity under the Eleventh Amendment. See App. to Pet. for Cert. 56a-60a. The State Board did not petition for certiorari, and the Eleventh Amendment issue is not before us.

5 Specifically, the "special education and related services" must

"(A) have been provided at public expense, under public supervision and direction, and without charge, (B) meet the standards of the State educational agency, (C) include an appropriate preschool, elementary, or secondary school education in the State involved, and (D) [be] provided in conformity with the individualized education program required under section 1414(a)(5) of this title." 1401(18).

6 Petitioner claims that courts deciding cases arising under the Education of the Handicapped Act are limited to inquiring whether a school district has followed the requirements of the state plan and has followed the Act's procedural requirements. However, we held in Board of Education of Hendrick Hudson Central School District v. Rowley, 458 U.S. 176, 206 , n. 27 (1982), that a court is required "not only to satisfy itself that the State has adopted the state plan, policies, and assurances required by the Act, but also to determine that the State has created an [individualized education plan] for the child in

question which conforms with the requirements of 1401(19) [defining such plans]." Judicial review is equally appropriate in this case, which presents the legal question of a school's substantive obligation under the "related services" requirement of 1401(17).

7 The Department of Education has agreed with this reasoning in an interpretive ruling that specifically found CIC to be a "related service." 46 Fed. Reg. 4912 (1981). Accord, Tokarcik v. Forest Hills School District, 665 F.2d 443 (CA3 1981), cert. denied sub nom. Scanlon v. Tokarcik, 458 U.S. 1121 (1982). The Secretary twice postponed temporarily the effective date of this interpretive ruling, see 46 Fed. Reg. 12495 (1981); id., at [468 U.S. 883, 891], and later postponed it indefinitely, id., at 25614. But the Department presently does view CIC services as an allowable cost under Part B of the Act. Ibid.

8 The obligation to provide special education and related services is expressly phrased as a "conditio[n]" for a state to receive funds under the Act. See 20 U.S.C. 1412; see also S. Rep. No. 94-168, p. 16 (1975). This refutes petitioner's contention that the Act did not "impos[e] an obligation on the States to spend state money to fund certain rights as a condition of receiving federal moneys" but "spoke merely in precatory terms," *Pennhurst State School and Hospital v. Halderman*, 451 U.S. 1, 18 (1981).

9 The Secretary of Education is empowered to issue such regulations as may be necessary to carry out the provisions of the Act. 20 U.S.C. 1417(b). This function was initially vested in the Commissioner of Education of the Department of Health, Education, and Welfare, who promulgated the regulations in question. This function was transferred to the Secretary of Education when Congress created that position, see Department of Education Organization Act, 301(a)(1), (2)(H), 93 Stat. 677, 20 U.S.C. 3441(a)(1), (2)(H).

10 The regulations actually define only those "medical services" that are owed to handicapped children: "services provided by a licensed physician to determine a child's medically related handicapping condition which results in the child's need for special education and related services." 34 CFR 300.13(b)(4) (1983). Presumably this means that "medical services" not owed under the statute are those "services by a licensed physician" that serve other purposes.

11 Children with serious medical needs are still entitled to an education. For example, the Act specifically includes instruction in hospitals and at home within the definition of "special education." See 20 U.S.C. 1401(16).

12 Petitioner attempts to distinguish the administration of prescription drugs from the administration of CIC on the ground that Texas law expressly limits the liability of school personnel performing the former, see Tex. Educ. Code Ann. 21.914(c) (Supp. 1984), but not the latter. This distinction, however, bears no relation to whether CIC is a "related service." The introduction of handicapped children into a school creates numerous new possibilities for injury and liability. Many of these risks are [468 U.S. 883, 894] more serious than that posed by CIC, which the courts below found is a safe procedure even

when performed by a 9-year-old girl. Congress assumed that states receiving the generous grants under the Act were up to the job of managing these new risks. Whether petitioner decides to purchase more liability insurance or to persuade the State to extend the limitation on liability, the risks posed by CIC should not prove to be a large burden.

13 We need not address respondents' claim that CIC, in addition to being a "related service," is a "supplementary ai[d] and servic[e]" that petitioner must provide to enable Amber to attend classes with nonhandicapped students under the Act's "mainstreaming" directive. See 20 U.S.C. 1412(5)(B). Respondents have not sought an order prohibiting petitioner from educating Amber with handicapped children alone. Indeed, any request for such an order might not present a live controversy. Amber's present individualized education program provides for regular public school classes with nonhandicapped children. And petitioner has admitted that it would be far more costly to pay for Amber's instruction and CIC services at a private school, or to arrange for home tutoring, than to provide CIC at the regular public school placement provided in her current individualized education program. Tr. of Oral Arg. 12.

JUSTICE BRENNAN, with whom JUSTICE MARSHALL joins, concurring in part and dissenting in part.

I join all but Part III of the Court's opinion. For the reasons stated in my dissenting opinion in *Smith v. Robinson*, post, p. 992, I would affirm the award of attorney's fees to the respondents.

JUSTICE STEVENS, concurring in part and dissenting in part.

The petition for certiorari did not challenge the award of attorney's fees. It contested only the award of relief on the merits to respondents. Inasmuch as the judgment on the merits is supported by the Court's interpretation of the Education of the Handicapped Act, there is no need to express any opinion concerning the Rehabilitation Act of 1973. * Accordingly, while I join Parts I and II of the Court's opinion, I do not join Part III.

[Footnote *] The "Statement of the Questions Presented" in the petition for certiorari reads as follows:

1. Whether 'medical treatment' such as clean intermittent catheterization is a 'related service' required under the Education for All Handicapped Children Act and, therefore, required to be provided to the minor Respondent.

2. Is a public school required to provide and perform the medical treatment prescribed by the physician of a handicapped child by the Education of All Handicapped Children Act or the Rehabilitation Act of 1973?

3. Whether the Fifth Circuit Court of Appeals misconstrued the opinions of this Court in *Southeastern Community College v. Davis, Pennhurst State School & Hospital v. Halderman,* and *State Board of Education v. Rowley.*" Pet. for Cert. i.

Because the Court does not hold that the Court of Appeals answered any of these questions incorrectly, it is not justified in reversing in part the judgment of that court. [468 U.S. 883, 897]

The Supreme Court of the United States

471 U. S. 359

BURLINGTON SCHOOL COMMITTEE, *et. al.*,

Petitioners

v.

MASSACHUSETTS DEPARTMENT OF EDUCATION

Respondent

No. 84-433

April 29, 1985

JUSTICE REHNQUIST delivered the opinion of the court.

The Education of the Handicapped Act (Act), 84 Stat. 175, as amended, 20 U.S.C. § 1401 *et seq.*, requires participating state and local educational agencies "to assure that handicapped children and their parents or guardians are guaranteed procedural safeguards with respect to the provision of free appropriate public education" to such handicapped children. § 1415(a). These procedures include the right of the parents to participate in the development of an "individualized education program" (IEP) for the child and to challenge in administrative and court proceedings a proposed IEP with which they disagree. § § 1401(19), 1415(b), (d), (e). Where as in the present case review of a contested IEP takes years to run its course – years critical to the child's development – important practical questions arise concerning interim placement of the child an financial responsibility for that placement. This case requires us to address some of those questions.

Michael Panico, the son of respondent Robert Panico, was a first grader in the public school system of petitioner Town of Burlington, Massachusetts, when he began experiencing serious difficulties in school. It later became evident that he had "specific learning disabilities" and thus was "handicapped" within the meaning of the Act, 20 U.S.C. § 1401(1). This entitled him to receive at public expense specially designed instruction to meet his unique needs, as well as related transportation. § § 1401(16), 1401(17). The negotiations and other proceedings between the Town and the Panicos, thus far spanning more than 8 years, are too involved to relate in full detail; the following are the parts relevant to the issues on which we granted certiorari.

In the spring of 1979, Michael attended the third grade of the Memorial School, a public school in Burlington, Mass., under an IEP calling for individual tutoring by a reading specialist for one hour a day individual and group counseling. Michael's continued poor performance and the fact that Memorial School encompassed only grades K through 3 led to much discussion between his parents and Town school officials about his difficulties and his future schooling. Apparently the course of these discussions did not run smoothly; the upshot was that the Panicos and the Town agreed that Michael was generally of above average to superior intelligence, but had special educational needs calling for a placement in a school other than Memorial. They disagreed over the source and exact nature of Michael's learning difficulties, the Town believing the source and exact nature of Michael's learning difficulties, the Town believing the source to be emotional and the parents believing it to be neurological.

In late June, the Town presented the Panicos with a proposed IEP for Michael for the 1979-1980 academic year. It called for placing Michael in a highly structured class of six children with special academic and social needs, located at another Town public school, the Pine Glen School. On July 3, Michael's father rejected the proposed IEP and sought review under § 1415(b)(2) by respondent Massachusetts Department of Education's Bureau of Special Education Appeals (BSEA). A hearing was initially scheduled for August 8, but was apparently postponed in favor of a mediation session on August 17. The mediation efforts proved unsuccessful.

Meanwhile, the Panicos received the results of the latest expert evaluation of Michael by specialists at Massachusetts General Hospital, who opined that Michael's "emotional difficulties are secondary to a rather severe learning disorder characterized by perceptual difficulties" and recommended "a highly specialized setting for children with learning handicaps . . . such as the Carroll School, "a state approved private school for special education located in Lincoln, Mass. App. 26, 31. Believing that the Town's proposed placement of Michael in the Carroll School in mid-August at his own expense, and Michael started there in September.

The BSEA held several hearings during the fall of 1979, and in January 1980 the hearing officer decided that the Town's proposed placement at the Pine Glen School was inappropriate and that the Carroll School was "the least restrictive adequate program within the record" for Michael's educational needs. The hearing officer ordered the Town to pay for Michael's tuition and transportation of the Carroll School for the 1979-1980 school year, including reimbursement the Panicos for their expenditures on these items for the school year to date.

The Town sought judicial review of the State's administrative decision in the United States District Court for the District of Massachusetts pursuant to 20 U.S.C. § 1415(e)(2) and a parallel state statute, naming Mr. Panico and the State Department of Education as defendants. In November 1980, the District Court granted summary judgment against the Town on the state-law claim under a "substantial evidence" standard or review, entering a final judgment on this claim under Federal Rule of Civil Procedure 54(b). The Court also set the federal claim for future trial. The Court of Appeals vacated the judgment on he state-law claim, holding that review under the state statute was preempted by 1415(e)(2), which establishes a "preponderance of the evidence" standard of review and which permits the reviewing court to hear additional evidence.

In the meantime, the Town had refused to comply with the BSEA order, the District Court had denied a stay of that order, and the Panicos and the State had moved for preliminary injunctive relief. The State also had threatened outside of the judicial proceedings to freeze all of the Town's special education assistance unless it complied with the BSEA order. Apparently in response to this treat, the Town agreed in February 1981 to pay for Michael's Carroll School placement and related transportation for the 1980-1981 term, none of which had yet been paid, and to continue paying for these expenses until the case was decided. But the Town persisted in refusing to reimburse Mr. Panico for the expenses of the 1979-1980 school year. When the Court of Appeals disposed of the state claim, it also held that under this status quo, none of the parties could show irreparable injury and thus none was entitled to a preliminary injunction. The court reasoned that the Town had not shown that Mr. Panico would not be able to repay the tuition and related costs borne by the Town if he ultimately lost on the merits, and Mr. Panico had not shown that he would be irreparably harmed if not reimbursed immediately for past payments which might ultimately be determined to be the Town's responsibility.

On remand, the District Court entered an extension pretrial order on the Town's federal claim. In denying the Town summary judgment, it rules that 20 U.S.C. § 1415(e)(3) did not bar reimbursement despite the Town's insistence that the Panicos violated that provision by changing Michael's placement to the Carroll School during the pendency of the administrative proceedings. The court reasoned that § 1415(e)(3) concerned the physical placement of the child and not the right to tuition reimbursement or to procedural review of a contested IEP. The court also dealt with the problem that no IEP had been developed for the 1980-1981 or 1981-1982 school years. It held that its power under § 1415(e)(2) to grant appropriate" relief upon reviewing the contested IEP for the 1979-1980 school year included the power to grant relief for subsequent school years despite the lack of IEPs for those years. In this connection, however, the court interpreted the statute to place the burden of proof on the Town to upset the BSEA decision that the IEP was inappropriate for 1979-1980 and on the Panicos and the State to show that the relief for subsequent terms was appropriate.

After a 4-day trial, the District Court in August 1982

overturned the BSEA decision, holding that the appropriate 1979-1980 placement for Michael was the one proposed by the Town in the IEP and that the parents had failed to show that this placement would not also have been appropriate for subsequent years. Accordingly, the court concluded that the Town was "not responsible for the cost of Michael's education at the Carroll School for the academic years 1979-80 through 1982-82."

In contesting the Town's proposed form of judgment embodying the court's conclusion, Mr. Panico argued that, despite finally losing on the merits of the IEP in August 1982, he should be reimbursed for his expenditures in 1979-1980, that the Town should finish paying for the recently completed 1981-1982 term, and that he should not be required to reimburse the Town for its payments to date, apparently because the school terms in question fell within the pendency of the administrative and judicial review contemplated by § 1415(e)(2). The case was transferred to another District Judge and consolidated with two other cases to resolve similar issues concerning the reimbursement for expenditures during the pendency of review proceedings.

In a decision on the consolidated cases, the court rejected Mr. Panico's argument that the Carroll School was the "current educational placement" during the pendency of the review proceedings and thus that under § 1415(e)(3) the Town was obligated to maintain that placement. *Doe v. Anrig*, 561 F. Supp. 121 (1983). The court reasoned that the Panicos' unilateral action in placing Michael at the Carroll School without the Town's consent could not "confer thereon the imprimatur of continued placement," *id.* at 129, n. 5, even though strictly speaking there was no actual placement in effect during the summer of 1979 because all parties agreed Michael was finished with the Memorial School and the Town itself proposed in the IEP to transfer him to a new school in the fall.

The District Court next rejected an argument, apparently grounded at least in part on a state regulation, that the Panicos were entitled to rely on the BSEA decision upholding their placement contrary to the IEP, regardless of whether that decision were ultimately reversed by a court. With respect to the payments made by the Town after the BSEA decision, under the State's threat to cut off funding, the court criticized the State for resorting to extrajudicial pressure to enforce a decision subject to further review. Because this "was not a case where the town was legally obliged under section § 1415(e)(3) to continue payments preserving the status quo," the State's coercion could not be viewed as "the basis for a final decision on liability" and it could only be "regarded as other than wrongful . . . on the assumption that the payments were to be returned if the order was ultimately reversed." *Id.*, at 130. The court entered a judgment ordering the Panicos to reimburse the Town for its payments for Michael's Carroll placement and related transportation in 1980-1981 and 1981-1982.

The Panicos appealed.

In a broad opinion, most of which we do not review, the Court of Appeals for the First Circuit remanded the case a second time. 736 F.2d 773 (1984). The court ruled, among other things, that the District Court erred in conducting a full trial de novo, that it gave insufficient weight to the BSEA findings, and that in other respects it did not properly evaluate the IEP. The court also considered several questions about the availability of reimbursement for interim placement. The Town argued that § 1415(e)(3) bars the Panicos from any reimbursement relief, even if on remand they were to prevail on the merits of the IEP, because of their unilateral change of Michael's placement during the pendency of the § 1415(e)(2) proceedings. The court held that such unilateral parental change of placement would not be "a bar to reimbursement of the parents if their actions are held to be appropriate at final judgment." Id., at 799. In dictum, the court suggested, however, that a lack of parental consultation with the Town or "attempt to achieve a negotiated compromise and agreement on a private placement," as contemplated by the Act, "may be taken into account in a district court's computation of an award of equitable reimbursement." Ibid. To guide the District Court on remand, the court stated that "whether to order reimbursement, and at what amount, is a question determined by balancing the equities." Id., at 801. The court also held that the Panicos' reliance on the BSEA decision would estop the Town from obtaining reimbursement "for the period of reliance and requires that where parents have paid the bill for the period, they must be reimbursed." Ibid.

The town filed a petition for a writ of certiorari in this Court challenging the decision of the Court of Appeals on numerous issues, including the scope of judicial review of the administrative decision and the relevance to the merits of an IEP of violations by local school authorities of the Act's procedural requirements. We granted certiorari, 469 U.S. __ (1984), only to consider the following two issues: whether the potential relief available under § 1415(e)(2) includes reimbursement to parents for private school tuition and related expenses, and whether § 1415(e)(3) bars such reimbursement to parents who reject a proposed IEP and place a child in a private school without the consent of local school authorities. We express no opinion on any of the many other views stated by the Court of Appeals.

Congress stated the purpose of the Act in these words:

"to assure that all handicapped children have available to them . . . a free appropriate public education which emphasized special education and related services designed to meet their unique needs [and] to assure that the rights of handicapped children and their parents or guardians are protected." 20 U.S.C. § 1400(c).

The Act defines a "free appropriate public education" to mean:

"special education and related services which (A) have been provided at public expense, under public supervision and direction, and without charge, (B) meet the standards of the State educational agency, (C) include an appropriate preschool, elementary, or secondary school education in the State involved, and (D) are provided in conformity with [an] individualized education program." 20 U.S.C. § 1401(18).

To accomplish this ambitious objective, the Act provides federal money to state and local educational agencies that undertake to implement the substantive and procedural requirements of the Act. See Hendrick Hudson District Bd. of Education v. Rowley, 458 U.S. 176, 179-184 (1982).

The modus operandi of the Act is the already mentioned "individualized educational program." The IEP is in brief a comprehensive statement of the educational needs of a handicapped child and the specially designed instruction and related services to be employed to meet those needs. § 1401(19). The IEP is to be developed jointly by a school official qualified in special education, the child's teacher, the parents or guardian, and, where appropriate, the child. In several places, the Act emphasizes the participation of the parents in developing the child's educational program and assessing its effectiveness. See §§ 1400(c), 1401(19), 1412(7), 1415(b)(1)(A), (C), (D), (E), and 1415(b)(b)(2); 34 CFR § 300.345 (1984).

Apparently recognizing that this cooperative approach would not always produce a consensus between the school officials and the parents, and that in any disputes the school officials would have a natural advantage, Congress incorporated an elaborate set of what it labeled "procedural safeguards" to insure the full participation of the parents and proper resolution of substantive disagreements. Section 1415(b) entitles the parents "to examine all relevant records with respect to the identification, evaluation, and educational placement of the child," to obtain an independent educational evaluation of the child, to notice of any decision to initiate or change the identification, evaluation, or educational placement of the child, and to present complaints with respect to any of the above. The parents are further entitled to "an impartial due process hearing," which in the instant case was the BSEA hearing, to resolve their complaints.

The Act also provides for judicial review in state or federal court to "[a]ny party aggrieved by the findings and decision" made after the due process hearing. The Act confers on the reviewing court the following authority:

"[T]he court shall receive the records of the administrative proceedings, shall hear additional evidence at the request of a party, and, basing its decision on the preponderance of the evidence, shall grant such relief as the court determines is appropriate." § 1415(e)(2)

The first question on which we granted certiorari requires us to decide whether this grant of authority includes the power to order school authorities to reimburse parents for their expenditures on private special education for a child, if the court ultimately determines that such placement rather than a proposed IEP, is proper under the Act.

We conclude that the Act authorizes such reimbursement. The statute directs the court to "grant such relief as [it] determines is appropriate." The ordinary meaning of these words confers broad discretion on the court. The type of relief is not further specified, except that it must be "appropriate." Absent other reference, the only possible interpretation is that the relief is to be "appropriate" in light of the purpose of the Act. As already noted, this is principally to provide handicapped children with "a free appropriate public education which emphasizes special education and related services designed to meet their unique needs." The Act contemplates that such education will be provided where possible in regular public schools, with the child participating as much as possible in the same activities as non-handicapped children, but the Act also provides for placement in private schools at public expense where this is not possible. See § 1412(5); 34 CFR §§ 300.132, 300.227, 300.307(B), 300.347 (1984). In a case where a court determines that a private placement desired by the parents was proper under the Act and that an IEP calling for placement in a public school was inappropriate, it seems clear beyond cavil that "appropriate" relief would include a prospective injunction directing the school officials to develop and implement at public expense an IEP placing the child in a private school.

If the administrative and judicial review under the Act could be completed in a matter of weeks, rather than years, it would be difficult to imagine a case in which such prospective injunctive relief would not be sufficient. As this case so vividly demonstrates, however, the review process is ponderous. A final judicial decision on the merits of an IEP will in most instances come a year or more after the school term covered by that IEP has passed. In the meantime, the parents who disagree with the proposed IEP are faced with a choice: go along with the IEP to the detriment of their child if it turns out to be inappropriate or pay for what they consider to be the appropriate placement.

If they choose the latter course, which conscientious parents who have adequate means and who are reasonably confident of their assessment normally would, it would be an empty victory to have a court tell them several years later that they were right but that these expenditures could not in a proper case be reimbursed by the school officials. If that were the case, the child's right to a free appropriate public education, the parents' right to participate fully in developing a proper IEP, and all of the procedural safeguards would be less than complete. Because Congress undoubtedly did not intend this result, we are confident that by empowering the court to grant "appropriate" relief Congress meant to include retroactive reimbursement to parents as an available remedy in a proper case.

In this Court, the Town repeatedly characterizes reimbursement as "damages," but that simply is not the case. Reimbursement merely requires the Town to belatedly pay expenses that it should have paid all along and would have borne in the first instance had it developed a proper IEP. Such a post-hoc determination of financial responsibility was contemplated in the legislative history:

"If a parent contends that he or she has been forced, at that parent's own expense, to seek private schooling for the child because an appropriate program does not exist within the local educational agency responsible for the child's education and the local educational agency disagrees, that disagreement and **the question of who remains financially responsible** is a matter to which the due process procedures established under [the predecessor to 1415] appl[y]." S. Rep. No. 94-168, p. 32 91975) (emphasis added).

See 34 CFR § 300.403(b) (1984) (disagreements and question of financial responsibility subject to the due process procedures).

Regardless of the availability of reimbursement as a form of relief in a proper case, the Town maintains that the Panicos have waived any right they otherwise might have to reimbursement because they violated § 1415(e)(3), which provides:

"During the pendency of any proceedings conducted pursuant to [1415], unless the State or local educational agency and the parents or guardian otherwise agree, the child remain in the then current educational placement of such child . . ."

We need not resolve the academic question of what Michael's "then current placement" was in the summer of 1979, when both the Town and the parents had agreed that a new school was in order. For the purposes of our decision, we assume that the Pine Glen School, proposed in the IEP, was Michael's current placement and, therefore, that the Panicos did "change" his placement after they had rejected the IEP and had set the administrative review in motion. In so doing, the Panicos contravened the conditional command of § 1415(e)(3) that "the child shall remain in the then current educational placement."

As an initial matter, we note that the section calls for agreement by **either** the **State or** the **local educational agency**. The BSES's decision in favor of the Panicos and the Carroll School placement would seem to constitute agreement by the State to the change of placement. The decision was issued in January 1980, so from then on the Panicos were no longer in violation of § 1415(e)(3). This conclusion, however, does not entirely resolve the instant dispute because the Panicos are also seeking reimbursement for Michael's expenses during the fall of 1979, prior to the State's concurrence in the Carroll School placement.

We do not agree with the Town that a parental violation of § 1415(e)(3) constitutes a waiver of reimbursement. The provision says nothing about financial responsibility, waiver, or parental right to reimbursement at the conclusion of judicial proceedings. Moreover, if the provision is interpreted to cut off parental rights to reimbursement, the principal purpose of the Act will in many cases be defeated in the same way as if reimbursement were never available. As in this case, parents will often notice a child's learning difficulties while the child is in a regular public school program. If the school officials disagree with the need for special education or the adequacy of the public school's program to meet the child's needs, it is unlikely they will agree to an interim private school placement while the review process runs its course. Thus, under the Town's reading of § 1415(e)(3), the parents are forced to leave the child in what may turn out to be an inappropriate educational placement or to obtain the appropriate placement only by sacrificing any claim for reimbursement. The Act was intended to give handicapped children both an appropriate education and a free one; it should not be interpreted to defeat one or the other of those objectives.

The legislative history supports this interpretation, favoring a proper interim placement pending the resolution of disagreements over the IEP:

"The conferees are cognizant that an impartial due process hearing may be required to assure that the rights of the child have been completely protected. We did feel, however, that the placement, or change of placement should not be unnecessarily delayed while long and tedious administrative appeals were being exhausted. Thus the conference adopted a flexible approach to try to meet the needs of both the child and the State." 121 Cong. Rec. 37412 (1975) (Sen. Stafford).

We think at least one purpose of § 1415(e)(3) was to prevent school officials from removing a child from the regular public school classroom over the parents' objection pending completion of the review proceedings. As we observed in *Rowley*, 458 U.S., at 192, the impetus for the Act came from two federal court decisions, *Pennsylvania Assn. for Retarded Children v. Commonwealth*, 334 F. Supp. 1257 (ED Pa. 1971), and 343 F. Supp. 279 (1972), and *Mills v. Board of Education of District of Columbia*, 348 F. Supp.

866 (D.C. 1972), which arose from the efforts of parents of handicapped children to prevent the exclusion or expulsion of their children from the public school. Congress was concerned about the apparently widespread practice of relegating handicapped children to private institutions or warehousing them in special classes. See § 1400(4); 34 CFR § 300.347(a) (1984). We also note that § 1415(e)(3) is located in a section detailing procedural safeguards which are largely for the benefit of the parents and the child.

This is not to say that § 1415(e)(3) has no effect on parents. While we doubt that this provision would authorize a court to order parents to leave their child in a particular placement, we think it operates in such a way that parents who unilaterally change their child's placement during the pendency of review proceedings, without the consent of state or local school officials, do so at their own financial risk. If the courts ultimately determine that the IEP proposed by the school officials was appropriate, the parents would be barred from obtaining reimbursement for any interim period in which their child' placement violated § 1415(e)(3). This conclusion is supported by the agency's interpretation of the Act's application to private placements by the parents:

(a) If a handicapped child has available a free appropriate public education and the parents choose to place the child in a private school or facility, the public agency is not required by this part to pay for the child's education at the private school or facility . . .

(b) Disagreements between a parent and a public agency regarding the availability of a program appropriate for the child, and the question of financial responsibility, are subject to the due process procedures under [§ 1415]. 34 CFR § 300.403 (1984).

We thus resolve the questions on which we granted certiorari; because the case is here in an interlocutory posture, we do not consider the estoppel ruling below or the specific equitable factors identified by the Court of Appeals for granting relief. We do think that the court was correct in concluding that "such relief as the court determines is appropriate," within the meaning of § 1415(e)(2), means that equitable considerations are relevant in fashioning relief.

The judgment of the Court of Appeals is **Affirmed**.

The Supreme Court of the United States

484 U. S. 305

HONIG, California Superintendent of Public Instruction,
Plaintiff

v.

DOE, et al.,
Respondents

No. 86-728

January 20, 1988

JUSTICE BRENNAN delivered the opinion of the Court as to holdings in number 1 and 2, in which Rehnquist, C.J., and White, Marshall, Blackmun, and Stevens, J.J joined. Rehquist, C.J., filed a concurring opinion. Scalia, J. filed a dissenting opinion, in which O'Connor, J. joined.

As a condition of federal financial assistance, the Education of the Handicapped Act requires States to ensure a "free appropriate public education" for all disabled children within their jurisdictions. In aid of this goal, the Act establishes a comprehensive system of procedural safeguards designed to ensure parental participation in decisions concerning the education of their disabled children and to provide administrative and judicial review of any decisions with which those parents disagree. Among these safeguards is the so-called "stay-put" provision, which directs that a disabled child "shall remain in [his or her] then current educational placement" pending completion of any review proceedings, unless the parents and state or local educational agencies otherwise agree. 20 U.S.C. 1415(e)(3). Today we must decide whether, in the face of this statutory proscription, state or local school authorities may nevertheless unilaterally exclude disabled children from the classroom for dangerous or disruptive conduct growing out of their disabilities. In addition, we are called upon to decide whether a district court may, in the exercise of its equitable powers, order a State to provide educational services directly to a disabled child when the local agency fails to do so.

I

In the Education of the Handicapped Act (EHA or the Act), 84 Stat. 175, as amended, 20 U.S.C. 1400 *et seq.*, Congress sought "to assure that all handicapped children have available to them . . . a free appropriate public education which emphasizes special education and related services designed to meet their unique needs, [and] to assure that the rights of handicapped children and their parents or guardians are protected." 1400(c). When the law was

passed in 1975, Congress had before it ample evidence that such legislative assurances were sorely needed: 21 years after this Court declared education to be "perhaps the most important function of state and local governments," *Brown v. Board of Education*, 347 U.S. 483, 493 (1954), Congressional studies revealed that better than half of the Nation's eight million disabled children were not receiving appropriate educational services. 1400(b)(3). Indeed, one out of every eight of these children was excluded from the public school system altogether, 1400(b)(4); many others were simply "warehoused" in special classes or were neglectfully shepherded through the system until they were old enough to drop out. See H. R. Rep. No. 94-332, p. 2 (1975). Among the most poorly served of disabled students were emotionally disturbed children: Congressional statistics revealed that for the school year immediately preceding passage of the Act, the educational needs of 82 percent of all children with emotional disabilities went unmet. See S. Rep. No. 94-168, p. 8 (1975) (hereinafter S. Rep.).

Although these educational failings resulted in part from funding constraints, Congress recognized that the problem reflected more than a lack of financial resources at the state and local levels. Two federal-court decisions, which the Senate Report characterized as "landmark," see *id.*, at 6, demonstrated that many disabled children were excluded pursuant to state statutes or local rules and policies, typically without any consultation with, or even notice to, their parents. See *Mills v. Board of Education of District of Columbia*, 348 F. Supp. 866 (DC 1972); *Pennsylvania Assn. for Retarded Children v. Pennsylvania*, 334 F. Supp. 1257 (ED Pa. 1971), and 343 F. Supp. 279 (1972) (*PARC*). Indeed, by the time of the EHA's enactment, parents had brought legal challenges to similar exclusionary practices in 27 other states. See S. Rep., at 6.

In responding to these problems, Congress did not content itself with passage of a simple funding statute. Rather, the EHA confers upon disabled students an enforceable substantive right to public education in participating States, see *Board of Education of Hendrick Hudson Central School Dist. v. Rowley*, 458 U.S. 176 (1982)[1], and conditions federal financial assistance upon a State's compliance with the substantive and procedural goals of the Act. Accordingly, States seeking to qualify for federal funds must develop policies assuring all disabled children the "right to a free appropriate public education," and must file with the Secretary of Education formal plans mapping out in detail the programs, procedures and timetables under which they will effectuate these policies. 20 U. S. C. 1412(1), 1413(a). Such plans must assure that, "to the maximum extent appropriate," States will "mainstream" disabled children, i.e., that they will educate them with children who are not disabled, and that they will segregate or otherwise remove such children from the regular classroom setting "only when the nature or severity of the handicap is such that education in regular classes . . . cannot be achieved satisfactorily." 1412(5).

The primary vehicle for implementing these congressional goals is the "individualized educational program" (IEP), which the EHA mandates for each disabled child. Prepared at meetings between a representative of the local school district, the child's teacher, the parents or guardians, and, whenever appropriate, the disabled child, the IEP sets out the child's present educational performance, establishes annual and short-term objectives for improvements in that performance, and describes the specially designed instruction and services that will enable the child to meet those objectives. 1401(19). The IEP must be reviewed and, where necessary, revised at least once a year in order to ensure that local agencies tailor the statutorily required "free appropriate public education" to each child's unique needs. 1414(a)(5).

Envisioning the IEP as the centerpiece of the statute's education delivery system for disabled children, and aware that schools had all too often denied such children appropriate educations without in any way consulting their parents, Congress repeatedly emphasized throughout the Act the importance and indeed the necessity of parental participation in both the development of the IEP and any subsequent assessments of its effectiveness. See 1400(c), 1401(19), 1412(7), 1415(b)(1)(A), (C), (D), (E), and 1415(b)(2). Accordingly, the Act establishes various procedural safeguards that guarantee parents both an opportunity for meaningful input into all decisions affecting their child's education and the right to seek review of any decisions they think inappropriate. These safeguards include the right to examine all relevant records pertaining to the identification, evaluation and educational placement of their child; prior written notice whenever the responsible educational agency proposes (or refuses) to change the child's placement or program; an opportunity to present complaints concerning any aspect of the local agency's provision of a free appropriate public education; and an opportunity for "an impartial due process hearing" with respect to any such complaints. 1415(b)(1), (2).

At the conclusion of any such hearing, both the parents and the local educational agency may seek further administrative review and, where that proves unsatisfactory, may file a civil action in any state or federal court. 1415(c), (e)(2). In addition to reviewing the administrative record, courts are empowered to take additional evidence at the request of either party and to "grant such relief as [they] determine[] is appropriate." 1415(e)(2). The "stay-put" provision at issue in this case governs the placement of a child while these often lengthy review procedures run their course. It directs that:

"During the pendency of any proceedings conducted pursuant to [1415], unless the State or local educational agency and the parents or guardian otherwise agree, the child shall remain in the then current educational placement of such child . . ." 1415(e)(3).

The present dispute grows out of the efforts of certain officials of the San Francisco Unified School District (SFUSD) to expel two emotionally disturbed children from school indefinitely for violent and disruptive conduct related to their disabilities. In November 1980, respondent John Doe assaulted another student at the Louise Lombard School, a developmental center for disabled children. Doe's April 1980 IEP identified him as a socially and physically awkward 17 year old who experienced considerable difficulty controlling his impulses and anger. Among the goals set out in his IEP was "[i]mprovement in [his] ability to relate to [his] peers [and to] cope with frustrating situations without resorting to aggressive acts." App. 17. Frustrating situations, however, were an unfortunately prominent feature of Doe's school career: physical abnormalities, speech difficulties, and poor grooming habits had made him the target of teasing and ridicule as early as the first grade, *id.*, at 23; his 1980 IEP reflected his continuing difficulties with peers, noting that his social skills had deteriorated and that he could tolerate only minor frustration before exploding. *Id.*, at 15-16.

On November 6, 1980, Doe responded to the taunts of a fellow student in precisely the explosive manner anticipated by his IEP: he choked the student with sufficient force to leave abrasions on the child's neck, and kicked out a school window while being escorted to the principal's office afterwards. *Id.*, at 208. Doe admitted his misconduct and the school subsequently suspended him for five days. Thereafter, his principal referred the matter to the SFUSD Student Placement Committee (SPC or Committee) with the recommendation that Doe be expelled. On the day the suspension was to end, the SPC notified Doe's mother that it was proposing to exclude her child permanently from SFUSD and was therefore extending his suspension until such time as the expulsion proceedings were completed.2 The Committee further advised her that she was entitled to attend the November 25 hearing at which it planned to discuss the proposed expulsion.

After unsuccessfully protesting these actions by letter, Doe brought this suit against a host of local school officials and the state superintendent of public education. Alleging that the suspension and proposed expulsion violated the EHA, he sought a temporary restraining order cancelling the SPC hearing and requiring school officials to convene an IEP meeting. The District Judge granted the requested injunctive relief and further ordered defendants to provide home tutoring for Doe on an interim basis; shortly thereafter, she issued a preliminary injunction directing defendants to return Doe to his then current educational placement at Louise Lombard School pending completion of the IEP review process. Doe re-entered school on December 15, 5 1/2 weeks, and 24 school days, after his initial suspension.

Respondent Jack Smith was identified as an emotionally disturbed child by the time he entered the second grade in 1976. School records prepared that year indicated that he was unable "to control verbal or physical outburst[s]" and exhibited a "[s]evere disturbance in relationships with peers and adults." *Id.*, at 123. Further evaluations subsequently revealed that he had been physically and emotionally abused as an infant and young child and that, despite above average intelligence, he experienced academic and social difficulties as a result of extreme hyperactivity and low self-esteem. *Id.*, at 136, 139, 155, 176. Of particular concern was Smith's propensity for verbal hostility; one evaluator noted that the child reacted to stress by "attempt[ing] to cover his feelings of low self worth through aggressive behavior [,] . . . primarily verbal provocations." *Id.*, at 136.

Based on these evaluations, SFUSD placed Smith in a learning center for emotionally disturbed children. His grandparents, however, believed that his needs would be better served in the public school setting and, in September 1979, the school district acceded to their requests and enrolled him at A. P. Giannini Middle School. His February 1980 IEP recommended placement in a Learning Disability Group, stressing the need for close supervision and a highly structured environment. *Id.*, at 111. Like earlier evaluations, the February 1980 IEP noted that Smith was easily distracted, impulsive, and anxious; it therefore proposed a half-day schedule and suggested that the placement be undertaken on a trial basis. *Id.*, at 112, 115.

At the beginning of the next school year, Smith was assigned to a full-day program; almost immediately thereafter he began misbehaving. School officials met twice with his grandparents in October 1980 to discuss returning him to a half-day program; although the grandparents agreed to the reduction, they apparently were never apprised of their right to challenge the decision through EHA procedures. The school officials also warned them that if the child continued his disruptive behavior—which included stealing, extorting money from fellow students, and making sexual comments to female classmates—they would seek to expel him. On November 14, they made good on this threat, suspending Smith for five days after he made further lewd comments. His principal referred the matter to the SPC, which recommended exclusion from SFUSD. As it did in John Doe's case, the Committee scheduled a hearing and extended the suspension indefinitely pending a final disposition in the matter. On November 28, Smith's counsel

protested these actions on grounds essentially identical to those raised by Doe, and the SPC agreed to cancel the hearing and to return Smith to a half-day program at A. P. Giannini or to provide home tutoring. Smith's grandparents chose the latter option and the school began home instruction on December 10; on January 6, 1981, an IEP team convened to discuss alternative placements.

After learning of Doe's action, Smith sought and obtained leave to intervene in the suit. The District Court subsequently entered summary judgment in favor of respondents on their EHA claims and issued a permanent injunction. In a series of decisions, the District Judge found that the proposed expulsions and indefinite suspensions of respondents for conduct attributable to their disabilities deprived them of their congressionally mandated right to a free appropriate public education, as well as their right to have that education provided in accordance with the procedures set out in the EHA. The District Judge therefore permanently enjoined the school district from taking any disciplinary action other than a two- or five-day suspension against any disabled child for disability-related misconduct, or from effecting any other change in the educational placement of any such child without parental consent pending completion of any EHA proceedings. In addition, the judge barred the State from authorizing unilateral placement changes and directed it to establish an EHA compliance-monitoring system or, alternatively, to enact guidelines governing local school responses to disability-related misconduct. Finally, the judge ordered the State to provide services directly to disabled children when, in any individual case, the State determined that the local educational agency was unable or unwilling to do so.

On appeal, the Court of Appeals for the Ninth Circuit affirmed the orders with slight modifications. *Doe v. Maher*, 793 F.2d 1470 (1986). Agreeing with the District Court that an indefinite suspension in aid of expulsion constitutes a prohibited "change in placement" under 1415(e)(3), the Court of Appeals held that the stay-put provision admitted of no "dangerousness" exception and that the statute therefore rendered invalid those provisions of the California Education Code permitting the indefinite suspension or expulsion of disabled children for misconduct arising out of their disabilities. The court concluded, however, that fixed suspensions of up to 30 school days did not fall within the reach of 1415(e)(3), and therefore upheld recent amendments to the state education code authorizing such suspensions.[3] Lastly, the court affirmed that portion of the injunction requiring the State to provide services directly to a disabled child when the local educational agency fails to do so.

Petitioner Bill Honig, California Superintendent of Public Instruction,[4] sought review in this Court, claiming that the Court of Appeals' construction of the stay-put provision conflicted with that of several other courts of appeals which had recognized a dangerousness exception, compare *Doe v. Maher*, 793 F. 2d 1470 (1986) (case below), with *Jackson v. Franklin County School Board*, 765 F. 2d 535, 538 (CA5 1985); *Victoria L. v. District School Bd. of Lee County, Fla.*, 741 F.2d 369, 374 (CA 11 1984); *S-1 v. Turlington*, 635 F.2d 342, 348, n. 9 (CA5), cert. denied, 454 U.S. 1030 (1981), and that the direct services ruling placed an intolerable burden on the State. We granted certiorari to resolve these questions, 479 U.S. ___ (1987), and now affirm.

II

At the outset, we address the suggestion, raised for the first time during oral argument, that this case is moot.[5] Under Article III of the Constitution this Court may only adjudicate actual, ongoing controversies. *Nebraska Press Assn v. Stuart*, 427 U.S. 539, 546 (1976); *Preiser v. Newkirk*, 422 U.S. 395, 401 (1975). That the dispute between the parties was very much alive when suit was filed, or at the time the Court of Appeals rendered its judgment, cannot substitute for the actual case or controversy that an exercise of this Court's jurisdiction requires. *Steffel v. Thompson*, 415 U.S. 452, 459, n. 10 (1974); *Roe v. Wade*, 410 U.S. 113, 125 (1973). In the present case, we have jurisdiction if there is a reasonable likelihood that respondents will again suffer the deprivation of EHA-mandated rights that gave rise to this suit. We believe that, at least with respect to respondent Smith, such a possibility does in fact exist and that the case therefore remains justiciable.

Respondent John Doe is now 24 years old and, accordingly, is no longer entitled to the protections and benefits of the EHA, which limits eligibility to disabled children between the ages of three and 21. See 20 U.S.C. Sec. 1412(2)(B). It is clear, therefore, that whatever rights to state educational services he may yet have as a ward of the State, see Tr. of Oral Arg. 23, 26, the Act would not govern the State's provision of those services, and thus the case is moot as to him. Respondent Jack Smith, however, is currently 20 and has not yet completed high school. Although at present he is not faced with any proposed expulsion or suspension proceedings, and indeed no longer even resides within the SFUSD, he remains a resident of California and is entitled to a "free appropriate public education" within that State. His claims under the EHA, therefore, are not moot if the conduct he originally complained of is "'capable of repetition, yet evading review.'" *Murphy v. Hunt*, 455 U.S. 478, 482 (1982). Given Smith's continued eligibility for educational services under the EHA[6], the nature of his disability, and petitioner's insistence that all local school districts retain residual authority to exclude disabled children for dangerous conduct, we have little difficulty concluding that there is a "reasonable expectation," *ibid.*, that Smith would once again be subjected to a unilateral "change in placement" for

conduct growing out of his disabilities were it not for the state-wide injunctive relief issued below.

Our cases reveal that, for purposes of assessing the likelihood that state authorities will re-inflict a given injury, we generally have been unwilling to assume that the party seeking relief will repeat the type of misconduct that would once again place him or her at risk of that injury. See *Los Angeles v. Lyons*, 461 U.S. 95, 105-106 (1983) (no threat that party seeking injunction barring police use of chokeholds would be stopped again for traffic violation or other offense, or would resist arrest if stopped); *Hunt v. Murphy, supra*, at 484 (no reason to believe that party challenging denial of pre-trial bail "will once again be in a position to demand bail"); *O'Shea v. Littleton*, 414 U.S. 488, 497 (1974) (unlikely that parties challenging discriminatory bond-setting, sentencing, and jury-fee practices would again violate valid criminal laws). No such reluctance, however, is warranted here. It is respondent Smith's very inability to conform his conduct to socially acceptable norms that renders him "handicapped" within the meaning of the EHA. See 20 U.S.C. 1401(1); 34 CFR 300.5(b)(8) (1987). As noted above, the record is replete with evidence that Smith is unable to govern his aggressive, impulsive behavior -- indeed, his notice of suspension acknowledged that "Jack's actions seem beyond his control." App. 152.

In the absence of any suggestion that respondent has overcome his earlier difficulties, it is certainly reasonable to expect, based on his prior history of behavioral problems, that he will again engage in classroom misconduct. Nor is it reasonable to suppose that Smith's future educational placement will so perfectly suit his emotional and academic needs that further disruptions on his part are improbable. Although Justice Scalia suggests in his dissent, post, at 3, that school officials are unlikely to place Smith in a setting where they cannot control his misbehavior, any efforts to ensure such total control must be tempered by the school system's statutory obligations to provide respondent with a free appropriate public education in "the least restrictive environment," 34 CFR 300.552(d) (1987); to educate him, "to the maximum extent appropriate," with children who are not disabled, 20 U.S.C. 1412(5); and to consult with his parents or guardians, and presumably with respondent himself, before choosing a placement. 1401(19), 1415(b). Indeed, it is only by ignoring these mandates, as well as Congress' unquestioned desire to wrest from school officials their former unilateral authority to determine the placement of emotionally disturbed children, see *infra*, at 15-16, that the dissent can so readily assume that respondent's future placement will satisfactorily prevent any further dangerous conduct on his part. Overarching these statutory obligations, moreover, is the inescapable fact that the preparation of an IEP, like any other effort at predicting human behavior, is an inexact science at best.

Given the unique circumstances and context of this case, therefore, we think it reasonable to expect that respondent will again engage in the type of misconduct that precipitated this suit.

We think it equally probable that, should he do so, respondent will again be subjected to the same unilateral school action for which he initially sought relief. In this regard, it matters not that Smith no longer resides within the SFUSD. While the actions of SFUSD officials first gave rise to this litigation, the District Judge expressly found that the lack of a state policy governing local school responses to disability-related misconduct had led to, and would continue to result in, EHA violations, and she therefore enjoined the state defendant from authorizing, among other things, unilateral placement changes. App. 247-248. She of course also issued injunctions directed at the local defendants, but they did not seek review of those orders in this Court. Only petitioner, the State Superintendent of Public Instruction, has invoked our jurisdiction, and he now urges us to hold that local school districts retain unilateral authority under the EHA to suspend or otherwise remove disabled children for dangerous conduct. Given these representations, we have every reason to believe that were it not for the injunction barring petitioner from authorizing such unilateral action, respondent would be faced with a real and substantial threat of such action in any California school district in which he enrolled. Cf. *Los Angeles v. Lyons, supra*, at 106 (respondent lacked standing to seek injunctive relief because he could not plausibly allege that police officers choked all persons whom they stopped, or that the City "AUTHORIZED police officers to act in such manner" (emphasis added)). Certainly, if the SFUSD's past practice of unilateral exclusions was at odds with state policy and the practice of local school districts generally, petitioner would not now stand before us seeking to defend the right of all local school districts to engage in such aberrant behavior.[7]

We have previously noted that administrative and judicial review under the EHA is often "ponderous," *Burlington School Committee v. Massachusetts Dept. of Education*, 471 U.S. 359, 370 (1985), and this case, which has taken seven years to reach us, amply confirms that observation. For obvious reasons, the misconduct of an emotionally disturbed or otherwise disabled child who has not yet reached adolescence typically will not pose such a serious threat to the well-being of other students that school officials can only ensure classroom safety by excluding the child. Yet, the adolescent student improperly disciplined for misconduct that does pose such a threat will often be finished with school or otherwise ineligible for EHA protections by the time review can be had in this Court. Because we believe that respondent Smith has demonstrated both "a sufficient likelihood that he we will again be wronged in a similar way," *Los Angeles v. Lyons*, 461 U.S., at 111, and that any re-

sulting claim he may have for relief will surely evade our review, we turn to the merits of his case.

III

The language of 1415(e)(3) is unequivocal. It states plainly that during the pendency of any proceedings initiated under the Act, unless the state or local educational agency and the parents or guardian of a disabled child otherwise agree, "the child **shall** remain in the then current educational placement." 1415(e)(3) (emphasis added). Faced with this clear directive, petitioner asks us to read a "dangerousness" exception into the stay-put provision on the basis of either of two essentially inconsistent assumptions: first, that Congress thought the residual authority of school officials to exclude dangerous students from the classroom too obvious for comment; or second, that Congress inadvertently failed to provide such authority and this Court must therefore remedy the oversight. Because we cannot accept either premise, we decline petitioner's invitation to re-write the statute.

Petitioner's arguments proceed, he suggests, from a simple, common-sense proposition: Congress could not have intended the stay-put provision to be read literally, for such a construction leads to the clearly unintended, and untenable, result that school districts must return violent or dangerous students to school while the often lengthy EHA proceedings run their course. We think it clear, however, that Congress very much meant to strip schools of the unilateral authority they had traditionally employed to exclude disabled students, particularly emotionally disturbed students, from school. In so doing, Congress did not leave school administrators powerless to deal with dangerous students; it did, however, deny school officials their former right to "self-help," and directed that in the future the removal of disabled students could be accomplished only with the permission of the parents or, as a last resort, the courts.

As noted above, Congress passed the EHA after finding that school systems across the country had excluded one out of every eight disabled children from classes. In drafting the law, Congress was largely guided by the recent decisions in *Mills v. Board of Education of District of Columbia*, 348 F. Supp. 866 (1972), and *PARC*, 343 F. Supp. 279 (1972), both of which involved the exclusion of hard-to-handle disabled students. *Mills* in particular demonstrated the extent to which schools used disciplinary measures to bar children from the classroom. There, school officials had labeled four of the seven minor plaintiffs "behavioral problems," and had excluded them from classes without providing any alternative education to them or any notice to their parents. 348 F. Supp., at 869-870. After finding that this practice was not limited to the named plaintiffs but affected in one way or another an estimated class of 12,000 to 18,000 disabled students, *id.*, at 868-869, 875, the District Court enjoined future exclusions, suspensions, or expulsions "on grounds of discipline." *Id.*, at 880.

Congress attacked such exclusionary practices in a variety of ways. It required participating States to educate all disabled children, regardless of the severity of their disabilities, 20 U.S.C. 1412(2)(c), and included within the definition of "handicapped" those children with serious emotional disturbances. 1401(1). It further provided for meaningful parental participation in all aspects of a child's educational placement, and barred schools, through the stay-put provision, from changing that placement over the parent's objection until all review proceedings were completed. Recognizing that those proceedings might prove long and tedious, the Act's drafters did not intend 1415(e)(3) to operate inflexibly, see 121 Cong. Rec. 37412 (1975) (remarks of Sen. Stafford), and they therefore allowed for interim placements where parents and school officials are able to agree on one. Conspicuously absent from 1415(e)(3), however, is any emergency exception for dangerous students. This absence is all the more telling in light of the injunctive decree issued in *PARC*, which permitted school officials unilaterally to remove students in "'extraordinary circumstances.'" 343 F. Supp., at 301. Given the lack of any similar exception in *Mills*, and the close attention Congress devoted to these "landmark" decisions, see S. Rep., at 6, we can only conclude that the omission was intentional; we are therefore not at liberty to engraft onto the statute an exception Congress chose not to create.

Our conclusion that 1415(e)(3) means what it says does not leave educators hamstrung. The Department of Education has observed that, "[w]hile the [child's] placement may not be changed [during any complaint proceeding], this does not preclude the agency from using its normal procedures for dealing with children who are endangering themselves or others." Comment following 34 CFR 300.513 (1987). Such procedures may include the use of study carrels, time-outs, detention, or the restriction of privileges. More drastically, where a student poses an immediate threat to the safety of others, officials may temporarily suspend him or her for up to 10 school days.[8] This authority, which respondent in no way disputes, not only ensures that school administrators can protect the safety of others by promptly removing the most dangerous of students, it also provides a "cooling down" period during which officials can initiate IEP review and seek to persuade the child's parents to agree to an interim placement. And in those cases in which the parents of a truly dangerous child adamantly refuse to permit any change in placement, the 10-day respite gives school officials an opportunity to invoke the aid of the courts under 1415(e)(2), which empowers courts to grant any appropriate relief.

Petitioner contends, however, that the availability of judicial relief is more illusory than real, because a party seeking review under 1415(e)(2) must exhaust time-consuming administrative remedies, and because under the Court of Appeals' construction of 1415(e)(3), courts are as bound by the stay-put provision's "automatic injunction," 793 F.2d, at 1486, as are schools.[9] It is true that judicial review is normally not available under 1415(e)(2) until all administrative proceedings are completed, but as we have previously noted, parents may by-pass the administrative process where exhaustion would be futile or inadequate. See *Smith v. Robinson*, 468 U.S. 992, 1014, n. 17 (1984) (citing cases); see also 121 Cong. Rec. 37416 (1975) (remarks of Sen. Williams) ("[E]xhaustion . . . should not be required . . . in cases where such exhaustion would be futile either as a legal or practical matter"). While may of the EHA's procedural safeguards protect the rights of parents and children, schools can and do seek redress through the administrative review process, and we have no reason to believe that Congress meant to require schools alone to exhaust in all cases, no matter how exigent the circumstances. The burden in such cases, of course, rests with the school to demonstrate the futility or inadequacy of administrative review, but nothing in 1415(e)(2) suggests that schools are completely barred from attempting to make such a showing. Nor do we think that 1415(e)(3) operates to limit the equitable powers of district courts such that they cannot, in appropriate cases, temporarily enjoin a dangerous disabled child from attending school.

As the EHA's legislative history makes clear, one of the evils Congress sought to remedy was the unilateral exclusion of disabled children by **schools**, not courts, and one of the purposes of 1415(e)(3), therefore, was "to prevent **school** officials from removing a child from the regular public school classroom over the parents' objection pending completion of the review proceedings." *Burlington School Committee v. Massachusetts Dept. of Education*, 471 U.S., at 373 (emphasis added). The stay-put provision in no way purports to limit or pre-empt the authority conferred on courts by 1415(e)(2), see *Doe v. Brookline School Committee*, 722 F.2d 910, 917 (CA1 1983); indeed, it says nothing whatever about judicial power.

In short, then, we believe that school officials are entitled to seek injunctive relief under 1415(e)(2) in appropriate cases. In any such action, 1415(e)(3) effectively creates a presumption in favor of the child's current educational placement which school officials can overcome only by showing that maintaining the child in his or her current placement is substantially likely to result in injury either to himself or herself, or to others. In the present case, we are satisfied that the District Court, in enjoining the state and local defendants from indefinitely suspending respondent or otherwise unilaterally altering his then current placement, properly balanced respondent's interest in receiving a free appropriate public education in accordance with the procedures and requirements of the EHA against the interests of the state and local school officials in maintaining a safe learning environment for all their students.[10]

IV

We believe the courts below properly construed and applied 1415(e)(3), except insofar as the Court of Appeals held that a suspension in excess of 10 school days does not constitute a "change in placement."[11] We therefore affirm the Court of Appeals' judgment on this issue as modified herein. Because we are equally divided on the question whether a court may order a State to provide services directly to a disabled child where the local agency has failed to do so, we affirm the Court of Appeals' judgment on this issue as well.

Affirmed.

Chief Justice Rehnquist, **concurring**.

I write separately on the mootness issue in this case to explain why I have joined Part II of the Court's opinion, and why I think reconsideration of our mootness jurisprudence may be in order when dealing with cases decided by this Court.

The present rule in federal cases is that an actual controversy must exist at all stages of appellate review, not merely at the time the complaint is filed. This doctrine was clearly articulated in *United States v. Munsingwear*, 340 U.S. 36 (1950), in which Justice Douglas noted that "[t]he established practice of the Court in dealing with a civil case from a court in the federal system which has become moot while on its way here or pending our decision on the merits is to reverse or vacate the judgment below and remand with a direction to dismiss." *Id.*, at 39. The rule has been followed fairly consistently over the last 30 years. See, e.g., *Preiser v. Newkirk*, 422 U.S. 395 (1975); *SEC v. Medical Committee for Human Rights*, 404 U.S. 403 (1972).

All agree that this case was "very much alive," *ante*, at 10, when the action was filed in the District Court, and very probably when the Court of Appeals decided the case. It is supervening events since the decision of the Court of Appeals which have caused the dispute between the majority and the dissent over whether this case is moot. Therefore, all that the Court actually holds is that these supervening events do not deprive this Court of the authority to hear the case. I agree with that holding, and would go still further in the direction of relaxing the test of mootness where the events giving rise to the claim of mootness have occurred after our decision to grant certiorari or to note probable jurisdiction.

The Court implies in its opinion, and the dissent expressly states, that the mootness doctrine is based upon Art. III of the Constitution. There is no doubt that our recent cases have taken that position. See *Nebraska Press Assn. v.*

Stuart, 427 U.S. 539, 546 (1976); *Preiser v. Newkirk, supra*, at 401; *Sibron v. New York*, 392 U.S. 40, 57 (1968); *Liner v. Jafco, Inc.*, 375 U.S. 301, 306, n. 3 (1964). But it seems very doubtful that the earliest case I have found discussing mootness, *Mills v. Green*, 159 U.S. 651 (1895), was premised on constitutional constraints; Justice Gray's opinion in that case nowhere mentions Art. III.

If it were indeed Art. III which—by reason of its requirement of a case or controversy for the exercise of federal judicial power—underlies the mootness doctrine, the "capable of repetition, yet evading review" exception relied upon by the Court in this case would be incomprehensible. Article III extends the judicial power of the United States only to cases and controversies; it does not except from this requirement other lawsuits which are "capable of repetition, yet evading review." If our mootness doctrine were forced upon us by the case or controversy requirement of Art. III itself, we would have no more power to decide lawsuits which are "moot" but which also raise questions which are capable of repetition but evading review than we would to decide cases which are "moot" but raise no such questions.

The exception to mootness for cases which are "capable of repetition, yet evading review," was first stated by this Court in *Southern Pacific Terminal Co. v. ICC*, 219 U.S. 498 (1911). There the Court enunciated the exception in the light of obvious pragmatic considerations, with no mention of Art. III as the principle underlying the mootness doctrine:

"The questions involved in the orders of the Interstate Commerce Commission are usually continuing (as are manifestly those in the case at bar) and their consideration ought not to be, as they might be, defeated, by short-term orders, capable of repetition, yet evading review, and at one time the Government and at another time the carriers have their rights determined by the Commission without a chance of redress." *Id.*, at 515.

The exception was explained again in *Moore v. Ogilvie*, 394 U.S. 814, 816 (1969):

"The problem is therefore 'capable of repetition, yet evading review.' The need for its resolution thus reflects a continuing controversy in the federal-state area where our 'one man, one vote' decisions have thrust" (citation omitted).

It is also worth noting that *Moore v. Ogilvie* involved a question which had been mooted by an election, just as did *Mills v. Green* some 70 years earlier. But at the time of *Mills*, the case originally enunciating the mootness doctrine, there was no thought of any exception for cases which were "capable of repeition, yet evading review."

The logical conclusion to be drawn from these cases,

and from the historical development of the principle of mootness, is that while an unwillingness to decide moot cases may be connected to the case or controversy requirement of Art. III, it is an attenuated connection that may be overridden where there are strong reasons to override it. The "capable of repetition, yet evading review" exception is an example. So too is our refusal to dismiss as moot those cases in which the defendant voluntarily ceases, at some advanced stage of the appellate proceedings, whatever activity prompted the plaintiff to seek an injunction. See, e.g., *City of Mesquite v. Aladdin's Castle, Inc.*, 455 U.S. 283, 289, n. 10 (1982); *United States v. W.T. Grant Co.*, 345 U.S. 629, 632 (1953).

I believe that we should adopt an additional exception to our present mootness doctrine for those cases where the events which render the case moot have supervened since our grant of certiorari or noting of probable jurisdiction in the case. Dissents from denial of certiorari in this Court illustrate the proposition that the roughly 150 or 160 cases which we decide each year on the merits are less than the number of cases warranting review by us if we are to remain, as Chief Justice Taft said many years ago, "the last word on every important issue under the Constitution and the statutes of the United States." But these unique resources—the time spent preparing to decide the case by reading briefs, hearing oral argument, and conferring—are squandered in every case in which it becomes apparent after the decisional process is underway that we may not reach the question presented. To me the unique and valuable ability of this Court to decide a case—we are, at present, the only Art. III court which can decide a federal question in which a way as to bind all other courts—is a sufficient reason either to abandon the doctrine of mootness altogether in cases which this Court has decided to review, or at least to relax the doctrine of mootness in such a manner as the dissent accuses the majority of doing here. I would leave the mootness doctrine as established by our cases in full force and effect when applied to the earlier stages of a lawsuit, but I believe that once this Court has undertaken a consideration of a case, an exception to that principle is just as much warranted as where a case is "capable of repetition, yet evading review."

Justice Scalia, with whom Justice O'Connor joins, **dissenting.**

Without expressing any views on the merits of this case, I respectfully dissent because in my opinion we have no authority to decide it. I think the controversy is moot.

I

The Court correctly acknowledges that we have no power under Art. III of the Constitution to adjudicate a case that no longer presents an actual, ongoing dispute between the named parties. Ante, at 10, citing *Nebraska Press Assn. v.*

Stuart, 427 U.S. 539, 546 (1976); *Preiser v. Newkirk*, 422 U.S. 395, 401 (1975). Here, there is obviously no present controversy between the parties, since both respondents are no longer in school and therefore no longer subject to a unilateral "change in placement." The Court concedes mootness with respect to respondent John Doe, who is now too old to receive the benefits of the Education of the Handicapped Act (EHA). *Ante*, at 11. It concludes, however, that the case is not moot as to respondent Jack Smith, who has two more years of eligibility but is no longer in the public schools, because the controversy is "capable of repetition, yet evading review." *Ante*, at 11-16.

Jurisdiction on the basis that a dispute is "capable of repetition, yet evading review" is limited to the "exceptional situatio[n]," *Los Angeles v. Lyons*, 461 U.S. 95, 109 (1983), where the following two circumstances simultaneously occur: "'(1) the challenged action [is] in its duration too short to be fully litigated prior to its cessation or expiration, and (2) there [is] a reasonable expectation that the same complaining party would be subjected to the same action again.'" *Murphy v. Hunt*, 455 U.S. 478, 482 (1982) (per curiam), quoting *Weinstein v. Bradford*, 423 U.S. 147, 149 (1975) (per curiam). The second of these requirements is not met in this case.

For there to be a "reasonable expectation" that Smith will be subjected to the same action again, that event must be a "demonstrated probability." *Murphy v. Hunt, supra*, at 482, 483; *Weinstein v. Bradford, supra*, at 149. I am surprised by the Court's contention, fraught with potential for future mischief, that "reasonable expectation" is satisfied by something less than "demonstrated probability." Ante, at 11-12, n. 6. No one expects that to happen which he does not think probable; and his expectation cannot be shown to be reasonable unless the probability is demonstrated. Thus, as the Court notes, our cases recite the two descriptions side by side ("a 'reasonable expectation' or a 'demonstrated probability,'" Hunt, supra, at 482). The Court asserts, however, that these standards are "described . . . in the disjunctive," ante, at 11-12, n. 6 -- evidently believing that the conjunction "or" has no accepted usage except a disjunctive one, i.e., "expressing an alternative, contrast, or opposition," *Webster's Third New International Dictionary* 651 (1981). In fact, however, the conjunction is often used "to indicate . . . (3) the synonymous, equivalent, or substitutive character of two words or phrases fell over a precipice [or] cliff the off [or] far side lessen [or] abate; (4) correction or greater exactness of phrasing or meaning these essays, [or] rather rough sketches the present king had no children--[or] no legitimate children . . ." *Id.*, at 1585. It is obvious that in saying "a reasonable expectation or a demonstrated probability" we have used the conjunction in one of the latter, or nondisjunctive, senses. Otherwise (and according to the Court's exegesis), we would have been saying that a controversy is sufficiently likely to recur if either a certain degree of probability exists or a higher degree of probability exists. That is rather like a statute giving the vote to persons who are "18 or 21." A bare six years ago, the author of today's opinion and one other member of the majority plainly understood "reasonable expectation" and "demonstrated probability" to be synonymous. Cf. *Edgar v. MITE Corp.*, 457 U.S. 624, 662, and n. 11 (1982) (Marshall, J., dissenting, joined by Brennan, J.) (using the two terms here at issue interchangeably, and concluding that the case is moot because "there is no DEMONSTRATED PROBABILITY that the State will have occasion to prevent MITE from making a takeover offer for some other corporation") (emphasis added).

The prior holdings cited by the Court in a footnote, see *ante*, at 12, n. 6, offer no support for the novel proposition that less than a probability of recurrence is sufficient to avoid mootness. In *Burlington Northern R. Co. v. Maintenance of Way Employees*, __ U.S. __ , __, n. 4 (1987), we found that the same railroad and union were "reasonably likely" to find themselves in a recurring dispute over the same issue. Similarly, in *California Coastal Comm'n v. Granite Rock Co.*, __ U.S. ___, ___ (1987), we found it "likely" that the plaintiff mining company would submit new plans which the State would seek to subject to its coastal permit requirements. See *Webster's Third New International Dictionary* 1310 (1981) (defining "likely" as "of such a nature or so circumstanced as to make something probable[] . . . seeming to justify belief or expectation[] . . . in all probability"). In the cases involving exclusion orders issued to prevent the press from attending criminal trials, we found that "[i]t can reasonably be assumed" that a news organization covering the area in which the defendant court sat will again be subjected to that court's closure rules. *Press-Enterprise Co. v. Superior Court of Cal., Riverside County*, __ U.S. __, __ (1986); *Globe Newspaper Co. v. Superior Court of Norfolk County*, 457 U.S. 596, 603 (1982). In these and other cases, one may quarrel, perhaps, with the accuracy of the Court's probability assessment; but there is no doubt that assessment was regarded as necessary to establish jurisdiction.

In *Roe v. Wade*, 410 U.S. 113, 125 (1973), we found that the "human gestation period is so short that the pregnancy will come to term before the usual appellate process is complete," so that "pregnancy litigation seldom will survive much beyond the trial stage, and appellate review will be effectively denied." *Roe*, at least one other abortion case, see *Doe v. Bolton*, 410 U.S. 179, 187 (1973), and some of our election law decisions, see *Rosario v. Rockefeller*, 410 U.S. 752, 756, n. 5 (1973); *Dunn v. Blumstein*, 405 U.S. 330, 333, n. 2 (1972), differ from the body of our mootness jurisprudence not in accepting less than a probability that the issue will recur, in a manner evading review, between the same parties; but in dispensing with the same-party requirement

entirely, focusing instead upon the great likelihood that the issue will recur between the defendant and the other members of the public at large without ever reaching us. Arguably those cases have been limited to their facts, or to the narrow areas of abortion and election rights, by our more recent insistence that, at least in the absence of a class action, the "capable of repetition" doctrine applies only where "there [is] a reasonable expectation that the SAME COMPLAINING PARTY would be subjected to the same action again." *Hunt*, 455 U.S., at 482 (emphasis added), quoting *Weinstein*, 423 U.S., at 149; see *Burlington Northern R. Co., supra*, at __, n. 4; *Illinois Elections Bd. v. Socialist Workers Party*, 440 U.S. 173, 187 (1979). If those earlier cases have not been so limited, however, the conditions for their application do not in any event exist here. There is no extraordinary improbability of the present issue's reaching us as a traditionally live controversy. It would have done so in this very case if Smith had not chosen to leave public school. In sum, on any analysis, the proposition the Court asserts in the present case—that probability need not be shown in order to establish the "same-party-recurrence" exception to mootness—is a significant departure from settled law.

II

If our established mode of analysis were followed, the conclusion that a live controversy exists in the present case would require a demonstrated probability that all of the following events will occur: (1) Smith will return to public school; (2) he will be placed in an educational setting that is unable to tolerate his dangerous behavior; (3) he will again engage in dangerous behavior; and (4) local school officials will again attempt unilaterally to change his placement and the state defendants will fail to prevent such action. The Court spends considerable time establishing that the last two of these events are likely to recur, but relegates to a footnote its discussion of the first event, upon which all others depend, and only briefly alludes to the second. Neither the facts in the record, nor even the extra-record assurances of counsel, establish a demonstrated probability of either of them.

With respect to whether Smith will return to school, at oral argument Smith's counsel forthrightly conceded that she "cannot represent whether in fact either of these students will ask for further education from the Petitioners." Tr. of Oral Arg. 23. Rather, she observed, respondents would "look to [our decision in this case] to find out what will happen after that." *Id.*, at 23-24. When pressed, the most counsel would say was that, in her view, the 20-year-old Smith could seek to return to public school because he has not graduated, he is handicapped, and he has a right to an education. *Id.*, at 27. I do not perceive the principle that would enable us to leap from the proposition that Smith could reenter public school to the conclusion that it is a demonstrated probability he will do so.

The Court nevertheless concludes that "there is at the very least a reasonable expectation" that Smith will return to school. *Ante*, at 12, n. 6. I cannot possibly dispute that on the basis of the Court's terminology. Once it is accepted that a "reasonable expectation" can exist without a demonstrable probability that the event in question will occur, the phrase has been deprived of all meaning, and the Court can give it whatever application it wishes without fear of effective contradiction. It is worth pointing out, however, how slim are the reeds upon which this conclusion of "reasonable expectation" (whatever that means) rests. The Court bases its determination on three observations from the record and oral argument. First, it notes that Smith has been pressing this lawsuit since 1980. It suffices to observe that the equivalent argument can be made in every case that remains active and pending; we have hitherto avoided equating the existence of a case or controversy with the existence of a lawsuit. Second, the Court observes that Smith has "as great a need of a high school education and diploma as any of his peers." *Ibid*. While this is undoubtedly good advice, it hardly establishes that the 20-year-old Smith is likely to return to high school, much less to public high school. Finally, the Court notes that counsel "advises us that [Smith] is awaiting the outcome of this case to decide whether to pursue his degree." *Ibid*. Not only do I not think this establishes a current case or controversy, I think it a most conclusive indication that no current case or controversy exists. We do not sit to broaden decision-making options, but to adjudicate the lawfulness of acts that have happened or, at most, are about to occur.

The conclusion that the case is moot is reinforced, moreover, when one considers that, even if Smith does return to public school, the controversy will still not recur unless he is again placed in an educational setting that is unable to tolerate his behavior. It seems to me not only not demonstrably probable, but indeed quite unlikely, given what is now known about Smith's behavioral problems, that local school authorities would again place him in an educational setting that could not control his dangerous conduct, causing a suspension that would replicate the legal issues in this suit. The majority dismisses this further contingency by noting that the school authorities have an obligation under the EHA to provide an "appropriate" education in "the least restrictive environment." *Ante*, at 14. This means, however, the least restrictive environment appropriate for the particular child. The Court observes that "the preparation of an [individualized educational placement]" is "an inexact science at best," *ante*, at 14, thereby implying that the school authorities are likely to get it wrong. Even accepting this assumption, which seems to me contrary to the premises of the Act, I see no reason further to assume that they will get it wrong by making the same mistake they did last time—assigning Smith to too unrestrictive an environment, from which he will thereafter be suspended—rather than by assigning him to too restrictive an environment. The latter, which seems to me more likely than the former (although both combined are much less likely than a correct placement), might produce a lawsuit, but not a lawsuit involving the issues that we have before us here.

III

The Chief Justice joins the majority opinion on the ground, not that this case is not moot, but that where the events giving rise to the mootness have occurred after we have granted certiorari we may disregard them, since mootness is only a prudential doctrine and not part of the "case or controversy" requirement of Art. III. I do not see how that can be. There is no more reason to intuit that mootness is merely a prudential doctrine than to intuit that initial standing is. Both doctrines have equivalently deep roots in the common-law understanding, and hence the constitutional understanding of what makes a matter appropriate for judicial disposition. See *Flast v. Cohen*, 392 U.S. 83, 95 (1968) (describing mootness and standing as various illustrations of the requirement of "justiciability" in Art. III).

The Chief Justice relies upon the fact that an 1895 case discussing mootness, *Mills v. Green*, 159 U.S. 651 (1895), makes no mention of the Constitution. But there is little doubt that the Court believed the doctrine called into question the Court's power and not merely its prudence, for (in an opinion by the same Justice who wrote *Mills*) it had said two years earlier:

"[T]he court is not EMPOWERED to decide moot questions or abstract propositions, or to declare . . . principles or rules of law which cannot affect the result as to the thing in issue in the case before it. No stipulation of parties or counsel . . . can enlarge the POWER, or affect the duty, of the court in this regard." *California v. San Pablo & Tulare R. Co.*, 149 U.S. 308, 314 (1893) (Gray, J.) (emphasis added).

If it seems peculiar to the modern lawyer that our 19th century mootness cases make no explicit mention of Art. III, that is a peculiarity shared with our 19th century, and even our early 20th century, standing cases. As late as 1919, in dismissing a suit for lack of standing we said simply:

"Considerations of propriety, as well as long-established practice, demand that we refrain from passing upon the constitutionality of an act of Congress unless obliged to do so in the proper performance of our judicial function, when the question is raised by a party whose interests entitle him to raise it." *Blaire v. United States*, 250 U.S. 273, 279 (1919).

See also, e.g., *Standard Stock Food Co. v. Wright*, 225 U.S. 540, 550 (1912); *Southern Ry. Co. v. King*, 217 U.S. 524, 534 (1910); *Turpin v. Lemon*, 187 U.S. 51, 60-61 (1902); *Tyler v. Judges of Court of Registration*, 179 U.S. 405, 409 (1900). The same is also true of our early cases dismissing actions lacking truly adverse parties, that is, collusive actions. See, e.g., *Cleveland v. Chamberlain*, 1 Black 419, 425-426 (1862); *Lord v. Veazie*, 8 How. 251, 254-256 (1850). The explanation for this ellipsis is that the courts simply chose to refer directly to the traditional, fundamental limitations upon the powers of common-law courts, rather than referring to Art. III which in turn adopts those limitations through terms ("The judicial Power"; "Cases"; "Controversies") that have virtually no meaning except by reference to that tradition. The ultimate circularity, coming back in the end to tradition, is evident in the statement by Justice Field:

> "By cases and controversies are intended the claims of litigants brought before the courts for determination by such regular proceedings as are established by law or custom for the protection or enforcement of rights, or the prevention, redress, or punishment of wrongs. Whenever the claim of a party under the constitution, laws, or treaties of the United States takes such a form that the judicial power is capable of acting upon it, then it has become a case." *In re Pacific R. Commn.*, 32 F. 241, 255 (CCND Cal. 1887).

See also 2 M. Farrand, *Records of the Federal Convention of 1787*, p. 430 (rev. ed. 1966):

> "Docr. Johnson moved to insert the words 'this Constitution and the' before the word 'laws'

> "Mr. Madison doubted whether it was not going too far to extend the jurisdiction of the Court generally to cases arising Under the Constitution, & whether it ought not to be limited to cases of a Judiciary Nature. The right of expounding the Constitution in cases not of this nature ought not to be given to that Department.

> "The motion of Docr. Johnson was agreed to nem: con: it being generally supposed that the jurisdiction given was constructively limited to cases of a Judiciary nature—"

In sum, I cannot believe that it is only our prudence, and nothing inherent in the understood nature of "The judicial Power," U.S. Const., Art. III, 1, that restrains us from pronouncing judgment in a case that the parties have settled, or a case involving a nonsurviving claim where the plaintiff has died, or a case where the law has been changed so that the basis of the dispute no longer exists, or a case where conduct sought to be enjoined has ceased and will not recur. Where the conduct has ceased for the time being but there is a demonstrated probability that it will recur, a real-life controversy between parties with a personal stake in the outcome continues to exist, and Art. III is no more violated than it is violated by entertaining a declaratory judgment action. But that is the limit of our power. I agree with The Chief Justice to this extent: the "yet evading

review" portion of our "capable of repetition yet evading review" test is prudential; whether or not that criterion is met, a justiciable controversy exists. But the probability of recurrence between the same parties is essential to our jurisdiction as a court, and it is that deficiency which the case before us presents.

* * * *

It is assuredly frustrating to find that a jurisdictional impediment prevents us from reaching the important merits issues that were the reason for our agreeing to hear this case. But we cannot ignore such impediments for purposes of our appellate review without simultaneously affecting the principles that govern district courts in their assertion or retention of original jurisdiction. We thus do substantial harm to a governmental structure designed to restrict the courts to matters that actually affect the litigants before them.

Endnotes

1 Congress' earlier efforts to ensure that disabled students received adequate public education had failed in part because the measures it adopted were largely hortatory. In the 1966 amendments to the Elementary and Secondary Education Act of 1965, Congress established a grant program "for the purpose of assisting the States in the initiation, expansion, and improvement of programs and projects . . . for the education of handicapped children." Pub. L. 89-750, 161, 80 Stat. 1204. It repealed that program four years later and replaced it with the original version of the Education of the Handicapped Act, Pub. L. 91-230, 84 Stat. 175, Part B of which contained a similar grant program. Neither statute, however, provided specific guidance as to how States were to use the funds, nor did they condition the availability of the grants on compliance with any procedural or substantive safeguards. In amending the EHA to its present form, Congress rejected its earlier policy of "merely establish[ing] an unenforceable goal requiring all children to be in school." 121 Cong. Rec. 37417 (1975) (remarks of Sen. Schweiker). Today, all 50 states and the District of Columbia receive funding assistance under the EHA. U.S. Dept. of Education, Ninth Annual Report to Congress on Implementation of Education of the Handicapped Act (1987).

2 California law at the time empowered school principals to suspend students for no more than five consecutive school days, Cal. Educ. Code Ann. 48903(a) (West 1978), but permitted school districts seeking to expel a suspended student to "extend the suspension until such time as [expulsion proceedings were completed]; provided, that [it] has determined that the presence of the pupil at the school or in an alternative school placement would cause a danger to persons or property or a threat of disrupting the instructional process." 48903(h). The State subsequently amended the law to permit school districts to impose longer initial periods of suspension. See n. 3, *infra*.

3 In 1983, the State amended its Education Code to permit school districts to impose initial suspensions of 20, and in certain circumstances, 30 school days. Cal. Educ. Code Ann.

48912(a), 48903 (West Supp. 1988). The legislature did not alter the indefinite suspension authority which the SPC exercised in this case, but simply incorporated the earlier provision into a new section. See 48911(g).

4 At the time respondent Doe initiated this suit, Wilson Riles was the California Superintendent of Public Instruction. Petitioner Honig succeeded him in office.

5 We note that both petitioner and respondents believe that this case presents a live controversy. See Tr. of Oral Arg. 6, 27-31. Only the United States, appearing as amicus curiae, urges that the case is presently nonjusticiable. *Id.*, at 21.

6 Notwithstanding respondent's undisputed right to a free appropriate public education in California, Justice Scalia argues in dissent that there is no "demonstrated probability" that Smith will actually avail himself of that right because his counsel was unable to state affirmatively during oral argument that her client would seek to re-enter the state school system. See *post*, at 2. We believe the dissent overstates the stringency of the "capable of repetition" test. Although Justice Scalia equates "reasonable expectation" with "demonstrated probability," the very case he cites for this proposition described these standards in the distinctive, see *Murphy v. Hunt*, 455 U.S., at 482 ("[T]here must be a 'reasonable expectation' OR a 'demonstrated probability' that the same controversy will recur" (emphasis added)), and in numerous cases decided both before and since *Hunt* we have found controversies capable of repetition based on expectations that, while reasonable, were hardly demonstrably probable. See e.g., *Burlington Northern R. Co. v. Maintenance of Way Employees*, 481 U.S. ____, ___, n. 4 (1987) (parties "reasonably likely" to find themselves in future disputes over collective bargaining agreement); *California Coastal Comm'n v. Granite Rock Co.*, 480 U.S. ____, _____ (1987) (O'Connor, J.) ("likely" that respondent would again submit mining plans that would trigger contested state permit requirement); *Press-Enterprise Co. v. Superior Court of Cal., Riverside County*, 478 U.S. 1, 6 (1986) ("It can reasonably be assumed" that newspaper publisher will be subjected to similar closure order in the future); *Globe Newspaper Co. v. Superior Court of Norfolk County*, 457 U.S. 596, 603 (1982) (same); *United States Parole Comm'n v. Geraghty*, 445 U.S. 388, 398 (1980) (case not moot where litigant "faces some likelihood of becoming involved in same controversy in the future") (dicta). Our concern in these cases, as in all others involving potentially moot claims, was whether the controversy was capable of repetition and not, as the dissent seems to insist, whether the claimant had demonstrated that a recurrence of the dispute was more probable than not. Regardless, then, of whether respondent has established with mathematical precision the likelihood that he will enroll in public school during the next two years, we think there is at the very least a reasonable expectation that he will exercise his rights under the EHA. In this regard, we believe respondent's actions over the course of the last seven years speak louder than his counsel's momentary equivocation during oral argument. Since 1980, he has sought to vindicate his right to an appropriate public education that is not only

free of charge, but free from the threat that school officials will unilaterally change his placement or exclude him from class altogether. As a disabled young man, he has as at least as great a need of a high school education and diploma as any of his peers, and his counsel advises us that he is awaiting the outcome of this case to decide whether to pursue his degree. Tr. Oral Arg. 23-24. Under these circumstances, we think it not only counterintuitive but unreasonable to assume that respondent will forgo the exercise of a right that he has for so long sought to defend. Certainly we have as much reason to expect that respondent will re-enter the California school system as we had to assume that Jane Roe would again both have an unwanted pregnancy and wish to exercise her right to an abortion. See *Roe v. Wade*, 410 U.S. 113, 125 (1973).

7 Petitioner concedes that the school district "made a number of procedural mistakes in its eagerness to protect other students from Doe and Smith." Reply Brief for Petitioner 6. According to petitioner, however, unilaterally excluding respondents from school was not among them; indeed, petitioner insists that the SFUSD acted properly in removing respondents and urges that the stay-put provision "should not be interpreted to require a school district to maintain such dangerous children with other children." *Id.*, at 6-7.

8 The Department of Education has adopted the position first espoused in 1980 by its Office of Civil Rights that a suspension of up to 10 school days does not amount to a "change in placement" prohibited by 1415(e)(3). U.S. Dept. of Education, Office of Special Education Programs, Policy Letter (Feb. 26, 1987), Ed. for Handicapped L. Rep. 211:437 (1987). The EHA nowhere defines the phrase "change in placement," nor does the statute's structure or legislative history provide any guidance as to how the term applies to fixed suspensions. Given this ambiguity, we defer to the construction adopted by the agency charged with monitoring and enforcing the statute. See *INS v. Cardoza-Fonseca*, 480 U.S. ____, _____ (1987). Moreover, the agency's position comports fully with the purposes of the statute: Congress sought to prevent schools from permanently and unilaterally excluding disabled children by means of indefinite suspensions and expulsions; the power to impose fixed suspensions of short duration does not carry the potential for total exclusion that Congress found so objectionable. Indeed, despite its broad injunction, the District Court in *Mills v. Board of Education of District of Columbia*, 348 F. Supp. 866 (DC 1972), recognized that school officials could suspend disabled children on a short-term, temporary basis. See *id*, at 880. Cf. *Goss v. Lopez*, 419 U.S. 565, 574-576, (1975) (suspension of 10 school days or more works a sufficient deprivation of property and liberty interests to trigger the protections of the Due Process Clause). Because we believe the agency correctly determined that a suspension in excess of 10 days does constitute a prohibited "change in placement," we conclude that the Court of Appeals erred to the extent it approved suspensions of 20 and 30 days' duration.

9 Petitioner also notes that in California, schools may not suspend any given student for more than a total of 20, and in certain special circumstances 30, school days in a single

year, see Cal. Educ. Code Ann. 48903 (West Supp. 1988); he argues, therefore, that a school district may not have the option of imposing a 10-day suspension when dealing with an obstreperous child whose previous suspensions for the year total 18 or 19 days. The fact remains, however, that state law does not define the scope of 1415(e)(3). There may be cases in which a suspension that is otherwise valid under the stay-put provision would violate local law. The effect of such a violation, however, is a question of state law upon which we express no view.

10 We therefore reject the United States' contention that the District Judge abused her discretion in enjoining the local school officials from indefinitely suspending respondent pending completion of the expulsion proceedings. Contrary to the Government's suggestion, the District Judge did not view herself bound to enjoin any and all violations of the stay-put provision, but rather, consistent with the analysis we set out above, weighed the relative harms to the parties and found that the balance tipped decidedly in favor of respondent. App. 222-223. We of course do not sit to review the factual determinations underlying that conclusion. We do note, however, that in balancing the parties' respective interests, the District Judge gave proper consideration to respondent's rights under the EHA. While the Government complains that the District Court indulged an improper presumption of irreparable harm to respondent, we do not believe that school officials can escape the presumptive effect of the stay-put provision simply by violating it and forcing parents to petition for relief. In any suit brought by parents seeking injunctive relief for a violation of 1415(e)(3), the burden rests with the school district to demonstrate that the educational status quo must be altered.

11 See n. 8, *supra.*

The Supreme Court of the United States

510 U. S. 7

FLORENCE COUNTY SCHOOL DISTRICT FOUR, et al.

Petitioners

v.

SHANNON CARTER, a minor by and through her father, and next friend, Emory D. Carter

Respondent

No. 91-1523

November 9, 1993

On Writ of Certiorari to the U.S. Court of Appeals for the Fourth Circuit.

Counsel for Petitioners: Donald B. Ayer, Esq., Washington, DC.

Counsel for Respondent: Peter W.D. Wright, Esq., Richmond, VA.

Counsel for the United States, as Amicus Curiae supporting Respondent: Amy L. Wax, Esq., Assistant to the Solicitor General, Department of Justice, Washington, DC.

Before Rehnquist, C.J., and Blackmun, Stevens, O'Connor, Scalia, Kennedy, Souter, Thomas, and Ginsburg, JJ.

SANDRA DAY O'CONNOR, Associate Justice.

The Individuals with Disabilities Education Act (IDEA), 84 Stat. 175, as amended, 20 U.S.C. § 1400 et seq. (1988 ed. and Supp. IV), requires States to provide disabled children with a "free appropriate public education," § 1401(a)(18). This case presents the question whether a court may order reimbursement for parents who unilaterally withdraw their child from a public school that provides an inappropriate education under IDEA and put the child in a private school that provides an education that is otherwise proper under IDEA, but does not meet all the requirements of § 1401(a)(18). We hold that the court may order such reimbursement, and therefore affirm the judgment of the Court of Appeals.

I

Respondent Shannon Carter was classified as learning disabled in 1985, while a ninth grade student in a school operated by petitioner Florence County School District Four. School officials met with Shannon's parents to formulate an individualized education program (IEP) for Shannon, as required under IDEA. 20 U.S.C. §§ 1401(a)(18) and (20), 1414(a)(5) (1988 ed. and Supp. IV). The IEP provided that Shannon would stay in regular classes except for three periods of individualized instruction per week, and established specific goals in reading and mathematics of four months' progress for the entire school year. Shannon's parents were dissatisfied, and requested a hearing to challenge the appropriateness of the IEP. See § 1415(b)(2). Both the local educational officer and the state educational agency hearing officer rejected Shannon's parents' claim and concluded that the IEP was adequate. In the meantime, Shannon's parents had placed her in Trident Academy, a private school specializing in educating children with disabilities. Shannon began at Trident in September 1985 and graduated in the spring of 1988.

Shannon's parents filed this suit in July 1986, claiming that the school district had breached its duty under IDEA to provide Shannon with a "free appropriate public education," § 1401(a)(18), and seeking reimbursement for tuition and other costs incurred at Trident. After a bench trial, the District Court ruled in the parents' favor. The court held that the school district's proposed educational program and the achievement goals of the IEP "were wholly inadequate" and failed to satisfy the requirements of the Act. App. to Pet. for Cert 27a. The court further held that "[a]lthough [Trident Academy] did not comply with all the procedures outlined in [IDEA]," the school "provided Shannon an excellent education in substantial compliance with all the substantive requirements" of the statute. Id. at 37a. The court found that Trident "evaluated Shannon quarterly, not yearly as mandated in [IDEA], it provided Shannon with low teacher-student ratios, and it developed a plan which allowed Shannon to receive passing marks and progress from grade to grade." Ibid. The court also credited the findings of its own expert, who determined that Shannon had made "significant progress" at Trident and that her reading comprehension had risen three grade levels in her three years at the school. Id., at 29a. The District Court concluded that Shannon's education was "appropriate" under IDEA, and that Shannon's parents were entitled to reimbursement of tuition and other costs. Id., at 37a.

The Court of Appeals for the Fourth Circuit affirmed. 950 F.2d 156 (1991). The court agreed that the IEP proposed by the school district was inappropriate under IDEA. It also rejected the school district's argument that reimbursement is never proper when the parents choose a private school that is not approved by the State or that does not comply with all the terms of IDEA. According to the Court of Appeals, neither the text of the Act nor its legislative history imposes a "requirement that the private school be approved by the state in parent-placement reimbursement cases." Id., at 162. To the contrary, the Court of Appeals concluded, IDEA's state-approval requirement applies only when a child is placed in a private school by public school officials. Accordingly, "when a public school system had defaulted on its obligations under the Act, a private school placement is 'proper under the Act' if the education provided by the private school is 'reasonably calculated to enable the child to receive educational benefits.'" *Id.*, at 163, quoting *Board of Ed. of Hendrick Hudson Central School Dist. v. Rowley*, 458 U.S. 176, 207 (1982).

The court below recognized that its holding conflicted with *Tucker v. Bay Shore Union Free School Dist.*, 873 F.2d 563, 568 (1989), in which the Court of Appeals for the Second Circuit held that parental placement in a private school cannot be proper under the Act unless the private school in question meets the standards of the state education agency. We granted certiorari, 507 U.S. __ (1993), to resolve this conflict among the Courts of Appeals.

II

In *School Comm. of Burlington v. Department of Ed. of Mass.*, 471 U.S. 359, 369 (1985), we held that IDEA's grant of equitable authority empowers a court "to order school authorities to reimburse parents for their expenditures on private special education for a child if the court ultimately determines that such placement, rather than a proposed IEP, is proper under the Act." Congress intended that IDEA's promise of a "free appropriate public education" for disabled children would normally be met by an IEP's provision for education in the regular public schools or in private schools chosen jointly by school officials and parents. In cases where cooperation fails, however, "parents who disagree with the proposed IEP are faced with a choice: go along with the IEP to the detriment of their child if it turns out to be inappropriate or pay for what they consider to be the appropriate placement." *Id.* at 370. For parents willing and able to make the latter choice, "it would be an empty victory to have a court tell them several years later that they were right but that these expenditures could not in a proper case be reimbursed by the school officials." *Ibid.* Because such a result would be contrary to IDEA's guarantee of a "free appropriate public education," we held that "Congress meant to include retroactive reimbursement to parents as an available remedy in a proper case." *Ibid.*

As this case comes to us, two issues are settled: 1) the school district's proposed IEP was inappropriate under IDEA, and 2) although Trident did not meet the § 1401(a)(18) requirements, it provided an education otherwise proper under IDEA. This case presents the narrow question whether Shannon's parents are barred from reimbursement because the private school in which Shannon enrolled did not meet the § 1401(a)(18) definition of a "free appropriate public education."[1] We hold that they are not, because § 1401(a)(18)'s requirements cannot be read as applying to parental placements.

Section 1401(a)(18)(A) requires that the education be "provided at public expense, under public supervision and direction." Similarly, § 1401(a)(18)(D) requires schools to

provide an IEP, which must be designated by "a representative of the local educational agency," 20 U.S.C. § 1401(a)(20) (1988 ed., Supp. IV), and must be "establish[ed]," and "revise[d]" by the agency, § 1414(a)(5). These requirements do not make sense in the context of a parental placement. In this case, as in all Burlington reimbursement cases, the parents' rejection of the school district's proposed IEP is the very reason for the parents' decision to put their child in a private school. In such cases, where the private placement has necessarily been made over the school district's objection, the private school education will not be under "public supervision and direction." Accordingly, to read the § 1401(a)(18) requirements as applying to parental placements would effectively eliminate the right of unilateral withdrawal recognized in Burlington. Moreover, IDEA was intended to ensure that children with disabilities receive an education that is both appropriate and free. *Burlington, supra*, at 373. To read the provisions of § 1401(a)(18) to bar reimbursement in the circumstances of this case would defeat this statutory purpose.

Nor do we believe that reimbursement is necessarily barred by a private school's failure to meet state education standards. Trident's deficiencies, according to the school district, were that it employed at least two faculty members who were not state-certified and that it did not develop IEPs. As we have noted, however, the § 1401(a)(18) requirements—including the requirement that the school meet the standards of the state educational agency, § 1401(a)(18)(B) —do not apply to private parental placements. Indeed, the school district's emphasis on state standards is somewhat ironic. As the Court of Appeals noted, "it hardly seems consistent with the Act's goals to forbid parents from educating their child at a school that provides an appropriate education simply because that school lacks the stamp of approval of the same public school system that failed to meet the child's needs in the first place." 950 F.2d. at 164. Accordingly, we disagree with the Second Circuit's theory that "a parent may not obtain reimbursement for a unilateral placement if that placement was in a school that was not on [the State's] approved list of private" schools. *Tucker*, 873 F.2d, at 568 (internal quotation marks omitted). Parents' failure to select a program known to be approved by the State in favor of an unapproved option is not itself a bar to reimbursement.

Furthermore, although the absence of an approved list of private schools is not essential to our holding, we note that parents in the position of Shannon's have no way of knowing at the time they select a private school whether the school meets state standards. South Carolina keeps no publicly available list of approved private schools, but instead approves private school placements on a case-by-case basis. In fact, although public school officials had previously placed three children with disabilities at Trident, see

App. to Pet. for Cert. 28a, Trident had not received blanket approval from the State. South Carolina's case-by-case approval system meant that Shannon's parents needed the cooperation of state officials before they could know whether Trident was state-approved. As we recognized in *Burlington*, such cooperation is unlikely in cases where the school officials disagree with the need for the private placement. 471 U.S., at 372.

III

The school district also claims that allowing reimbursement for parents such as Shannon's puts an unreasonable burden on financially strapped local educational authorities. The school district argues that requiring parents to choose a state-approved private school if they want reimbursement is the only meaningful way to allow States to control costs; otherwise States will have to reimburse dissatisfied parents for any private school that provides an education that is proper under the Act, no matter how expensive it may be. There is no doubt that Congress has imposed a significant financial burden on States and school districts that participate in IDEA. Yet public educational authorities who want to avoid reimbursing parents for the private education of a disabled child can do one of two things: give the child a free appropriate public education in a public setting, or place the child in an appropriate private setting of the State's choice. This is IDEA's mandate, and school officials who conform to it need not worry about reimbursement claims.

Moreover, parents who, like Shannon's, "unilaterally change their child's placement during the pendency of review proceedings, without the consent of the state or local school officials, do so at their own financial risk." *Burlington*, *supra*, at 373-374. They are entitled to reimbursement only if a federal court concludes both that the public placement violated IDEA, and that the private school placement was proper under the Act.

Finally, we note that once a court holds that the public placement violated IDEA, it is authorized to "grant such relief as the court determines is appropriate." 20 U.S.C. § 1415(e)(2). Under this provision, "equitable considerations are relevant in fashioning relief," *Burlington*, 471 U.S., at 374, and the court enjoys "broad discretion" in so doing, *id.*, at 369. Courts fashioning discretionary equitable relief under IDEA must consider all relevant factors, including the appropriate and reasonable level of reimbursement that should be required. Total reimbursement will not be appropriate if the court determines that the cost of the private education was unreasonable.

Accordingly, we **affirm** the judgment of the Court of Appeals.

So Ordered.

Endnotes

1 Section 1401(a)(18) defines "free appropriate public education" as, special education and related services that

(A) have been provided at public expense, under public supervision and direction, and without charge,

(B) meet the standards of the State educational agency,

(C) include an appropriate preschool, elementary, or secondary school education in the State involved, and

(D) are provided in conformity with the individualized education program ...

The Supreme Court of the United States
526 U.S. 66 (1999)

CEDAR RAPIDS COMMUNITY SCHOOL DISTRICT,

Petitioners

v.

GARRET F., a minor, by his mother and next friend, CHARLENE F.,

Respondents

No. 96-1793.

Certiorari to the United States Court of Appeals for the Eighth Circuit

Decided March 3, 1999

Stevens, J., delivered the opinion of the Court, in which Rehnquist, C. J., and O'Connor, Scalia, Souter, Ginsburg, and Breyer, JJ., joined. Thomas, J., filed a dissenting opinion, in which Kennedy, J., joined.

The Individuals with Disabilities Education Act (IDEA), 84 Stat. 175, as amended, was enacted, in part, "to assure that all children with disabilities have available to them . . . a free appropriate public education which emphasizes special education and related services designed to meet their unique needs." 20 U. S. C. §1400(c). Consistent with this purpose, the IDEA authorizes federal financial assistance to States that agree to provide disabled children with special education and "related services." See §§1401(a)(18), 1412(1). The question presented in this case is whether the definition of "related services" in §1401(a)(17)[1] requires a public school district in a participating State to provide a ventilator-dependent student with certain nursing services during school hours.

I

Respondent Garret F. is a friendly, creative, and intelligent young man. When Garret was four years old, his spinal column was severed in a motorcycle accident. Though paralyzed from the neck down, his mental capacities were unaffected. He is able to speak, to control his motorized wheelchair through use of a puff and suck straw, and to operate a computer with a device that responds to head movements. Garret is currently a student in the Cedar Rapids Community School District (District), he attends regular classes in a typical school program, and his academic performance has been a success. Garret is, however, ventilator dependent,[2] and therefore requires a responsible individual nearby to attend to certain physical needs while he is in

school.[3]

During Garret's early years at school his family provided for his physical care during the school day. When he was in kindergarten, his 18-year-old aunt attended him; in the next four years, his family used settlement proceeds they received after the accident, their insurance, and other resources to employ a licensed practical nurse. In 1993, Garret's mother requested the District to accept financial responsibility for the health care services that Garret requires during the school day. The District denied the request, believing that it was not legally obligated to provide continuous one-on-one nursing services.

Relying on both the IDEA and Iowa law, Garret's mother requested a hearing before the Iowa Department of Education. An Administrative Law Judge (ALJ) received extensive evidence concerning Garret's special needs, the District's treatment of other disabled students, and the assistance provided to other ventilator-dependent children in other parts of the country. In his 47-page report, the ALJ found that the District has about 17,500 students, of whom approximately 2,200 need some form of special education or special services. Although Garret is the only ventilator-dependent student in the District, most of the health care services that he needs are already provided for some other students.[4] "The primary difference between Garret's situation and that of other students is his dependency on his ventilator for life support." App. to Pet. for Cert. 28a. The ALJ noted that the parties disagreed over the training or licensure required for the care and supervision of such students, and that those providing such care in other parts of the country ranged from non-licensed personnel to registered nurses. However, the District did not contend that only a licensed physician could provide the services in question.

The ALJ explained that federal law requires that children with a variety of health impairments be provided with "special education and related services" when their disabilities adversely affect their academic performance, and that such children should be educated to the maximum extent appropriate with children who are not disabled. In addition, the ALJ explained that applicable federal regulations distinguish between "school health services," which are provided by a "qualified school nurse or other qualified person," and "medical services," which are provided by a licensed physician. See 34 CFR §§300.16(a), (b)(4), (b)(11) (1998). The District must provide the former, but need not provide the latter (except, of course, those "medical services" that are for diagnostic or evaluation purposes, §1401(a)(17)). According to the ALJ, the distinction in the regulations does not just depend on "the title of the person providing the service"; instead, the "medical services" exclusion is limited to services that are "in the special training, knowledge, and judgment of a physician to carry out." App. to Pet. for Cert. 51a. The ALJ thus concluded that the IDEA required the District to bear financial responsibility for all of the services in dispute, including continuous nursing services.[5]

The District challenged the ALJ's decision in Federal District Court, but that Court approved the ALJ's IDEA ruling and granted summary judgment against the District. *Id.*, at 9a, 15a. The Court of Appeals affirmed. 106 F. 3d 822 (CA8 1997). It noted that, as a recipient of federal funds under the IDEA, Iowa has a statutory duty to provide all disabled children a "free appropriate public education," which includes "related services." See *id.*, at 824. The Court of Appeals read our opinion in *Irving Independent School Dist. v. Tatro*, 468 U. S. 883 (1984), to provide a two-step analysis of the "related services" definition in §1401(a)(17) -- asking first, whether the requested services are included within the phrase "supportive services"; and second, whether the services are excluded as "medical services." 106 F. 3d, at 824-825. The Court of Appeals succinctly answered both questions in Garret's favor. The Court found the first step plainly satisfied, since Garret cannot attend school unless the requested services are available during the school day. *Id.*, at 825. As to the second step, the Court reasoned that *Tatro* "established a bright-line test: the services of a physician (other than for diagnostic and evaluation purposes) are subject to the medical services exclusion, but services that can be provided in the school setting by a nurse or qualified layperson are not." *Ibid.*

In its petition for certiorari, the District challenged only the second step of the Court of Appeals' analysis. The District pointed out that some federal courts have not asked whether the requested health services must be delivered by a physician, but instead have applied a multi-factor test that considers, generally speaking, the nature and extent of the services at issue. See, e.g., *Neely v. Rutherford County School*, 68 F. 3d 965, 972-973 (CA6 1995), cert. denied, 517 U. S. 1134 (1996); *Detsel v. Board of Ed. of Auburn Enlarged City School Dist.*, 820 F. 2d 587, 588 (CA2) (per curiam), cert. denied, 484 U. S. 981 (1987). We granted the District's petition to resolve this conflict. 523 U. S. __ (1998).

II

The District contends that §1401(a)(17) does not require it to provide Garret with "continuous one-on-one nursing services" during the school day, even though Garret cannot remain in school without such care. Brief for Petitioner 10. However, the IDEA's definition of "related services," our decision in *Irving Independent School Dist. v. Tatro*, 468 U. S. 883 (1984), and the overall statutory scheme all support the decision of the Court of Appeals.

The text of the "related services" definition, see n. 1, *supra*, broadly encompasses those supportive services that "may be required to assist a child with a disability to benefit from special education." As we have already noted, the District does not challenge the Court of Appeals' conclusion that the in-school services at issue are within the covered category of "supportive services." As a general matter, services that enable a disabled child to remain in school during the day provide the student with "the meaningful access to education that Congress envisioned." *Tatro*, 468 U. S., at 891 ("'Congress sought primarily to make public education available to handicapped children' and 'to make such access meaningful'" (quoting *Board of Ed. of Hendrick Hudson Central School Dist., Westchester Cty. v. Rowley*, 458 U. S. 176, 192 (1982)).

This general definition of "related services" is illuminated by a parenthetical phrase listing examples of particular services that are included within the statute's coverage. §1401(a)(17). "Medical services" are enumerated in this list, but such services are limited to those that are "for diagnostic and evaluation purposes." *Ibid.* The statute does not contain a more specific definition of the "medical services" that are excepted from the coverage of §1401(a)(17).

The scope of the "medical services" exclusion is not a matter of first impression in this Court. In *Tatro* we concluded that the Secretary of Education had reasonably determined that the term "medical services" referred only to services that must be performed by a physician, and not to school health services. 468 U. S., at 892-894. Accordingly, we held that a specific form of health care (clean intermittent catheterization) that is often, though not always, performed by a nurse is not an excluded medical service. We referenced the likely cost of the services and the competence of school staff as justifications for drawing a line between physician and other services, *ibid.*, but our endorsement of that line was unmistakable.[6] It is thus settled that the phrase "medical services" in §1401(a)(17) does not embrace all forms of care that might loosely be described as "medical" in other contexts, such as a claim for an income tax deduction. See 26 U. S. C. §213(d)(1) (1994 ed. and Supp. II) (defining "medical care").

The District does not ask us to define the term so broadly. Indeed, the District does not argue that any of the items of care that Garret needs, considered individually, could be excluded from the scope of §1401(a)(17).[7] It could not make such an argument, considering that one of the services Garret needs (catheterization) was at issue in *Tatro*, and the others may be provided competently by a school nurse or other trained personnel. See App. to Pet. for Cert. 15a, 52a. As the ALJ concluded, most of the requested services are already provided by the District to other students, and the in-school care necessitated by Garret's ventilator dependency does not demand the training, knowledge, and judgment of a licensed physician. *Id.*, at 51a-52a. While more extensive, the in-school services Garret needs are no more "medical" than was the care sought in *Tatro*.

Instead, the District points to the combined and continuous character of the required care, and proposes a test under which the outcome in any particular case would "depend upon a series of factors, such as [1] whether the care is continuous or intermittent, [2] whether existing school health personnel can provide the service, [3] the cost of the service, and [4] the potential consequences if the service is not properly performed." Brief for Petitioner 11; see also *id.*, at 34-35.

The District's multi-factor test is not supported by any recognized source of legal authority. The proposed factors can be found in neither the text of the statute nor the regulations that we upheld in *Tatro*. Moreover, the District offers no explanation why these characteristics make one service any more "medical" than another. The continuous character of certain services associated with Garret's ventilator dependency has no apparent relationship to "medical" services, much less a relationship of equivalence. Continuous services may be more costly and may require additional school personnel, but they are not thereby more "medical." Whatever its imperfections, a rule that limits the medical services exemption to physician services is unquestionably a reasonable and generally workable interpretation of the statute. Absent an elaboration of the statutory terms plainly more convincing than that which we reviewed in *Tatro*, there is no good reason to depart from settled law.[8]

Finally, the District raises broader concerns about the financial burden that it must bear to provide the services that Garret needs to stay in school. The problem for the District in providing these services is not that its staff cannot be trained to deliver them; the problem, the District contends, is that the existing school health staff cannot meet all of their responsibilities and provide for Garret at the same time.[9]

Through its multi-factor test, the District seeks to establish a kind of undue-burden exemption primarily based on the cost of the requested services. The first two factors can be seen as examples of cost-based distinctions: intermittent care is often less expensive than continuous care, and the use of existing personnel is cheaper than hiring additional employees. The third factor-the cost of the service-would then encompass the first two. The relevance of the fourth factor is likewise related to cost because extra care may be necessary if potential consequences are especially serious.

The District may have legitimate financial concerns, but our role in this dispute is to interpret existing law. Defining "related services" in a manner that accommodates the cost concerns Congress may have had, cf. *Tatro*, 468 U.

S., at 892, is altogether different from using cost itself as the definition. Given that §1401(a)(17) does not employ cost in its definition of "related services" or excluded "medical services," accepting the District's cost-based standard as the sole test for determining the scope of the provision would require us to engage in judicial lawmaking without any guidance from Congress. It would also create some tension with the purposes of the IDEA. The statute may not require public schools to maximize the potential of disabled students commensurate with the opportunities provided to other children, see *Rowley*, 458 U. S., at 200; and the potential financial burdens imposed on participating States may be relevant to arriving at a sensible construction of the IDEA, see *Tatro*, 468 U. S., at 892. But Congress intended "to open the door of public education" to all qualified children and "require[d] participating States to educate handicapped children with non-handicapped children whenever possible." *Rowley*, 458 U. S., at 192, 202; see *id.*, at 179-181; see also *Honig v. Doe*, 484 U. S. 305, 310-311, 324 (1988); §§1412(1), (2)(c), (5)(B).[10]

This case is about whether meaningful access to the public schools will be assured, not the level of education that a school must finance once access is attained. It is undisputed that the services at issue must be provided if Garret is to remain in school.

Under the statute, our precedent, and the purposes of the IDEA, the District must fund such "related services" in order to help guarantee that students like Garret are integrated into the public schools.

The judgment of the Court of Appeals is accordingly **Affirmed.**

Endnotes

1 "The term 'related services' means transportation, and such developmental, corrective, and other supportive services (including speech pathology and audiology, psychological services, physical and occupational therapy, recreation, including therapeutic recreation, social work services, counseling services, including rehabilitation counseling, and medical services, except that such medical services shall be for diagnostic and evaluation purposes only) as may be required to assist a child with a disability to benefit from special education, and includes the early identification and assessment of disabling conditions in children." 20 U. S. C. §1401(a)(17).

Originally, the statute was enacted without a definition of "related services." See Education of the Handicapped Act, 84 Stat. 175. In 1975, Congress added the definition at issue in this case. Education for All Handicapped Children Act of 1975, §4(a)(4), 89 Stat. 775. Aside from nonsubstantive changes and added examples of included services, see, e.g., Individuals with Disabilities Education Act Amendments of 1997, §101, 111 Stat. 45; Individuals with Disabilities Education Act

Amendments of 1991, §25(a)(1)(B), 105 Stat. 605; Education of the Handicapped Act Amendments of 1990, §101(c), 104 Stat. 1103, the relevant language in §1401(a)(17) has not been amended since 1975. All references to the IDEA herein are to the 1994 version as codified in Title 20 of the United States Code—the version of the statute in effect when this dispute arose.

2 "Included are such services as care for students who need urinary catheterization, food and drink, oxygen supplement positioning, and suctioning." *Id.*, at 28a; see also *id.*, at 53a.

3 In addition, the ALJ's opinion contains a thorough discussion of "other tests and criteria" pressed by the District, *id.*, at 52a, including the burden on the District and the cost of providing assistance to Garret. Although the ALJ found no legal authority for establishing a cost-based test for determining what related services are required by the statute, he went on to reject the District's arguments on the merits. See *id.*, at 42a-53a. We do not reach the issue here, but the ALJ also found that Garret's in-school needs must be met by the District under an Iowa statute as well as the IDEA. *Id.*, at 54a-55a.

4 "Included are such services as care for students who need urinary catheterization, food and drink, oxygen supplement positioning, and suctioning." *Id.*, at 28a; see also *id.*, at 53a.

5 In addition, the ALJ's opinion contains a thorough discussion of "other tests and criteria" pressed by the District, id., at 52a, including the burden on the District and the cost of providing assistance to Garret. Although the ALJ found no legal authority for establishing a cost-based test for determining what related services are required by the statute, he went on to reject the District's arguments on the merits. See *id.*, at 42a-53a. We do not reach the issue here, but the ALJ also found that Garret's in-school needs must be met by the District under an Iowa statute as well as the IDEA. *Id.*, at 54a-55a.

6 "The regulations define 'related services' for handicapped children to include 'school health services,' 34 CFR §300.13(a) (1983), which are defined in turn as 'services provided by a qualified school nurse or other qualified person,' §300.13(b)(10). 'Medical services' are defined as 'services provided by a licensed physician.' §300.13(b)(4). Thus, the Secretary has [reasonably] determined that the services of a school nurse otherwise qualifying as a 'related service' are not subject to exclusion as a 'medical service,' but that the services of a physician are excludable as such.

" . . . By limiting the 'medical services' exclusion to the services of a physician or hospital, both far more expensive, the Secretary has given a permissible construction to the provision." 468 U. S., at 892-893 (emphasis added) (footnote omitted); see also *id.*, at 894 ("[T]he regulations state that school nursing services must be provided only if they can be performed by a nurse or other qualified person, not if they must be performed by a physician").

Based on certain policy letters issued by the Department of Education, it seems that the Secretary's post-Tatro view of the statute has not been entirely clear. E.g., App. to Pet. for Cert. 64a. We may assume that the Secretary has authority under the

IDEA to adopt regulations that define the "medical services" exclusion by more explicitly taking into account the nature and extent of the requested services; and the Secretary surely has the authority to enumerate the services that are, and are not, fairly included within the scope of §1407(a)(17). But the Secretary has done neither; and, in this Court, she advocates affirming the judgment of the Court of Appeals. Brief for United States as Amicus Curiae; see also *Auer v. Robbins*, 519 U. S. 452, 462 (1997) (an agency's views as amicus curiae may be entitled to deference). We obviously have no authority to rewrite the regulations, and we see no sufficient reason to revise *Tatro*, either.

7 See Tr. of Oral Arg. 4-5, 12.

8 At oral argument, the District suggested that we first consider the nature of the requested service (either "medical" or not); then, if the service is "medical," apply the multi-factor test to determine whether the service is an excluded physician service or an included school nursing service under the Secretary of Education's regulations. See Tr. of Oral Arg. 7, 13-14. Not only does this approach provide no additional guidance for identifying "medical" services, it is also disconnected from both the statutory text and the regulations we upheld in *Irving Independent School Dist. v. Tatro*, 468 U. S. 883 (1984). "Medical" services are generally excluded from the statute, and the regulations elaborate on that statutory term. No authority cited by the District requires an additional inquiry if the requested service is both "related" and non-"medical." Even if §1401(a)(17) demanded an additional step, the factors proposed by the District are hardly more useful in identifying "nursing" services than they are in identifying "medical" services; and the District cannot limit educational access simply by pointing to the limitations of existing staff. As we noted in *Tatro*, the IDEA requires schools to hire specially trained personnel to meet disabled student needs. *Id.*, at 893.

9 See Tr. of Oral Arg. 4-5, 13; Brief for Petitioner 6-7, 9. The District, however, will not necessarily need to hire an additional employee to meet Garret's needs. The District already employs a one-on-one teacher associate (TA) who assists Garret during the school day. See App. to Pet. for Cert. 26a-27a. At one time, Garret's TA was a licensed practical nurse (LPN). In light of the state Board of Nursing's recent ruling that the District's registered nurses may decide to delegate Garret's care to an LPN, see Brief for United States as Amicus Curiae 9-10 (filed Apr. 22, 1998), the dissent's future-cost estimate is speculative. See App. to Pet. for Cert. 28a, 58a-60a (if the District could assign Garret's care to a TA who is also an LPN, there would be "a minimum of additional expense").

10 The dissent's approach, which seems to be even broader than the District's, is unconvincing. The dissent's rejection of our unanimous decision in *Tatro* comes 15 years too late, see *Patterson v. McLean Credit Union*, 491 U. S. 164, 172-173 (1989) (stare decisis has "special force" in statutory interpretation), and it offers nothing constructive in its place. Aside from rejecting a "provider-specific approach," the dissent cites unrelated statutes and offers a circular definition of "medical

services." Post, at 3-4 ("'services' that are 'medical' in 'nature'").
Moreover, the dissent's approach apparently would exclude most ordinary school nursing services of the kind routinely provided to nondisabled children; that anomalous result is not easily attributable to congressional intent. See *Tatro*, 468 U. S., at 893.

In a later discussion the dissent does offer a specific proposal: that we now interpret (or rewrite) the Secretary's regulations so that school districts need only provide disabled children with "health-related services that school nurses can perform as part of their normal duties." Post, at 7. The District does not dispute that its nurses "can perform" the requested services, so the dissent's objection is that District nurses would not be performing their "normal duties" if they met Garret's needs. That is, the District would need an "additional employee." Post, at 8. This proposal is functionally similar to a proposed regulation—ultimately withdrawn—that would have replaced the "school health services" provision. See 47 Fed. Reg. 33838, 33854 (1982) (the statute and regulations may not be read to affect legal obligations to make available to handicapped children services, including school health services, made available to nonhandicapped children). The dissent's suggestion is unacceptable for several reasons. Most important, such revisions of the regulations are better left to the Secretary, and an additional staffing need is generally not a sufficient objection to the requirements of §1401(a)(17). See n. 8, *supra*.

Justice Thomas, with whom Justice Kennedy joins, **dissenting**.

The majority, relying heavily on our decision in *Irving Independent School Dist. v. Tatro*, 468 U. S. 883 (1984), concludes that the Individuals with Disabilities Education Act (IDEA), 20 U. S. C. §1400 *et seq.*, requires a public school district to fund continuous, one-on-one nursing care for disabled children. Because *Tatro* cannot be squared with the text of IDEA, the Court should not adhere to it in this case. Even assuming that *Tatro* was correct in the first instance, the majority's extension of it is unwarranted and ignores the constitutionally mandated rules of construction applicable to legislation enacted pursuant to Congress' spending power.

I

As the majority recounts, *ante*, at 1, IDEA authorizes the provision of federal financial assistance to States that agree to provide, *inter alia*, "special education and related services" for disabled children. §1401(a)(18). In *Tatro, supra*, we held that this provision of IDEA required a school district to provide clean intermittent catheterization to a disabled child several times a day. In so holding, we relied on Department of Education regulations, which we concluded had reasonably interpreted IDEA's definition of "related services"[a] to require school districts in participating States to provide "school nursing services" (of which we as-

sumed catheterization was a subcategory) but not "services of a physician." *Id.*, at 892-893. This holding is contrary to the plain text of IDEA and its reliance on the Department of Education's regulations was misplaced.

A

Before we consider whether deference to an agency regulation is appropriate, "we first ask whether Congress has 'directly spoken to the precise question at issue. If the intent of Congress is clear, that is the end of the matter; for the court, as well as the agency, must give effect to the unambiguously expressed intent of Congress.' "*National Credit Union Admin. v. First Nat. Bank & Trust Co.*, 522 U. S. 479, 499-500 (1998) (quoting *Chevron U. S. A. Inc. v. Natural Resources Defense Council, Inc.*, 467 U. S. 837, 842-843 (1984)).

Unfortunately, the Court in *Tatro* failed to consider this necessary antecedent question before turning to the Department of Education's regulations implementing IDEA's related services provision. The Court instead began "with the regulations of the Department of Education, which," it said, "are entitled to deference." *Tatro, supra*, at 891-892. The Court need not have looked beyond the text of IDEA, which expressly indicates that school districts are not required to provide medical services, except for diagnostic and evaluation purposes. 20 U. S. C. §1401(a)(17). The majority asserts that *Tatro* precludes reading the term "medical services" to include "all forms of care that might loosely be described as 'medical.' " *Ante*, at 8. The majority does not explain, however, why "services" that are "medical" in nature are not "medical services." Not only is the definition that the majority rejects consistent with other uses of the term in federal law,[2] it also avoids the anomalous result of holding that the services at issue in *Tatro* (as well as in this case), while not "medical services," would nonetheless qualify as medical care for federal income tax purposes. *Ante*, at 8.

The primary problem with *Tatro*, and the majority's reliance on it today, is that the Court focused on the provider of the services rather than the services themselves. We do not typically think that automotive services are limited to those provided by a mechanic, for example. Rather, anything done to repair or service a car, no matter who does the work, is thought to fall into that category. Similarly, the term "food service" is not generally thought to be limited to work performed by a chef. The term "medical" similarly does not support *Tatro*'s provider-specific approach, but encompasses services that are "of, relating to, or concerned with physicians or the practice of medicine." See *Webster's Third New International Dictionary* 1402 (1986) (emphasis added); see also *id.*, at 1551 (defining "nurse" as "a person skilled in caring for and waiting on the infirm, the injured, or the sick; specif: one esp. trained to carry out such duties under the supervision of a physician").

IDEA's structure and purpose reinforce this textual interpretation. Congress enacted IDEA to increase the educational opportunities available to disabled children, not to provide medical care for them. See 20 U. S. C. §1400(c) ("It is the purpose of this chapter to assure that all children with disabilities have . . . a free appropriate public education"); see also §1412 ("In order to qualify for assistance . . . a State shall demonstrate . . . [that it] has in effect a policy that assures all children with disabilities the right to a free appropriate public education"); *Board of Ed. of Hendrick Hudson Central School Dist., Westchester Cty. v. Rowley*, 458 U. S. 176, 179 (1982) ("The Act represents an ambitious federal effort to promote the education of handicapped children"). As such, where Congress decided to require a supportive service—including speech pathology, occupational therapy, and audiology—that appears "medical" in nature, it took care to do so explicitly. See §1401(a)(17). Congress specified these services precisely because it recognized that they would otherwise fall under the broad "medical services" exclusion. Indeed, when it crafted the definition of related services, Congress could have, but chose not to, include "nursing services" in this list.

B

Tatro was wrongly decided even if the phrase "medical services" was subject to multiple constructions, and therefore, deference to any reasonable Department of Education regulation was appropriate. The Department of Education has never promulgated regulations defining the scope of IDEA's "medical services" exclusion. One year before *Tatro* was decided, the Secretary of Education issued proposed regulations that defined excluded medical services as "services relating to the practice of medicine." 47 Fed. Reg. 33838 (1982). These regulations, which represent the Department's only attempt to define the disputed term, were never adopted. Instead, "[t]he regulations actually define only those 'medical services' that are owed to handicapped children," *Tatro*, 468 U. S., at 892, n. 10) (emphasis in original), not those that are not. Now, as when Tatro was decided, the regulations require districts to provide services performed " 'by a licensed physician to determine a child's medically related handicapping condition which results in the child's need for special education and related services.' " *Ibid.* (quoting 34 CFR §300.13(b)(4) (1983), recodified and amended as 34 CFR §300.16(b)(4) (1998).

Extrapolating from this regulation, the *Tatro* Court presumed that this meant "that 'medical services' not owed under the statute are those 'services by a licensed physician' that serve other purposes." *Tatro, supra*, at 892, n. 10 (emphasis deleted). The Court, therefore, did not defer to the regulation itself, but rather relied on an inference drawn from it to speculate about how a regulation might read if the Department of Education promulgated one. Deference in those circumstances is impermissible. We cannot defer to a regulation that does not exist. (c)

II

Assuming that *Tatro* was correctly decided in the first instance, it does not control the outcome of this case. Because IDEA was enacted pursuant to Congress' spending power, *Rowley, supra*, at 190, n. 11, our analysis of the statute in this case is governed by special rules of construction. We have repeatedly emphasized that, when Congress places conditions on the receipt of federal funds, "it must do so unambiguously." *Pennhurst State School and Hospital v. Halderman*, 451 U. S. 1, 17 (1981). See also *Rowley, supra*, at 190, n. 11; *South Dakota v. Dole*, 483 U. S. 203, 207 (1987); *New York v. United States*, 505 U. S. 144, 158 (1992).

This is because a law that "condition[s] an offer of federal funding on a promise by the recipient ... amounts essentially to a contract between the Government and the recipient of funds." *Gebser v. Lago Vista Independent School Dist.*, 524 U. S. 274, 276 (1998). As such, "[t]he legitimacy of Congress' power to legislate under the spending power . . . rests on whether the State voluntarily and knowingly accepts the terms of the 'contract.' There can, of course, be no knowing acceptance if a State is unaware of the conditions or is unable to ascertain what is expected of it." *Pennhurst, supra*, at 17 (citations omitted). It follows that we must interpret Spending Clause legislation narrowly, in order to avoid saddling the States with obligations that they did not anticipate.

The majority's approach in this case turns this Spending Clause presumption on its head. We have held that, in enacting IDEA, Congress wished to require "States to educate handicapped children with nonhandicapped children whenever possible," *Rowley*, 458 U. S., at 202. Congress, however, also took steps to limit the fiscal burdens that States must bear in attempting to achieve this laudable goal. These steps include requiring States to provide an education that is only "appropriate" rather that requiring them to maximize the potential of disabled students, see 20 U. S. C. §1400(c) *Rowley, supra*, at 200, recognizing that integration into the public school environment is not always possible, see §1412(5), and clarifying that, with a few exceptions, public schools need not provide "medical services" for disabled students, §§1401(a)(17) and (18).

For this reason, we have previously recognized that Congress did not intend to "impos[e] upon the States a burden of unspecified proportions and weight" in enacting IDEA. *Rowley, supra*, at 176, n. 11. These federalism concerns require us to interpret IDEA's related services provision, consistent with *Tatro*, as follows: Department of Education regulations require districts to provide disabled children with health-related services that school nurses can perform as part of their normal duties. This reading of *Tatro*, although less broad than the majority's, is equally plausible and certainly more consistent with our obligation to interpret Spending Clause legislation narrowly. Before concluding that the district was required to provide clean intermittent catheterization for Amber Tatro, we observed that school nurses in the district were authorized to perform services that were "difficult to distinguish from the provision of [clean intermittent catheterization] to the handicapped." *Tatro*, 468 U. S., at 893. We concluded that "[i]t would be strange indeed if Congress, in attempting to extend special services to handicapped children, were unwilling to guarantee them services of a kind that are routinely provided to the nonhandicapped." *Id.*, at 893-894.

Unlike clean intermittent catheterization, however, a school nurse cannot provide the services that respondent requires, see *ante*, at 3, n. 3, and continue to perform her normal duties. To the contrary, because respondent requires continuous, one-on-one care throughout the entire school day, all agree that the district must hire an additional employee to attend solely to respondent. This will cost a minimum of $18,000 per year. Although the majority recognizes this fact, it nonetheless concludes that the "more extensive" nature of the services that respondent needs is irrelevant to the question whether those services fall under the medical services exclusion. *Ante*, at 9. This approach disregards the constitutionally mandated principles of construction applicable to Spending Clause legislation and blindsides unwary States with fiscal obligations that they could not have anticipated.

For the foregoing reasons, I respectfully dissent.

Footnotes - Dissent

[a] The Act currently defines "related services" as "transportation and such developmental, corrective, and other supportive services (including speech pathology and audiology, psychological services, physical and occupational therapy, recreation, including therapeutic recreation, social work services, counseling services, including rehabilitation counseling, and medical services, except that such medical services shall be for diagnostic and evaluation purposes only) as may be required to assist a child with a disability to benefit from special education...." 20 U. S. C. §1401(a)(17) (emphasis added).

[b] See, e.g., 38 U. S. C. §1701(6) ("The term 'medical services' includes, in addition to medical examination, treatment and rehabilitative services ... surgical services, dental services ... optometric and podiatric services, ... preventive health services, ... [and] such consultation, professional counseling, training, and mental health services as are necessary in connection with the treatment"); §101(28) ("The term 'nursing home care' means the accommodation of convalescents ... who require nursing care and related medical services"); 26 U. S. C. §213(d)(1) ("The term 'medical care' means amounts paid-- ... for the diagnosis, cure, mitigation, treatment, or prevention of disease").

[c] Nor do I think that it is appropriate to defer to the Department of Education's litigating position in this case. The agency has had ample opportunity to address this problem but has failed to do so in a formal regulation. Instead, it has maintained conflicting positions about whether the services at issue in this case are required by IDEA. See *ante*, at 7-8, n. 6. Under these circumstances, we should not assume that the litigating position reflects the "agency's fair and considered judgment." *Auer v. Robbins*, 519 U. S. 452, 462 (1997).

The Supreme Court of the United States

546 U. S. __ (2005)

BRIAN SCHAFFER, A MINOR, BY HIS PARENTS AND NEXT FRIENDS, JOCELYN AND MARTIN SCHAFFER, ET AL., PETITIONERS

v.

JERRY WEAST, SUPERINTENDENT, MONTGOMERY COUNTY PUBLIC SCHOOLS, ET AL.

No. 04-698

On Writ Of Certiorari to The United States Court Of Appeals for The Fourth Circuit Court

Decided: November 14, 2005

O'Connor, J., delivered the opinion of the Court, in which Stevens, Scalia, Kennedy, Souter, and Thomas, JJ., joined. Stevens, J., filed a concurring opinion. Ginsburg, J., and Breyer, J., filed dissenting opinions. Roberts, C. J., took no part in the consideration or decision of the case.

The Individuals with Disabilities Education Act (IDEA or Act), 84 Stat. 175, as amended, 20 U. S. C. A. §1400 *et seq.* (main ed. and Supp. 2005), is a Spending Clause statute that seeks to ensure that "all children with disabilities have available to them a free appropriate public education," §1400(d)(1)(A). Under IDEA, school districts must create an "individualized education program" (IEP) for each disabled child. §1414(d). If parents believe their child's IEP is inappropriate, they may request an "impartial due process hearing." §1415(f). The Act is silent, however, as to which party bears the burden of persuasion at such a hearing. We hold that the burden lies, as it typically does, on the party seeking relief.

I.

A.

Congress first passed IDEA as part of the Education of the Handicapped Act in 1970, 84 Stat. 175, and amended it substantially in the Education for All Handicapped Children Act of 1975, 89 Stat. 773. At the time the majority of disabled children in America were "either totally excluded from schools or sitting idly in regular classrooms awaiting the time when they were old enough to 'drop out,' " H. R. Rep. No. 94-332, p. 2 (1975). IDEA was intended to reverse this history of neglect. As of 2003, the Act governed the provision of special education services to nearly 7 million children across the country. See Dept. of Education, Office of Special Education Programs, Data Analysis System, www.ideadata.org/tables27th/ar_ aa9.htm (as visited Nov. 9, 2005, and available in Clerk of Court's case file).

IDEA is "frequently described as a model of 'cooperative federalism.' " *Little Rock School Dist. v. Mauney*, 183 F. 3d 816, 830 (CA8 1999). It "leaves to the States the primary responsibility for developing and executing educational programs for handicapped children, [but] imposes significant requirements to be followed in the discharge of that responsibility." *Board of Ed. of Hendrick Hudson Central School Dist., Westchester Cty. v. Rowley*, 458 U. S. 176, 183 (1982). For example, the Act mandates cooperation and reporting between state and federal educational authorities. Participating States must certify to the Secretary of Education that they have "policies and procedures" that will effectively meet the Act's conditions. 20 U. S. C. §1412(a). (Unless otherwise noted, all citations to the Act are to the pre-2004 version of the statute because this is the version that was in effect during the proceedings below. We note, however, that nothing in the recent 2004 amendments, 118 Stat. 2674, appears to materially affect the rule announced here.) State educational agencies, in turn, must ensure that local schools and teachers are meeting the State's educational standards. 20 U. S. C. §§1412(a)(11), 1412(a)(15)(A). Local educational agencies (school boards or other administrative bodies) can receive IDEA funds only if they certify to a state educational agency that they are acting in accordance with the State's policies and procedures. §1413(a)(1).

The core of the statute, however, is the cooperative process that it establishes between parents and schools. *Rowley, supra*, at 205-206 ("Congress placed every bit as much emphasis upon compliance with procedures giving parents and guardians a large measure of participation at every stage of the administrative process . . . as it did upon the measurement of the resulting IEP against a substantive standard"). The central vehicle for this collaboration is the IEP process. State educational authorities must identify and evaluate disabled children, §§1414(a)-(c), develop an IEP for each one, §1414(d)(2), and review every IEP at least once a year, §1414(d)(4). Each IEP must include an assessment of the child's current educational performance, must articulate measurable educational goals, and must specify the nature of the special services that the school will provide. §1414(d)(1)(A).

Parents and guardians play a significant role in the IEP process. They must be informed about and consent to evaluations of their child under the Act. §1414(c)(3). Parents are included as members of "IEP teams." §1414(d)(1)(B). They have the right to examine any records relating to their child, and to obtain an "independent educational evaluation of the[ir] child." §1415(b)(1). They must be given written prior notice of any changes in an IEP, §1415(b)(3), and be notified in writing of the procedural safeguards available to them under the Act, §1415(d)(1). If parents believe that an IEP is not appropriate, they may seek an administrative "impartial due process hearing." §1415(f). School districts may also seek such hearings, as Congress clarified in the 2004 amendments. See S. Rep. No. 108-185, p. 37 (2003). They may do so, for example, if they wish to change an existing IEP but the parents do not consent, or if parents refuse to allow their child to be evaluated. As a practical matter, it appears that most hearing requests come from parents rather than schools. Brief for Petitioners 7.

Although state authorities have limited discretion to determine who conducts the hearings, §1415(f)(1)), and responsibility generally for establishing fair hearing procedures, §1415(a), Congress has chosen to legislate the central components of due process hearings. It has imposed minimal pleading standards, requiring parties to file complaints setting forth "a description of the nature of the problem," §1415(b)(7)(B)(ii), and "a proposed resolution of the problem to the extent known and available . . . at the time," §1415(b)(7)(B)(iii). At the hearing, all parties may be accompanied by counsel, and may "present evidence and confront, cross-examine, and compel the attendance of witnesses." §§1415(h)(1)-(2) After the hearing, any aggrieved party may bring a civil action in state or federal court. §1415(i)(2) Prevailing parents may also recover attorney's fees. §1415(i)(3)(B) Congress has never explicitly stated, however, which party should bear the burden of proof at IDEA hearings.

B.

This case concerns the educational services that were due, under IDEA, to petitioner Brian Schaffer. Brian suffers from learning disabilities and speech-language impairments. From pre-kindergarten through seventh grade he attended a private school and struggled academically. In 1997, school officials informed Brian's mother that he needed a school that could better accommodate his needs. Brian's parents contacted respondent Montgomery County Public Schools System (MCPS) seeking a placement for him for the following school year.

MCPS evaluated Brian and convened an IEP team. The committee generated an initial IEP offering Brian a place in either of two MCPS middle schools. Brian's parents were not satisfied with the arrangement, believing that Brian needed smaller classes and more intensive services. The Schaffers thus enrolled Brian in another private school, and initiated a due process hearing challenging the IEP and seeking compensation for the cost of Brian's subsequent private education.

In Maryland, IEP hearings are conducted by administrative law judges (ALJs). See Md. Educ. Code Ann. §8-413(c)(Lexis 2004). After a 3-day hearing, the ALJ deemed the evidence close, held that the parents bore the burden of persuasion, and ruled in favor of the school district. The parents brought a civil action challenging the result. The United States District Court for the District of Maryland reversed and remanded, after concluding that the burden of persuasion is on the school district. *Brian S. v. Vance*, 86 F. Supp. 2d 538 (2000). Around the same time, MCPS offered Brian a placement in a high school with a special learning center. Brian's parents accepted, and Brian was educated in that program until he graduated from high school. The suit remained alive, however, because the parents sought compensation for the private school tuition and related expenses.

Respondents appealed to the United States Court of Appeals for the Fourth Circuit. While the appeal was pending, the ALJ reconsidered the case, deemed the evidence truly in "equipoise," and ruled in favor of the parents. The Fourth Circuit vacated and remanded the appeal so that it could consider the burden of proof issue along with the merits on a later appeal. The District Court reaffirmed its ruling that the school district has the burden of proof. 240 F. Supp. 2d 396 (Md. 2002). On appeal, a divided panel of the Fourth Circuit reversed. Judge Michael, writing for the majority, concluded that petitioners offered no persuasive reason to "depart from the normal rule of allocating the burden to the party seeking relief." 377 F. 3d 449, 453 (2004). We granted certiorari, 543 U. S. 1145 (2005), to resolve the following question: At an administrative hearing assessing the appropriateness of an IEP, which party bears the burden of persuasion?

II.

A.

The term "burden of proof" is one of the "slipperiest member[s] of the family of legal terms." 2 J. Strong, *McCormick on Evidence* §342, p. 433 (5th ed. 1999) (hereinafter McCormick). Part of the confusion surrounding the term arises from the fact that historically, the concept encompassed two distinct burdens: the "burden of persuasion," i.e., which party loses if the evidence is closely balanced, and the "burden of production," i.e., which party bears the obligation to come forward with the evidence at different points in the proceeding. *Director, Office of Workers' Compensation Programs v. Greenwich Collieries*, 512 U. S. 267, 272 (1994). We note at the outset that this case concerns only the burden of persuasion, as the parties agree, Brief for Respondents 14; Reply Brief for Petitioners 15, and when we speak of burden of proof in this opinion, it is this to which we refer.

When we are determining the burden of proof under a statutory cause of action, the touchstone of our inquiry is, of course, the statute. The plain text of IDEA is silent on the allocation of the burden of persuasion. We therefore begin with the ordinary default rule that plaintiffs bear the risk of failing to prove their claims. *McCormick* §337, at 412 ("The burdens of pleading and proof with regard to most facts have and should be assigned to the plaintiff who generally seeks to change the present state of affairs and who therefore naturally should be expected to bear the risk of failure or proof or persuasion"); C. Mueller & L. Kirkpatrick, *Evidence §3.1*, p. 104 (3d ed. 2003) ("Perhaps the broadest and most accepted idea is that the person who seeks court action should justify the request, which means that the plaintiffs bear the burdens on the elements in their claims").

Thus, we have usually assumed without comment that plaintiffs bear the burden of persuasion regarding the essential aspects of their claims. For example, Title VII of the Civil Rights Act of 1964, 42 U. S. C. §2000e-2 *et seq.*, does not directly state that plaintiffs bear the "ultimate" burden of persuasion, but we have so concluded. *St. Mary's Honor Center v. Hicks*, 509 U. S. 502, 511 (1993); *id.*, at 531 (Souter, J., dissenting). In numerous other areas, we have presumed or held that the default rule applies. See, e. g., *Lujan v. Defenders of Wildlife*, 504 U. S. 555, 561 (1992) (standing); *Cleveland v. Policy Management Systems Corp.*, 526 U. S. 795, 806 (1999) (Americans with Disabilities Act); *Hunt v. Cromartie*, 526 U. S. 541, 553 (1999) (equal protection); *Wharf (Holdings) Ltd. v. United Int'l Holdings, Inc.*, 532 U. S. 588, 593 (2001) (securities fraud); *Doran v. Salem Inn, Inc.*, 422 U. S. 922, 931 (1975) (preliminary injunctions); *Mt. Healthy City Bd. of Ed. v. Doyle*, 429 U. S. 274, 287 (1977) (First Amendment). Congress also expressed its approval of the general rule when it chose to apply it to administrative proceedings under the Administrative Procedure Act, 5 U. S. C. §556(d); see also *Greenwich Collieries, supra*, at 271.

The ordinary default rule, of course, admits of exceptions. See *McCormick §337*, at 412-415. For example, the burden of persuasion as to certain elements of a plantiff's claim may be shifted to defendants, when such elements can fairly be characterized as affirmative defenses or exemptions. See, e.g., *FTC v. Morton Salt Co.*, 334 U. S. 37, 44-45 (1948). Under some circumstances this Court has even placed the burden of persuasion over an entire claim on the defendant. See *Alaska Dept. of Environmental Conservation v. EPA*, 540 U. S. 461, 494 (2004). But while the normal default rule does not solve all cases, it certainly solves most of them. Decisions that place the entire burden of persuasion on the opposing party at the outset of a proceeding—as petitioners urge us to do here—are extremely rare. Absent some reason to believe that Congress intended otherwise, therefore, we will conclude that the burden of persuasion lies where it usually falls, upon the party seeking relief.

B.

Petitioners contend first that a close reading of IDEA's text compels a conclusion in their favor. They urge that we should interpret the statutory words "due process" in light of their constitutional meaning, and apply the balancing test established by *Mathews v. Eldridge*, 424 U. S. 319 (1976). Even assuming that the Act incorporates constitutional due process doctrine, *Eldridge* is no help to petitioners, because "[o]utside the criminal law area, where special concerns attend, the locus of the burden of persuasion is normally not an issue of federal constitutional moment." *Lavine v. Milne*, 424 U. S. 577, 585 (1976).

Petitioners next contend that we should take instruction from the lower court opinions of *Mills v. Board of Education*, 348 F. Supp. 866 (D. C. 1972), and *Pennsylvania Association for Retarded Children v. Commonwealth*, 334 F. Supp. 1257 (ED Pa. 1971) (hereinafter *PARC*). IDEA's drafters were admittedly guided "to a significant extent" by these two landmark cases. *Rowley*, 458 U. S., at 194. As the court below noted, however, the fact that Congress "took a number of the procedural safeguards from *PARC* and *Mills* and wrote them directly into the Act" does not allow us to "conclude . . . that Congress intended to adopt the ideas that it failed to write into the text of the statute." 377 F. 3d, at 455.

Petitioners also urge that putting the burden of persuasion on school districts will further IDEA's purposes because it will help ensure that children receive a free appropriate public education. In truth, however, very few cases will be in evidentiary equipoise. Assigning the burden of persuasion to school districts might encourage schools to put more resources into preparing IEPs and presenting their evidence. But IDEA is silent about whether marginal dollars should be allocated to litigation and administrative expenditures or to educational services. Moreover, there is reason to believe that a great deal is already spent on the administration of the Act. Litigating a due process complaint is an expensive affair, costing schools approximately $8,000-to-$12,000 per hearing. See Department of Education, J. Chambers, J. Harr, & A. Dhanani, What Are We Spending on Procedural Safeguards in Special Education 1999-2000, p. 8 (May 2003) (prepared under contract by American Institute for Research, Special Education Expenditure Project). Congress has also repeatedly amended the Act in order to reduce its administrative and litigation-related costs. For example, in 1997 Congress mandated that States offer mediation for IDEA disputes. Individuals with Disabilities Education Act Amendments of 1997, Pub. L. 105-17, §615(e), 111 Stat. 90, 20 U. S. C. §1415(e). In 2004, Congress added a mandatory "resolution session" prior to any due process hearing. Individuals with Disabilities Education Improvement Act of 2004, Pub. L. 108-446, §615(7)(f)(1)(B), 118 Stat. 2720, 20 U. S. C. A. §1415(f)(1)(B) (Supp. 2005). It also made new findings that "[p]arents and schools should be given expanded opportunities to resolve their disagreements in positive and constructive ways," and that "[t]eachers, schools, local educational agencies, and States should be relieved of irrelevant and unnecessary paperwork burdens that do not lead to improved educational outcomes." §§1400(c)(8)-(9).

Petitioners in effect ask this Court to assume that every IEP is invalid until the school district demonstrates that it is not. The Act does not support this conclusion. IDEA relies heavily upon the expertise of school districts to meet its goals. It also includes a so-called "stay-put" provision, which requires a child to remain in his or her "then-current educational placement" during the pendency of an IDEA hearing. §1415(j). Congress could have required that a child be given the educational placement that a parent requested during a dispute, but it did no such thing. Congress appears to have presumed instead that, if the Act's procedural requirements are respected, parents will prevail when they have legitimate grievances. See *Rowley, supra*, at 206 (noting the "legislative conviction that adequate compliance with the procedures prescribed would in most cases assure much if not all of what Congress wished in the way of substantive content in an IEP").

Petitioners' most plausible argument is that "[t]he ordinary rule, based on considerations of fairness, does not place the burden upon a litigant of establishing facts peculiarly within the knowledge of his adversary." *United States v. New York, N. H. & H. R. Co.*, 355 U. S. 253, 256, n. 5 (1957); see also *Concrete Pipe & Products of Cal., Inc. v. Construction Laborers Pension Trust for Southern Cal.*, 508 U. S. 602, 626 (1993). But this "rule is far from being universal, and has many qualifications upon its application." *Greenleaf's Lessee v. Birth*, 6 Pet. 302, 312 (1832); see also McCormick §337, at 413 ("Very often one must plead and prove matters as to which his adversary has superior access to the proof"). School districts have a "natural advantage" in information and expertise, but Congress addressed this when it obliged schools to safeguard the procedural rights of parents and to share information with them. See *School Comm. of Burlington v. Department of Ed. of Mass.*, 471 U. S. 359, 368 (1985). As noted above, parents have the right to review all records that the school possesses in relation to their child. §1415(b)(1). They also have the right to an "independent educational evaluation of the[ir] child." *Ibid.* The regulations clarify this entitlement by providing that a "parent has the right to an independent educational evaluation at public expense if the parent disagrees with an evaluation obtained by the public agency." 34 CFR §300.502(b)(1) (2005). IDEA thus ensures parents access to an expert who can evaluate all the materials that the school must make available, and who can give an independent opinion. They are not left to challenge the government without a realistic opportunity to access the necessary evidence, or without an expert with the firepower to match the opposition.

Additionally, in 2004, Congress added provisions requiring school districts to answer the subject matter of a complaint in writing, and to provide parents with the reasoning behind the disputed action, details about the other options considered and rejected by the IEP team,

and a description of all evaluations, reports, and other factors that the school used in coming to its decision. Pub. L. 108-446, §615(c)(2)(B)(i)(I), 118 Stat. 2718, 20 U. S. C. A. §1415(c)(2)(B)(i)(I) (Supp. 2005). Prior to a hearing, the parties must disclose evaluations and recommendations that they intend to rely upon. 20 U. S. C. §1415(f)(2). IDEA hearings are deliberately informal and intended to give ALJs the flexibility that they need to ensure that each side can fairly present its evidence. IDEA, in fact, requires state authorities to organize hearings in a way that guarantees parents and children the procedural protections of the Act. See §1415(a). Finally, and perhaps most importantly, parents may recover attorney's fees if they prevail. §1415(i)(3)(B). These protections ensure that the school bears no unique informational advantage.

III.

Finally, respondents and several States urge us to decide that States may, if they wish, override the default rule and put the burden always on the school district. Several States have laws or regulations purporting to do so, at least under some circumstances. See, e.g., Minn. Stat. §125A.091, subd. 16 (2004); Ala. Admin. Code Rule 290-8-9-.08(8)©(6) (Supp. 2004); Alaska Admin. Code tit. 4, §52.550(e)(9) (2003); Del. Code Ann., Tit. 14, §3140 (1999). Because no such law or regulation exists in Maryland, we need not decide this issue today. Justice Breyer contends that the allocation of the burden ought to be left entirely up to the States. But neither party made this argument before this Court or the courts below. We therefore decline to address it.

We hold no more than we must to resolve the case at hand: The burden of proof in an administrative hearing challenging an IEP is properly placed upon the party seeking relief. In this case, that party is Brian, as represented by his parents. But the rule applies with equal effect to school districts: If they seek to challenge an IEP, they will in turn bear the burden of persuasion before an ALJ. The judgment of the United States Court of Appeals for the Fourth Circuit is, therefore, affirmed.

It is so **ordered**.

The Chief Justice took no part in the consideration or decision of this case.

Justice Stevens, **concurring**.

It is common ground that no single principle or rule solves all cases by setting forth a general test for ascertaining the incidence of proof burdens when both a statute and its legislative history are silent on the question. See *Alaska Dept. of Environmental Conservation v. EPA*, 540 U. S. 461, 494, n. 17 (2004); see also *ante*, at 7; post, at 1-2 (Ginsburg, J., dissenting). Accordingly, I do not understand the majority to disagree with the proposition that a court, taking into account "'policy considerations, convenience, and fairness,'" post, at 1 (Ginsburg, J., dissenting), could conclude that the purpose of a statute is best effectuated by placing the burden of persuasion on the defendant. Moreover, I agree with much of what Justice Ginsburg has written about the special aspects of this statute. I have, however, decided to join the Court's disposition of this case, not only for the reasons set forth in Justice O'Connor's opinion, but also because I believe that we should presume that public school officials are properly performing their difficult responsibilities under this important statute.

Justice Ginsburg, **dissenting**.

When the legislature is silent on the burden of proof, courts ordinarily allocate the burden to the party initiating the proceeding and seeking relief. As the Fourth Circuit recognized, however, "other factors," prime among them "policy considerations, convenience, and fairness," may warrant a different allocation. 377 F. 3d 449, 452 (2004) (citing 2 J. Strong, *McCormick on Evidence §337*, p. 415 (5th ed. 1999) (allocation of proof burden "will depend upon the weight . . . given to any one or more of several factors, including . . . special policy considerations . . . [,] convenience, . . . [and] fairness")); see also 9 J. Wigmore, *Evidence §2486*, p. 291 (J. Chadbourn rev. ed. 1981) (assigning proof burden presents "a question of policy and fairness based on experience in the different situations"). The Court has followed the same counsel. See *Alaska Dept. of Environmental Conservation v. EPA*, 540 U. S. 461, 494, n. 17 (2004) ("No 'single principle or rule ... solve[s] all cases and afford[s] a general test for ascertaining the incidence' of proof burdens." (quoting Wigmore, *supra*, §2486, p. 288; emphasis deleted)). For reasons well stated by Circuit Judge Luttig, dissenting in the Court of Appeals, 377 F. 3d, at 456-459, I am persuaded that "policy considerations, convenience, and fairness" call for assigning the burden of proof to the school district in this case.

The Individuals with Disabilities Education Act (IDEA), 20 U. S. C. §1400 *et seq.*, was designed to overcome the pattern of disregard and neglect disabled children historically encountered in seeking access to public education. See §1400(c)(2) (congressional findings); S. Rep. No. 94-168, pp. 6, 8-9 (1975); *Mills v. Board of Ed. of District of Columbia*, 348 F. Supp. 866 (DC 1972); *Pennsylvania Assn. for Retarded Children v. Pennsylvania*, 334 F. Supp. 1257 (ED Pa. 1971), and 343 F. Supp. 279 (ED Pa. 1972). Under typical civil rights and social welfare legislation, the complaining party must allege and prove discrimination or qualification for statutory benefits. See, e.g., *St. Mary's Honor Center v. Hicks*, 509 U. S. 502, 511 (1993) (Title VII of the Civil Rights Act of 1964, 42 U. S. C. §2000e *et seq.*); *Director, Office of Workers' Compensation Programs v. Greenwich Collieries*, 512 U. S. 267, 270 (1994) (Black Lung Benefits Act, 30 U. S. C. §901 *et seq.*). The IDEA is atypical in this respect: It casts an affirmative, beneficiary-specific obligation on providers of public education. School districts are charged

with responsibility to offer to each disabled child an individualized education program (IEP) suitable to the child's special needs. 20 U. S. C. §§1400(d)(1), 1412(a)(4), 1414(d). The proponent of the IEP, it seems to me, is properly called upon to demonstrate its adequacy.

Familiar with the full range of education facilities in the area, and informed by "their experiences with other, similarly-disabled children," 377 F. 3d, at 458 (Luttig, J., dissenting), "the school district is . . . in a far better position to demonstrate that it has fulfilled [its statutory] obligation than the disabled student's parents are in to show that the school district has failed to do so," *id.*, at 457. Accord *Oberti v. Board of Ed. of Borough of Clementon School Dist.*, 995 F. 2d 1204, 1219 (CA3 1993) ("In practical terms, the school has an advantage when a dispute arises under the Act: the school has better access to relevant information, greater control over the potentially more persuasive witnesses (those who have been directly involved with the child's education), and greater overall educational expertise than the parents."); *Lascari v. Board of Ed. of Ramapo Indian Hills Regional High School Dist.*, 116 N. J. 30, 45-46, 560 A. 2d 1180, 1188-1189 (1989) (in view of the school district's "better access to relevant information," parent's obligation "should be merely to place in issue the appropriateness of the IEP. The school board should then bear the burden of proving that the IEP was appropriate. In reaching that result, we have sought to implement the intent of the statutory and regulatory schemes.").[1]

Understandably, school districts striving to balance their budgets, if "[l]eft to [their] own devices," will favor educational options that enable them to conserve resources. *Deal v. Hamilton County Bd. of Ed.*, 392 F. 3d 840, 864-865 (CA6 2004). Saddled with a proof burden in administrative "due process" hearings, parents are likely to find a district-proposed IEP "resistant to challenge." 377 F. 3d, at 459 (Luttig, J., dissenting). Placing the burden on the district to show that its plan measures up to the statutorily mandated "free appropriate public education," 20 U. S. C. §1400(d)(1)(A), will strengthen school officials' resolve to choose a course genuinely tailored to the child's individual needs.[2]

The Court acknowledges that "[a]ssigning the burden of persuasion to school districts might encourage schools to put more resources into preparing IEPs." *Ante*, at 9. Curiously, the Court next suggests that resources spent on developing IEPs rank as "administrative expenditures" not as expenditures for "educational services." *Ibid.* Costs entailed in the preparation of suitable IEPs, however, are the very expenditures necessary to ensure each child covered by IDEA access to a free appropriate education. These outlays surely relate to "educational services." Indeed, a carefully designed IEP may ward off disputes productive of large administrative or litigation expenses.

This case is illustrative. Not until the District Court ruled that the school district had the burden of persuasion did the school design an IEP that met Brian Schaffer's special educational needs. See *ante*, at 5; Tr. of Oral Arg. 21-22 (Counsel for the Schaffers observed that "Montgomery County . . . gave [Brian] the kind of services he had sought from the beginning once . . . [the school district was] given the burden of proof."). Had the school district, in the first instance, offered Brian a public or private school placement equivalent to the one the district ultimately provided, this entire litigation and its attendant costs could have been avoided.

Notably, nine States, as friends of the Court, have urged that placement of the burden of persuasion on the school district best comports with IDEA's aim. See *Brief for Virginia et al.* as Amici Curiae. If allocating the burden to school districts would saddle school systems with inordinate costs, it is doubtful that these States would have filed in favor of petitioners. Cf. Brief for United States as Amicus Curiae Supporting Appellees Urging Affirmance in 00-1471 (CA4), p. 12 ("Having to carry the burden of proof regarding the adequacy of its proposed IEP . . . should not substantially increase the workload for the school.").[3]

One can demur to the Fourth Circuit's observation that courts "do not automatically assign the burden of proof to the side with the bigger guns," 377 F. 3d, at 453, for no such reflexive action is at issue here. It bears emphasis that "the vast majority of parents whose children require the benefits and protections provided in the IDEA" lack "knowledg[e] about the educational resources available to their [child]" and the "sophisticat[ion]" to mount an effective case against a district-proposed IEP. Id., at 458 (Luttig, J., dissenting); cf. 20 U. S. C. §1400(c)(7)-(10). See generally M. Wagner, C. Marder, J. Blackorby, & D. Cardoso, *The Children We Serve: The Demographic Characteristics of Elementary and Middle School Students with Disabilities and their Households* (Sept. 2002), available at www.seels.net/designdocs/SEELS_Children We Serve Report.pdf (as visited Nov. 8, 2005, and available in Clerk of Court's case file). In this setting, "the party with the 'bigger guns' also has better access to information, greater expertise, and an affirmative obligation to provide the contested services." 377 F. 3d, at 458 (Luttig, J., dissenting). Policy considerations, convenience, and fairness, I think it plain, point in the same direction. Their collective weight warrants a rule requiring a school district, in "due process" hearings, to explain persuasively why its proposed IEP satisfies IDEA's standards. Ibid. I would therefore reverse the judgment of the Fourth Circuit.

Justice Breyer, **dissenting**.

As the majority points out, the Individuals with Disabilities Education Act (Act), 20 U. S. C. §1400 *et seq.*, requires school districts to "identify and evaluate disabled children, . . . develop an [Individualized Education Program] for each one . . . , and review every IEP at least once a year." *Ante*, at 3 (opinion of the Court). A parent dissatisfied with "any matter relating [1] to the identification, evaluation, or educational placement of the child," or [2] to the "provision of a free appropriate public education," of the child, has the opportunity "to resolve such disputes through a mediation process." 20 U. S. C. §§1415(a), (b)(6)(A), (k) (Supp. 2005). The Act further provides the parent with "an opportunity for an impartial due process hearing" provided by the state or local education agency. §1415(f)(1)(A). If provided locally, either party can appeal the hearing officer's decision to the state educational agency. §1415(g). Finally, the Act allows any "party aggrieved" by the results of the state hearing(s), "to bring a civil action" in a federal district court. §1415(i)(2)(A). In sum, the Act provides for school board action, followed by (1) mediation, (2) an impartial state due process hearing with the possibility of state appellate review, and, (3) federal district court review.

The Act also sets forth minimum procedures that the parties, the hearing officer, and the federal court must follow. See, e.g., §1415(f)(1) (notice); §1415(f)(2) (disclosures); §1415(f)(3) (limitations on who may conduct the hearing); §1415(g) (right to appeal); §1415(h)(1) ("the right to be accompanied and advised by counsel"); §1415(h)(2) ("the right to present evidence and confront, cross-examine, and compel the attendance of witnesses"); §1415(h)(3) (the right to a transcript of the proceeding); §1415(h)(4) ("the right to written . . . findings of fact and decisions"). Despite this detailed procedural scheme, the Act is silent on the question of who bears the burden of persuasion at the state "due process" hearing.

The statute's silence suggests that Congress did not think about the matter of the burden of persuasion. It is, after all, a relatively minor issue that should not often arise. That is because the parties will ordinarily introduce considerable evidence (as in this case where the initial 3-day hearing included testimony from 10 witnesses, 6 qualified as experts, and more than 50 exhibits). And judges rarely hesitate to weigh evidence, even highly technical evidence, and to decide a matter on the merits, even when the case is a close one. Thus, cases in which an administrative law judge (ALJ) finds the evidence in precise equipoise should be few and far between. Cf. *O'Neal v. McAninch*, 513 U. S. 432, 436-437 (1995). See also Individuals with Disabilities Education Improvement Act of 2004, Pub. L. 108-446, §§615(f)(3)(A)(ii)-(iv), 118 Stat. 2721, 20 U. S. C. A. §§1415(f)(3)(A)(ii)-(iv) (Supp. 2005) (requiring appointment of ALJ with technical capacity to understand Act).

Nonetheless, the hearing officer held that before him was that rara avis—a case of perfect evidentiary equipoise. Hence we must infer from Congress' silence (and from the rest of the statutory scheme) which party—the parents or the school district—bears the burden of persuasion.

One can reasonably argue, as the Court holds, that the risk of nonpersuasion should fall upon the "individual desiring change." That, after all, is the rule courts ordinarily apply when an individual complains about the lawfulness of a government action. E.g., *ante*, at 6-11 (opinion of the Court); 377 F. 3d 449 (CA4 2004) (case below); *Devine v. Indian River County School Bd.*, 249 F. 3d 1289 (CA11 2001). On the other hand, one can reasonably argue to the contrary, that, given the technical nature of the subject matter, its human importance, the school district's superior resources, and the district's superior access to relevant information, the risk of nonpersuasion ought to fall upon the district. E.g., *ante*, at 1-5 (Ginsburg, J., dissenting); 377 F. 3d, at 456-459 (Luttig, J., dissenting); *Oberti v. Board of Ed.*, 995 F. 2d 1204 (CA3 1993); *Lascari v. Board of Ed.*, 116 N. J. 30, 560 A. 2d 1180 (1980). My own view is that Congress took neither approach. It did not decide the "burden of persuasion" question; instead it left the matter to the States for decision.

The Act says that the "establish[ment]" of "procedures" is a matter for the "State" and its agencies. §1415(a). It adds that the hearing in question, an administrative hearing, is to be conducted by the "State" or "local educational agency." 20 U. S. C. A. §1415(f)(1)(A) (Supp. 2005). And the statute as a whole foresees state implementation of federal standards. §1412(a); *Cedar Rapids Community School Dist. v. Garret F.*, 526 U. S. 66, 68 (1999); *Board of Ed. of Hendrick Hudson Central School Dist., Westchester Cty. v. Rowley*, 458 U. S. 176, 208 (1982). The minimum federal procedural standards that the Act specifies are unrelated to the "burden of persuasion" question. And different States, consequently and not surprisingly, have resolved it in different ways. See, e.g., Alaska Admin. Code, tit. 4, §52.550(e)(9) (2003) (school district bears burden); Ala. Admin. Code Rule 290-8-9.08(8)(c)(6)(ii)(I) (Supp. 2004); (same); Conn. Agencies Regs. §10-76h-14 (2005) (same); Del. Code Ann., tit. 14, §3140 (1999) (same); 1 D. C. Mun. Regs., tit. 5, §3030.3 (2003) (same); W. Va. Code Rules §126-16-8.1.11(c) (2005) (same); Ind. Admin. Code, tit. 511, 7-30-3 (2003) (incorporating by reference Ind. Code §4-21.5-3-14 (West 2002)) (moving party bears burden); 7 Ky. Admin. Regs., tit. 707, ch. 1:340, Section 7(4) (2004) (incorporating by reference Ky. Rev. Stat. Ann. §13B.090(7) (Lexis 2003)) (same); Ga. Comp. Rules & Regs., Rule 160-4-7-.18(1)(g)(8) (2002) (burden varies depending upon remedy sought); Minn. Stat. Ann. §125A.091, subd. 16 (West Supp. 2005) (same). There is no indication that this lack of uniformity has proved harmful.

Nothing in the Act suggests a need to fill every interstice of the Act's remedial scheme with a uniform federal rule. See *Kamen v. Kemper Financial Services, Inc.*, 500 U. S. 90, 98 (1991) (citations omitted). And should some such need arise—i.e., if non-uniformity or a particular state approach were to prove problematic—the Federal Department of Education, expert in the area, might promulgate a uniform federal standard, thereby limiting state choice. 20 U. S. C. A. §1406(a) (Supp. 2005); *Irving Independent School Dist. v. Tatro*, 468 U. S. 883, 891-893 (1984); see also *Barnhart v. Walton*, 535 U. S. 212, 217-218 (2002); *NationsBank of N. C., N. A. v. Variable Annuity Life Ins. Co.*, 513 U. S. 251, 256-257 (1995); *Chevron U. S. A. Inc. v. Natural Resources Defense Council, Inc.*, 467 U. S. 837, 842-845 (1984).

Most importantly, Congress has made clear that the Act itself represents an exercise in "cooperative federalism." See *ante* (opinion of the Court), at 2-3. Respecting the States' right to decide this procedural matter here, where education is at issue, where expertise matters, and where costs are shared, is consistent with that cooperative approach. See *Wisconsin Dept. of Health and Family Servs. v. Blumer*, 534 U. S. 473, 495 (2002) (when interpreting statutes "designed to advance cooperative federalism[,] . . . we have not been reluctant to leave a range of permissible choices to the States"). Cf. *Smith v. Robbins*, 528 U. S. 259, 275 (2000); *New State Ice Co. v. Liebmann*, 285 U. S. 262, 311 (1932) (Brandeis, J., dissenting). And judicial respect for such congressional determinations is important. Indeed, in today's technologically and legally complex world, whether court decisions embody that kind of judicial respect may represent the true test of federalist principle. See *A T & T Corp. v. Iowa Utilities Bd.*, 525 U. S. 366, 420 (1999) (Breyer, J., concurring in part and dissenting in part).

Maryland has no special state law or regulation setting forth a special IEP-related burden of persuasion standard. But it does have rules of state administrative procedure and a body of state administrative law. The state ALJ should determine how those rules, or other state law applies to this case. Cf., e.g., Ind. Admin. Code, tit. 511,7-30-3 (2003) (hearings under the Act conducted in accord with general state administrative law); 7 Ky. Admin. Regs., tit. 707, ch. 1:340, Section 7(4) (2004) (same). Because the state ALJ did not do this (i.e., he looked for a federal, not a state, burden of persuasion rule), I would remand this case.

Endnotes

1 The Court suggests that the IDEA's stay-put provision, 20 U. S. C. §1415(j), supports placement of the burden of persuasion on the parents. Ante, at 10. The stay-put provision, however, merely preserves the status quo. It would work to the advantage of the child and the parents when the school seeks to cut services offered under a previously established IEP. True, Congress did not require that "a child be given the educational placement that a parent requested during a dispute." Ibid. But neither did Congress require that the IEP advanced by

the school district go into effect during the pendency of a dispute.

2   The Court observes that decisions placing "the entire burden of persuasion on the opposing party at the outset of a proceeding ... are extremely rare." *Ante*, at 8. In cases of this order, however, the persuasion burden is indivisible. It must be borne entirely by one side or the other: Either the school district must establish the adequacy of the IEP it has proposed or the parents must demonstrate the plan's inadequacy.

3   Before the Fourth Circuit, the United States filed in favor of the Schaffers; in this Court, the United States supported Montgomery County.

The Supreme Court of the United States

548 U. S. _____ (2006)

ARLINGTON CENTRAL SCHOOL DISTRICT BOARD OF EDUCATION,

Petitioner

v.

PEARL MURPHY AND THEODORE MURPHY,

Respondents

No. 05-18

On Writ Of Certiorari to The United States Court Of Appeals For The Second Circuit Court: 402 F. 3d 332, reversed and remanded.

June 26, 2006

Alito, J., delivered the opinion of the Court, in which Roberts, C. J., and Scalia, Kennedy, and Thomas, JJ., joined.

Ginsburg, J., filed an opinion concurring in part and concurring in the judgment. Souter, J., filed a dissenting opinion. Breyer, J., filed a dissenting opinion, in which Stevens and Souter, JJ., joined.

The Individuals with Disabilities Education Act (IDEA or Act) provides that a court "may award reasonable attorneys' fees as part of the costs" to parents who prevail in an action brought under the Act. 111 Stat. 92, 20 U. S. C. §1415(i)(3)(B). We granted certiorari to decide whether this fee-shifting provision authorizes prevailing parents to recover fees for services rendered by experts in IDEA actions. We hold that it does not.

I.

Respondents Pearl and Theodore Murphy filed an action under the IDEA on behalf of their son, Joseph Murphy, seeking to require petitioner Arlington Central School District Board of Education to pay for their son's private school tuition for specified school years. Respondents prevailed in the District Court, 86 F. Supp. 2d 354 (SDNY 2000), and the Court of Appeals for the Second Circuit affirmed, 297 F. 3d 195 (2002).

As prevailing parents, respondents then sought $29,350 in fees for the services of an educational consultant, Marilyn Arons, who assisted respondents throughout the IDEA proceedings. The District Court granted respondents' request in part. It held that only the value of Arons' time spent between the hearing request and the ruling in respondents' favor could properly be considered charges incurred in an "action or proceeding brought" under the Act, see 20 U. S. C. §1415(i)(3)(B). 2003 WL 21694398, *9 (SDNY, July 22,

2003). This reduced the maximum recovery to $8,650. The District Court also held that Arons, a non-lawyer, could be compensated only for time spent on expert consulting services, not for time spent on legal representation, id., at *4, but it concluded that all the relevant time could be characterized as falling within the compensable category, and thus allowed compensation for the full $8,650, id., at *10.

The Court of Appeals for the Second Circuit affirmed. 402 F. 3d 332 (2005). Acknowledging that other Circuits had taken the opposite view, the Court of Appeals for the Second Circuit held that "Congress intended to and did authorize the reimbursement of expert fees in IDEA actions." Id., at 336. The court began by discussing two decisions of this Court holding that expert fees could not be recovered as taxed costs under particular cost- or fee-shifting provisions. See Crawford Fitting Co. v. J. T. Gibbons, Inc., 482 U. S. 437 (1987) (interpreting Fed. Rule Civ. Proc. 54(d) and 28 U. S. C. §1920); West Virginia Univ. Hospitals, Inc. v. Casey, 499 U. S. 83 (1991) (interpreting 42 U. S. C. §1988 (1988 ed.)). According to these decisions, the court noted, a cost- or fee-shifting provision will not be read to permit a prevailing party to recover expert fees without " 'explicit statutory authority' indicating that Congress intended for that sort of fee-shifting." 402 F. 3d, at 336.

Ultimately, though, the court was persuaded by a statement in the Conference Committee Report relating to 20 U. S. C. §1415(i)(3)(B) and by a footnote in Casey that made reference to that Report. 402 F. 3d, at 336-337 (citing H. R. Conf. Rep. No. 99-687, p. 5 (1986)). Based on these authorities, the court concluded that it was required to interpret the IDEA to authorize the award of the costs that prevailing parents incur in hiring experts. 402 F. 3d, at 336.

We granted certiorari, 546 U. S. _____ (2006), to resolve the conflict among the Circuits with respect to whether Congress authorized the compensation of expert fees to prevailing parents in IDEA actions. Compare Goldring v. District of Columbia, 416 F. 3d 70, 73-77 (CADC 2005); Neosho R-V School Dist. v. Clark ex rel. Clark, 315 F. 3d 1022, 1031-1033 (CA8 2003); T. D. v. LaGrange School Dist. No. 102, 349 F. 3d 469, 480-482 (CA7 2003), with 402 F. 3d 332 (CA2 2005). We now reverse.

II.

Our resolution of the question presented in this case is guided by the fact that Congress enacted the IDEA pursuant to the Spending Clause. U. S. Const., Art. I, §8, cl. 1; see Schaffer v. Weast, 546 U. S. ___ (2005). Like its statutory predecessor, the IDEA provides federal funds to assist state and local agencies in educating children with disabilities "and conditions such funding upon a State's compliance with extensive goals and procedures." Board of Ed. of Hendrick Hudson Central School Dist., Westchester Cty. v. Rowley, 458 U. S. 176, 179 (1982).

Congress has broad power to set the terms on which it disburses federal money to the States, see, e.g., *South Dakota v. Dole*, 483 U. S. 203, 206-207 (1987), but when Congress attaches conditions to a State's acceptance of federal funds, the conditions must be set out "unambiguously," see *Pennhurst State School and Hospital v. Halderman*, 451 U. S. 1, 17 (1981); *Rowley, supra*, at 204, n. 26. "Legislation enacted pursuant to the spending power is much in the nature of a contract," and therefore, to be bound by "federally imposed conditions," recipients of federal funds must accept them "voluntarily and knowingly." *Pennhurst*, 451 U. S., at 17. States cannot knowingly accept conditions of which they are "unaware" or which they are "unable to ascertain." *Ibid.* Thus, in the present case, we must view the IDEA from the perspective of a state official who is engaged in the process of deciding whether the State should accept IDEA funds and the obligations that go with those funds. We must ask whether such a state official would clearly understand that one of the obligations of the Act is the obligation to compensate prevailing parents for expert fees. In other words, we must ask whether the IDEA furnishes clear notice regarding the liability at issue in this case.

III.

A.

In considering whether the IDEA provides clear notice, we begin with the text. We have "stated time and again that courts must presume that a legislature says in a statute what it means and means in a statute what it says there." *Connecticut Nat. Bank v. Germain*, 503 U. S. 249, 253-254 (1992). When the statutory "language is plain, the sole function of the courts—at least where the disposition required by the text is not absurd—is to enforce it according to its terms." *Hartford Underwriters Ins. Co. v. Union Planters Bank, N. A.*, 530 U. S. 1, 6 (2000) (quoting *United States v. Ron Pair Enterprises, Inc.*, 489 U. S. 235, 241 (1989), in turn quoting *Caminetti v. United States*, 242 U. S. 470, 485 (1917); internal quotation marks omitted).

The governing provision of the IDEA, 20 U. S. C. §1415(i)(3)(B), provides that "in any action or proceeding brought under this section, the court, in its discretion, may award reasonable attorneys' fees as part of the costs" to the parents of "a child with a disability" who is the "prevailing party." While this provision provides for an award of "reasonable attorneys' fees," this provision does not even hint that acceptance of IDEA funds makes a State responsible for reimbursing prevailing parents for services rendered by experts.

Respondents contend that we should interpret the term "costs" in accordance with its meaning in ordinary usage and that §1415(i)(3)(B) should therefore be read to "authorize reimbursement of all costs parents incur in IDEA proceedings, including expert costs." Brief for Respondents 17.

This argument has multiple flaws. For one thing, as the Court of Appeals in this case acknowledged, "'costs' is a term of art that generally does not include expert fees." 402 F. 3d, at 336. The use of this term of art, rather than a term such as "expenses," strongly suggests that §1415(i)(3)(B) was not meant to be an open-ended provision that makes participating States liable for all expenses incurred by prevailing parents in connection with an IDEA case—for example, travel and lodging expenses or lost wages due to time taken off from work. Moreover, contrary to respondents' suggestion, §1415(i)(3)(B) does not say that a court may award "costs" to prevailing parents; rather, it says that a court may award reasonable attorney's fees "as part of the costs" to prevailing parents. This language simply adds reasonable attorney's fees incurred by prevailing parents to the list of costs that prevailing parents are otherwise entitled to recover. This list of otherwise recoverable costs is obviously the list set out in 28 U. S. C. §1920, the general statute governing the taxation of costs in federal court, and the recovery of witness fees under §1920 is strictly limited by §1821, which authorizes travel reimbursement and a $40 per diem. Thus, the text of 20 U. S. C. §1415(i)(3)(B) does not authorize an award of any additional expert fees, and it certainly fails to provide the clear notice that is required under the Spending Clause.

Other provisions of the IDEA point strongly in the same direction. While authorizing the award of reasonable attorney's fees, the Act contains detailed provisions that are designed to ensure that such awards are indeed reasonable. See §§1415(i)(3)(C)-(G). The absence of any comparable provisions relating to expert fees strongly suggests that recovery of expert fees is not authorized. Moreover, the lack of any reference to expert fees in §1415(d)(2) gives rise to a similar inference. This provision, which generally requires that parents receive "a full explanation of the procedural safeguards" available under §1415 and refers expressly to "attorneys' fees," makes no mention of expert fees.

B.

Respondents contend that their interpretation of §1415(i)(3)(B) is supported by a provision of the Handicapped Children's Protection Act of 1986 that required the General Accounting Office (GAO) to collect certain data, §4(b)(3), 100 Stat. 797 (hereinafter GAO study provision), but this provision is of little significance for present purposes. The GAO study provision directed the Comptroller General, acting through the GAO, to compile data on, among other things: "(A) the specific amount of attorneys' fees, costs, and expenses awarded to the prevailing party" in IDEA cases for a particular period of time, and (B) "the number of hours spent by personnel, including attorneys and consultants, involved in the action or proceeding, and expenses incurred by the parents and the State educational agency and local educational agency." *Id.*, at 797-798.

Subparagraph (A) would provide some support for respondents' position if it directed the GAO to compile data on awards to prevailing parties of the expense of hiring consultants, but that is not what subparagraph (A) says. Subparagraph (A) makes no mention of consultants or experts or their fees.[1]

Subparagraph (B) similarly does not help respondents. Subparagraph (B), which directs the GAO to study "the number of hours spent in IDEA cases by personnel, including ... consultants," says nothing about the award of fees to such consultants. Just because Congress directed the GAO to compile statistics on the hours spent by consultants in IDEA cases, it does not follow that Congress meant for States to compensate prevailing parties for the fees billed by these consultants.

Respondents maintain that "Congress' direction to the GAO would be inexplicable if Congress did not anticipate that the expenses for 'consultants' would be recoverable," Brief for Respondents 19, but this is incorrect. There are many reasons why Congress might have wanted the GAO to gather data on expenses that were not to be taxed as costs. Knowing the costs incurred by IDEA litigants might be useful in considering future procedural amendments (which might affect these costs) or a future amendment regarding fee shifting. And, in fact, it is apparent that the GAO study provision covered expenses that could not be taxed as costs. For example, the GAO was instructed to compile statistics on the hours spent by all attorneys involved in an IDEA action or proceeding, even though the Act did not provide for the recovery of attorney's fees by a prevailing state or local educational agency.[2] Similarly, the GAO was directed to compile data on "expenses incurred by the parents," not just those parents who prevail and are thus eligible to recover taxed costs.

In sum, the terms of the IDEA overwhelmingly support the conclusion that prevailing parents may not recover the costs of experts or consultants. Certainly the terms of the IDEA fail to provide the clear notice that would be needed to attach such a condition to a State's receipt of IDEA funds.

IV.

Thus far, we have considered only the text of the IDEA, but perhaps the strongest support for our interpretation of the IDEA is supplied by our decisions and reasoning in *Crawford Fitting*, 482 U. S. 437, and *Casey*, 499 U. S. 83. In light of those decisions, we do not see how it can be said that the IDEA gives a State unambiguous notice regarding liability for expert fees.

In *Crawford Fitting*, the Court rejected an argument very similar to respondents' argument that the term "costs" in §1415(i)(3)(B) should be construed as an open-ended reference to prevailing parents' expenses. It was argued in *Crawford Fitting* that Federal Rule of Civil Procedure 54(d), which provides for the award of "costs" to a prevailing party, authorizes the award of costs not listed in 28 U. S. C. §1821. 482 U. S., at 439. The Court held, however, that Rule 54(d) does not give a district judge "discretion to tax whatever costs may seem appropriate"; rather, the term "costs" in Rule 54(d) is defined by the list set out in §1920. *Id.*, at 441. Because the recovery of witness fees, see §1920(3), is strictly limited by §1821, the Court observed, a broader interpretation of Rule 54(d) would mean that the Rule implicitly effected a partial repeal of those provisions. *Id.*, at 442. But, the Court warned, "we will not lightly infer that Congress has repealed §§1920 and 1821, either through Rule 54(d) or any other provision not referring explicitly to witness fees." *Id.*, at 445.

The reasoning of *Crawford Fitting* strongly supports the conclusion that the term "costs" in 20 U. S. C. §1415(i)(3)(B), like the same term in Rule 54(d), is defined by the categories of expenses enumerated in 28 U. S. C. §1920. This conclusion is buttressed by the principle, recognized in *Crawford Fitting*, that no statute will be construed as authorizing the taxation of witness fees as costs unless the statute "refers explicitly to witness fees." 482 U. S., at 445; see also *ibid.* ("absent explicit statutory or contractual authorization for the taxation of the expenses of a litigant's witness as costs, federal courts are bound by the limitations set out in 28 U. S. C. §1821 and §1920").

Our decision in *Casey* confirms even more dramatically that the IDEA does not authorize an award of expert fees. In *Casey*, as noted above, we interpreted a fee-shifting provision, 42 U. S. C. §1988, the relevant wording of which was virtually identical to the wording of 20 U. S. C. §1415(i)(3)(B). Compare *ibid.* (authorizing the award of "reasonable attorneys' fees as part of the costs" to prevailing parents) with 42 U. S. C. §1988(b) (1988 ed.) (permitting prevailing parties in certain civil rights actions to be awarded "a reasonable attorney's fee as part of the costs"). We held that §1988 did not empower a district court to award expert fees to a prevailing party. *Casey, supra,* at 102. To decide in favor of respondents here, we would have to interpret the virtually identical language in 20 U. S. C. §1415 as having exactly the opposite meaning. Indeed, we would have to go further and hold that the relevant language in the IDEA unambiguously means exactly the opposite of what the nearly identical language in 42 U. S. C. §1988 was held to mean in *Casey*.

The Court of Appeals, as noted above, was heavily influenced by a *Casey* footnote, see 402 F. 3d, at 336-337 (quoting 499 U. S., at 91-92, n. 5), but the court misunderstood the footnote's meaning. The text accompanying the footnote argued, based on an analysis of several fee-shifting statutes, that the term "attorney's fees" does not include expert fees. *Id.*, at 88-91. In the footnote, we commented on petitioners' invocation of the Conference Committee Report relating to 20 U. S. C. §1415(i)(3)(B), which stated: "'The conferees intended that the term "attorneys' fees as part of the costs" include reasonable expenses and fees of expert witnesses and the reasonable costs of any test or evaluation which is found to be necessary for the preparation of the ... case.' " 499 U. S., at 91-92, n. 5 (quoting H. R. Conf. Rep. No. 99-687, at 5; ellipsis in original). This statement, the footnote commented, was "an apparent effort to depart from ordinary meaning and to define a term of art." 499 U. S., at 92, n. 5. The footnote did not state that the Conference Committee Report set out the correct interpretation of §1415(i)(3)(B), much less that the Report was sufficient, despite the language of the statute, to provide the clear notice required under the Spending Clause. The thrust of the footnote was simply that the term "attorneys' fees," standing alone, is generally not understood as encompassing expert fees. Thus, *Crawford Fitting* and *Casey* strongly reinforce the conclusion that the IDEA does not unambiguously authorize prevailing parents to recover expert fees.

V.

Respondents make several arguments that are not based on the text of the IDEA, but these arguments do not show that the IDEA provides clear notice regarding the award of expert fees.

Respondents argue that their interpretation of the IDEA furthers the Act's overarching goal of "ensuring that all children with disabilities have available to them a free appropriate public education," 20 U. S. C. §1400(d)(1)(A) as well as the goal of "safeguarding the rights of parents to challenge school decisions that adversely affect their child." Brief for Respondents 20. These goals, however, are too general to provide much support for respondents' reading of the terms of the IDEA. The IDEA obviously does not seek to promote these goals at the expense of all other considerations, including fiscal considerations. Because the IDEA is not intended in all instances to further the broad goals identified by the respondents at the expense of fiscal considerations, the goals cited by respondents do little to bolster their argument on the narrow question presented here.[3]

Finally, respondents vigorously argue that Congress clearly intended for prevailing parents to be compensated for expert fees. They rely on the legislative history of §1415 and in particular on the following statement in the Conference Committee Report, discussed above: "The conferees intend that the term 'attorneys' fees as part of the costs' include reasonable expenses and fees of expert witnesses and the reasonable costs of any test or evaluation which is found to be necessary for the preparation of the ... case." H. R. Conf. Rep. No. 99-687, at 5.

Whatever weight this legislative history would merit in another context, it is not sufficient here. Putting the legislative history aside, we see virtually no support for respondents' position. Under these circumstances, where everything other than the legislative history overwhelming suggests that expert fees may not be recovered, the legislative history is simply not enough. In a Spending Clause case, the key is not what a majority of the Members of both Houses intend but what the States are clearly told regarding the conditions that go along with the acceptance of those funds. Here, in the face of the unambiguous text of the IDEA and the reasoning in Crawford Fitting and Casey, we cannot say that the legislative history on which respondents rely is sufficient to provide the requisite fair notice.

We reverse the judgment of the Court of Appeals for the Second Circuit and remand the case for further proceedings consistent with this opinion.

It is so **ordered**.

Justice Ginsburg, concurring in part and concurring in the judgment.

I agree, in the main, with the Court's resolution of this case, but part ways with the Court's opinion in one respect. The Court extracts from *Pennhurst State School and Hospital v. Halderman*, 451 U. S. 1, 17 (1981), a "clear notice" requirement, and deems it applicable in this case because Congress enacted the Individuals with Disabilities Education Act (IDEA), as it did the legislation at issue in *Pennhurst*, pursuant to the Spending Clause. Ante, at 3-4. That extraction, in my judgment, is unwarranted. *Pennhurst's* "clear notice" requirement should not be unmoored from its context. The Court there confronted a plea to impose "an unexpected condition for compliance—a new programmatic obligation for participating States." *Bell v. New Jersey*, 461 U. S. 773, 790, n. 17 (1983). The controversy here is lower key: It concerns not the educational programs IDEA directs school districts to provide, but "the remedies available against a non-complying district." *Ibid*; see post, at 9-11 (Breyer, J., dissenting).

The Court's repeated references to a Spending Clause derived "clear notice" requirement, see *ante*, at 3-4, 6, 8, 11, and n. 3, 12, are questionable on other grounds as well. For one thing, IDEA was enacted not only pursuant to Congress' Spending Clause authority, but also pursuant to §5 of the Fourteenth Amendment. See *Smith v. Robinson*, 468 U. S. 992, 1009 (1984) (IDEA's predecessor, the Education of the Handicapped Act, was "set up by Congress to aid the States in complying with their constitutional obligations to provide public education for handicapped children."). Furthermore, no "clear notice" prop is needed in this case given the twin pillars on which the Court's judgment securely rests. First, as the Court explains, *ante*, at 4-6, the specific, attorneys'-fees-oriented, provisions of IDEA, i.e., 20 U. S. C. §1415(i)(3)(B)-(G); §1415(d)(2)(L), "overwhelmingly support the conclusion that prevailing parents may not recover the costs of experts or consultants," *ante*, at 8. Those provisions place controls on fees recoverable for attorneys' services, without mentioning costs parents might incur for other professional services and controls geared to those costs. Second, as the Court develops, prior decisions closely in point "strongly support," even "confirm ... dramatically," today's holding that IDEA trains on attorneys' fees and does not authorize an award covering amounts paid or payable for the services of an educational consultant. *Ante*, at 9 (citing *Crawford Fitting Co. v. J. T. Gibbons, Inc.*, 482 U. S. 437 (1987), and *West Virginia Univ. Hospitals, Inc. v. Casey*, 499 U. S. 83 (1991)).

For the contrary conclusion, Justice Breyer's dissent relies dominantly on a Conference Report stating the conferees' view that the term "attorneys' fees as part of the costs" includes "expenses and fees of expert witnesses" and payments for tests necessary for the preparation of a case. H. R. Conf. Rep. No. 99-687, p. 5 (1986) (internal quotation marks omitted).[4] Including costs of consultants and tests in §1415(i)(3)(B) would make good sense in light of IDEA's overarching goal, i.e., to provide a "free appropriate public education" to children with disabilities, §1400(d)(1)(A). See *post*, at 5-8 (Breyer, J., dissenting). But Congress did not compose §1415(i)(3)(B)'s text,[5] as it did the texts of other statutes too numerous and varied to ignore, to alter the common import of the terms "attorneys' fees" and "costs" in the context of expense-allocation legislation. See, e.g., 42 U. S. C. §1988(c) (2000 ed. and Supp. III) (added in 1991 specifically to "include expert fees as part of the attorney's fee"); *Casey*, 499 U. S., at 88-92, and n. 4 (citing variously composed statutes that "explicitly shift expert ... fees as well as attorney's fees"). Given the constant meaning of the formulation "attorneys' fees as part of the costs" in federal legislation, we are not at liberty to rewrite "the statutory text adopted by both Houses of Congress and submitted to the President," *id.*, at 98, to add several words Congress wisely might have included. The ball, I conclude, is properly left in Congress' court to provide, if it so elects, for consultant fees and testing expenses beyond those IDEA and its implementing regulations already authorize[6], along with any specifications, conditions, or limitations geared to those fees and expenses Congress may deem appropriate. Cf. §1415(i)(3)(B)-(G); §1415(d)(2)(L) (listing only attorneys' fees, not expert or consulting fees, among the procedural safeguards about which school districts must inform parents).

In sum, although I disagree with the Court's rationale to the extent that it invokes a "clear notice" requirement tied to the Spending Clause, I agree with the Court's discussion of IDEA's terms, *ante*, at 4-6, and of our decisions in *Crawford* and *Casey, ante*, at 8-11. Accordingly, I concur in part in the Court's opinion, and join the Court's judgment.

Dissents

Justice Souter, dissenting.

I join Justice Breyer's dissent and add this word only to say outright what would otherwise be implicit, that I agree with the distinction he draws between this case and *Barnes v. Gorman*, 536 U. S. 181 (2002). See *post*, at 10-11 (citing *Barnes, supra*, at 191 (Souter, J., concurring)). Beyond that, I emphasize the importance for me of §4 of the Handicapped Children's Protection Act of 1986, 100 Stat. 797, as amended, 20 U. S. C. A. §1415 note, which mandated the study by what is now known as the Government Accountability Office. That section, of equal dignity with the fee-shifting provision enacted by the same statute, makes Justice Breyer's resort to the related Conference Report the reasonable course.

Justice Breyer, with whom Justice Stevens and Justice Souter join, dissenting.

The Individuals with Disabilities Education Act (IDEA or Act), 20 U. S. C. A. §1400 *et seq.*, (Supp. 2006), says that a court may "award reasonable attorneys' fees as part of the costs to the parents" who are prevailing parties. §1415(i)(3)(B). Unlike the Court, I believe that the word "costs" includes, and authorizes payment of, the costs of experts. The word "costs" does not define its own scope. Neither does the phrase "attorneys' fees as part of costs." But Members of Congress did make clear their intent by, among other things, approving a Conference Report that specified that "the term 'attorneys' fees as part of the costs' includes reasonable expenses of expert witnesses and reasonable costs of any test or evaluation which is found to be necessary for the preparation of the parent or guardian's case in the action or proceeding." H. R. Conf. Rep. No. 99-687, p. 5 (1986); Appendix A, *infra*, at 19. No Senator or Representative voiced *any* opposition to this statement in the discussion preceding the vote on the Conference Report—the last vote on the bill before it was sent to the President. I can find no good reason for this Court to interpret the language of this statute as meaning the precise opposite of what Congress told us it intended.

I.

There are two strong reasons for interpreting the statutory phrase to include the award of expert fees. First, that is what Congress said it intended by the phrase. Second, that interpretation furthers the IDEA's statutorily defined purposes.

A.

Congress added the IDEA's cost-shifting provision when it enacted the Handicapped Children's Protection Act of 1986 (HCPA), 100 Stat. 796. Senator Lowell Weicker introduced the relevant bill in 1985. 131 Cong. Rec. 1979-1980 (1985). As introduced, it sought to overturn this Court's determination that the then-current version of the IDEA (and other civil rights statutes) did not authorize courts to award attorneys' fees to prevailing parents in IDEA cases. See *Smith v. Robinson*, 468 U. S. 992 (1984). The bill provided that "in any action or proceeding brought under this subsection, the court, in its discretion, may award a reasonable attorney's fee as part of the costs to a parent or legal representative of a handicapped child or youth who is the prevailing party." 131 Cong. Rec. 1980; see S. Rep. No. 99-112, p. 2 (1985).

After hearings and debate, several Senators introduced a new bill in the Senate that would have put a cap on attorneys' fees for legal services lawyers, but at the same time would have explicitly authorized the award of "a reasonable attorney's fee, reasonable witness fees, *and other reasonable expenses of the civil action,* in addition to the costs to a parent . . . who is the prevailing party." *Id.,* at 7 (emphasis added). While no Senator objected to the latter provision, some objected to the cap. See, e.g., *id.,* at 17-18 (Additional Views of Senators Kerry, Kennedy, Pell, Dodd, Simon, Metzenbaum and Matsunaga) (accepting cost-shifting provision, but objecting to cap and other aspects of the bill). A bipartisan group of Senators, led by Senators Hatch and Weicker, proposed an alternative bill that authorized courts to award "a reasonable attorney's fee in addition to the costs to a parent" who prevailed. *Id.,* at 15-16 (Additional Views of Senators Hatch, Weicker, Stafford, Dole, Pell, Matsunaga, Simon, Kerry, Kennedy, Metzenbaum, Dodd, and Grassley); 131 Cong. Rec. 21389.

Senator Weicker explained that the bill: *"will enable courts to compensate parents for whatever reasonable costs they had to incur to fully secure what was guaranteed to them by the EHA.* As in other fee shifting statutes, it is our intent that such awards will include, at the discretion of the court, reasonable attorney's fees, *necessary expert witness fees, and other reasonable expenses which were necessary for parents to vindicate their claim to a free appropriate public education for their handicapped child." Id.,* at 21390 (emphasis added).

Not a word of opposition to this statement (or the provision) was voiced on the Senate floor, and S. 415 passed without a recorded vote. *Id.,* at 21393.

The House version of the bill also reflected an intention to authorize recovery of expert costs. Following the House hearings, the Committee on Education and Labor produced a substitute bill that authorized courts to "award reasonable attorneys' fees, *expenses and costs*" to prevailing parents. H. R. Rep. No. 99-296, pp. 1, 5 (1985) (emphasis added). The House Report stated that

"The phrase 'expenses and costs' *includes expenses of expert witnesses; the reasonable costs of any study, report, test, or project which is found to be necessary for the preparation of the parents' or guardian's due process hearing, state adminis-*

trative review or civil action; as well as traditional costs and expenses incurred in the course of litigating a case (e.g., depositions and interrogatories)." *Id.,* at 6 (emphasis added).

No one objected to this statement. By the time H. R. 1523 reached the floor, another substitute bill was introduced. 131 Cong. Rec. 31369 (1985). This new bill did not change in any respect the text of the authorization of expenses and costs. It did add a provision, however, that directed the General Accounting Office (GAO) -- now known as the Government Accountability Office, see 31 U. S. C. A. §731 note (Supp. 2006) -- to study and report to Congress on the fiscal impact of the cost-shifting provision. See *id.,* at 31369-31370. The newly substituted bill passed the House without a recorded vote. *Id.,* at 31377.

Members of the House and Senate (including all of the primary sponsors of the HCPA) then met in conference to work out certain differences. At the conclusion of those negotiations, they produced a Conference Report, which contained the text of the agreed-upon bill and a "Joint Explanatory Statement of the Committee of the Conference." See H. R. Conf. Rep. No. 99-687 (1986), Appendix A, *infra.* The Conference accepted the House bill's GAO provision with "an amendment expanding the data collection requirements of the GAO study to include information regarding the amount of funds expended by local educational agencies and state educational agencies on civil actions and administrative proceedings." *Id.,* at 7. And it accepted (with minor changes) the cost-shifting provisions provided in both the Senate and House versions. The conferees explained:

"With slightly different wording, both the Senate bill and the House amendment provide for the awarding of attorneys' fees in addition to costs. The Senate recedes to the House and the House recedes to the Senate with an amendment clarifying that 'the court, in its discretion, may award reasonable attorneys' fees as part of the costs . . .' This change in wording incorporates the Supreme Court's *Marek v. Chesny* decision 473 U. S 1 (1985). *The conferees intend that the term 'attorneys' fees as part of the costs' include reasonable expenses and fees of expert witnesses and the reasonable costs of any test or evaluation which is found to be necessary for the preparation of the parent or guardian's case in the action or proceeding, as well as traditional costs incurred in the course of litigating a case." Id.,* at 5 (emphasis added; citation omitted).

The Conference Report was returned to the Senate and the House. A motion was put to each to adopt the Conference Report, and both the Senate and the House agreed to the Conference Report by voice votes. See Appendix B, *infra,* at 22 (Senate); Appendix C, *infra,* at 23 (House). No objection was raised to the Conference Report's statement that the cost-shifting provision was intended to authorize expert costs. I concede that "sponsors of the legislation did not mention anything on the floor about expert or consultant fees" at the time the Conference Report was submitted. *Ante*, at 3, n. 2 (Ginsburg, J., concurring in part and concurring in judgment). But I do not believe that silence is significant in light of the fact that every Senator and three of the five Representatives who spoke on the floor had previously signed his name to the Conference Report—a Report that made Congress' intent clear on the first page of its explanation. See Appendix A, *infra*, at 19. And every Senator and Representative that took the floor preceding the votes voiced his strong support for the Conference Report. 132 Cong. Rec. 16823-16825 (1986) (Senate); *id.*, at 17607-17612 (House). The upshot is that Members of both Houses of Congress voted to adopt both the statutory text before us and the Conference Report that made clear that the statute's words include the expert costs here in question.

B.

The Act's basic purpose further supports interpreting the provision's language to include expert costs. The IDEA guarantees a "free" and "appropriate" public education for "all" children with disabilities. 20 U. S. C. A. §1400(d)(1)(A) (Supp. 2006); see also §1401(9)(A) (defining "free appropriate public education" as one "provided at public expense," "without charge"); §1401(29) (defining "special education" as "specially designed instruction, at *no cost* to parents, to meet the unique needs of a child with a disability" (emphasis added)).

Parents have every right to become involved in the Act's efforts to provide that education; indeed, the Act encourages their participation. §1400(c)(5)(B) (IDEA "ensures that families of disabled children have meaningful opportunities to participate in the education of their children at school"). It assures parents that they may question a school district's decisions about what is "appropriate" for their child. And in doing so, they may secure the help of experts. §1415(h)(1) (parents have "the right to be accompanied and advised by counsel and by individuals with special knowledge or training with respect to the problems of children with disabilities"); see generally *Schaffer v. Weast*, 546 U. S. ___, ___ (2005) (slip op., at 3-4) (detailing Act's procedures); *Board of Ed. of Hendrick Hudson Central School Dist., Westchester Cty. v. Rowley*, 458 U. S. 176, 205-206 (1982) (emphasizing importance of Act's procedural guarantees).

The practical significance of the Act's participatory rights and procedural protections may be seriously diminished if parents are unable to obtain reimbursement for the costs of their experts. In IDEA cases, experts are necessary. See Kuriloff & Goldberg, Is Mediation a Fair Way to Resolve Special Education Disputes? First Empirical Findings, *2 Harv. Negotiation L. Rev. 35*, 40 (1997) (detailing findings

of study showing high correlation between use of experts and success of parents in challenging school district's plan); Kuriloff, Is Justice Served by Due Process?: Affecting the Outcome of Special Education Hearings in Pennsylvania, *48 Law & Contemp. Prob. 89*, 100-101, 109 (1985) (same); see also Brief for National Disability Rights Network et al. as *Amici Curiae* 6-15 (collecting sources); cf. *Schaffer, supra*, at ___ (slip op., at 5) (Ginsburg, J., dissenting) ("The vast majority of parents whose children require the benefits and protections provided in the IDEA lack knowledge about the educational resources available to their child and the sophistication to mount an effective case against a district-proposed IEP" (internal quotation marks and alterations omitted)).

Experts are also expensive. See Brief for Respondents 28, n. 17 (collecting District Court decisions awarding expert costs ranging from $200 to $7,600, and noting three reported cases in which expert awards exceeded $10,000). The costs of experts may not make much of a dent in a school district's budget, as many of the experts they use in IDEA proceedings are already on the staff. Cf. *Oberti v. Board of Ed. Clementon School Dist.*, 995 F. 2d 1204, 1219 (CA3 1993). But to parents, the award of costs may matter enormously. Without potential reimbursement, parents may well lack the services of experts entirely. See Department of Education, M. Wagner et al., *The Individual and Household Characteristics of Youth With Disabilities: A Report from the National Longitudinal Transition Study-2 (NLTS-2)*, pp. 3-5 (Aug. 2003) (finding that 25% of disabled children live in poverty and 65% live in households with incomes less than $50,000); see Department of Education, M. Wagner et al., *The Children We Serve: The Demographic Characteristics of Elementary and Middle School Students with Disabilities and Their Households*, p. 28 (Sept. 2002), available at http: // www.seels.net / designdocs / SEELS _ Children _ We _Serve_Report.pdf (as visited June 23, 2006, and available in Clerk of Court's case file) (finding that 36% of disabled children live in households with incomes of $25,000 or less).

In a word, the Act's statutory right to a "free" and "appropriate" education may mean little to those who must pay hundreds of dollars to obtain it. That is why this Court has previously avoided interpretations that would bring about this kind of result. See *School Comm. of Burlington v. Department of Ed. of Mass.*, 471 U. S. 359 (1985) (construing IDEA provision granting equitable authority to courts to include the power to order reimbursement for parents who switch their child to private schools if that decision later proves correct); *id.*, at 370 (without cost reimbursement for prevailing parents, "the child's right to a free appropriate public education, the parents' right to participate fully in developing a proper individualized education plan (IEP), and all of the procedural safeguards would be less than complete"); *Florence County School Dist. Four v. Carter*, 510 U. S. 7, 13 (1993) (holding that prevailing parents are not barred from reimbursement for switching their child to a private school that does not meet the IDEA's definition of a free and appropriate education). In *Carter*, we explained: "IDEA was intended to ensure that children with disabilities receive an education that is both appropriate and free. To read the provisions of §1401(a)(18) to bar reimbursement in the circumstances of this case would defeat this statutory purpose." *Id.*, at 13-14 (citation omitted).

To read the word "costs" as requiring successful parents to bear their own expenses for experts suffers from the same problem. Today's result will leave many parents and guardians "without an expert with the firepower to match the opposition," *Schaffer, supra*, at __ (slip op., at 11), a far cry from the level playing field that Congress envisioned.

II.

The majority makes essentially three arguments against this interpretation. It says that the statute's purpose and "legislative history is simply not enough" to overcome: (1) the fact that this is a Spending Clause case; (2) the text of the statute; and (3) our prior cases which hold that the term "costs" does not include expert costs. *Ante*, at 12. I do not find these arguments convincing.

A.

At the outset the majority says that it "is guided by the fact that Congress enacted the IDEA pursuant to the Spending Clause." *Ante*, at 3. "In a Spending Clause case," the majority adds, "the key is not what a majority of the Members of both Houses intend but what the States are clearly told regarding the conditions that go along with the acceptance of those funds." *Ante*, at 12. Thus, the statute's "conditions must be set out 'unambiguously.'" *Ante*, at 3-4 (citing *Pennhurst State School* and *Hospital v. Halderman*, 451 U. S. 1, 17 (1981) and *Rowley*, 458 U. S., at 204, n. 26). And "we must ask" whether the statute "furnishes clear notice regarding the liability at issue in this case." *Ante*, at 4.

I agree that the statute on its face does not *clearly* tell the States that they must pay expert fees to prevailing parents. But I do not agree that the majority has posed the right question. For one thing, we have repeatedly examined the nature and extent of the financial burdens that the IDEA imposes without reference to the Spending Clause or any "clear-statement rule." See, e.g., *Burlington, supra*, at 369 (private school fees); *Carter, supra*, at 13 (same); *Smith*, 468 U. S., at 1010-1011 (attorneys' fees); *Cedar Rapids Community School Dist. v. Garret F.*, 526 U. S. 66, 76-79 (1999) (continuous nursing service); but see *id.*, at 83 (Thomas, J., joined by Kennedy, J., dissenting). Those cases did not ask whether the statute "furnishes clear notice" to the affirmative obligation or liability at issue.

For another thing, neither *Pennhurst* nor any other case suggests that *every spending detail* of a Spending Clause statute must be spelled out with unusual clarity. To the contrary, we have held that *Pennhurst's* requirement that Congress "unambiguously" set out "a condition on the grant of federal money" *does not* necessarily apply to legislation setting forth "*the remedies available against a non-complying State.*" *Bell v. New Jersey*, 461 U. S. 773, 790, n. 17 (1983) (emphasis added) (rejecting *Pennhurst*-based argument that Elementary and Secondary Education Act of 1965 did not unambiguously provide that the Secretary could recover federal funds that are misused by a State). We have added that *Pennhurst* does not require Congress "specifically" to "identify" and "proscribe *each condition* in Spending Clause legislation." *Jackson v. Birmingham Bd. of Ed.*, 544 U. S. 167, 183 (2005) (rejecting argument that *Pennhurst* precluded interpreting Title IX's private cause of action to encompass retaliation (internal quotation marks and alterations omitted)); see also *Bennett v. Kentucky Dept. of Ed.*, 470 U. S. 656, 665-666 (1985). And we have denied any implication that "suits under Spending Clause legislation are suits in contract, or that contract-law principles apply to *all* issues that they raise." *Barnes v. Gorman*, 536 U. S. 181, 188-189, n. 2 (2002) (emphasis added).

These statements and holdings are not surprising. After all, the basic objective of *Pennhurst's* clear-statement requirement does not demand textual clarity in respect to every detail. That is because ambiguity about the precise nature of a statutory program's details—particularly where they are of a kind that States might have anticipated—is rarely relevant to the basic question: Would the States have accepted the Federal Government's funds *had they only known* the nature of the accompanying conditions? Often, the later filling-in of details through judicial interpretation will not lead one to wonder whether funding recipients would have agreed to enter the basic program at all. Given the nature of such details, it is clear that the States would have entered the program regardless. At the same time, to view each statutory detail of a highly complex federal/state program (involving say, transportation, schools, the environment) simply through the lens of linguistic clarity, rather than to assess its meanings in terms of basic legislative purpose, is to risk a set of judicial interpretations that can prevent the program, overall, from achieving its basic objectives or that might well reduce a program in its details to incoherence.

This case is about just such a detail. Permitting parents to recover expert fees will not lead to awards of "indeterminate magnitude, untethered to compensable harm" and consequently will not "pose a concern that recipients of federal funding could not reasonably have anticipated." *Barnes*, 536 U. S., at 191 (Souter, J., joined by O'Connor, J., concurring) (citation and internal quotation marks omitted). Unlike, say, punitive damages, an award of costs to expert parties is neither "unorthodox" nor "indeterminate," and thus does not throw into doubt whether the States would have entered into the program. *Id.*, at 188. If determinations as to whether the IDEA requires States to provide continuing nursing services, *Cedar Rapids, supra*, or reimbursement for private school tuition, *Burlington, supra*, do not call for linguistic clarity, then the precise content of recoverable "costs" does not call for such clarity here *a fortiori*.

B.

If the Court believes that the statute's language is unambiguous, I must disagree. The provision at issue says that a court "may award reasonable attorneys' fees as part of the costs" to parents who prevail in an action brought under the Act. 20 U. S. C. A. §1415(i)(3)(B) (Supp. 2006). The statute neither defines the word "costs" nor points to any other source of law for a definition. And the word "costs," alone, says nothing at all about which costs falls within its scope.

Neither does the statutory phrase—"as part of the costs to the parents of a child with a disability who is the prevailing party"—taken in its entirety unambiguously foreclose an award of expert fees. I agree that, read literally, that provision does not clearly grant authority to award any costs at all. And one might read it, as the Court does, as referencing another federal statute, 28 U. S. C. §1920, which provides that authority. See *ante*, at 5; see also §1920 (federal taxation of cost statute). But such a reading is not inevitable. The provision (indeed, the entire Act) says nothing about that other statute. And one can, consistent with the language, read the provision as both embodying a general authority to award costs while also specifying the inclusion of "reasonable attorneys' fees" as part of those costs (as saying, for example, that a court "may award reasonable attorneys' fees as part of a costs award ").

This latter reading, while linguistically the less natural, is legislatively the more likely. The majority's alternative reading, by cross-referencing only the federal general cost-awarding statute (which applies solely in *federal courts*), would produce a jumble of different cost definitions applicable to similar IDEA administrative and state-court proceedings in different States. See §1920 ("A judge or clerk of *any court of the United States* may tax as costs the following. . . ." (emphasis added)). This result is particularly odd, as all IDEA actions must begin in state due process hearings, where the federal cost statute clearly does not apply, and the overwhelming majority of these actions are never appealed to *any* court. See GAO, Report to the Ranking Minority Member, Committee on Health, Education, Labor and Pensions, U. S. Senate, Special Education: Numbers of Formal Disputes are Generally Low and States Are Using Mediation and Other Strategies to Resolve Conflicts (GAO-

03-897), p. 13 (2003) (approximately 3,000 administrative hearings annually; under 10% appealed to state or federal court); see also *Moore v. District of Columbia*, 907 F. 2d 165, 166 (CADC 1990) (en banc) (joining other Circuits in holding that IDEA authorizes an "award of attorney fees to a parent who prevails in IDEA administrative proceedings"). And when parents do appeal, they can file their actions in either state or federal courts. 20 U. S. C. A. §1415(i)(2)(A) (Supp. 2006).

Would Congress "obviously" have wanted the content of the word "costs" to vary from State to State, proceeding to proceeding? *Ante*, at 5. Why? At most, the majority's reading of the text is plausible; it is not the only possible reading.

C.

The majority's most persuasive argument does not focus on either the Spending Clause or lack of statutory ambiguity. Rather, the majority says that "costs" is a term of art. In light of the law's long practice of excluding expert fees from the scope of the word "costs," along with this Court's cases interpreting the word similarly in other statutes, the "legislative history is simply not enough." *Ante*, at 12.

I am perfectly willing to assume that the majority is correct about the traditional scope of the word "costs." In two cases this Court has held that the word "costs" is limited to the list set forth in 28 U. S. C. §1920 and does not include fees paid to experts. See *Crawford Fitting Co. v. J. T. Gibbons, Inc.*, 482 U. S. 437 (1987) (interpreting Fed. Rule Civ. Proc. 54(d)); *West Virginia Univ. Hospitals, Inc. v. Casey*, 499 U. S. 83 (1991) (interpreting 42 U. S. C. §1988 (1988 ed.)). But Congress is free to redefine terms of art. See, e.g., *Casey*, 499 U. S., at 88-90 (citing examples of statutes that shift "'costs of litigation (including . . . expert witness fees)'"). And we have suggested that it might well do so through a statutory provision worded in a manner similar to the statute here—indeed, we cited the Conference Report language here at issue. *Id.*, at 91-92, n. 5 (characterizing language as an "apparent effort to *depart* from ordinary meaning and to define a term of art" and noting that Congress made no such "effort" in respect to 42 U. S. C. §1988).

Regardless, here the statute itself indicates that Congress did not intend to use the word "costs" as a term of art. The HCPA, which added the cost-shifting provision (in §2) to the IDEA, also added another provision (in §4) directing the GAO to "conduct a study of the impact of the amendments to the IDEA made by section 2" over a 312 year period following the Act's effective date. §4(a), 100 Stat. 797. To determine the fiscal impact of §2 (the cost-shifting provision), §4 ordered the GAO to submit a report to Congress containing, among other things, the following information:

"Data, for a geographically representative

select sample of States, indicating (A) *the specific amount of attorneys' fees, costs, and expenses awarded to the prevailing party*, in each action and proceeding under §2 from the date of the enactment of this Act through fiscal year 1988, *and the range of such fees, costs and expenses* awarded in the actions and proceedings under such section, categorized by type of complaint and (B) for the same sample as in (A) the *number of hours spent by personnel, including attorneys and consultants*, involved in the action or proceeding, and expenses incurred by the parents and the State educational agency and local educational agency." §4(b)(3), *id.*, at 797-798 (emphasis added).

If Congress intended the word "costs" in §2 to authorize an award of only those costs listed in the federal cost statute, why did it use the word "expenses" in §4(b)(3)(A) as part of the "amount awarded to the prevailing party"? When used as a term of art, after all, "costs" does not cover expenses. Nor does the federal costs statute cover any expenses—at least not any that Congress could have wanted the GAO to study. Cf. 28 U. S. C. §1920 (referring only once to "expenses," and doing so solely to refer to special interpretation services provided in actions initiated by the United States).

Further, why did Congress, when asking the GAO (in the statute itself) to study the "numbers of hours spent by personnel" include among those personnel both attorneys "*and consultants*"? Who but experts could those consultants be? Why would Congress want the GAO to study the hours that those experts "spent," unless it thought that it would help keep track of the "costs" that the statute imposed?

Of course, one might, through speculation, find other answers to these questions. One might, for example, imagine that Congress wanted the GAO to study the expenses that payment of expert fees engendered in state-court proceedings where state, but not federal, law requires that "'expenses' other than 'costs' might be receivable." *Ante*, at 7, n. 1; but see *supra*, at 12-13. Or one might think that the word "expenses" is surplusage. *Ante*, at 7, n. 1; but see *Duncan v. Walker*, 533 U. S. 167, 174 (2001) (expressing Court's "'reluctance to treat statutory terms as surplusage in any setting,'" but especially when they play "a pivotal role in the statutory scheme"). Or one might believe that Congress was interested in the hours these experts spent, but not in the fees they obtained. *Ante*, at 7. But these answers are not necessarily consistent with the purpose of the GAO study provision, a purpose revealed by the language of the provision and its position in the statute. Its placement and its reference to §2 indicate that Congress ordered the study to help it keep track of the magnitude of the reimbursements that an earlier part of the new statute (namely, §2) mandated. See 100 Stat. 797 (stating that purpose of GAO study

was to determine the "impact" of "section 2"). And the *only* reimbursement requirement that §2 mandates is the payment of "costs."

But why speculate about this? We *know* what Congress intended the GAO study to cover. It *told* the GAO in its Conference Report that the word "costs" included the costs of experts. And, not surprisingly, the GAO made clear that it understood precisely what Congress asked it to do. In its final report, the GAO wrote: "Parents can receive reimbursement from state or local education agencies for some or all of their attorney fees *and related expenses* if they are the prevailing party in part or all of administrative hearings or court proceedings. *Expert witness fees, costs of tests or evaluations found to be necessary during the case, and court costs for services rendered during administrative and court proceedings are examples of reimbursable expenses.*" GAO, Briefing Report to Congressional Requesters, Special Education: The Attorney Fees Provision of Public Law 99-372 GAO/HRD-22BR, p. 13 (Nov. 1989). At the very least, this amounts to *some* indication that Congress intended the word "costs," not as a term of art, not as it was used in the statutes at issue in *Casey and Crawford Fitting*, but rather as including certain additional "expenses." If that is so, the claims of tradition, of the interpretation this Court has given other statutes, cannot be so strong as to prevent us from examining the legislative history. And that history could not be more clear about the matter: Congress intended the statutory phrase "attorneys' fees as part of the costs" to include the costs of experts. See Part I, *supra*.

III.

For the reasons I have set forth, I cannot agree with the majority's conclusion. Even less can I agree with its failure to consider fully the statute's legislative history. That history makes Congress' purpose clear. And our ultimate judicial goal is to interpret language in light of the statute's purpose. Only by seeking that purpose can we avoid the substitution of judicial for legislative will. Only by reading language in its light can we maintain the democratic link between voters, legislators, statutes, and ultimate implementation, upon which the legitimacy of our constitutional system rests.

In my view, to keep faith with that interpretive goal, we must retain all traditional interpretive tools—text, structure, history, and purpose. And, because faithful interpretation is art as well as science, we cannot, through rule or canon, rule out the use of any of these tools, automatically and in advance. Cf. *Helvering v. Gregory*, 69 F. 2d 809, 810-811 (CA2 1934) (L. Hand, J.).

Nothing in the Constitution forbids us from giving significant weight to legislative history. By disregarding a clear statement in a legislative report adopted without opposition in both Houses of Congress, the majority has reached a result no Member of Congress expected or overtly desired. It has adopted an interpretation that undercuts, rather than furthers, the statute's purpose, a "free" and "appropriate" public education for "all" children with disabilities. See *Circuit City Stores, Inc. v. Adams*, 532 U. S. 105, 133 (2001) (Stevens, J., joined by Souter, Ginsburg, and Breyer, JJ., dissenting) ("A method of statutory interpretation that is deliberately uninformed, and hence unconstrained, may produce a result that is consistent with a court's own views of how things should be, but it may also defeat the very purpose for which a provision was enacted"). And it has adopted an approach that, I fear, divorces law from life. See *Duncan, supra*, at 193 (Breyer, J., joined by Ginsburg, J., dissenting).

For these reasons, I respectfully dissent.

Endnotes

1 Because subparagraph (A) refers to both "costs" and "expenses" awarded to prevailing parties and because it is generally presumed that statutory language is not superfluous, it could be argued that this provision manifests the expectation that prevailing parties would be awarded certain "expenses" not included in the list of "costs" set out in 28 U. S. C. §1920 and that expert fees were intended to be among these unenumerated "expenses." This argument fails because, whatever expectation this language might seem to evidence, the fact remains that neither 20 U. S. C. §1415 nor any other provision of the IDEA authorizes the award of any "expenses" other than "costs." Recognizing this, respondents argue not that they are entitled to recover "expenses" that are not "costs," but that expert fees are recoverable "costs." As a result, the reference to awards of both "expenses" and "costs" does not support respondents' position. The reference to "expenses" may relate to IDEA actions brought in state court, §1415(i)(2)(A), where "expenses" other than "costs" might be receivable. Or the reference may be surplusage. While it is generally presumed that statutes do not contain surplusage, instances of surplusage are not unknown.

2 In 2000, the attorneys' fees provision provided only an award to prevailing parents. See 20 U. S. C. §1415(i)(3)(B). In 2004, Congress amended §1415(i)(3)(B) to include two additional awards. See §101, 118 Stat. 2724. The amendments provided awards "to a prevailing party who is a State educational agency or local educational agency" where the complaint filed is frivolous or presented for an improper purpose, such as to harass, delay, or increase the cost of litigation. See 20 U. S. C. A. §§1415(i)(3)(B)(i)(II)-(III) (Supp. 2006).

3 Respondents note that a GAO report stated that expert witness fees are reimbursable expenses. See Brief for Respondents 19 (citing GAO, Special Education: The Attorney Fees Provision of Public Law 99-372, p. 13 (Nov. 1989)). But this passing reference in a report issued by an agency not

responsible for implementing the IDEA is plainly insufficient to provide clear notice regarding the scope of the conditions attached to the receipt of IDEA funds.

4 The relevant statement from the Conference Report reads in its entirety:

"The conferees intend that the term 'attorneys' fees as part of the costs' include reasonable expenses and fees of expert witnesses and the reasonable costs of any test or evaluation which is found to be necessary for the preparation of the parent or guardian's case in the action or proceeding, as well as traditional costs incurred in the course of litigating a case." H. R. Conf. Rep. 99-687, at 5.

Although the Conference Report goes on to consider other matters, including controls on attorneys' fees, nothing further is said on expert witness fees or test costs.

5 At the time the Conference Report was submitted to the Senate and House, sponsors of the legislation did not mention anything on the floor about expert or consultant fees. They were altogether clear, however, that the purpose of the legislation was to "reverse" this Court's decision in Smith v. Robinson, 468 U. S. 992 (1984). In *Smith*, the Court held that, under the statute as then designed, prevailing parents were not entitled to attorneys' fees. See 132 Cong. Rec. 16823 (1986) (remarks of Sen. Weicker) ("In adopting this legislation, we are rejecting the reasoning of the Supreme Court in Smith versus Robinson."); *id.*, at 16824 (remarks of Sen. Kerry) ("This vital legislation reverses a U. S. Supreme Court decision Smith versus Robinson."); *id.*, at 17608-17609 (remarks of Rep. Bartlett) ("I support those provisions in the conference agreement that, in response to the Supreme Court decision in ... Smith versus Robinson, authorize the awarding of reasonable attorneys' fees to parents who prevail in special education court cases."); id., at 17609 (remarks of Rep. Biaggi) ("This legislation clearly supports the intent of Congress back in 1975 and corrects what I believe was a gross misinterpretation of the law. Attorneys' fees should be provided to those individuals who are being denied access to the educational system.").

6 Under 34 C. F. R. §300.502(b)(1) (2005), a "parent has the right to an independent educational evaluation at public expense if the parent disagrees with an evaluation obtained by the public agency."

Note: Appendix A, B, and C in Justice Breyer's dissent have been omitted. Appendix A is the Conference Report that accompanied the Handicapped Children's Protection Act of 1986, which modified the special education law to include reimbursement for attorneys' fees. Appendix B and C consisted of a portion of the House and Senate testimony noting that "the Conference Report was agreed to." A pdf version of *Arlington Central School District Board of Education v. Pearl and Theodore Murphy* with these Appendices is available from the U. S. Supreme Court website at www.supremecourtus.gov/opinions/05pdf/05-18.pdf

Section Five

Resources and References

APPENDIX A

Resources and References

The Internet provides a vast library of publications and websites, but the quality of the information is uneven. In research and arguments, you should use information from the highest authority.

The links in this Appendix will take you to documents from government agencies, research authorities, and respected organizations. If you are looking for authoritative publications about "best practices" or guidance and clarification on an issue from the U.S. Department of Education, visit these websites first.

U. S Department of Education Websites

Office of Special Education and Rehabilitative Services
www.ed.gov/about/offices/list/osers/index.html?src=oc

Office of Elementary and Secondary Education www.ed.gov/about/offices/list/oese/index.html
Institute of Education Sciences
www.ed.gov/about/offices/list/ies/index.html?src=oc

IDEA 2004: News, Information and Resources

Individuals with Disabilities Education Act

IDEA 04 website from the U. S. Department of Education
http://idea.ed.gov/

Special Education and Rehabilitative Services
www.ed.gov/policy/speced/guid/idea/idea2004.html

IDEA Partnership Project
www.ideapartnership.org/

Federal Regulations

On August 14, 2006, the Department of Education published the Final Regulations for IDEA 2004 in the *Federal Register*. The Regulations begin at page 46540 and continue to page 46845 of the *Federal Register*.

Full text of the IDEA 2004 Regulations from the Government Printing Office http://a257.g.akamaitech. net/7/257/2422/01jan20061800/edocket.access.gpo.gov/2006/pdf/06-6656.pdf

"Major Changes in the Regulations" provides a quick overview of significant changes. The Table of Contents for the Regulations begins at page 46753. The Index begins at page 46817. We recommend that you download, print and save these documents on your computer so you can easily search for answers to a question.

Major Changes in the Regulations
www.wrightslaw.com/idea/comment/summary.pdf

Table of Contents
www.wrightslaw.com/idea/comment/regs.toc.pdf

IDEA Regulations
www.wrightslaw.com/idea/comment/46755-46817.actual.regs.all.pdf

Index
www.wrightslaw.com/idea/comment/regs.index.pdf

Commentary to the Federal Regulations

The Commentary to the Federal Regulations provides definitions and discussions of legal terms in the IDEA 2004 statute and regulations, and often clarifies the "plain meaning" of a term. If you are doing legal research or looking for the answer to a specific question, the Commentary will be an invaluable resource. The Commentary in the *Federal Register* begins at page 46547 and continues through page 46743.

You can download the full text of the IDEA 2004 Regulations and Commentary as one document: http://a257.g.akamaitech.net/7/257/2422/01jan20061800/edocket.access.gpo.gov/2006/pdf/06-6656.pdf

You can download the Commentary as eight files on different issues.

Definitions. Pages 46547 through 46579 (Regs 1-100)
www.wrightslaw.com/idea/comment/46547-46579.reg.001-100.definitions.pdf

ESY, LRE, etc. Pages 46579 through 46629 (Regs 101-230)
www.wrightslaw.com/idea/comment/46579-46629.reg.101-230.esy.lre.etc.pdf

Evaluations, reevaluations. Pages 46629 through 46661 (Regs 300-311)
www.wrightslaw.com/idea/comment/46629-46661.reg.300-311.evals.pdf

Individualized Education Programs. Pages 46661 through 46688 (Regs 320-328)
www.wrightslaw.com/idea/comment/46661-46688.reg.320-328.ieps.pdf

Procedures. Pages 46688 through 46713 (Regs 501-520)
www.wrightslaw.com/idea/comment/46688-46713.reg.501-520.procedures.pdf

Discipline. Pages 46713 through 46730 (Regs 530-537)
www.wrightslaw.com/idea/comment/46713-46730.reg.530-537.discipline.pdf

Monitoring. Pages 46730 through 46743 (Regs 600-815)
www.wrightslaw.com/idea/comment/46730-46743.reg.600-815.monitoring.pdf

Model Forms

Congress required the Education Department to develop and publish model IEP, IFSP, Procedural Safeguard Notice, and Prior Written Notice forms "no later than the date that the Secretary publishes final regulations. . ." (20 USC Section 1417(e)

Introduction to the IDEA 2004 Model Forms
www.ed.gov/policy/speced/guid/idea/modelform-intro.pdf

Individualized Education Program (IEP)
www.ed.gov/policy/speced/guid/idea/modelform-intro.pdf

Notice of Procedural Safeguards
www.ed.gov/policy/speced/guid/idea/modelform-safeguards.pdf

Prior Written Notice
www.ed.gov/policy/speced/guid/idea/modelform-notice.pdf

Special Education Technical Assistance and Dissemination Network

The Office of Special Education Programs (OSEP) supports a technical assistance network that is designed to improve results for children with disabilities. www.ed.gov/parents/needs/speced/resources.html

IDEA 2004 Topics

Access to the General Curriculum

National Center on Accessing the General Curriculum (NCAC)
www.cast.org/policy/ncac/index.html

The Access Center: Improving Outcomes for All Students K-8
www.k8accesscenter.org/

Autism

Professional Development in Autism (PDA) Center
http://depts.washington.edu/pdacent/

Deaf/Blind

The National Information Clearinghouse on Children Who are Deaf-Blind (DB-LINK)
www.tr.wou.edu/dblink/

National Technical Assistance Consortium for Children and Young Adults Who Are Deaf-Blind (NTAC)
www.tr.wou.edu/ntac/

Dispute Resolution and Mediation

Center for Appropriate Dispute Resolution in Special Education (CADRE)
www.directionservice.org/cadre/

Dropout Prevention

National Dropout Prevention Center for Students with Disabilities
www.dropoutprevention.org/

Early Childhood

National Early Childhood Technical Assistance Center (NECTAC)
www.ectac.org/

Educational Reform, Assessment and Accountability

National Center on Educational Outcomes (NCEO)
http://education.umn.edu/nceo/

General Information

National Dissemination Center for Children with Disabilities (NICHCY)
www.nichcy.org/

Higher Education

HEATH Resource Center
www.heath.gwu.edu/

Midwest Center for Postsecondary Outreach (MCPO)
www.mcpo.org/

Northeast Technical Assistance Center (NETAC)
www.netac.rit.edu/

PEPNet
www.pepnet.org/

Postsecondary Education Consortium (PEC)
http://sunsite.utk.edu/cod/pec/

Western Region Outreach Center and Consortia (WROCC)
http://wrocc.csun.edu/

Inclusion

National Institute for Urban School Improvement
www.urbanschools.org/

Florida State University Center for Prevention and Early Intervention Policy
www.cpeip.fsu.edu/resourceFiles/resourceFile_18.pdf

Juvenile Justice

National Center on Education, Disability, and Juvenile Justice
www.edjj.org/

Learning Disabilities

National Research Center on Learning Disabilities
http://nrcld.org/

Literacy

Reading Rockets
http://readingrockets.org/

The Center on Accelerating Student Learning (CASL)
http://kc.vanderbilt.edu/casl/

Minorities

Linking Academic Scholars to Educational Resources (LASER)
www.coedu.usf.edu/LASER/

National Center for Culturally Responsive Educational Systems
www.nccrest.org/

National Center for Personnel Preparation in Special Education at Minority Institutions of Higher Education (MONARCH Center)
www.monarchcenter.org/

Monitoring

National Center for Special Education Accountability Monitoring (NCSEAM)
www.monitoringcenter.lsuhsc.edu/

National Center on Student Progress Monitoring: Improving Proven Practices in the Elementary Grades
www.studentprogress.org/

Parents

Family Center on Technology and Disability
www.fctd.info/

Technical Assistance Alliance for Parent Center National TAC
www.taalliance.org/

Region 1 TAC - Statewide Parent Advocacy Network (SPAN)
www.spannj.org/

Region 2 TAC - Exceptional Children's Assistance Center (ECAC)
www.ecac-parentcenter.org/

Region 3 TAC – Family Network on Disabilities of Florida
www.fndfl.org/

Region 4 TAC - Ohio Coalition for the Education of Children with Disabilities (OCECD)
www.ocecd.org/

Region 5 TAC - PEAK Parent Center
www.peakparent.org/

Region 6 TAC - Matrix Parent Network and Resource Center
www.matrixparents.org/

Positive Behavioral Supports

OSEP Center on Positive Behavioral Interventions and Supports
www.pbis.org/main.htm

Post School Outcomes

National Post-School Outcomes Center
http://psocenter.org/

Professional Development

Center for Improving Teacher Quality
www.ccsso.org/projects/

IRIS Center for Faculty Enhancement
http://iris.peabody.vanderbilt.edu/

Professional Development in Autism (PDA) Center
http://depts.washington.edu/pdacent/

Reading

Guidance for the Reading First Program. This publication clearly defines the U.S. Department of Education standard for an effective reading program. If a child is falls behind his peers in a classroom program such as this one a more intensive program is necessary.
http://www.ed.gov/programs/readingfirst/guidance.pdf

Regional and Federal Resource Centerrs

The Regional Resource Centers and the Federal Resource Centers provide consultation, technical assistance, and training to State educational agencies, and to school districts and other agencies. Below are links to the Federal Resource Center Website and to a website that networks all of the Resource Centers:

The Federal Resource Center for Special Education (FRC)
www.rrfcnetwork.org/

Universal Design

Center for Applied Special Technology
www.cast.org/

National Consortium on Universal Design for Learning
www.cast.org/pd/consortium/index.html

Tool Kit on Teaching and Assessing Students with Disabilities

The U.S. Department of Education collected documents and published them as the ***Tool Kit on Teaching and Assessing Students with Disabilities*** (April 2006). The ***Tool Kit*** contains research briefs, technical assistance, and information for improving instruction, assessment, and accountability for students with disabilities. The information in the ***Tool Kit*** can be considered "best practice."
http://www.osepideasthatwork.org/toolkit/index.asp

Overview
www.osepideasthatwork.org/toolkit/pdf/letter.pdf

Introduction to the Tool Kit
www.osepideasthatwork.org/toolkit/pdf/Introduction.pdf

Departmental Investments Supporting Teaching and Assessing Students with Disabilities
www.osepideasthatwork.org/toolkit/pdf/Investments.pdf

Models for Large Scale Assessment

Including Students with Disabilities in Large-Scale Assessment: Executive Summary
www.osepideasthatwork.org/toolkit/pdf/LSAExecutiveSummary.pdf

Validating Assessments for Students with Disabilities
www.osepideasthatwork.org/toolkit/pdf/Validitating_Assessments.pdf

Reliability Issues and Evidence www.osepideasthatwork.org/toolkit/pdf/Reliability_Issues.pdf

Validity Evidence
www.osepideasthatwork.org/toolkit/pdf/Validitating_Assessments.pdf

Standards and Assessment Approaches for Students with Disabilities Using a Validity Argument
www.osepideasthatwork.org/toolkit/pdf/validity_argument.pdf

A Decision Framework for IEP Teams Related to Methods for Individual Student Participation in State Accountability Assessments
www.osepideasthatwork.org/toolkit/pdf/Framework.pdf

Professional Development on Assesment Systems
www.osepideasthatwork.org/toolkit/pdf/ProfessionalDev_Assessment.pdf

Glossary
www.osepideasthatwork.org/toolkit/pdf/Glossary.pdf

Technical Assistance - Assessment

Large-Scale Assessment

Online Accommodations Bibliography
www.osepideasthatwork.org/toolkit/pdf/Online_Accomm_Bib.pdf

Universal Design Applied to Large-Scale Assessments
www.osepideasthatwork.org/toolkit/pdf/Universal_Design_LSA.pdf

Progress Monitoring in an Inclusive Standards-Based Assessment and Accountability System
www.osepideasthatwork.org/toolkit/pdf/ProgressMonitoring_InclusiveStandards.pdf

Alternate Assessment

Distribution of Proficient Scores that Exceed the 1% Cap: Four Possible Approaches www.osepideasthatwork.org/toolkit/pdf/distibution_scores.pdf

Expectations for Students with Cognitive Disabilities: Is the Cup Half Empty or Half Full? Can the Cup Flow Over?
www.osepideasthatwork.org/toolkit/pdf/ExpectationsStudentsCogDisabilities.pdf

Massachusetts: One State's Approach to Setting Performance Levels on the Alternate Assessment
www.osepideasthatwork.org/toolkit/pdf/MA_ApproachPerformance.pdf

Designing from the Ground Floor: Alternate Assessment on Alternate Achievement Standards
www.osepideasthatwork.org/toolkit/pdf/DesigningGrndFloor.pdf

Alternate Assessment: Teacher and State Experiences
www.osepideasthatwork.org/toolkit/pdf/TeacherStateExperiences.pdf

Progress Monitoring

What is Scientifically-Based Research on Progress Monitoring?
www.osepideasthatwork.org/toolkit/pdf/ScientificallyBasedResearch.pdf

Response to Intervention

Responsiveness to Intervention in the SLD Process
www.osepideasthatwork.org/toolkit/pdf/RTI_SLD.pdf

Instructional Practices

K-3 Literacy

Proven Ideas from Research for Parents: A Child Becomes a Reader – K-3
www.osepideasthatwork.org/toolkit/pdf/Proven_Ideas.pdf

Put Reading First: The Research Building Blocks for Teaching Children to Read – K-3
www.osepideasthatwork.org/toolkit/pdf/PutReadingFirst.pdf

Adolescent Literacy
Never Too Late: Approaches to Reading Instruction for Secondary Students with Disabilities
www.osepideasthatwork.org/toolkit/pdf/NeverTooLate.pdf

Social Interaction and Communication

Tangible Symbol Systems: Making the Right to Communicate a Reality for Individuals with Severe Disabilities
www.osepideasthatwork.org/toolkit/pdf/TangibleSymbol%20Systems.pdf

Behavior

School-Wide Behavioral Interventions

School-wide Positive Behavior Support: Implementers' Blueprint and Self-Assessment
www.osepideasthatwork.org/toolkit/pdf/SchoolwideBehaviorSupport.pdf

Accommodations

Accommodations Manual: How to Select, Administer, and Evaluate Use of Accommodations for Instruction and Assessment of Students with Disabilities
www.osepideasthatwork.org/toolkit/pdf/AccommodationsManual.pdf

Topic Briefs

OSEP has developed a series of topic briefs around several high-interest areas of IDEA. Topic briefs include a summary of all relevant statutory language around that topic, the citations and a cross-reference, when applicable, to other related briefs.

Alignment with the No Child Left Behind Act
www.ed.gov/policy/speced/guid/idea/tb-nclb-align.pdf

Changes in Initial Evaluation and Reevaluation
www.ed.gov/policy/speced/guid/idea/tb-init-eval.pdf

Children Enrolled by Their Parents in Private Schools
www.ed.gov/policy/speced/guid/idea/tb-priv-school.pdf

Discipline
www.ed.gov/policy/speced/guid/idea/tb-discipline.pdf

Disproportionality and Overidentification
www.ed.gov/policy/speced/guid/idea/tb-overident.pdf

Early Intervening Services
www.ed.gov/policy/speced/guid/idea/tb-early-intervent.pdf

Highly Qualified Teachers
www.ed.gov/policy/speced/guid/idea/tb-qual-teachers.pdf

Individualized Education Program (IEP), Team Meetings and Changes to the IEP
www.ed.gov/policy/speced/guid/idea/tb-iep-meetings.pdf

Individualized Education Program (IEP)
www.ed.gov/policy/speced/guid/idea/tb-iep.pdf

Local Funding
www.ed.gov/policy/speced/guid/idea/tb-local-fund.pdf

National Instructional Materials Accessibility Standard (NIMAS)
www.ed.gov/policy/speced/guid/idea/tb-accessibility.pdf

Part C Amendments in IDEA 2004
www.ed.gov/policy/speced/guid/idea/tb-partc-ammend.pdf

Part C Option: Age 3 to Kindergarten Age
www.ed.gov/policy/speced/guid/idea/tb-partc-opt.pdf

Procedural Safeguards: Surrogates, Notice and Consent
www.ed.gov/policy/speced/guid/idea/tb-safeguards-1.pdf

Procedural Safeguards: Mediation and Resolution Sessions
www.ed.gov/policy/speced/guid/idea/tb-safeguards-2.pdf

Procedural Safeguards: Due Process Hearings
www.ed.gov/policy/speced/guid/idea/tb-safeguards-3.pdf

Secondary Transition
www.ed.gov/policy/speced/guid/idea/tb-second-trans.pdf

State Funding
www.ed.gov/policy/speced/guid/idea/tb-state-fund.pdf

Statewide and Districtwide Assessments
www.ed.gov/policy/speced/guid/idea/tb-assessments.pdf

Other Resources

Questions and Answers On Serving Children With Disabilities Placed by Their Parents at Private Schools. A series of questions and answers addressing the obligation, under IDEA 2004, of states and local education agencies to children with disabilities enrolled by their parents in private elementary schools and secondary schools. (March 2006)
www.ed.gov/policy/speced/guid/idea/faq-parent-placed.pdf

National Standards and Quality Indicators: Transition Toolkit for Systems Improvement by National Alliance for Secondary Education and Transition
www.nasetalliance.org/toolkit/index.htm

Identifying & Implementing Educational Practices Supported by Rigorous Evidence: A User Friendly Guide by Institute of Education Sciences, U.S. Department of Education
www.ed.gov/rschstat/research/pubs/rigorousevid/rigorousevid.pdf

National Institute of Child Health and Human Development
Locate facts and resources for virtually every health condition, syndrome, and disorder.
www.nichd.nih.gov/health/topics/

Funding Sources
Finding things to spend money on isn't hard but finding money can be!. On this site, you will find resources and information to help you navigate through federal and state funding opportunities. Mocrosoft.com has published a free template to follow to help school districts locate all available funds.
www.microsoft.com/education/K12Funding.mspx

National Center for Education Evaluation and Regional Assistance

The National Center for Education Evaluation and Regional Assistance (NCEE) is one of the four centers of the Institute of Education Sciences. NCEE is responsible for conducting rigorous evaluations of federal programs, synthesizing and disseminating information from evaluation and research, and providing technical assistance to improve student achievement through the work of the evaluation division and the knowledge utilization division that includes the Regional Educational Laboratory Program; the What Works Clearinghouse, the Educational Resources and Information Center (ERIC), and the National Library of Education.
http://ies.ed.gov/ncee/aboutus/

Statistics

These websites will be continuously updates as current statistics become available.

School Matters
www.schoolmatters.com/

National Center for Education Statistics
http://nces.ed.gov/

422 • Appendix A. Resources and References

School Personnel

The Secretary's Fourth Annual Report on Teacher Quality
https://www.title2.org/titleIIreport05.pdf

Educating School Leaders
www.edschools.org/reports_leaders.htm

Educating School Teachers
www.edschools.org/teacher_report.htm

What Education Schools Aren't Teaching About Reading--and What Elementary Teachers Aren't Learning (National Center for Teacher Quality)
www.nctq.org/nctq/

Other Federal Statutes

Section 504 of the Rehabilitation Act

Office of Civil Rights
www.ed.gov/about/offices/list/ocr/index.html?src=mr

Frequently Asked Questions About Section 504 and the Education of Children with Disabilities
www.ed.gov/about/offices/list/ocr/504faq.html

Comparison of IDEA, Section 504 and ADA
www.cde.state.co.us/cdesped/download/pdf/504Comparison.pdf

An Overview of ADA, IDEA and Section 504
http://ericec.org/digests/e606.html

No Child Left Behind Act of 2001

NCLB and IDEA: What Parents of Students with Disabilities Need to Know and Do by the National Center on Educational Outcomes in collaboration with the Council of Chief State School Officers (CCSSO) and the National Association of State Directors of Special Education (NASDSE). Supported by the U.S. Department of Education
www.education.umn.edu/NCEO/OnlinePubs/Parents.pdf

Family Educational Rights and Privacy Act

Family Educational Rights and Privacy Act (FERPA) Model Notice for Directory Information
www.ed.gov/policy/gen/guid/fpco/pdf/ht100902a.pdf

McKinney-Vento Homeless Assistance Act

National Center for Homeless Education
www.serve.org/nche/

Education for Homeless Children and Youth Program – Title VII-B of the McKinney-Vento Homeless Assistance Act, as amended by the No Child Left Behind Act of 2001 Non-Regulatory Guidance (July 2004)
www.ed.gov/programs/homeless/guidance.pdf

APPENDIX B

Special Education Acronyms, Abbreviations and Terms

A

Accommodations. Changes in how test is administered that do not substantially alter what the test measures; includes changes in presentation format, response format, test setting or test timing. Appropriate accommodations are made to level the playing field, i.e., to provide equal opportunity to demonstrate knowledge.

Achievement test. Test that measures competency in a particular area of knowledge or skill; measures mastery or acquisition of skills.

Adversarial system. The system of trial practice in which each of the opposing parties has an opportunity to present and establish opposing contentions before the court.

Alternate assessment. Alternate assessments may be used to assess no more than 1 percent of students with the most severe cognitive impairments who are described as "students whose intellectual functioning and adaptive behavior are three or more standard deviations below the mean."

Alternative dispute resolution. See mediation.

Americans with Disabilities Act of 1990 (ADA). Legislation enacted to prohibit discrimination based on disability.

Appeal. Procedure in which a party seeks to reverse or modify a judgment or final order of a lower court or administrative agency, usually on grounds that lower court misinterpreted or misapplied the law, rather than on the grounds that it made an incorrect finding of fact.

Assessment. Systematic method of obtaining information from tests or other sources; procedures used to determine child's eligibility, identify the child's strengths and needs, and services child needs to meet these needs. See also evaluations.

Assistive technology device. An item, piece of equipment, or product used to maintain or improve the functional capabilities of a child with a disability.

Assistive technology service. A service that assists a child in selecting, acquiring or using an assistive technology device including evaluations of the child's needs; includes selecting, fitting, customizing, adapting, maintaining, repairing, and replacing assistive technology devices.

Attention deficit disorder/attention deficit hyperactivity disorder (ADD/ADHD). Child with ADD or ADHD may be eligible for special education under other health impairment, specific learning disability, and/or emotional disturbance categories if ADD/ADHD condition adversely affects educational performance.

Audiology. Related service; includes identification, determination of hearing loss, and referral for habilitation of hearing.

Autism. Developmental disability that affects communication and social interaction, adversely affects educational performance, is generally evident before age 3. Children with autism often engage in and have unusual responses to sensory experiences.

B

Basic skills. Skills in subjects like reading, writing, spelling, and mathematics.

Behavior disorder (BD). See emotional disturbance.

Behavior intervention plan. A plan of positive behavioral interventions in the IEP of a child whose behaviors interfere with his/her learning or that of others.

Brief. Written argument that supports a case; usually contains a statement of facts and a discussion of law.

Bodily injury. See serious bodily injury.

Burden of proof. Duty of a party to substantiate its claim against the other party; in civil actions, the weight of this proof is usually described as a preponderance of the evidence.

Business day. Means Monday through Friday, except for federal and state holidays.

C

Calendar day. See day.

Case law. Decisions issued by a court.

Charter school. Independent public schools that operate under public supervision but outside traditional public school systems; are exempt from many state and local rules, do not charge tuition, have a performance contract that specifies how the school will measure student performance, and complies with federal civil rights and education laws.

Child find. Requirement that states ensure that all children with disabilities are identified, located and evaluated, and determine which children are receiving special education and related services.

Child with a disability. A child who has a disability and who "needs special education and related services."

C.F.R. Code of Federal Regulations

Class action. A civil action filed in a court on behalf of a named plaintiff and on behalf of other individuals similarly situated.

Classroom-based instructional reading assessment. A reading assessment that relies on teacher observations.

Complaint. Legal document that outlines plaintiff's claim against a defendant.

Comprehension. The ability to understand and gain meaning from reading.

Confidential file. File maintained by the school that contains evaluations conducted to determine whether child is handicapped, other information related to special education placement; parents have a right to inspect the file and have copies of any information contained in it.

Consent. Requirement that the parent be fully informed of all information that relates to any action that school wants to take about the child, that parent understands that consent is voluntary and may be revoked at any time. See also Procedural safeguards notice and prior written notice.

Controlled substance. Means a drug or other substance identified under schedules I, II, III, IV, or V of the Controlled Substances Act; does not include a substance that is legally possessed or used under the supervision of a licensed health care provider.

Core academic subjects. English, reading or language arts, mathematics, science, foreign languages, civics and government, economics, arts, history, and geography.

Counseling services. Related service; includes services provided by social workers, psychologists, guidance counselors, or other qualified personnel.

Cumulative file. General file maintained by the school; parent has right to inspect the file and have copies of any information contained in it.

D

Damages. Monetary compensation that may be recovered by a person who has suffered loss, detriment or injury to his person, property or rights, through the unlawful act or negligence of another; damages are not generally available under the IDEA.

Day. Means calendar day unless otherwise indicated as school day or business day.

Deaf-blindness. IDEA disability category; includes hearing and visual impairments that cause severe communication, developmental and educational problems that adversely affects educational performance.

Deafness. IDEA disability category; impairment in processing information through hearing that adversely affects educational performance.

Department. The Department of Education.

Diagnostic reading assessment. A valid, reliable assessment based on scientifically based reading research that is used to identify a child's areas of strengths and weaknesses so the child learns to read by the end of third grade. A diagnostic reading assessment determines difficulties a child has in learning to read, the cause of these difficulties, and possible reading intervention strategies and related special needs.

Disability. In Section 504 and ADA, defined as impairment that substantially affects one or more major life activities; an individual who has a record of having such impairment, or is regarded as having such an impairment.

Discovery. Term for methods of obtaining evidence in advance of trial; includes interrogatories, depositions and inspection of documents.

Due process complaint notice. Notice filed to request a due process hearing; must include specific information including the child's name and address, name of the school the child attends, a description of the nature of the problem including facts relating to the problem, and a proposed resolution of the problem.

Due process hearing (impartial due process hearing). Procedure to resolve disputes between parents and schools; administrative hearing before an impartial hearing officer or administrative law judge.

Dyslexia. A specific learning disability (SLD) that is neurological in origin. It is characterized by difficulties with accurate and/or fluent word recognition and by poor spelling and decoding abilities. These difficulties typically result from a deficit in the phonological component of language that is often unexpected in relation to other cognitive abilities and the provision of effective classroom instruction. Dyslexia is listed as a "specific learning disability" in IDEA.

E

Early intervention (EI). Special education and related services provided to children until age 3 or, in some cases, until they enter kindergarten or elementary school.

Early intervening services. New program that allows at-risk children to receive additional academic and behavioral support, including scientifically-based reading instruction, without being identified as needing special education; should be used as short-term solutions, not replace special education services when a child needs them.

Education records. All records about students that are maintained by an educational agency or institution; includes instructional materials, teacher's manuals, films, tapes, test materials and protocols.

Educational consultant/diagnostician. An individual who may be familiar with school curriculum and requirements at various grade levels: may or may not have a background in learning disabilities; may conduct educational evaluations.

Emotional disturbance (ED). Disability category under IDEA; includes depression, fears, schizophrenia; adversely affects educational performance.

EMR. Educable mentally retarded.

ESY. Extended school year services.

Essential components of reading instruction. Explicit and systematic instruction in phonemic awareness, phonics, vocabulary development, reading fluency, oral reading skills, and reading comprehension strategies.

Evaluation. Procedures used to determine whether a child has a disability and the nature and extent of the special education and related services that the child needs.

Exhibit. Anything tangible that is produced and admitted in evidence during a trial.

F

Fluency. The capacity to read text accurately and quickly.

Free appropriate public education (FAPE). Special education and related services provided in conformity with an IEP; are without charge; and meets standards of the SEA.

Family Educational Rights and Privacy Act (FERPA) statute about confidentiality and access to education records.

Functional performance. Generally refers to activities and skills that are not academic or related to a child's academic achievement as measured on achievement tests.

G

General curriculum. Curriculum adopted by LEA or SEA for all children from preschool through high school.

Guardian ad litem. Person appointed by the court to represent the rights of minors.

H

Hearing impairment. Disability category under IDEA; permanent or fluctuating impairment in hearing that adversely affects educational performance.

Highly qualified teacher. Teachers who are certified by the state or pass the state teacher examination, demonstrate competence in the subject area they teach, and hold a license to teach. Elementary school teachers must demonstrate knowledge of teaching math and reading. Middle and high school teachers must have majors in the subjects they teach or demonstrate knowledge of that subject.

Highly qualified paraprofessional. A paraprofessional hired after NCLB was enacted must have a high school diploma or equivalent, complete two years of study at a college or university, have an associate's degree (minimum), or take a rigorous skills test.

Homeless children and youth. Children and youth who do not have a fixed, regular, nighttime residence; includes children who live in motels, hotels, trailer parks, or campgrounds; children who live in emergency shelters; children who are abandoned or are waiting for foster care placement; children who live in cars, parks, public spaces, abandoned buildings, substandard housing, bus or train stations; and migratory children who are homeless.

HOUSSE. High Objective Uniform State Standard of Evaluation

I

IDEA. The Individuals with Disabilities Education Act of 2004

IDELR. Individuals with Disabilities Law Reporter

IEE. Independent educational evaluation

IEP. Individualized Educational Plan

IFSP. Individualized family service plan for children with disabilities under age 3.

Illegal drug. A controlled substance; does not include substances that are legally possessed or used under the supervision of a licensed health-care professional.

Immigrant children and youth. Individuals between the ages of 3 and 21 who were not born in the United States and have not attended school in a state for more than three full academic years.

Impartial due process hearing. See due process hearing.

Inclusion. An effort to make sure students with disabilities go to school with their friends and neighbors, while also receiving the "specially designed instruction and support" they need to achieve high standards and succeed as learners.

Instructional material. Instructional content provided to a student; includes print and audio-visual materials and electronic or digital materials.

Interpreting services. Related service; includes oral transliteration services, cued language transliteration services, sign language, transliteration and interpreting services, and transcription services for children who are deaf or hard of hearing.

Interrogatories. Written questions served on a party that must be answered under oath before trial; method of discovery.

J

Judgment. Order by a court.

L

Learning disability. See specific learning disability (SLD).

Least restrictive environment (LRE). Legal requirement to educate children with disabilities in general education classrooms with children who are not disabled to the maximum extent possible.

LEA. Local education agency or school district

Limited English proficient (LEP). An individual between the ages of 3 and 21 who attends an elementary school or secondary school, who was not born in the United States or whose native language is not English, or a migratory child whose native language is not English. The individual's difficulties in speaking, reading, writing, or understanding English may not permit the individual to be proficient on state assessments.

M

Mainstreaming. Attempts to move students from special education classrooms to regular education classrooms only in situations where they re able to keep up with their typically developing peers without specially designed instruction or support. See also least restrictive environment and inclusion.

Manifestation determination review. If child with disability engages in behavior or breaks a rule or code of conduct that applies to nondisabled children and the school proposes to remove the child, the school must hold a hearing to determine if the child's behavior was caused by the disability.

Mediation. Procedural safeguard to resolve disputes between parents and schools; must be voluntary, cannot be used to deny or delay right to a due process hearing; must be conducted by a qualified and impartial mediator who is trained in effective mediation techniques.

Medical services. Related service; includes services provided by a licensed physician to determine a child's medically related disability that results in the child's need for special education and related services.

Mental retardation. Disability category under IDEA; refers to significantly sub-average general intellectual functioning with deficits in adaptive behavior that adversely affects educational performance.

Migratory child. A child who is, or whose parent is, a migratory agricultural worker or a migratory fisher. In the preceding 36 months, in order to obtain employment in agricultural or fishing work, the child has moved from one school district to another, or from one administrative area to another. (See Section 1309 of NCLB Act)

Modifications. Substantial changes in what the student is expected to demonstrate; includes changes in instructional level, content, and performance criteria, may include changes in test form or format; includes alternate assessments.

Multiple disabilities. Disability category under IDEA; concomitant impairments (such as mental retardation-blindness, mental retardation-orthopedic impairment, etc.) that cause such severe educational problems that problems cannot be accommodated in special education programs solely for one of the impairments; does not include deaf-blindness.

N

National Assessment of Educational Progress (NAEP). Assessments in reading, mathematics, science, writing, U.S. history, geography, civics, and the arts; is the only nationally representative, continuing assessment of what American students know and can do in various subjects.

Native language. Language normally used by the child's parents. When used to refer to an individual who has limited English proficiency, refers to the language normally used by the individual, or by the parents of a child or youth.

NIMAS. National Instructional Materials Accessibility Standard

Norm-referenced test. See standardized test.

O

OCR. Office of Civil Rights

Occupational therapy. Related service; includes therapy to remediate fine motor skills. **Opinion.** Formal written decision by judge or court; contains the legal principles and reasons upon which the decision was based.

Orientation and mobility services. Related service; includes services to visually impaired students that enable students to move safely at home, school, and community.

Orthopedic impairment. Disability category under IDEA; orthopedic impairment that adversely affects child's educational performance.

OSERS. Office of Special Education and Rehabilitative Services

OSEP. Office of Special Education Programs

Other health impairment. Disability category under IDEA; refers to limited strength, vitality or alertness due to chronic or acute health problems that adversely affects educational performance.

P

Paraprofessional. An individual employed in a public school who is supervised by a certified or licensed teacher; includes individuals who work in language instruction educational programs, special education, and migrant education.

Parent. Parent, guardian, or surrogate parent; may include grandparent or stepparent with whom a child lives, and foster parent.

Personal information. Individually identifiable information; includes name, home or physical address, telephone number, or Social Security identification number.

Phonemic awareness. The ability to hear and identify individual sounds, or phonemes.

Phonics. The relationship between the letters of written language and the sounds of spoken language.

Proficient. Solid academic performance for the grade, demonstrates competence in subject matter.

PTI. Parent training and information center

Physical therapy. Related service; includes therapy to remediate gross motor skills.

Precedent. A court decision that will influence similar cases in the future.

Prior written notice. Required written notice to parents when school proposes to initiate or change, or refuses to initiate or change, the identification, evaluation, or educational placement of the child.

Pro se. Representing oneself without assistance of legal counsel

Procedural safeguards notice. Requirement that schools provide full easily understood explanation of procedural safeguards that describe parent's right to an independent educational evaluation, to examine records, to request mediation and due process.

Psychological services. Related service; includes administering psychological and educational tests, interpreting test results, interpreting child behavior related to learning.

Public Law (P.L.) 94-142. The Education for All Handicapped Children Act that was enacted in 1975.

R

Reading. A complex system of deriving meaning from print that requires all of the following:

The skills and knowledge to understand how phonemes, or speech sounds, are connected to print.

The ability to decode unfamiliar words.

The ability to read fluently.

Sufficient background information and vocabulary to foster reading comprehension.

The development of appropriate active strategies to construct meaning from print.

The development and maintenance of a motivation to read. (20 U. S. C. § 6368)

Reasonable accommodation. Adoption of a facility or program that can be accomplished without undue administrative or financial burden.

Recreation. Related service; includes therapeutic recreation services, recreation programs, and leisure education.

Rehabilitation Act of 1973. Civil rights statute designed to protect individuals with disabilities from discrimination; purposes are to maximize employment, economic self-sufficiency, independence, inclusion and integration into society.

Rehabilitation counseling services. Related service; includes career development, preparation for employment, vocational rehabilitation services funded under the Rehabilitation Act of 1973.

Related services. Services that are necessary for child to benefit from special education; includes speech language pathology and audiology services, psychological services, physical and occupational therapy, recreation, early identification and assessment, counseling, rehabilitation counseling, orientation and mobility services, school health services, school nurse services, social work services, parent counseling and training.

Remediation. Process by which an individual receives instruction and practice in skills that are weak or nonexistent in an effort to develop/strengthen these skills.

Response to intervention (RTI). In determining if a child has a specific learning disability, refers to the child's response to scientific, research-based intervention.

S

School day. A day when children attend school for instructional purposes.

School health services. Related service; services provided by a qualified school nurse or other qualified person.

School nurse services. Related service; services provided by a qualified school nurse that are designed to enable a child with a disability to receive FAPE as described in the child's IEP.

Scientifically Based Research. Research that applies rigorous, systematic, and objective procedures to obtain reliable, valid knowledge about education activities and programs. Includes research that employs systematic, empirical methods that draw on observation or experiment, involves rigorous data analyses to test hypotheses and justify conclusions, relies on methods that provide reliable and valid data across evaluators and observers, and studies that are accepted by a peer-reviewed journal or approved by a panel of independent experts through rigorous, objective, and scientific review.

SEA. State department of education.

Section 504. Section 504 of the Rehabilitation Act protects individuals with disabilities from discrimination due to disability by recipients of federal financial assistance.

Serious bodily injury. Means bodily injury which involves a substantial risk of death; extreme physical pain; protracted and obvious disfigurement; or protracted loss or impairment of the function of a bodily member, organ, or mental faculty . . ."

Settlement. Conclusion of a legal matter by agreement of opposing parties in a civil suit before judgment is made.

Special education. Specially designed instruction, at no cost to the parents, to meet the unique needs of a child with a disability.

Specific learning disability (SLD). Disability category under IDEA; includes disorders that affect the ability to understand or use spoken or written language; may manifest in difficulties with listening, thinking, speaking, reading, writing, reading fluency, spelling, and doing mathematical calculations; includes minimal brain dysfunction, dyslexia, and developmental aphasia.

Speech-language pathology services. Related service; includes identification and diagnosis of speech or language impairments, speech or language therapy, counseling and guidance.

Speech or language impairment. Disability category under IDEA; includes communication disorders, language impairments, voice impairments that adversely educational performance.

Statutory rights. Rights protected by statute, as opposed to constitutional rights that are protected by the Constitution.

Statute of limitations. Time within which a legal action must be commenced; two-year statute of limitations to request a due process hearing added to IDEA 2004.

Statutory law. Written law enacted by legislative bodies.

Stay-put. During the pendency of any administrative or judicial proceeding regarding a due process complaint notice requesting a due process hearing, the child must remain in his or her current educational placement.

Supplemental educational services. Means tutoring and other supplemental academic enrichment services that are in addition to instruction provided during the school day and are high quality, research-based, and specifically designed to increase the academic achievement of eligible children on state academic assessments and attain proficiency in meeting the State's academic achievement standards.

Supplementary aids and services. Means aids, services, and supports that are provided in regular education classes that enable children with disabilities to be educated with nondisabled children to the maximum extent appropriate.

T

Technology. See assistive technology.

Testimony. Evidence given by a person as distinguished from evidence from writings and other sources.

Tourette syndrome. A neurological or neurochemical disorder characterized by involuntary, rapid, sudden movements or vocalizations (tics) that occur repeatedly; included as a disability category in IDEA 2004.

Transcript. Official record taken during a trial or hearing by an authorized stenographer.

Transition services. IEP requirement; designed to facilitate movement from school to the workplace or to higher education.

Transportation. Related service about travel; includes specialized equipment (i.e., special or adapted buses, lifts, and ramps) if required to provide special transportation for a child with a disability.

Traumatic brain injury. Disability category under IDEA; includes acquired injury caused by external physical force and open or closed head injuries that result in impairments; does not include congenital or degenerative brain injuries or brain injuries caused by birth trauma.

Travel training. See orientation and mobility services.

U

Universal design. New curricular materials and learning technologies are designed to be flexible enough to accommodate the unique learning styles of a wide range of individuals, including children with disabilities. Examples include electronic versions of textbooks, captioned and/or narrated videos, accessible websites, and voice recognition.

U.S.C. United States Code

V

Visual impairment including blindness. Disability category under IDEA; impaired vision that adversely affects educational performance.

Vocabulary. Words that students must know to read effectively.

W

Ward of the state. A child is a foster child, a ward of the State, or in the custody of a public child welfare agency.

Weapon. Means a "dangerous weapon" which is a weapon, device, instrument, material, or substance, animate or inanimate, that is used for, or is readily capable of, causing death or serious bodily injury, except that the term does not include a pocket knife with a blade of less than 2 1/2 inches in length.

Bibliography

Church, Robert L. (1976) *Education in the United States.* New York: The Free Press.

Cremin, Lawrence A. (1967) *The Transformation of the School: Progressivism in American Education, 1876-1957.* New York: Knopf.

Hallahan, Daniel P. and Cecil D. Mercer (2001) Learning Disabilities: Historical Perspectives. *Learning Disabilities Summit: Building a Foundation for the Future* at www.nrcld.org/html/information/articles/ldsummit/hallahan.html

Johnson, Scott. (2003) Reexamining Rowley: A New Focus in Special Education Law. *The Beacon: Journal of Special Education Law and Practice*, 2(2). www.harborhouselaw.com/articles/rowley.reexamine.johnson.htm

Kerr, Sonja. (2000) *Special Education Due Process Hearings.* www.harborhouselaw.com/articles/dp.kerr.htm

Kathleen S. Mehfoud (2004) *Special Education Law: The School Board Perspective.* www.harborhouselaw.com/articles/dp.mehfoud.htm

Sperry, David, Philip T. K. Daniel, Dixie Snow Huefner, E. Gordon Gee. (1998) *Education Law and the Public Schools: A Compendium* Norwood, MA: Christopher-Gordon Publishers, Inc.

Togut, Torin. (2004) High Stakes Testing: Barometer for Success, or Prognosticator for Failure? *The Beacon: Journal of Special Education Law and Practice*, 2(3). www.harborhouselaw.com/articles/highstakes.togut.htm

Weber, Mark C. (2002) *Special Education Law and Litigation Treatise, 2nd Edition.* Horsham PA: LRP Publications

Wright, Pamela and Peter Wright (2005) *Wrightslaw: From Emotions to Advocacy.* Hartfield VA: Harbor House Law Press, Inc.

Wright, Peter W. D. and Pamela Darr Wright (2005) *Wrightslaw: IDEA 2004.* Hartfield VA: Harbor House Law Press, Inc.

Wright, Peter W. D., Pamela Wright and Suzanne Heath (2004) *Wrightslaw: No Child Left Behind.* Hartfield, VA: Harbor House Law Press, Inc.

Wright, Peter W. D. and Pamela Darr Wright (2004) *Representing the Special Education Child: A Manual for the Attorney and Advocate.* www.harborhouselaw.com/articles/dp.wright.htm

Wright, Peter W. D. (2004) High Stakes Testing: The Next Wave of Special Education Litigation. *The Beacon: Journal of Special Education Law and Practice*, 2(3). www.harborhouselaw.com/articles/highstakes.litigation.wright.htm

Index